Local Networks

Lexington Books Series in Computer Science

Kenneth J. Thurber, General Editor

Computing in the Humanities
Peter C. Patton and *Renee A. Holoien*

Data Base Computers
Olin H. Bray and *Harvey A. Freeman*

Data Structures and Computer Architecture
Kenneth J. Thurber and *Peter C. Patton*

Distributed Database Management Systems
Olin H. Bray

Distributed-Processor Communications Architecture
Kenneth J. Thurber and *Gerald M. Masson*

Requirements-Oriented Computer System Design
Kenneth J. Thurber

Interconnection Networks for Large-Scale Parallel Processing
Howard J. Siegel

Microcomputer Interfacing
G. Jack Lipovski

Basic Computer Logic
John Scott

Local Networks
W.R. Franta and *Imrich Chlamtac*

Database Management System Anatomy
James A. Larson

Local Networks

Motivation, Technology, and Performance

W.R. Franta
Imrich Chlamtac
University of Minnesota

LexingtonBooks
D.C. Heath and Company
Lexington, Massachusetts
Toronto

Library of Congress Cataloging in Publication Data

Franta, W.R.
Local networks.

Includes bibliographical references and index.
1. Computer networks. I. Chlamtac, Imrich. II. Title.
TK5105.5.F73 001.64′404 80-7725
ISBN 0-669-03779-6 AACR2

Published simultaneously in Canada

Printed in the United States of America

International Standard Book Number: 0-669-03779-6

Library of Congress Catalog Card Number: 80-7725

venujeme našim rodičom

dedicated to our parents and wives

Contents

List of Figures

List of Tables

Preface

A *network* is loosely defined as an interconnected set of elements. Interconnection is effected by a communication subnetwork that allows the elements to exchange information to support the intent or applications of the network. In the past few years, a great deal has been written about "long-haul" networks, in which the communication subnetwork generally employs common-carrier offerings to interconnect usually widely dispersed elements consisting of one or more computer systems.

More recently, considerable attention has been given to local networks. Local networks are generally geographically compact (that is, contained in a room, building, or complex of buildings); usually employ privately owned subnetworks of very high bandwidth; and interconnect both active elements, such as computer systems, and passive elements, such as large-capacity secondary-storage devices. Additionally, local networks are generally owned and operated by a single organization. For reasons such as these, local networks are characteristically different from long-haul networks.

Isolated instances of local networks have existed since the early 1960s. These networks generally employed ad hoc point-to-point subnetwork links to interconnect a small number of "compatible" elements. In recent years, significant advances have been made in both the hardware and the software technology needed to support local networks.

In this book, we first examine the nature of local networks, the reasons for the growth in interest in them, and the applications they are intended to support. We then turn to local network-design issues, and, by way of a general model of local networks, we examine the extant hardware and software technology available as responses to design questions. These issues and resolution options relate to network topology, subnetwork hardware (including access protocols), element-to-element protocols, reliability, ease of realization, and so forth.

Next, we define measures of performance and discuss the development and use of both simulation and analytic performance models in assessing local-network performance. We discuss local-network instrumentation approaches and interpret available measured-performance data. We then review a series of existing networks as examples of design alternatives that have been employed.

Finally, we discuss the motivation for, and the problems associated with *internetting*, the interconnection of local networks and the connection of local networks to long-haul networks.

Our intention is to present a picture of what local networks are and how they are realized. We do not pretend to give a definitive treatment, for one does not yet exist. Further, we concentrate as much as possible on material that is unique to local networks, avoiding restatement of material that is also relevant to long-haul networks and is therefore available in a number of other books.

Glossary of Abbreviations

ACK acknowledgment
ADCCP Advanced Data Communication and Control Procedure (ANSI)
BRAM broadcast-recognizing access method
BSN back-end storage network
BTMA busy-tone multiple access
CCITT Consultative Committee for International Telephony and Telegraphy
CHORS Computer Hardcopy Storage System
CIU communication-interface unit
CMDS Cambridge Model Distributed System
CP control portion
CPU central processing unit
CRC character-redundancy check
CSMA carrier-sense multiple access
CSMA-CD carrier-sense multiple access with collision detection
DCM distance-control matrix
DDB distributed database
DLCN distributed-loop computer network
DMA direct memory access
FDMA frequency division multiple access
GDM global data manager
GTM global task master
HDLC higher data link control
HXDP Honeywell experimental distributed processing
I/O input-output
IP information portion
IPC interprocess communication
LBT listen-before-transmit
LDM local data manager
LLL Lawrence Livermore Laboratories
LNI local-network interface
LOS line of sight
LWT listen-while-transmit
MASS Multi-Access Storage System
MSAP mini-slot alternating priorities
NAD network access device
NAK negative acknowledgment
PODA priority-oriented demand assignment (FPODA, CPODA)
PPB prioritized parametric BRAM
PSD prioritized staggered delays

REJ reject
RJE remote job entry
SDLC synchronous data-link control (IBM)
SNA systems network architecture (IBM)
SREJ selective reject
SUPBRAM supervisory-node broadcast-recognizing access method
TCI trunk-control interface
TCU trunk-control unit
TDMA time-division multiple access
TH terminal-peripheral handler
VA virtual architecture
VDPA vector-determined proportional access
VDU visual display unit
VPE virtual processing elements

Local Networks

1 Local Networks: Nature and Need

Introduction

A local network is composed of an interconnected set of active elements, such as computers, and passive elements, such as disks. The interconnection supports digital communication among the elements, which are dispersed over a limited geographic area that is typically less than a kilometer in diameter. The interconnection medium is wideband, usually in the 1–50 megabits per second (Mb/s) range, and is essentially error-free. Finally, the network is private, as it usually is owned and operated by a single organization; in many cases, it has also been designed and implemented by the owning organization.

Local networks have many properties in common with the more familiar long-haul networks, such as ARPANET and TELENET [8], and yet are unlike them in a variety of ways. They are the same in the sense that both support physical-network topology (that is, a physical interconnection of elements by communication links or channels, with the physical connection supporting a complete logical connectivity of the elements, such that information can physically be sent from any element to any other element. From this point of view, local networks differ from long-haul networks only by the values they assign to certain network-design variables. For example, local networks:

1. Employ high-bandwidth channels (generally in the megabit range), whereas long-haul networks employ low-bandwidth channels (generally in the kilobit range);
2. Exhibit transmission delays that are shorter than those in long-haul networks (primarily because of the use of high-bandwidth channels);
3. Employ channels with very low error rates, not only compared with those of long-haul channels but in an absolute sense as well;
4. Can easily employ state-of-the-art technology, as their construction is not subject to the constraints, especially legal, often associated with long-haul networks that use common carriers [1]; and
5. Are more closely and easily controlled (managed), as they are generally owned and operated by a single organization.

To amplify further, it has been suggested [2] that there are five classes of computer-communication problems:

1. The central-computer-facility problem: the organization of the several mainframe computers and large peripheral devices operated by a particular organization into a coherent set of commonly accessible (shared) resources.
2. The satellite or remote-computing problem: interconnection of a wide variety of minicomputer-based equipment and associated peripheral devices, located over a limited geographical area up to several kilometers in diameter, to the central computing facility (usually termed *distributed data processing* or *local intelligence*)
3. The terminal-access problem: general interconnection of any terminal device, intelligent or unintelligent, to any computer system, usually a satellite computer but sometimes a mainframe in the central computing facility. These terminals include traditional keyboard terminals, as well as office automation devices, digital voice terminals, and other microcomputer-based equipment.
4. The standard computer-network problem: interconnecting the computing equipment of one organization—typically its central computing facility—through a single transparent, application-independent computer network, to some set of other computing resources. This can be accomplished through a public data network, through a private or dedicated packet-switching network, through the use of one of the network architectures offered by computer vendors, or by various other strategies.
5. The internetwork-communications problem: linking together a number of separate and independent computer networks by means of gateway computers, so that messages can be exchanged from one network to the destination network possibly through several intermediate networks.

Networks in the first three categories are local networks. The problems identified in those three categories also give some idea as to why there is widespread interest in local networks.

Local networks allow a random collection of elements to become a coordinated system. This ability allows an organization to expand a facility with a degree of vendor independence (freedom from recoding applications); to incorporate special-purpose elements, such as database machines or vector processors, into a system using the general-purpose software of another mainframe; and to supply the user interface for the special-purpose device. In the latter case, the local network can also mitigate the system-integration task by obviating the development of extensive general-purpose software (editors, compilers, terminal handlers, and so forth) for the special-purpose device.

Local networks promote and facilitate both resource sharing and reliability. A network element composed of a battery of disks, for example, is available to all mainframe elements on the network; that is, they can share the files and file space on the battery. Additionally, local networks promote reliability through element redundancy.

Local networks may also promote a uniformity of user access. This uniformity is supported by an element that uses a uniform, single gateway or entrance to the network and transforms user requests to accommodate the particular hardware and software attributes of other elements of the network. We shall elaborate on this point in chapter 4.

Local networks permit amplification of the dispersion of functionality found in the classic time-sharing system. Thus, a mainframe element may be in one place, a high-speed printing element in another, a sensor controller in another, a terminal or work station [9] in yet another, and so on.

Local networks allow the functionality that is traditionally associated with large, centalized systems—for example, a time-sharing system—to be realized through a collection of dedicated minicomputers (conceivably, microcomputers), with orchestration supported by the local-network-supplied connectivity.

Our listing is meant to be not exhaustive but rather indicative. It should convey, however, the idea that local networks signal a drawing together of wideband communications and computers in a manner that permits new ways of providing traditional functionality and ways of providing new functionality.

Thus, local networks support a wide variety of applications and exhibit a spectrum of functionality. In chapter 2, we give several examples of local networks that support applications systems ranging from real-time control to the integrated electronic office.

The Generic Local Network

It is obvious that a hardware device is needed to physically connect the elements that make up the local network. We call such connection devices communication-interface units (CIUs). The functionality of a CIU will be considered in the next chapter. Here, it suffices to say that a CIU serves to physically connect an element to the wideband communications network and that its functionality is dependent on such factors as the nature of the element it attaches, the technology and rate of the communications channel, the topology of the network, and the communications protocols (that is, rules) employed. Generically, a local network has the structure shown in figure 1–1, and its hardware and software architecture is likely to support the following functional guidelines.

1. It should be possible to transmit data directly between any two elements without involving store-and-forward at a third element, even for a short time.

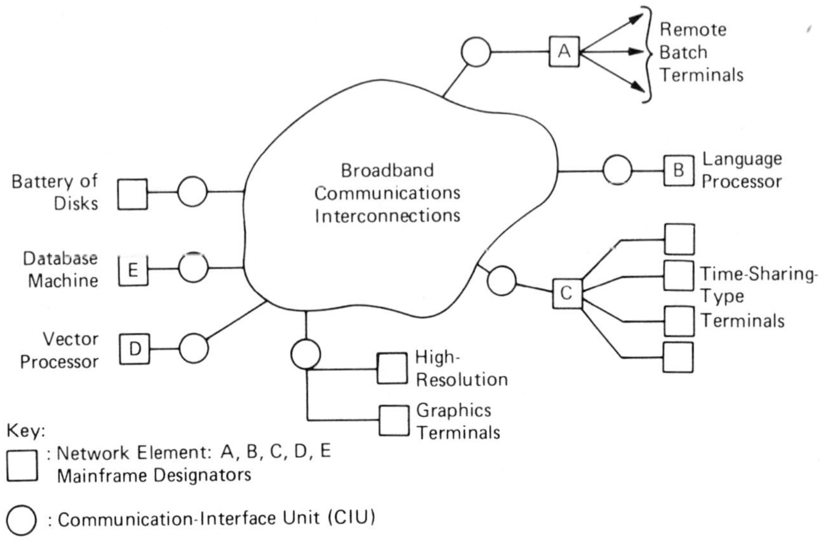

Figure 1–1. Generic Local Network

2. The network should provide data communications between elements separated by as much as 4 kilometers and at a link-data rate of at least 1 megabit per second (Mb/s).

3. The network should be such that it can easily be changed or extended after installation (within the limitation of the network to include or delete elements). Also, the network should be such that the connection to or disconnection of an element from the network would not introduce more than a transient fault in network operation.

4. Each element should be connected to the network in such a way that a failure in the element would not cause more than a transient failure of the network as a whole, except as related only to the functionality of the failed element. Also, the network should be capable of recovering from the effects of transient failures.

5. The local network should be such that it is possible to construct translation equipment so that the network can be interfaced to other networks or to common-carrier facilities. Direct compatibility with any other communications facilities or equipment is not required.

6. The network should include features that facilitate network maintenance, diagnostics, and service.

7. The network should conform to the mandatory requirements of relevant licensing agencies (applicable when satellite, radio, or microwave channels are employed).

8. The network should be defined in terms of layered protocols (see chapter 2).

9. Where possible and appropriate, the network should be defined in terms of other standards, such as protocol and electrical (physical-interface) standards.

These guidelines are, in fact, consistent with the needs of the spectrum of applications for which local networks are attractive. They have served as the basis of a functional description for the purpose of standards work [10], and they deserve elaboration, which will be given in chapter 2.

Technological and Economic Motivations

The recent widespread interest in local networks is in response to the conjunction of the needs identified earlier with recent technological and economic developments. In particular, local networking is driven by the well-documented [3], rapidly falling cost of very large scale integration (VLSI) digital logic and the attendant rapid increase in complexity supported by VLSI chips, the availability of inexpensive off-the-shelf cable television, radio [7], and satellite-communications technology [6], and the promise of fiber-optics-communications technology [4,5]. In fact, we speak in terms of these techniques when we mention the fortuitous "drawing together" of digital and communications developments that makes local networking viable.

In the following chapters, we examine the technology of local networking, including network topology, the media used for the physical connection of elements, the hierarchy of protocols employed, and predicted and measured performance. Along the way, we will reinforce and elaborate on our preceding remarks. We will present several sample networks—designed by both research and development communities—and we will review the CIUs that are commercially available. We will discuss the impact of VLSI on local networking, the need for and movement toward local network standards, and the current and future need for encryption schemes and devices. We devote an entire chapter to internetting—the interconnection of local networks and the connection of local to long-haul networks. We also devote a chapter to the software (operating) systems associated with local networks, and in this regard we suggest that local networks represent an evolutionary step toward distributed systems.

References

1. Wilkes, Maurice V. "The Impact of Wideband Local Area Communication Systems on Distributed Computing." Keynote address, First

International Conference on Distributed Computing, Huntsville, Alabama, October 1979.

2. McQuillan, John M. "Understanding the New Local Network Technologies." Report No. 3927. Cambridge, Mass.: Bolt Beranek and Newman, September 1978.
3. Stefferud, Einar. "Economic Background for Computer Mail: A Review of Fundamental Issues." *Proceedings of COMPCON*, 1980, pp. 94–97.
4. Evans, Scott, and Herman, Jim. "Fiber Optics Successfully Links Microcomputers." *Digital Design*, April 1978, pp. 36–37.
5. "Growth of the Fiber Optics Market." *Digital Design*, April 1980, p. 16.
6. Martin, James. *Communications Satellite Systems*. New York: Prentice-Hall, 1978.
7. Abramson, N. "The Aloha System." TR B72-1, University of Hawaii, January 1972.
8. Roberts, L.G., The Evolution of Packet Switching, *Proceedings of the IEEE* 66 (November 1978): 1307–1313.
9. Thacker, C. P., et al. "ALTO: A Personal Computer. In *Computer Structures: Readings and Examples*. New York: McGraw-Hill, forthcoming.
10. Graube, Maris. "IEEE to Establish Local Networking Standards." *Computer Business News*, December 17, 1979, p. 3.

2 Local-Network Organization and Structure

Introduction

As figure 1–1 showed, local networks require CIUs to support element interconnection and transport of information. The selected CIU design determines the class of allowable networks by directly or indirectly determining the classes of elements that may be interconnected. The key CIU-design parameters are:

1. Transmission-mode selection, that is, analog or digital mode;
2. Selection of allowable topologies, including the allowable distances between adjacent elements and the allowable diameter of the whole network;
3. Transmission medium or media and bandwidth selection;
4. Selection of the classes of elements for which interconnection is possible;
5. Selection of reliability attributes; and
6. Determination of cost constraints, both on a per-element interface and for the network as a whole.

Furthermore, decisions regarding these design parameters must be made with consideration of the functional guidelines given in chapter 1. We will discuss, in turn, the options and issues for each design parameter.

Transmission Mode

The choice between analog and digital transmission modes is simple; the digital mode is selected. This choice is consistent with the trends in digital voice transmission as well as the availability of reliable, off-the-shelf, high-bandwidth media and components.

Topology

To simplify our characterization of topologies, we call a CIU and its associated elements a node. A node is shown graphically in figure 2–1a. The characterization is not complete, in the sense that it does not handle all possible circumstances unambiguously. For example, we would consider the

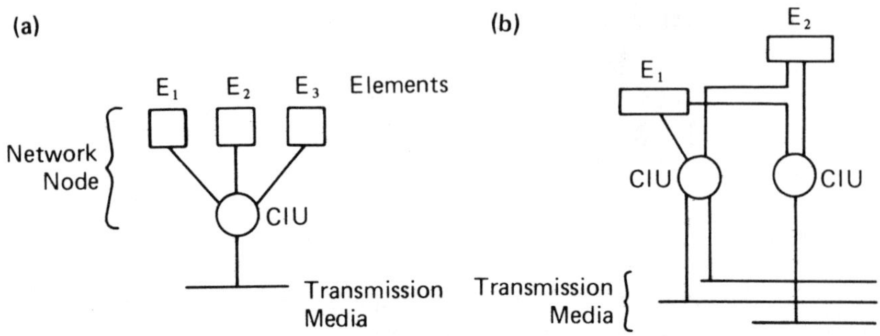

Figure 2–1. Network Node Structure

circumstance depicted in figure 2–1b to represent two nodes, although it could also be considered one.

Network topology is concerned basically with the pattern of node interconnections. The most general topology is an unconstrained graph structure, as shown in figure 2–2. The unconstrained graph topology is generally associated with long-haul networks, in which, because of geographic dispersion, the transmission links are generally low-bandwidth (less than 50 Kb/s) common-carrier lines. It is also possible to realize local networks that exhibit the same topology. In fact, the local network at Lawrence Livermore Laboratories had evolved into such a topology [72], as shown in figures 2–3 and 2–4. The Lawrence network has since been redesigned to exhibit the topology shown in figure 2–5.

Generally, local networks are seldom realized as an unconstrained graph.

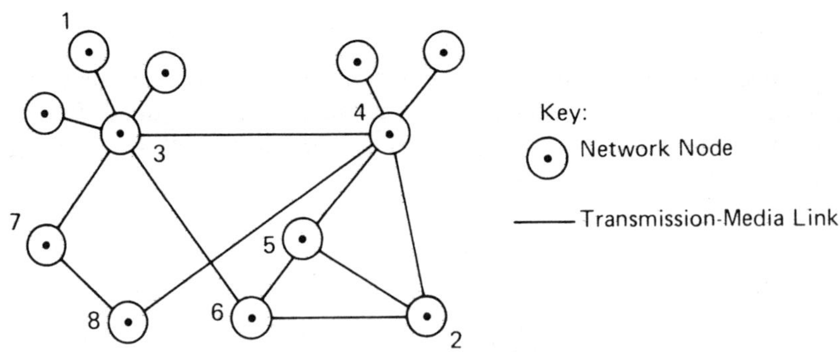

Figure 2–2. Unconstrained Topology

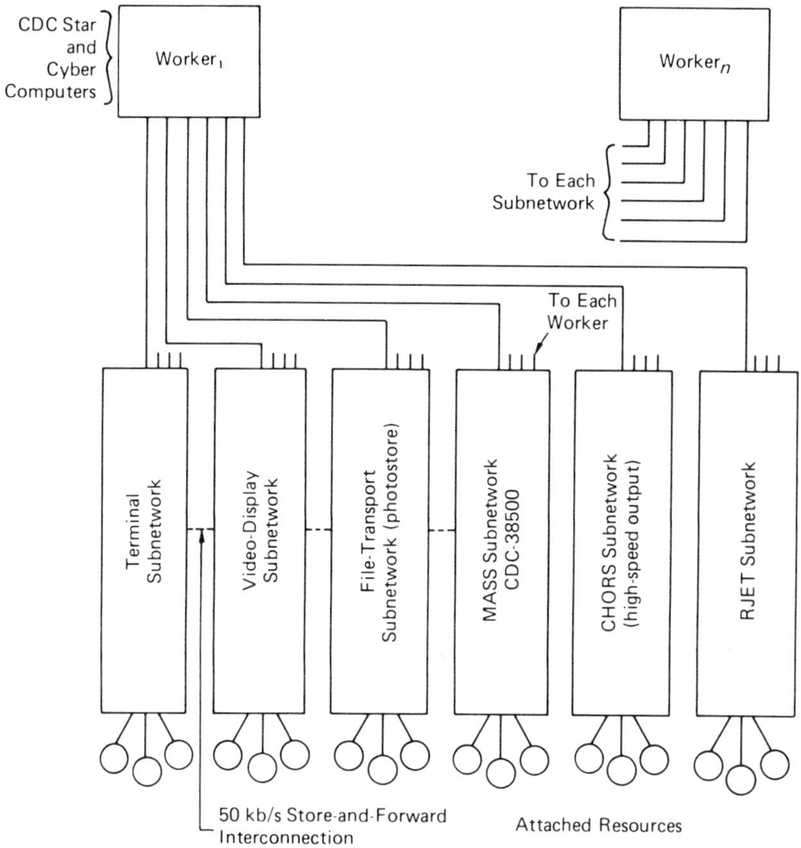

Figure 2–3. Functional Organization for Evolved Lawrence Livermore Laboratories Local Network

The basic reason for avoidance of the general-graph topology is that it does not promote certain of the desirable functional guidelines listed in chapter 1. In particular, guidelines 1, 2, and 4 are not usually possible with the unconstrained topology. Providing other functional capabilities, particularly those given by guidelines 3, 5, and 6, is more complex for an unconstrained topology than for the more prevalent controlled topologies to be discussed.

To elaborate still further, the links that connect the nodes in figure 2–2 are generally point-to-point links, that is, from one node only to one other node, and such networks therefore require a routing strategy. For example, transmitting a message originating at node 1 in figure 2–2, with node 2 as

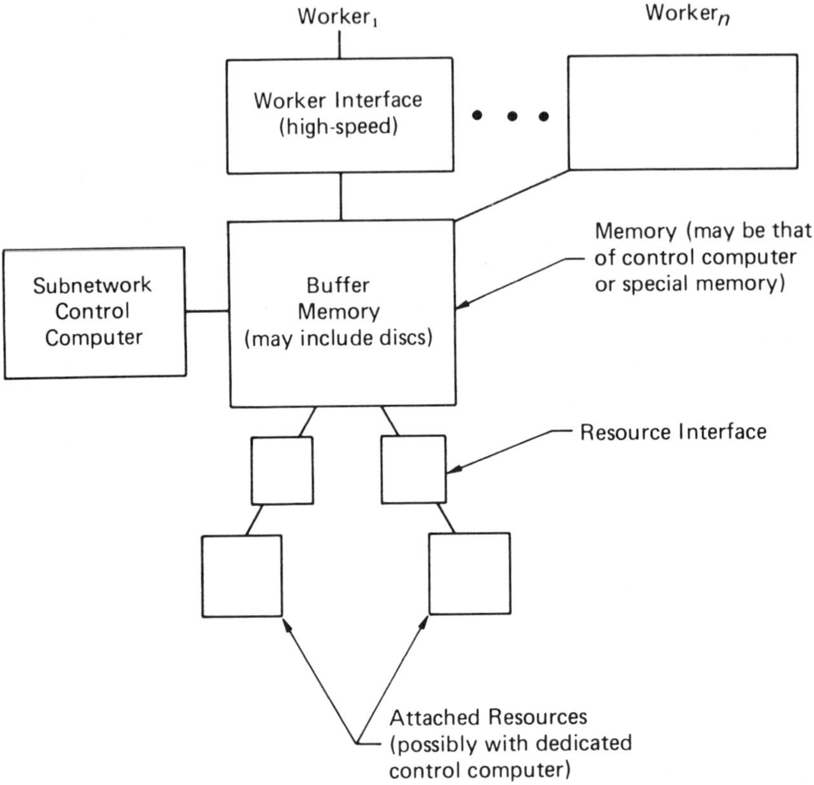

Figure 2–4. Typical Subnetwork for Evolved Lawrence Livermore Laboratories Local Network

destination, requires that the message be received by node 3 and forwarded to node 4 or node 6 or node 7 for subsequent forwarding to node 1. A routing strategy refers to the decisions a node makes regarding messages received that must be forwarded. These decisions generally concern (1) whether or not the message should be forwarded if the receiving node is not the final destination of the message; and (2) if forwarding is to be done, determination of the link (or links) over which the message should be forwarded.

The controlled topologies discussed next obviate the need for complex routing strategies and better serve local networks by more directly supporting functional guidelines 1 through 9 in chapter 1.

The Star Network

Two variants of the star-network topology are shown in Figures 2–6a and 2–6b. Star networks evolved as the first controlled-topology networks because

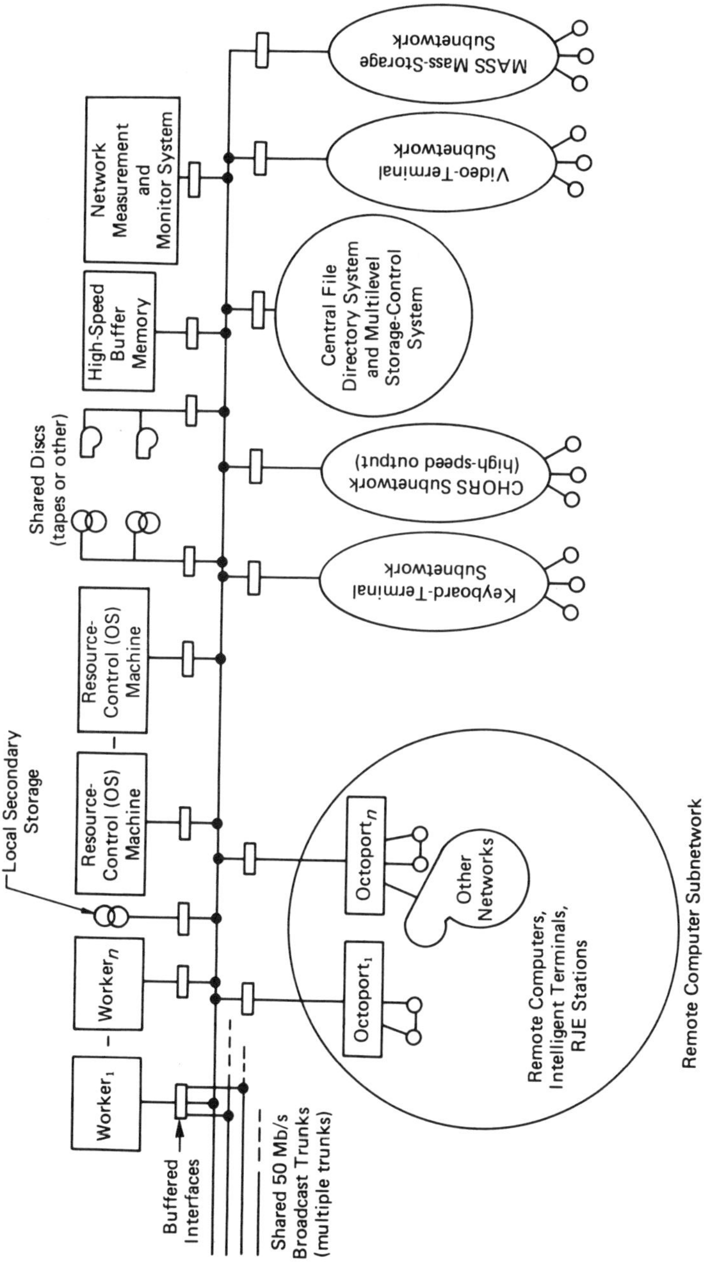

Figure 2–5. Future Lawrence Livermore Laboratories Network Based on Functional Partitioning

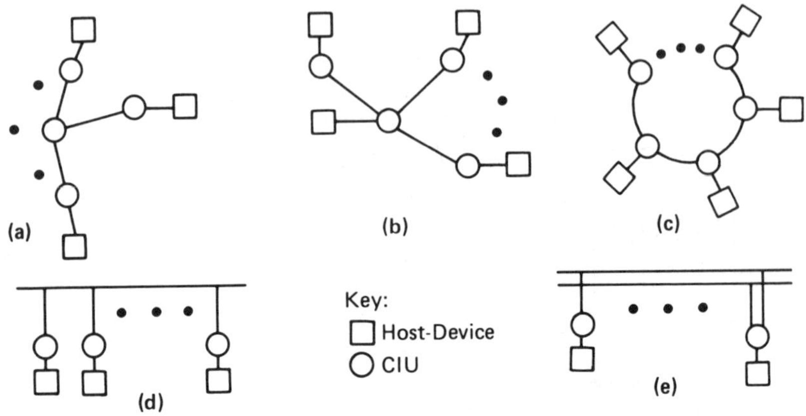

Figure 2–6. Common Local-Network Topologies: (**a**) Passive Hub Star; (**b**) Active Hub Star; (**c**) Ring; (**d**) Simple Bus; (**e**) Multiple Bus

they are the simplest. Furthermore, this topology is natural if the majority of the messages transmitted are between a primary node (the hub) and secondary nodes (the nodes on the periphery). If that is not the pattern, however, the hub must serve a routing function by forwarding messages that originate at a periphery node and are destined for another periphery node. This topology is reminiscent of a central-node time-sharing system, wherein the periphery nodes are terminals, clusters of terminals, or remote batch stations that are connected by point-to-point links.

Clearly, operation of the network requires correct operation of the hub node; by *correct*, we mean that the central node must be operational and it must have sufficient capacity so as not to be a bottleneck to the responsiveness of the network. In any case, the central node represents a single point of network failure; that is, the network fails when the central node fails, a feature not consistent with functional guideline 4. Furthermore, it is likely that the star topology offers special difficulties in certain cases of expansion and thus will not be responsive to functional guideline 3.

The remaining two controlled topologies do not suffer from the drawbacks of the unconstrained graph or star networks, and thus they best serve the given local-network functional guidelines.

The Ring Topology

The ring topology is shown in figure 2–6c. In the ring, messages are passed unidirectionally (for example, clockwise). Generally, a transmitted message circulates around the ring in such a manner that it can be thought of as having been placed on the ring by the transmitting node, received and forwarded by each intermediate node, and received by the destination node. Thus, as with the star topology, there are no routing decisions. Unlike the star network, however, the ring supports arbitrary message-traffic patterns (including the primary-to-secondary-node pattern described for the star network).

The Bus Topology

The simple bus topology is shown in figure 2–6d. With the bus, transmitted messages flow away from the originating node in both directions, and each other node can test message content as it passes by to determine if that node is the itended destination of a transmission. Thus, bus-oriented networks obviate the need for routing (forwarding) altogether.

Bus and ring topologies exhibit similar characteristics in many respects. They differ primarily in that (1) the bus topology offers, at least theoretically, a more reliable network, in that forwarding is not required; (2) the ring topology is more receptive to fiber-optic links than is the bus (a point discussed later in this chapter); and (3) the ring offers the possibility of a so-called automatic-acknowledging feature, as discussed in chapter 3.

The bus topology predominates for a variety of reasons, including (1) its inherent resistance to single-point failures, a feature resulting from the absence of a need to relay messages; (2) the availability of technology, such as cable television, to reliably support bus-oriented high-bandwidth local networks; and (3) the ease of accommodation of the topology in a room, building, or complex of buildings in which the local network is to be realized. Oddly, the last factor is often the deciding one in topology selection, especially when we note that the technology that supports busses can also support rings.

Sample Systems

In this section we present a sampling of local networks that employ the bus or ring structure. The examples given here were designed for one or more of the reasons given in chapter 1.

The University of Minnesota Network

The topology of the University of Minnesota network is a bus, as shown in figure 2–7. In the figure, the broken lines represent the local-network interconnections, the solid lines are conventional mainframe channel-to-device connections, and the dash-and-dot line is a special-purpose link

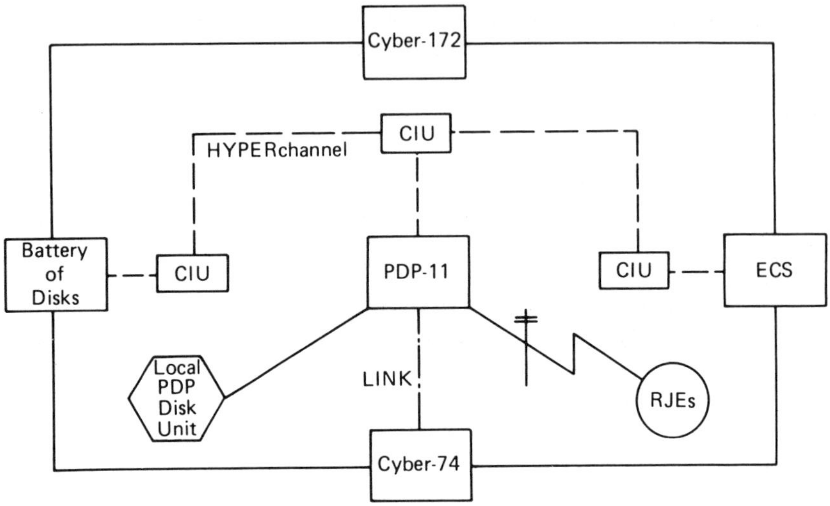

Note: The Cyber-172 is used primarily as an interactive machine, the Cyber-74 primarily as a batch machine.

Figure 2–7. The University of Minnesota Network

connection that aided development of the local network by allowing down-line loading of PDP programs from the Cyber-74. The configuration can be viewed as a back-end storage network (BSN), with the battery of disks as the back-end store.

The network developed at the University of Minnesota indicates the power of the BSN approach, a power perhaps not yet fully appreciated. For some years, the university has been operating a remote job-entry system, using a PDP-11 as a front-end communications device. Data are transmitted to and received from the PDP-11 by numerous remote job entry (RJE) stations. The front end communicates with a university-designed interface, called LINK, connected to a Cyber-74 channel. The data are passed over this channel to the Cyber peripheral processor units and, after several passes through the Cyber, find their way to disk storage. After job completion, the output, which is on disk, goes through several levels of storage transmission internal to the Cyber-74 and, finally, wends its way to the PDP-11 and thence to the RJE station. This procedure is being replaced by the network operation shown in figure 2–7.

The configuration in figure 2–7 reduces not only most of the PDP-to-Cyber data-transfer times but also practically all of the software overhead needed to get the data to and from the RJE stations. Data will be transferred directly from the PDP-11 to the appropriately selected disk via the CIUs of the local network. An additional benefit results from the storage of disk-track tables outside the Cyber-74 main memory; when the Cyber-74 or Cyber-172 goes down, the current disk-storage indexes are not lost, and communication with the RJE sites may continue. This situation illustrates the data-transfer efficiency and fail-safe nature of the approach. Load balancing between the Cyber-74 and the Cyber-172 is also possible. Finally, as the configuration saturates, additional mainframes, either general or special-purpose, can be added to the network to increase installation computing capacity.

A Large Shared-Database System

Figure 2–8 shows a complex bus-oriented topology in which multiple busses and multiple CIUs are used (1) to enhance network reliability and (2) to decompose the network into segments. The figure shows work stations that are connected to and share a Cyber-203 pipeline processor as well as a large secondary-storage system managed by a Cyber-18.

The Lawrence Livermore Laboratories System[a]

The Lawrence Livermore Laboratories (LLL) system, known as Octopus, has evolved over the last fourteen years. It may be the oldest example of a local network. It was originally conceived as a star network, with a central switching node, but for a variety of reasons it evolved into a network based on functional partitioning.

The basic idea of the functional approach, as shown in figure 2–3, is a separate subnetwork for each function that is shared by the worker computers. Figure 2–4 is a diagram of the generic form of a typical subnetwork. Each subnetwork consists of a connection to each worker computer, a buffer memory, and a subnetwork control computer. The buffer memory may be the same as that of the subnetwork control computer or it may be a separate high-performance, high-capacity memory (possibly including disks). The subnetwork control computer and buffer memory are replicated for redundancy or to provide increased capacity to handle the many attached devices, as in the case of the terminal subnetwork. These replicated systems are interconnected for their appropriate function. The interfaces to the worker computers from the buffer memories are bit-parallel (the older interfaces can operate at 10 Mb/s). The new mass-memory Multi Access Storage System (MASS) subnetwork-to-worker interface can operate at 40 Mb/s, and the Computer Hardcopy Output System (CHORS) subnetwork interface is a simulated tape drive. The bandwidth of the buffer

[a]Adapted from Watson [72], with permission.

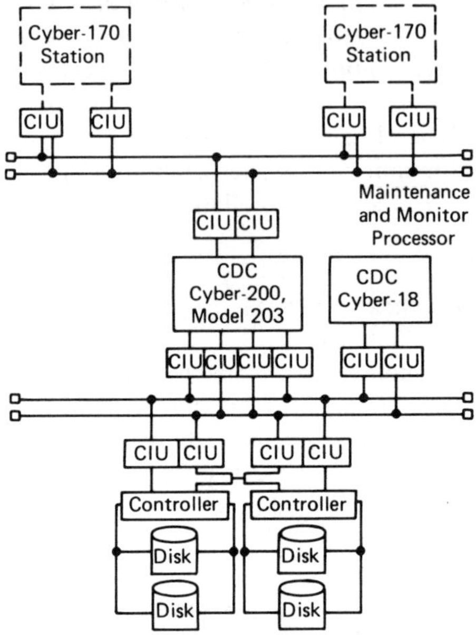

Figure 2–8. A Network Supporting a Shared, Managed Data Base

memory ranges from 16 Mb/s in the terminal subnetwork to 270 Mb/s in the MASS subnetwork. As shown in figure 2–3, the interconnections between the computers in the terminal subnetwork and between the control computers in the subnetworks are via 50 Kb/s serial store-and-forward packet-switching technology.

The various subnetworks shown in figure 2–3 were developed at different times during the evolution of Octopus. Using this approach, each new subnetwork can be introduced into the system with minimal interference with the existing network. In this way, problems within a subnetwork can be isolated from the rest of the network, and the communications technology and control computers can be sized for their application.

The subnetwork approach provides a good safety margin of excess average bandwidth. The functional separation of shared resources and associated control computers has been very successful and will be continued with modifications, as will be described.

The main problem with the functional-subnetwork approach is that, as time has elapsed, the desired cross-communications between subnetwork functions are awkward because of the enforced hardware topology (high-speed paths between the networks exist only through the worker computers).

The CPU cycles and main memory space of worker computers are always in short supply, and to use them as switching nodes is undesirable. For example, the movement of files between an older mass-storage-system subnetwork to a newer one cannot take place directly. Files cannot be moved from RJE terminals directly to mass storage or high-speed, high-capability output, nor from central-file storage to high-speed output devices. To provide more flexibility, the store-and-forward technology used within the terminal subnetwork has been extended, as previously mentioned, to interconnect several of the subnetworks for control-message transmission. An even more serious limitation on cross-communication between subnetworks has been the communications-protocol architecture. There is no clearly layered set of protocols to separate interprocess and application functions, although there are some family resemblances in several of the subnetworks. Generally, for efficiency and because each subnetwork was developed by different groups at different times, the subnetworks are not fully protocol-compatible. (This lack of modularity and layered design in the protocol structure is one of the most serious restrictions on the ease of evolution of the current Octopus network.) The hardware and software architecture in several of the subnetworks is not symmetrical, which creates additional difficulties.

The worker computers are interconnected via each subnetwork, but they currently contain only software for interworker file transfer. This restriction limits the ways that users can develop their application systems for multiprocessing among the worker computers. There is no easy way within the existing framework for worker computers to share high-performance secondary storage, such as disk drives or other emerging technology. It would be useful in case of a crash of a worker computer to be able to access the secondary storage of the crashed machine so that a wider range of work could be moved and continued elsewhere.

When the hundreds of microcomputers and minicomputers within the laboratory are interconnected with each other and the central Octopus network, the need for cross-communication between subnetworks will increase further as these remote systems attempt to use various central resources. If all high-speed subnetwork data intercommunication must go through the workers, their prime computation function will be seriously degraded.

In addition to the lack of a high-speed communications path and uniform protocol family between subnetworks, it is also time-consuming, expensive, and difficult to add new worker computers or subnetworks to the system using the current approach. New workers must have interfaces custom-designed and built for each subnetwork. In turn, each new subnetwork must have interfaces built between each type of worker and subnetwork buffer memory and between each attached resource and buffer memory. For example, the CDC Star computers cannot be finally, fully integrated into the network until a three- to four-year lag from time of delivery. The result is considerable inconvenience to users whose tools and mode of working are dependent on full-network interconnections for maximum effectiveness. As a result of manpower limitations and the technical problems previously described, major new subnetworks, such as MASS and CHORS, have required several years to become operational. It is believed that the bus approach not only will simplify worker-computer interface but also will allow functional separation to be more easily performed.

As a result of this history and current state, LLL is evolving its network into the bus topology shown in figure 2–5. Figure 2–5 also shows a high-speed buffer-memory element, which consists of a large-word-addressable, random-access bulk-memory device as well as an element whose sole function is to monitor network status and collect performance data (an issue to be discussed in chapter 5).

The Cambridge Model Distributed System

The Cambridge Model Distributed System (CMDS) [73] is organized as a ring, as shown in figure 2–9. CMDS sets out to provide, by means of interconnected minicomputers and microcomputers, facilities similar to those commonly provided by a conventional time-sharing system. In CMDS, terminals called visual display units (VDUs) [73] are connected to the system via concentrators. On log-in, a user is assigned a computer from among the pool of computers available for assignment. The user has exclusive use of that computer for the duration of his session, that is, until log-off. To support the time-sharing environment, special-purpose elements are also included on the ring. The purpose of some of these elements—for

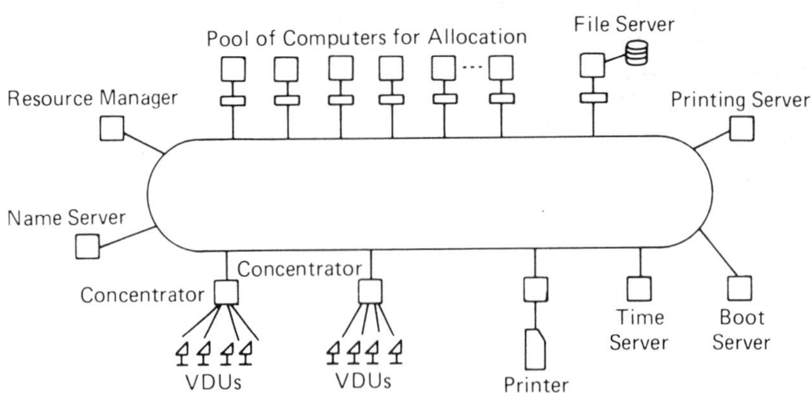

Figure 2–9. The Cambridge Model Distributed System

example, the printer and the file server—is obvious, while others, such as the name server, time server, resource manager, and host server, require explanation.

VDU Concentrator. The VDU concentrator communicates with other parts of the system. There is sufficient memory space in the Z80A microcomputer in the VDU concentrator to buffer a line being typed on each VDU and, similarly, to buffer lines received for display. The VDU program is responsible for character echoing and also provides local line-editing facilities.

Name Server. The name server plays a fundamental role in the concept of CMDS. When presented with the name of a service, a process, or a computer anywhere in the system, the name server returns the appropriate location of that item. It is also capable of performing the converse translation. The user is thus provided with a flexible system for naming and is completely freed from the need to know the physical placement on the ring of services, processes, and so forth.

File Server. The file server provides a complete filing system, which holds both user and system files in the normal manner. It can also be used as a backing store; that is, it can be used for swapping or overlaying the contents of the high-speed memory of a computer, with the transfer speed limited, of course, by the speed at which the ring operates.

Printing Server. The printing server provides spooling facilities and facilities for printing files. It also provides certain formatting services. It can receive documents to be printed from a number of users in an interleaved manner and is responsible for scheduling their ultimate printing. In short, the printing server provides services similar to those provided by the supervisor in a time-sharing system. It makes use of the file server for storage. The printer itself is not connected directly to the printing server but is separately interfaced to the ring. The arguments that led to the adoption of this somewhat nonobvious division of labor will be explained in chapter 6.

Time Server. The time server is a Z80A microcomputer connected to a radio receiver that receives continuous date and time signals (including pulses at one-second intervals) transmitted on 60 kilocycles per second (kHz) from a nearby radio station. On request, the time server supplies the date and time to the nearest millisecond.

Boot Server. All the servers in the system are provided with a bootstrap routine in read-only memory. This routine is automatically activated when a server is switched on and causes an application to be made to the boot server, which holds the programs required for the initial loading of the various computers in the system. The boot server recognizes (from tables) what the function of each server is and delivers to it along the ring a program (normally, the initial program required), which it proceeds to load into its memory. It may happen, however, that the initial program is too long to be stored conveniently in the boot server; in these circumstances, the server uses the program it obtains from the boot server to enable it to obtain the initial program from the file server. In addition to bootstrapping automatically when it is switched on, a server can be caused to reboot itself at any time by being sent a special message along the ring, which is recognized by the server CIU. This feature is especially useful when recovering from system failure.

Resource Manager. The resource manager is responsible for validation of user log-in information, assignment of other servers to users, and integrity of the system.

The Electronic Office

The electronic office is typified by bus-topology systems, as depicted in figure 2–10. Users interface to the network via work stations, which generally consist of microcomputer-based systems with a raster-oriented display and several megabytes of secondary storage. These work stations directly support a language processor, such as Pascal, and are sufficient for a variety of computational tasks. In an environment in which users are scientists or engineers, the work stations' programming-language tools would be used directly, whereas, in an environment in which the users are not programmers (for example, clerks in an office), the language tools probably would not be

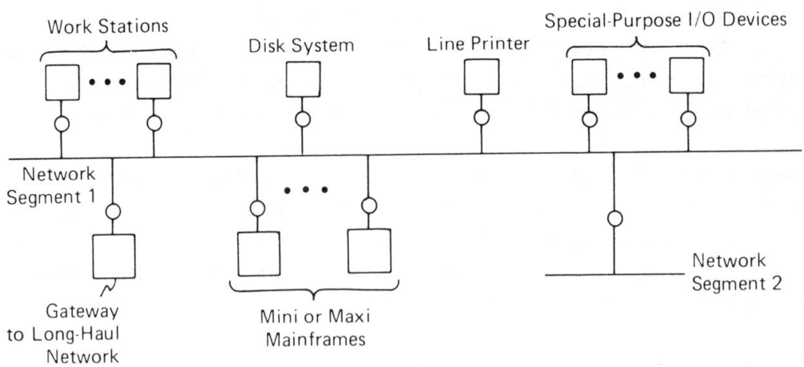

Figure 2–10. Generic Electronic Office Network

used directly. Rather, users in the latter category would interact with systems and programs prepared by programmers and resident either on the work-station local store or on a shared-network secondary store.

Office systems might also contain (1) large computers, which can be accessed by users for computationally demanding tasks; (2) a collection of shared input-output devices (for example, typesetters); and (3) access paths, or gateways, to long-haul networks. Finally, special CIUs are generally provided to connect segments of the local network, as shown in figure 2–10. Networks in this class clearly represent the largest market for local networks.

Other Examples

Many other examples are available, including a number of pioneering efforts that were realized by the in-house development of both hardware and software by a number of universities, contract-research companies, and industrial organizations. Some of these efforts are summarized in table 2–1 (the column labeled *protocol* will be discussed in chapter 3). Additional general discussions can be found in [2, 3, 4, 5, 8, 9, 10] and extensive bibliographies are given in [1, 11]. Several of these and other commercial networks are discussed in detail in chapter 6.

Transmission Media

As a network presupposes communication, a word is in order about the media which carries that communication. Local networks are generally supported by coaxial cable, radio, satellite, and fiber-optics based communication channels. Most networks employ only one of the named media, the most prevelant being coaxial cable, although some employ two or more media, for example, satellite and coaxial cable, or coaxial cable and radio. Adequate coverage of the technology associated with each medium requires a separate volume. Here we briefly characterize each medium.

Coaxial Cable

The transmission medium most often used in local networks is coaxial cable. Its popularity is due to its moderate cost, high bandwidth, and low bit error rate. It is used either to support a baseband channel, or a broadband channel.

With baseband, the coaxial cable is used to provide a single channel. With this approach baseband (square wave) signaling is used to place digital signals directly on the cable; signals which propagate in both directions along the length of the cable from the point of origin. Baseband coax has been used

Table 2–1
Summary of Experimental Local-Network Systems

System	*Topology*	*Protocol*	*Bandwidth*	*Node Cost ($)*	*Vintage*
Star Nets					
C.mmp/Carnegie [29]	Star	Ad hoc	?	?	1976
Pluribus/BBN [51]	Star	Packet switching	250 kb/s	5,000	1976
Ring Nets					
CDS/Irvine [32]	Ring	Marker	2.3 Mb/s	1,000	1973
Cambridge [73]	Ring	Marker	10 Mb/s	300	1977
MIT-LCS [7, 15]	Ring or bus	Contention	1–8 Mb/s	2,000	1977
Spider/Bell Labs [16]	Ring	Central			
Bus Nets					
Ethernet/Xerox [54]	Bus	CSMA-CD	3 Mb/s	500	1974
Fibernet/Xerox [19]	Bus	CSMA-CD	150 Mb/s	0	1978
Ford [38]	Bus	CSMA-CD	1.3 Mb/s	1,000	
NBS [57]	Bus		1–2 Mb/s	2,500	1977
ENET/Queen Mary College [114]	Bus	CSMA-CD	3–5 Mb/s	500	1977
CNET/Queen Mary College [114]	Bus	CSMA-CD	100 kb/s	200	1977
HYPERchannel/NCS [100, 112]	Bus	CSMA	50 Mb/s	25,000	1975
BATNET/PNL [39]	Bus	CSMA	3 Mb/s	2,000	1977
Distributed Nets					
Argonne National Lab [113]	Net	Packet switching	50 kb/s	10,000	1976
ICN/LASL [66]	Net	Message switching	150 kb/s	?	1976
Octopus/LLL [69, 72]	Net	Packet switching	10 Mb/s	?	1970s

Source: John M. McQuillan, "Understanding the New Local Network Technologies," Report No. 3927. (Cambridge, Mass.: Bolt Beranek and Newman, 1978). Reprinted with permission.

to support data rates up to 50 Mbs, over distances of a few thousand feet. Lower data rates can be carried over distances of a few kilometers.

Coaxial cable provides low error rates, typically between one bit in 10^7 and one bit in 10^{11} bits, depending on the network configuration. As with most transmission media, errors tend to occur in bursts rather than at random. In practice (that is, in actual local networks) the medium seems to be essentially error free. Signal propagation delay may be as low as 1.3 nanoseconds/foot or 78% the speed of light. Multi-drop configurations can be easily and inexpensively implemented with coaxial cable. Taps (device connections) for coaxial cable are inexpensive, easily installed and easily removed, generally without disturbance to the traffic on the cable. This simplicity of installation and removal of taps allows devices to be added to, deleted from, and moved with relative ease, and without impact on the operational network. Most extant local networks based on coaxial cable are baseband in nature.

Broadband-based local networks employ techniques associated with (borrowed from) the cable television (CATV), industry. Broadband CATV is a directional broadcast transmission system employing frequency division multiplexing (FDM) to divide the cable bandwidth into a number of independent channels. Local networks employing CATV techniques also employ directional transmissions. Given that transmissions are directional (instead of bidirectional as with baseband) network connectivity is obtained by having nodes transmit messages in one frequency range (upstream) to a master (head) node that retransmits them (downstream) in another frequency range for reception by all network connected nodes. The head node acts very much like a satellite transponder (discussed below) in that it continually retransmits, in a second frequency range, all incoming signals (without buffering, and so on) in a first frequency range.

Broadband has been used to support channels of up to 12 Mb/s with error rates like those for baseband.

Broadband is qualitatively different from baseband in several ways:

1. With broadband a head or master node must relay all transmissions, with baseband no master node is necessary.
2. With broadband, messages generally travel farther than with baseband in going from source node to destination node, thus increasing delays. (With baseband, the distance traveled is the distance between the source and destination node. With broadband, the distance traveled is the distance between source node and head node plus the distance between the head node and the destination node.)
3. Broadband networks may directly span up to 50km (20 km being more likely) while baseband networks generally span less than 1 km.
4. Broadband supports multiple channels on a single cable (via FDM), baseband supports only one. The collection of broadband channels can be of different bandwidth, thus facilitating the effective mixing of different kinds of traffic. (The head node maps different upstream frequencies into different downstream frequencies.) Thus broadband directly facilitates simultaneous transmission of digital, analog voice and analog video signals over a single cable, whereas baseband carries digital only. (We realize, of course, that video and voice can be digitized for transmission.) Additionally, with broadband some frequency ranges can be allocated to point-to-point connections with a degree of security (non-interference) not found with baseband.

Broadband-based networks are only discussed in this volume, in our Epilogue (chapter 8).

Optic Fibers

A fiber-optic channel possesses several attributes which make it the preferred transmission medium for some applications. First, fiber-optic channels can achieve very high transmission rates; rates in excess of 1 Giga-bit/s are possible, with error rates on the order of one bit in 10^9 bits (an experimental result for ring networks). Propagation delay is $2 \cdot 10^8$ m/s or nearly 70% the speed of light, with the channel immune to electrical interference. As fiber-optic channels have been widely used for point-to-point communications their use in ring networks is straightforward. Their use as a replacement for coaxial cable in a multidrop or multiaccess bus configuration is more difficult. The difficulty centers on the ease with which a signal originating at one node on the bus can be routed to all other connected nodes. Simple taps, as used with coaxial cable, are not viable with fiber-optic channels necessitating logically equivalent physical alternatives. One alternative calls for a physical star network (logically a bus) with the star reflecting the light incoming as one path to all other paths (and hence nodes). A second alternative "taps" are had by literally melting fiber strands together to achieve reflection. Neither approach is completely satisfactory and as a result multidrop fiber optic networks are not yet cost effective. Fiber-optic-based bus networks are not commercially available, although an experimental fiber-optic version of the Ethernet System (see chapter 6), known as Fibernet does exist. Ring-oriented fiber-optic-based networks are available.

Satellite

The class of communication satellites of interest are geo-stationary (rotating the same rate as the earth), orbiting at approximately 23,300 miles (generally in the plane of the equator) above the earth. These satellites incorporate a number of *transponders*, which receive earth-originating signals (ground station originating up-link signals) in one frequency range and broadcast them (down link signals) back to earth in a second frequency range. Most satellite transponders operate in the 3,400-6,425 MHZ range (the C band) although some operate in the 10-15 GHZ range (the Ku band). A modern satellite generally has several transponders; between 10 and 25 being typical, with each transponder having a bandwidth between 30–50 MHZ, directing its downlink signal beam to cover a designated geographic area. (As mentioned earlier, the satellite functions in a manner analagous to the head-end node used in broadband-coaxial-cable-based channels.) The most noticeable attribute of a satellite channel is the rather long delay of .24 to .27 seconds necessary for a signal to propagate from an earth station to a satellite and then back to another earth station. This delay makes satellite channels, in some sense, qualitatively different from earth-based channels (including coaxial cable) which exhibit node-to-node delays in the microsecond or millisecond range.

Satellite channel error rates are determined by a number of factors including weather conditions, activity on the sun, obstruction by the moon, orientation of the satellite relative to the earth stations (earthstation antenna elevation being a key factor), and the frequency band used by the satellite. Furthermore, errors may occur independently or in bursts. None the less, bit error rates of one bit in between 10^6 and 10^7 bits can be expected 95% to 99% of the time. Under poor conditions, such as heavy rain storms or heavy cloud cover, error rates can be expected to be much higher, say one bit in 10^4 bits, or worse.

Satellite channels are attractive because of the large geographic area that can be covered by an uplink/downlink pair (for example, nearly the entire continental United States) and the constantly falling cost of satellite channels, and ground stations made possible by rapidly improving technology.

Radio

Local networks employ two kinds of radio channels. The first kind is point-to-point in nature and is used, for example, to extend a cable-based local network segments, or connect two cable-based segments. Most channels in this category operate in the 4 and 6–11 GHz band (that is, the C band, hence potentially interfering with some satellite channels) and have bandwidths in the 1–45 Mb/s range. Equipment for this class of channels is commercially available at reasonable cost.

The second form of radio channel is broadcast in nature, with a single channel being shared (in a multi-access manner) by a collection of nodes.

These nodes may be stationary or mobile, and if mobile, may be ground, sea or air based. To keep propagation delays reasonable, say $\leq .1$s, a network must occupy less than a 100-mile area. Additionally, in order to transmit reasonably sized messages (say on the order of 2000 bits) within the delay limit mentioned above, the channel must have a data rate of a few hundred Kb/s, necessitating a channel with a bandwidth of a few hundred KHz. For realistic implementations this requires radio frequencies in at least the MHz range, and the 300 MHz–3 GHz and 3 GHz–30 GHz ranges are generally used. Because of interference, bit error rates are typically higher than with other media.

The Layered View of Network Functionality

In local networks, active elements may communicate with both passive elements and other active elements. To accommodate this exchange, elements must be compatibly interconnected to their associated CIUs, and CIUs must be compatibly connected to the network link; compatibility has both physical and logical components.

Physical compatibility concerns the rules regarding the number and nature of the electrical signals that pass from one network component (CIU or element) to another, while logical compatibility relates to the agreements under which network components exchange information, agreements that allow components to properly interpret the intent and content of received information. As mentioned in chapter 1, these rules are called *protocols*. The contemporary view of networks organizes protocols into a hierarchy of protocol layers. The lowest layer specifies the rules for the physical interconnection of network components, and the highest layer specifies the rules governing the interface to and interactions with the network by active element processes. The hierarchical layering may be either a conceptual model of the network for purposes of intellectual manageability in design and presentation or a blueprint for realization of the network, or both.

The dual nature is obviously of most interest; with it, not only does the hierarchical organization promote intellectual manageability of the network design but observance of its structure in realization gives modularity, which contributes to reliability, maintainability, and alterability (for both change in functionality and addition of functionality).

These attributes obtain from the need in a hierarchical organization to have well-defined interfaces between the layers, such that a layer's internal organization and operation can remain private to that layer. The extant hierarchical protocol models, generally developed for long-haul networks, have between five and seven layers. Figure 2–11 is a typical model.

Level 1, the physical layer, specifies the mechanical, electrical, and functional characteristics required to connect, maintain, and disconnect a physical circuit between the CIU and the element or between the CIU and the communication link.

The level-2 link layer adds addresses to outgoing messages and decodes them on incoming messages. It also provides the ability to detect and correct errors and otherwise control the flow of data across the physical link.

Levels 3 and 4 handle network control. They specify the network addressing and routing through the network, control errors, and account for services received. At these levels, the lack of established standards becomes obvious, as almost every vendor handles this in a different manner. Long-haul networks using the CCITT X.25 protocol [74] are forming a basis for

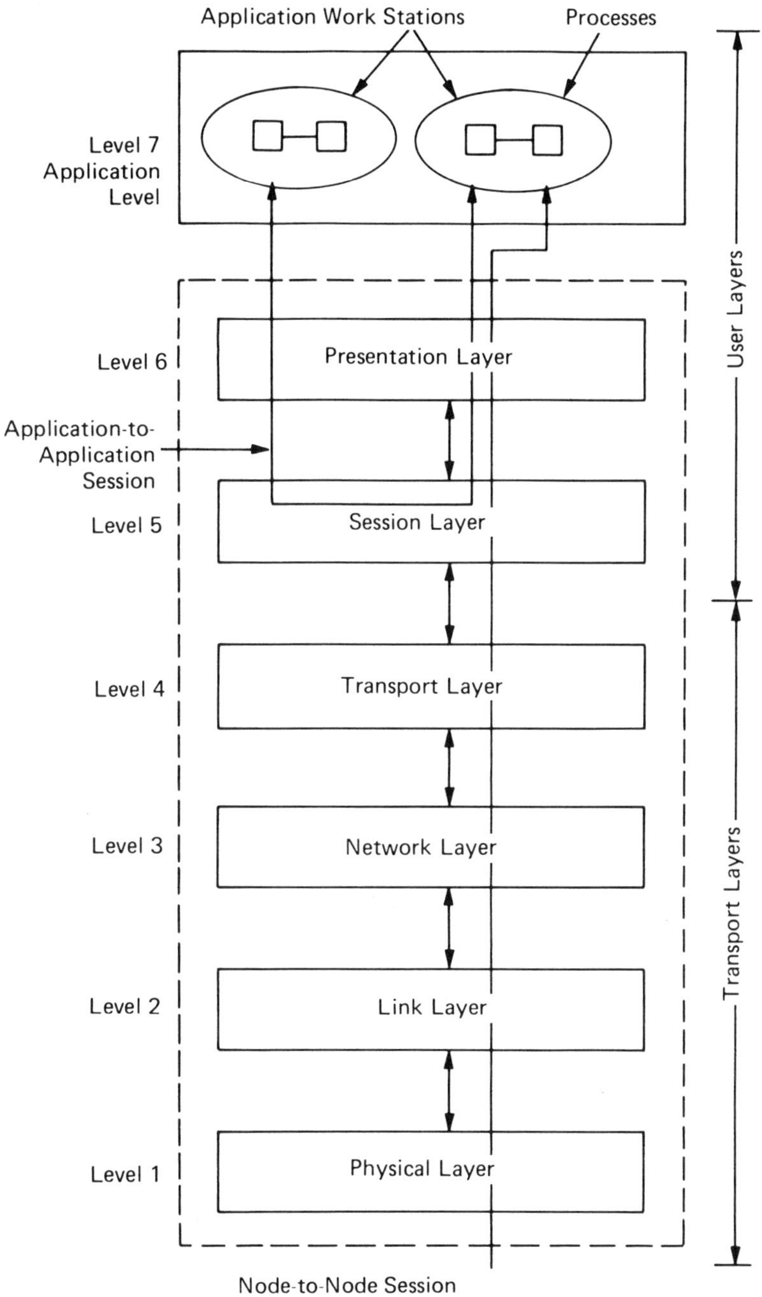

Source: *Electronics*, December 7, 1978, p. 120.

Figure 2–11. Hierarchical Network-Protocol Layers

implementing this layer, but X.25 is actually a link protocol and does not provide network-control functions.

The next three levels provide the control for application programs or jobs running in a particular element interfaced to the network. Level 5, for session control, supports a dialog, or structured message exchange, between two such programs. Level 6, the presentation layer, translates various network service-request and data formats and handles the transformation between formats. Level 7, the only one seen by the user, is the application layer, where application processes either generate or receive and interpret the messages handled by the other six levels.

As figure 2–11 indicates, the lower four layers provide a basic network-communication facility, while the top three layers are concerned with the application-processes use of the network-communication facility. For long-haul networks, there is reasonable agreement on the functionality of and interfaces to the layers 1 through 3. There is not such widespread agreement for the remaining levels. For all the obvious benefits, it is desirable to have a well-defined standard functional and interface specification for all layers, especially the lower three, because such a standard allows all vendors to produce equipment that is easily attached to a network. Five standards organizations are attacking the problem:

1. International standards organizations (ISO), a cooperative venture of more than seventy member nations.
2. Consultative Committee for International Telephony and Telegraphy (CCITT), a cooperative venture in which most countries hold membership under United Nations arrangements. (This organization is responsible for the X.25 packet-protocol standard, which standardizes levels 1 through 3.)
3. American National Standards Institute (ANSI), a well-recognized body that has published numerous national standards on a variety of subjects (the body through which the United States participates in ISO).
4. Electronics Industry Association, a trade association of U.S. electronic-equipment manufacturers, which has produced a variety of industry standards, notable among them the RS-232C standard for attaching a terminal to a computer.
5. The Institute of Electronic and Electrical Engineers Local Network Standards Committee (see reference [10] in chapter 1).

Draft standards, such as the X.25 standard, have been drawn up by these groups. These draft standards are now being circulated to the member countries, but voting on agreement with the proposed standards probably will not occur until late 1981, although pressures to network may hurry the procedure.

For local networks, the process is not so well advanced, especially when we consider that the levels and interfaces suited to long-haul networks are not well suited to local networks. For example, consider the lowest-level layer. In long-haul networks, nodes are connected to low-bandwidth point-to-point links, whereas in local networks, nodes are connected to high-bandwidth bus-oriented nets. As a consequence, local networks employ protocol options that are not viable in long-haul networks, and the reverse.

Nonetheless, it is both possible and desirable to produce a hierarchial layering of protocols for local networks. This layering in all likelihood would remain much like the layering of figure 2–11 for its user levels and would be unique to local networks in its transport levels. The need for such a local-network protocol standard is no less urgent than it is for long-haul networks, since the standard holds the key to the compatibility of different manufacturers' equipment, especially CIUs, so that, at the very least, it is possible to employ CIUs from several manufacturers on a single local network.

Transport-Layer Protocols

The transport-service layers for a local network might include:

Level 1, the physical layer, which specifies the electrical and functional characteristics necessary to interface an element to a CIU and a CIU to the network channel;

Level 2, the access layer, which specifies the mechanisms for CIU access to the channel, message format, transmission rules for outgoing messages, channel-monitoring and message-receipt rules, received-message error-detection rules, and transmission-acknowledgement rules;

Level 3, a combination of levels 2 and 3 in figure 2–11, which specifies addressing-information rules for outgoing messages, monitoring and regulation rules to control the flow of messages to nodes, and rules to initiate and terminate extended-message transfer sequences (often called *virtual circuits*).

Although our layering is typical, it is not definitive, as a standard does not exist.

Level-1 Protocols. It is desirable to organize the protocols so that host-to-CIU and CIU-to-channel message transfers can overlap in time. The host-to-CIU and CIU-to-channel interfaces, however, are generally half-duplex. The suggested overlap insures that messages coming in to a CIU will not be rejected or lost because of ongoing CIU-to-host activity, and the half-duplex measure represents the lowest-cost practical option.

CIUs must connect to mainframe or device elements. For device elements, they generally connect to the device controller. For mainframe elements, they connect either to a direct memory access (DMA) interface or to a channel interface with the information (message) transfer interrupt-driven, programmed, or under direction of a channel program. We clarify these options by the following characterizations:

> Channel-program information transfer: an option found on many large-scale hosts in which host-to-CIU transfers are under the direction of a channel program executed by a channel processor, which executes the channel program in parallel with central processing unit (CPU) execution, with transfers to or from the CIU and central-processor memory.
>
> Interrupt-driven information transfer: an option by which, each time the CIU has a unit of information to transmit to the host or the CIU is ready to accept a unit of information from the host, the CPU is interrupted and (generally) actively participates in the transfer of information, which may be to or from host-memory or host-processor registers (termed *programmed input-output*), depending on the host input-output instructions employed.
>
> Direct memory access: an option in which host-to-CIU transfers are initiated by the CPU, after which the actual transfer is made to or from CPU memory (via the processor-memory bus) by the DMA controller that is (generally) resident in the CIU, with CPU and controller interleaving use of the memory bus and memory unit.

We have hedged our explanations with "generally," because several variants of these three schemes are possible. Generally, channel-program or DMA transfers can accommodate high-speed transfers and are therefore employed with large CPUs. Interrupt-driven (including programmed) and DMA transfers are usually employed with minicomputers and microcomputers, with DMA providing the greater speed. These options require both complex and high-speed CIU logic, as found in the HYPER channel and examples in chapter 6, for large-scale mainframes. For microprocessors, slower, less-complex logic suffices as found, for example, in the PERQ example in chapter 6.

Similar observations are true for CIUs that attach to device elements via the device controller, which regulates the transfer of information to or from the device. The controller may be very simple (virtually nonexistent) for such devices as a terminal or very complex for such devices as a battery of large-capacity, high-speed disks. Generally, speaking, the CIU must interface to the device controller in the same manner as a host must when the device is directly connected. Thus, the CIU must accommodate a DMA, programmed, and so on, connection to the device controller, as appropriate.

Level-2 Protocols. We have described local networks as resulting from the interconnection of elements via a shared communication channel. The shared channel may be coaxial-cable-based, fiber-based, microwave-based, satellite-based, or radio-based.

Multimedia networks, such as the one depicted in figure 2–12, do not change this basic characteristic. The figure depicts a network that is composed of three cable-based segments interconnected by satellite and microwave links. Two circumstances are possible. Either the link nodes forward all local-segment messages, so that they may be considered segment extenders, or they forward only those messages addressed to elements that are attached to other segments, in which case they may be considered gateways. In either case, the channels are shared by multiple nodes. The basic task of the level-2 access protocol is to multiplex use of the shared channel over the set of nodes that are logically connected to it, in a manner that provides an acceptable level of service to those nodes. The measures of acceptability vary. Frequently employed measures concentrate on:

1. The presence or absence of fairness in allowing the nodes channel access;
2. The amount of information the channel must carry to allow shared channel use;
3. The reliability or robustness of the protocol in the face of channel noise and CIU and element failure;
4. The CIU requirements that are imposed;

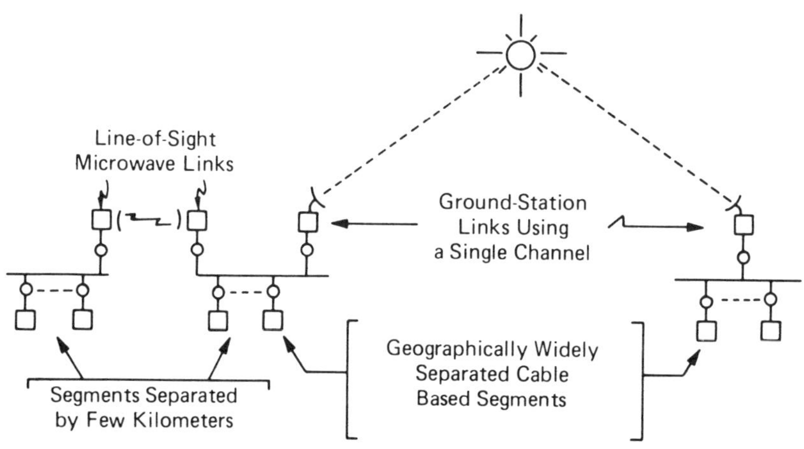

Figure 2–12. Multiple-Segment Multimedia Local Network

5. The delay suffered by a node in attempting to transmit a message; and
6. The channel utilization, that is, the fraction of channel bandwidth used to transmit application messages, achievable as a function of the total node-transmission demand on the channel.

Furthermore, not all access protocols are applicable to all network topologies, environments, or channels. Some, for example, are suited to the long delays associated with satellite channels. Some requirc a simultaneous transmit-and-receive capability, found only with cables. Some require CIU random-number generation or interval-timer capabilities, which may not be appropriate for reasons of cost, reliability, and the like. Some are applicable only to ring networks. Some only work well under specific node-to-node message-traffic patterns. These issues play a key role in CIU access-protocol selection, the topic discussed in chapters 3 and 5.

Control Strategy. Many familiar access strategies are variants on the notion of polling, wherein a single CIU is designated the master (the others are slaves), which in some order signals each CIU that it may transmit a message. CIU designs have tended to avoid poling-based access protocols for two reasons: (1) the master represents a potential single point of network failure; and (2) other strategies (to be discussed) are demonstrably more acceptable (or at least as acceptable), as gauged by the measures of acceptability listed previously.

It is true that, after a finite delay, slaves can notice the failure of the master and, by prearrangement or some form of election, can agree on a new master and proceed. The point is that failure detection and reassignment of master status requires CIU functionality and introduces network delays that are avoidable if other strategies are used.

The other strategies are based on notions of node homogeneity. That is, a node is not assigned the right to transmit by a master; rather, all nodes obey the same (or very similar) access strategy and individually determine when they may transmit. The degree to which and manner whereby the strategy forces node cooperation determines the overall characteristics of the strategy.

Strategies by which nodes cooperate to some degree and individually determine when they might transmit are said to exhibit distributed control, whereas those that require a master exhibit centralized control. "Other" category schemes generally exhibit distributed control. These schemes may or may not be fair, in the sense of giving each node an equal number of opportunities to transmit. (Fairness does not imply that equal channel bandwidth is used by each node but rather that consecutive assignments of the channel to a node are bound by a finite number of assignments to all other nodes, independent of the transmission demands or needs of the other nodes.)

Bursty Traffic. In many local networking environments, the transmission needs of a node obey some kind of statistical process. That is, for certain idle periods, a node may have no need to transmit. These idle periods alternate with busy or ready periods during which a node has one or more messages to transmit. The durations of idle periods, as well as the number and length of the messages transmitted during ready periods, are often best characterized by random variables. The term *bursty* is used to capture the seemingly inherent random (or probabilistic) qualities of the node message-transmission needs. We say "seemingly inherent," because some deep (usually unreachable) understanding of network interactions may reveal that node idle and ready patterns are very deterministic. As in the case of queuing theory and the waiting-line system, however, probabilistic assumptions nicely serve to characterize node (and hence network) behavior. From probabilistic assumptions, we may conclude, for example, at least approximately, that the instantaneous demand for the shared channel will be equal to the sum of the average demands of the nodes (as characterized by the averages of the random variables previously described, and hence we can determine an adequate channel bandwidth for the given local-network environment.

Many of the access protocols that are most often used in local networks are well suited to nodes exhibiting bursty behavior. We must note, however, that, although bursty behavior is prevalent, it is not pervasive. In certain process-control environments, message traffic is more regular or cyclic than bursty, and in these environments it is best to avoid use of certain access strategies that are best suited to bursty environments.

A Taxonomy of Access Strategies. The protocols that multiplex node accesses to a shared channel are known as *multiaccess protocols*. They can be classified according to a number of criteria, including:

1. The amount of information necessary to protocol operation;
2. Whether they exhibit centralized or distributed control;
3. Whether or not they exhibit a measure of fairness;
4. The degree to which their multiplexing scheme adapts to changes in node demands for the channel; and
5. The level of node cooperation demanded by the protocol.

Based on criteria 4 and 5, we can characterize access protocols as fixed assignment, random assignment, demand assignment, or adaptive assignment [75]. A taxonomy of access protocols organized along these lines is shown in table 2–2.

Fixed-Assignment Protocols. Fixed-assignment protocols allocate channel bandwidth to nodes in a static fashion. A classic example is given by the

Table 2–2
Taxonomy of Distributed-Control Access Protocols, with Typical Protocols for Each Class.

		Demand Assignment		
Fixed Assignment	*Random Assignment*	*Centralized Control*	*Distributed Control*	*Adaptive Assignment*
ATDMA [86] FDMA TDMA [85]	ALOHA [20, 21, 87, 88, 89] BTMA [91] (R) CSMA [54, 90] (several variants) CSMA-CD [92] Slotted-ALOHA [88] SSMA [93, 94] (R, S)	TDMA CSMA [43] (L) Polling [23, 41] Probing [42] SRMA [23] TDMA	BRAM [98] FIFO-R [96] MSAP [99] PSD [100] R-ALOHA [95] Register Insertion [102, 103, 104] RRR [97] Slotting [105, 106, 107] SUPBRAM [108] (R) Token Passing [101] VDPA [33]	A SUPBRAM [110] (R) P-BRAM [98] PODA [120] (S) RUC [111] (R, S) SRUC [111] Urn Scheme [109]

A-SUPBRAM: Adaptive SUPBRAM
ATDMA: Asynchronous Time-Division Multiple Access (also known as statistical multiplexing)
BRAM: Broadcast-Recognizing Access Method
BTMA: Busy-Tone Multiple Access
CSMA: Carrier-Sense Multiple Access
CSMA-CD: Carrier-Sense Multiple Access with Collision Detection
FDMA: Frequency-Division Multiple Access
GSMA: Global-Scheduling Multiple Access
MSAP: Minislotted Alternating Priorities
P-BRAM: Parametric BRAM
PODA: Priority-Oriented Demand Assignment
Probing: Adaptive Polling
PSD: Prioritized Staggered Delay
R-ALOHA: Reservation ALOHA
RRR: Round-Robin Reservation
RUC: Reservation upon Collision
SRMA: Split-Channel Reservation Multiple Access
SRUC: Split RUC
SSMA: Spread-Spectrum Multiple Access
SUPBRAM: Supervisory-Node BRAM
TDMA: Time-Division Multiple Access
VDPA: Vector-Driven Proportional Access

Only applicable to or intended for:
(L) = Cable-based channels
(R) = Radio channels
(S) = Satellite channels

time-division multiple-access (TDMA) protocol, which segments time into slots of a width sufficient to transmit a fixed-sized message. Slots are assigned to nodes in a fixed order, such as "round robin," such that a node transmits when its slot passes (in the time sense) if it is ready. If the node is not ready when its slot passes, the channel bandwidth remains unused for the duration of the slot. TDMA exhibits distributed control, fairness, no adaptability, and a high level of node cooperation. As might be imagined, it is not well suited to bursty traffic.

Random-Assignment Protocols. Random-assignment protocols attempt to be responsive to bursty node-transmission needs by allowing nodes to individually determine when they might transmit by observing channel state (busy or idle). The simplest example is the ALOHA protocol, wherein nodes completely ignore channel state and transmit whenever a need arises. Obviously, a time-overlapped use of the shared channel by two or more nodes can result, and overlapped channel use destroys the integrity of the overlapped messages. The messages involved in the overlapped channel use are said to collide. All colliding messages are destroyed by the collision and must be retransmitted. To avoid continual additional collisions, nodes randomize retransmission attempts by delaying retransmission, following collision, by a randomly determined interval. A number of variants on this theme are possible. Those wherein nodes actually examine channel state and refrain from transmission so long as the channel is busy are more acceptable. The refraining node is said to defer to an ongoing transmission. A node having exercised deference—a listen-before-transmit (LBT) feature—may continually monitor the channel until it becomes idle or periodically recheck channel state until it is found idle, each option favoring a different strategy on when transmission might be attempted. We note that deference does not eliminate collisions, for, even with deference, multiple nodes may detect that the channel is idle and transmit.

For all variants, in order to insure retransmission of colliding messages, collision must be detected. Collision may be detected in two ways: nodes either use an interval timer and acknowledgment messages or employ a listen-while-transmit (LWT) feature. With the first option, after transmission, a transmitting node waits a specified period for an acknowledgment message to be returned from the node addressed in its previous transmission. If an acknowledgment is received, the transmission arrived intact. If no acknowledgment arrives within the specified period, the transmitting node assumes that the integrity of its transmission was destroyed, by either channel noise or collision, and it initiates its retransmission sequence. Furthermore, if acknowledgment messages are not given special priority, as they are in some protocols, they, too, can be involved in collisions, and a receiving node must also be able to identify and discard multiple copies of a received message after having transmitted an acknowledgment for each copy received.

The interval-timer technique requires that a receiving node be able to detect receipt of defective messages, that is, messages destroyed by channel noise or collision. (Note that a node may not attempt receipt if the address portion of the message is destroyed by collision.) The technique generally employed is the so-called cyclic-redundancy check (CRC) scheme, whereby (1) the transmitting node calculates a unique, real-valued function $f(.)$, using the message M as argument, and transmits $f(M)$ as a portion of the message; and (2) the receiving node calculates $f(M')$, using the received message M' as argument, and compares $f(M)$ with $f(M')$. If $f(M')$ as calculated equals $f(M)$ as received, the message is declared intact, and an acknowledgment is issued; otherwise, no acknowledgment is issued. Note that the technique is sufficient to detect message destruction from either noise or collision if $f(.)$ is properly selected, a matter to be discussed in chapter 3.

The LWT detection option has a transmitting node receiving its own transmission on the fly. If, at anytime during transmission, the transmitted and received signals disagree, collision is declared, the transmission is discontinued, and the retransmission sequence is initiated. The LWT feature allows the duration of overlapped channel use to be sharply curtailed, thus nicely limiting the bandwidth that is wastefully consumed by collision. LWT is best suited to the cable medium, and its use does not obviate the use of acknowledgment messages, as it does not account for channel noise affecting the destination node (that is, the receiver) but not affecting the transmitting node.

In summary, random-access techniques exhibit distributed control, fairness, a degree of cooperation, and some adaptability.

Demand-Assignment Protocols. Demand-assignment protocols require that the communication channel, or an ancillary channel, explicitly carry the control information issued by the nodes that the nodes use to determine the access order for the communication channel. The information exchanged is either a sequence of node channel-reservation requests, confirmations, or releases. The control information may be a normal part of messages or additional information, such as a channel-ownership token. The protocols are termed *demand assignment* in that, unlike TDMA, they attempt to avoid wasted channel bandwith by avoiding assignment of the channel to idle nodes.

Adaptive-Access Protocols. Adaptive-access protocols control migration of the access mechanism as the collective node demand for the shared channel changes, so as to maintain the most acceptable level of service possible under the constraints imposed by the migration strategy and options.

As discussed in chapter 3, certain access protocols are easily identified as best suited to very low collective node demand (that is, where only a single node is ready at any time), while others are suited to very high collective node demand (that is, where each node is always ready). Access mechanisms most acceptable for midrange collective node demands are more difficult to identify, which makes the generation of migration mechanisms more difficult. Nonetheless, a few adaptive-access protocols have been described.

Stability Consideration. Random-access protocols and adaptive protocols with a large adaptive time constant exhibit an inherent instability, resulting from a positive-feedback loop created by collisions. More specifically, collisions create a need for retransmissions. Thus, from a service point of view, the channel has effectively been removed from service for the duration of the colliding-message channel-overlap time. In any service system, temporary removal of the server can only cause the queue of units awaiting service (in this case, messages) to grow beyond what it would have been if the server had remained in service.

With random-access techniques such as ALOHA, units independently and randomly assign themselves to the server (the channel), so that collisions cause an increasingly larger number of attempts to use the channel, because of the queue-lengthening phenomena, until collapse occurs, that is, until all transmission attempts result in collisions and effective channel bandwidth goes to zero.

A number of control strategies that have been developed to avoid the collapse of random-access protocols are discussed in chapter 5. The circumstance with adaptive protocols is not as well understood.

Level-3 Protocols. There is a tight coupling between level-2 and level-3 protocol functionality. In fact, the functionality we assign to each level is, in part, the result of a subjective decision. The important point, however, is that the total functionality, no matter how it is divided between levels 2 and 3, is provided by the transport level. By our partitioning of functionality, level 3 is concerned with message enveloping, message addressing, flow control, and error control, so that the transport level can provide a reliable (essentially error-free) information-transmission service. The unit of information transmitted is the frame. Frames may be of variable length either to accommodate (contain) entire messages that are of variable length or to accommodate different classes of fixed-length messages, or to accommodate both needs.

Most local networks employ variable-length frames that accommodate multiple classes of messages, with each class having a class-dependent length distibution. A few local-network designs always transmit fixed-length frames, that is, packets, such that messages larger in length than a packet must be divided into multiple frames, each of which is separately transmitted, as in packet-switched long-haul networks. Frames have a well-defined format, generally a variant of the format depicted in figure 2–13.

In figure 2–13, physical address refers to the unique integer index

Preamble	Destination Address	Source Address	Type Field	Data Field	Error-Check Field	Trailer

Figure 2–13. Frame Format

assigned to each CIU, generally by switches on the CIU, or to a logical address that is recognized as equivalent to the unique physical address by a group of CIUs. Via the group address, a node is able to broadcast a message that will be received by a known subset of the network nodes. Via broadcast, a node can, for example, broadcast a request for information or broadcast information of interest. Requests may be for a service or resources, and one or more nodes may respond to the requesting node as being willing to supply that service or resource. Information broadcasts may contain, for example, status information that the broadcasting node believes is of interest to the set of nodes in the group designated by the address used.

The data-field length depends on message type and the particular instance of message of that type. The CIU handling of the data-field contents depends on message type. A CIU may receive data from an attached element, place it in a frame, and transmit it without interpretation. Alternatively, a CIU may receive a frame and interpret the data field as a sequence of commands. We discuss these alternatives more fully in chapter 4.

The width of the addressing and type fields in a frame may be as small as six or eight bits or as large as forty-eight bits. Use of narrower bandwidths is a carry-over from frame structures used in long-haul networks, where there is a need, imposed by modest-bandwidth channels, to be concerned about the amount of overhead carried in a frame. With local networks, with wideband channels, we can be more relaxed about overhead and can provide for larger widths.

The width of the CRC field is generally taken to be sixteen bits, which is sufficient to contain the check-character sequence generated by the CCITT polynomial generator, as discussed in the previous section. CRC fields with widths as large as thirty-two bits have been proposed [76], with larger CRC fields improving control of errors.

Flow Control. Flow control is concerned with regulating the rate at which a stream of frames passes from one node (the transmitting node) to another node (the receiving or destination node). Flow control is employed to assure that streams of frames are not sent to a node at a rate too fast for the receiving node to handle the frames, that is, at a rate too fast to properly dispose of the frames according to type or at a rate in excess of that at which buffering capacity can be freed. In long haul networks complex mechanisms have been designed to realize flow control.

In local networks, because of the high channel bandwidth and the relatively low delays suffered to transmit a frame (relative to long-haul networks), simpler schemes are possible. In particular, it is often sufficient for a transmitting node not to send the next frame in a stream until (1) the receiving node has explicitly acknowledged receipt of the last-transmitted frame (via a returned acknowledgment frame), (2) the receiving node explicitly requests the next frame or frames, or (3) the sending node has knowledge of some combination of these alternatives. These mechanisms are sufficient, for example, for flow regulation precipitated by the differences in the inherent speeds of communications elements.

Mechanisms that satisfy the foregoing requirements are based on the "sliding window" concept, as discussed in chapter 3.

Error Handling. Error-handling mechanisms are designed to insure that frame transmission is reliable. Error-handling schemes must therefore be able to detect faulty frame transmission and to take appropriate action when errors occur. The detection process is associated with the level-2 protocol when the mechanism employed is the CRC or an LWT feature. When acknowledgment frames provide the assurance of proper frame delivery, interval timers must be used to determine how long the transmitting node should wait for an acknowledgment frame before deciding that the previously transmitted frame did not arrive intact at its intended destination.

Generally, proper action on faulty transmissions is a retransmission attempt, an attempt precipitated by the level-2 or level-3 protocol. Because of the low error-rate characteristics of the local network channel and the ability of the randomization techniques associated with the access protocols to sort out collisions, the retry mechanism is generally sufficient.

Continued inability to transmit a frame successfully generally signals a failed CIU or faulty channel, and proper procedure under such a circumstance is application- or network-environment-dependent.

Summary. In summary, it is the function of the network-transport protocol to provide a so-called datagram service, a basic service providing reliable delivery of a group-addressed message or frame, without regard to whether or not the message (frame) is one in an ordered stream of frames. Additionally, the network-level protocols must provide the flow-control and sequencing capabilities necessary to properly regulate the flow of long sequences of frames. These stream-support mechanisms are referred to as virtual connections or virtual circuits; in addition to regulating frame flow between connected nodes, they provide mechanisms to establish connections and mechanisms to terminate connections, and they support frame-sequence-number schemes to guarantee a properly ordered sequence of delivered frames.

The X.25 protocol, the proposed long-haul network standard, contains all the features we have described. A detailed description of X.25 may be found in Davies et al. [74].

User-Layer Protocols

User-level protocols directly support applications and, as figure 2–11 indicates, are realized using functionality associated with the lower-level protocols. Whereas a single transport-level protocol serves all nodes, multiple user-level protocols, each serving a specialized need, are in order. In a local network, each node need not support the full complement of user-level protocols supported in the network, but only those germane to the element type that constitutes the node. As with the transport protocols, design of user-level protocols involves resolution of issues relating to addressing, flow control (synchronization), and error control. For user-level protocols, the issues revolve about application processes (rather than network-support processes), and the designer of user-level protocols may assume, that is, employ as building blocks, the reliable datagram and virtual-connection mechanisms provided by the lower levels.

Sometimes, the user level is no more complex than a direct application of the transport-level datagram service. For example, for the network depicted in figure 2–9, a simple datagram would be sufficient to inform the resource manager of a release-of-resource intent. Securing of a resource is only slightly more complex, requiring a request-resource datagram, a confirmation-of-assignment datagram, and the understanding by the requesting process that the resource must not be used until the confirmation datagram is received. Thus, securing a resource may be accomplished directly by multiple invocations of the network datagram service. It may also be had by single use of a proper interprocess communication (IPC) primitive, which has been realized using the datagram service. We shall examine this latter alternative in chapter 4.

More elaborate protocols are also necessary to support, for example virtual terminals, giving uniform network or host access; file transfer; remote job entry; digital voice transmission; graphics-display information exchanges; distributed-database (DDB) queries and updates [78]; electronic mail [77], and electronic conferencing [77]. Protocols for some of these needs—such as DDB updates—are realized by direct use of the network datagram service. Others—for example, a file-transfer protocol applicable to heterogeneous mainframe elements—are realized only by elaborations over and above the datagram or virtual-connection service. For example, a file-transfer protocol as described must accept multiple data formats and must transform information from one format to another.

Examples of many of these protocols have been devised for long-haul networks. As these protocols have been much written about [74], and as our intention is to avoid here material found in a number of other books, we do not present material on these protocols. This posture also offers a convenient escape mechanism, as the merits of direct use in local networks of protocols, which have been designed for long-haul networks, are not yet clear. There are some indications, however, that some or all of these protocols should be more closely integrated into a local-network operating system, a subject to be discussed in chapter 4.

A Model for CIUs

Whatever their final form, the protocol layers must be distributed between the components of a node, that is, between the CIU and its attached element. When formulating the distribution, we must remember that all nodes request the services of the transport layers but not all nodes will require the same user levels. As the extremes of distribution we can relegate all the protocol functionality to the CIUs or relegate all the protocol functionality, except layer 1, to the attached element. The second alternative results in the simplest, hence lowest-cost CIU. Additionally, it is expensive in terms of software-development needs for local networks with elements that are host computers, originally developed for stand-alone operation under complex extant operating-system software. The first alternative results in the most complex, expensive CIU but most completely relieves the attached element of network-support activity and hence reserves its capabilities for its intended native purpose.

A more balanced view results by observing that all elements require the services of the transport layers, however; and it therefore makes sense for the CIU to contain functionality for some or all of the requirements of those layers. As all elements may not require user layers, or as different elements require different user layers, it may not be necessary or desirable to include the functionality of these layers in the CIU (a circumstance that may change). On the basis of these observations, our generic CIU model is shown in figure 2–14.

CIUs have been realized that contain only level-1 functionality, for example, ALTOS [79], and that contain all functionality associated with layers 1 through 3, for example HYPER channel adaptors [80]. CIU cost, complexity, and reliability, the last of our design parameters (see chapter 2), increase not only with the bandwidth of the channel but also with the complexity of the level-1 functionality, a complexity that is determined, in turn, by the nature of the element to which the CIU attaches, and with the degree to which the functionality of protocol layers 2 and 3 are served by the CIU and the options employed within those layers. Cost increases with bandwidth, as the protocol functionality must be provided by faster CIU components. Faster components are required for a 50 Mb/s link than for a 1 Mb/s link. CIU cost, however, is dominated by the hardware and firmware necessary to interface the CIU to an element class. For example, it is far

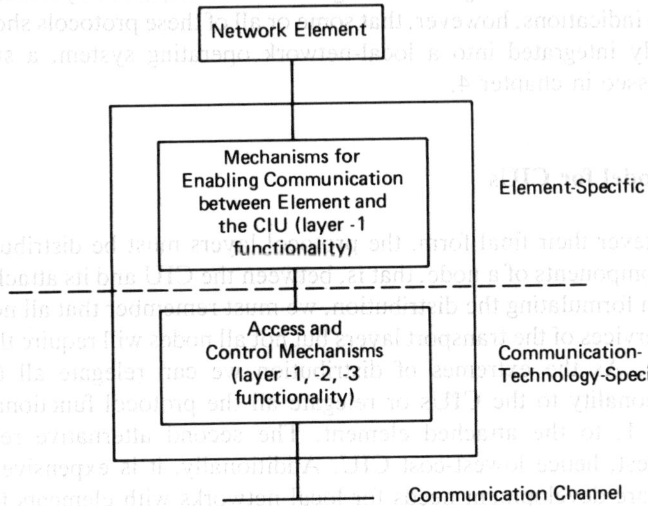

Figure 2–14. The Generic CIU Model

more complex and costly to interface a CIU to a Cyber mainframe channel than to a PDP-11/40 DMA interface or a terminal.

Hence, CIU cost is proportional to attached element cost, and, to be a viable device, CIU cost must be significantly less than the cost of elements in the class to which it connects.

The functionality shown in the block diagram in figure 2–14 is generally provided by equipping each CIU with a microprocessor with working registers and program, memory, buffer memory, and a basic sensing mechanism to detect network- or host-originated activity.

Example 2.1

Figure 2–15 gives a block diagram of the CIUs (known as network access devices, or NADs) being offered by Control Data Corporation for use in their bus-oriented Loosely Coupled Network [121]. The NAD has six functional parts:

1. The bus control interface (hardware and microcode to connect the NAD logically and electrically to the 50 Mb/s bus). This part is divided into two parts, the bus-control interface (TCI) (busses are referred to as trunks in Control Data nomenclature) and from one to four trunk-control units (TCUs), depending on the number of busses to which the CIU is attached.

2. The data set, which provides the modulation and demodulation associated with transmission of data over the coaxial cable.
3. The memory, which serves as a buffer for incoming and outgoing data and code to be executed by the processor.
4. The processor, which controls CIU resources and manages data flow.
5. The device interface to connect elements of a given class to the CIU.,
6. The serial-maintenance interface to connect a maintenance-control terminal or a device to inject an artificial message-transfer loading.

Each CIU employs a variant of BRAM for access mechanism [98]. A reference to a description of the algorithm is given in chapter 6.

Example 2.2

Figure 2–16 shows a more detailed block diagram, this time of the local-network interface (LNI) CIU being developed at the Laboratory for

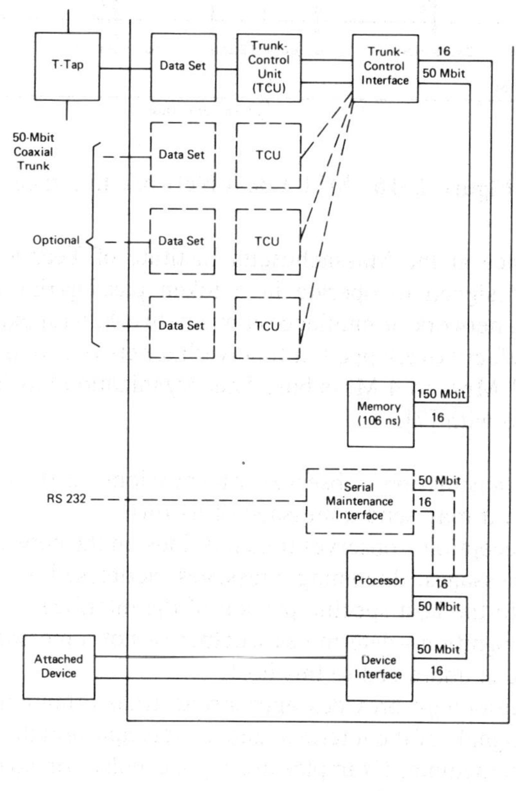

Figure 2–15. Network Access Device: Typical Loosely Coupled Network

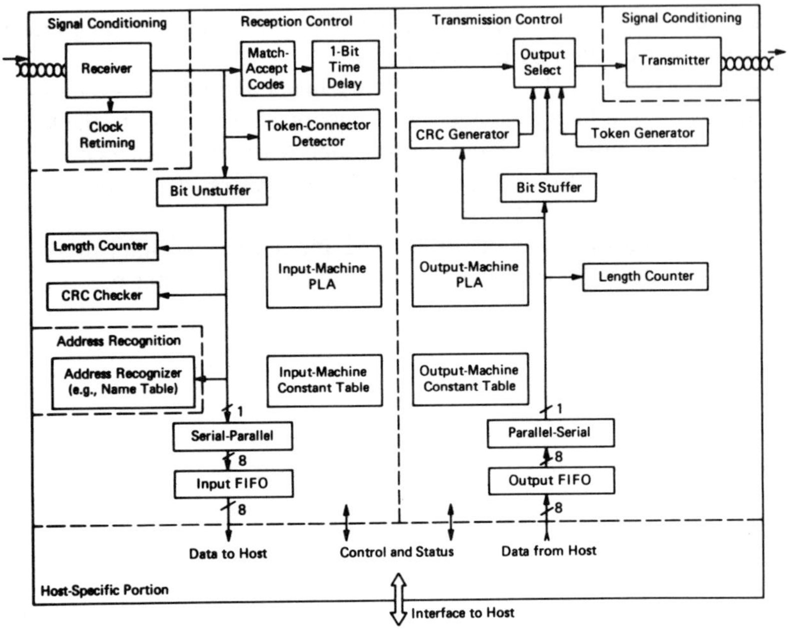

Figure 2–16. MIT Local Network Interface

Computer Science at the Massachusetts Institute of Technology [7]. The LNI is being designed to operate in a token passing-ring network or a multiaccess ring network or multiaccess bus network, with exchanges (via a DMA-host interface) overlapped in time with a network transmit or receive sequence on a 1 Mb/s to 4 Mb/s bus. This organization has four functional parts, associated with [7]:

1. Control of transmission—observes transmissions on the network, determining when it may send a message of its own.
2. Control of reception—observes transmissions on the network, looking for incoming messages. Incoming messages addressed to this host are transferred to the host-specific portion of the interface.
3. Address recognition—determines whether or not a message detected by the interface is addressed to this host.
4. Signal conditioning—provides appropriate transformations between the logic-level signals of the interface and signals appropriate to the network transmission medium. Examples are bipolar pulses on coaxial cable and light pulses on optical fibers.

Reliability

Local-network hardware promotes reliability by employing simple bus or loop topologies (perhaps with multiple busses or rings) and by employing special logic and protocols to insure that an aberrant CIU does not monopolize or logically sever the bus or ring.

Simple distributed-access-control algorithms disallow network failure to follow from failure of a central controlling CIU. When token algorithms are employed (see chapter 3), they must be able to regenerate lost tokens (caused by noise or CIU failure) and eliminate multiple tokens (resulting from lost-token regeneration algorithms). Distributed-multiaccess-control mechanisms obviously do not require recovery algorithms, which contributes to network reliability.

The bus topology at least has the potential of being more reliable than rings; in rings each CIU must regenerate each message to pass it on, whereas in bus systems all CIUs except the CIU transmitting the message remain passive, as regeneration is not necessary. Additionally, software mechanisms can be employed to enhance network reliability, a topic discussed in chapter 4.

Discussion

Various combinations of protocol levels 1, 2, and 3 can be used to realize a CIU harmoniously. Although some combinations are better than others, it is difficult to talk about a best combination, even though various options can be compared quantitatively in terms of overall channel use, delays in transmitting frames, and so forth, as we do in chapter 5. However, because various protocol combinations require different CIU functionality, which affects CIU cost and reliability, or combinations that are difficult to realize, such as the LWT feature and high-bandwidth channels, a definite best combination is illusive.

There is argument, in fact, that suggests that the entire development process has been done backwards, in the sense that local networks have been designed by first selecting the lower-level protocols, then designing and building a CIU, and then finally coupling the design with an application, rather than by developing networks from the top down [81], beginning with the application. Although top-down design is laudable, the mold is set, and it's too late to cry foul. In fact, much activity is currently under way to give certain protocol combinations the status of a local networking standard. The groups involved in this activity are those mentioned earlier, plus the IEEE Computer Society's Local Network Standards Committee [82], which is attempting to develop standards on cables used, connectors (CIU to cable), electrical signals, protocols employed (transport level), and error-checking methods. Vendor pressures have a tendency to produce de facto standards, which result from a large number of networks having been realized using a given vendor-supplied CIU. De facto standards also come about from the efforts of a conglomerate of vendors, as exemplified by the cooperative effort of Digital Equipment Corporation, Intel, and Xerox Corporation to produce a standard protocol to be realized on a chip, in which each of the partners is contributing experience or a production capability [76].

The ability to realize complete CIUs on a chip (or chip set) is in fact a strong driving force to settle on standards, as it aids in ensuring a high volume in sales for the resulting chip. As of this writing, several chips exist that support simple access-level protocols and network interfaces, but none that directly interface to elements (with the exception, perhaps, of an RS-232 interface) [116].

The prospects for local networking are enormous, and the prospect of a low-cost CIU on a chip has enormous implications, especially for the office environment, which is likely to employ CIUs connected to a 1–10 Mb/s bus. According to Doll [83]: "Essentially every business machine we have in our offices today will become a potential candidate for interconnection to the intelligent networks of the middle 1980s." Via these interconnections, teleconferencing and electronic mail [77] will take on new dimensions, and new services and functions will evolve to use them. In essence, every major office supplier, microelectronic firm, and mainframe company is either engaged in a scramble for dominance in the field or is anxiously awaiting developments before jumping in with attendant devices or ancillary services [115, 116, 117, 118, 119].

Outside the office, the high-bandwidth local network will alter the composition of the traditional computer room irrevocably. The stand-alone machine will disappear, and interconnections to promote large-scale resource sharing will predominate. In short, not only are the technological needs available to mate computing and communication, but they are available at such attractive costs as to make the psychological need for interconnection (sharing) overwhelming as a way of solving problems and providing capabilities (see chapter 1).

Local Networks and Distributed Systems

We feel compelled before closing this chapter to make a few remarks regarding how local networks and distributed systems [84] are the same and

Table 2–3
Local Computer Network Taxonomy and Systems

Evolution Context	*New System or Subsystem Concepts*				*Existing-System Improvement*		
Reason	*Distributed Processing*				*Communication Bound*	*I/O or Memory-Bound*	
Subnetwork Communication Technology	*Packet Switch (Category 1)*	*Circuit Switch (Category 2)*	*Bus Structure (Category 3)*	*I/O Channels (Category 4)*	*Packet Switch (Category 5)*	*Bus Structure (Category 6)*	*I/O Channels (Category 7)*
Major System Concepts	CMI[13] ICS[14] LCS[15] Spider[16] MITRIX[17] Ringnet[18] Fibernet[19] HMINET[20] MININET[21] Cablenet[22] DATAKIT[23] Data Ring[24] MICRONET[25] RIT Network[26] PRL Network[27]	DDN[28] C.mmp[29] PRIME[30] AN/USQ-67[31]	DCS[32] HXDP[33] DLCN[34] ADCS[35] ORION[36] DDLCN[37] FordNet[38] BATNET[39] TECHNEC[40] EPIC-DPS[41] SHINPADS[42]	DCN[43] IRCN[44] MISS[45] Iowa State-Network[46]	ISUnet[47] PRRMP[48] PROMIS[49] VICNET[50] Pluribus[51] KUIPNET[52] ARGONNE[53] ETHERNET[54] CYBERNET[55] ALOHANET[56] NBS Network[57] Computer Cells[58] Acknowledging Ethernet[59]	MITRENET[60] HYPERchannel[61] University of Delaware Network[62] University of Minnesota Network[63] Star-Shaped-Ring Network[64]	RIG[65] LASL[66] CERN[67] Labolink[68] OCTOPUS[69] GMAD Network[70] Liverpool Network[71]

how they are different. Our remarks must be taken as our own and therefore as subjective; there is no agreed-upon relationship between the two kinds of systems. First, the two notions are alike in that they employ the interconnection of intelligent elements. Both forms require CIUs and protocols, as discussed in this chapter. The two forms may differ in the sense that local networks represent an evolutionary step toward true distributed systems.

The elements in a local network are often heterogeneous and have traditionally operated under the direction of incompatible software, with the local network "patching" nodes together to work in concert. The glue is the CIU and its protocol functionality, together with software changes in extant-element resident software systems. Distributed systems are more homogeneous, especially in their software structures, and are designed rather than patched systems. With distributed systems, the CIU often assumes many operating-system functions relegated to element software in local networks. As a result of these attitudes, the system depicted in figure 2–8 is a local network, and the system depicted in figure 2–9 may be called a distributed system.

As an alternative to our comparative guidelines, we offer the taxonomy developed by Thurber and Freeman [6], shown in table 2–3, which is based on a systems-evolution context, reasons for development, and communication technology employed.

References

1. Thurber, K.J., and Freeman, H.A. "A Bibliography of Local Computer Network Architectures." *Computer Architecture News* 7 (February 1979):22–27; and *Computer Communication Review* (April 1979):1–6.
2. *Local Area Networking*. Report of a Workshop Held at the National Bureau of Standards, 22–23 August 1977. Ira W. Cotten, editor. U.S. Dept. of Commerce, National Bureau of Standards, April 1978.
3. *Proceedings of the University of Minnesota Workshop on Local Computer Networks*, 16–17 September 1976, 13–14 October 1977, and 23–24 October 1978. P.C. Patton and A. Franck, editors. University of Minnesota.
4. *Proceedings of the Local Area Communications Network Symposium*, Boston, May 1979.
5. *Proceedings of the Fourth Conference on Local Computer Networks*, Minneapolis 22–23 October 1979.
6. Thurber, K.J., and Freeman, H.A. "Architecture Considerations for Local Computer Networks." *Proceedings of the First International*

Conference on Distributed Computing Systems, October 1979, pp. 131–142.

7. Clark, D.D., Pogran, K.T., and Reed, D.P. "An Introduction to Local Area Networks." *Proceedings of the IEEE* 66 (November 1978): 1497–1517.
8. Cotton, I.W. "Technologies for Local Area Computer Networks." *Proceedings of the Local Area Communications Network Symposium*, May 1979, pp. 25–45.
9. Anderson, R.J. "Local Data Networks—Traditional Concepts and Methods." *Proceedings of the Local Area Communications Network Symposium*, May 1979, pp. 127–149.
10. Fraser, A.G. "The Present Status and Future Trends in Computer/Communication Technology." *Communications* (September 1976): 10–19, 27.
11. Shoch, J.F. "An Annotated Bibliography on Local Computer Networks." Xerox Parc Technical Report SSL-79-5, October 1979.
12. "Back-End Storage Networks." *Computer* 13 (February 1980):7–58.
13. Swan, R.J., Fuller, S.H., and Sieworek, D.P. "Cm*—A Modular Multi-microprocessor." *AFIPS Conference Proceedings* 46 (1977 National Computer Conference):637–644.
14. Hinton, O.R., et al. "Distributed Industrial Control Using a Network of Microcomputers." *COMPCON 77 Fall*, September 1977, pp. 316–319.
15. Pogran, K.T., and Reed, D.P. "The MIT Laboratory for Computer Science Network." *Local Area Networking*, NBS Special Publication 500-31, April 1978, pp. 20–22.
16. Fraser, A.G. "Spider—An Experimental Data Communications System." *ICC 74 Conference Record*, June 1974, pp. 21F-1–21F-10.
17. Willard, D.G. "A Time Division Multiple Access System for Digital Communication." *Computer Design*, June 1974.
18. Gordon, R.L., Farr, W.W., and Levine, P. "Ringnet: A Packet Switched Local Network with Decentralized Control." *Proceedings of the Fourth Conference on Local Computer Networks*, October 1979, pp. 13–19.
19. Rawson, E.G., and Metcalfe, R.M. "Fibernet: Multimode Optical Fibers for Local Computer Networks," *IEEE Transactions on Communications*, July 1978, pp. 983–990.
20. Popescu-Zeletin, R. "The Data Access and Transfer Support in a Local Heterogeneous Network (HMINET)." *Proceedings of the Sixth Data Communications Symposium*, November 1979, pp. 147–152.
21. Manning, E.G., and Peebles, R.W. "A Homogeneous Network for Data Sharing—Communications," *Computer Networks* (May 1977): 211–224.

22. Wood, D.C., et al. "A Cable-Bus Protocol Architecture." *Proceedings of DATACOM 79*, November 1979, pp. 137–146.
23. Fraser, A.G. "DATAKIT—A Modular Network for Synchronous and Asynchronous Traffic." *ICC 79 Conference Record* 2 (June 1979): 20.1.1–20.1.3.
24. Hopper, A. "Data Ring at Computer Laboratory, University of Cambridge." *Local Area Networking*, NBS Special Publication 500-31, April 1978, pp. 11–17.
25. Wittie, L.D. "MICRONET: A Reconfigurable Microcomputer Network for Distributed Systems Research." *Simulation* vol. 33, (November 1978):145–153; and 9 (April 1979):1–6.
26. Lin, K. "Design of a Packet-Switched Micro-Subnetwork," *COMPCON 78 Fall*, September 1978, pp. 184–193.
27. Burnett, D.J., and Sethi, H.R. "Packet Switching at Philips Research Laboratories." *Computer Networks* 1 (1977):341–348.
28. Springer, J.F. "The Distributed Data Network, Its Architecture and Operation." *COMPCON 78 Fall*, September 1978, pp. 221–228.
29. Wulf, W., and Levin, R. "A Local Network," *DATAMATION*, February 1975, pp. 47–50.
30. Quatse, J.T., Gaulene, Pierre, and Dodge Donald, "The External Access Network of a Modular Computer System." *AFIPS Conference Proceedings* 40 (1972 Spring Joint Conference, May 1972):783–790.
31. Sperry Univac, "AN/USQ-67 Converter—Switching System, Signal Data." Sperry Univac Product Description Bulletin, June 1977.
32. Farber, D.J. "A Ring Network." *DATAMATION*, February 1975, pp. 44–46.
33. Jensen, E.D. "The Honeywell Experimental Distributed Processor-An Overview." *Computer* 11 (January 1978):28–38.
34. Liu, M.T. "Distributed Loop Computer Networks," *Advances in Computers*, vol. 17, edited by M. Rubinoff and M.C. Yovits, pp. 163–221. New York: Academic Press, 1978.
35. Aramis, E., et al "ADCS: Aramis Distributed Computer System." *Computer Networking Symposium Proceedings*, December 1978, pp. 139–155.
36. Aramis, E., Cabanel, J.P., Dssouli, R., and Sazbon, R.D. "ORION: A New Distributed Loop Computer Network." *Computer Networking Symposium Proceedings*, December 1979, pp. 164–168.
37. Wolf, J.J., and Liu, M.T. "A Distributed Double-Loop Computer Network (DDLCN)." *Proceedings of the Seventh Texas Conference on Computing Systems*, October 1978, pp. 6-19–6-34.
38. Biba, K.J., and Yeh, J.W. "FordNet: A Front-End Approach to Local Computer Networks." *Proceedings of the Local Area Communications Network Symposium*, May 1979, pp. 199–215.

39. Gerhardstein, L.H., et al. "The Pacific Northwest Laboratory Minicomputer Network." *Proceedings of the Third Berkeley Workshop on Distributed Data Management and Computer Networks*. August 1978, pp. 144–158.
40. Huen, W., Greene, P., Hochsprung, R., and El-Dessouki, O., "A Network Computer for Distributed Processing." *COMPCON 77 Fall*, September 1977, pp. 326–330.
41. Anderson, D.R. "The EPIC-DPS: A Distributed Network Experiment." *FASCON '75 Record*, September 1975, pp. 121A–121G.
42. Kuhns, R.C., and Shoquist, M.C. "A Serial Data Bus System for Local Processing Networks." *COMPCON 79 Spring*, February 1979, pp. 266–271.
43. Mills, D.L. "An Overview of the Distributed Computer Network." *AFIPS Conference Proceedings* 45 (1976 National Computer Conferen):523–531.
44. Rosen, S., and Steele, J.M. "A Local Computer Network." *COMPCON 73 Digest*, February 1973, pp. 129–132.
45. Ashenhurst, R.L., and Vonderohe, R.H. "A Hierarchical Network." *DATAMATION*, February 1975, pp. 40–44.
46. Pohm, A.V., Davis, J.A., Christiansen, S. Bridges, G.D., and Horton, R.E. "A Network of Mini and Microcomputers for Experimental Support." *Proceedings of the Fourth Conference on Local Computer Networks*, October 1979, pp. 91–96.
47. Lee, C.C., and Pohm, A.V. "Interface Processor for High Speed Recirculating Data Network." *COMPCON 78 Fall*, September 1978, pp. 194–200.
48. Mehra, S.K., and Majithia, J.C. "A Modified Ethernet for Multiprocessor Intercommunications." *Proceedings of the Computer Networking Symposium*, December 1979, pp. 132–138.
49. Hertzberg, R.Y., Schultz, Jan R., and Wanner, James F. "The PROMIS Network." *Proceedings of the Local Area Communications Network Symposium*, May 1979, pp. 87–111.
50. Bowles, S.W. "VICNET: An X.25 Packet Switching Network." *Proceedings of the Sixth New Zealand Computer Conference* 1 (1978):83–99.
51. Mann, W.F., et al. "A Network-Oriented Multiprocessor Front-End Handling Many Hosts and Hundreds of Terminals." *AFIPS Conference Proceedings* 45 (1976 National Computer Conference):533–540.
52. Sakai, T., Hayashi, T., Kitazawa, S., Tabata, K., and Kadade, T. "Inhouse Computer Network KUIPNET." *Information Processing ZZ*, edited by B. Gilchrist pp. 161–166. North-Holland, Amsterdam, 1977.

53. Lidinsky, W.P. "The Argonne Intra-Laboratory Network." Proceedings of the Berkeley Workshop on Distributed Data Management and Computer Networks, May 1976, pp. 263–275.
54. Metcalfe, R.M., and Boggs, D.R. "ETHERNET: Distributed Packet Switching for Local Computer Networks." *CACM* 19 (July 1976): 395–404.
55. Sherman, R.H., et al. "Current Summary of Ford Activities in Local Networking." *Local Area Networking*, NBS Special Publication 500–31, April 1978, pp. 22–23.
56. Binder, R., et al. "ALOHA packet broadcasting—A Retrospect," *AFIPS Conference Proceedings* 44 (1975 National Computer Conference):203–215.
57. Carpenter, R.J., et al. "A Microprocessor-Based Local Network Node." *COMPCON 78 Fall*, September 1978, pp. 104–109.
58. Nelson, D.L., and Gordon, R.L. "Computer Cells—A Network Architecture for Data Flow Computing." *COMPCON 78 Fall*, September 1978, pp. 296–301.
59. Tokoro, M., and Tamaru, K. "Acknowledging Ethernet." *COMPCON 77 Fall*, September 1977, pp. 320–325.
60. Hopkins, G.T. "Multimode Communications on the MITRENET." *Proceedings of the Local Area Communications Network Symposium*, May 1979, pp. 169–177.
61. Thorton, J.E. "Back-End Network Approaches." *Computer*, February 1980, pp. 10–17.
62. Szurkowski, E. "A High Bandwidth Local Computer Network." *COMPCON 78 Fall*, September 1978, pp. 98–103.
63. Franck, A., et al. "Some Architectural and System Implications of Local Computer Networks." *COMPCON 78 Spring*, February 1979, pp. 272–276D.
64. Saltzer, J.H., and Pogran, K.T. "A Star-Shaped Ring Network with High Maintainability." *Proceedings of the Local Area Communications Network Symposium*, May 1979, pp. 179–190.
65. Ball, J.E., et al, "RIG, Rochester's Intelligent Gateway: System Overview." *IEEE Transactions on Software Engineering* SE-2 (December 1976):321–328.
66. Christman, R.D. "Development of the LASL Computer Network." *COMPCON 73 Digest*, February 1973, pp. 239–242.
67. Altaber, J. "Real-time Network for the Control of a Very Large Machine." *Local Area Networking*, NBS Special Publication 500-31, April 1978, pp. 5–6.
68. Yajima, S., et al. "Labolink: An Optically Linked Laboratory Computer Network." *Computer*, November 1977, pp. 52–59.
69. Fletcher, J.G., et al. "Computer Storage Structure and Utilization at a

Large Scientific Laboratory." *Proceedings of the IEEE* 63 (August 1975):1104–1113.
70. Smith, S.M. "Use of Broadband Coaxial Cable Networks in an Assembly Plant Environment." *Proceedings of the Local Area Communications Network Symposium*, May 1979. pp. 67–74.
71. Innes, D.R., and Alty, J.L. "An Intra University Network." *Proceedings of the Fourth Data Communications Symposium*, October 1975, pp. 1-8–1-13.
72. Watson, Richard W. "The LLL Octopus Network: Some Lessons and Future Directions." *Proceedings of the Third USA-Japan Computer Conference*, 1978, pp. 12–21.
73. Wilkes, Maurice V., and Needham, Roger M. "The Cambridge Model Distributed System." *Operating Systems Review* 14 (January, 1980): 21–29.
74. Davies, D.W.; Barber, D.L.A.; Price, W.L.; and Solomonides, C.M. *Computer Networks and Their Protocols*. New York: Wiley, 1979.
75. Kleinrock, L. *Queueing Systems, Volume 2: Applications*. New York: Wiley-Interscience, 1975.
76. Durniak, Anthony. "Local Networking Grabs NCC Spotlight." *Electronics* 5 June 1980, pp. 98–90.
77. Uhlig, Ronald; Farber, David J.; and Bair, James H. *The Office of the Future*. Amsterdam, North-Holland, 1979.
78. Mohan, C. "Distributed Database Management: Some thoughts and Analyses." TR-129. Department of Computer Science, University of Texas at Austin, May 1979.
79. Thacker, C.P.; McCreight, E.M.; Lampson, B.W.; Sproull, R.F.; and Boggs, D.R. "ALTO: A Personal Computer." In *Computer Structures: Readings and Examples*. New York: McGraw-Hill, forthcoming.
80. Network Systems Corporation. HYPERchannel Adaptor Product Description, 1978.
81. McQuillan, John M. "Understanding the New Local Network Technologies." Report No. 3927. Cambridge, Mass.: Bolt Beranek and Newman, September 1978.
82. Graube, Maris. "IEEE to Establish Local Networking Standards." *Computer Business News*, December 17, 1979, p. 3.
83. Doll, Dixon R. "Data Communications Forecast for the '80s." *Computer World*, 5 January 1980, p. 8.
84. Enslow, Philip H. "What Is a Distributed Processing System?" *Computer* 11 (January 1978):13–21.
85. Kosovych, O. "Fixed Assignment Access Technique." *IEEE Transactions on Communications* COM-26 (September 1978).
86. Chu, W.W. "A Study of Asynchronous Time Division Multiplexing

for Time-sharing Computer Systems." *Proceedings of the SJCC* 35 (1969):669–678.

87. Abramson, N. "The ALOHA system—Another Alternative for Computer Communications," *AFIPS Conference Proceedings* 37 (1970 Fall Joint Computer Conference):281–85.
88. Roberts, L.G. "ALOHA Packet System with and without Slots and Capture." *Computer Communications Review* 5 (April 1975):28–42.
89. Kleinrock, L., and Lam, S. "Packet-switching in a Slotted Satellite Channel." *AFIPS Conference Proceedings* 42 (1973 National Computer Conference):703–710.
90. Kleinrock, L., and Tobagi, F.A. "Packet Switching in Radio Channels: Part I—Carrier Sense Multiple Acces Modes and Their Throughput-Delay Characteristics." *IEEE Transactions in Communications*, COM-23 (December 1975):1400–1416.
91. Tobagi, F., and Kleinrock, L. "Packet Switching in Radio Channels: Part II—The Hidden Terminal Problem in Carrier Sense Multiple Access and the Busy Tone Solution." *IEEE Transactions Communications* COM-23 (December 1975):1417–1433.
92. Tobagi, F., and Hunt, V.B. "Performance Analysis of Carrier Sense Multiple Access with Collision Detection." *Proceedings of the Local Area Communications Network Symposium*, May 1979; and Stanford Electronics Laboratory, Computer Systems Laboratory Technical Report 173, 30 June 1979.
93. Kahn, R.E.; Gronemeyer, S.A.; Burchfiel, J.; and Kunzelman, R.C. "Advances in Packet Radio Technology." *Proceedings of the IEEE* 66 (November 1978).
94. Special Issue on Spread Spectrum Communications, *IEEE Transactions on Communications* COM-25 (August 1977):
95. Crowther, W.R.; Rettbert, R.; Walden, D.; Ornstein, S.; and Heart, F. "A System for Broadcast Communication: Reservation-ALOHA." *Proceedings of the Sixth Hawaii International System Science Conference*, January 1973.
96. Roberts, L. "Dynamic Allocation of Satellite Capacity through Packet Reservation." *AFIPS Conference Proceedings* (June 1973):
97. Binder, R. "A Dynamic Packet Switching System for Satellite Broadcast Channels", *Proceedings of the ICC 75*, San Francisco, June 1975, pp. 41-1–41-5.
98. Chlamtac, I., Franta, W.R., and Levin, D. "BRAM: The Broadcast Recognizing Access Method." *IEEE Transactions on Communications*. COM-27 (August 1979):1183–1190.
99. Kleinrock, L., and Scholl, M. "Packet Switching in Radio Channels: New Conflict-free Multiple Access Schemes for a Small Number of

Data Users." *ICC Conference Proceedings*, June 1977, pp. 22.1-105–22.1-111.
100. Franta, W.R., and Bilodeau, Mark Benedict. "Analyses of a Prioritized CSMA Protocol Based on Staggered Delays." *ACTA INFORMATICA* 13 (1980):299–324.
101. Loomis, D.C. "Ring Communication Protocols." Technical Report, University of California, Irvine, Department of Information and Computer Science, 26 January 1973.
102. Liu, M.T., and Reames, C.C. "Communication Protocol and Network Operating System Design for the Distributed Loop Computer Network (DLCN)." *Proceedings of the Fourth Annual Symposium on Computer Architecture*, March 1977, pp. 193–200.
103. Hafner, E.R., Nenadal, F., and Tschanz, M., "A Digital Loop Communication System." *IEEE Transactions on Communications*, June 1974, p. 877.
104. Wilkes, M.V., "Communication Using a Digital Ring." *Proceedings of the PACNET Conference*, Sendai, Japan, August 1975, pp. 217–255.
105. Pierce, J.R. Network for Block Switching of Data." *Bell System Technical Journal* 51 (July/August 1972):1133–1143.
106. Hopper, A. "Data Ring at Computer Laboratory, University of Cambridge." *Local Area Networking*, NBS Special Publication 500-31, August 22–23, 1977, pp. 11–16.
107. Zafiropoulo, P., and Rothauser, E.H. "Signalling and Frame Structures in Highly Decentralized Loop Systems." *Proceedings of the International Conference on Computer Communication*, Washington, D.C., IMB Research Laboratory, Zurich, pp. 309–315.
108. Chlamtac, I., and Franta, W.R. "SUPBRAM Description and Performance Analysis with 1-Optimization." TR 79-4. University of Minnesota, Department of Computer Science, February 1979.
109. Kleinrock, L., and Yemini, Y. "An Optimal Adaptive Scheme for Multiple Access Broadcast Communication." *ICC Conference Proceedings*, June 1977.
110. Chlamtac, I., and Franta, W.R. "Generalized SUPBRAM: Protocol and Performance Analysis." TR-79-9. University of Minnesota, Department of Computer Science, April 1979.
111. Borgonovo, F., and Fratta, L. "SRUC: A Technique for Packet Transmission on Multiple Access Channels." *Proceedings of the International Conference on Computer Communication*, Kyoto, Japan, 1978.
112. Christensen, G., and Franta, W.R. "Design and Analysis of the HYPERchannel Protocol." *Proceedings of the Third USA–Japan Computer Conference*, October 1978.

113. Fortune, P.J.; Lidinsky, W.P.; and Zelle, B.R. "Design and Implementation of a Local Computer Network." Proceedings of the *ICC*, 1977.
114. West, A.R. "A Broadcast Packet-Switched Computer Communications Network—Design Progress Report." Department of Computer Science, Queen Mary College, University of London, February 1977.
115. "Exxon Targets Office Systems, Local Networks." *Computer Business News*, 14 April 1980, p. 17.
116. Greitzer, John "Clamor for Local Network Chips Spurs Developments in Industry." *Computer Business News*, 31 March 1980, pp. 1, 6.
117. Greitzer, John. "Zilog to Unveil System for Local Network Mart." *Computer Business News*, 5 May 1980, p. 2.
118. Ungerman-Bass, Inc. NET/ONE Product Announcement. 1980.
119. Rosen, Brian, "PERQ Packet Strem Network." *Proceedings of COMPCON 80*, February 1980, pp. 317–318.
120. Jacobs, I., and Lee, I. "A Priority-Oriented Demand Assignment (PODA) Protocol and an Error Recovery Algorithm for Distributively Controlled Packet Satellite Communication Network." *Proceedings of EASCON 77*, 1977, pp. 14-1A, 14-1F.
121. Hohn, William C. "The Control Data Loosely Coupled Network Lower Level Protocols" Proceedings of the National Computer Conference, June 1980, pp. 129–134.
122. Watson, Bruce, W. "Configuration-Dependent Performance of a Prioritized CSMA Broadcast Network", *Computer*, February 1981, pp. 51–60.

3 Protocol Options

Access-Protocol Options

A number of (level-2) access protocols can be used in local networks, especially those using coaxial cable channels. They differ in the degree to which they force nodes to cooperate in assigning the channel and the means by which they assign the channel. (Throughout this chapter, we will assume that all nodes are directly connected to all other nodes, unless we say otherwise.)

The "no-cooperation" protocols are the easiest to realize but always yield the poorest performance measures. The ALOHA scheme [1], for example, allows a node to transmit whenever it chooses. Should the transmissions of two or more nodes overlap in time, both or all transmissions collide; they become unintelligible to the receiving nodes and consequently must be retransmitted. Collisions can be detected either by the failure of an acknowledgment message to arrive (after a suitable delay) from the intended receiver node or by equipping a node so that it receives its own transmissions. To avoid repeated collisions, nodes engaged in collision use random-number generators to determine a delay interval that must elapse before retransmission is attempted. If messages are assumed to be of constant length, that is, packets requiring T units of time for transmission, then a slotted version of ALOHA can be had, in which transmissions may only be initiated at the beginning of a T slot. Slotting, which may be considered a type of minimal cooperation, reduces the potential for collision and improves performance characteristics.

At the opposite end of the control spectrum are access protocols providing total cooperation among nodes. With total cooperation, collisions can be avoided, of course. The simplest total-control protocol is TDMA [2], the time-division multiple-access scheme in which T slots are assigned the K nodes in a round-robin fashion. Each node, when its slot occurs, either transmits, if ready, or allows its assigned T slot to go unused. Other total-cooperation protocols can be obtained if the information required to achieve total cooperation is transmitted on the channel.

It is instructive to compare these extremes in terms of performance. A number of models have appeared that predict and compare the performances of various access protocols. These models make the following assumptions:

1. There are K nodes in the network.
2. Node generation of messages is random (bursty), so that intergeneration times may be assumed to be exponential, with mean $1/\lambda$.
3. This message traffic is generated equally by the K nodes (that is, the nodes are homogeneous in terms of their transmission requirements), so that the mean message intergeneration time at a node may be assumed to be $1/K\lambda$.
4. Messages are of constant length (that is, they are packets requiring T time units for transmission).
5. The channel-propagation delay between the remotest pair of nodes is given by d.
6. If required by the protocol, all nodes can hear messages transmitted by all other nodes (that is, the broadcast capability can be used).

Performance is usually given in terms of (1) the channel throughout S (the number of messages transmitted per unit of time); (2) the channel capacity C (the maximum S value achievable with a given access protocol); and (3) the expected delay D (the time elapsing between the generation of a message and its successful transmission). If T is taken as the time unit, as is usually done, then we effectively have $T = 1$; with $a = d/T$ we have $0 < a < 1$ (the normalized propagation delay); and D, S, and G become the normalized delay, throughput, and message loading (the total number of new and retransmitted messages offered to the channel per unit of time), respectively.

These measures and assumptions yield performance curves for a variety of representative access protocols (figures 3–1 and 3–2). Notice that the ALOHA scheme has a very small capacity ($C = 0.18$), while TDMA has a large capacity ($C = 1$). For low S, however, TDMA has D values much larger than those for Aloha. Thus, we may conclude that Aloha performs reasonably well for small S values (small loading), whereas TDMA does not. However, TDMA performs well for large S values (large loadings), whereas ALOHA collapses. For large loadings, ALOHA collapses because of a large number of collisions, while TDMA allows full use of the channel. For small loadings, ALOHA yields few collisions and hence small D values, whereas TDMA wastes the channel bandwidth (by forcing ready nodes to wait for unused T slots to pass before transmitting) and hence yields large D values.

Viewed differently, to obtain small D values, no-cooperation protocols are preferred for small loadings, while total-cooperation protocols are preferred for large loadings. For mid-range loadings, neither seems desirable, especially when compared to delays predicted by $M/D/1$ queuing theory, the theoretical limit against which comparisons can be made. This $M/D/1$ model represents the ideal for comparison, since it assumes no collisions and no channel idle time (for control purposes) so long as there are messages to transmit. It is clearly ideal in that it assumes an omniscient control

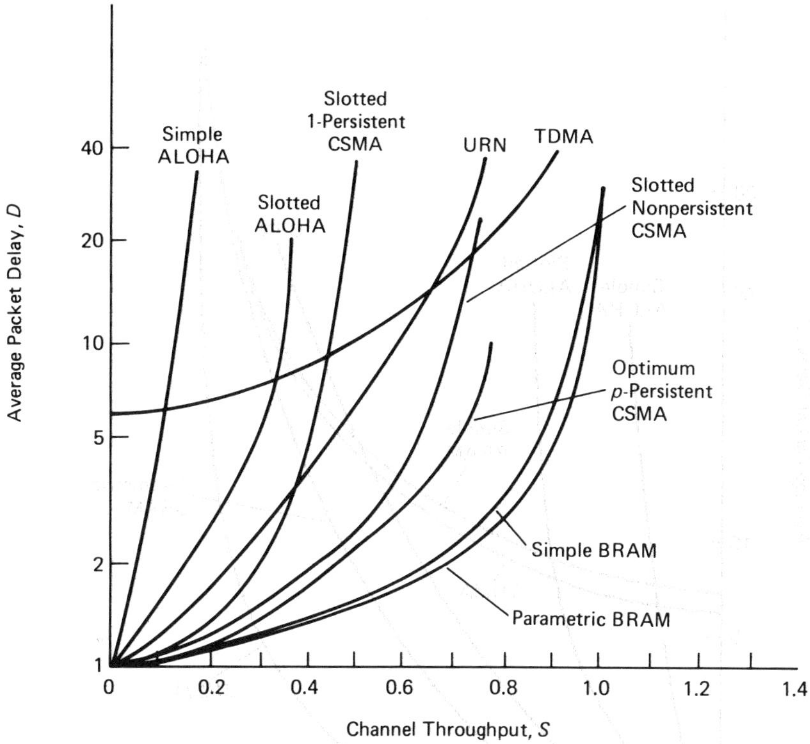

Source: I. Chlamtac et al., "Performance Issues in Back-End Storage Networks," *Computer*. February 1980, p. 23. Reprinted with permission.
$K = 10$; $a = 0.01$.

Figure 3–1. Access-Protocol Delay Curves; $a = 0.01$

mechanism requiring (at transmission termination) zero time to select and inform the node that will transmit next.

The situation for mid-range S values (hence, moderate loadings) is improved by the inclusion of slightly more control in the form of node deference to ongoing transmissions. We imagine a scheme like ALOHA, but in which nodes sense the channel before transmitting and refrain from transmitting if an ongoing transmission can be "heard." With deference, a number of protocol variants emerge, depending upon the action taken by the deferring ready nodes at the termination of the ongoing transmission. Specifically, at termination of an ongoing transmission, a ready node may transmit with probability p. Collectively, these protocols are known as carrier-sense multiple-access (CSMA) schemes, and the value of p serves to further characterize the variants [3, 4]. When $p = 1$, we have 1-persistent

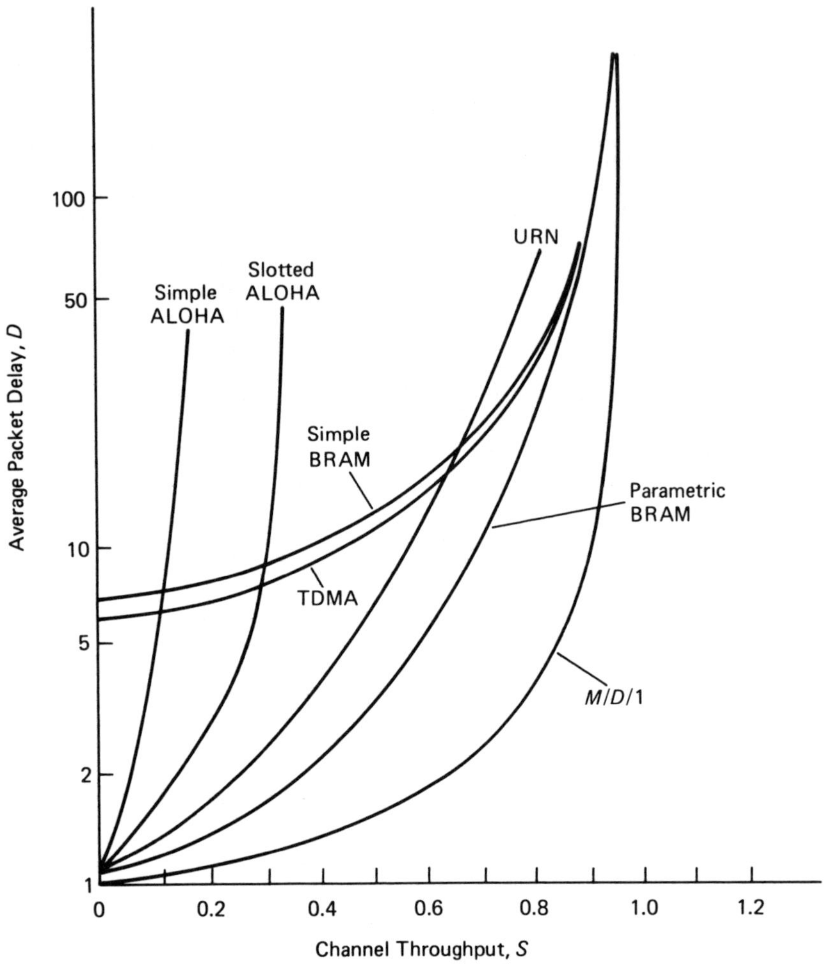

Source: I. Chlamtac et al., "Performance Issues in Back-End Storage Networks," *Computer*. February 1980, p. 23. Reprinted with permission.
$K = 10$; $a = 1$.

Figure 3–2. Access-Protocol Delay Curves: $a = 1$

CSMA; for $0 < p < 1$, we have p-persistent CSMA; and for $p = 0$ (implying a transmission attempt after a random delay interval), we have nonpersistent CSMA. As can be seen in figures 3–1 and 3–2, CSMA schemes yield more acceptable D values for mid-range loadings (S values). The improvement afforded by deference is caused by a reduction in the size of the "collision window," that is, with CSMA, collisions can only occur if multiple nodes transmit following termination of a sensed ongoing transmission or if multiple nodes sense that the channel is idle and transmit. Multiple nodes will only sense that the channel is idle in a time interval of width a, the normalized propagation-delay time. This observation also indicates why 1-persistent CSMA exhibits poorer performance than nonpersistent CSMA. For the majority of local networks, $a \ll 1$ (generally in the range $0.01 < a < 0.2$), so that CSMA greatly improves delay performance (CSMA yields C values as high as 0.85).

CSMA schemes are important because certain variants of them are used in a number of networks [5,6,7]. A prioritized CSMA variant used in a commercially available product, for example, has been described and analyzed [6,7]. The Ethernet variant [5] minimizes the bandwidth wasted because of collisions by having nodes receive and transmit in parallel, so that a comparison failure between the transmitted and received messages signals collision. (Without comparison hardware, collision can be detected via the absence,after an appropriate delay, of an acknowledgment message.) When a comparison failure occurs, the node sensing collision jams the channel to guarantee that all currently transmitting nodes sense collision. After jamming, transmission is terminated and reattempted after a random delay interval. (The retransmission delay distribution is usually taken to be uniform [3,4].) This CSMA variant, known as CSMA-CD (CD for collision detection), allows C values near 0.98 [3,4].

The schemes described so far are simple to realize in that they are based on no information, as in ALOHA, or on minimal timing information, as in slotted ALOHA and TDMA, or on minimal information available from the channel, as in the CSMA variants. Of the three approaches, those in the latter category yield the lowest D values and highest C values by avoiding the preallocation waste of TDMA and the large collision potential of ALOHA.

It is natural to wonder if protocols yielding still lower D values can be constructed. The answer is yes, of course, and schemes in this new category are generally dynamic in nature and adapt in some way to changing loadings, that is, demand for channel use. Two examples are urn schemes [8] and parametric broadcast-recognizing access method (BRAM) [10]. Both schemes use information readily available on the channel, at no or little overhead, to assess message-loading levels so as to dynamically adjust to changing values in those levels. As we see in figure 3–1 and 3–2, they are very effective in improving performance (both allow C values of 1 to be reached), especially if a is not extremely small or loadings are large. All these protocols are structurally similar, and all can be described with a few basic concepts (for example, scheduling and grouping functions) [9].

Protocols with reasonable performance characteristics can be realized, then, without high-overhead control schemes. CSMA-CD, as used in Ethernet, is one example, and HYPERchannel is another. Protocols with still better performance can be had with small increases in overhead; the urn scheme and parametric BRAM typify this group.

This short comparison of approaches gives an indication of the link between the access protocol and its performance. Certain conclusions on these matters are immediate, the most important among them being that trade-offs exist. That is, no protocol can be claimed as the ultimate solution for all network configurations and traffic environments. Different protocols not only exhibit different performance measures but also require different information for their realization, information that may or may not be easily obtained in a given environment. As table 2–2 showed, a large number of access protocols have been invented. In this chapter, we will present one or two examples from each of the four classes.

Fixed-Assignment Strategies

The best-known fixed-assignment strategy is TDMA, described in the opening section of this chapter. A statistical version of TDMA, wherein nodes are assigned slots on the basis of demand has also been developed [12].

Random-Assignment Strategies

Random-assignment strategies range from the no-cooperation ALOHA through various CSMA variants that use deference as a cooperation mechanism.

ALOHA. The ALOHA access strategy is a very simple access protocol, originally designed for use in a system using a radio channel [13]. With ALOHA, ready nodes transmit whenever they desire. The strategy is not truly viable for cable-based systems unless collision detection is used, as, otherwise, delivery of acknowledgments is difficult. The strategy exhibits the very low capacity of $C = 1/2e = 0.18$, because the duration of overlapped channel use can be high.

A slotted version of ALOHA segments the time axis into slots of size T (the packet-transmission time) and insures that transmissions are attempted only on slot boundaries. Slotting tends to reduce the level of overlapped channel use by a factor of two; hence, slotted ALOHA has a capacity of $C = 1/e = 0.36$. Overlapped messages (collisions) are serialized by randomizing retransmission times to occur Δt units after termination of the colliding packet, with Δt drawn from a probability distribution.

ALOHA exemplifies strategies that exhibit instability. The level or degree of instability is a function of the collective node backlog of packets, and its detrimental effects may be controlled, to some degree, by proper selection of the parameters and distribution of the random variable Δt (see also [14]).

Carrier-Sense Multiple Access (CSMA). CSMA refers to a family of protocols, with all members employing deference. The family members are differentiated by the action they take upon encountering a busy channel [4].

With the nonpersistent CSMA, a ready node senses the channel and transmits a packet (or message) if the channel is idle, that is, if no carrier signal is present. If a carrier is present, the node waits Δt time units, with Δt drawn from a probability distribution called the retransmission delay distribution. After the Δt delay, the node repeats the sequence described. Nodes sending acknowledgment messages must vie for the channel in the same fashion. If, after a reasonable time, an acknowledgment is not returned, it is assumed that channel noise or collision destroyed the transmission, and the sequence is repeated. The length of the Δt delays is randomly drawn so as to serialize the transmission attempts of nodes that become ready during a transmission, hence avoiding collisions.

With 1-persistent CSMA, a ready node senses the channel and transmits if it is sensed idle. If the channel is sensed busy, the node persists in sensing the channel until it goes idle, at which time the node transmits. Acknowledgments, noise, and collisions are handled in the same manner as in nonpersistent CSMA.

With p-persistent CSMA, a ready node senses the channel and transmits with probability p if it is idle and delays a time units with probability $1-p$. If, after the a time-unit delay, the channel is again sensed idle, the decision process is repeated. If, after the a delay, the channel is sensed busy, a retransmission attempt is scheduled after a Δt delay (as in nonpersistent CSMA). If the ready node initially senses the channel busy, it persists in sensing the channel until it becomes idle, at which time it transmits with probability p and delays its point of decision by a time units with probability $1-p$. Collisions, noise, and acknowledgments are handled as previously described.

Nonpersistent CSMA attempts to avoid collisions by having ready nodes that sense the channel busy and reschedule their transmission attempts for randomly determined future times, the random drawings serving to serialize their reattempts.

CSMA that is 1-persistent attempts to avoid channel idle time (and reduce message-transmission delay) by having ready nodes persist. If only one ready node persists, a successful transmission follows when the channel becomes idle (having been busy because of a single or overlapped transmission). If multiple nodes persist, collision is a guarantee. CSMA that is p-persistent attempts to avoid the guaranteed collisions caused by multiple persisting nodes, through the parameter p.

Other CSMA variants are possible, including slotted versions of non- and 1-persistent CSMA.

Protocols with Collision Detection (CSMA-CD). As we stated earlier, protocol performance is affected by the size of the collision window (that is, with deference, the magnitude of the intervals over which collisions can occur) and by the duration of overlapped channel use. For the access protocols described so far (and excluding ALOHA), the magnitude v of the overlapped channel-use interval is in the range $0 \leq v \leq T$, with $T + a$ the packet transmission time or the transmission time of the largest possible (or likely) message. Collision detection via listen-while-transmit (LWT) reduces the level of overlapped use to ζ, the time required to correctly sense collision, jam the channel, and terminate transmission. The value for ζ may be as small as one bit transmission time, but, in any case, we surely have $\zeta \ll T$. A nonpersistent CSMA with collision detection has been devised and analyzed [15]. With CSMA-CD, then, a ready node senses the channel and transmits if it is idle. If a collision is detected, using LWT, the channel is jammed, and a transmission attempt is rescheduled to occur after a delay of Δt (see nonpersistent CSMA). The procedure if a busy channel is sensed is as in nonpersistent CSMA.

Demand-Assignment Strategies

As with protocols in other categories, we wish the nodes to execute identical algorithms to determine channel access, and demand-assignment algorithms require considerably more cooperation than do algorithms in the previous two categories. Mechanisms for cooperation include *deference*, *scheduling periods*, and *synchronization*. Deference, as we stated, refers to a node's observation of channel busy or idle state and its adherence to a rule whereby it does not attempt to transmit a message on an observably busy channel. (The busy or idle state is usually detected by the presence or absence, respectively, of a carrier signal.) Scheduling periods alternate with transmission periods (and idle periods) and use the channel to determine which ready node will next obtain control of the shared channel. To be effective, nodes must synchronize their scheduling-period decisions with respect to a commonly known time epoch; and the end of a transmission is usually taken as the beginning of the next scheduling period. Scheduling periods are of variable length and, for the class of protocols of interest, are based on dynamically or statically assigned node priorities. With certain demand protocols, if, following a transmission, no nodes are ready, a maximal (but finite) length scheduling period elapses, after which a state known as *contention* is entered. The contention mode is terminated when one or more nodes attempt transmissions. If two or more nodes quasi-simultaneously attempt transmissions, their overlapped use of the shared channel destroys their transmissions. Overlapped transmissions are said to collide, and colliding messages must be retransmitted. The retransmission is sorted out by the scheduling period that follows the termination of the last-started transmission involved in the collision.

The Broadcast-Recognizing Access Method (BRAM). The BRAM protocol is designed for use in networks exhibiting complete connectivity, as found, for example, in bus-topology local networks [10,16]. In BRAM, ready-node transmission starting points are staggered in the schedulng period by integral multiples of a, the channel end-to-end propagation delay. The assigned staggerings are calculated by each node via a scheduling function, $S(i,j)$, with i the node index of a node wishing to transmit and j the index of the node that successfully transmitted last. (The value of j is usually contained in the message header, so that, when a message is transmitted, that is, logically speaking, broadcast, the value may be recognized, that is, received by all nodes.) At the end of a transmission, ready node i waits $a \cdot S(i,j)$ time units, captures the channel if it is found idle at that time, and defers if it is not. Thus the ready node i that has calculated the smallest value for $S(i,j)$ captures the channel. Thus, the function $S(i,j)$ assigns, for each scheduling period, a priority value to each node. The S function presented in Chlamtac and Franta [10] provides a rotating priority mechanism by using

$$S(i,\ j) = \begin{cases} (i - j + K) \bmod K, & i \neq j \\ K, & i = j \end{cases} \tag{3.1}$$

which gives lowest priority to the node that broadcast last, or by using $S(i,j) = (i - j + K) \bmod K$, which gives highest priority to the node that broadcast last with K the number of nodes in the network.

Certain additional points are in order. First, a maximal-length period is of lengh $K \cdot a$ and obtains when, following a transmission, no nodes are ready. For simplicity, in BRAM, maximal-length scheduling periods repeat until one or more nodes become ready and one node captures the channel and transmits. Thus, BRAM is a collision-free access protocol. Second, the scheduling functions rotate priorities in a round-robin fashion. Third, the first scheduling function is fair, by strictly rotating the priorities, and the second is selfish. The first is best suited to interactive traffic, the second to file-transfer traffic.

Prioritized Staggered Delays (PSD). The PSD access protocol is, logically speaking, a variant of BRAM in which the scheduling function $S(i,.) = i$ is used; that is, PSD statically assigns priority values to nodes. PSD differs from BRAM in two other respects. First, priority is given to acknowledgment messages. This is accomplished, logically speaking, by using the scheduling function $S(i,.) = i + 1$, with the first starting point in the scheduling period assigned to the node that received the last transmission for initiating transmission of an acknowledgment message. Second, with PSD, a contention mode is entered if a maximal-length scheduling period elapses, that is, if there are no ready nodes. (A maximal-length scheduling period is of length $(K + 1)a$.) Nodes becoming ready during a contention mode may freely transmit, and if two or more transmit quasi-simultaneously, collision results. Collisions are serialized not by randomization of retransmission attempts but by the normal selection process that occurs in the scheduling period following termination of the last-begun transmission involved in the transmission collision.

Example 3.1

We must make it clear that the assigned priorities are not governed by placement of the nodes on the shared cable.

To clarify, we give an example in which a bus-propagation delay of 2 nanoseconds (ns) per foot is employed and a zero generation time for acknowledgments (ACKs) is assumed.

The fixed delay (that is, the delay giving priority to acknowledgments) is given by the product of 4 ns and the total bus length in feet, that is by two round-trip propagation-delay times for the total bus length. A 1,000-foot cable therefore requires a 4-microsecond (μs) fixed delay.

The time slot assigned to each CIU in the network depends on the priority it is to be given and on its position on the cable. The CIU with highest priority has a delay equal to the fixed delay. The time-slot delay for each of the lower-priority CIUs is calculated by the equation:

$$\text{delay}(N) = \text{delay}(N - 1) + (4 \text{ ns} \times \text{distance})$$

where N refers to the CIU with priority $N (N = 0$ has highest priority), and distance gives the length, measured in feet, between the CIU with priority index N and the CIU with priority index $N - 1$.

Figure 3–3 shows a four-node network with the assigned CIU priorities and the distances between CIUs. The unique time-slot delay calculations for each of the CIUs are:

$$\text{delay}(0) = \text{fixed delay} + (4\text{ ns} \times 1{,}000\text{ ft}) = 4\ \mu\text{s}$$

$$\begin{aligned}\text{delay}(1) &= \text{delay}(0) + (4\text{ ns} \times 200\text{ ft})\\ &= 4\ \mu\text{s} + 800\text{ ns} = 4.8\ \mu\text{s}\end{aligned}$$

$$\begin{aligned}\text{delay}(2) &= \text{delay }(1) + (4\text{ ns} \times 200\text{ ft})\\ &\ 4.8\ \mu\text{s} + 3.2\ \mu\text{s} = 8\ \mu\text{s}\end{aligned}$$

$$\begin{aligned}\text{delay}(3) &= \text{delay}(2)\ + (4\text{ ns} \times 500\text{ ft})\\ &\ 8\ \mu\text{s} + 2\ \mu\text{s} = 10\ \mu\text{s}\end{aligned}$$

When node j captures the channel, by implication, the channel has been idle at least delay(j) time units, as measured from the end of the previous transmission. The channel-idle time represented by delay(j) is called the scheduling period. The length of any given scheduling period is obviously dependent on j, that is, on the node that captures the channel.

After a 12 μs delay, all CIUs are enabled to transmit if none have captured the channel. At this point, any CIU wishing to transmit has immediate access to the channel. It is during this period that there is a potential for message collision. For two messages to collide, the originating CIUs would have to begin transmission within a small collision window, the width of which is given by the propagation-delay time between them. In figure 3–3, for example, CIUs 0 and 2 have a 2 μs window in which collision could occur. Because of the proximity of CIUs 0 and 1, there is only a 400 ns collision window between them. The first description of this protocol is given in [6].

The Mini-Slot Alternating Priorities (MSAP) Protocol. MSAP is an adaptation of hub-polling [18], and has elements of both BRAM and PSD. Logically, like PSD, MSAP assigns static priorities to nodes and logically uses the scheduling function $S(i,.) = i$ to stagger node starting points in the scheduling period. Unlike PSD, a contention mode is not entered when a maximal-length scheduling period elapses. Instead, scheduling periods are repeated until some node becomes ready, as with BRAM. As we might expect, MSAP performs well when $K \cdot a$ is small and node demand for channel use is high.

Controlling the Channel Access in Ring (Loop) Systems. Over the last decade, dozens of ring and loop networks have been developed in experimental and commerical environments [19–45,55]. The distinction between loops and rings is fuzzy at best, and for the most part they are interchangeable. If a distinction has to be made between them, it relates to the type of control used. Loops are considered to have centralized control, while rings have distributed control [46].

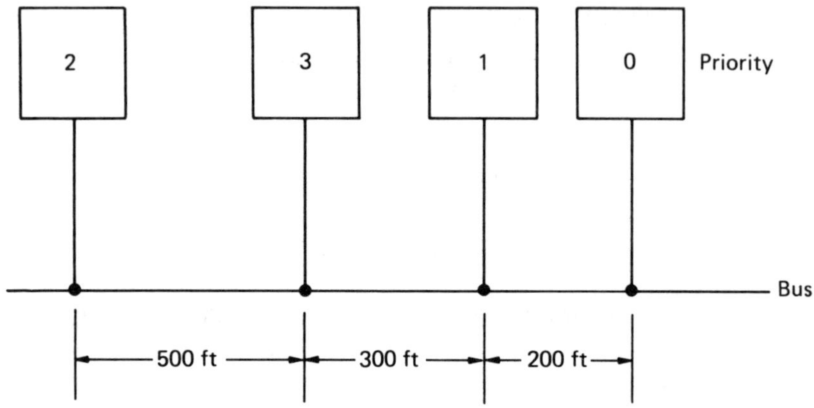

Figure 3–3. Unique-Time-Slot Timing Example

In the ring network, nodes are connected by a one-way transmission channel along which messages are passed from one node to the next until they are returned and removed by the initiating node. Failures by malfunctioning nodes can be overcome by node-bypass logic in the CIU. To control ring communication, we are faced with a problem similar to that for busses; that is, we wish to determine transmission rights in a distributed manner. Access mechanisms can be had either by augmenting the data ring by a dedicated control ring or by having control information transmitted on the data channel. In practice, both approaches have been used; the latter, however, is most prevalent.

Multiaccess schemes for rings include fixed-assignment time-division techniques, demand-assignment techniques, random-access techniques, polling variants, and reservation schemes. Many of these schemes can be realized by minor modifications of their bus-oriented counterparts [47]. The most popular techniques for rings fall into the control-token, message-passing, and register-insertion categories, each of which we summarize in this section. An exhaustive discussion of techniques and systems can be found in Penney and Baghdadi [48,49] and Kanakia and Thomasian [50]. In designing control structures for rings, certain characteristics play key roles:

1. Messages are passed in one direction from node to node;
2. Propagation delays are small;
3. The ring gives an inherent ordering of nodes, corresponding to their physical placement on the ring;
4. The connectivity of the network is minimal, requiring $K-1$ transmissions (relays) to send a message to all nodes in a K-node network;

5. The ring interface is an active element, with a capability to identify the address of messages passing along the ring;
6. The number of messages traveling around the ring at a given time is always limited.

The *control-token-passing* scheme [51] is based on a control token that is passed from node to node around the ring. Upon receiving the token, each node can take one of two actions: either it passes the token (when it has no message to transmit) or retains the token, transmits a message (or messages), and then passes the token.

In the *message-passing* protocol, a series of message slots are passed continuously around the ring [20,37,52]. Nodes may interrogate the empty-full state of a slot as it passes. If a node has a message to transmit, it identifies the first empty slot, marks it full, and transmits its message in the slot.

The third well-known strategy, *register insertion* [34,36,53] derives its name from the fact that a shift register resides at each node. The strategy can provide a fair-share allocation of the channel bandwidth [36] to the nodes, and under certain circumstances also provides improved performance as compared to the two previously discussed techniques [54]. With register insertion, a message awaiting transmission is first loaded into the shift register. When the channel turns idle, or between the transmissions of two consecutive messages, the message is inserted into the ring by shifting it from the register onto the ring, while any incoming message is shifted into the register. Following this action, the register becomes an extension of the ring, blocking the node from further transmissions until the outgoing message is removed from the ring after its return following its circuit. If the message is not returned for any reason (for example, if it was damaged in transit), the node has to wait until the register is again free (empty) before retransmission is attempted. This characterization of ring-control structures is not exhaustive, only demonstrative. As pointed out in previous sections, techniques applicable to busses can also be adapted, with minor changes to rings.

Message-Based Priorities and PSD. Certain network applications necessitate that dynamic priorities be assigned to messages rather than nodes [17]. This situation is exemplified, for example, by networks carrying both short control messages and a sustained stream of long background traffic. In such situations, it is often necessary that a guaranteed service level be given the short control messages at the expense, of course, of a degraded level (slight, it is hoped) of service for the messages relegated to background.

For these reasons, it is desirable to provide for a message-associated access protocol. One approach that satisfies both objectives is the replication of the access mechanism associated with the PSD protocol. Specifically, n message-priority classes can be provided by a small amount of new hardware

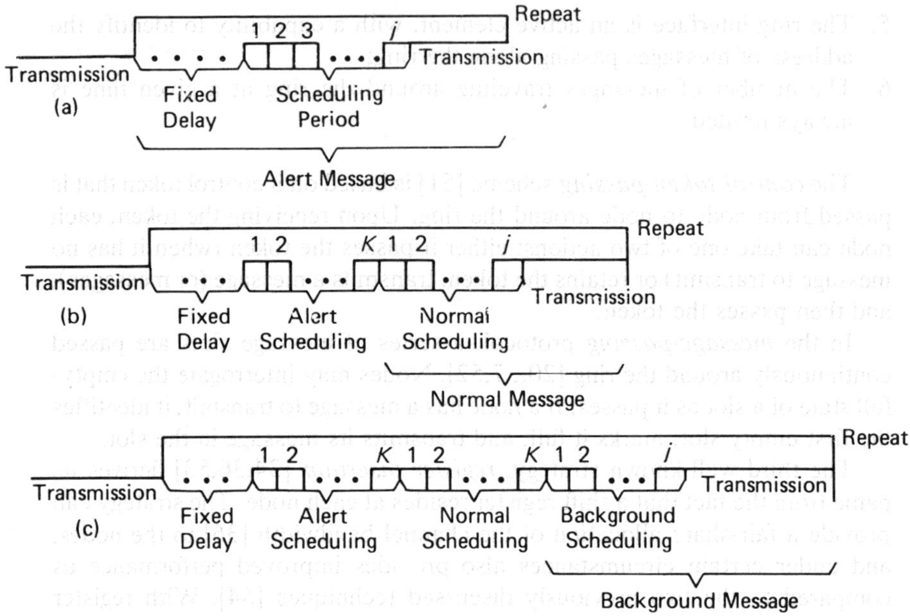

(a) Node j captures the channel to transmit an alert message.
(b) Node j captures the channel to transmit a normal message.
(c) Node j captures the channel to transmit a background message.
(d) Contention mode begins only if no transmission occurs when $J = K$ in situation (c).

Figure 3–4. Message-Based Priority-Access Mechanism

and the hardware, which realizes the PSD access scheme. With this approach, each node is assigned the same unique delay in each replicaton and, following transmission of a message, the channel-access selection process repeats from the beginning of the highest-priority replication. The situation with $n = 3$ is depicted in figure 3–4.

With $n = 3$, the associated message classes are labeled as alert, normal, and background. Alert messages are generally short, have a low incidence rate, and must be guaranteed quick delivery. At the other extreme, background messages are generally long, and their prompt delivery is not critical.

A still-better scheme would be a multilevel parametric BRAM (see later in this chapter), wherein we would organize the nodes into m_1 groups for alert messages, m_2 groups for normal messages, and m_3 groups for background messages. With these groupings values, m_1^*, m_2^*, m_3^* can be determined to balance delay against the probability of collision for each class. Delay performance would be improved, as likely values would have $m_1^* \sim 1$ (or $m_1^* << k$), $m_2^* \sim m^*$ and $m_3^* \sim m^*$, with m^* as in parametric BRAM.

Other Variants. A number of other schemes, mostly hybrid reservation or contention schemes, have been devised.

The assigned-slot listen-before-transmission (LBT) protocol [56] is similar to the BRAM schemes [10] in that it assigns transmission priorities to nodes in a conceptual scheduling period, which is followed by a transmission period. As one or more nodes can be assigned to a single scheduling point, an optimization much like parametric BRAM can be performed. The protocol differs from others in that the nodes that were scheduled for transmission, but had to defer to an ongoing transmission, do not reschedule in the following scheduling period but rather reschedule to a period according to a specified randomizing delay-distribution function—similar to that used in nonpersistent CSMA node.

A modification of BRAM [10] and HYPERchannel protocol [6], which uses a single scheduling period followed by a contention node, was proposed in Spaniol [57]. The ordering of priorities in the scheduling period is node-determined. Unlike other schemes, this protocol can guarantee a fairer use of the channel by the nodes, by limiting each node to an optimal number of transmissions when it gains access rights, as opposed to a single transmission allocted to each user in the BRAM protocol.

A generalized TDMA scheme, the so-called multi-accessing tree protocol [58,59], has also been proposed as a solution to the instability problem that is inherent in many protocols. Rather than resolving collisions by randomizing retransmissions, the nodes are arranged on leaves of a tree, for example, a binary tree. The channel is assumed to be slotted, and the slots are arranged in pairs. Each pair corresponds to one of the two subtrees (in a binary tree). By starting with the root of the tree, nodes corresponding to the two subtrees may transmit in their left or right slots. If a collision obtains in a slot, the subtree is accessed again in the same way until, eventually, either a collision-free transmission is obtained or the leaves are reached and the nodes are actually separated. Although the utilization of the method is limited ($C = 0.347$), the message delay is guaranteed to be finite. By providing for dynamic use of binary and nonbinary trees, the utilization can be slightly improved ($C = 0.430$ in the optimal case).

A protocol that is a combination of CSMA and TDMA has also been studied, [60], and simulation has showed a certain performance improvement over either of the two individual schemes. Polling [61] and explicit reservation schemes [62] can also be used as access schemes in local networks, although random-access schemes provide better performance under the expected bursty communication patterns found in most local networks. In certain process-control environments, where bursty traffic does not occur, these latter options become attractive. The vector-determined proportional access (VDPA) or protocol is also attractive in these cases [125].

Adaptive-Assignment Strategies

Urn Scheme. The urn scheme partitions time into a sequence of packet-transmission slots and attempts to assign only one ready node to each slot, in a manner that effectively uses channel bandwidth [8]. Specifically, suppose n of the K nodes are ready to transmit in a given transmission slot. A successful transmission obtains if l nodes are assigned to transmit in a given slot and there is only one ready node among them. The urn protocol derives its name from the sampling strategy it employs to assign a value to l. The strategy that is adapted views the situation as an attempt to draw l nodes from the K nodes in such a way as to maximize the probability that there is only one ready node among them. The probability of there being only one of n ready nodes in a collection of l nodes drawn from K is

$$\frac{\binom{l}{1}\binom{K-l}{n-1}}{\binom{K}{n}}$$

an element of the hypergeometric distribution. This probability is maximized when $l = [K/n]$; $[x]$ gives the integer part of x. Three problems remain: (1) estimating n by information transmitted on the channel, (2) determining which l of the K nodes are assigned to a given slot, and (3) informing the l nodes of the assignment. The protocol is adaptive in the sense that l adapts dynamically to changes in n.

To ensure distributed control, estimation of the number of ready nodes must be done in a distributed fashion. In Kleinrock and Yemini [8], a single-reservation mini-slot is suggested. Nodes use the mini-slot to announce their transition from idle to ready by broadcasting a standard bit pattern. If the mini-slot is empty, no additional nodes have become ready. If one node becomes ready, the mini-slot announces that fact, and all nodes can increment $\hat{n}$, the estimate of n, by 1. If two or more nodes become ready, collision occurs in the mini-slot, an event that we assume is detectable by all nodes. In this case, the nodes may increment $\hat{n}$ by 2, assuming a Poisson message source, as the probability of more than two becoming ready during a transmission slot is small (shown to be less than 0.08 [8]). Decrements of $\hat{n}$ can be made when acknowledgment messages are detected.

The remaining issue—selection of the nodes that will compete for the channel in a given period—can be accomplished in several ways [8]. One way assumes the nodes to be numbered with indexes 1 to K. A window of size n (actually $\hat{n}$) is then rotated around the network so that a subset of nodes is allowed access to the channel for each transmission cycle. This scheme is doubly attractive as it serves to control collisions, which obviously can occur in transmission slots. Specifically, if collisions occur, the window can be successively reduced until collisions are eliminated, after which it can again be expanded.

Parametric BRAM. The performance of BRAM deteriorates as the product $K \cdot a$ increases. It does so as the length of scheduling periods increases, both in average length and in maximal length. Intuitively, we observe that the length of scheduling periods can introduce considerable channel idle time for low and medium-loading values and nonnegligible a values. Specifically, when the collection of ready nodes becomes small, the probability of there being, for a given scheduling period, a ready node with small $S(.,.)$, see equation 3.1, value is small.

Since the propagation delay a is a parameter of the network, it cannot be shortened. It is possible, however, to force the allowable S values to be drawn from a smaller range, say $S \in \{1,m\}$ instead of $\{1,K\}$, with $m < K$. Forcing the S's to be drawn from the range $\{1,m\}$ has the potential to shorten the length of scheduling periods, but at a price. The price is the introduced possibility of collisions brought about by the fact that, with K reduced to m, we can no longer guarantee $S(j,n_2) \neq S(k,n_2)$ for $j \neq k$, as is true with equation 3.1.

For parametric BRAM, we collect the K nodes into m groups; that is, we construct a grouping function $g(i)$ such that $1 \leq g(i) \leq m$ for each node i, $1 \leq i \leq K$. Next, we replace the scheduling function, equation 3.1, by

$$R(n_1,n_2) = \begin{cases} (n_1 - n_2 + m) \bmod m & n_1 \neq n_2 \\ m & n_1 = n_2 \end{cases} \qquad (3.2)$$

where n_1 is the group index associated with a ready node, and n_2 is the group index for the node that last broadcast successfully. The scheduling function equation, 3.2, yields a protocol that remains fair to the groups. Alternatively, we can use

$$R(n_1,n_2) = (n_1 - n_2 + m) \bmod m \;\; \forall\, n_1 \qquad (3.3)$$

for a protocol that gives priority to the group of which the last node to transmit successfully is a member (prioritized parametric BRAM, or PPB).

Using equation 3.2 or equation 3.3, the starting times for transmissions from nodes in different groups are staggered by at least a, so that collisions between nodes in different groups cannot occur. Collisions between two or more ready nodes within the same group can occur, however, if the group index (for a given scheduling period) for those nodes results in the minimum S value for ready nodes; all ready nodes in that group will simultaneously sense the channel idle and will transmit. All nodes involved in the transmission collision must retransmit their packets. To avoid the continual recurrence of collisions, subsequent transmission attempts for the colliding nodes must be randomized. This is easily accomplished by having colliding nodes not attempt subsequent schedulings of transmissions until a time X has elapsed, with X a drawing from a specified distribution. (For performance measures given in chapter 5, we have used $X = n \cdot a$, with n a uniformly distributed integer as described in Kleinrock and Tobagi [4].)

Thus, we must note that, to properly account for collisions, the BRAM protocol must be amended to include the following: If node j is involved in collision, then node j draws a variate for X and waits for a time interval equal to the variable value to elapse, whereupon the node attempts to reschedule the transmission.

Using the parametric scheduling functions, equation 3.2 or equation 3.3, we can select m to achieve a balance, for decreasing m values, between the desirable likelihood of smaller scheduling periods and the undesirable increasing probability of collision. Thus, with R, protocol performance will be a function of K, m, a, and the loading level. Smaller m values tend to reduce the lengths of scheduling periods but increase the probability of collisions, while larger m values tend to increase the length of scheduling periods but reduce the probability of intergroup collisions. We call that value of m—say, m^*—optimal that balances these tendencies with respect to a given loading, so as to yield the best throughput S or lowest delay D possible over the set of allowable m values, the allowable set of m values being, of course, in the range $1 \leq m \leq K$. The m^* values can be found by a limited search procedure and simulation, based on the fact that $m^* = 1$ for low loadings, that m^* increases as the loading does, and that $m^* = K$ for large loading levels.

Other Media and Topologies

In previous sections, we discussed various approaches to sharing a single multiaccess channel among a number of nodes. We have assumed that all nodes are able to detect (hear) all transmissions emanating from all other nodes, and that the channel end-to-end propagation delay, a, is small and certainly less than T, the packet-transmission time. In this section, we consider radio and satellite channels, in which one or the other of these assumptions is violated.

Radio Channels. Most of the protocols presented in the previous sections are applicable to multiaccess radio channels so long as all nodes can hear the transmissions emanating from all other nodes. One exception is CSMA-CD, which is not viable, because a node that simultaneously transmits and receives on a radio channel will always correctly receive its own transmission. That is, the transmission of a node completely overwhelms transmissions from other nodes insofar as the node receiver is concerned. The situation becomes more interesting when the so-called hidden-node environment is considered.

The hidden-node environment obtains when the shared channel is a radio channel and, because of obstacles (buildings, mountains, and so forth) or signal strengths, some nodes cannot directly detect or receive transmissions emanating from certain other nodes. In this respect, certain nodes are hidden from other nodes. Transmissions from one node to another node hidden from the first can be effected only if the transmission is received by one or more other nodes and by some pattern of relays forwarded to the hidden node. Thus, the hidden-node environment assumes a network in which each node may be aware of the existence of all other nodes even though direct communication with all other nodes is not possible. The networks of interest can be more formally characterized by the following considerations. We call two nodes connected if they can directly receive each other's transmissions. We say two nodes are disconnected if they are hidden from each other. The connectivity of a network of stationary nodes can be depicted by a connectivity graph, as shown in figure 3–5, by linking connected nodes by lines. Thus, for example, figure 3–5 reflects a network in which nodes 1 and 2 are connected but nodes 1 and 3 are hidden from each other (nodes are identified by a node index within a circle). A network with K nodes and some connectivity graph can be further characterized by K', the maximal number of relays necessary to forward a message from any one node to every other node in the network. Examination of figure 3–5 for example, reveals a value of $K' = 4$ for the network depicted.

With hidden nodes, we can still employ protocols such as ALOHA, BRAM, or CSMA. In the hidden-node environment, however, carrier sensing does not always work. As a consequence, hidden nodes may cause collisions that would have been avoided in the fully connected environment (for example, cable). For example, imagine three nodes, two of which are hidden from each other but connected to the third. The two hidden nodes, unable to hear each other, may generate overlapped transmissions, causing a collision at the third node. The collision may be significant, as the third node may be needed to relay a message between two disconnected nodes. Thus,

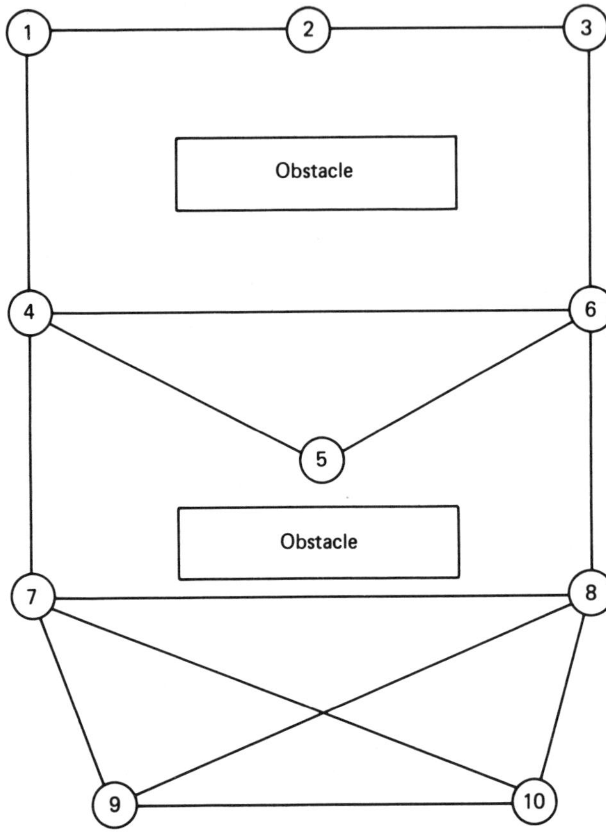

Figure 3–5. Sample Network with Hidden Nodes

we might expect that, although access strategies designed for fully connected networks can be employed in the hidden-node environment, their performance characteristics will deteriorate rapidly (because of collisions) as the degree of disconnectivity grows. This intuition has been demonstrated for CSMA in Tobagi [3] and Tobagi and Kleinrock [63], on BRAM in Chlamtac and Franta [64].

A number of strategies have been developed to overcome the performance degradations caused by hidden nodes.

Busy-Tone Multiple Access (BTMA). The BTMA protocol is limited to star-oriented networks with hidden nodes [3,63]. With BTMA, a central station is assumed to be connected to all other nodes, while the other nodes may have arbitrary connectivity relationships. The channel bandwidth is split into a message channel (over which data are transmitted) and a control or "busy-tone" channel. The busy-tone channel is used to simulate the carrier signal that is available in fully connected networks. As the central node is connected to all other nodes, it broadcasts a busy tone wherever it senses an ongoing data-channel transmission. Using the busy tone to represent carrier, any protocol using deference can, for example, be used on the data channel, including CSMA or ALOHA (which does not need the busy tone). Furthermore, nodes other than the control node can be mobile (dynamic connectivity pattern) or stationary (static connectivity pattern).

A Strategy that Allows Simultaneous Transmissions. BTMA and most other access protocols designed for the hidden-node environment only tolerate sequential use of the data channel by the nodes. A different approach, which places no restrictions on connectivity patterns, allows simultaneous noninterfering transmissions. The strategy uses the ALOHA protocol repeatedly for different groups of nodes [65]. In the sample network of figure 3–5, transmissions between the two pairs of nodes 1, 2 and 6, 8 can both be successfully completed simultaneously. (A similar effect can be achieved in a fully connected network by limiting the transmission power of the nodes, thus obtaining a partially connected multihop network.) In Kleinrock and Silvester [65], the channel access is controlled by a slotted ALOHA scheme. When the transmission-radius signal strength of nodes in such a network is reduced, two things happen. First, the level of collisions in the network is reduced (by having fewer nodes competing for the channel in a given region); second, the average number of relays necessary to forward a message from any source to any destination increases. The capacity of the slotted ALOHA channel, which is $1/e$ for a fully connected network, can be multiplied here by the average number of simultaneous transmissions that can be accommodated when the transmission radius is decreased. However, the increased number of required relays for a message effectively decreases the network capacity. What results is a clear trade-off, which can be controlled by changing the transmission radius, and an optimal radius size can be found. Kleinrock and Silvester [65] demonstrated the existence of an optimal value, which leads to a network in which the network capacity is proportional to the square root of the number of nodes.

A different approach to increasing utilization by channel reuse is obtained by frequency division [66,67], in which the resulting subchannels are arranged into cells. The frequencies are then managed by a central agent, which allocates them to mobile users as they move from one cell to another. Both the Dyna Tac [66] and AMPS [67] systems yield good performance results in the mobile-telephone-system environment, which is characterized as more stream-like than bursty.

The BRAM Hidden-Node Case. The description of adjusting the BRAM scheme to account for hidden nodes is illustrative of the additional problems that result when controlling a multiaccess channel in the presence of hidden nodes.

To determine the effect of hidden nodes on BRAM, we must examine its operation. Specifically, for simple BRAM, collision-free channel access is guaranteed by the following conditions of the ability of each ready node:

C1. To recognize the beginning of a scheduling period;

C2. To calculate its projected transmission time via the S function (which requires an ability to secure the identity of the node that successfully transmitted last);

C3. To defer to a node that gained access to the channel by virtue of having an earlier scheduled transmission time.

Each condition can be violated by the presence of hidden nodes in the network, with the consequences of potential message collision. Specifically, because of the absence of complete connectivity, the following violations may occur:

V1. One node may fail to recognize the end of a transmission of another node and hence will fail to recognize the beginning of the next scheduling period (a node may, in fact, think a busy channel idle and interfere with the scheduling period);

V2. Two nodes may have different identities for the last node to transmit, so that two evaluations of the scheduling function S can give the same value;

V3. One node may fail to sense that another has captured the channel (by virtue of having an earlier starting time) and may begin transmission when its (later) scheduled starting point epoch occurs.

Each violation results in message collision and other combinatoric violations (each of the points above are based on violations of one and only one of the protocol requirements) are possible.

To assess the effect of hidden nodes on BRAM performance, we calculate a connectivity value, R, as follows. First, we construct the node-to-node connectivity matrix, x:

$$x = \begin{bmatrix} x_{11} & \cdots & x_{1k} \\ \vdots & & \vdots \\ x_{k1} & \cdots & x_{kk} \end{bmatrix}$$

with $x_{ij} = 1$ if $i \nleftrightarrow j$, and $x_{ij} = 0$ if $i \leftrightarrow j$ (the notation $\leftrightarrow$ is used to denote line-of-sight (LOS) connectivity, $\nleftrightarrow$ denotes its absence). Then, for the case of homogeneous message arrivals, we let

$$R = \frac{\Sigma x_{ij}}{K^2} \tag{3.4}$$

so that R gives the ratio of hidden node pairs to all node pairs in the network. The value of R given by equation 3.4 is used in figure 3–6. In the figure, we notice the rapid deterioration in throughput as loading, G, and R increase. As R approaches 1, BRAM approaches in function, and therefore in performance, simple unslotted ALOHA.

The definition given by equation 3.4 is not sufficient for networks with node-dependent message-arrival rates. Rather, it becomes necessary to define $R(\lambda_i,x_{ij})$ where the λ_i reflects the message-arrival rate to node i and the x_{ij} are as defined earlier. The reason becomes obvious when one considers the simple case of a network, first with only two high-traffic nodes (relative to the other nodes) not in LOS with each other, and then with two very low traffic nodes (relative to the other nodes) not in LOS with each other. Obviously, the first situation causes more degradation in network performance than does the second. To generalize the definition of R, we reconsider violations V1 through V3 of the required BRAM conditions C1 through C3 and assess their impact in terms of their probability of occurence. By expressing V1 through V3 in terms of a mutually exclusive and exhaustive set of conditions we can relatively easily calculate their probability of occurrence. Once calculated, these probabilities suggest that

$$R = \frac{1}{\lambda^2} \sum_{i,j=1}^{K} \lambda_i \lambda_j x_{ij}$$

with

$$\lambda = \sum_{i=1}^{K} \lambda_i,$$

as the generalized definition of R [64].

The best-grouping algorithm adapts BRAM to the hidden-node environment, noting that the inability to observe staggered starting times is the major cause of performance degradation when hidden nodes are present. Parametric BRAM [10], uses random grouping of nodes, with the number of groups determined so as to optimally balance the inserted channel idle times against the probability of message collision, as a function of channel load. The collisions introduced in this case are between nodes belonging to the same group, and it is easily seen that, for parametric BRAM, the connectivity relationship between nodes in the same group does not affect the occurrence

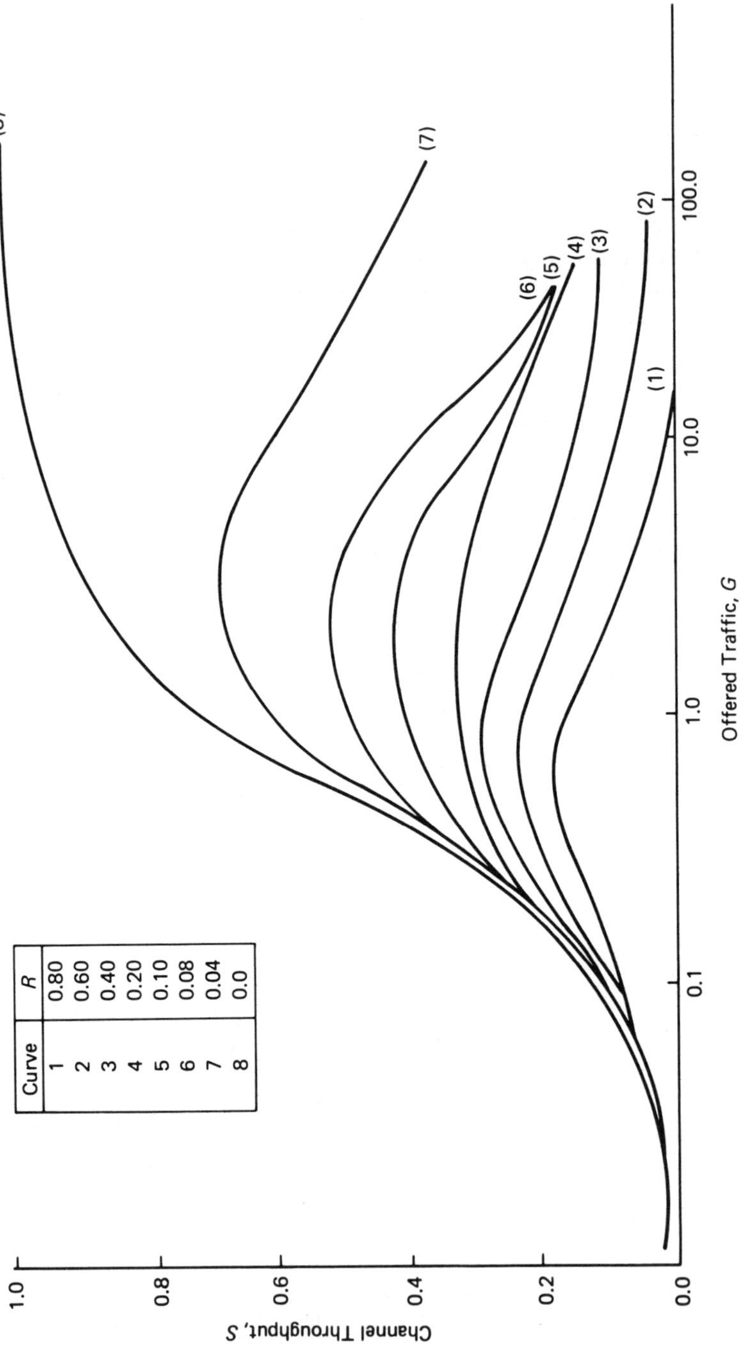

Figure 3–6. Effect of *R* on Throughput (equation 3.4)

of collisions. The connectivity of nodes in different groups, however, does affect the occurrence of collisions.

On the basis of these observations, we apply parametric BRAM to networks with hidden nodes via the best-grouping algorithm:

Definition: A node is considered to be connected to a group of nodes if it is connected with all nodes belonging to the group.

Algorithm:

1. Choose one of the nodes and create the first group.
2. Choose any other node that does not yet belong to anyone of the existing groups. If this node is connected to all existing groups, then create a new group by collapsing all the groups not connected with the given node and include the given node in this group.
3. If all nodes already belong to one of the created groups, stop; otherwise, return to step 2.

Remark: The algorithm assumes at least two nodes in a network.

Theorem:

a. Each node belongs to exactly one group.
b. The number of created groups is in the range $[1,K]$.
c. The algorithm yields the maximal number of groups, with all groups being connected to each other.
d. The groupings obtained are uniquely independent of the node-selection order.

The algorithm therefore gives g groups, $1 \leq g \leq K$, resulting from the connectivity matrix X. In a full, connected environment, $X = 0$, and parametric BRAM requires that g assume all the values between 1 and K. It is also easily seen that, by any union of some of the g groups, any number of groups, $m^* \leq g$, can be obtained, still fulfilling the connectivity property across groups. Thus, behavior of parametric BRAM in a hidden-node environment will be similar to its behavior in a fully connected environment up to that traffic-load value, G, that dictates a number of groups g. Figure 3–7 shows throughput performance for a suboptimal and *the* optimal groupings,as determined by the best-grouping-algorithm for the network in figure 3–5.

The Supervisory-Node Broadcast-Recognizing Access (SUPBRAM) Strategy. The SUPBRAM protocol is designed for networks with stationary nodes and an arbitrary connectivity graph, and in which constant-length

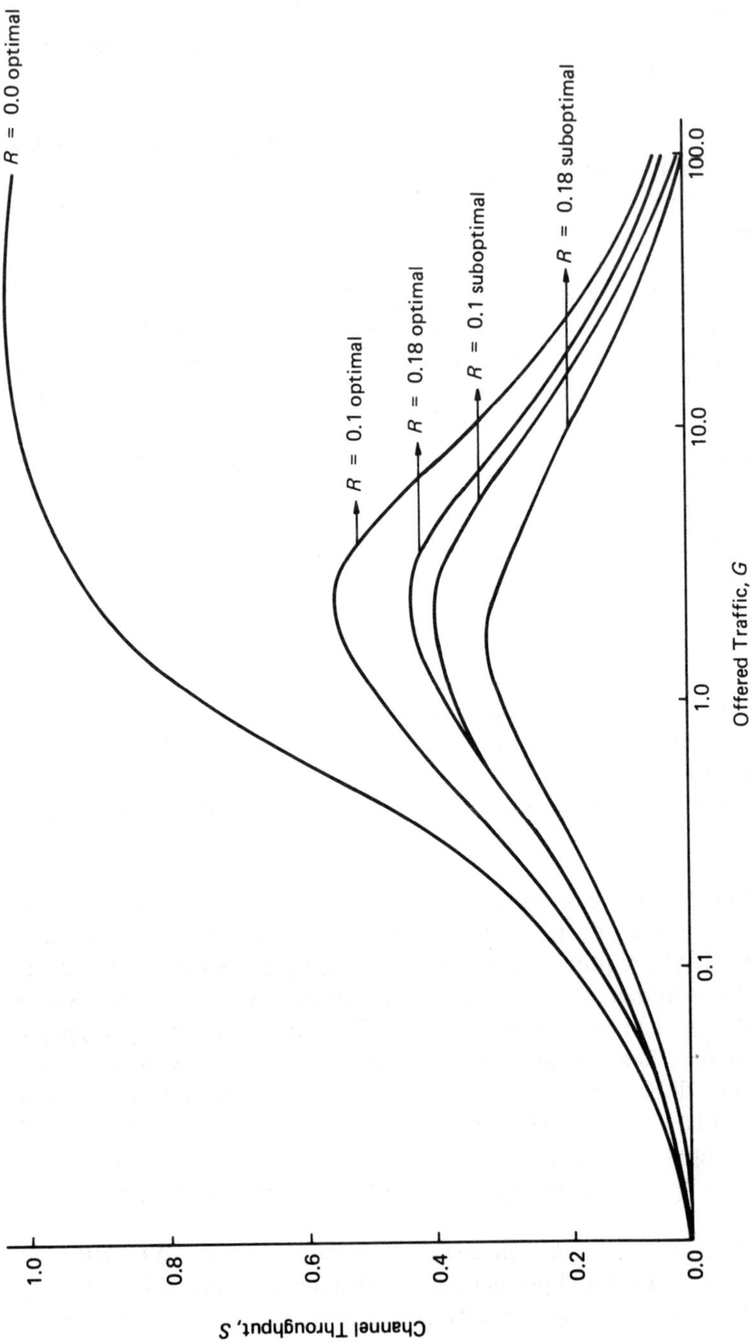

$a = 0.01$

Figure 3–7. Performance Effect of Optimal Grouping Algorithm

packets are the units of information transmitted. As we shall see, it is viable in networks for which K' is small, for example, less than ten or fifteen. When K' is large, a protocol that allows simultaneous transmissions in regions that do not cause collisions may offer better performance. To allow for simultaneous transmissions under SUPBRAM, the protocol should be implemented independently in each region with region-specific K and K' values. Little is known about protocols in this latter category [65]. Among those protocols that do not accommodate simultaneous transmissions, SUPBRAM yields excellent performance measures. It does so by avoiding collisions and by providing an algorithm for adjustment of one of its parameters, denoted by l, so as to yield best-possible performance (as measured in terms of channel throughput and average message delay) over all allowable values of that parameter for each value of the collective backlog of messages awaiting transmission. The SUPBRAM protocol can be considered a logical extension of the BRAM protocol presented earlier [68,69].

Although, as we have shown, BRAM can be used in a network with hidden nodes [64], its performance is much affected by the absence of complete connectivity. Two causes in particular contribute to performance degradation: (1) a node's possible inability to synchronize, that is, recognize the beginning of a scheduling period, and (2) the inability of the collection of nodes to have a commonly agreed-upon value for the index of the node that transmitted last. SUPBRAM overcomes these problems in the ways described next.

First, we imagine packets to be composed of a fixed-length control portion (CP) and a fixed-length information portion (IP). The control portion contains the index of the originating node. In SUBPRAM, transmission of the CP and IP is always separated by a delay, the magnitude of which is determined by a function of packet-traffic intensity. That is, a packet is transmitted in two distinct portions, with transmission of the IP being done after a delay following the transmission of the CP that successfully captures the channel for exclusive use by the node originating the CP. (Capture is effected in much the same manner as with BRAM, as discussed later.)

Nodes transmit CPs during a scheduling period, and, as in BRAM, the node with smallest scheduled CP transmission time for a given scheduling period, as determined by the scheduling function, is allowed to transmit its IP in the information-transfer period that follows the scheduling period by the load-dependent delay. We refer to the two-stage transmission of a packet as split-packet transmission. The scheduling periods are of variable length for the same reasons as in BRAM, with the length of a given scheduling period determined by the indexes of the ready nodes that are attempting to schedule transmissions in that period, and by network parameters.

Further, node synchronization, that is, collision-free channel use for both CP and IP transmissions, is obtained by having certain nodes serving as superivising nodes for others and relaying CPs so that a given CP will propagate to all nodes in the network, particularly to those nodes that are not connected to the node at which the CP originated. When a node receives a CP (either by being connected to the node of origin of the CP or by being connected to a node that served as a supervising node and relayed the CP), it decides if it, too, should serve as a supervisory node and relay the CP to all nodes to which it is connected. Relay decisions are based on (1) the index of the originating node as contained within the CP; (2) the time of arrival of the CP; and (3) information contained in the distance-control vector (DCV), which is constructed at network initialization on the basis of the network connectivity graph. Thus, CP information is propagated to all network nodes by the relaying action of, perhaps, a chain of supervising nodes.

The split-packet delay must be of sufficient width to allow relevant CPs, as originated at any and all network nodes during a scheduling period, to be relayed to all network nodes. During the delay process, ready nodes that have transmitted a CP determine whether or not they have captured the channel for subsequent IP transmission by examining the indexes of the nodes contained in all CPs received, either directly or by relay during the delay period, and noting (calculating) the time at which the CP was transmitted by the node of origin.

To formalize these notions, imagine a network with $K \geq 2$ nodes identified by unique indexes 1,2, . . . ,K, for which $K \geq 2$ is as defined earlier. Let a represent the propagation delay between the remotest pair of connected nodes in the network. (The channel end-to-end delay, as defined earlier, is not useful in a hidden-node network, because its value is infinity.)

To extend BRAM to the hidden node environment we must (1) provide for node synchronization, (2) revise the scheduling function, (3) devise a viable CP-relay algorithm, and (4) quantify the value for the split-packet delay. We consider each requirement in turn.

The Distance-Control Matrix. Before proceeding to an explanation of the mechanisms for the foregoing requirements, we define the distance-control matrix (DCM) on which they depend. The DCM is a $K \times K$ matrix, D, with entries

$$d_{ji} = \begin{cases} \pm d & i \neq j \\ -0 & i = j \end{cases}$$

where $d = |d_{ji}|$ gives the minimal number of relays necessary to relay information from node i to node j (along source-based graphs of diameter K^1), and the sign of $d_{ji} = +$ if node j must consider relaying node i-originated CPs, or the sign of $(d_{ji}) = -$ if node j should never relay node j-originated CPs.

CP Source Node Index

Receiving Node Index	1	2	3	4	5	6	7	8	9	10
1	-0	-1	-2	+1	+2	-3	+2	-4	-3	-4
2	+1	-0	+1	+2	+3	+2	+3	+3	-4	-4
3	-2	+1	-0	-3	-4	+1	-4	+2	-4	+3
4	+1	+2	-2	-0	+1	-1	+1	+2	+2	+2
5	-2	-3	-2	-1	-0	-1	-2	-2	-3	-3
6	-2	+2	+1	-1	-1	-0	-2	+1	+3	+2
7	+3	-3	-3	+1	+2	-2	-0	+1	+1	-1
8	-3	+3	+2	-2	-3	+1	-1	-0	-1	+1
9	-3	-4	-3	-2	-3	-2	-1	-1	-0	-1
10	-3	-4	-3	-2	-3	-2	-1	-1	-1	-0

Figure 3–8. DCM for Sample Network with Hidden Nodes

Thus the sign of d_{ji} informs node j if it is a supervisory node for node i-originated CPs. The relay algorithm requires that each node j use only its row of the DCM, as given by the values d_{jn}, $n = 1, \ldots, k$; we call the rows of the DCM distance-control vectors (DCVs). Chlamtac and Franta [68] give an algorithm for the construction of the DCM, which uses the connectivity graph as input. Figure 3–8 shows the DCM for the network depicted in figure 3–5.

Node Synchronization. Node synchronization can be effected given that nodes can count the passage of intervals of width a, that is, a-slots. Synchronization requires, as for BRAM, a common understanding among the nodes of the epochs that mark the beginning of scheduling periods and adherence to a rule that requires CPs to be transmitted completely within the boundaries of a single a-slot, as counted from the beginning of a scheduling period. The particular a-slot in which a CP is transmitted is determined by the scheduling function, as will be given later. In SUPBRAM, as in BRAM, the node that captures the channel is the node that is given the smallest value (highest priority) by the scheduling function, and it is that node which transmits a CP earliest in a given scheduling period.

To agree upon the identity of the node that first transmitted a CP (for a given scheduling period), each node maintains the tuple (t_f, id_f), where t_f = the minimum over all CPs received, or the index of the a-slot within the current scheduling period in which the CP was transmitted, and id_f = the node index of the node associated with t_f, as extracted from the CP. This tuple is maintained as follows. For node j, let t represent the index of the a-slot in which a CP containing index i is received. The time at which the CP was transmitted is then given by $t - |d_{ji}|$. If initially we have $(t_f, id_f) =$

$(+\infty, 0)$, the tuple is maintained by the following algorithm (executed by node j each time a CP-containing index i is received):

If $t - |d_{ji}| < t_f$, *then* $id_f \leftarrow i$; $t_f \leftarrow t - |d_{ji}|$; set alarm for $t_f + K' \cdot a$ (at alarm, execute $t_f \leftarrow \infty$), with only the last scheduled alarm in effect.

Given the tuple (t_f, id_f), all nodes are able to agree upon the index of the node that will capture the channel. Furthermore, the tuple is sufficient, given T_{n-1}, the epoch marking the beginning of the current scheduling period, to calculate the beginning of the next scheduling period. We have

$$T_n = T_{n-1} + (t_f - |d_{ji}|)a + la + \mathrm{IP}_{\mathrm{time}}$$

where l is the width of the split-packet delay, in a-slots, and $\mathrm{IP}_{\mathrm{time}}$ is the time, in a-slots, required to transmit an IP. Thus, the scheduling-period boundaries are easily calculated, so long as scheduling periods and transmission periods strictly alternate. It may happen, however, that a maximal-length scheduling period passes following a transmission, that is, no CPs are transmitted, as there are no ready nodes. When this happens, an idle period is entered. For completely connected networks with a shared channel, this usually signals entry to a contention mode, as discussed earlier. With SUPBRAM, we avoid a contention mode and maintain synchronization as follows. Let t' be the index of the a-slot, counted from the beginning of the maximal-length scheduling period that passed unused at which node j becomes ready. (To account for countered (clock) drift, artificial messages can be generated to prevent t' from becoming too large.) Node j then calculates the beginning of the next scheduling period by finding the minimal r—say, r^*—such that

$$T_{n-1} + r^* (K' - l)a + q_j \cdot a \leq t'$$

and setting

$$T_n = T_{n-1} + r^*(K' - l)a$$

where q_j is the output of node j evaluation of the scheduling function. Thus, if we associate T_0 with network initialization, the nodes remain synchronized for the duration of network operation. (We note that nodes may drop from and later rejoin the network by simply waiting for a CP to resynchronize.) It is not difficult to show that this procedure minimizes $(T_n - t')$, that is, that the first possible scheduling period is used. We may put these two pieces together so that node j, which becomes ready at time t', with t' counted in a-slots from T_{n-1}, calculates T_n by

$$Z \leftarrow (t_f - |\ d_{jid_f}\ |\ )a + la + \mathrm{IP}_{\mathrm{time}} + T_{n-1}$$

if $t' < Z$ *then* $T_n \leftarrow Z$; otherwise,

$$T_n \leftarrow T_{n-1} + r^* \ (K' - l)a$$

with r^* as defined.

The Scheduling Function. The SUPBRAM scheduling function serves to stagger node CP-transmission starting times within a scheduling period, in a manner analagous to its use in BRAM. The intention, as in BRAM, is to assign the channel to the node that is assigned by the scheduling function as the minimal starting point (a-slot index) among all ready nodes. Although scheduling functions of the form given earlier for BRAM can be used, the situation is complicated by the need to relay CPs because of hidden nodes. Specifically, the scheduling function calculates, for a node, the index of the a-slot in which the node may transmit its CP if it has not (by relay) received information of a ready node with a smaller assigned index by the time its assigned a-slot passes. If such information is received by the node, it refrains from transmitting its CP; if no such information is received, the node transmits its CP in its assigned a-slot. After transmission of a CP, the node is still not certain it has captured the channel, for CPs with smaller indexes may arrive (as the result of relays) during the split delay. If none do arrive, the node has captured the channel; if one does arrive, the node defers. The point of the matter is simple: the spacing (staggering) given by the scheduling function together with the split-packet delay must be of sufficient width for all ready nodes to receive relevant CPs and to determine whether or not they have captured the channel. In a manner analogous to BRAM, we take the scheduling function, with $d = K' - l$, to be

$$S(i,id_f) = \begin{cases} [(i - id_f + K)\bmod K - 1) \cdot d + 1, & i \neq id_f \\ (K - 1) \cdot d + 1, & i = id_f \end{cases} \tag{3.5}$$

to give lowest priority to the node id_f that transmitted last, and

$$S(i,id_f) = [(i - id_f + K)\bmod K] \cdot d, \qquad \forall i \tag{3.6}$$

to give highest priority to the node that transmitted last. As in BRAM, the function (equation 3.5) rotates the priority assignments among the nodes in a fair manner. The potential CP-transmission time for node i within the scheduling period marked by T_n is determined by

$$\bar{\bar{t}} = T_n + S(i,id_f) \cdot a$$

as in BRAM. Node action at $\bar{\bar{t}}$ is determined by CPs received between T_n and $\bar{\bar{t}}$. Specifically, if, during $(T_n,\bar{\bar{t}})$, t_f takes on a value less than $\bar{\bar{t}}$, node i refrains (defers); if t_f does not take on such a value, node i transmits its CP in the a-slot marked by $\bar{\bar{t}}$.

Obviously we must have $d > 0$, which implies $1 \leq l < K'$; and d together with the value l guarantee a collision-free relay of CPs, as discussed next.

The Relay Algorithm. The relay algorithm serves to forward CPs about the network so that nodes can come to a common understanding of the index of the node that has, in a given scheduling period, captured the channel. The relay algorithm employed in SUPBRAM is designed (1) to avoid collisions among CPs, among CPs and IPs, and among IPs; (2) to relay relevant CPs to nodes in the minimum possible number of a-slot delays; and (3) to avoid unnecessary relays of IPs. The relay algorithm relies heavily on both the multiplier d used in the scheduling function S (.,.) and the split delay given by la.

As stated earlier, the sign of the element d_{ji} serves to determine if node j should consider relaying CPs received from node i. The DCM construction algorithm [68] assigns signs so as to minimize the number of relays required. There are two reasons, however, why CPs are not blindly relayed if the sign of d_{ji} signals relay. First, there is no need to relay CPs emanating from nodes that cannot be contenders for capturing the channel. Second, relay of multiple copies of CPs must be avoided (a node could receive multiple copies of a CP that have traveled different routes) to minimize scheduling-period lengths and avoid possibly infinite relay loops. These needs are nicely served by the information contained in the tuple (t_f,id_f). Specifically, received CPs with origin time greater than t_f should not be relayed. Thus, we may couple relay decisions with updates of the tuple (t_f, id_f) to obtain (executed by node j each time a CP with index i is received:

if $t - | d_{ji} | < t_f$, *then*

$$[id_f \leftarrow i; t_f \leftarrow t - | d_{ji} | \tag{3.7}$$

if the sign of $(d_{ji}) = +$, *then* relay (CP $\equiv i$); set alarm for $t_f + K' \cdot a$,

with t as before, the index of the a-slot within the current scheduling period in which the CP is received by node j. It can be shown that the procedure in equation 3.7, together with the DCM, avoids unnecessary relays and minimizes path-relay delays, while serving to relay all relevant information to the nodes.

Collisions are avoided and delays are further reduced by the following considerations. First, we wish relays to occur as soon as possible after CPs are received. Second, if CPs are always transmitted at the beginning of an a-slot, collisions can occur. (A collision occurs, for example, if two CPs originate at two nodes and travel two different relay routes of different lengths, such that the difference in lengths of the routes cancels the staggering in starting times, as given by the scheduling function, and they arrive at a third node in the same a-slot.) To circumvent this potentiality for the purposes of scheduling, we divide a-slots into a series of subslots, which we assign to the nodes in a variant of a TDMA scheme. Each a-slot is decomposed into $K' \cdot K'$ subslots, each of sufficient width to transmit or receive a CP (assumed to require CP_{time} time units). As CP_{time} is very small, the interval $K' \cdot K' \cdot CP_{time}$ remains small.

Formally we define as follows: $a \equiv$ maximum a (the propagation delay between the remotest pair of connected nodes) and $K' \cdot K'$ CP_{time}. The subslots are organized into K' blocks with each block containing K' subslots. Subslots within a block are assigned to nodes in a "TDMA" fashion. Node i always transmits its CPs using the $(S(i_j id_f) mod\ K')$th subslot of a block and relays node j's CPs in the $(S(j_i id_f) mod\ K')$th subslot. To minimize delays, node i always transmits its CPs in the first block of the a-slot assigned it by $S(i, id_f)$ and relays CPs in the block directly following the block in which the CP is received. An example with $K' = 4$ is shown in figure 3–9.

Thus, although multiple CPs can be received in a block, only one (if any)

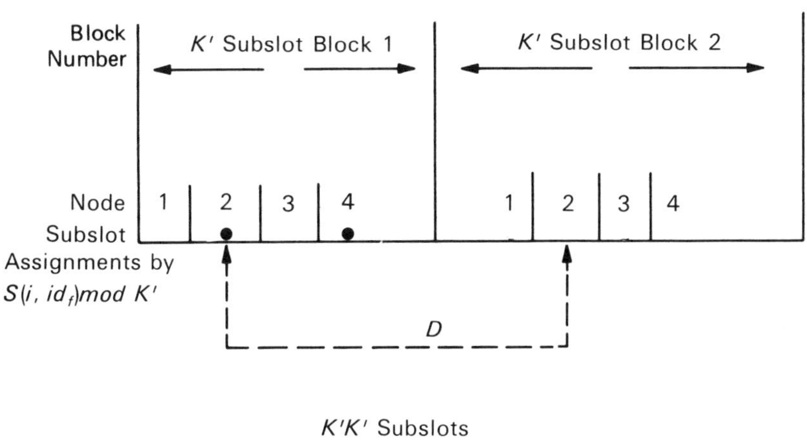

• indicates CPs received. D implies decision process given in equation 3.7. View is from node 3's perspective.

Figure 3–9. A Subslot-Assignment Example

will be relayed. For example, figure 3–9 shows two CPs (in subslots 2 and 4) received, for example, by node 3 in the first block. suppose those CPs contain indexes $\hat{i}$ and $\hat{\hat{i}}$. Since one of the pair, $(t - | d_{j\hat{\hat{i}}} |)$ or $(t - | d_{j\hat{i}} |)$ is smaller, only one CP need be relayed. The subslot scheme directly avoids collisions. The d value used in the scheduling function and the l delay guarantee adequate time to relay CPs so that nodes may cooperate and a single IP transmission can ensue. These ideas can now be brought together to formally characterize the SUPBRAM protocol.

Formalized Protocol Description (executed by node i when ready):

1. Compute $\bar{\bar{t}} = T_n + S(i,id_f) \cdot a$ + TDMA offset ($\bar{\bar{t}}$ is node i's next potential CP transmission time).
2. *If* at $\bar{\bar{t}}$, $t_f < S(i,id_f) \cdot a$, *then* repeat from 1 (CP of a higher priority node has arrived); *else* transmit node i CP at $\bar{\bar{t}}$.
3. *If* at $\hat{t} = T_n + [S(i,id_f) + l) \cdot a, t_f < S(i,id_f) \cdot a$, *then* repeat from 1 (CP of a higher priority node has arrived); *else* transmit node i IP at $\hat{t}$.

In SUPBRAM, two protocol parameters can be adjusted to improve its performance: the split-packet-delay value l and the number of scheduling points in the scheduling period. First, any l value in the range $1 \leq l \leq K^1 - 1$ works, and it has been shown that optional selections exist (to minimize delay)[68]. Second, we note that, in n a-slots, a transmitted reservation packet will reach all nodes within a radius n of the origin. Subsequently, each subset of nodes that are separated by no more than n hops can compete in a collision-free manner for a single scheduling period, which allows reduction in the length of scheduling periods. For more detail, consult Chlamtac and Franta [68,69].)

Satellite Channels. Satellite channels are qualitatively different from cable and radio channels [71]. First, for satellites, the propagation a is large rather than small, so that often $a > T$, with T the packet-transmission time. In fact, a is so large that 270 ms must elapse for a signal to travel from earth to satellite and then back to earth. Second, satellite channels are more prone to errors than cable channels are; in fact, the error characteristics are affected by weather. Finally, since the satellite is a transponder, a node can use correct reception of its own transmission as an acknowledgment (at least knowing that it was not interfered with by a collision).

The approximately quarter-second propagation delay makes carrier-sense schemes less than viable for satellite channels. Random-assignment, demand-assignment, and adaptive-assignment strategies, however, are available. In particular, the ALOHA (slotted or unslotted) random-access strategies can be used, with nodes sensing collisions in the manner described earlier.

Reservation ALOHA (R-ALOHA). R-ALOHA [70] is a variant of slotted ALOHA in which nodes can reserve slots. In R-ALOHA, slots are collected into frames with n slots per frame. Nodes keep a record of slot use for the most recent frame. The record notes, for each slot, whether it was successfully used, unused, or contained a collision. Successfully used slots are reserved, in the next frame, for exclusive use by the nodes that used them successfully in the last frame. Slots that went unused or were involved in collision may be vied for, in the next frame, by the normal ALOHA mechanism, with some randomization strategy to serialize previous collisions. In R-ALOHA, acknowledgments are treated as normal messages; R-ALOHA performance is much like that of slotted ALOHA.

Roberts Reservation ALOHA (or FIFO protocol). As described by Roberts [72], slots are organized into frames, with each frame containing one ALOHA reservation frame and n data-transfer frames. The slots are of a width sufficient so that each ALOHA reservation slot can be divided into a sequence of K' subslots. Each subslot is vied for in an ALOHA fashion (with some randomization across the K' slots if $K' < K$). Subslots are used by nodes to reserve data slots. Specifically, each node maintains a counter, which gives a systemwide count of the number of reserved but not yet used data slots. Reservation subslots carry the count of the number of data slots a node wishes to reserve. (Reservation requests that are destroyed by collision are retransmitted in subsequent frame-reservation-slot subslots after randomization; collisions are detected in the manner described earlier.) If data slots are used by nodes in the order in which they are reserved, simple arithmetic allows a node that has reserved l data slots to know which consecutive l data slots it can use to transmit its l packets collision-free. Acknowledgments are sent in reservation subslots. TDMA reservation variants [73] have also been devised.

Satellite ALOHA (S-ALOHA). S-ALOHA [75] has the flavor of p-persistent CSMA. In the S-ALOHA channel-access protocol, each node maintains two output queues: the new queue (for new packets) and the retransmit queue (for packets that need to be retransmitted because of previous conflict). All nodes follow the same rules for transmission. At the beginning of a slot, a node will transmit a packet from the retransmit queue, with probability PR (retransmit gate). Only if the retransmit queue is empty will a node transmit a packet from the new queue, with probability PN (new gate). If two or more nodes transmit in the same slot, their packets will collide and will destroy each other. The senders detect the conflict by monitoring the channel after a round-trip time and promptly return a copy of the collided packet to the retransmit queue.

Priority-Oriented Demand Assignment (PODA). PODA [74–76] is a demand-assignment protocol designed to efficiently support both datagram and stream traffic, with multiple-delay classes and priorities and variable message lengths. Its design represents an integration of several demand-assignment and control techniques:

1. Explicit reservations are used for datagram messages, generally resulting in delays of at least two satellite hops.
2. A single explicit reservation is used to set up each stream, with subsequent packets automatically scheduled at predetermined intervals, thus generally yielding one-hop delays.
3. Very high reliability, when desired, is provided by the use of scheduled acknowledgments and packet retransmissions.
4. High availability and improved performance are achieved by the use of distributed-control techniques.
5. Robustness and mixed-receiving-rate operation are achieved by the integrated use of both distributed- and centralized-control techniques.

The design described here assumes a TDMA channel, although the PODA approach could be used to allocate channel capacity with other channel-assignment techniques. Channel time is divided into two basic subframes, an information subframe and a control subframe (see figure 3–10). The information subframe is used for scheduled datagram and stream transmissions, which also contain control information, such as reservations and acknowledgments, in their headers. In normal operation, the control subframe is used exclusively to send reservations that cannot be sent in the information subframe in a timely manner. The information subframe is further divided into a section for centralized assignments and a section for distributed assignments. Details on the use of these sections and the other aspects of PODA are described in the following paragraphs.

The control subframe must be used for initial reservation access by a node that has no impending scheduled transmissions, and it may also need to be used at times to make reservations for traffic whose urgency does not allow waiting for the next opportunity to use the header of a scheduled message.

The access method used for this subframe depends on the particular characteristics of the system in which PODA is being used. If the total number of nodes is small, then fixed assignments of one slot per station are typically used within the control subframe, and the system is referred to as FPODA. For large populations of nodes with low demands, mixed

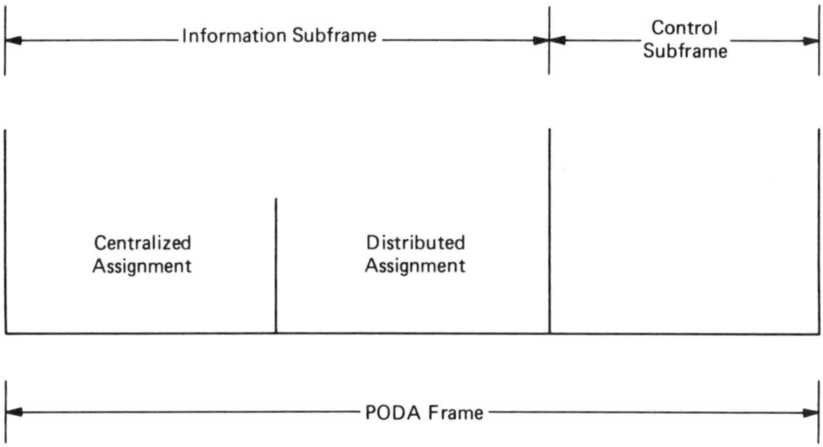

Figure 3–10. PODA Frame Structure

demands, or situations in which traffic requirements are not well known, random access (slotted ALOHA) is used, and the system is referred as CPODA. Combinations of fixed assignment and random access in the control subframe are also possible. In either case, subframe time is divided into fixed-sized slots equal to the (constant) length of the control packets.

The slotted ALOHA transmissions in CPODA create potential stability and fairness problems in the control subframe. Since the desirable operating point for contention subframe loading is considerably less than $1/e$ for best overall system performance, however, instability problems are rare relative to a typical ALOHA channel. In addition to the usual slotted ALOHA control techniques, the following mechanisms enhance stability and fairness.

1. The size of the control subframe is varied according to current scheduling requirements. If no reservations are outstanding, the control subframe occupies almost the entire CPODA frame; as loading increases, the control subframe is reduced to a value determined by the urgency of the messages being scheduled until a minimum value is reached.

2. New reservation transmissions are constrained at all nodes, allowing only higher-priority traffic to compete in the contention subframe when the channel is heavily scheduled.

CPODA does have a potential fairness problem relative to FPODA, caused by the ability of heavy-traffic nodes to obtain continued use of the channel via reservations made in their scheduled transmissions. This is reasonably resolved, however, by enlarging the control subframe when excessive conflicts occur (temporarily increasing the delay of messages waiting to be scheduled).

All datagram reservations received successfully in the satellite downlink are entered into a scheduling queue, maintained by all stations using distributed scheduling. These entries are ordered according to reservation urgency, which is a function of potential lateness (relative to the node-specified delay class) and priority. Reservations with the same urgency are further ordered to provide fairness to the nodes involved. Channel time in the information subframe is then assigned to messages according to the latest ordering of reservations in the scheduling queue.

A reservation for a stream is made only once, at the beginning of the stream use, and is retained at each node in a separate stream queue when received in the downlink. Each stream reservation contains information defining the stream-repetition interval, desired maximum delay relative to the interval, and priority. Whenever the interval starting time is near, a reservation is created for that stream's next message and is entered into the scheduling queue; the reservation urgency is calculated according to the stream-queue information and is treated in the same way as datagram-reservation urgency. Thus, all channel-time requests, whether for datagrams or for streams, are ordered according to a single set of rules. In particular, high-priority datagram traffic can preempt lower-priority stream allocations for an indefinite period, possibly resulting in termination of the streams.

Link-Level Protocols

The level-2 access protocol monitors the channel before and during transmission (as appropriate), and, for a ready node, sends a "bucket-of-bits" message out on the channel, in accordance with agreed-upon access rules. Correspondingly, it captures (receives) a bucket-of-bits message from the channel and disposes of the received message according to the destination address it contains. In local networks, the level-3 link-level protocol is tightly coupled with the access protocol, especially when certain access options, such as LWT, are employed. For purposes of exposition, however, we imagine clean functionality boundaries between the two protocol layers. From this somewhat imaginary position, we can charge the level-3 protocol with providing (1) a service for the reliable delivery of individual variable-length messages and (2) aids for regulating the flow of a stream of messages between two communicating nodes. The essence of the first provision is a reliable datagram service; that of the second is maintenance of a virtual circuit. Providing these services is mitigated by the wideband, reliable, low-delay nature of local-network hardware technology. These attributes allow use of simple routing, flow, and error-control strategies.

For example, since the channel is both wideband and nearly error-free, long messages can be transmitted without excessive penalty. As the medium is wideband, one transmission does not unduly delay the transmission of subsequent messages. As the mechanism is error-free, few messages need be transmitted multiple times. In short, many of the arguments that lead to packetization of messages in long-haul networks become weak or vacuous in local networks. The simplicities afforded contribute, in turn, to economy in the realization of level-3 protocols, an economy that again contributes to low delays and simple, compact software. The wideband, reliable nature of the channel also allows us to freely add overhead bits to transmitted messages. Thus, for example, address and CRC fields can be as wide as is convenient without compromising performance (see figure 2–13).

A partial exception to some of these observations is found in multihop radio networks (wherein efficient routing of messages is still necessary) or mixed-media networks, which employ microwave or satellite links (wherein extensive buffering and packetization may remain necessary).

A Diversion: Radio Routing

The object of routing in radio-channel networks is effective use of the channel and avoidance of collisions. In broadcast-radio networks, a forwarding of a packet must always be omnidirectional. That is, in radio networks one has to achieve a sense of direction for routed packets and avoid infinite looping of forwarded packets. Several solutions have been suggested [77]. One of them, broadcast routing, consists of transmitting all received packets by all nodes, unless either a "hop counter" in the received packet indicates that the packet has already been forwarded the maximum allowable number of times or the packet is recognized by the nodes as one that has been forwarded in the past. The choice of the number of hops a packet is allowed to make before being discarded by a receiving node is closely related to network reliability and effective channel utilization. Large hop counts give high probability that a packet will reach its destination by alternative routing paths in case of intermediate node failure. However, a large number of duplicate copies of a packet floating around the network reduces the effective channel throughput. Small hop-count values have the opposite effect. The ability of nodes to recognize previously transmitted packets provides some bandwidth-utilization improvement, in that received packets can be discarded long before their hop count is exhausted. Altogether, broadcast routing is simple and robust, and it does not use any knowledge of network topology, which is convenient in radio networks of mobile nodes.

Another technique suitable for the mobile environment is directed broadcast routing. With this approach, the nodes are aware of their relative distances, in terms of the minimal number of hops that connect them, via information that is updated and kept in a distance table. The routing decision is a simple one. A receiving node forwards a received packet if the receiver node is closer to the destination than to the sending node; otherwise, it is discarded. This approach, similar to the approach used in the ARPANET, provides a guaranteed delivery of packets to the destination node, with low delays resulting from the shortest-path routes.

Other approaches are also possible. Hierarchical routing [77], for example, requires that the central site be aware of the complete topological layout. Using this knowledge, a shortest path to each node is determined. The nodes are organized along these routes into a tree, with a central site serving as root. Each packet transmitted from the central site contains a label that details the path description. At each relay node, the label of the packet is checked, and the packet is forwarded only if the repeater node is designated to do so as a result of being on the packet's route.

Routing along the shortest-path route in radio networks can cause collisions, possibly requiring several retransmissions and thus offsetting the advantages of choosing shortest routes. Thus, although shortest-route forwarding is optimal in point-to-point networks (when the delays are identical in both directions [78]), in radio networks, because of collisions, shortest-path routing may be suboptimal. Alternate strategies remain an open question.

Error Control

Each frame transmitted may contain enough information for the receiver simply to detect errors or enough information for the receiver to detect and correct errors. Obviously, detection requires a simpler mechanism than does detection and correction. Detection and correction is attractive when the transmission delays are long and the channel is unreliable. With local networks where delays are low (and the channel is very reliable), detection and retransmission is simple and is more effective than detection and correction. As described in chapter 2, the usual detection mechanism is the so-called cyclic-redundancy check, which is calculated and appended to each frame transmitted (each frame being viewed as simply a string of bits). A receiving node calculates its own value of the check for comparison with the transmitted value, as is also explained in chapter 2. The essence of the method is the function $f(.)$, which should be simple to calculate, unique for a given message M, adequate to allow detection of a single-bit error, and adequate to allow detection of multiple-bit errors, whether they occur in a single string or scattered throughout M. The function $f(.)$ most commonly used is a binary polynomial, which requires that we also view the message M as generating a polynomial. For example, the message M given by the bit string 1010010001 can be thought to correspond to the coefficients of the binary polynomial

$$P_M^9(x) = 1 + x^2 + x^5 + x^9$$

and any binary message can be viewed as giving the coefficients of a binary polynomial $P_M^n(x)$, for some degree n, dependent on message length. Throughout this presentation we use modulo-2 binary arithmetic, so that there are no borrows or carries, that is, $1 + 1 = 0$, $0 + 1 = 1$, $1 + 0 = 1$, $0 + 0 = 0$, and $-1 = +1$, so that addition and subtraction are equivalent.) The function $f(.)$ is calculated by selecting a binary polynomial $P_l(x)$, of degree l, forming

$$\frac{P_M^n(x)}{P_l(x)} = Q(x) + R(x)^*$$

where $Q(x)$ is the quotient polynomial and $R(x)$ is the remainder polynomial, and using

$$f(M) \equiv R(x)$$

We have, of course, by the rules of division, that the degree of $R(x)$ is less than l and is furthermore unique for a given $P_M^n(x)$, hence a given message M.

Example 3.2

If M is the string 1010010001, such that $P_M^n(x) = P_M^9(x)$, as given, and $P_l(x) = P_5(x) = 1 + x^2 + x^4 + x^5$ then

$$\frac{P_M^9(x)}{P_5(x)} = Q(x) + R_2(x)$$

with $R_2(x) = 1 + x$. As the degree of $R(x)$ may be anything less than l, it makes sense to reserve l bits in the message header for the value of $R(x)$. Thus, with $P_5(x)$ the CRC field must be at least five bits wide.

To be effective, $P_l(x)$ must be properly selected. To gain insight into the selection criteria, consider a transmitted message M that is received in error. The message is transmitted as $P_M^n(x) + E(x)$, where $E(x)$ contains one 1 bit for each error in the transmitted version of $P_M^n(x)$. The receiving node forms

$$\frac{P_M^n(x) + E(x)}{P_l(x)} + Q(x) + R(x) + \frac{E(x)}{P_l(x)}$$

so that the remainder is $R(x) + E(x)/P_l(x)$. Obviously, those errors for which $E(x)/P_l(x) = 0$ will pass by unnoticed. For a single-bit error,

$E(x) = x^i$; for two isolated errors, $E(x) = x^i + x^j = x^j(x^{i-j} + 1)$ if $i \geq j$. A burst error of k bits will produce $E(x) + x^i(x^{k-1} + \ldots + 1)$, with i indicating how far from the beginning of the message the error occurs. Based on observations such as these, $P_l(x)$ should be chosen so as not to have these terms as factors, so that division of these terms by $P_l(x)$ is nonzero. As for machine arithmetic, an amazing amount of theory has been developed regarding selection of $P_l(x)$. It turns out, for example, that $P_l(x)$ should have $(x + 1)$ as a factor in order to ferret out all errors consisting of an odd number of inverted bits. Furthermore, detection of a burst error of length k is facilitated by having the degree of $P_l(x)$ greater than k, that is, by insuring that $l > k$.

Several polynomials $P_l(x)$ have the status of standards. Among them are

$$P_{16}(x) = x^{16} + x^{12} + x^5 + 1$$

the CCITT standard, which has $(x + 1)$ as a factor and is often employed. It can be shown by examining $E(x)$ and $P_{16}(x)$ that $P_{16}(x)$ will unveil all single and double-bit errors, all errors involving an odd number of bits, all burst errors of with $k \leq 16$, and over 99.9 percent of the burst errors with $k = 17$ and $k = 18$. A polynomial of higher degree, such as $P_{32}(x)$ [126], would serve to reveal all burst errors with $k \leq 32$.

Although calculation of $R(x)$ may seem complex (requiring division and multiplication), it is not. In fact, a simple shift register and a set of l modulo-2 adders is all that is needed to capture the calculation in hardware [89]. As a result, hardware is usually used.

Flow Control

By definition, a datagram service allows one node to send a message to another node with no prior reservation of buffer space or other form of announcement. If, when a datagram message is received, there is not sufficient storage to retain it, the message is rejected. If nothing more is done, the sending node will assume that the message did not arrive intact and will retransmit the message according to the prevailing retry strategy. Alternatively, the receiving node can send a negative acknowledgment (NAK), with an indicator giving the reason for rejection. The latter strategy can regulate the flow of retrys better than can the normal retry strategy, which is not designed to cope with a shortage of storage (buffer) space in destination nodes. Additionally, the NAK strategy may mean the difference between eventual delivery of the message or discard. If, for example, the retry strategy dictates discard after n retrys, and n retrys are met with n rejects, the datagram may be discarded or at least unduly delayed as a result of processing by another (perhaps application-level) error-handling layer. A NAK, on the other hand, can be used to space the retrys to allow time for the destination node to complete processing of previous commitments.

This latter strategy (using NAKs) is essentially one in which a datagram-requested action is never truly rejected but is only deferred, and, in essence, a buffer is always reserved in each node to receive datagrams.

Regulation of the flow of messages in a stream of messages requires slightly more complex handling, and some variant of the *sliding-window* mechanism is usually used. The sliding-window mechanism associates a sequence number i, $0 \leq i \leq \infty$, with each frame in a stream of frames. At any time after initiation of the stream transmission, the receiving node has received m frames and the sending node has transmitted n frames and has received acknowledgments for l of them, $0 \leq l \leq n$. Thus, as described, the sending node is able to continue to transmit frames without awaiting receipt of acknowledgments for previously transmitted frames. Frame flow is regulated by having a maximum number, w, of outstanding unacknowledged, frames, such that $0 \leq (n - l) \leq w$. If, at any, time $(n - l) = w$, the sending node must wait for an acknowledgment (or acknowledgments) before sending additional frames. The allowed number of unacknowledged frames, w, is known as the width of a sliding window. Proper setting of w allows a receiving node to properly allocate buffer storage and regulate the rate at which messages are received from the sender (by withholding acknowledgments). The window is bounded by the indexes m and $m + w$, or l and $l + w$. Usually, an acknowledgment for frame j, $m < j \leq (m + w)$, is also sufficient to imply acknowledgments for frames $(m + 1), (m + 2), \ldots, (j - 1)$ if they were not explicitly sent. When the acknowledgment for frame j is sent, the receiving-node window slides to the right from $(m, m + w)$ to $(j + 1, j + 1 + w)$. A similar sliding occurs at the sending node when an acknowledgment is received.

The magnitude of w is determined by: (1) the speed of sending node; (2) the amount of (buffer) memory in a CIU; and (3) the rate at which a receiving node can consume, act on, or dispose of received frames. The frame header field that contains the sequence number i must, furthermore, be of infinite width, at least theoretically. As this is not possible, the frame header usually is of sufficient width to contain a finite set of indexes, such as $0 \leq i \leq K$. With this restriction, frames in a sequence are numbered 0 through $K - 1$, and the Kth frame is again numbered zero, the $(K + 1)$st is numbered one, and so on, in a modulo-K cyclic fashion. If, because of retransmissions, frames can be delivered out of order, confusion can result as to the cycle to which a given frame belongs. To avoid confusion on which frame is which—that is, to identify the cycle to which a frame belongs—the window mechanism must be synchronized with the modulo-K assignment of indexes to frames. No confusion results if $w \leq K/2$.

Example 3.3

That $w \leq K/2$ is sufficient is shown as follows. Imagine that the transmitting node has received acknowledgment for all frames to l of the current cycle. It may then freely transmit frames $(l + 1)\text{mod}\, K$, $(l + 2)\text{mod}\, K, \ldots$, $(l + w)$ mod K, which may contain indexes in several cycles. Suppose, further, that the receiving node has received and acknowledged frames to m. It is therefore expecting frames $(m + 1)\text{mod}\ K, \ldots$, $(m + w)\text{mod}\ K$, which again may involve multiple cycles. Clearly, at most two cycles will be involved if $w \leq K$. Assuming $w \leq K$, our next objective is to further limit w so that the receiver can have no difficulty determining the cycle of a frame no matter what the retransmission policy of the sender is. Unique identification is had if a received frame can possibly belong to only one cycle. Thus, we must avoid the circumstance where retransmissions of frames in the range $l + 1, \ldots, m$ can be misinterpreted by the receiver. In the worst case, $m - l$ can differ by $w - 1$, so that the receiver is expecting frames in a next cycle and possibly receiving them (as a result of retransmissions) from a last cycle. From the receiver's view, then, it is possibly receiving frames in a window of width $2w$. We avoid confusion if we have $2w \leq K$, which gives $w \leq k/2$.

For cable-based local networks, we generally have $w = 1$, as the delay in delivering acknowledgments is low. With a satellite channel, where delay is long, however, n and l may differ as discussed. Note, also, that $w = 1$ is viable with a wideband channel but not so viable with a satellite channel.

Example 3.4

To effect a stream with a satellite channel, it is necessary that the time required to receive an acknowledgment, on, for example, a first frame, be less than $w - 1$, the remaining window width, times the round-trip time. If this constraint is not met, a node will transmit w frames and then wait for an acknowledgment for the first of the w frames. For a satellite, we can say that the delay to receive an acknowledgement is at least 0.7 second, the likely roundtrip propagation delay. If s is the speed of the channel, and each frame contains f bits, then streaming is effected if

$$(w - 1)\,\frac{f}{s} > .7 \tag{3.8}$$

Given any two of the quantities f, s, w, this relationship allows setting the third so as to effect streaming. For example, given w and s, we can calculate the minimum allowable frame size for streaming.

With satellite channels, we may be more concerned about the cost of overhead or header fields than we would be for cable-based systems. For a frame with n_h header bits and n_0 data bits, we can define efficiency, e, to be

$$e = \frac{n_0}{n_0 + n_h} \tag{3.9}$$

Coupling equation 3.9 with equation 3.8 we can obtain [127]

$$e = \frac{n_0}{n_0 + n_h}$$

if equation 3.8 is true, and

$$e = \frac{n_0 w}{n_0 + n_h + s(.7)}$$

if equation 3.8 is violated, from which we can plot e versus n_0 for given w to assess the efficiency of a chosen strategy. Generally, satellite channels require large w, as, for example $w \geq 128$ rather than $w = 7$. Consult Martin [127] for additional information.

Addressing and Frame Enveloping

Frame Structure. Figure 2–13 depicted a suggested frame-enveloping format, with to and from addresses, and CRC and frame type fields. The type field designates the type of frame, and, for example, may label a frame as a control-datagram message or as the *i*th frame in a sequence of frames, or the like. At the very least, the type field should separate frames into the two categories of data frames and control frames. Doing so helps CIUs quickly interpret frame type and consequently decide the appropriate frame handling; permits control frames to be freely interspersed with data frames from a sequence of data frames; and promotes use of fixed control-frame structures and multiple data-frame formats. Furthermore, as has been suggested [128], for complete generality, control frames may be structured to consist of a series of variable-length tokens, as depicted in figure 3–11. Most framing structures currently in use are one of several semistandard variants of structures proposed for long-haul networks. All these variants more or less abide by the frame structure shown in figure 2–13, use 8- or 16-bit address and CRC fields, and support frame streaming. These variants include:

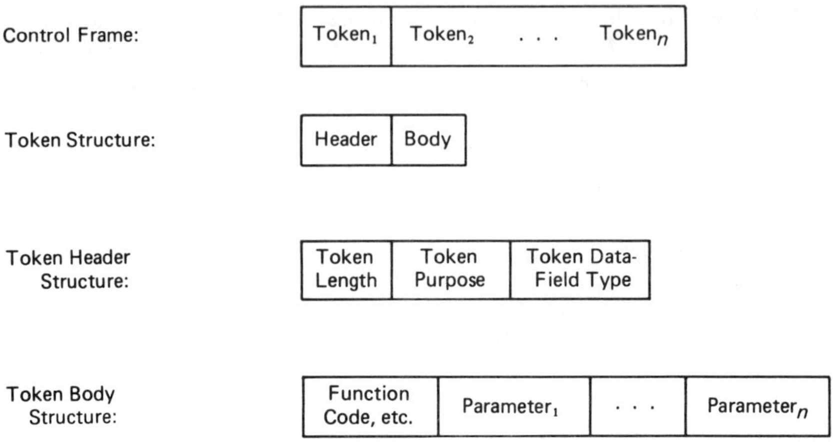

Figure 3–11. Control-Frame Structure

IBM's synchronous data-link control (SDLC), which is employed in their systems network architecture (SNA), for which $w = 8$;

Digital Equipment Corporations DECNET protocol, for which $w = 225$;

The American National Standards Institute's proposed Advanced Data Communication and Control Procedure (ADCCP), for which $w = 8$ or $w = 128$.

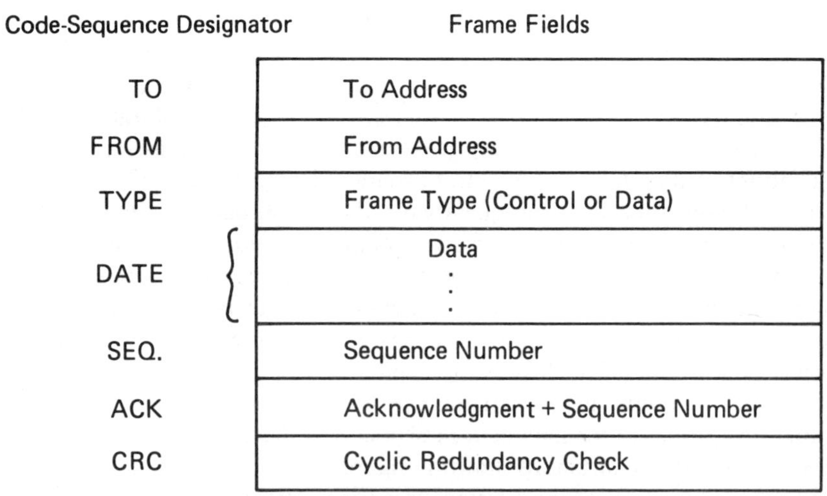

Figure 3–12. Frame Format

Details on these protocols, including frame types, exist elsewhere [79–84].

Addressing. Typically, the to and from addresses have referred to unique physical CIU addresses. Occasionally, a special address has been reserved to imply all CIUs to effect broadcasting. Experience has shown, however, that a more versatile addressing structure is required (see chapter 4), so that it becomes desirable for a CIU to recognize a multiplexity of addresses as referring to it. (Group addressing and broadcast both require this capability.) A form of associative addressing nicely serves this need, in that each CIU maintains a table of addresses, such that for each frame sensed on the channel the CIU compares the frame address in parallel with all addresses in the table. A match signals a need to receive the message. Certain CIUs have been built to recognize multiple addresses [47,125]. The price to be paid for multiple-address recognition is added CIU hardware and, at least in the contemporary CIUs, added CIU cost.

Example 3.5

The following code sequence sketches the realization of a protocol that supports bidirectional traffic and streaming and is intended for use by a CIU. As sketched, acknowledgments are expected to arrive within an interval of known duration; if they do not, frames are retransmitted. Thus, the code sequence sketched assumes use of an access protocol that does not automatically retransmit frames or await and monitor acknowledgments. Each frame is assumed to have the format depicted in figure 3–12. For presentation, we assume that frames can be named (like Pascal records), and that fields of named frames can be accessed by the dot notation. A frame to be transmitted will be named s, a frame received will be named r, so that, for example, s. type and r. type refers to the type field of the named records. The protocol allows acknowledgments to be "piggybacked" on data frames via the acknowledgment field, and, as written, the protocol employs the variables n and l and function $f(.)$, as defined earlier, and w is used to denote the sequence-number-cycle width.

<u>Begin</u>
We ignore the problem of a CIU having only finite number of frame buffers.)

address: = address of this node;

n. buffered: = (number of frames buffered awaiting acknowledgment)

seq. expected: = (sequence number of the next frame expected)

ack. expected: = (sequence number associated with next expected acknowledgment, that is, $l + 1$)

```
seq. next:      = (sequence number for next frame transmitted, that is,
                   n + 1)
s. from:        = address;
while true
begin
await (event)(an event is either a timeout, arrival of a frame, or availability of
              a frame to send)
case event of
frame to send:
    begin
        get frame from element, placing frame in
        buffer [seq. next];
        s. to:        = ______;
        s. type:      = "data";
        s. data:      = buffer [seq.next];
        s. seq.:      = seq.next;
        s. ack.:      = (seq.expected + w) mod w
        send (s) (have access protocol transmit frame);
        start timer;
        n. buffered: = n.buffered + 1;
        seq. next:    = seq. next + 1) mod w
    end
timeout:
    begin
        seq. next:        = ack. expected;
        for i:            = 1,..., n. buffered do
            begin
            s. to:     = ______;
            s. type:   = data;
            s. data:   = buffer [seq. next];
            s. seq.:   = seq. next;
            s. ack.:   = (seq. expected + w) mod w
            send (s);
```

```
        start timer;
        seq. next: = (seq. next + 1) mod w
    end
frame arrival:
    begin
        get frame from channel, place in r;
        if r. to    = address then begin (ignore frames not addressed to this
                      node)
        if r. crc =   f(r) then begin (ignore frames with errors)
        if (r. type = data) and (r. seq. = seq. expected) then
            begin
            pass r. info to element;
            seq. expected: = (seq. expected + 1) mod w
            end
        if (ack. expected ≤ r. ack and r. ack < seq. next) or
        (seq. next < ack. expected and ack. expected ≤ r. ack) or
        (r. ack < seq. next and seq. next < ack. expected) then
            begin
            n. buffered:     = n. buffered − 1;
            ack. expected:  = (ack. expected + 1) mod w
            if ack. expected = seq. next then stop timer;
    end;
    end;
end while
end;
```

Virtual Circuits

A virtual circuit derives its name from its likeness to a telephone circuit. A telephone circuit must be established (connected), exist for a time, and be disconnected at termination of the call. For the duration of the connection, information is transmitted bidirectionally between the (generally) two connected parties. By analogy, a virtual circuit logically connects two communicating nodes in a network. The connection must be established and disconnected, as with a telephone call, and during the connection streams of sequenced frames flow between the connected nodes (as in example 3.5). Establishment and disconnection of virtual circuits is done via messages, and their use facilitates the management (reservation) of resources within the connected nodes for extended message-transfer sequences.

A number of issues arise when we consider virtual circuits:

1. How are they established?
2. How are they terminated?
3. What sequencing and error-control strategy should be used?
4. Among how many virtual-circuit connections should a node (generally the CIU) be able to multiplex?
5. How can a high-priority message be passed to a node outside the sequenced stream of messages that constitute the virtual circuit?
6. What node element is addressed in a virtual circuit?

A complete listing of design issues (for long-haul networks) is given in Wecker [85] and Tannenbaum [86].

We must imagine that, in local networks, virtual circuits are established to facilitate the rapid flow of a sizeable number of frames between the connected node pairs. A typical example might involve the transfer of a file of information between an active node and a passive node consisting of a battery of disks. A virtual circuit facilitates such transfers by allowing acknowledgments to be deferred (for example, via a sliding-window protocol) and, depending on the window size, allows connected nodes to responsibly manage frame buffer space.

Virtual circuits are established by call requests, whereby the calling node requests establishment of a circuit between itself and the (addressed) called node. (The circuit may be established using the physical CIU address or the address of a process managed by the CIU. Several possible addressing schemes are discussed in chapter 4 in connection with interprocess communication mechanisms.) The called CIU or CIU process can accept or reject the call, depending on its internal state. Accepted calls are confirmed, after which the streaming of data may occur. Circuits are disconnected by a clear, and established connections can be reset and restarted. The best-known virtual-circuit procotol is contained in the specification of the X.25 protocol [87,88]; as an extensive, well-documented description of its provisions and formats exists in the references cited, they are not repeated here.

Contemporary CIUs, for reasons of cost, support a small number of virtual connections, as discussed earlier in this chapter, but usually support a datagram service in parallel with virtual-circuit mechanisms. For virtual-circuit stream transfer, they generally employ a sliding-window mechanism to realize flow and error control. Additional comments will be made with regard to examples in chapter 6.

User-Level Protocols

As discussed in chapter 2, user-level protocols directly support applications and are realized by building on the datagram and virtual-circuit mechanisms provided by the transport-protocol layers. These protocols support applications by supporting resource sharing, interprocess communication, and distributed computation. User level-protocols used in local networks do not really differ from those used in long-haul networks. As these protocols are well documented for long-haul networks [83,86,89–92], their descriptions need not be repeated here.

Protocol Specification and Verification

Protocols can become complex algorithms, especially when they incorporate machinery to effect timeouts and manage sliding-window flow- and error-control mechanisms. Complex algorithms require precise specification, and their implementations must be verified. Specification provides a formal, unambiguous, functional statement of what the algorithm does, including all that is essential to its description and omitting all that is not. Verification is a formal guarantee that an implementation of the algorithm (for example, in a programming language) is in consonance with its specification. (Testing can never guarantee correctness.)

Without formal specification, we cannot be sure that we have a commonly agreed-upon functional description of an algorithm. Without verification of an implemented algorithm, we cannot be sure that implementation faithfully realizes the algorithm as set forth in its specification.

In the last several years, much work has been done to provide tools and tehcniques for the specification and verification of algorithms; Berg et al. [129] contains a summary.

A protocol is an algorithm involving a source node and a receiving node; that is, we may view a protocol as involving two processes (in the operating-system sense) that execute in parallel. For example, the algorithm depicted in example 3.5 is executed by both nodes of a communicating pair and, within a given node may be replicated (by multiple-process instantiations) or multiplexed to accommodate multiple streams. Among the classes of algorithms we might attempt to specify and verify, parallel algorithms, involving parallel programs or processes, offer the most difficulty [129].

Consequently, specification and verification of protocols is difficult. Nevertheless, much progress has been made. To begin, the layering of protocols somewhat simplifies the task, for we can attempt to specify and verify each layer separately, keeping in mind the interactions of one layer with the others [93,94].

Formal specification techniques for protocols include:

Transition models, including state transition diagrams [95,96], formal grammars [97,98], Petri nets [99,100], so called 1-systems [101], graphs [102, 108], colloquies [103], high-level languages [104–107], and

Programming languages

Transition models involve the identification of states and the allowable transitions (events) between states.

Example 3.6

A state diagram shows states as circles and transitions, that is, events, by directed arrows that are labeled to indicate the event. To demonstrate, imagine a simple sliding-window protocol with $w = 1$, so that sender and receiver alternate transmissions. State-transition diagrams are shown in figures 3–13 and 3–14. The major drawback of transition models lies in coping with the large number of states and transitions that they may contain. The approach is useful, however, in specifying protocols with a small number of states [117–124]. Petri nets may partially relieve the explosive number of states and transitions, particularly so-called extended Petri nets [114,115].

Use of high-level languages to specify protocols is of mixed merit. The approach offers a specification that may be the same as or close to an implementation, so that, if the specification can be assumed to be correct, so can the implementation. (Generally, specifications cannot formally be shown to be correct. Rather, they are and can only be declared correct after careful scrutiny by a knowledgeable committee, all of whom agree that the formal specification captures the functional behavior of the protocol. Implementations are generally shown to correspond to a formal specification by formal methods [129].) However, it has proved difficult to specify protocols using high-level languages. It has been particularly difficult to capture the interactions of the parallel programs that constitute the protocol using high-level languages [104–107]. This disadvantage is partially alleviated by using a hybrid approach, which combines high-level languages with graphs or transition diagrams [106,116,117]. (Other approaches may be found by consulting the references.)

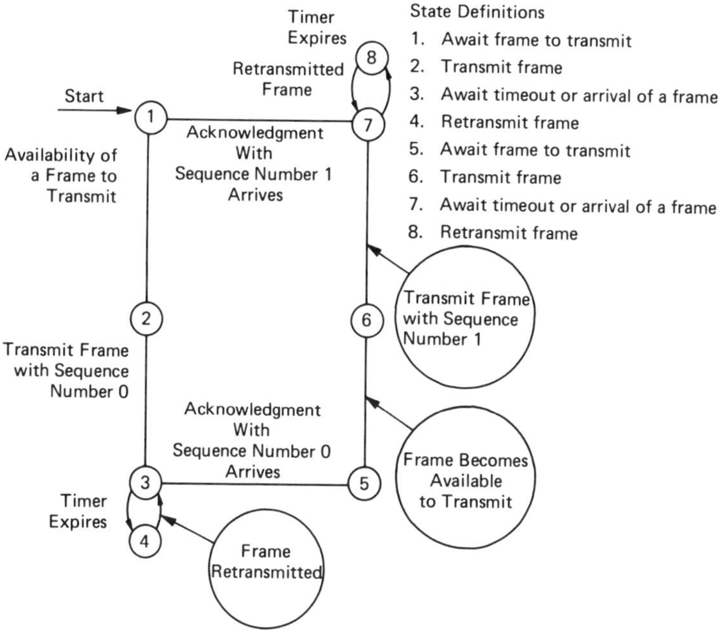

Figure 3–13. Sending-Node Transition Diagram

The formal specification of a protocol serves not only to unambiguously capture protocol functional behavior but also to serve as a description and framework in which we may prove properties about the protocol and to serve as a formal statement of proper behavior against which a proof of the correctness of an implementation can be made. We will not discuss proof of protocols, although the task parallels, in spirit, the proof of programs generally. Instead, we discuss the use of protocol specifications to prove properties of protocols. (Generally, properties of protocols are proved by showing the formal functional specification to possess those properties rather than directly proving that an implementation possesses the properties. The former approach is generally more tenable, as the specification is a more abstract model of the protocol than is the implementation, and, given that an implementation has been formally proved to be in consonance with the specification, it too must exhibit the properties.).

Desirable properties include [118–121]:

1. Freedom from deadlock, that is, a guarantee that the parallel programs that constitute the protocol will not all enter states wherein each is waiting for an action (an event) by another;

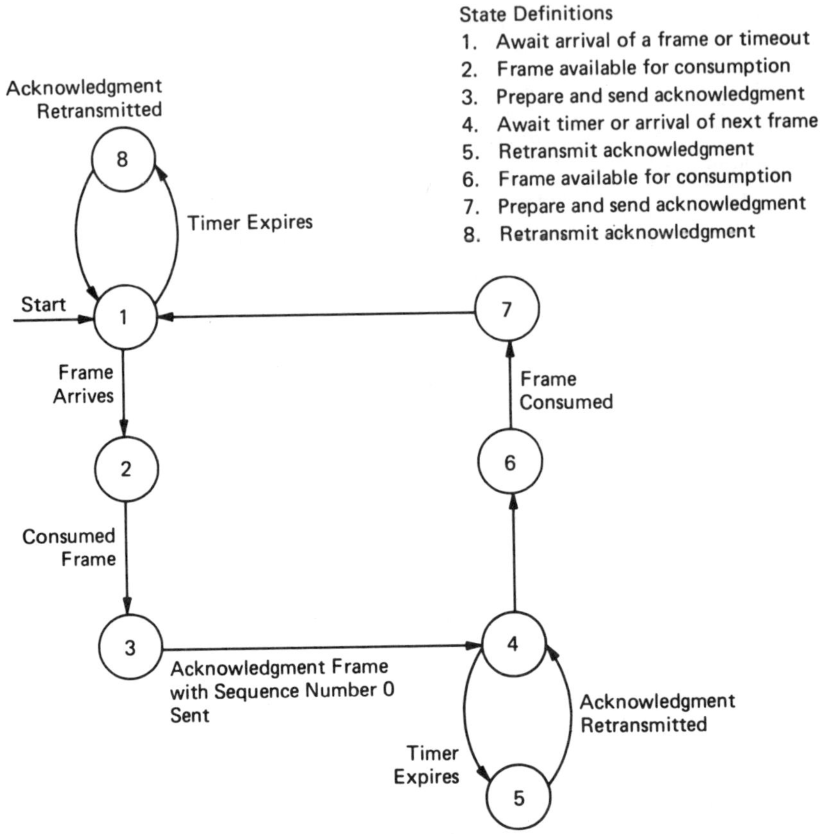

Figure 3–14. Receiving-Node Transition Diagram

2. Completeness, that is, the ability of the parallel programs to handle all situations or conditions that might arise;
3. Freedom from saturation or starvation, wherein a receiving node is not supplied frames at a rate fast enough to keep it busy or is supplied frames at too fast a rate;
4. Freedom from infinite loops, that is, loops wherein the parallel programs uselessly cycle through a sequence of states;
5. Possession of self-synchronization, such that a node or program in the parallel set returns to normal states from abnormal (error) states in a finite time;
6. Reachability, that is, assurance that a given set of states is reachable from another set of states;
7. Termination, that is, that a deserved final state is reached.

Proofs of properties follow two major approaches: reachability analysis for specifications given via transition models and program proofs for specifications given in language form.

Reachability analysis proceeds by constructing a global transition diagram (by combining the state diagrams of the interacting parallel programs).

Example 3.7

As a very simple example, consider the protocol transition diagrams in figure 3–15, derived from Davies et al. [89], wherein we have numbered the states to facilitate creation of the global transition diagram, shown in figure 3–16. Construction of the global diagram proceeds by determining possible combinations of (sender and receiver) states and the transitions among them. For example, an allowable combined state is one in which the sender is awaiting a frame to send (state 1) and the receiver is awaiting arrival of a frame from the sender (state 3), a state that we can denote by 1,3 in a global state-transition diagram. The culmination of this effort for the simple pair of parallel programs modeled in figure 3–15 is shown in figure 3–16. The global diagram for the protocol shown in figures 3–13 and 3–14 would contain sixty-four states (resulting from the 8×8 states in the individual parallel programs of the sender and receiver).

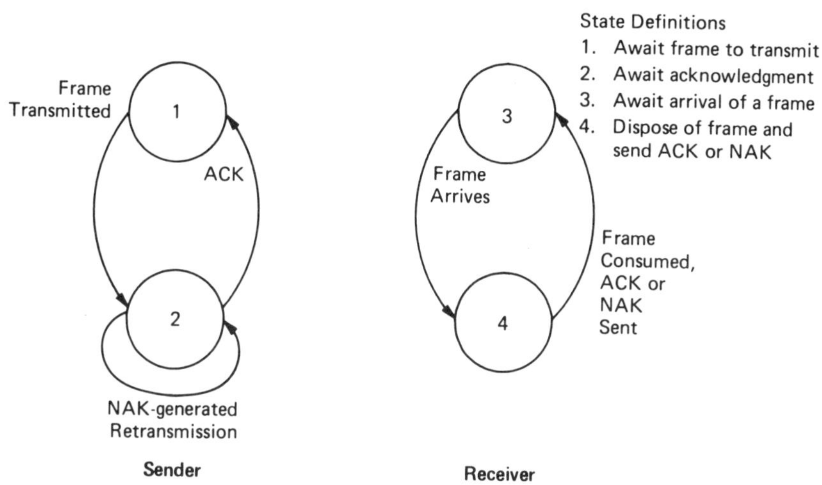

Figure 3–15. Transition Diagram for Simple Protocol

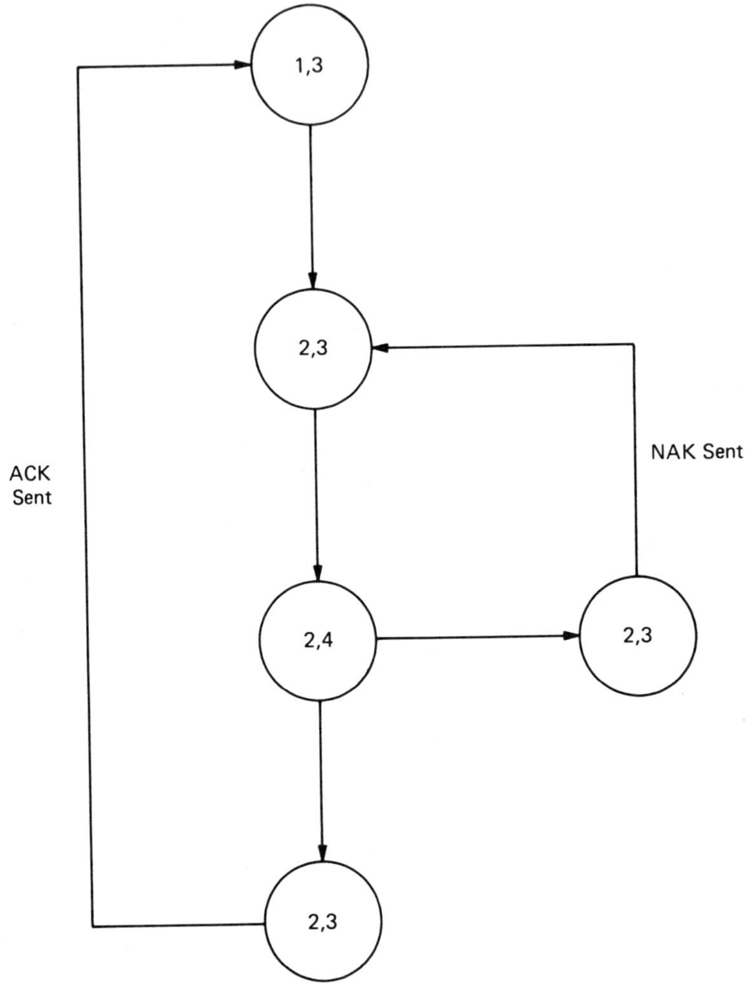

Figure 3–16. Global State-Transition Diagram

Reachability is a viable tool for proving properties such as those listed earlier. For example, global states with no exit-transition arcs signal deadlock. Additionally, any incompleteness becomes apparent during construction of the global diagram.

Example 3.8

From the global diagram for the protocol of figures 3–13 and 3–14, it can be shown that the protocol is self-synchronizing, with the cost of a single last frame. That is, if the sender and receiver portions of the parallel program are not initialized so that both segments begin operation in state 1, then, after one frame transmission, which will be discarded, they will become synchronized. Reachability analysis can be automated [122–124], but the approach suffers from the often explosive number of states that must be considered.

Program proof techniques for use with language-based protocol specifications follow the same pattern as those for proof of programs generally. That is, execution is assumed to begin in some known state, and a description of that state is captured in a predicate calculus assertion (given in terms of the protocol's descriptive variables). From that initial assertion and the semantics of protocol program statements, we prove (using predicate calculus rules and logic) other predicate calculus theorems that characterize various properties of the protocol. The approach does not suffer from a need to cope with an explosive number of states, but it suffers instead the problems that attend parallel program proofs generally [129]. Examples of the use of the technique can be had by consulting Sunshine [93] and Davies et al. [89].

Other techniques that assist in (but cannot guarantee) showing properties of protocols include simulation and testing [129]. A number of specifications of real protocols have been done, including the HDLC link-level protocol and the SNA link-level protocol [93], and a variety of protocol properties have been proved.

Summary

Our coverage has not been complete or particularly detailed, but we hope it has been sufficient to convey an image of the approaches and techniques used in local-network protocols. Details and additional material may be found by consulting the references.

References

1. Abramson, N. "The ALOHA-System." In *Computer Communication Networks*, edited by N. Abramson and F. Kuo. pp. 501–518. Englewood Cliffs, N.J.: Prentice-Hall, 1973.
2. Martin, J. *Teleprocessing Network Organization*. Englewood Cliffs, N.J.: Prentice-Hall, 1970.
3. Tobagi, F. "Random Access Techniques for Data Transmission Over Packet Switched Radio Networks." Ph.D. dissertation, University of California at Los Angeles (Report No. UCLA-ENG 7499), December 1974.
4. Kleinrock, L, and Tobagi, F. "Packet Switching in Radio Channels: Part I—Carrier Sense Multiple Access Modes and Their Throughput-

Delay Characteristics." *IEEE Transactions on Communications* COM-23 (December 1975):1400–1416.

5. Metcalfe, R.M., and Boggs, D.R. "ETHERNET: Distributed Packet Switching for Local Computer Networks." *Communications of the ACM* 19, (July 1976):395–404.
6. Christensen, G., and Franta, W.R. "Design and Analysis of the Access Protocol for HYPERchannel Networks." *Proceedings of the Third USA-Japan Computer Conference*, Montvale, N.J., March 1979, sections 4–4–1 to 4–4–8.
7. Franta, W.R., and Bilodeau, M.B. "Analysis of a Prioritized CSMA Protocol Based on Staggered Delays." *ACTA Information* 13 (1980): 299–329.
8. Kleinrock, L., and Yemini, Y. "An Optimal Adaptive Scheme for Multiple Access Broadcast Communication." *Proceedings of the ICC*, 1978, paper 7.2.
9. Chlamtac, I., and Franta, W.R. "Aids to the Development of Network Simulators." *AFIPS Conference Proceedings* 48 (1979 National Computer Conference):57–66.
10. Chlamtac, I.; Franta, W.R.; and Levin, D. "BRAM: The Broadcast Recognizing Access Method." *IEEE Transactions on Communications* COM-27 (August 1979):1183–1190.
11. Thornton, J.E.; Christensen, G.E.; and Jones, P. "A New Approach to Network Storage Management." *Computer Design* 14 (November 1975):81–85.
12. Chu, W.W. "A Study of Asynchronous Time Division Multiplexing for Time-sharing Computer Systems." *AFIPS Conference Proceedings* 35 (1969 Spring Joint Computer Conference):669–678.
13. Abramson, N. "The ALOHA-System—Another Alternative for Computer Communications." *AFIPS Conference Proceedings* 37 (Proceedings 1970 Fall Joint Computer Conference): pp. 281–285.
14. Lam, S.S., and Kleinrock, S. "Packet Switching in a Multi Access Broadcast Channel: Dynamic Control Procedures." *IEEE Transactions on Communications* COM-23 (September 1975):891–904.
15. Tobagi, F.A., and Hunt, V.B. "Performance Analysis of Carrier Sense Multiple Access with Collision Detection." *Proceedings of the Local Area Communications Network Symposium*, Boston, May 1979.
16. Chlamtac, I. "Radio Packet Broadcasted Computer Network—The Broadcast Recognizing Access Method." M.S. thesis, Tel Aviv University, 1976.
17. Chlamtac, I., and Franta, W.R. "Message-Based Priority Access to Local Networks." *Computer Communications* 3 (April 1980):77–8.

18. Schwartz, M. *Computer-Communication Network Design and Analysis*. Englewood Cliffs, N.J.: Prentice-Hall, 1977.
19. Farmer, W.D., and Newhall, E.E. "An Experimental Distributed Switching System to Handle Bursty Computer Traffic." *Proceedings of the ACM Symposium on Problems in the Optimization of Data Communications*, October 1969, pp. 1–33.
20. Pierce, J.R. "Network for Block Switches of Data." *Bell System Technical Journal* 51 (July/August 1972):1133–1145.
21. Farber, D.J., and Larson, K.C. "The Structure of a Distributed Computer System-Software." *Symposium on Computer Communications Networks and Teletraffic*, Polytechnic Institute of Brooklyn, April 1972, pp. 539–545.
22. Farber, D.J., and Larson, K.C. "The System Architecture of the Distributed Computer System—The Communications System." *Symposium on Computer Communications Networks and Teletraffic*, Polytechnic Institute of Brooklyn, April 1972, pp. 21–27.
23. Farber, D.J., and Heinrich, F.R. "The Structure of a Distributed Computer System—the Distributed File System." *Proceedings of the ICCC*, October 1972, pp. 364–370.
24. Farber, D.J. "The Systems Architecture of the Distributed Computer System-Reliability." Technical Report, University of California, Irvine, 1972.
25. Loomis, D.C. "Ring Communication Protocols." Technical Report No. 26, University of California, Irvine, January 1973.
26. Farber, D.J., Feldman, J., Heinrich, F.R., Hopwood, M.D., Larson, K.C., Loomis, D.C. and Rowe, L.A. "The Distributed Computer System." *Proceedings of the Seventh IEEE Computer Society International Conference*, February 1973, pp. 31–34.
27. Farber, D.J. "Extendability Considerations in the Design of the Distributed Computer Systems (DCS)." *1973 National Telecommunications Conference* 1, Atlanta, November 1973, pp 15E.1–15E.6.
28. Farber, D.J. "A Ring Network." *Datamation* 21 (February 1975): 44–46.
29. Farber, D.J. "The Design of the Distributed Computer System." *International Meeting on Minicomputers and Data Communications*, Liege, Belgium, January 1976, pp. 161–163.
30. Fraser, A.G. "Spider—A Data Communications Experiment." Computing Science Technical Report No. 23, Bell Laboratories, Murray Hill, N.J., 1974.
31. Reames, C.C., and Liu, M.T. "A Loop Network for Simultaneous Transmission of Variable Length Messages." *Proceedings of the*

Second Annual Symposium on Computer Architecture, Houston, January 1975, pp. 7–12.

32. Liu, M.T., and Reames, C.C. "The Design of the Distributed Loop Computer Network." *Proceedings of the 1975 International Computer Symposium* 1, Taipei, August 1975, pp. 273–282.
33. Reames, C.C., and Liu, M.T. "Design and Simulation of the Distributed Loop Computer Network (DLCN)." *Proceedings of the Third Annual Symposium on Computer Architecture*, Florida, January 1976, pp. 124–129.
34. Liu, M.T., and Reames, C.C. "Message Communication Protocol and Operating System Design for the Distributed Loop Computer Network (DLCN)." *Proceedings of the Fourth Annual Symposium on Computer Architecture*, March 1977, pp. 193–200.
35. Oh, Y., and Liu, M.T. "Interface Design for Distributed Control Loop Networks." *Proceedings of the 1977 National Telecommunications Conference*, Los Angeles, December 1977.
36. Wilkes, M.V. "Communication Using a Digital Ring." *PACNET Conference*, Sendai, Japan, August 1975, pp. 47–55; plus addendum, December 1976.
37. Hopper, A. "Data Ring at Computer Laboratory." *University of Cambridge Conference on Local Area Networking*, NBS Special Publication 500-31, Washington, D.C., April 1978.
38. Hassing, T.E., Hampton, Raymond M., Bailey, G.W., and Gardella, R.S. "A Loop Network for General Purpose Data Communications in a Heterogeneous World. Data Networks: Analysis and Design." *Third Data Communications Symposium*, St. Petersburg, November 1973.
39. Heger, D. "Computer Control System With Distributed Microcomputers." *Fifth Meeting of European Distributed Intelligence Study Group*, Brussels, November 1977, unpublished.
40. Steward, E.H. "A Loop Transmission System." *Proceedings of the Sixth ICC*, June 1970, pp. 36/1–36/9.
41. Hippert, R.O. "IBM 2790 Digital Transmission Loop." *IBM Journal of Research and Development*, November 1970, pp. 662–667.
42. Weller, D.R. "A Loop Communication System for I/O to a Small Multi-user Computer." *Proceedings of the Fifth Annual IEEE Conference on Hardware, Software, Firmware and Tradeoffs*, Boston, September 1971, pp. 49–50.
43. IEEE Standard Serial Highway Interface System (CAMAC) IEEE Standard 595-1976. ESONE Standard EUR 6100.
44. Gordon, R.L.; Farr, W.W.; and Levine, P. "Ringnet: A Packet Switched Local Network with Decentralized Control." *Fourth Conference on Local Computer Networks*, Minneapolis, October 1979, pp. 13–19.

45. Pohn, A. "Local Network of Microcomputers for Experiment Support." *Fourth Conference on Local Computer Networks*, Minneapolis, October 1979, pp. 91–96.
46. Cotton, I.W. "Technologies for Local Area Computer Networks." *Proceedings of the Local Area Communications Network Symposium*, Boston, May 1979, pp. 25–46.
47. Clark, D.C.; Progran, K.T.; and Reed, D.P. "An Introduction to Local Area Networks." *Proceedings of the IEEE* 66 (November 1978): 1497–1517.
48. Penny, B.K., and Baghdadi, A.A. "Survey of Computer Communications Loop Networks: Part 1." *Computer Communications* 2 (August 1979).
49. Penney, B.K., and Baghdadi, A.A. "Survey of Computer Communications Loop Networks:Part 2" *Computer Communications* 2 (October 1979).
50. Kanakia, H., and Thomasian, A. "A Comparative Study of Access Control Mechanisms in Loop Networks." *Fourth Conference on Local Computer Networks*, Minneapolis, October 1979.
51. Loomis, D.L. "Ring Communication Protocols." Technical Report No. 26, University of California, Irvine, January 1973.
52. Zafiropoulo, P., and Rothauser, E.H. "Signalling and Frame Structures in Highly Decentralized Loop Systems." *Proceedings of the International Conference on Computer Communications*, Washington, D.C., IBM Research Laboratory, Zurich, pp. 309–315.
53. Hafner, E.R., Nenadal, Z., and Tschanz, M. "A Digital Loop Communications System." *IEEE Transactions on Communications* COM-22 (June 1974):877–881.
54. Babic, G., and Ming, T.L. "A Performance Study of the Distributed Loop Computer Network (DLCN)." *Proceedings of the Computer Networking Symposium*, December 1977, pp. 66–76.
55. Mockapetris, A.P., and Farber, D.J. "Experiences With the Distributed Computer System." Submitted to *Journal of Distributed Processing*, 1979.
56. Hansen, L.W., and Schwartz, M. "An Assigned-Slot-Listen-Before-Transmission Protocol for a Multiaccess Data Channel." *IEEE Transactions on Communications* COM-27 (June 1979):846–857.
57. Spaniol, D. "Analysis and Performance Evaluation of Some Hyperchannel Access Protocols." *Performance Evaluation*, in press.
58. Capetanakis, J.I. "The Multiple Access Broadcast Channel: Protocol and Capacity Considerations." Ph.D. thesis, Massachusetts Institute of Technology, August 1977.
59. Capetanakis, J.I. "Generalized TDMA: The Multi-Accessing Tree Protocol." *IEEE Transactions of Communications* COM-27 (October 1979).

60. Ricart, G., and Agrawala, A. "Dynamic Management of Packet Radio Slots." *Third Berkeley Workshop on Distributed Data Management and Computer Networks*. August 1978.
61. Rubin, I. "A Group Random Access Procedure for Math-Access Communication Channels." *NTC 77 Conference Record, National Telecommunications Conference*, Los Angeles, December 1977, pp. 12:5–1 to 12:5–7.
62. Tobagi, F.A., and Kleinrock, L. "Packet Switching in Radio Channels: Part III—Polling and (Dynamic) Split-Channel Reservation Multiple Access." *IEEE Transactions on Communications* COM-24 (August 1976):832–845.
63. Tobagi, F., and Kleinrock, L. "Packet Switching in Radio Channels: Part II—The Hidden Terminal Problem in Carrier Sense Multiple-Access and the Busy Tone Solution." *IEEE Transactions on Communications* COM-23 (December 1975):1417–1433.
64. Chlamtac, I., and Franta, W.R. "The Operational Performance of the Broadcast Recognizing Access Method in a Network with Hidden Nodes." Proceedings of the ICC, Denver, 1981.
65. Kleinrock, L., and Silvester, J. "Optimum Transmission Radii for Packet Radio Networks or Why Six is a Magic Number." Proceedings of the *NTC 1978*, Birmingham, 1978.
66. Stern, M., and Grasiano, V. "Dyna Tac Update." Proceedings of the *ICC 1978*, pp. 4.1.1 to 4.1.4.
67. Erlich, N. "The Advanced Mobile Phone Service." *IEEE Communications Magazine* 17, (March 1979).
68. Chlamtac, I., and Franta, W.R. "SUPBRAM Performance Analysis: Simple SUPBRAM and *l*-optimized SUPBRAM", University of Minnesota, Department of Computer Science, TR-79-4, February 1979.
69. Chlamtac, I., and Franta, W.R. "Generalized SUPBRAM: Protocol and Performance Analysis", University of Minnesota, Department of Computer Science, TR-79-7, April 1979.
70. Crowther, W.; Rettberg, R.; Walden, D.; Orenstein, S.; and Heart, F. "A System for Broadcast Communication: Reservation ALOHA." *Proceedings of the Sixth Hawaii International System Science Conference*, January 1973, pp. 371–374.
71. Martin, J. *Communications Satellite Systems*, Englewood Cliffs, N.J.: Prentice-Hall, 1978.
72. Roberts, L. "Dynamic Allocation of Satellite Capacity Through Packet Reservation", *AFIPS Conference Proceedings* 42 (June 1973): 329–344.
73. Binder, R. "A Dynamic Packet Switching System for Satellite

Broadcast Channels", *Proceedings of the ICC 1975*, San Francisco, June 1975, pp. 41–1 to 41–5.

74. Jacobs, I., et al. "CPODA—A Demand Assignment Protocol for SATNET." *Procedings of the Fifth Data Communications Symposium*, Snowbird, Utah, September 1977, pp. 2–5 to 2–9.
75. Gerla, M.L.; Nelson, L.; and Kleinrock, L. "Packet Satellite Multiple Access: Models and Measurements." *Conference Record, NTC*, Los Angeles, December 1977, paper 12:2.
76. Chu, W.W., and Naylor, W.E. "Measurement and Simulation Results of C-PODA Protocol Performance." *NTC 78 Conference Record*, Birmingham, December 1978.
77. Gitman, I.; Van Slyke, R.M.; and Frank, H. "Routing in Packet Switching Broadcast Radio Networks." *IEEE Transactions on Communications* COM-24 (August 1976):926–930.
78. Dalal, Y.K., and Metcalfe, R.M. "Reverse Path Forwarding of Broadcast Packets." *Communications of the ACM* 21 (December 1978):1040–1048.
79. ISO High Level Data Link Control—Elements of Procedure, IS 4335, 1977.
80. Proposed American National Standard for Advanced Data Communication Control Procedures (ADCCP) Seventh Draft, American Nation Stand. Inst., December 1977.
81. ISO High Level Data Link Control—Elements of Procedure, IS 4335, 1977.
82. Cypser, R. *Communications Architecture for Distributed Systems*. Reading, Mass.: Addison-Wesley, 1979.
83. Corr, F.P., and Neal, D.H. "SNA and Emerging International Standards." *IBM Systems Journal* 18 (1979):244–262.
84. "DNA: Data Access Protocol Functional Specification." Digital Equipment Corporation. Maynard, Mass., AA-D601B-TC, 1980.
85. Wecker, S. "Computer Network Architecture." *Computer*, August 1979.
86. Tannenbaum, Andrew S. *Computer Networks*. Englewood Cliffs, N.J.: Prentice-Hall, 1981.
87. Johnson, J.P., and Gleap, J.M. "Designing an X.25 Network-to-Host Interface." *Computer Communications* 1 (February 1978):13–18.
88. Provisional Recommendations X.3, X.25, X.28 and X.29 on Packet Switched Data Transmission Services, CCITT, Geneva, 1978.
89. Davies, D.W.; Barber, D.L.A.; Price, W.L.; and Solomonides, C.M. *Computer Networks and Their Protocols*. New York: Wiley, 1979.
90. Day, J.D. "Resource Sharing Protocols." *Computer* 12 (September 1979):47–56.

91. "Back-End Storage Networks." *Computer*, February 1980, special issue.
92. Sproull, Robert F., and Cohen, D. "High-Level Protocols." *Proceedings of the IEEE* 66 (November 1978):1371–1386.
93. Sunshine, C. "Formal Techniques for Protocol Specification and Verification." *Computer* 12 (September 1979):20–27.
94. Reference Model of Open Systems Architecture (Version 3), TC 9/SCIG N117, International Organization for Standardization, November 1978.
95. Bochman, G.R. "Finite State Description of Communication Protocols." *Computer Networks* 2 (October 1978):361–372.
96. Zafiropulo, P.; West, C.H.; Rudin, H.; Cowan, D.D.; and Brand, D. "Towards Analyzing and Synthesizing Protocols." *IEEE Transactions on Communications* COM-28 (April 1980):651–660.
97. Harangoso, J. "An Approach to Describing a Link Level Protocol With a Formal Language." *Proceedings of the Fifth Data Communications Symposium*, Utah, 1977, pp. 4–37 to 4–49.
98. Teng, A.Y., and Liu, M.T. "A Formal Model for Automatic Implementation and Logical Validation of Network Communication Protocols." *Proceedings of the Computer Networking Symposium*, National Bureau of Standards, December 1978, pp. 114–123.
99. Merlin, P.M., and Farber, D.J. "Recoverability of Communication Protocols—Implications of a Theoretical Study." *IEEE Transactions on Comunications* COM-24 (September 1976):1036–1043.
100. Symons, F.J.W. "Modeling and Analysis of Communications Protocols Using Numerical Petri Nets." Department of Electrical Engineering, University of Essex, England, Technical Report 152, May 1978.
101. Ellis, C.A. "Consistency and Correctness of Duplicate Database Systems." *Proceedings of the Sixth ACM Symposium on Operating Systems Principles*, Purdue University, November 1977. *ACM Operation Systems Review* 11 (1977):67–84.
102. Postel, J.B. "A Graph Model Analysis of Computer Communications Protocols." Ph.D. dissertation, University of California at Los Angeles (Report No. UCLA-ENG 7410), 1974.
103. LeMolli, G. "A Theory of Colloquies." *Proceedings of the First European Workshop on Computer Networks*, Arles, France, April 1973, pp. 153–173.
104. Bochmann, G.V. "Logical Verification and Implementation of Protocols." *Proceedings of the Fourth Data Communications Symposium*, Quebec City, October 1975 (IEEE). (Also Publication No. 190, Department d'Informatique, University of Montreal.)
105. Stenning, N.V. "A Data Transfer Protocol." *Computer Networks* 1 (1976):99–110.

106. Danthine, A., and Bremer, J. "Modeling and Verification of End-to-End Transport Protocols." *Proceedings of the Computer Network Protocols Symposium*, Liege, Belgium, 13–15 February 1978.
107. Krogdahl, S. "Verification of Some Link-Level Protocols." *Computer Science Reports*, University of Tromso, Computer Science Department, N-9001, Tromso, Norway, June 1977.
108. Postel, J., and Farber, D. "Graph Modelling of Computer Communication Protocols." *Fifth Texas Conference on Computing Systems,* Austin, 1976, pp. 65–77.
109. Keller, R.M. "Formal Verification of Parallel Programs." *Communications of the ACM* 7(1976):371–384.
110. Merlin, P.M. "A Study of the Recoverability of Computing Systems." Ph.D. dissertation, University of California, Irvine, December 1974. Also Merlin and Farber, "A Note on Recoverability of Modular Systems." *Proceedings of the AFIPS National Computer Conference* 44 (May 1975):695–699.
111. Merlin, P.M., and Farber, D.J. "Recoverability of Communication Protocols—Implications of a Theoretical Study." *IEEE Transactions on Communications* COM-24 (September 1976):1036–1043. Also Merlin and Farber *1976 International Conference on Communications*, Philadelphia (IEEE) 14–16 June 1976,; and *IEEE Transactions on Communications* COM-24 (June 1976):614–621.
112. Merlin, P.M. "A Methodology for the Design and Implementation of Communication Protocols." *IEEE Transactions on Communications* COM-24 (June 1976):614–621.
113. Ellis, C.A. "Consistency and Correctness of Duplicate Database Systems." *Proceedings of the Sixth ACM Symposium on Operating Systems Principles*, Purdue University, November 1977, 67–84.
114. Yoeli, M., and Barzilai, Z. "Behavioral Descriptions of Communication Switching Systems Using Extended Petri Nets." *Digital Processes* 3(1977):307–320.
115. Symons, F.J.W. "Modelling and Analysis of Communication Protocols Using Petri Nets." Telecommunications Systems Group, Department of Electrical Engineering, University of Essex, Report No. 140, September 1976. Also "A General Graphical Model of Processing Systems Using NPNs, A Generalization of Petri Nets." Report No. 141, October 1976.
116. Merlin, P.M., and Segall, A. "A Failsafe Distributed Routing Protocol." *IEEE Transactions on Communications* COM-27 (September 1979):1230–1237. Also Segall, Merlin, and Gallager, *1978 ICC*, Toronto, June 1978 (IEEE).
117. Bochmann, G.V. and Gecsei, J. "A Unified Method for Specification and Verification of Protocols." *Proceedings of the IFIP Congress*,

Toronto, August 1977, pp. 229–234. Also Publication No. 247, Department d'Informatique, University of Montreal.

118. Bochmann, G.V. "Finite State Description of Communication Protocols." *Computer Networks* 2 (October 1978):361–372.
119. Hajek, J. "Automatically Verified Data Transfer Protocols." *Proceedings of the Fourth International Computer Communications Conference*, Kyoto, September 1978, pp. 749–756.
120. Rudin, H.; West, C.H.; and Zafiropulo, P. "Automated Protocol Validation: One Chain of Development." *Computer Networks* 2 (October 1978):373–380.
121. Merlin, P.M. "Specification and Validation of Protocols." *IEEE Transactions on Communications* COM-27 (November 1979): 1671–1680.
122. Rudin, H.; West, C.H.; and Zafiropulo, P. "Automated Protocol Validation: One Chain of Development." *Proceedings of the Computer Network Protocols Symposium*, Liege, Belgium, 13–15 February 1978.
123. West, C.H., and Zafiropulo, P. "Automated Validation of a Communication Protocol: the CCITT X.21 Recommendation." *IBM Journal of Research and Development* 22 (January 1978).
124. West, C.H., "General Technique for Communication Protocol Validation." *IBM Journal of Research and Development* 22 (July 1978).
125. Franta, W.R.; Kain, R.Y.; Jensen, E.D.; and Marshal, G. "Real-Time Distributed Computer Systems." In *Advances in Computers*, Vol 20. New York: Academic Press, 1981.
126. Digital Equipment Corporation, Intel Corporation, Xerox Corporation, *The Ethernet: A Local Area Network*, Data Link Layer and Physical Layer Specifications, Version 1.0, September 30, 1980.
127. Martin, James. *Communications Satellite Systems*. Englewood Cliffs, N.J.: Prentice-Hall, 1978.
128. Watson, R.W., and Fletcher, J.G. "An Architecture for Support of Network Operating System Services." *Computer Networks* (February 1980):33–49.
129. Berg, H.K.; Boebert, W.E.; Franta, W.R.; and Make, T. *Formal Methods of Program Verification and Specification*. Englewood Cliffs, N.J.: Prentice-Hall, 1981.

4 Network Operating Systems

The Stand-Alone Machine

In the traditional sense, operating systems consist of a series of programs heaped upon the raw hardware and firmware capabilities of a mainframe to create a virtual machine for use by applications programs. The virtual machine adds to and subtracts from the raw machine in a manner designed to make the application-program interface to the virtual machine friendly, powerful, and efficient. Thus, from the application viewpoints, the operating system's purpose is to support applications and application-program development. To do so, the operating system must turn a collection of hardware/software resources into a coherent set of abstract *objects* or resources and support their naming, access, sharing, protection, synchronization, error control, intercommunication, allocation, and for process objects creation and cancellation [1]. To accomplish this task, the operating system employs a variety of synchronization, scheduling, allocation, error-handling, access-control, and protection mechanisms. These mechanisms, in turn, support a variety of crucial ancillary program packages, including file systems, editors, language translators, command languages, and interpreters. The nature and extent of use of the mechanisms employed depend, at least in part, on the raw machine on which the system is realized. Minicomputers and large-scale machine systems generally employ a variety of complex mechanisms; however, microcomputers, important mainframes in the local network environment, often support simple operating systems, which are sufficient to support the single user that is often associated with the microcomputer.

The Network Case

In a local network, each node executes code that we can characterize as being associated with operating-system functions or mechanisms. In a sense, we can take that collection of code, which is distributed across all nodes in the network that perform operating-system functions, to constitute the network operating system. The network operating system code essentially serves the same purpose in the network environment that operating system code serves in the traditional single, stand-alone machine environment. Because the environment associated with a network is somewhat different from the environment associated with stand-alone machines, however, we might expect the mechanisms that support the network to be different from those that support the stand-alone operating system. The network environment exhibits multiple loci of control, spread over multiple nodes of varying power and configuration; the absence of shared memory; partitioned system state; and nondeterminism. These are generally not found collectively in stand-alone systems.

To elaborate, there is a locus of control at each node, such that in an *n*-node network, there are *n* loci of control. Thus, the network environment exhibits true execution parallelism and not simply concurrency.

To realize coherency, communication is required among the loci of the nodes. In networks, the communication mechanism is messages, which must actually be transmitted rather than placed in a shared memory, as would be the case in a shared-memory multiprocessor system. For reasons of reliability, expandability, and the like, and excluding necessary master-slave arrangements between active and passive nodes, node autonomy is the order of the day in local networks. Autonomy makes nodes equal and allows them to progress independently of but in concert with other network nodes. Viewed differently, autonomy guarantees that no node will be forced to alter its loci of control because of demands (messages) from other nodes [2].

System-state variables (and hence their values) are distributed among the nodes. For example, if resource *j* is attached to node *k*, only node *k* may have knowledge of the backlog of requests for and the current user of resource *j*. Thus, certain node decisions may be made only after requesting information, or without certain information, or on the basis of estimates or historical versions of the information. Put differently, node software may have incomplete or slightly different notions of total system state in hand against which to determine future execution paths.

Node autonomy, partitioned systsem state, and the uncertainty in the delays associated with message transmission signal nondeterminism, that is, uncertainty in the order in which events will occur, as perceived by the network nodes. For example, node *a* may not be able to assume that its request to node *b* will be the next one honored by node *b*, that the next message received will be from node *c*, or that it will be able to transmit a message to node *d* before node *e* does. The network transport-protocol layers (layers 1 through 3, as discussed in chapters 2 and 3) are at the heart of the mechanisms used to achieve coherency in the network environment. That is, the local network operating system mechanisms are built using the datagram and virtual-circuit mechanisms provided by the transport protocol.

A Model of Network or Distributed Computation

A conceptual framework for discussing network and distributed systems is provided by a model that captures the essence of the network circumstance.

We believe that the model described by Svobodova, Liskoff, and Clarka [3] is both simple and proper in the sense of capturing the essence of local-network (or distributed-systems) architecture.

The crux of the model is the *guardian*, an abstraction of a physical node in the network. A guardian is a local address space supporting one or more *processes* and containing, it is hoped, strongly typed data *objects*. The guardian address space is private, and guardians communicate only by message objects. A network or distributed system is composed of multiple guardians. A *process* is a sequential execution of a *program object*. Within a guardian, processes share memory, share objects, and may communicate with each other via shared objects. The location (address) of objects within a guardian is private to the containing guardian and cannot be made public in a message. *Tokens*, that is, external names for objects, can be sent and referenced in messages. Via tokens, guardian processes may request manipulation of objects contained in other guardians. As the objects are strongly typed, the allowed requestable manipulations are well defined, and thus the object can be viewed as an abstract data type [4,17]. Nonrequestable manipulations are disallowed by processes of the guardian containing the object, hence the guardian guards the objects it contains. As described, guardians are completely autonomous, but cooperative, in that nonrequestable manipulations are prohibited and the model makes no statement about the order in which legal manipulation requests, as contained in received messages, are honored.

The model thus provides a first-level specification of the behavior of a local network or distributed system, by providing information on (1) system modularity, that is, guardian processes and objects, and (2) object manipulations for which a guardian will honor requests.

The model must make some statement about coherency, that is, about how guardians interact and synchronize their activities. What we need is information about the order in which requests will or will not be honored. Information on the order in which they *will* be honored is often useful but tends to limit parallelism and stifle the inherent nondeterministic nature of distributed sysems, which stems, for example, from the unknown order in which external stimuli will be received or from the unpredictable order in which the access protocol will handle the collective set of node-transmission requests. Thus, it may also be useful to make statements about the ordering of requests that will *not* be honored. Coherency information can be conveyed by considering the honoring of a request to constitute an *event*, and providing information on legal or illegal event orderings. Consistent with our notions of node autonomy is the specification of legal or illegal orderings for individual guardians, rather than for the collection of guardians. Further, from guardian-event orderings, statements can be made about systemwide event orderings (at least theoretically).

Several proposals have been made for specifying orders [2,3,5], but none has received widespread acceptance. Some proposals specify constraints on legal orders [2], while others specify legal orders directly [3].

Network Operating System Organization and Mechanisms

The two preceding sections have attempted to characterize the network environment. The characterization is admittedly an incomplete representation of reality, but it is nonetheless indicative. Here we attempt to characterize proposed network and distributed operating system mechanisms. We say "proposed" because local networking and distributed system development is in its infancy. No proposal has received widespread use or acceptance. Further, for local networks there are two "flies in the ointment" of development. One is the need to integrate a network using heterogeneous extant operating systems operating on heterogeneous mainframe elements. The other is the need to incorporate nodes in which the CIU alone is guardian. This latter circumstance is reflected in the master-slave relationships that must exist between active and passive nodes, as is the case, for example, between the PDP (active) node and disk (passive) node shown in figure 2–7.

Ignoring these potentially anomalous circumstances, we discuss proposed network mechanisms for resource sharing, that is, remote access of resources, and for synchronization and intercommunication of guardian processes that are applicable to application environments that include real-time (or time-critical), operating-system, and distributed computations.

Interprocess Communication Mechanisms

Interprocess communication (IPC) mechanisms support interguardian communication and synchronization. They do so by allowing copies of named (and typed) objects of one guardian to be transferred to the local address spaces of one or more other guardians. The transfer is initiated by an IPC command executed by a process in the source node.

The executed command must explicitly or implicitly convey enough information to:

1. Identify the destination guardians;
2. Specify the objects into which the copies are to be deposited within the destination guardians;
3. Specify the action sequence to be taken if delivery cannot be made;

4. Specify the effect that command execution is to have on the continued progress of the initiating process.

To give an idea of IPC proposals, we present a few examples.

Example 4.1 (abstracted from [3,5])

As sketched [3,5], processes in one guardian send messages to typed objects, known as ports, in other guardians. Ports are abstract data types with declarations of the form:

$$
\begin{aligned}
\text{portname} = \underline{\text{port}}\ [\, & c_1\ (\text{args}_1) \\
& \quad \underline{\text{replies}}\ (\hat{c}_1, \overline{\text{args}_1}) \\
& c_2\ (\text{args}_2) \\
& \quad \underline{\text{replies}}\ (\hat{c}_2, \overline{\text{args}_2})\ ] \\
& \cdot \\
& \cdot \\
& \cdot \\
& c_n\ (\text{args}_n) \\
& \quad \underline{\text{replies}}\ (\hat{c}_n, \text{args}_n)]
\end{aligned}
$$

where c_i are commands (action sequences) that can be remotely requested; args_i are the dummy arguments associated with each invocation; $\hat{c}_i$ is a named command in another port, whose invocation constitutes the reply resulting from the invocation of c_i, and args_i are the arguments (messages) associated with the reply invocation. A port is instantiated by a separate statement of the form

$$x := \underline{\text{create}}\ \text{portname}$$

Port commands are remotely invoked via

$$\underline{\text{send}}\ c_i\ (\text{args})\ \underline{\text{to}}\ \langle\, x \,\rangle\ [\underline{\text{replies}}\ \text{to}\ \langle y \rangle],$$

where args is the message associated with the requested invocation of c_i. The replies port is optional, but, if used, y refers to a command in a named port.

It is assumed the system (protocol layers 1 through 3) will guarantee delivery of the message (which contains C_i, args, y) and the process executing the send is allowed to continue execution, that is, it is not blocked awaiting either successful transmission of the message or a reply. Failure to deliver, for example, because of queuing limitations in the destination guardian, will be signaled to the sender via the replies port, if specified.

Processes in the guardian in which a port is created may execute:

```
receive on X
   when C_1 (args_1) [reply to ⟨args_1⟩]:  S_1
                    .
                    .
                    .
   when C_n (args_n) [reply to ⟨args_n⟩]:  S_n
   when failure (S:string)            :  S_failure
   when timeout: ⟨expression⟩         :  S_timeout
end
```

which means that, if there are messages waiting on ports in the port list, the oldest message, that is, the one that arrived at this node longest ago, is removed. (A way of giving ports priority must also be provided.) The line containing the command identifier of this message is selected (such a line must exist). The objects in the message are decoded left to right and assigned to the formals in the formal arg-list, and the reply port, if any, is assigned to the formals, args. Then the associated statement is executed. If no messages are waiting, the receiving process waits for one to arrive, or times out, whichever happens first.

The message failure string is automatically and implicitly associated with each port type. Failure messages are mostly generated by the system and convey such information as transmission problems or nonexistence of the target port or guardian.

To illustrate, we consider a process named *buffer*, which manages a buffer into which a producer deposits information units and from which consumer units extract information units. The producer deposits units via

```
send put (message) to X.
```

Consumers extract units via

```
send get (Z) to X replies to Y
```

Guardian buffer contains the declaration

```
buf = port [put (m)
            get ( )
                replies (got, m)],
```

the creation statement

X: = create buf,

and a receive statement of the form

```
receive on X
    when put (m): {put m in buffer} ;
    when get ( ) reply to (m)        : {got m for reply};
```

where the second when clause assumes a port declared in the consumer with a command named *got*. Synchronization, that is, delay in the consumer awaiting a message is not shown. Several other details are also ignored.

Example 4.2 (abstracted from [6,7,8,9])

The communicating sequential process proposal [6] receives much attention. Two command types are proposed: a "receive" command of the form,

process_name? target_ variable

and a "send" command of the form

process_name! expression

Communication is between named processes of one or more guardians and occurs when attempted execution of a statement of the form

$$P_1?\ v$$

in P_2 can be matched (paired) with attempted execution of a statement of the form

$$P_2!\ e$$

in P_1. When such a pairing occurs, the value of expression e is transferred from P_1 to P_2 (as a message) and becomes the new value of the variable v, completing execution of the pair of statements. Thus, process A may attempt execution of either $B\ ?\ v$ or $B\ !\ e$ at any time, but process execution is suspended, that is, the process is blocked, until execution of the companion statement $A!\ e$ or $A?\ v$ is attempted in process B. That process is blocked which first attempts execution of the statement requiring a pairing. The mechanism may be said to require a "rendezvous" as originally proposed by Walden [10].

Nondeterminism and flexibility are obtained by allowing ? to appear in the guards of Dijkstra guarded commands [11] (! may not appear in a guard). A guarded command has the form:

$$\langle \text{guard} \rangle \rightarrow \langle \text{command-list} \rangle$$

A guard consists of a list of declarations, Boolean expressions, and an input command (each of these is optional). A guard fails if any of its Boolean expressions have the value "false," or if the process named in its input command has terminated. If a guard fails, then the guarded command has no effect; control is transferred to the statement following that command. If a guard does not fail, then the command-list is executed. This takes place only after the input command (if present) has been completed.

Guarded commands may be combined into an alternative command that has the form:

$$[G_1 \rightarrow C_1 \square G_2 \rightarrow C_2 \square \ldots \square G_n \rightarrow C_n]$$

An alternative command specifies execution of one of its constituent guarded commands. Consequently, if all guards fail, the alternative command fails. If more than one guarded command can be executed successfully, an arbitrary one is selected for execution.

Alternative commands can be executed as many times as possible by using the repetitive command that has the form:

$$*[G_1 \rightarrow C_1 \square G_2 \rightarrow C_2 \square \ldots \square G_n \rightarrow C_n]$$

The alternative command is executed repeatedly so long as it does not fail. When the alternative command fails because all its guards fail, then the repetitive command terminates and control is transferred to the following statement.

These mechanisms are illustrated by sketching, again, the process called *process buffer*, which serves as manager of information units. For simplicity, we illustrate the circumstance for a single producer process and a single consumer process. The producer process deposits information units in the buffer, and the consumer process removes the unit. The producer process deposits units by executing

buffer! insert (x),

the consumer process extracts information units by executing buffer! move ( ); buffer? extract (*y*)

and the process buffer has the structure:

```
process buffer:
   var b [0 . . 99]: some type;
      in,out: integer;
   in: = 0; out: = 0;

 *[in-out <100, producer? insert (b [in mod 100])
                   → in: = in + 1
                 □ 0 < in-out,consumer?move ( )
                        → consumer! extract (b [out mod 100]);
                                        out 1 = out + 1
 ]
```

The guarded command nondeterministically selects between insertion and extraction as determined by the truth of the guards. As stated, the guard containing ? cannot be true until the Boolean expression is true and a ! matching the input signaled by ? has been identified, that is, until a rendezvous is possible.

Example 4.3 (abstracted from [12])

The Ada language is designed for real-time, system, and other application processes. A number of compilers for the language will be available in 1981. The IPC mechanisms it provides can be considered extensions of the ?,! commands presented in example 4.2. The mechanisms have the flavor of remote procedure invocations, require the same synchronization between communicating processes, called tasks, as required by ? and !, and, via ancillary constructs, provide for nondeterminism and timeouts.

In Ada, a statement with the appearance of a procedure call plays the role of ?, and a statement with the appearance of a procedure declaration header preceded by the keyword accept plays the role of identifying a sequence to be executed when rendezvous occurs. The keyword select with ors delineates nondeterministic selection alternatives, and Boolean guards are introduced by when. Given these mappings and ignoring certain declarations, the producer task, as identified in example 4.2, could be written to execute

send (inmail)

and the consumer task could be written to execute

receive (outmail).

Task buffer could then have the task body that follows, which is consonant with the communication "call" statements send and receive, as identified earlier. task body buffer is

```
    b: array (0 . . 99) of message;
      in,out: integer range 1 . .99: = 1 (initial value 1)
     count: integer range 0 . . 99: = 0

begin
   loop
      select
         when in-out < 100
            accept send (in mail: in message) do
                        b(in mod 100): = in mail;
            end;
            in:=in+1;
      or
         when   in-out > 0
            accept receive (outmail: out message) do
                outmail: = b(out mod 100);
            end;
            out:=out +1;
      end select
   end loop
end buffer;
```

Example 4.4 (abstracted from [13,14])

The Honeywell experimental distributed processing (HXDP) system, is a distributed system designed for real-time control applications. The communication primitives were constructed to promote the separation of guardian realization and the logical linking of guardians, by communication, to realize a coherent system.

Kernel Primitives. In keeping with an objective of language independence, we will emphasize the semantics of the primitives and largely ignore syntax; the reader should visualize the primitives as calls to separately compiled procedures. The primitives are presented in this section without motivation; the design issues and the reasons for the design choices are in [13,14].

Modules. Application modules known to the HXDP executive are called virtual processing elements (VPEs). A VPE has a visible part and a hidden part.

Visible Part. The visible part of a VPE consists of an information interface and a signal interface. The information interface is a set of objects of type *rawstorage* (the basic hardware-storage type, such as bytes or words), called *windows*. The signal interface is a set of objectives of type *Boolean*, called *events*.

Hidden Part. The hidden part of a VPE consists of the implementation of the VPE semantics in some programming language. This language will be able to reference three primitives supported by the kernel: display, view, and wait. These primitives manage the visible interface; display and view are the only means by which the VPE implementation can operate on windows, and wait enables the VPE to halt its virtual program until an event becomes true. The VPE implementation can also use events freely as Boolean variables. The complete semantics of the primitives and the interface will be given later by an example of message movement.

Structures of Modules. Application structures constructed from interconnected VPEs are called virtual architectures (VAs). A VA may be redefined as a VPE at a still higher level of abstraction, in which case its constituent VPEs and all their associated parallelism and interactions become hidden, and a new visible interface (containing events and windows) is defined to permit interconnection of the VA to other VPEs.

Interconnection. The act of constructing a VA, or programming-in-the-large, begins by relating a source window on one VPE unidirectionally to another, destination window, generally in another VPE. In addition, the VA constructor may specify a set of related windows to serve as alternate destinations. The use of alternate destinations will be described after normal message handling is presented.

Module Interaction. Consider two VPEs. Suppose VPE_1 has an interface consisting of an output window (window_1) and an event (event_1), and its implementation defines some hidden object (object_1), such as a table or an array. Furthermore, VPE_2 has an interface consisting of an input window (window_2) and an event (event_2), and has a hidden object (object_2). Suppose event_2 has been associated with window_2.

Now assume that these two VPEs have been combined into an elementary VA by relating window_1 unidirectionally to window_2. Window_1 will be the

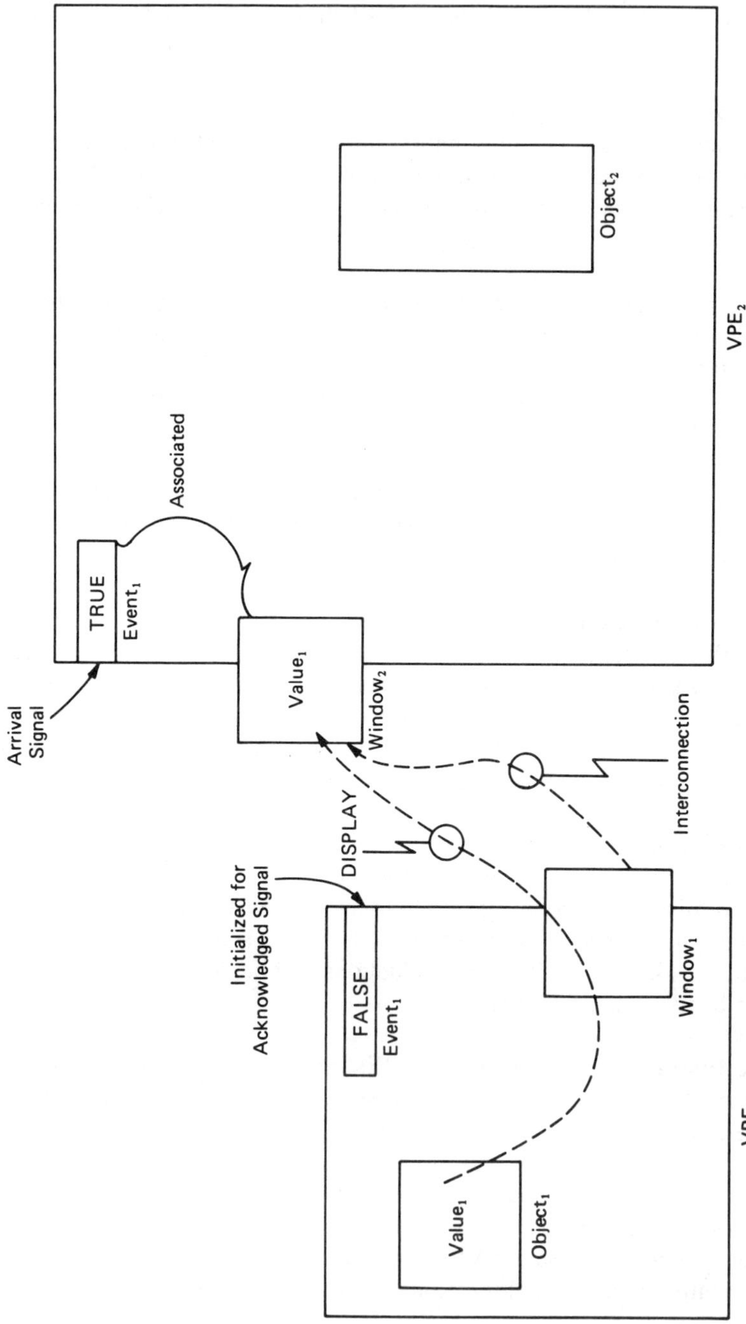

Figure 4–1. Consequences of a DISPLAY

message source, as indicated by the interconnection arrow shown in figure 4–1.

A message interaction begins when VPE_1 invokes the following primitive (we express our primitives in an arbitrary self-defining syntax): display $object_1$ as $window_1$, acknowledge event is $event_1$.

This causes the value of $object_1$ to be moved in *rawstorage* form through $window_1$ to $window_2$, The acknowledge event ($event_1$) is reset to false immediately, and the arrival event ($event_2$) is set to *true* when the message arrives in $window_2$, producing the situation shown in figure 4–1.

VPE_2 detects the arrival of the message by means of $event_2$, either by executing a clause of a conditional statement governed by $event_2$ or by resuming execution after a wait primitive that has $event_2$ as a parameter.

After detecting the arrival of a message, VPE_2 invokes the primitive view $window_2$ as $objective_2$. This causes the rawstorage message in $window_2$ to be moved to the storage area assigned to $object_2$. Invocation of the view by VPE_2 eventually causes $event_1$ to be set to true; this is the acknowledgment signal, which VPE_1 can detect in the same ways that VPE_2 detected the arrival event. Also, the view sets $event_2$ to false, ready for arrival of the next message. This sequence of events produces the status shown in figure 4–2.

If VPE_1 invokes a second display through $window_1$ and the second

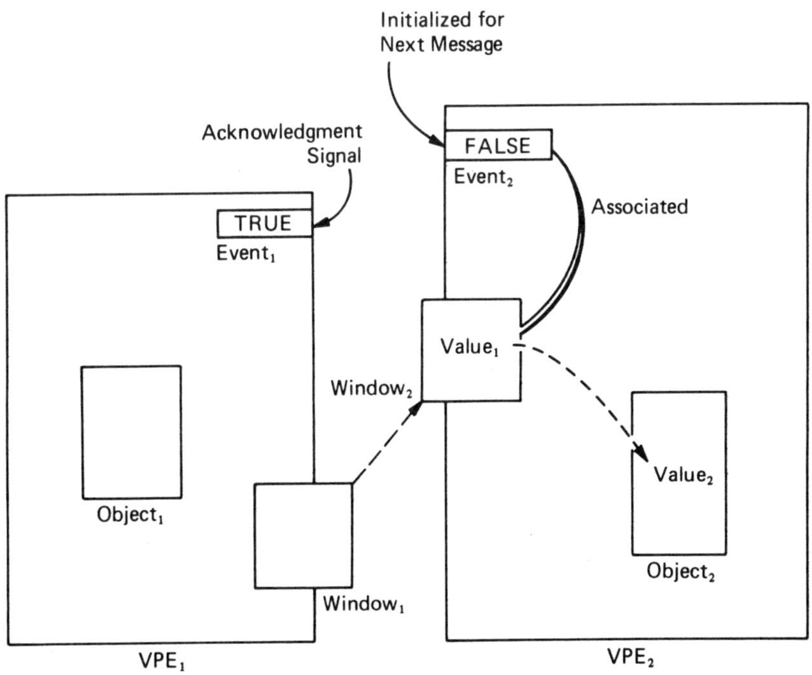

Figure 4–2. Consequences of a VIEW

message arrives at window$_2$ before VPE$_2$ invokes the first view, the second message replaces the first one in window$_2$ and the first will thereby be lost. This circumstance can be guarded against during module implementation by using the acknowledgment events to serialize views and displays; alternatively it can be guarded against during VA construction by inserting an intermediary VPE, which implements a desired queuing discipline.

The use of the arrival event and the acknowledgment event is optional. If the acknowledgment event is not used, messages may be lost and are delivered on a most-recently-arrived basis, as noted earlier. If, however, the arrival event is not used, the receiving VPE must test for message arrival by executing repeated views and examining the results; this will generally be a complex and unreliable practice.

Since events (from the point of view of the VPE implementation) are Boolean variables, they may be manipulated directly by the VPE. Such usage might occur if a VPE expects a message that will act as stimulus or signal with no associated message; in this case, setting the arrival event to true represents the complete information transfer to the receiving VPE. Since there is no message body, the receiving VPE does not need to view it, and can complete the transaction (from its viewpoint) by resetting the event by assigning it the value false. This coding, however, subverts the synchronization mechanism, because the sender never sees an acknowledgment; that can be produced only by a view executed by the receiving VPE.

Undeliverable Messages. Three degrees of certainty can be associated with each attempt by the transport layers to deliver a message:

Case 1: The transport protocol can be certain that the message arrived;

Case 2: The transport protocol can be certain that the message did not arrive; or

Case 3: The transport protocol cannot be certain whether or not the message arrived.

One transport layer may send a message and receive, instead of an acknowledgment, an indication that the destination has failed. The sending transport system cannot know whether the message arrived before or after the failure.

If it is certain that the message arrived (case 1), the display is complete. If either of the other two cases occurs, the transport protocol will examine the VA definition to see if a set of alternate windows has been related to the source window. All alternate windows are included within oralternate groups. The first window in an oralternate group is declared to be an oralternate window. Other windows within each oralternate group are declared to be andalternate windows. The transport layer will try successive alternate windows according to the following rules.

1. If it is certain that the message arrived at a window, the display is complete.
2. If there are no remaining alternate windows, the display is complete.
3. If the next alternate window is an andalternate window, the transport layer will try to send the message to that window if case 2 or case 3 applied to the previous attempt.
4. If the next alternate window is an oralternate window, and if case 1 or case 3 applied to any previous attempt, the display is complete; otherwise, the transport layer will try to send the message to that window.

The andalternate/oralternate qualifiers are required because strategies that minimize the probability of message loss (for example, retransmit to an andalternate window) raise the probability of message duplication and those that minimize the probability of message duplication (for example, not retransmit to an oralternate window) raise the probability of message loss.

Extended Functionality. The three kernel primitives display, view, and wait can be used in intermediary VPEs to provide functionality (such as timing, queuing, or broadcast) that is not in the kernel. Certain intermediary VPEs perform functions (such as copying messages for broadcast) that are independent of the meaning that applications VPEs associate with message contents. Such intermediary VPEs may be catalogued and reused in a variety of applications. Providing enhanced functionality by means of intermediary VPEs is not much more expensive than incorporating those functions directly in the kernel, if the number of VPEs per processor is small.

To evaluate IPC proposals, criteria are necessary. Proposals can be compared by a number of *specific* criteria, some of which were presented earlier in this chapter, as well as a number of more *general* evaluation criteria, such as are summarized in table 4–1. The criteria listed in table 4–1 relate not only to IPC mechanisms but also to the languages in which the IPC mechanism is imbedded and the system that supports the language, if specified. Criteria specifically relevant to IPC mechanisms include their provisions for

Naming message recipients;

Associating action sequences with received messages;

Sender-receiver synchronization and nondeterminism;

Static, dynamic guardian structures;

Table 4–1
IPC and Language-Evaluation Criteria

Expressive Power or Richness	This refers to the ability of the language IPC mechanism to express certain behaviors—that is, the ability to model certain nondeterminism, and the like. This property is also referred to as *completeness* or *adequacy*. An increase in experssive power is likely to be accompanied by an increase in the difficulty of determining the correctness of usages. Although it is desirable to have simplicity as one of the goals, it is not advisable to make it the overriding criterion.
Provability	One may be interested in proving [17] many properties, such as partial correctness, freedom from deadlocks, termination, and fairness. Some constructs would make proofs of certain properties extremely difficult, if not impossible. For example, at the current state of the art of program proving, the presence of timeouts makes the tractability of proofs almost impossible. Of course, an important consideration is the power of the language used for specifying assertions about program properties. The assertion language or the logic used should be rich enough to be able to specify various desired properties formally. Formalization of the semantics of constructs is an important prerequisite to program proving.
Ease of Implementation	The implementation of certain features may be very difficult. For example, a discussion of the difficulties using both input and output statements (that is, message SEND and RECEIVE statements) in the guards of guarded commands in CSP [6] (see example 4.2) can be found in [8,9].
Efficiency of Implementation	It is not sufficient merely to define IPC primitives whose functionality suggests that they are worth implementing. It must also be possible to deliver that functionality with reasonable efficiency, as in most applications efficiency is likely to be an important consideration. Although constructs can be easily implemented, the efficiency of the implementations may be low. Practicality of mechanisms includes a measure of their efficiency. Compile-time, type-checking, and so on, are more efficient than run-time checking.
Ease of Use	Powerful features are not necessarily easy to use. Normally, high-level constructs and good abstraction capabilities contribute to ease of use. Ease of use and expressive power are complementary criteria. IPC mechanism and language mechanisms rich enough to express a variety of computations do not automatically imply that they can be easily expressed; certain ingenious, awkward, and obscure ways may be necessary. Language primitives should be combinable in coherent ways. Orthogonality should be exhibited by them. Avoidance of subtle interactions among primitives makes them easier to use and helps avoid errors. Flexibility in the use of the constructs is also an important factor.
Understandability of Resulting Programs	Any proposal for new language mechanisms should be closely scrutinized to determine their effect on program structure. Mechanisms that discourage complex and confusing structures should be encouraged. Very powerful high-level constructs often lead to easily understandable programs. Of course, this may not always be the case. Mechanisms promoting hierarchical structures are beneficial. In general, constructs that are easily verified are likely to be easily understood.
Impact of Change	Constructs that encourage a high degree of modularity are desirable Permitting a good deal of autonomy in the definition of processes helps in reducing and localizing the impact of changes.
Maximization of Possible Parallelism	The greater the degree of concurrency permitted by the constructs, the better. The overhead required to support concurrency must not offset the advantages gained by parallelism.

Note: A similar listing of criteria appeared in Mohan [16].

Failure handling;

Compile-time and run-time checking possibilities; and

The number of object movements required to effect a communication.

Naming. Two naming procedures are possible. Sending processes either name an object in the destination processes or name an object in the sending processes. The IPC mechanisms in examples 4.1, 4.2, and 4.3 imply *destination-object naming*, the mechanisms in example 4.4 use *source-object naming*.

Source-object naming promotes separate development and compilation of guardian realizations, but requires, as in example 4.4, a separate linking step to associate source-named objects with destination-named objects. Additionally, destination-object naming promotes compile-time type checking (comparison of the type of source objects against the type of destination objects to insure legal message transfers), whereas source-object naming requires run-time or link-time type checking.

Naming conventions may be symmetric or asymmetric. Symmetric mechanisms require the source and destination process guardians each to know object names in the other. Example 4.2 exemplifies symmetric naming, as communicating processes must know the identity of each other. Examples 4.1, 4.2, and 4.4 are asymmetric mechanisms. None of the sample mechanisms directly support multidestination or broadcast naming (see chapter 2), although it is easily associated with the mechanisms of example 4.4. Furthermore, a receive-from-any kind of naming is occasionally desirable [15].

Nondeterminism and Synchronization. Many IPC mechanisms generally accommodate nondeterminism. The mechanisms in examples 4.2 and 4.3 support it directly. Synchronization relates to whether or not a communication blocks initiating or destination processes until some stage of the communication is completed.

For the initiating process, candidate blocking stages include:

1. Blocking the initiating process until the message is formatted and passed to the transport-level protocols for transmission.
2. Blocking the initiating process until the resulting message has been successfully received by the destination guardian and associated with the proper destination object.
3. Blocking the initiating process until the communication sequence is completed, including destination-guardian action sequences and replies, if any.

All IPC mechanisms block through stage 1.

Destination processes may be blocked when awaiting the arrival of an object value from a source process. Blocking continues until an object arrives.

Four possible synchronization modes are possible [15]:

1. Fully synchronous: both source and destination processes are blocked (generally through stage 3 above).
2. Half-synchronous: the source process only is blocked.
3. Half-synchronous: the destination process only is blocked.
4. Nonsynchronous: neither is blocked through stage 3.

Examples 4.2 and 4.3 give fully synchronous mechanisms, example 4.1 half-synchronous mechanisms (the receiver may be blocked), and example 4.4 nonsynchronous mechanisms. The following points are worth noting:

1. Half-synchronous and fully sunchronous mechanisms can be realized using nonsynchronous mechanisms (see Example 4.4).
2. Half-synchronous mechanisms with source blocking are necessary to implement sliding-window schemes (see chapter 3).
3. Nonblocking single-destination send mechanisms can be used to construct a broadcast mechanism.
4. Fully synchronous and nonsynchronous mechanisms alone are not adequate [15].

Action Sequences. A communication-object value generally requires an action sequence by a destination process. Most IPC mechanisms directly associate that action sequence with a destination-guardian object. The mechanisms of example 4.4 are static as presented, but are extendable to be do not.

Static and Dynamic Structures. A static structure implies process and object naming (either source-object naming or destination-object naming) to remain static for the duration of system existence. The mechanisms of example 4.2 require a static structure. Dynamic structures allow either a dynamic naming convention or dynamic processes. The mechanisms of example 4.3 allow dynamic process structures but static namings. The mechanisms of example 4.4 are static as presented, but are extendable to be dynamic with respect to both process structure and object naming [18]. Static structures may be analyzed at compile to avoid circular blocking possibilities, such as deadlocks [16], whereas dynamic structures may not. Dynamic structures are useful to effect dynamic reconfigurations of communication structures as a means of achieving reliability [18].

Failure Handling. The IPC mechanisms of examples 4.1, 4.3, and 4.4 provide some level of support for certain anomalous situations. The mechanisms of examples 4.1 and 4.3 provide direct support, example 4.4 mechanisms provide indirect support. Mechanisms of examples 4.1 and 4.3 also provide timeout mechanisms, so that failure to receive object values can be signaled within destination guardians and action can be taken.

Oddly enough, only example 4.1 reference sources give even a word to the concept of message priorities, which is an important concept, especially in real-time systems.

We repeat our opening caveat: The IPC mechanisms discussed must be considered proposals; none has received widespread adaptation. Many other proposals, including remote-procedure invocations [19] and serializers and sequencers [20,21], have also been proposed. Although the proposals are tentative, the evaluation criteria are general and applicable to all proposals. A summary of other proposals is given in table 4–2.

Resource Management

To achieve coherency, the network operating system must provide for the management of resources, including naming and access functions, and support for multiplexed use. Network topology much influences the means by which network operating systems support resources management. Two basic presentations are possible: either resources are presented directly to the network or they are presented to the network through active nodes. These basic presentations are depicted in figure 4.3. The presentation shown in figure 4–3a is often associated with a local network, that of figure 4–3b with distributed systems. A mixed presentation, that is, some mix of the two views in figure 4–3 is possible, of course, as is a network presentation with some node-private devices. The view in figure 4–3a, a kind of "computer-cell" approach, is also employed in long-haul networks, such as Arpanet [22]. An instance of the view in figure 4–3b is found in figure 2–10. The differences in presentation affect the level of uniformity in the naming, access, and allocation of resources, and the difficulty of integrating the resource into the network.

Active-Element Presentation of Resources. Node active-element-presented resources result when the network is constructed by interconnecting computer cells, that is, computer systems, with direct connected devices, operating under an extant operating system. Node-presented resource systems require fewer CIUs and less software development than do network-presented resource systems. (The network in figure 4–3a requires two CIUs, that in figure 4–3b requires six.)

Active-element presentations result, however, in two dichotomies: the *dual-access dichotomy* and the *dual-service dichotomy*. The dual-access dichotomy results because computer-cell active elements must support access to both direct-connected resources and resources presented to the

Table Table 4–2
Summary of Distributed-System IPC Mechanisms and Languages

System	*No Blocking Send Primitive*	*Or Waits Nondeterminism*	*Destination Object Communication*	*Process/Link/ Port Name Propagation Possible*	*Shared Objects*	*Only Self-Destruction of Processes*	*Process Types*	*Dynamic, Static Process Structures*	*IPC Mechanism, Language, System, or Model*
Distributed Processes [19]	N	Y	Y	N	N	1	Y	N	M
Synchronizing Resources [24]	N	Y	Y		Y	Y	Y	Y	M
PLITS/ZENO [25]	Y	Y	2	Y	N	Y	Y	Y	L
Extended PDP-2 [26]	Y	N	N	Y	N	Y	Y	Y	L
ACTORS [27]	Y	Y	Y	Y	N	Y	Y	Y	M
PARLANCE [28]	N	N	N	N	N	Y	Y	N	L
FLOWGRAPHS [29]	N	Y	N				Y	Y	M
Roscoe [30]	Y	Y	N	Y	N	N		Y	
E-CLU [5]	Y		N	Y	Y	Y	Y	Y	M/L
PCL [31]	Y	Y	N	N	Y	N	Y	Y	L
TASK [32]	Y	Y	2	Y	Y	N	Y	Y	L
NSL [33]	N	Y	Y	N	Y	N	Y	Y	M
LIMP [34]	N	N	N	Y	N	Y	Y	Y	M
CSP [6]	N	Y	Y	N	N	Y	Y	N	M/L
*MOD [35]	N	N	Y	N	Y	Y	Y	Y	L
ADA [12]	N	Y	Y		Y	N	Y	Y	L
HXDP [13,14]	Y	Y	2	N	Y	N	Y		S

1 = processes exist forever; 2 = both destination address and source object addressed communications are possible.

Y = yes; N = no; blanks indicate lack of information.
M = mechanism; L = language; S = system

Much of the information contained in this table originally appeared in Mohan [16].

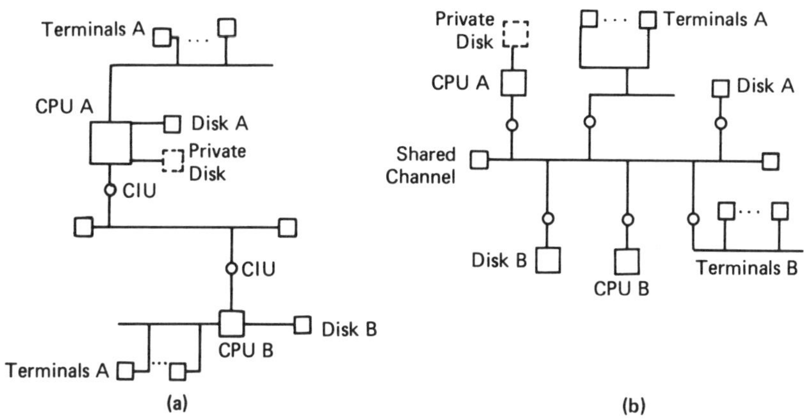

Figure 4–3. Possible Network-Device Presentations: (**A**) Active-Element Presentation; (**B**) Network Presentation

network by another computer cell. Support for the first kind of resource is a matter of channel programs, controller commands, process activations, and so forth. Support for the second kind is a matter of message exchanges. Generally, the extant operating systems under which most active elements operate have not been constructed to handle both direct-connected resources and network-connected resources. The circumstance is shown is figure 4–4. For direct-connected resources, the operating system resource manager maps application-process resource requests (logical names) to physical names, addresses, and so forth, and maps application requests to process generators, device drivers, and so forth. For coherency (in networks), the resource manager must be augmented to handle requests directed to resources in other cells. The required augmentation can often be sizeable and difficult to incorporate into the extant system, with naming, IPC, network delay, and protection problems compounding the difficulty.

The other side of the problem requires the cell-operating system to accommodate resource-manipulation requests that have originated in other computer cells.

These remotely generated requests also require augmentation of the resource manager (figure 4–5), a message handler, and perhaps a few resource-manager-activated processes to assist in the remotely generated requests. Again, the situation is often exacerbated by cell-operating systems that are designed for direct-connected resources only, and a resource manager that is possibly distributed over several system modules. The latter situation often obtains, for example, for requested file-manager operations, file access, and transfer. Nonhomogeneous cells operating under dissimilar operating systems further complicate the situation.

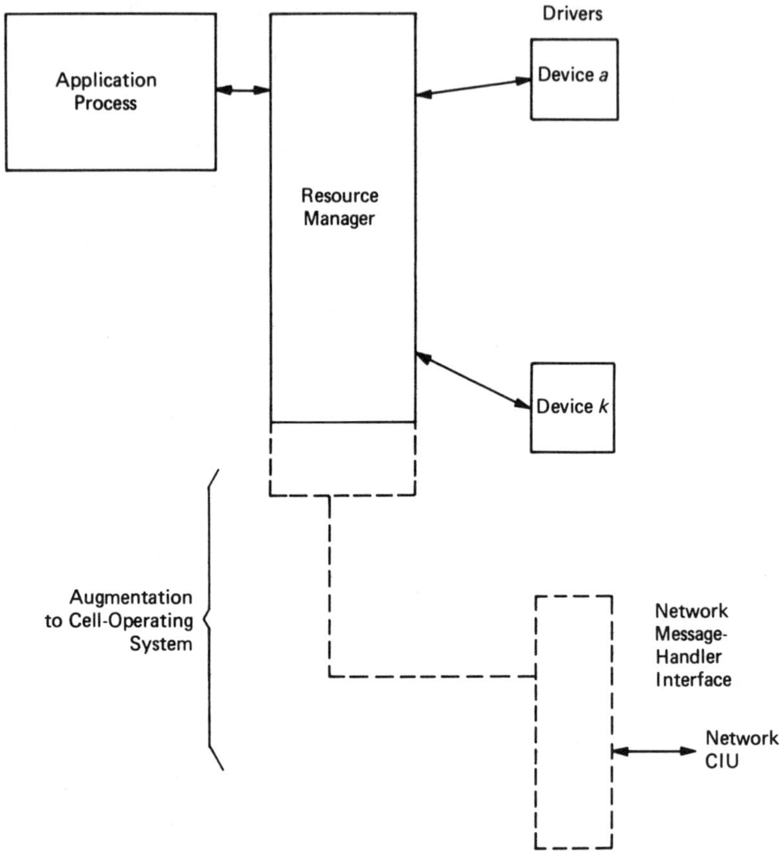

Figure 4–4. The Dual-Access Dichotomy

The Lawrence Livermore system shown in figures 2–3 and 2–4 clearly exhibits these difficulties. The solution, of course, is to design the cell or network operating systems so that all resources appear only as direct-connected or network-connected.

Network CIU Presentation of Resources. Network presentation of resources requires more CIUs, as shown in figure 4–3, but has several advantages, including a uniform scheme for naming resources (hence uniformity in access to resources) and reduced overhead on active elements. Specifically, in figure 4–3a, terminal A's use of cell B devices requires intervention (help) by both CPU A and CPU B. Similar use in figure 4–3b

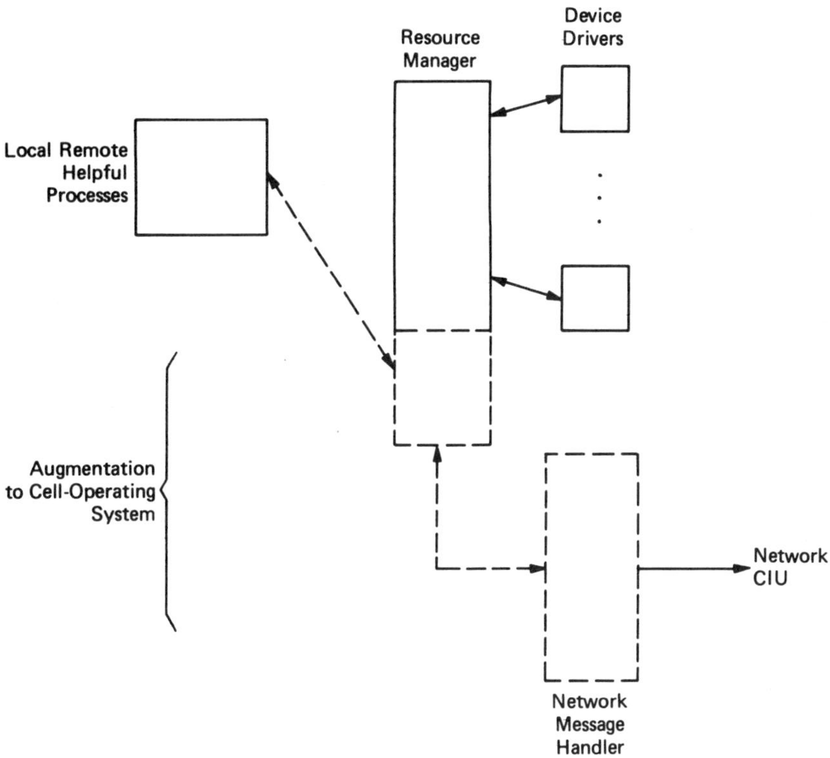

Figure 4–5. The Dual-Service Dichotomy

does not require CPU A or CPU B. The topology in figure 4–3b does, however, increase the traffic on the shared bus over and above that required by the configuration in figure 4–3a.

Network-presented resource systems can exhibit, furthermore, many of the problems described for active-element presentation, especially if heterogeneous mainframes and devices populate the network. They have the potential, however, to shift overhead functions to the CIUs (and away from the elements), to promote uniformity of access, and to relieve elements from a need to support devices directly.

The local networks shown in figures 2–7 and 2–10 are based on network presentations of resources.

A Contemporary Problem with Network-Connected Devices. The network shown in figure 2–7 does not require augmentation of the cell-operating systems for the Cybers, but for two reasons requires major augmentation of the PDP-11 system. First, coherency among active elements is achieved by a common understanding of the format and locking mechanisms for the shared system tables in extended core storage (ECS), the allowed manipulations of the tables, the organization of the disks, and the serial access to the disks enforced by their controller. On the negative side, contemporary CIUs attempt to control cost and insure reliability by having small main memories and no secondary storage. Consequently, they exist in a master-slave relationship with the active elements and, because of their limited capability, must often be instructed.

We can group hosts that communicate with direct-attached devices into two classes for purposes of discussion: those communicating via memory-mapped mechanisms and those communicating via channel-mapped mechanisms. Almost all hosts marketed today fit into one of these two categories. Memory-mapped input-output (I/O) associates the device with specified memory cells. With this scheme, status, for example, is obtained by reading a specified memory location, whereas device functions are sent by writing other locations. Memory-mapped I/O is characterized, especially for high-speed devices, by the fact that data transfer is effected by a direct memory-access mechanism, activated by first storing a device function code and parameters (for example, starting address and word count for the transfer) in specified memory locations and then setting a "start" bit. By implication, each setting of the start bit requires a function setting.

Under the channel-mapped I/O scheme, the host processor must either first reserve the appropriate channel and then communicate with the device over that channel by using processor instructions expressly designed for that purpose, or prepare a channel program, which is passed to a channel processor for execution. Different instructions are normally included for issuing functions and for transferring data. Thus, channel-mapped I/O allows a device function to be followed by multiple transfers of data, since functions are passed differently from data. This permits a mixture of function and data (reading and writing) operations to be done in any sequence.

Both memory and channel mapping therefore require that a function designator be first passed to the device (actually to the device controller), after which data may be transferred. The two schemes are distinguished by the fact that memory-mapped schemes require a function for each data transfer, whereas channel-mapped ones do not. This difference can affect the number of messages required for host-device communication in local networks.

To explain host-device communication, we will use the disk as an example (a likely candidate for sharing by multiple active elements in a network).

For directly connected host-device communications (figure 4–6a), it is first necessary to select the proper disk unit and start the heads moving to the

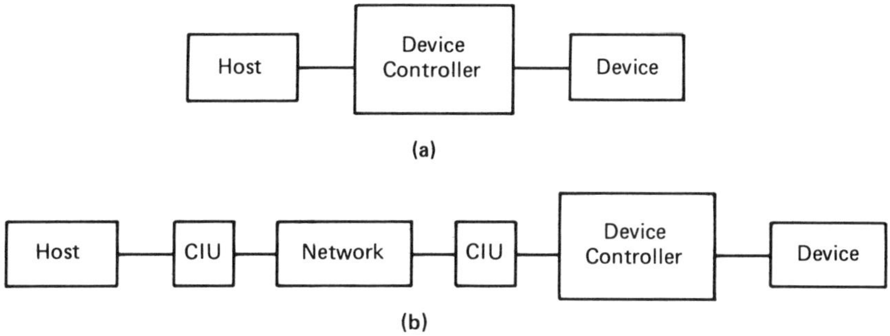

Figure 4–6. Configurations for (**a**) Directly Connected and (**b**) Remotely Connected Network Devices

desired location. This is effected by either setting the disk-location and seek function into the memory registers and waiting for the seek to be completed (often via a processor interrupt), or by placing a seek function on the channel, followed by an output of the seek parameters. In the latter case, status must be obtained to determine when the seek is complete. This is accomplished by placing a status function on the channel (and inputting the status) or by using an interrupt. Once the seek is complete, a similar sequence is employed to transfer data between the disk unit and the host.

The network complicates matters by requiring the host to "talk through" two CIUs before accessing the disk unit (figure 4–6b). Thus, the functional design of the CIUs plays an important role in determining the overhead (defined to include steps required to access the disk, over and above those required by direct connection) of host-device communication via the local network. Two approaches are possible—either the host can directly control the device (through the local network) via a virtual circuit connecting it to the device, or the CIU can be instructed to control the device by giving it a sequence of instructions requested (parameterized) by the host).

Using the virtual connection established between the host and device CIUs, all functions or data and their corresponding responses are automatically routed to the device as if the device were directly connected to a channel-I/O-based computer and all channel manipulations (except the one used to break the connection) are passed immediately to the remote CIU, which performs the identical manipulations on its channel. In like manner, any action taken by the device is immediately passed to the host CIU. This approach allows a networked device to be driven without modification to the host software, except for initial establishment and breaking of the CIU-to-CIU connection. In practice, a virtual circuit is impractical for several reasons, among them the fact that the time required to send a change in channel state through two CIUs and the network may be too large for effective host-device communication. This situation is true, for example, if head positioning is followed by data write, and local network message-transfer delays cause the data to arrive (at the device CIU) after the heads have rotated past proper position. Additionally, device speed can cause, at the host or device CIU, either an unmanageable backlog of data or an unacceptable starvation for data.

We can instruct a CIU in how to communicate with a device by making it able to receive a message, decode and interpret the control information or function-designator field of the message, and execute the functions. For generality (flexibility), the CIU actions associated with a function designator are generally defined by microcode. Additionally, the memory size and sophistication of the CIU determine the number of host connections, n, that it can honor simultaneously. When $n = 1$, a host generally must reserve the CIU for device communication; that host has mutually exclusive control over the device CIU. Reservation requests received while the CIU is reserved are rejected. When $n = k$, with $1 < k < \infty$, k host reservations can be honored simultaneously. With $n = \infty$, a host can transmit a request at any time (a datagram-type service) and can rightfully expect it to be honored. The memory capacity required for the CIU increases with n. The value of n can affect local network performance, since the number of rejects is apt to increase with decreasing n; this happens if, for example, the CIU interfaces multiple hosts to a battery of disks.

Given these considerations, the most effective approach is instructing the device CIU on how to communicate with the device and providing the CIU with a buffering capability. Consequently, host software assigned for direct coupling must be modified to accommodate host-device communication via CIUs. For existing systems, the level of host software alteration necessary to accommodate networked devices is dependent on the power and flexibility of the CIUs employed. Specifically, with instructed CIUs, the host must transmit functions, parameters, and data through two CIUs to communicate with the device. Thus, the host must package instructions for interpretation by the device CIU. These packages must be transmitted by the host to the host CIU, with instructions for forwarding to the device CIU. In many instances the device CIU must interpret a channel program, which must be "downloaded" to it in one of the packages. (Only a single downloading is necessary if the device CIU requires only a single channel program.) If the channel programs could be stored reliably in the device CIU, downloading would be unnecessary. To eliminate downloading, the device CIU must have adequate local storage; however, most do not. Consequently, the host needs four sets of commands to communicate with a remotely connected device, whereas it needs only one—the hardware command set—to communicate with a directly connected device. The four sets consist of host-to-host CIU commands, host-CIU-to-device-CIU commands, device-program commands, and hardware commands (the last two for use by the device CIU). The effort necessary for a host to communicate with a remote device is therefore a function of (1) the host interface to, and the power of, the host-CIU commands, (2) the host-to-host protocol, (3) the power of the device-CIU commands, and (4) the simplicity of the device program sequences required.

Table 4–3 contains an illustrative set of CIU functions (in actual practice, additional functions would be required). The host-CIU list contains three functions—STATUS and two that access the network. The reason for having two accessing functions is simple. The SEND function normally sends a relatively small block to another CIU. The block has two important characteristics. First, it is small enough so that it can always be received by the destination CIU, that is, it need never be rejected for lack of storage. Second, it requests the destination CIU to perform a function or informs the CIU to expect additional information. Should the function require transmission of a large block of data, such as a device program, that larger block is sent immediately following the SEND function block by means of the SEND DATA function. This mechanism allows the device CIU to reject the communication if it is unable to process the function because of the unavailability of a large block of memory, which is allocated to another task, that is, connections exist.

The device CIU has several functions (requested in control messages) for managing device programs. The LOAD DEVICE PROGRAM function instructs the CIU to define the next incoming message as a device program. This implies that memory space for the program will be allocated and maintained. The EXECUTE function is used to invoke execution of a stored device program and to pass data to the program relevant to that invocation (such as the SEEK parameters for a disk unit). However, not all data can be

Table 4–3
Typical CIU Functions

Host-CIU Functions	*Remote-CIU Functions*	*Device-Program Instructions*
STATUS	LOAD DEVICE PROGRAM from host	SEND FUNCTION TO DEVICE
	EXECUTIVE DEVICE PROGRAM	SEND DATA TO DEVICE
SEND remote CIU function (and any parameters) to another CIU	TERMINATE DEVICE PROGRAM	READ DATA from device
	REMOTE DEVICE PROGRAM	TEST DATA
SEND DATA associated with previous functions	SEND DATA TO DEVICE	

passed to the device CIU with the EXECUTE function. For example, the information to be written onto a disk unit is often too large to fit entirely into the CIU's memory. For this reason, the SEND DATA TO DEVICE (or DATA) function is included. The DATA function is of special interest, since it typifies the additional overhead caused by the network. As noted earlier, without the network (that is, with direct connection), data transfers are initiated by a handful of instructions. With the network, the host must send a control function to the device CIU containing the DATA function and, immediately thereafter, send the data, using the SEND DATA function. Thus, in addition to the downloading and invocation of the device program, the local-network overhead includes transmission of two additional functions and one additional data transfer (the control message).

It is possible to reduce the overhead in several ways. First, it is apparent that the host-CIU interface, whether driven by a memory-mapped or a channel-mapped I/O scheme, should be designed to resemble direct connection as closely as possible. For example, most devices using memory-mapped I/O contain a bit indicating "ready for next function," that is, not busy, or idle. The CIU interface should contain a similar bit. Likewise, most memory-mapped computers also contain processor-interrupt capabilities; the host-CIU interface should also contain such capabilities.

Second, two of the three additional command sets required by the local network—the host-CIU and device-CIU sets—should be merged in some cases. For example, computers using channel-based I/O do not have to issue a function each time a new data transfer is initiated. The normal host sequence for sending data to a network device is to first issue a SEND function along with the control message to the device CIU, and then issue a SEND DATA function along with the desired data for the device. As the channel-based I/O scheme distinguishes between functions (such as SEND) and data (the control message), the intermediate SEND DATA function can be omitted, since the device CIU can detect that another data block is present, rather than a function.

Third, by similar reasoning, the device-CIU functions (such as DATA and LOAD DEVICE PROGRAM) could be moved to the host CIU in name only. With proper design, this would allow a simplified control message to be passed by the host to the host CIU. The host CIU could then add the device-CIU function as needed, thereby forming a standard control message. This would allow nearly identical control messages to be used for every networked device. (The control messages would differ in destination and device selection only.)

Finally, regardless of I/O scheme, the host CIU could remember the last control message sent. Subsequent SEND DATA functions (or data on the I/O channel) would automatically cause the host CIU to reissue the last control message before transmitting the data. If, for example, twenty blocks were to be written to a disk unit, the host (and network) overhead incurred by SEND functions would apply only to the first block, and subsequent blocks would be sent consecutively without the need for the host to interface explicitly to the host CIU. This option is similar to that of the virtual circuit, although there are several important distinctions. First, there is no virtual circuit, that is, changes in the I/O channel state are not reflected by identical changes at the device. Second, the data are buffered in the CIUs to ease any mismatch in equipment speeds. Finally, and most important, the device becomes controlled by the device program. Thus, the device program, rather than the host, assumes responsibility for checking device status. Error processing may still be passed to the host, however.

There are basically two ways the device CIU may be made to execute the instructions forming a device program. One is to build CIU hardware that can directly execute instruction set, and the other is to emulate the instruction set with a general-purpose processor in the device CIU. The latter option is the most commonly selected, since it contributes to the realization of a general-purpose CIU, thus reducing costs and, in a sense, contributing to the ease with which a CIU may be adapted to a new device. It also allows the instruction set to be composed of extremely powerful instructions. The one potentially serious drawback to emulation is the time it requires.

To summarize, remote use of devices imposes additional overhead on the host in that such use generally involves the composing of messages for interpretation by the device CIU and then the communicating of those messages to the host CIU with forwarding instructions. Preliminary counts indicate, for example, that for the network in figure 2–7, up to thirty-two messages are required to download a program (and verify that it was received correctly, plus twenty more to transfer a disk sector and cancel a host reservation of the device CIU. Additional overhead is incurred because responses (device to device CIU to host CIU to host) are in a format dissimilar to that encountered in direct connection. Host software must be written (or altered) to account for both of these requirements, and the magnitude of the task depends upon the complexity and organization of the host operating system and the division of labor between the host and the CIUs. These considerations affect performance not only in terms of ease of local network realization but also in terms of the number and length of the messages needed to transfer data and handle device errors.

These problems can easily be solved by more-capable CIUs, and CIUs can be made more capable by the addition of memory, reliable secondary storage, such as bubbles, and more capable processors. Developing more-capable CIUs is thus more a matter of cost than of technology, and as hardware costs fall, more-capable CIUs will surely become available at reasonable cost.

A major advantage offered by the network view of devices is the ability to tailor the CIUs to a particular resource and to move certain operating-system functions to the CIU.

Example 4.5

Consider the network shown in figure 4–7, in which the node types computer, database storage, terminal (peripherals), and interface to long-haul network are displayed. Given this configuration, we can imagine an operating system structured as shown in figure 4–8, wherein the CIU software has been layered into levels. In figure 4–8, levels 0 to 3 realize the transport-layer protocols and level 5 the IPC mechanisms, as discussed earlier in this chapter. Levels 0 to 5 are common to all CIUs, independent of the attached resource type, and provide basic service functions required by the operating system. The composition of levels 6 through 9, however, is not unique, but depends on the node type; and, in this sense, the functionality normally associated with a computer cell is distributed. Each CIU contains only those layers necessary to accommodate the node type. We summarize the functionality for the levels shown:

Terminal-peripheral handler (TH): serves I/O, editing, log-in, log-out, command-language interpretation functions.

Common hosts interface: serves log-in and mapping operations to accommodate host-generated network-service requests and network-generated host requests.

Global data manager (GDM): serves to interpret database update requests, and formulate update programs, which are passed to the appropriate local database manager for execution.

Local data manager (LDM): applies updates formulated by the GDM, engaging in distributed database update algorithms [23], as necessary.

Global task manager (GTM): manages tasks associated with its attached resource that are of network interest. Makes task initiation, termination, requests of other node task managers as required.

Network Control. The network-control layer in figure 4–8 is concerned with diagnostic and monitoring functions. Monitoring serves to give each node a world view of the system, that is, a picture of which nodes are operable and which are off-line, an estimate of the level of system and channel loadings, and a picture of the status of resources. Network control operates by monitoring normal message traffic on the channel, by special messages sent to and received from the network-control layers of other

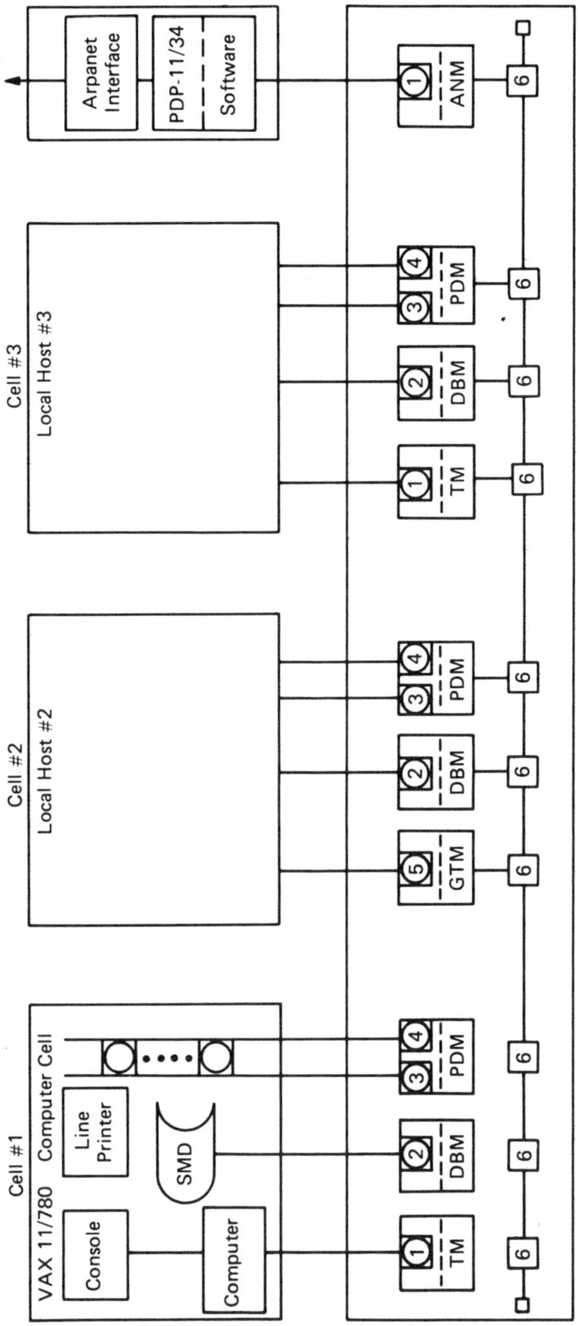

Figure 4–7. Sample Network

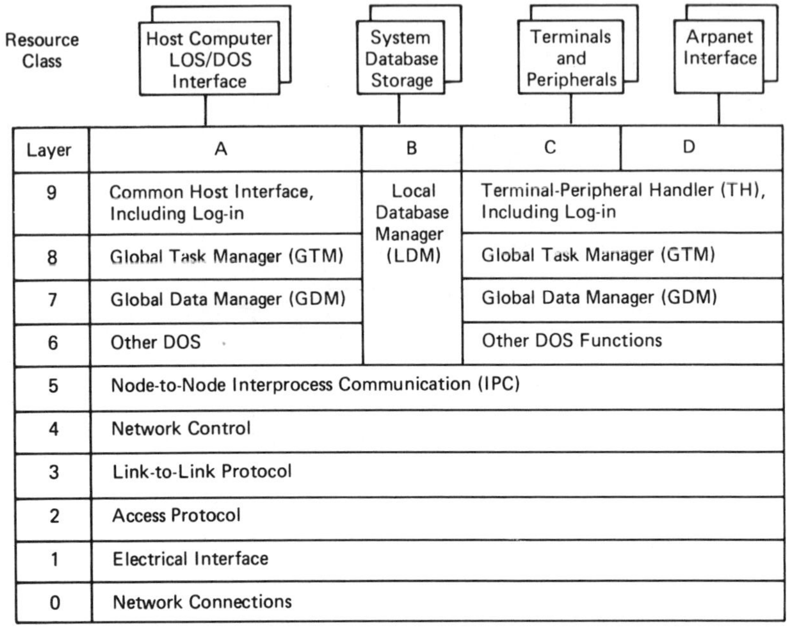

Figure 4–8. Operating-System Structure

nodes, and by cooperation with and use of other system layers in the node. Monitoring also implies data collection to facilitate performance measurement; diagnostic functions may also be initiated by the network-control layer.

Passive monitoring of normal message traffic by each node serves to provide each node with information on the fraction of channel bandwidth used by each node, retransmission patterns, noise and collision patterns, and resource-request and resource-allocation patterns (if permitted).

Passive monitoring by each node, though not increasing the total channel message loading, tends to place a burden on each CIU, in that it is acting on each message that appears on the channel. Thus, passive monitoring by each node may slow operation of the system. Alternatively, special passive monitoring nodes can be employed. The primary purpose of the nodes is to collect operational performance data by monitoring channel traffic. The approach is attractive in that, unlike the case with software monitoring in centralized systems, the data-collection task does not perturb the data being collected; that is, no "Heisenberg or interference effects" result. As a result of information contained in the message header (plus the message itself), the monitoring node can easily monitor the distribution of message lengths, the utilization of the channel, and collision and retransmission patterns and can collect data to construct a histogram matrix of source-destination pairs and the like. Additionally, the monitoring node can broadcast information on system state that can be useful to all system nodes, such as information suggesting or ordering a change in the parameters of an adaptive-access algorithm (see chapter 3) or announcing that a given node has apparently failed and left the network. Finally, the monitoring node can use messages directed at one or more network CIUs requesting return of information on node state.

Not all state or performance information can be collected passively. In particular, element-specific information can only be collected by the CIU attached to the element. Element-specific information may include operational data, such as whether the element is available or unavailable (perhaps failed), and performance data, such as the message-traffic pattern (inter-arrival time distribution—see chapter 5) of element-to-element attached CIU messages, including or excluding those messages that do not subsequently appear on the channel (discussed earlier in this chapter). Information in this category must be collected by the individual CIUs but can be passed to the passive monitoring node for assembly, analysis, and display.

A Generic System Organization. The system organization shown in figure 4–8 is but an instance of the general organization structure shown in figure 4–9, which segments the network operating system into three layers. (Figure 4–9 is very much like a figure in Watson and Fletcher [1].) As in figure 4–8, in the organization depicted in figure 4–9, various common needs are collected together and handled by a common standardized layer in each node, with each layer in the hierarchy of layers using the services of the layers beneath it.

Several addressing modes must be supported by the IPC layer, including:

Physical addressing: composed of a CIU physical address and port identifier within the CIU;

Logical addressing: symbolic reference to a resource or object;

Broadcast addressing: addressing of a designated port in each and every CIU; and

Generic and group addressing: with a generic address referring to a possible sequence of logical addresses.

For all but the first addressing mode, the IPC maps the logical or generic address into the proper physical address before sending the message. Logical addressing is analogous, for example, to symbolic references to files in centralized systems, and allows an addressing independent of the physical placement (that is, the node, and port node address pair) of the object

Application-Program Layer	Application process, creation, cancellation, etc.
Service Layer	File transfers, database updates, terminal support, RJE support, process scheduling, resource management support including clocks, files, directories, etc.
Service-Support Layer	Data translation support, world view of resources, capability and security support, data end-control message modes and format support.
IPC Layer	Interprocess communication (IPC), primitives, datagram service, resource-naming-convention support, link-level protocol (level-3 protocol), access protocol (level-2 protocol).

Figure 4–9. Network Operating System Architecture

addressed. Generic addressing allows symbolic reference to an object or resourc type, and the IPC layer must generally map such addresses to a group (or broadcast) physical address.

The service-support layer creates a uniform interface for commonly needed services, such as resource acquisitions, releases, interval timers, and data translation. To facilitate its function, it defines message request, reply, and data-transfer formats, dividing messages into the classes of data and control as discussed in chapter 3. It supports a series of data types (and mappings), capability forms (a protected-resource name—see following section), and a methodology (message sequence) for acquiring, using, and releasing resources. Details may be found in Watson and Fletcher [1].

Capabilities. The classic operating-system mechanism for insuring only authorized use of system resources is the capability. In its basic form, a capability is nothing more than an unforgeable resource identifier that must be presented when attempting to address (that is, gain access to) a resource.

Generally, the capability has or implies associated access rights, that is, legal manipulations, or uses that the presenter of the capability is allowed to make against the resource. Capabilities thus protect against illegal use of a resource, so that possession of a resource capability is the key to using a resource. Most stand-alone machine systems go to great pains to prevent one user process from passing an obtained resource capability to another user process. Generally, a capability is obtained from a process that controls use of the resource.

In the local-network environment, a resource is guarded by the node that contains it. We shall call that node the server node for the given resource. The nodes containing the process attempting to use the resource will be referred to as user nodes. To effect a viable protection mechanism in the network environment, capabilities must be passed from the server node to the user nodes in a manner that prevents arbitrary monitoring nodes from gaining access to the resource by stealing the capability.

Donnelly and Fletcher [36] discuss a series of protocols that insure that (1) the capabilities can be validated when used as authorization for resource-use requests, and (2) the capabilities can be communicated or passed between any processes that can communicate data. (The following material closely parallels material presented in Donnelley and Fletcher [36].)

Capability-Passing Rights. Since the right to access any resource must originate from within the serving process, all capabilities must be passed at least once (from the server node to a using process) to be of any use at all. To handle this first-pass situation, some operating systems have used the expedient of a pass-once capability [37]. Since a stand-alone system can arrange to monitor capability passing, it can mark pass-once capabilities as unpassable after they have once been passed from their service process to a user.

The difficulty of restricting capability passing in local networks can be seen by considering the process A, B, and S, pictured in figure 4–10. Suppose that A has a capability of a resource serviced by S. Also suppose that A can communicate with B (if not, then A clearly cannot pass capabilities or anything else to B; so no special capability-passing restriction is necessary). If the mechanism used to pass direct access to a resource from A to B has been denied by a monitoring-system kernel, A can still give B the right (indirectly) access the resource. A can simply have B send all its service requests to A for forwarding to S. A will also have to return the results of such requests to B.

In some cases, this sort of indirect capability passing is a useful mechanism, for example, in cases where A wishes to monitor B's access to the resource or where A wishes to be able to cut off B's access at a later time. In many other cases, however, the inability to pass direct access to a resource

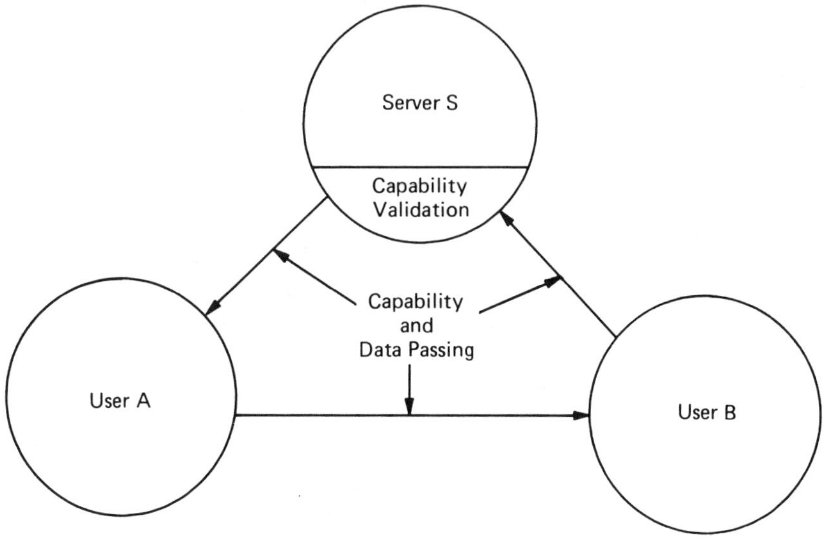

Figure 4–10. The Distributed-Resources-Sharing Problem

simply places an unnecessary additional communication burden on the passing process.

As a result of these observations, the capability-management protocols given in Donnelley and Fletcher [36] *all* allow passing of capabilities.

Tools Available for Capability Validation. In choosing a capability-management protocol, it is convenient to consider available validation mechanisms first, as the capability-passing mechanisms seem to follow naturally from the validation techniques chosen.

When a service process receives a request for resource access, it receives two pieces of information that can be used for capability validation: (1) the resource-access-request message data (the string of bits) and (2) the address of the sender. These two pieces of information give rise to two basic approaches to capability validation—the *data-authorization* and *address-authorization* approaches.

Address Authorization. A service process using data authorization gives some secret information to processes authorized to access the resource and believes that other unauthorized processes will not be able to guess or surreptitiously obtain the secret information.

The simplest form of data authorization is given by a password protocol. To create a password-protected capability, a service process creates a block of data containing the resource identification and a secret password to authorize resource access. To validate an access request authorized by a password-protected capability, the service process need only compare the password in the received capability data block with the valid authorizing password. The authorizing password either can be chosen at random and stored with the resource or can be computed from the resource identification by a secret algorithm known only to the server (for example, encrypted with a secret key). To pass the right to access, a password-protected capability, from one process to another, it suffices to pass the capability data block (including its password) in a message.

The ease of communicating password-protected capabilities also gives rise to their most significant problem. A process with a password-protected capability must be careful not to reveal the secret password.

Address Authorization. A service process using address authorization utilizes the address of the requesting process (as supplied in the header of the received request) to determine whether or not to allow a resource-access request.

The simplest form of address authorization is given by an access-list protocol. To create an access-list-validated capability, a service process creates and maintains a list of the addresses (names) of processes that are allowed to access the resource. Service processes for access-list-protected capabilities need only pass resource-identification information to authorized using processes. This information is not used for authorization, however. To validate an access request authorized by an access-list-protected capability, the service process checks to see if the sender's address is in the access list for the resource. Communicating access-list-protected capabilities is more difficult than communicating password-protected capabilities. The basic difficulty stems from the fact that the service process must update its access list every time a capability is passed from one using process to another. To insure update, the service process must be notified that the capability transfer has occurred.

At first glance, it might appear that the passing of an access-list-protected capability could be accomplished by two steps: (S1) request the service process to add the address of the process that is to receive the capability to the access list; and (S2) send the resource identification to the receiving process. Unfortunately, these two steps do not suffice to insure secure capability passing. The problem that exists is characterized as *capability reflection*.

The essence of the capability-reflection problem is the situation that can arise if a process, D, can be duped into falsely believing that it received a capability from another process, B. If D can then be called upon to send (reflect) the capability back to B, B may receive an unauthorized capability.

To illustrate the capability-reflection problem for the two-step access-list

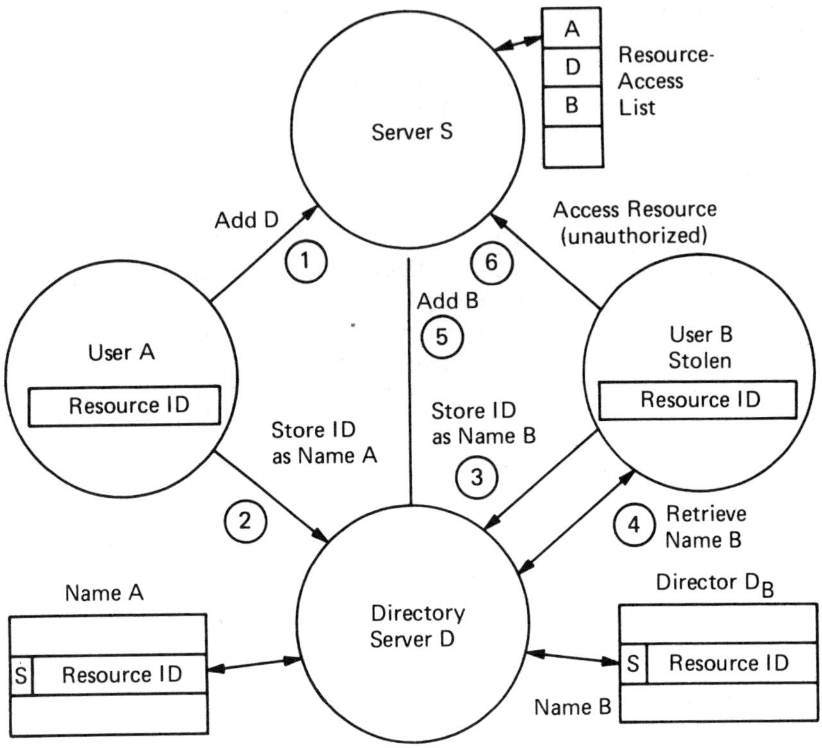

Figure 4–11. The Capability-Reflection Problem

protocol, imagine a directory server D, as depicted in figure 4–11. The function of the directory server is the storage and retrieval of capabilities. It allows processes to store capabilities in directories so that they may later be retrieved and used by any process with a capability to the directory. A directory server allows processes to store and share capabilities in a manner analogous to the way a file server allows storage and sharing of information.

Suppose, for example, that process A has the only capability to an access-list-protected resource serviced by S. Suppose, also, that A has a capability to directory D_A and that B has a capability to D_B (but not to D_A). Consider what must happen if A is to store its capability in D_A. Following steps (S1) and (S2), it first requests S to add D to the access list for the resource (1). A then sends the resource identification to D and requests that the capability be stored in D_A (2). If, at a later time, some other process with access to D_A requests retrieval of the stored capability, D must go through steps (S1) and (S2) to satisfy the request. That is, it must have S add the retrieving process to the resource-access list and then must return the resource identification to the retrieving process.

The capability-reflection problem appears when we consider the sequence that obtains if process B sends the resource identification (which we assume A has not kept secret because it trusts the access-list mechanism) to D and requests that its capability be stored in D_B (3). At this point, the situation appears to D as if B were authorized to access the resource. All B need do is ask D to retrieve the capability from its directory (4) and it will have duped D into placing it on the access list without proper authorization. A similar reflection problem appears in conjunction with data theft when we consider public-key-encryption protection of capabilities.

To supply an access-list-based capability-management protocol that is safe from the reflection problem, the given two-step protocol must be amended. One method of bolstering the two-step protocol is by requiring that all capabilities be received from the resource-service process. By this procedure, a process sending a capability to another merely notifies the receiver to expect the actual capability from the resource-service process. The sender also requests the server to add the receiver to the resource-access list and to send the capability identification to the receiver on the sender's behalf. The fact that the process receiving the capability actually receives the resource identification from the service process along with the address of the sending process guarantees that the sender was authorized to access the resource. This access-list protocol is somewhat awkward, requires a significant amount of message traffic, and requires servers to maintain access lists.

There are a number of methods for combining data and address authorization in a capability management protocol [36]. One employs encrypted addresses, another encrypted capabilities.

This brief excursion serves to characterize contemporary thinking about capability-based access mechanisms in networks and to show how they differ from schemes used with stand-alone machines.

The two schemes presented, as well as the remaining two given in Donnelley and Fletcher [36], each have strengths and weaknesses; finding a best scheme seems remote, although all proposals have much in common.

A Note on Distributed Control

Earlier in this chapter, we sketched a model of distributed systems. In that model, each node encompassed certain resources, and we considered that a node guards the resources it encompassed, in that it regulates the use of the resources it guards.

It is desirable to have a corresponding qualitative model of distributed or decentralized control, one that identifies the elements and parameters of distributed control and contributes to an understanding of options and mechanisms. A possible genesis for such a model is given in Jensen [38], where distributed control is equated to resource management. The elements of the model are abstract *resources* (data, objects, programs, processes, devices, and so forth) that are managed by active entities called *controllers*. A resource may be managed by a single controller, as in the guardian model, with different resources managed by different controllers, which cooperate as necessary. Control is decentralized in the sense that different resources are managed by different controllers, with each controller having exclusive control over the resources it manages. The multiaccess channel represents an instance of a different organization. With the multiaccess channel a collection of equal controllers (represented by the CIU-access protocol) cooperate in allocating the channel resource, and no single controller has exclusive authority to manage the channel. The model given by Jensen [38] attempts to capture these differences and characterize distributed control in terms of the number of controllers that manage a resource and the manner by which they do so. Possible points in the control space include a cooperative manner (as with the multiaccess channel) and an exclusive-control manner (as in the case of a guardian).

Other views of distributed control are possible, however. For example, rather than viewing a distributed system as composed of a series of abstract resources, it can be viewed as composed of a set of *services* [39]. This view emphasizes the vehicles by which a resource is accessed rather than the resource object, as was the case with the previous view. In terms of the guardian model, the emphasis would be on the guardian, not on the objects it guards. Still another model is given in Chandy and Misra [40].

Summary

The material in this chapter is neither definitive not complete, but it is indicative of trends in the development of local-network mechanisms and operating systems. Our intent was to provide an awareness of those trends (with extensive links to the literature). A definitive treatment of local-network operating systems will have to wait until sufficient time has passed to complete and then assess the results of the myriad of ongoing local-network operating-system development efforts.

References

1. Watson, Richard W., and Fletcher, J.G. "An Architecture for Support of Network Operating System Services." *Computer Networks* 4 (February 1980).

2. Boebert, W.E.; Franta, W.R.; and Berg, H.K. "NPN: A Finite State Specification Technique for Distributed Software." *Proceedings Specifications of Reliable Software*, 1979, pp. 139–149.
3. Svobodova, Liba; Liskov, Barbara; and Clarka, David. "Distributed Computer Systems: Structure and Semantics." MIT/LCS/TR-215, March 1979.
4. Liskov, B.; Snyder, A.; Atkinson, R.; and Schaffert, C. "Abstraction Mechanisms in CLU." *CACM* 20 (August 1977):564–576.
5. Liskov, Barbara. "Primitives for Distributed Computing." Industrial Liaison program report, 8-20-79, Massachusetts Institute of Technology, 1979.
6. Hoare, C.A.R. "Communicating Sequential Processes." *CACM* 21 (August 1978):666–677.
7. Bernstein, Arthur J. "Output Guards and Non-Determinism in Communicating Sequential Processes." *ACM Transactions on Programming Languages and Systems* 2 (April 1980):234–238.
8. Kieburtz, Richard B., and Silberschatz, Abraham. "Comments on Communicating Sequential Processes." *ACM Transactions on Programming Languages and Systems* 1 (October 1979):218–225.
9. Silberschatz, Abraham. "Communication and Synchronization in Distributed Systems." *IEEE Transactions on Software Engineering* SE-5 (November 1979):542–546.
10. Walden, David C. "A System for Interprocessing Communication in a Resource Sharing Network." *CACM* 15 (April 1972):221–230.
11. Dijkstra, E.W. "Guarded Commands, Non-Determinancy, and Formal Derivation of Programs." *CACM* 18 (August 1975):453–457.
12. Wagner, Peters. *Programming with Ada: An Introduction by Means of Graduated Examples*. Englewood Cliffs, N.J.: Prentice-Hall, 1980.
13. Boebert, W.E.; Cornhill, D.P.; Franta, W.R.; Jensen, E.D.; and Kain, R.Y. "Kernel Primitives of the HXDP Executive." *Proceedings of the COMPSAC Conference*, November 1978.
14. Boebert, W.E.; Cornhill, D.P.; Franta, W.R.; Jensen, E.D.; and Kain, R.Y. "Design Issues in a Distributed Executive." *Proceedings of the COMPSAC Conference*, November 1978.
15. Manning, Eric; Livesey, N.J.; and Tokudea, H. "Interprocess Communication in Distributed Systems: One View." *Proceedings of IFIP 80*, October 1980.
16. Mohan, C. "Perspective of Distributed Computing in Models, Languages, Issues and Applications." Working Paper DSG-8001, Department of Computer Sciences, University of Texas at Austin, February 1980.
17. Franta W.R.; Berg, H.; Boebert, W.E.; and Moher, T. *Formal Methods of Program Verification and Specification*. Englewood Cliffs, N.J.: Prentice-Hall, 1981.

18. Kain, R.Y., and Franta, W.R. "Interprocess Communication Schemes Supporting System Reconfiguration." *Proceedings of the COMPSAC Conference*, November 1980.
19. Brinch Hansen, P. "Distributed Processes: A Concurrent Programming Language." *CACM* 21 (November 1978):934–941.
20. Reed, David, and Kanodia, Rajendra. "Synchronization with Event Counts and Sequencers." *CACM* 22 (February 1979):115–123.
21. Bullis, K., and Franta, W.R. "Implementation of Event Counts and of Broadcast Network." *Computer Networks* 4 (April 1980):57–69.
22. Thomas, R.,H. "A Resource Sharing Executive for the Arpanet." *AFIPS Conference Proceedings* 42 (1973 SJCC):155–163.
23. Thomas, R.H. "A Majority Consensus Approach to Concurrency Control for Multiple Copy Databases." *ACM Transactions on Database Systems* 4 (June 1979):180–209.
24. Thomas, R.H. "Rationale for the Design of the Ada Programming Language." *ACM Sigplan Notices*, June 1979.
25. Deball, J.; Williams, G.; and Low, J. "Preliminary Zeno Language Description." TR 41, University of Rochester, January 1979.
26. Kahn, G., and MacQueen, D. "Coroutines and Networks of Communicating Processes." *Proceedings of IFIP 77*, 1977.
27. Hewitt, C.; Attardi, G.; and Liberman, H. "Specifying and Proving Properties of Guardians for Distributed Systems." *Proceedings of the International Symposium on Semantics of Concurrent Processes*, Evion, France, 1979.
28. Reynolds, P. "Parallel Processing Structures: Languages, Schedules, and Performance Results," Ph.D. thesis, University of Texas at Austin, 1979.
29. Milne, G., and Milner, R. "Concurrent Processes in Their Syntax." *JACM*, April 1979.
30. Solomon, M., and Finkle, R. "The Roscoe Distributed Operating System." *Proceedings of the Seventh Symposium on Operating Principles*, December 1979.
31. Lesser, V.; Serrain, V.; and Bonar, J. "PCL: Process-Oriented Job Control Language." *Proceedings of the First International Conference on Computing Systems*, Huntsville, Alabama, October 1979.
32. Jones, A., and Schwans, K. "Taskforces: Distributed Software for Solving Problems of Substantial Size." *Proceedings of the Fourth International Conference on Software Engineering*, September 1979.
33. Tarrini, F.; Sharp, R.; Martinelli, M.; and Endrizzi, A. "A Network System Language." *Proceedings of the First International Conference on Distributed Computing Systems*, Huntsville, Alabama, October 1979.

34. Hunt, J.G. "Messages in Type Languages." *ACM Sigplan Notices*, January 1979.
35. Cook, R. "Mod-A Language for Distributed Programming." *Proceedings of the First International Conference for Distributed Computing Systems*, Huntsville, Alabama October 1979.
36. Donnelley, J.E., and Fletcher, J.G., "Resource Access Control in a Network Operating System." Unpublished manuscript, Lawrence Livermore Laboratory, 1980.
37. Basket, Forrest; Howard, John H.; and Montague, John T. "Task Communication in Demos." *Proceedings of the Sixth Symposium on Operating System Principles*, Purdue University 1977, pp. 23–31.
38. Jensen, E.D. Decentralized Control, Distributed Systems: An Advanced Course. Springer-Verlag, 1980.
39. Abraham, Steven M., and Dalal Yogen, K. "Techniques for Decentralized Management of Distributed Systems." *Proceedings of COMPCON 80, Spring*, February 1980, pp. 430–437.
40. Chandy, K.M., and Misra, J. "A Simple Model of Distributed Programs Based on Implementation-Hiding and Process Autonomy." *ACM Sigplan Notices*, October 1980, pp. 26–35.

5 Modeling and Measurement

Introduction

Evaluation of local networks is a continuous process, dictated by changing computational needs and technological advances in both computing and communication. The evaluation of local-network performance is determined by the interplay between application requirements, the functionality of the machinery supporting the network, and its operational environment. Performance is generally characterized by quantitative operational measures, such as expected-message delay, channel utilization, the number of messages required for a given class of node-to-node interactions, and error rates for frame transmissions, and by nonfunctional, partially qualitative measures, such as the ease with which nodes can be added to or deleted from the network, the extent to which new operating-system code must be designed, written and tested to accommodate new applications, and ease of use of the network.

Each class of measures is affected, in turn, by design choices made with respect to the devices that constitute both the elements and the CIUs. Proper evaluation requires both models to predict performance and network instrumentation to measure performance. We will discuss each issue in turn.

As with any modeling effort, modeling of local networks requires a proper abstraction process, one that results in capturing in the model the driving forces of the system being modeled. Only by capturing the driving forces, that is, those that essentially determine system behavior, and by omitting ancillary forces, which do not significantly contribute to behavior, can we realize viable, tractable models. All modeling efforts require identification of system components and component attributes (state variables) and characterization of the rules of interaction between components. With local networks, this task is facilitated by the hierarchical organization of the network into protocol levels (or layers). This is particularly true since protocol functionality of one layer is supplied as a service to higher layers, such that performance of one is dependent on both its design and the performance characteristics associated with services obtained from the lower-level supporting protocols.

Example 5.1

To achieve proper real-time support for a terminal process, it is not sufficient to guarantee high-priority fast processing by the node active element, as extensive delays at the access level might preclude any adequate level of service regardless of terminal-process design, a circumstance that may only be cured by a message-based priority scheme at the access-protocol level.

In some sense, the measures associated with the various protocol levels migrate from a more quantitative nature to a more qualitative nature as we move from the lowest to the highest protocol levels. Additionally, lower-level protocols are in many ways simpler than their higher-level brothers. Taking these two remarks together serves to indicate why, in fact, there are more models of low-level protocols than there are of high-level protocols, a circumstance reflected in the attentions given to each layer in the following sections.

Models based on queuing theory, including networks of queues, probability theory, network-optimization theory, and heuristics have all been developed; no single analytic tool is viable for all models. The structural nature of local networks, particularly the use of a multiaccess channel, may, furthermore, prevent direct use to predict local-network performance of models developed for long-haul networks. Consequently, new queuing theory, renewal theory, Markov chain, and Markov decision-process models have been developed. Additionally, as with long-haul networks, models based on simulation have been extremely useful in the evaluation of all levels of local-network protocols. In all these modeling efforts, a number of simplifying assumptions about the system has to be made. With analytic models, these assumptions tend to be extremely constraining but necessary in obtaining solutions. Simulation tools, being based on procedural descriptions, offer more latitude than do analytic tools in expressing component attributes and interactions. Even simulation models, however, cannot encompass all the component interactions found in a real system. Thus, assessment of system behavior also requires system instrumentation and the collection of operational data. System instrumentation is at least as important as modeling, providing collected data that can be used to validate model assumptions and predictions, to suggest system-operational parameter settings, and to monitor component failures and error rates, and so forth. As discussed later in this chapter, instrumentation may be passive or active.

In subsequent sections of this chapter we will report on local-network modeling, instrumentation, and data-collection efforts.

Measures of Performance

Measures are selected to characterize the behavior of a single network, to compare the behavior of a set of networks, or to compare the behavior of various alternatives that might be employed within a layer or layers of the protocol hierarchy of a network [82]. Certain measures may also serve either to compare measured performance with model-predicted performance or to validate certain assumptions associated with available models.

As a result of this myriad of uses, it is difficult to specify a small or canonical set of measures that serves all needs. It is easy to say, however, that measures are generally concerned with delays (of messages), in gaining channel access, and so forth; utilizations (of channels, of message buffers, and so on); reliability or robustness (of components, CIU software packages, and the like); usability of the network; extendability; and so forth.

Definitions of these measures depend on many factors, including the intent of the model, the level of the protocol hierarchy addressed by the model, and the tools employed to develop the model. No matter the circumstance, however, the measures are dependent on certain system features. For example, the unit of information transmitted is usually called a frame. In most local networks, frames are variable in length, and hence, for modeling purposes, they have an associated distribution. For several reasons, models are often developed with all frames assumed to be of a fixed length, such that all frame-transmission times are equal to a constant. Fixed-size frames are assumed because the system employs packet transmissions, or the model only remains tractable if the assumption is used, or fair comparison of results produced by several models demands the assumption. The channel end-to-end propagation delay, defined as the time required for a transmission signal to travel between the remotest pair of connected nodes, also plays a key role. The value of this parameter is determined by the communication medium, the speed of light, and, of course, the distance between the remotest pair of nodes.

As suggested in chapter 3, many performance measures are quantitative in nature. Typical measures include:

1. Channel utilization (U): the long-run fraction of time the channel is engaged in the transfer of data. Generally, all forms of overhead detract from utilization; header information, overlapped channel use (because of collisions), and scheduling periods are all examples of overhead. Additionally, for nonsaturated channels, utilization is generally equivalent to throughput, the rate at which frames are successfully transmitted.
2. Channel capacity (C): the maximum possible value of U allowed by the operational characteristics of the protocols employed (especially the access protocol).
3. Expected message delay (D): the average delay experienced by a message following its arrival to a node until its successful transmission, assuming a homogeneous set of nodes, that is, with the arrival process of all nodes being governed by the same exponential distribution, and a single distribution governing the lengths of all messages. If nonhomo-

geneous processes are involved, D must be replaced by node-dependent mean values $D_i, i = 1, \ldots, K$ for a K-node system.

4. Buffer occupancy: the length of the node queues of messages awaiting transmission.

Other measures may also be of interest and applicable, depending on the protocols employed. For example, with access protocols in which collisions may occur, we may also be interested in the expected number of collisions that precede successful transmission of a frame and the delay associated with acknowledgments, as a function, for example, of the retry distribution and its parameters. Additionally, for virtual circuits, we may be interested in the number of rejects encountered during attempts to establish virtual circuit. Although these quantities often appear directly as model variables, when they do not, they are derived from measures that do; for example, by Little's formula:

$$L = \lambda W$$

relating mean arrival rate λ, mean delay W, and mean queue length L. Qualitative measures [1] include (1) the robustness of the protocols, CIUs, and so forth, to failures, sudden fluctuations in traffic, and the like; and (2) the ease of adding or deleting nodes, functionality, capacity, and so forth, to the network, including software developments, and the security the network guarantees to frames.

Instrumentation Possibilities

Instrumentation is concerned with the collection of operational data from which estimates of performance measures may be derived. Local networks offer the possibility of collecting operational data in both an active and a passive fashion. Passive data collection is generally done by having a node passively monitor all channel traffic, from which estimates of utilization, the frame-length distribution, collision characteristics, and so forth, can be obtained. The beauty of passive monitoring is its natural ability to provide operational data without disturbance, that is, without perturbation to the data being observed and collected. With local networks, software operating in the passive node can be used for passive monitoring, whereas, in traditional, centralized systems, hardware monitors must be employed. The extent to which passive monitoring can be relegated to the passive-node CIU depends on the power and functionality of the CIU. Passive CIUs can keep account of node status (operational, failed, and so on); serve to regulate experiments (for example, introduce noise on the channel); logically turn CIUs on and off;

and initialize, monitor, record, and display the results of diagnostic-program executions.

Certain operational data, such as the node-message interarrival distribution (histogram), cannot really be collected passively. In this case, active monitoring (processing by each node actively involved in network operation) must be used. The data-collection activity of these active nodes can, however, be activated and deactivated by commands from the passive monitoring node, which therefore also serves a control function.

It should be obvious that the extent to which a CIU can monitor and control data collection and engage in diagnostic function depends on its processing capability, storage capability, and the bandwidth of the shared channel. CIUs that are designed to connect a terminal to a network simply aren't likely (for reasons of cost) to have the horsepower to engage in actual monitoring, whereas those designed to connect a major mainframe are likely to have such power.

Not much has been published about instrumentation and monitoring in local networks, whereas much literature exists on long-haul network instrumentation [3,4,5]. A few exceptions exist.

In Tobagi, Lieberson, and Kleinrock [3] and Tobagi et al. [6], instrumentation for experiments in long-haul and radio networks is described, including artificial traffic generators and capabilities to collect data on cumulative statistics of events occurring at a node and to produce snapshots to indicate a node's state, such as buffer occupancy, at random times.

Measured Performance

There are few reports on the operational performance of local networks. A notable exception is a report on Ethernet [7]. This report and our own experience suggest that:

1. Channel errors (detected by the CRC mechanism) may be almost nonexistent with cable-based local networks (errors of one in two million messages are reported for Ethernet [7]).
2. Message lengths form a bimodal distribution, with the mix determined by the local-network functionality and application (a fact derived from the traffic mix of function-request messages and data-transfer messages and contrary to the analyses resulting from most modeling efforts, which assume messages of fixed length).
3. The packing efficiency, that is, the ratio of the number of data bits to total bits in a frame, can be high (being determined by the placement of the peaks in the bimodal distribution of message length). It has been

measured at around 0.8 for Ethernet [7], but it is generally much lower in high-speed applications, such as in the network shown in figure 2–7.

As more local networks become operational, more reports on performance will become available, including ones on mixed-media networks, that is, networks using cable, microwave, or satellite channels.

Data on the ease of constructing local networks around existing operating systems are also lacking. Preliminary information [8] suggests that hosts (active elements) using channel programs are easiest to accommodate, whereas hosts with limited memory [such as Cyber Peripheral Processor Units, (PPUs)] are the most difficult. Measured performance of satellite systems can be found in Gerla, Nelson, and Kleinrock [5] and in Chu and Naylor [10]. Given the dearth of reports on measured performance, subsequent comparison of alternatives will rely primarily on model-predicted results.

Models and Quantifiable Measures

To obtain predictive information about a system, one builds a model of the system from which certain measures can be obtained. At the initial design stages of a computer network, models are in fact the only source of available performance data. Different modeling techniques exist, and they differ in their scope of applicability, in the constraints and assumptions they make about the system being studied, and in the type and number of measures on which they provide information. Analytic models, simulation models, hybrid (simulation and analytic) models, and network testbeds represent different classes of predictive techniques. However, all of them view the modeled system, existing or projected, as consisting of components with attributes and rules that govern the interactions between components. (In a local network, for example, the channel, the CIU, and the element are components that can be functionally described by attributes such as transmission rate, CIU storage capacity, and processing speed.) The various modeling techniques differ first in the way the rules of interaction are accounted for in the model. In analytic models, the interactions are given by rules of formal mathematics. In simulation or numeric models [35,37], the rules of interaction are given in a looser form, that is, procedurally, by algorithms. With the testbed approach, the rules, and also the components, are simulated by software or hardware components of the tested system. The major difference between a testbed and a real-world system relates to size and flexibility, with testbed systems often smaller and more flexible than real-world systems.

The main restriction on analytic models comes from the need to use formal descriptions of interaction rules. Thus, analytic models tend to be simple accounting for a small number of components and specifying interaction rules in a relatively concise mathematical manner. Analytic models are generally used for relative-performance assessment (that is, comparison of performance for various parameter settings, and the like) but not to directly quantify actual system behavior. With simulation, the allowable model complexity is significantly increased, and simulation models are used to predict actual system performance, in addition to providing relative-performance comparisons.

A simulation modeling effort is almost sure to yield results (valid or not), whereas one based on analysis may not, because of the mathematical sophistication the approach requires and the inherent limitations the approach possesses (by virtue of its insistance on adherence to formal mathematical rules). Analytic-model development tends to be expensive in terms of people (the developer's time); simulation models tend to be expensive in terms of computer time (and possibly also people time). Testbed systems are expensive in terms of people time and equipment costs, but may be more flexible than analytic or simulation models and may be cheaper than simulation models in terms of computer time. In the following sections, we discuss each class of model-development tools.

Analytic Models

Analytic models are generally more difficult to develop than simulation models (or even testbed models), but, once developed, they usually offer results for a variety of parameter settings at a low cost. Furthermore, they show qualitative relationships between parameters and variables more clearly than do models developed by other techniques. For networks, analytic models require that the message-arrival process and variations in message length be described by probability distributions, that is, by random variables. Generally, mathematical tractability dictates that the message-arrival process be based on infinite or finite source processes such that the time between consecutive arrivals (for each process) is governed by an exponential random variable (an exponential random variable, $\bar{X}$, has density function $\lambda e^{-\lambda x}$, distribution function $1 - e^{-\lambda x}$, with $0 < x < \infty$, and mean $1/\lambda$). In infinite-source processes, the pool of messages available for arrival is inexhaustible; with finite-source processes, there exist, at most, M available messages, and the supply is depleted by one for each arrival and incremented by one by return of successfully transmitted messages to the source pool. Each arrival process is convenient in different circumstances, and each will be used in subsequent sections. The simplest (most tractable) mechanism is one in which there are K homogeneous nodes and one exponentially driven message source, such that message arrival is associated with a particular node in an equally likely random manner.

Although message lengths may be assumed to be variable (governed by a random variable), most modeling efforts have proceeded by assuming messages of constant length.

Given the options available for source processes and message-length distributions, as well as the variations possible in defining performance measues, it is sometimes difficult to directly compare predicted behavior of two different models, a circumstance that will face us in the following sections.

Queuing Models. Queuing models are probably the most-often applied tool for network-performance evaluation. Queuing theory views a system as composed of one or more service centers to which customers come for service. (The customers may be tasks in an operating-system model, messages requiring transmission, or the like, and the server may be a CPU or a communication channel, or the like). The queuing-theory description of a service center requires specification of:

1. The interarrival-time distribution of customers to the service center;
2. The distribution of service time the customers require of the server;
3. The discipline by which the service node selects customers from a queue in which they wait, after arrival, for attention by one of possibly a set of servers in the service node.

Example 5.2

With a multiaccess channel, the customers are messages that the collection of nodes wish to transmit over the shared channel—the server in this case. The service time for a customer is given by the time required to send the message over the channel, a time determined by the length of the message (in bits) and the speed of the channel (in bits per second).

The messages requiring transmission come to the CIUs from their attached elements or are generated directly by the CIUs (as is the usual case, for example, with acknowledgments). Characterization of the pattern of message arrival to and generation within a CIU can be difficult. Generally, it is convenient and adequate to assume that the CIUs represent random sources of messages, with the message-generation process at work within one CIU statistically independent from the similar processes at work within the other CIUs.

Given these assumptions, we can assume that CIU i generates messages for transmission with exponentially distributed intergeneration times with rate parameter λ_i. (Thus, the mean intergeneration time for node i is $1/\lambda_i$.) By the laws associated with exponentially driven processes, the rate of arrival of messages to the channel (over all nodes) is given by

$$\lambda = \sum_{i=1}^{K} \lambda_i$$

and the time between arrivals is exponential (with parameter λ, of course).

Alternatively, with homogeneous nodes, we may say that the arrival process regulating arrival of messages (for transmission) to the system is exponential with parameter λ, such that the arrival rate at any CIU is λ/K, with the CIU-dependent processes also exponential.

Finally, characterization of the multiaccess channel as a queuing model requires specification of the queuing discipline, that is, the process that governs the selection of messages for transmission. This specification comes, nontrivially perhaps, from the multiaccess protocol. With multiaccess protocols, complications can arise in that the system is not always a work-conserving system. (In work-conserving queuing systems, the server is always gainfully serving a customer so long as customers exist to serve). Thus, work required can be both created and destroyed in a multiaccess system model. For example, collision of transmissions with the required retransmission attempt represents work destruction. However, if nodes are polled to determine message-transmission order, and polling times are nonzero, the server will not be used to transmit messages while the polling process is taking place—a work-creation circumstance. Many results exist for work-conserving queuing systems [12,13,14,15], some for work-creating systems [5,6], but few or none for work-destroying systems.

Having characterized the elements of a queuing station, analysis proceeds by defining the state of the system as given by the number of customers it contains (and perhaps the remaining service time for the customer being served), and by attempting to determine and characterize operational behavior via determination of the queue-length distribution, the customer-delay distribution, server utilization, and server idle- and busy-period distributions. If distributions cannot be found, the moments of these distributions are sought.

We can attempt to characterize behavior for the transient period following network startup or the steady-state period that obtains after the network has been in operation for a very long time. Steady-state behavior is easier to obtain than transient behavior, and most queuing-theory results are for the steady-state situation. Single service centers are labeled *M/M/K*, *M/G/K*, G/G/K, and so forth, where the first designator characterizes the customer interarrival-time distribution, the second is the customer service-time distribution, and the third is the number of (identical) servers in the center. (The designator M denotes the exponential distribution, with M meaning Markovian or memoryless. G denotes a general, that is, arbitrary, distribution, such that analysis performed by assuming G is valid if the arbitrary G is replaced by the specific distribution denoted by M.) The complexity of queuing-theory analysis rises as we go from $M/M/K$ to $G/G/K$. Analysis of multiaccess protocols can occasionally employ $M/G/1$ models. The best-known result for $M/G/1$ queues is the Pollaczek-Khintchine mean-value formula:

$$L = \rho + \frac{\rho^2(1 + C_b^2)}{2(1 - \rho)} \tag{5.1}$$

where

$$\rho = \lambda \bar{X} = \lambda/\mu$$

gives server utilization, and where λ is mean arrival rate of customers to the system, $\bar{X}$ is the mean customer service time (also denoted by $1/\mu$), W is the mean customer waiting time (defined as the mean time that elapses between arrival of a customer and attention to it by the server), L is the mean number of customers in the system, and C_b^2 is the coefficient of variation for service time (given by the ratio $\sigma_b^2/\bar{X}^2$, with σ_b^2 the variance of the service-time distribution). The behavioral measures L and W are related by the general relationship

$$L = \lambda W \tag{5.3}$$

that is, by Little's result.

Example 5.3

Both $M/G/1$ and $M/M/1$ models can be applied to multiaccess-channel-protocol analysis. Assume the ideal case in which all nodes can immediately transmit arriving messages collision-free if the channel is free. If the channel is not free, they are queued. This situation implies complete cooperation between nodes in a distributed system, without the need for the communication overhead necessary to achieve that cooperation. Such a system is approximated if the cooperation-communication costs are so small as to become insignificant. Such is the case, for example, for simple BRAM, when the propagation delay a times the number of nodes K is relatively negligible as compared with the message (packet) transmission time T. To obtain the distribution of the number of messages in the system, we must account for the queue-selection discipline. Average results, however, are independent of this discipline, and we can use the well-known *M/D/*1 results to approximate the situation. (Note that, because of the assumed negligible propagation delay, no work is generated, since the scheduling periods become negligible, and no work is destroyed in the absence of collisions.)

To proceed, we let G denote the total traffic of messages entering the system for transmission; S denote channel throughput, as given by the number of messages successfully transmitted per unit of time; T denote the constant packet-transmission time; C denote channel capacity, defined as the maximum achievable value for S allowed by the multiaccess protocol; D denote expected transmission delay (queuing delay plus transmission time); and λ denote mean rate of arrival of new messages for transmission. Further, as in chapter 3, we normalize these measures by T. With these definitions and assumptions, we can approximate BRAM behavior by *M/D/*1 queueing-theory results. From equation 5.1 we then have:

$$L = \rho + \frac{\rho^2}{1 - \rho} \tag{5.4}$$

with L the expected number of packets in the system and $\rho = \lambda T \equiv \lambda$. Since $L = G$, we have, from equation 5.4,

$$G = \frac{S(2 - S)}{2(1 - S)} \tag{5.5}$$

or

$$S = 1 + G - \sqrt{1 + G^2} \tag{5.6}$$

and, from equation 5.3, we can obtain the expected average delay:

$$D = L/\lambda = \frac{2 - S}{2(1 - S)} \tag{5.7}$$

Further, we have $C = 1$, since, for sufficiently high loads, BRAM will operate as TDMA, fully utilizing the channel.

Under these assumptions of no cost for orderly cooperation, several other schemes that avoid collisions can be shown to exhibit similar behavior, particularly MSAP and MLMA [16,19]. If, however, the assumption of no-cost cooperation is not valid, then the *M/G/*1 queuing model no longer suffices as a viable tool to predict multiaccess protocol behavior.

Example 5.4

Queuing-theoretic models for work-creating roll-call polling systems have also been developed [20]. In Konheim and Meister [18], a network of K nodes with identical message-generation characteristics operating under a polling-access protocol is considered. A central station sends control (polling) messages to each of the nodes in turn, asking them if they have messages to transmit. If a queried node has messages (in this case, fixed-length packets) to transmit, it is allowed to control the channel for a time sufficient to transmit all its queued packets. When a queried node has transmitted all its queued packets (which may be none), the central node queries the next node, and the process is repeated in a cyclic fashion around the ordered set of nodes. In Konheim and Meister [18], it is assumed that polling messages are short, so that their transmission time is less than the channel end-to-end propagation delay. Given this assumption, each query is assumed to require two round-trip propagation-delay intervals. Thus, for the nth node in the polling sequence, a total delay of $2(n - 1)a$ time units will be necessary to poll that node in each polling cycle.

In Tobagi and Kleinrock [21], $E\ (Q_D)$, the expected queuing delay for node packets, and $E[Q_L]$, the expected value of the stationary queue length at each node, are derived. Specifically, we have:

$$E[Q_L] = \frac{1}{2}\frac{v}{1 - Km} + \frac{Krm(1 - m)}{2(1 - Km)} \qquad (5.8)$$

and

$$E[Q_D] = \frac{Kv}{2(1 - Km)} + \frac{1 - m}{2} + \frac{Kr(1 - m)}{2(1 - Km)} \qquad (5.9)$$

where Q_D is given in units of a, and Q_L as a number of packets, with m the expected number of packet-transmission times that pass before a packet that arrives during an a-slot is transmitted; v giving the variance of m; and r the integer number of a-slots that pass between queries of two consecutive nodes.

As in equations in 5.4 through 5.7, the expected delay given by equation 5.9 is normalized with respect to the packet-tranmission time T, so that the expected packet-transmission D, defined earlier, becomes:

$$D = E(Q_D) + \text{packet transmission time} = E(Q_D) + 1 \qquad (5.10)$$

Example 5.5

The results in equations 5.8 and 5.9 can also be applied to other multiaccess protocols [16,21,22]. In Tobagi and Kleinrock [21], equations 5.8 and 5.9 were interpreted to obtain expected delay for a multiaccess radio channel. Subsequently, the results were applied to simple prioritized BRAM and MSAP. From Tobagi and Kleinrock [21], we have

$$D = 1 + \frac{S}{2(1-S)} + \frac{a}{2}\left(1 - \frac{S}{K}\right)\left(1 + \frac{Kr}{1-S}\right) \tag{5.11}$$

with D, S, a, K, and r as defined before. Equation 5.11 is obtained by finding the analog of the relationship between roll-call polling-control message-transmission times and the two-way propagation-delay time for the multi-access-control mechanisms of BRAM and MSAP. From chapter 3 we know this time to be given by one a unit, giving $r = 1$, so that equation 5.11 becomes:

$$D = \frac{2-S}{2(1-S)} + \frac{a}{2}\left(1 - \frac{S}{K}\right)\left(1 + \frac{K}{1-S}\right) \tag{5.12}$$

It is also possible to obtain results giving the relationship between G and S for BRAM and MSAP using equations 5.8 and 5.9. From equations 5.8 and 5.9, in Chlamtac, Franta, and Levin [22] it is shown that:

$$G = \frac{S(2-S)}{2(1-S)} + \frac{aS}{K}\left(\frac{K-S}{1-S}\right) \tag{5.13}$$

Comparing equation 5.7 with equation 5.12 shows that equation 5.12 is the sum of expected delay for an *M/D/*1 system (Pollaczek-Khintchine formula) and the delay necessary to pass channel control from one node to another—the price paid for distributed control. Several conclusions are readily available. First, if the propagation delay becomes negligible, the price paid for distributed control becomes negligible, and no additional delay beyond that of *M/D/*1 need be accounted for. Second, the overall delay increases as the number of nodes increases and as the time, a, it takes to move control between them increases. Third, the best possible performance for multiaccess protocols that serialize channel use is given by *M/D/*1 queueing theory. Finally, as throughput approaches capacity, the average delay tends to infinity. (The foregoing analysis shows access schemes that are appealing when the $K \cdot a$ product is small and a collision-free access protocol is employed.

Models Based on Stochastic Processes and General Probabilistic Arguments. In some cases, basic probabilistic arguments serve to develop models for multiaccess protocols when direct use of queuing-theory results is not viable. Such is the case, for example, with the urn scheme presented in chapter 3.

Example 5.6

As another example where probability arguments serve, we consider the parametric BRAM protocol with node-dependent message-arrival rates λ_i. In particular, in parametric BRAM, the frequency of collisions can be controlled by the proper selection of node groups. (For homogeneous arrival rates, that is, when $\lambda_i = \lambda/K$, the grouping strategy wherein each group contains the same (or nearly the same) number of nodes is best.) When the λ_i are node-dependent, we can easily obtain groups for which the collision probabilities are severely imbalanced, such that collisions will occur very frequently in some groups and infrequently in others. Such imbalances can adversely affect performance. It is of interest, therefore, to ask how the nodes should be grouped so as to obtain the best performance possible when using parametric BRAM, under the assumption of node-dependent message arrival rates. The answer is given by the following theorem.

Theorem: The optimal grouping strategy, in the sense of reducing to a minimum the probability of intragroup collisions, is the one that divides the network nodes into groups of equal aggregated arrival rates.

Proof: Let

$$\lambda = \sum_{i=1}^{K} \lambda_i$$

Let us divide the K nodes into m disjoint groups, Is, $s = 1, \ldots, m$. Then the probability that a transmission is originated by node i, given that it originates in Is, is

$$\frac{\lambda_i}{\sum_{j \in Is} \lambda_j}$$

This transmission will be destroyed by collision if other nodes belonging to Is also become ready and transmit (by virtue of having generated a message during the previous transmission). The probability of collision in group *Is*, given that it originates a transmission, is therefore given by:

$$\sum_{\substack{j \in Is \\ j \neq i}} (1 - e^{-\lambda_j T}) \tag{5.14}$$

with T the packet-transmission time. Assuming the absence of a dominant λ_j, equation 5.14 becomes (approximately)

$$\sum_{\substack{j \in Is \\ j \neq i}} \lambda_j T + O(\lambda_j T)$$

which, since $T = 1$, becomes

$$\sum_{\substack{j \in Is \\ j \neq i}} [\lambda_j + O(\lambda_j)] \sim \sum_{\substack{j \in Is \\ j \neq i}} \lambda_j \tag{5.15}$$

The probability for a collision within group *Is* (recall that by construction there are only in-group collisions, and intergroup collisions do not occur) is therefore, at least approximately,

$$\sum_{i \in Is} \left[\frac{\lambda i}{\sum\limits_{i \in Is} \lambda i} \right] \sum_{\substack{j \in Is \\ j \neq i}} \lambda_j$$

which equals

$$\frac{1}{\sum\limits_{i \in Is} \lambda i} \sum_{i \in Is} \left[\sum_{j \in Is} \lambda_i \lambda_j - \lambda_i^2 \right]$$

or

$$\frac{1}{\sum\limits_{i \in Is} \lambda_i} \sum_{j \in Is} \lambda_i \lambda_j - \frac{1}{\sum\limits_{i \in Is} \lambda_i} \sum_{i \in Is} \lambda_i^2$$

Then, since the probability of a transmission originating in group *Is* is

$$\sum_{j \in Is} \lambda_j / \lambda$$

the probability, P, of a collision on any transmission is

$$P = \sum_{s=1}^{m} \left[\frac{1}{\sum_{i \in Is} \lambda_i} \sum_{i,j \in Is} \lambda_i \lambda_j - \frac{1}{\sum_{i \in Is} \lambda_i} \sum_{i \in Is} \lambda_i^2 \right] \left[\sum_{i \in Is} \lambda_i / \lambda \right]$$

which reduces to

$$P = \frac{1}{\lambda} \sum_{s=1}^{m} \sum_{i,j \in Is} \lambda_i \lambda_j - \frac{1}{\lambda} \sum_{i=1}^{K} \lambda_i^2 \tag{5.16}$$

To minimize the probability, P, of collision, we must minimize the right-hand side of equation 5.16. This is done by minimizing

$$\sum_{s=1}^{m} \sum_{i,j \in Is} \lambda_i \lambda_j = \sum_{s=1}^{m} \left(\sum_{i \in Is} \lambda_i \right)^2 = \sum_{s=1}^{m} (\lambda^{(s)})^2$$

with $\lambda(s)$ the aggregate arrival rate for group Is which is achieved by setting

$$\lambda^{(s)} = \frac{\lambda}{K}, \qquad s = 1,2,\ldots,m$$

establishing the theorem. The theorem remains true even if the assumption used to simplify equation 5.14 is not used, but the proof becomes more difficult.

Regenerative Processes. For many systems, one can identify a stochastic process that repeatedly restarts (regenerates) itself at certain states. For example, the behavior of an $M/G/1$ gueue is statistically regenerated each time the system passes through the idle state, where the queue is empty and the server is idle. All busy periods bounded by two consecutive idle states are statistically identical. Thus, system behavior is Markovian, that is, memory-less, from one busy period to another. Thus, by specifying behavior in a typical busy period and specifying the length of idle periods, we can obtain behavior of the system over the continuous time axis. Furthermore, if it is not possible to identify regeneration points, it may be possible to identify states in which the system approximately regenerates itself, although the validity of the approximation must be established by either simulation or other methods.

Example 5.7

An example of an application of this approach is provided by a model that establishes the throughput of the ALOHA protocol. As in Abramson [23], we assume that:

1. The interarrival times of all newly arrived and rearrived (for retransmission) packets, taken together, are given by an exponentially distributed random variable:
2. The retransmission-delay intervals are large, on the average, compared to packet-transmission times; and
3. The number of retransmissions required is small.

It has been shown, for example, by simulation [24] and analysis [25], that for slotted ALOHA assumption 1 is reasonably close to true when $X \to \infty$ (see assumption 2), where X is the mean retransmission-delay interval. The random-point process defined in assumption 1 clearly defines a regenerative process. Let the parameter associated with the exponential process given by assumption 1 be λ. Then the rate at which packets accumulate in the system is given by $G \equiv \lambda T$ packets per transmission period, with T the packet-transmission time. Given that only noncolliding packets are transmitted correctly, the rate of successful packet transmissions must be λ^1 with $\lambda^1 \leq \lambda$. We must have $S = \lambda^1 T$. If G and S are normalized by T (so that we have, effectively, $T = 1$) then $G = \lambda$ and $S = \lambda^1$. To relate G and S, we consider a typical transmission attempt. A packet is transmitted collision-free if no other packets arrive during its transmission and no other packet transmissions are in process when its transmission begins. These conditions are met if (1) no packets arrive during its transmission (an interval of width T) and no packets arrived in an interval less than T units before its arrival (so that their transmissions are not ongoing.) The probability of these events is given by using the well-known formula

$$Pr\{x \text{ arrivals in interval of length } y\} = G^x e^{-Gy}/x!$$

(which gives the probability that x customers arrive in an interval of length y, when the interarrival times are governed by an exponential distribution with parameter G), with the settings $x = 0$ and $y = 2T$ (with T normalized so that $T = 1$). With $x = 0$ and $y = 2$ we have:

$$Pr\ \{\text{successful transmission}\} = S = Ge^{-2G}. \tag{5.17}$$

With slotted ALOHA, y becomes T so that:

$$S = Ge^{-G} \tag{5.18}$$

Further, using equations 5.17 and 5.18, the point G at which S is maximized is easily had by solving $dG/dS = 0$, giving $C = 1/2e$ for ALOHA and $C = 1/e$ for slotted ALOHA.

Example 5.8

The model of example 5.7 proceeded by viewing the arrival of all packets (at all nodes) as constituting a single stream. Alternatively, we can consider a model wherein the identity of nodes is kept by considering K message streams [26]. Assume, for example, that G_i is the probability that the ith node transmits a packet in any slot (assuming a slotted ALOHA access scheme). Assume, also, that node actions are independent but statistically identical. For a K-node system, then, the normalized channel traffic rate is given by

$$G = \sum_{i=1}^{K} G_i$$

packets per slot. Again, for the packet of any node to be successfully transmitted in a given slot, it must be the only packet transmitted in that slot, and for each node the probability of a successful transmission S_i must obey $S_i \leq G_i$, such that the normalized channel throughput is given by:

$$S = \sum_{i=1}^{K} S_i$$

Under the assumption of independent nodes, the probability that a packet from node i will be the only one transmitted in a given slot is given by

$$\prod_{\substack{j=1 \\ j \neq i}}^{K} (1 - G_j)$$

so that we have:

$$S_i = G_i \prod_{\substack{j=1 \\ j \neq j}}^{K} (1 - G_j) \tag{5.19}$$

With K identical (homogeneous) nodes we have $S_i = S/K$ and $G_i = G/K$, so that equation 5.19 becomes:

$$S = G(1 - G/K)^{K-1} \tag{5.20}$$

In Abramson [27], it has also been shown that throughput is maximized if:

$$\sum_{i=1}^{K} G_i = 1$$

The result in equation 5.20 is related to the result in equation 5.18 in an obvious manner. Specifically, if we let $K \rightarrow \infty$ in equation 5.20, we obtain equation 5.18. In essence, then, equation 5.20 has assumed K nodes whereas equation 5.18 has assumed an infinite number of nodes. Thus, if K is small, equation 5.20 is viable; if K is large, equation 5.18 becomes viable.

Markov Chains. For the analysis approaches discussed to this point, a steady-state system was assumed, that is, the model results are representative of system behavior after the system has reached a certain equilibrium, generally the result of extended system operation. Simulations of slotted ALOHA [25] have indicated, however, that such an equilibrium condition may never be reached (especially in the case of infinite population systems). The same unstable behavior has also been shown for other access methods that allow collisions, such as CSMA [28] and parametric BRAM [22]. Thus, although the equilibrium results are important in understanding the behavior and performance of these methods under stable conditions, which may be prevalent over long periods of time, it is important to analyze the dynamic or nonequilibrium behavior of these systems, both to determine performance measures and to be able to define and evaluate dynamic control schemes for these methods. Markov chains, semi-Markov chains and Markov decision processes are among the approaches that can be applied when dynamic models are required [12,14,30], or when the underlying stochastic process is memoryless.

A Markov chain is a stochastic process, that is, a collection of random variables X_n, $n = 1, 2, \ldots$, if, for all n and all values of X_n,

$$Pr\{X_n = i_n \mid X_1 = i_1, X_2 = i_2, \ldots, X_{n-1} = i_{n-1}\} = Pr\{X_n = i_n \mid X_{n-1} = i_{n-1}\}$$

This statement is, in fact, a comprehensive definition of Markov chains, which states that the sequence $(X_n)\, n = 1, \ldots,$ has the so-called memoryless (or Markov) property, whereby the conditional probability of any future state, given any past states and the present state X_n, depends only on the present state and not on the past states. A more tractable tool results if, in addition to the preceding equation, we also have that:

1. The set of possible values of X_n is finite (and denoted by indices);
2. The values of the probabilities $P(X_n = j \mid X_{n-1} = i)$ are independent of n such that X_n becomes X; and
3. The transitions from one state, denoted by X_{n-1}, to another, denoted by X_n, occur at unit intervals.

Given these assumptions, we can write:

$$P_{ij} = Pr\ \{X_n = i \mid X_{n-1} = j\}$$

and refer to the set of P_{ij} as the transition probabilities, that is, of a transition from state $X = i$ to state $X = j$. Given the set of transition probabilities, we can represent the Markov transition process by the transition matrix:

$$P = \begin{bmatrix} P_{00}\ P_{01} & \cdots P_{0n} \\ P_{n1}\ P_{n2} & \cdots P_{nn} \end{bmatrix}$$

assuming n states. Given a set of initial probabilities $Pr\{x\} = i$, which denote the probability of being in a given state i at initiation of system operation and the transition probabilities, we can compute the probabilities of being in any given state after any given number of unit-interval transitions. Given certain rather general conditions, we can solve for the equilibrium probabilities Π_i, where Π_i is the long-run probability of the system being in state i. These probabilities can be determined from the equations:

$$\Pi_j = \sum_{i=1}^{n} \Pi_i P_{ij} \tag{5.21}$$

and

$$\sum_{i=1}^{n} \Pi_i = 1.$$

The important point is that, if a system moves around among a finite number of discrete states and displays the Markovian property in doing so, then it is a likely candidate for analysis using Markov chains.

Example 5.9

Markov-chain models were applied in Carleil and Hellman [31] and Kleinrock and Lam [32] to analyze slotted ALOHA throughput-delay behavior. We briefly summarize the developments. To begin, we note that, in multiaccess schemes wherein all nodes are able to sense transmissions from each other, delay is given by transmission time plus the number of retransmission times necessary for the packet to successfully reach its destination, plus the time the packet waits between retransmission attempts. We call the retransmission times plus the interretransmission delays the backlog delay; packets awaiting retransmission are said to be backlogged. In calculating delay, the propagation delay, a, plays an important role, since it takes at least a time units for each node to learn the destiny of packets it transmits. Each of the nodes in a K-node system may be in a packet-generation state or in a blocked state. A generation state occurs when a node is awaiting arrival of a new packet to transmit. Let the packet-generation rates (the packet-intergeneration times) be governed by an exponential distribution (Poisson process) with rate parameter σ, which is only in effect when the node is not blocked. A node is blocked once it has a packet to transmit, and it remains blocked until that packet is successfully transmitted. Thus, a node remains blocked during the initial transmission, during retransmission, if any, and during the intervals that separate retransmission attempts. The total traffic offered by the K nodes consists of all new and backlogged packets. If we denote the probability of transmitting a backlogged packet in a given slot by P, then we have, assuming bursty users, $P \geq \sigma$. Additionally, we must have $K\sigma < 1$, as one is the maximum throughput per slot. The state of the system is given by the channel backlog, that is, by N^t, a random variable representing the number of packets backlogged at time t. The descriptive random variable, N^t, is one that exhibits the Markov property at the beginning of each slot, a circumstance that is argued as follows. If $N^t = k$, that is, if k nodes are backlogged, and if each backlogged node transmits its packet in the next slot with probability p, the generation rate for the arrival of backlogged packets will be kp packets per slot. Given this assumption, a delay of n slots before transmission occurs with probability

$$P_n = (1 - P)^n P$$

so that the distribution of retransmission delays is geometric, with mean $1/P$. The number of nodes available to generate new traffic is therefore $K - k$, and their combined packet-generation rate is given by $(K - k)\sigma$ packets per slot. The system state will change from slot to slot as packets are transmitted either successfully or unsuccessfully, in which case the packets become (or remain) backlogged, requiring retransmission. All the probability distributions governing this process are easily seen to be memoryless, and the next state of the system depends only on the present state and on the probability of transmissions from the nodes. It is evident, therefore, that the system can be modeled by a discrete-state Markov process. As pointed out earlier, Markov models require definition of the state-transition probabilities, P_{ij}, which, in this case, are defined by $P_{ij} = Pr\{N^t = j \mid N^{t-1} = i\}$, with t and $t-1$ denoting two consecutive slots. Note that, unlike the case for collision-free protocols, we cannot conveniently use $M/M/1$ queuing models in this case, since, with slotted ALOHA, transitions occur only at slot boundaries, a circumstance that is argued as follows. If $N^t = k$, that is, if k nodes are based [12]. For the case being considered, any number of nodes can be ready for transmission or retransmission at the beginning of a slot. Thus, the number of backlogged nodes may increase by a number larger than one (at a transition point, although it will only decrease by one (if it decreases), since only one successful transmission can be accomplished in any given time slot.

To solve for the probabilities P_{ij}, we let S^t denote the channel-input rate of new packets, that is, $S^t = (K - N^t)\sigma$. N^t and S^t are clearly inversely proportional. Next, we assume all variable distributions to be time invariant. The discrete-state space consists of the th states N^t $[0,1,2,\ldots,K]$, and the state-transition probabilities associated with N^t become:

$$P_{ij} = Pr\{N^{t+1} = j \mid N^t = i\} =$$

$$\begin{cases} 0 & j \le i-2 \\ iP(1-P)^{i-1}(1-\sigma)^{K-i} & j = i-1 \\ (1-P)^i(K-i)\sigma(1-\sigma)^{K-i\;1} + [1 - iP(1-P)^{i-1}](1-\sigma)^{K-i} & j = i \\ (K-i)\sigma(1-\sigma)^{K-i-1}[1-(1-P)^i] & j = i+1 \\ \binom{K-i}{j-i}\sigma^{j-i}(1-\sigma)^{K-j} & j \ge i+2 \end{cases} \tag{5.22}$$

In the limit when $K \to \infty$ and $\sigma \to 0$, such that $K\sigma \to S$, a finite constant, equation 5.22 becomes:

$$P_{ij} = \begin{cases} 0 & j \leq i - 2 \\ iP(1 - P)^{i-1}\exp(-S) & j = i - 1 \\ (1 - P)^{i}s\ \exp(-S) + [1 - iP(1 - P)^{i-1}] \\ \quad \exp(-S) & j = i \\ S\ \exp(-S)[1 - (1 - P)^{i}] & j = i + 1 \\ \dfrac{S^{j-i}}{(j - i)!}\exp(S) & j \geq i + 2 \end{cases}$$

To find the stationary probabilities from equation 5.21 we formulate the equations:

$$\Pi_j = \sum_{i=0}^{K} \Pi_i P_{ij}$$
$$1 = \sum_{i=0}^{K} \Pi_i \qquad (5.23)$$

using equation 5.22, and solving the set of $K + 1$ equations (K of which are independent) that give the solution Π_i. Different methods exist for solving equation 5.23 [14,105]. To obtain the average delay for the system, one notes from previous definitions of delay that:

$$D = D_b + a + 1 \qquad (5.24)$$

where D_b is the average backlog time (the time a packet is backlogged) and $a + 1$ is the delay for a successful transmission (with the propagation delay).

To proceed, we note that we can apply equation 5.3, Little's result, to any part of a system. For the case at hand, we can apply it to the backlog mean time to obtain

$$D_b = \frac{\bar{N}}{\bar{S}} \qquad (5.25)$$

with $\bar{N}$ the mean number of backlogged packets, and $\bar{S}$ the mean rate at which backlogged packets are generated. By definition, we have:

$$\bar{N} = \sum_{i=0}^{K} i\Pi_i$$

To compute $\bar{S}$, we must compute the conditional probability of a successful transmission for each possible state and then compute the unconditional probability of a successful transition for each possible state and then compute the unconditional probability of a successful transition using the state probabilities. Specifically, we calculate:

$$s_i = Pr\{\text{number of new packets} = 1\}\, Pr\,\{\text{backlog} = 0\} + Pr\{\text{number of new packets} = 0\}\, Pr\,\{\text{backlog} = 1\}$$

and then compute:

$$\bar{S} = \sum_{i=0}^{K} s_i\, \Pi_i$$

Substituting these quantities into equation 5.25 gives the average delay value needed in equation 5.24. We note that delay-throughput analysis for the simple (unslotted) ALOHA protocol is not facilitated by the Markov-chain model. Instead, a semi-Markov model [30], as discussed next, is required.

Semi-Markov Chains. With discrete-time Markov chains, the transitions between different states are made at unit-time intervals according to specified transition probabilities. Consequently, the time spent in a given state follows the geometric distribution. If, however, the time between consecutive transitions is governed by a different stochastic process, we have a semi-Markov process. Semi-Markov processes are so named because, whereas the times between transitions are governed by an arbitrary distribution, the transitions themselves are governed by transition probabilities as in a Markov process. The class of semi-Markov processes is thus a generalization of Markov chains, and results similar to those discussed for Markov chains hold for semi-Markov processes. Consequently, the set of systems that can be modeled using semi-Markov chains is wider than those for Markov chains. We shall demonstrate the use of a semi-Markov model by looking at the analysis leading to an expression for average packet delay for slotted nonpersistent CSMA [33].

Example 5.10

Figure 5–1 shows the relationship between idle and busy periods, giving an imbedded Markov chain, for a channel that is accessed using slotted nonpersistent CSMA. In figure 5–1, imbedded slots are chosen to be the first slot of each idle period. This technique creates cycles (busy period plus idle period pairs) of random lengths, with lengths given by $I + T + 1$ a-slots, with I the number of slots in an idle period, T the number of slots in the busy

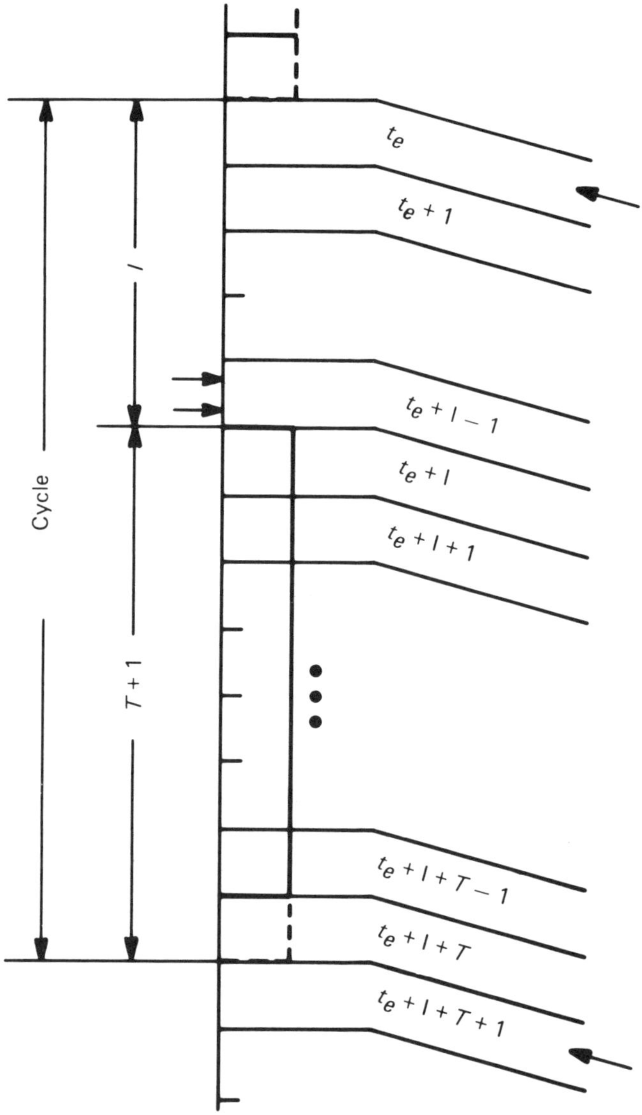

Figure 5–1. The Imbedded Markov Chain in Slotted Nonpersistent CSMA

(transmission) period, and 1 added in to account for the propagation delay necessary for the nodes to sense the channel. Let N^t denote the state of this system (the backlog in terms of number of packets to transmit) at time t, and let t_e denote the first slot in the idle period. N^{t_e} is a regenerative process embedded at the times t_e, in that the success of a transmission in each cycle depends only on the value of N^{t_e}. As a result, analysis of channel use can be made in a manner similar to the one described in the preceding section. First, the one-step transition matrices are derived, using probabilistic arguments over the different slots shown in figure 5–1. From them, the transition matrix P of the imbedded Markov chain N^{t_e} is derived as before, and stationary distributions are obtained using equation 5.23. Computation of the channel utilization is made by finding the probability of a successful transmission in a cycle and remembering that the average packet delay is the average backlog time. The detailed description of the derivation can be found in Tobagi et al. [6] and Tobagi and Kleinrock [33]. The method of imbedded Markov chains has also been used to derive expected message-delay equations for other slotted protocols [29].

Markovian Decision Processes. If we let $K \to \infty$ in equation 5.23, that is, use the equations obtained for P_{ij} by letting $K \to \infty$ in equation 5.22, we have a model that, unfortunately, does not admit a solution for the Π_i [34]. Consequently, we can no longer talk above a stationary system or a stable channel. The stability behavior of ALOHA has been analyzed [31,32], and it has been shown that the channel operates in a satisfactory manner, that is, with acceptable performance measures for only a finite period of time, and that eventually it may drift to a stable but unsatisfactory state from which it can recover only by outside intervention. An unsatisfactory state can seemingly be avoided by dynamically altering the packet-arrival rate or retransmission policy as the backlog of messages awaiting transmission changes [32]. The way in which the policy reacts to the change in message backlog constitutes a *control procedure*. To assess the impact and viability of a control procedure requires a model in which parameters and operating rules change with backlog, rather than remaining fixed as we have assumed so far.

For demonstration, let us concentrate on systems with underlying Markovian properties, so that we can use Markovian decision theory as a basis for dynamic analysis (modeling). Simply put, a Markovian decision process can be viewed as a stochastic process whose parameters evolve over time. Markovian decision theory requires, first, that we specify a sequence of decisions that determine which actions should be taken when the system is in a given state. Second, to compare decision processes, a cost structure has to be established, by which best decisions can be determined, for example, the one that minimizes a certain system performance measure, such as delay. Assume a Markovian decision model in which we have a finite number of possible states $[0,1,\ldots,M]$ and a policy R, which specifies the action to be taken when a given state is observed at a given time. If the policy is independent of time (that is, dependent only on state), it is called stationary, and, fortunately, stationary processes are often sufficient. With stationary processes, we can characterize the rule R by the parameter values (or actions) called for by a given state, such that we have $d_0(R)$, $d_1(R),\ldots,$ $d_M(R)$, with $d_i(R)$ giving the decision (action) taken when the system state is

i. With this view, a different transition matrix, P_{ij}, is used for each policy. In other words, given initial state, X_0 and decision rules $d_i(R)$, a transition from state i to state j is made according to the transition matrix P_{ij} associated with policy R and state i. The sequences of observed states and decisions taken together reflect a Markovian decision process.

To evaluate the goodness of different policies R, a cost C_{ik} is associated with each decision rule $d_i(R)$, and an expected cost measure is defined by:

$$E(c) = \sum_{i=0}^{M} C_{ik} \Pi_i$$

where k reflects $d_i(R)$ for each i and Π_i is the steady-state probability of being in state i under policy R. Namely, when the system is in state i, an expected cost C_{ik} occurs if the taken decision was $d_i(R) = k$. Consequently the expected cost $E(c)$ can be used to quantitatively characterize different policies.

Policies are compared by comparing expected costs. Under the model, the best policy is the one that minimizes the expected cost. To evaluate the optimal policy, linear programming techniques are often used [14,105].

Example 5.11

The study of the stability and control of the slotted ALOHA protocol is a classic example of the use of a Markovian decision model in the analysis of multiple-access schemes [31,32,33]. In previous models of slotted ALOHA protocols, we assumed that an equilibrium situation actually exists in the system. Using this assumption, we are able to derive mean values for delay, throughput, and channel load. Under closer inspection of the dynamic behavior of this protocol, no evidence can be found, however, to guarantee that a stable situation will exist or will even be attainable most of the time. If, for example, we observe the system under heavy load conditions, then clearly packet collisions will cause new ready nodes to enter the backlogged state. If the value of, say, p, which corresponds to times waited between retransmissions (see example 5.9 for definitions), is not subsequently adjusted, more and more backlogged nodes will attempt retransmission. Eventually, the sytem will be totally backlogged and new packets will be blocked from entering the system.

Remedy to this situation can be had by increasingly spacing the retransmissions of backlogged nodes as the backlog increases. With such a solution, two questions arise: what adjustment should be made to retransmission delays and in what way the benefit of increased throughput will be offset by increased delay.

To answer these questions, we observe the relation between the system

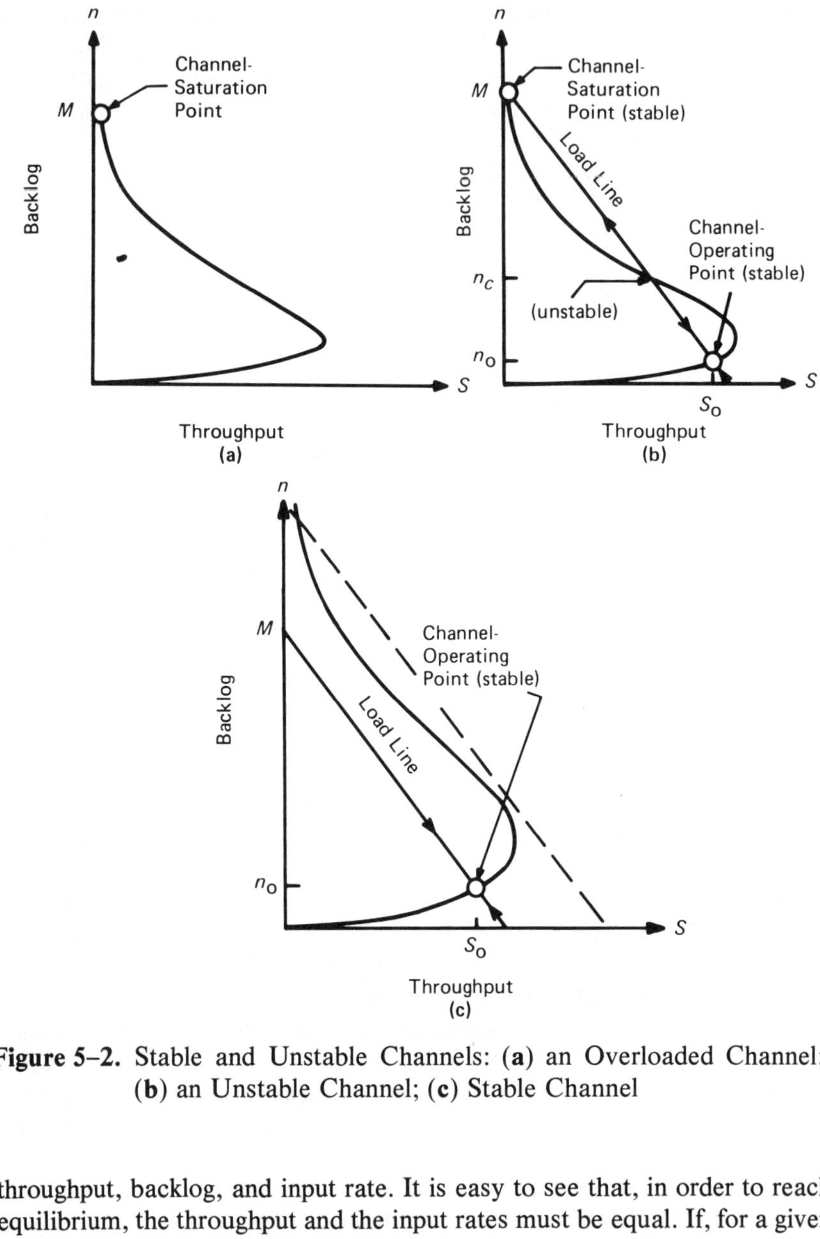

Figure 5–2. Stable and Unstable Channels: (**a**) an Overloaded Channel; (**b**) an Unstable Channel; (**c**) Stable Channel

throughput, backlog, and input rate. It is easy to see that, in order to reach equilibrium, the throughput and the input rates must be equal. If, for a given backlog value, the throughput exceeds the input rate, the backlog will be reduced. In the reverse circumstance, that of higher input than throughput rate, a backlog will unavoidably grow. Let us examine system states with respect to throughput, input rate, and backlog relationships. Figure 5–2a shows system throughput as a function of the system backlog. The mean throughput as a function of the mean backlog can be calculated [32] once the system-state probabilities are known, as shown in example 5.9. The calculation of the input rate as a function of the mean backlog with a finite number of nodes, M, is also straightforward and is given as a linear function of the number of nodes, the backlog, and the rate of new packet generation as follows:

$$\text{input rate} = (M - k)\sigma \tag{5.26}$$

To investigate the stability of the slotted ALOHA, we observe figure 5–26b, where it can be seen that throughput and input rates are equal at three different points. At the smallest backlog input-rate intersection point n_0, the system will be stable. In other words, despite limited fluctuations in input rate, the system will inherently tend toward returning to the same equilibrium point.

To verify this behavior, let us assume that, because of increased input rate, the system is pushed to a higher backlog situation. Since we are now in the situation of having the throughput rate higher than the input rate, the backlog will be quickly reduced and the system will move back to the equilibrium point. If, on the contrary, the backlog is suddenly reduced, the throughput will fall rapidly, causing significant increase in backlog and returning the system to the previous state of equilibrium. The situation is similar at the highest backlog equilibrium point. At the middle equilibrium point n_c, the input-throughput forces play a reverse role. If, for instance, the backlog is increased at this middle point, the input rate will become higher than the throughput, thus making the congested situation even worse. Eventually, the backlog will be sufficiently large to reach the stable but undesirable equilibrium point characterized by large backlog and low throughput.

The input and throughput curves do not necessarily intersect at more than one equilibrium point. A system is defined to be stable when it possesses only one equilibrium point [32]. Such a situation is depicted in figure 5–2c. In this case, the number of nodes is smaller than in the case given in figure 5–2b. With the assumption of constant and equal arrival rates in both cases, a smaller number of nodes results in smaller input rates, as seen in figure 5–2c. At the single equilibrium point n_o, the system behavior is identical to that of the low-backlog equilibrium point of figure 5–2b and is consequently stable. If, on the other hand, the number of nodes is increased sufficiently, as compared to figure 5–2b, the input-rate line will move above the peak of the throughput line, given by broken line in figure 5–2c. In this case, the only intersecton of input and throughput curves will occur for very large backlog values. From previous observations, this equilibrium point will be stable but undesirable, since both the input rate and the throughput rate will be almost zero because of a completely overloaded channel.

From previous discussion, it is clear that, to operate the system in a stable state, we have to limit the number of users to guarantee the case shown in figure 5–2c. (The case of a large number of nodes is dismissed immediately, since it overloads the channel). The operation of the system with a small number of users is far from optimal, as it requires a "play-it-safe" number of nodes—an outright waste of the channel resource. (Furthermore, studies have shown that, for an uncontrolled infinite population model, the channel is always unstable when p is kept constant [25,104].) The situation can be remedied, however, if we are willing to control the system dynamically. The simplest way to do this is to adjust the retransmission probability of the backlogged nodes according to the system backlog. For large-backlog situations, smaller p values will decrease the number of contending nodes, thus allowing backlog reduction. For small backlogs, p can be increased in order to reduce delay and increase throughput.

To analyze such control procedures requires that we find the correct value of p for various values of backlog. In other words, we must search for the optimal decision rule, which either will maximize throughput (under a given constraint on average delay) or will minimize average delay (given a constraint on throughput). It was shown [25] that a stationary control policy that simultaneously maximizes throughput and minimizes delay over the class of all policies always exists. This class of control policies permits each backlogged packet to be retransmitted independently with probabilities $p = p_0$ or p_1, with $p_0 > p_1$. The control policy uses p_0 or p_1 for all nodes, based on an estimate of network backlog. To find the best policy, interactive methods can be used [105] to produce stationary policies [25]. That is, there exists a backlog value n so that:

$$p = \begin{cases} p_0, & N^t < n \\ p_1, & N^t \geq n \end{cases} \tag{5.27}$$

This policy maximizes throughput and minimizes delay. Of course, for the policy to be effective, each node must know the channel state (the backlog). Although an exact and instantaneous knowledge cannot be expected, it has been shown that estimates serve well in achieving near-optimum performance. Various techniques for estimating the load from channel feedback are discussed in Lam [25] and Tanenbaum [102].

Clearly, the intersection points in figure 5–2b show such stable conditions. In Kleinrock and Lam [32], the channel is defined as stable if the two lines intersect at exactly one place, as in figure 5–2c. Each channel load line has at least one equilibrium point; however, two types of stable situations can be identified. If the equilibrium point is single, it is referred to as globally stable otherwise, it is only locally stable. In other words, in a globally stable equilibrium point, the system state (backlog) may occasionally fluctuate but will eventually drift back to its equilibrium position. With local stability, an excursion from this point will eventually lead to a new backlog equilibrium point—a globally stable one. In Kleinrock and Lam [32], the authors define a stability measure by looking at the average time it takes the system to drift from a safe channel state to an unsafe state of unstable channel. Subsequently, with a basically unstable channel, one can have a stable-channel situation, by operating it at very low loads, or an unstable channel, which gives better channel utilization, but at the price of unreliability. The solution to this problem lies in dynamically controlling the channel by keeping it in desirable states most of the time. This can be accomplished, for example, by controlling the retransmission delays or, in other words, the input rate. An excellent description of the developmentof the use of the Markovian decision model to achieve this objective can be found in Kleinrock and Lam [32] and Tanenbaum [102].

Simulation Models

The analysis discussed in the previous sections employed mathematical tools to yield tractable models. As demonstrated, in many instances a reasonable level of abstraction leads to models providing simple and easily employed solutions. Many times, however, mathematical models are too restrictive and rely on assumptions that are necessary for tractability but do not contribute to model validity. Simulation allows models that are more faithful to the system being modeled, but at a price. The price is increased difficulty, first, in determining the (internal) correctness of the model and, second, in determining the degree to which the model reflects the modeled system [35,58]. It remains, however, that simulation is often the only tool offering sufficient flexibility to adequately represent a given system. In many cases, moreover, the results obtained from simulation and those obtained from analytical models complement each other [59,60], each contributing information leading to an understanding of the workings of the system that is more complete than would be possible by either approach alone. Additionally, analytic-model results can be used to validate (that is, help determine the correctness of) complex simulation models.

The development, verification, and use (for experimentation) of simulation models is now relatively well understood and documented [35,37, 48–50].

Development of a simulation model encompasses several stages, including identification of goals, system analysis, system synthesis, model verification, model validation, and experimentation [11,35,36,37], as well as data collection and reduction [44–47].

A statement of goals and measures of interest (in the network context), was given earlier in this chapter. The second stage, system analysis is concerned with the dynamic behavior of the network system being modeled, including identification of components and interaction rules. Via system synthesis, these components are used to build a model, that is, a program executable on a computer. This stage involves choice of language (for example, general-purpose or special-purpose language) and choice of implementation of the model (for example, in a centralized or distributed manner). The model obtained is next verified against the conceptual model against which it was synthesized. Thus, the verification stage is concerned with assessing the internal correctness of the model and its faithfulness to its specification (a statement of its behavior.)

The final stage, validation, is concerned with determining, if possible, if the model-predicted measures are representative of or agree with those obtained from the real-world system. This is generally accomplished by statistical tests on model-and system-produced data.

Although these steps are essentially those of the scientific method, and hence germane to analytic models as well, adherence to the steps is more critical to the correct development of simulation models. Statistical tests, simulation languages, and software-development tools facilitate these tasks, and these techniques are well documented in simulation texts. What is not well known, however, is the availability of formal techniques for proving (in a sense) the correctness of model programs—the subject discussed next. This is followed by the description of two additional aids to the development of network simulators, concerned with event scheduling and input-traffic generation in the model.

Simplification and Formal Validation of Computer-Network Models. Typically, a model is validated by pilot runs and statistical tests. It is also possible, however, to formally compare model input-output behavior with actual system behavior, especially if the model faithfully mimics the details of the real network. Because a network has so many components and interactions, such comparisons are seldom feasible. What we need is a way to formally compare simple models and actual systems. This would allow correctness proofs for simulation models comparable to those for other computer programs. A methodology of the required kind exists [38], and, as an example, we apply it to a simple model of a network that employs the ALOHA transmission protocol [9].

Our approach is based on the concepts of base model, experimental frame, and lumped model. A *base model* is a model that can account for all the input-output behavior of the actual system. It must be a faithful, detailed, and consequently complex representation of the system. An *experimental frame* is a limited set of conditions under which the actual system is observed. Thus, the experimental frame defines the subset of the input-output behavior that is of interest. The *lumped model* is a simplification of the base model (by grouping or lumping components, and so on) that accounts for the input-output behavior in the given experimental frame but not necessarily outside it. Validation involves determining that the base model and the lumped model are equivalent for the given experimental frame. In the network context, the base model must account for all nodes, queues, protocols, and so forth, in the actual network.

To establish the equivalence of the base and lumped models, we need a formal machinery. The methodology of Zeigler [38] proceeds by first generating a qualitative description of the models in terms of system components, descriptive variables (describing the components), and rules for component interactions. From the qualitative description, we obtain a formal system specification. The formal description is given in terms of:

$\alpha_1, \alpha_2, \ldots, \alpha_n$—the input variables,

$\beta_1, \beta_2, \ldots, \beta_m$—the state variables, and

$\delta_1, \delta_2, \ldots \delta_n$—the output variables,

with the cross product of the ranges of these variables giving the set of inputs, states, and outputs of the system. To account for the discrete time points at which events occur, we introduce the notion of an event time. The next event time is specified by examining a nonordered subset of state variables, T_1, $T_2, \ldots, T_\kappa$ (event times), such that, at time t_i, the next event time is given by $t_{i+1} = t_i + \min\{T_1, T_2, \ldots, T_\kappa\}$. The function $t = \min\{T_1, T_2, \ldots, T_\kappa\}$ is called the time-advance function. The formalism is completed by specifying, first,

$$\delta_\phi : \text{STATES} \rightarrow \text{STATES}$$

which describes the internal state transition that occurs in going from time t_i to time t_{i+1}, and second,

$$\delta_{\text{ex}} : Q \times \text{INPUTS} \rightarrow \text{STATES}$$

which characterizes the transitions brought about by external events, with Q being the set of pairs (s,e) where s denotes system state and e is a real number in the range $[0,t(s)]$, which implicitly specifies the time of the next external event (and next event), and, finally, specifying

$$\lambda : Q \rightarrow \text{OUTPUTS}$$

which is the output function. Taken together, the set

$$\langle \text{INPUTS, STATES, OUTPUTS}, \delta_{\phi}, \delta_{ex}, \lambda, t \rangle$$

constitutes the system specification for the model (lumped or base).

To apply the methodology, we must first specify the base model and the experimental frame from which we can derive the lumped-model specification. We will not present here the specification of the base model. Instead, we will first informally describe how we derive the sample lumped model from the base model, then obtain the specification of lumped model, and finally informally establish lumped-model and base-model equivalence.

To proceed, we must specify an experimental frame. For simplicity, we consider the experimental frame given by the single variable, channel utilization (under the assumption of an ALOHA protocol). We then derive the lumped model by (1) omitting the variables, components, and interactions that account for user-host-node relationships and accounting for the omissions by replacing deterministic variables having to do with message length, and the like, by variates drawn from appropriate distributions; and (2) eliminating queues and certain variables that are not required for the experimental frame of interest. (For example, the base model must identify both the source and destination nodes for each message, whereas, in the lumped model, only source identity is necessary for the experimental frame composed solely of utilization.)

Informal Description of the Lumped Model.

Components. System components include the packet source, packet queue, retransmission queue, and channel, with their obvious interpretations.

Descriptive Variables. For the sources, we have the variables NEW. PACKET, which can assume values i in the range $i \in \{1,2,\ldots, K\}$ for a network with K nodes. We can write this specification compactly as

$$\text{NEW. PACKET}: i \in \{1,2,\ldots, K\}$$

(the notation employed was selected to be consistent with that used in Zeigler [38]).

For the packet queue, we have

$$\text{PACKET QUEUE}: y_i \in z^+, \qquad (z^+ = \{0,1,2,\ldots\})$$

where y_i is the length of the queue at node i. For the retransmission queue, we have

$$\text{RETR. QUEUE}: (z_i, T_i) \in z^+ \times R^+, \qquad (R^+ = \text{positive real number})$$

with z_i being the length of the retransmission queue at node i and T_i the scheduled retransmission-time delay, as drawn from a random-variate generator with seed $r_i \in [0,1]$.

For the channel, we have

TRANS. TIME. LEFT: $\sigma_i \in$ [0, packet-transmission time]

with packet transmission time, denoted by PTT, a system parameter.

Component Interactions. Component interactions are specified by noting that a newly arrived packet joins PACKET QUEUE according to i, with i the value asigned to NEW PACKET causing y_i to be incremented. If $y_i = 1$, the node transmits by increasing σ_i to the value given by the packet-transmission time. If $y_i > 1$, a transmission is scheduled at the time when σ_i becomes zero. The value of σ_i decreases from PTT until becoming zero at the end of the packet's transmission. If σ_i is reset while another σ_j, $j \neq i$, is nonzero, a retransmission time is drawn and z_i and T_i are adjusted.

Formal Description of the Lumped Model. The formal description constitutes the specification of the lumped model and contains the input variable NEW. PACKET such that

$$\text{INPUTS} = \{\Phi, 1, 2, \ldots, K\}$$

Furthermore, using the state variables from the informal description, we obtain:

$s \in$ STATES =

$$\left\{\begin{array}{llll} \text{RETR.TIME.SEED,} & \text{PACKET.QUEUE}_1 & \text{RETR.QUEUE}_1, & \text{TRANS.TIME.LEFT}_1 \\ & \text{PACKET QUEUE}_2, & \text{RETR.QUEUE}_2, & \text{TRANS.TIME.LEFT}_2 \\ & \vdots & \vdots & \vdots \\ & \text{PACKET.QUEUE}_K, & \text{RETR.QUEUE}_K, & \text{TRANS.TIME.LEFT}_K \end{array}\right\}$$

$$= \left\{\begin{array}{l} r_1, y_1, (z_1, T_1), \sigma_1 \\ \quad y_2, (z_2, T_2), \sigma_2 \\ \quad \vdots \\ \quad y_K, (z_K, T_K), \sigma_K \end{array}\right\}.$$

The time-advance function becomes:

$$t(s) = \min\{\sigma_1, \ldots, \sigma_k, T_1, \ldots, T_k\},$$

with σ_i, T_i as defined. For simultaneous events, we choose the tie-breaking rule function: If $\sigma_j = T_l$, then select σ_j. The next event time is therefore given by:

$$t_{i+1} = t_i + \min(\sigma_i, T_i).$$

If $T_l = \min T_i$, and $\sigma_{l'} = \min \sigma_i$, then δ_ϕ is given as follows:

If $T_l < \sigma_l$, (retransmission is the next event) *and if* $y_l = 0$

$$\textit{then } \delta_\phi(s) = \begin{pmatrix} \Gamma(r_1), y_1 & , (z_1, T_1 - T_l), \sigma_1 - T_l \\ & \vdots \qquad \vdots \\ y_l & , (z_l - 1, 0), \text{PTT} \\ & \vdots \qquad \vdots \\ y_K & , (Z_K, T_K - T_l), \sigma_K - T_l \end{pmatrix}$$

else $y_l > 0$ resulting in

$$\delta_\phi(s) = \begin{pmatrix} r_1, y_1 & , (z_1, T_1 - T_l), \sigma_1 - T_1 \\ y_l & , (z_l\, \Gamma(r_1)), \sigma_l - T_l \\ & \vdots \quad \vdots \quad \vdots \\ y_K & , (z_K, T_K - T_l), \sigma_K - T_l \end{pmatrix}$$

If $T_l > \sigma_{l'}$ (end of ongoing transmission is the next event) *and if* $y_l - 1 > 0$

$$\textit{then } \delta_\phi(s) = \begin{pmatrix} r_1, y_1, & (z_1, T_1 - \sigma_{l'}), \sigma_1 - \sigma_b \\ \vdots & \vdots \qquad \vdots \\ y_l - 1, & \vdots \qquad \text{PTT} \\ & \vdots \qquad \vdots \\ y_K, & (z_K, T_K - \sigma_{l'}), \sigma_K - \sigma_l, \end{pmatrix}$$

else $y_l - 1 = 0 \wedge z_l > 0$

$$\text{resulting in } \delta_\phi(s) = \begin{pmatrix} r_1, y_1, (z_1, T_1 - \sigma_{l'}), \sigma_1 - \sigma_l, \\ \vdots \quad\quad \vdots \quad\quad \vdots \\ 0, \ (z_l - 1, T_l - \sigma_{l'}), \text{PTT} \\ \vdots \quad\quad \vdots \quad\quad \vdots \\ y_K, (z_K, T_K - \sigma_{l'}), \sigma_K - \sigma_{l'} \end{pmatrix}$$

where $\Gamma(r_1)$ is drawing from a stream with seed r_1, and initially $\sigma_i = T_i = 0$. In the absence of external events, the next event time, t_{i+1}, is given by

$$t_{i+1} = t_i + \min(\sigma_l, T_l)$$

For external event times t at which NEW PACKET $\leftarrow m$, $1 \leq m \leq K$, the state at time $t \equiv t_{i+1} = t_i + e$ is given by:

$$\delta_{\text{ex}}(s,e,m) = \begin{pmatrix} r_1, \ y_1, \quad (z_1 \, T_1 - e), \sigma_1 - e \\ \vdots \quad\quad \vdots \quad\quad \vdots \\ y_m + 1, \quad \cdot \quad \text{PTT} \\ \vdots \quad\quad \vdots \\ y_K, \quad (z_k, T_k - e), \sigma_k - e \end{pmatrix}$$

with $0 \leq e \leq t(s)$.

Finally, using the experimental frame characterized by channel utilization, the output function becomes:

$$\lambda(s) = \begin{cases} \text{YES}, & \text{if } \exists\, m \in \sigma_m \neq 0 \wedge \sum_{\substack{i=0 \\ i \neq m}}^{K} \sigma_i = 0 \\ \text{NO}, & \text{if otherwise} \end{cases}$$

since, if $\sigma_i \neq 0$ for multiple values of i, collisions result. From $\lambda(s)$ we can easily obtain utilization.

Table 5–1
Equivalence of Grouped States of the Base Model and States of the Lumped Model

Grouped Base-Model States	*Lumped-Model States*
1. User → host → node → packet queue	Packet queue
2. Control unit → transmission buffer → channel	Channel
3. Receiver → buffer → retransmission queue	Retransmission queue
4. External sources	Packet source

Validation of the Lumped Model. Recall that our purpose is to validate the lumped model for an experimental frame by using the specifications of the base and lumped models. This validation is done by showing that the lumped model has the same input-output behavior as the base model for the given experimental frame.

We can demonstrate this equivalence by proving the existence of a mapping h: base-model states onto lumped-model states, which preserves the time-advance, transition, and output functions. This general approach requires a formal specification of the base model, which we have not supplied. We proceed informally, therefore, by suggesting that h has the form shown in table 5–1, in which grouped states of the base model correspond to states of the lumped model (assuming that both models are initialized identically.) As a result, the number of state variables has been reduced to four. The mapping h must ensure that each component interaction in the base model is a member of only one group in the lumped model, which we here assume to be true, but which can be demonstrated.

Preservation of the Time-Advance Function. For both base and lumped models, the next event time for the channel event is determined either by the end of a transmission or by an imminent retransmission time. Denoting the rows of the grouped base states by $g_1, \ldots g_4$ (from table 5–1) and the rows of the lumped states by $s_1, \ldots, s_4$, then $t(s) = \min(\sigma_i, T_i)$ for the lumped model, and $t'(g) = \min(\sigma_i, T_i)$ for the base model. Since we have assumed identical initial conditions for the two models, we have:

$$\begin{array}{lcl} g = (g_1, \ldots, g_4) & \xrightarrow{t'(g)} & \\ \downarrow h & & \min(\sigma_i, T_i) \\ s = (s_1, \ldots, s_4) & \xrightarrow[t(s)]{} & \end{array}$$

which guarantees the preservation of the time-advance function.

Preservation of the Transition Function. To formally prove that the transition function is perserved, we must show that, given initial correspondence between the states of the two models, any transition brings both models into corresponding states. Specifically, we must show that if $h(g) = s$ then $h(\delta_\phi(g)) = \delta_\phi\,(s)$.

Additionally, we must show that s_i represents g_i following all state transitions. Although we lack a specification for the base model, we can still show preservation by observation. We begin by recalling that the lumped-model states are, in fact, representatives of groups of base-model states. We assume all transitions within a group of base-model states to be zero-time transitions that do not affect σ_i, T_i. Thus, only transitions among states from different groups must be observed, which is done by observing the state changes in the corresponding states of the lumped model.

Because of the construction of the lumped model, the following holds: all transitions in the base model can be between two states either of the same group, g_i, or of two different groups g_i, g_j. In the first case, all transitions are zero-time transitions, and, since both states belong to the same group g_i, in the lumped model they are represented by the same state s_i. Zero-time transitions in the lumped model that leave the model in the same state s_i will thus still correspond to the same group g_i, as required. In the second case, where two states belong to groups g_i, g_j, we note that transitions between two different groups can only occur (when leaving the group through a series of zero-time transitions) through the right-most components of each group, that is, through packet queue, channel, retransmission queue, and packet source, respectively. But these components are also the ones that represent the four distinct states in the lumped model, and transitions between them are thus governed by exactly the same set of interactions rules. In summary, from observing the behavior of this specific example, one notes that in both models the sets of rules that affect observed behavior are the same.

Preservation of the Ouput Function. In this case, preservation dictates that corresponding states (in the two models) must produce the same output. The lumped model produces a YES value whenever a single node has a nonzero value of σ_m. In the base model, a receiving controller records reception, that is, a YES period if and only if the channel is busy with one transmission. It is easily seen that the two Yes periods correspond, so λ(lumped model) = λ(base model).

Commentary on Approach to Validation. Our purpose has been to demonstrate a formal approach to the validation of a network-simulation model. Our example was purposely chosen to be simple; generally, the complexity of the lumped model depends on the experimental frame and actual system. An experimental frame dealing only with channel utilization required only four state variables. Obviously, a more complex experimental frame would require a lumped model closer to the base model in complexity.

We find this approach helpful in structuring model programs (configurations, protocols, and so forth), even when we apply it only with the rigor used in the example. Specifically, its use promotes the same forethought and structuring for simulation programs that verification and specification techniques do for programming generally. Certainly, the structure of the base model cannot always be completely specified. However, by requiring a formal identification of components and component interactions in developing the lumped model, and by formally or informally proving the equivalence of the base and lumped models, the art of simulation modeling is brought a step closer to a rigorous discipline.

The base model gives a complete account of the real-world behavior, that is, for input-output and under all observed circumstances. By accounting for all known components and interactions, it is valid as a complete, exhaustive description of the real world, though at the expense of a level of complexity that cannot be realistically turned into a simulation model. Usually one validates a simulation model by comparing its outputs to those of experimental data. With this approach, however, one can only obtain replicative validity, that is, the model matches data already acquired from the real system (if such data exist). To be able to predict the behavior of a conceived system, or to observe the workings of a system, one requires a simulation model whose structure, in the sense of its components and rules of transition, does validly represent the system under investigation. Second, even if one is content with the level of validity obtained by matching inputs and outputs (that is, one sees the model as a black box), this kind of validation does not contribute to building an efficient simulator. The approach of formal validation described here is helpful in both these endeavors. It tells the modeler whether his simulator is valid in the strongest structural sense, and it also guides the construction of the simplest possible valid model. In other words, by defining the subset of output data that is of interest—the experimental frame—the user may eliminate model redundancy and thus obtain an efficient model. We must point out, though, that it is still the modeler who has to make the choice of how to simplify the model and has to verify that the simplification process conforms to rules that guarantee validity.

We believe we have avoided errors and have structured more highly lumped models in reasonable times as a result of only informal use of the methodology, that is, a use wherein a formal lumped model is not produced and consequently the equivalence proof is also informal. Doing so serves as a guide to the abstraction process (always difficult) and is consistent with the view of simulation we believe most natural [35].

Event Scheduling. A modular model structure, as allowed by use of scheduling and grouping functions (see table 5–2) makes the program easy

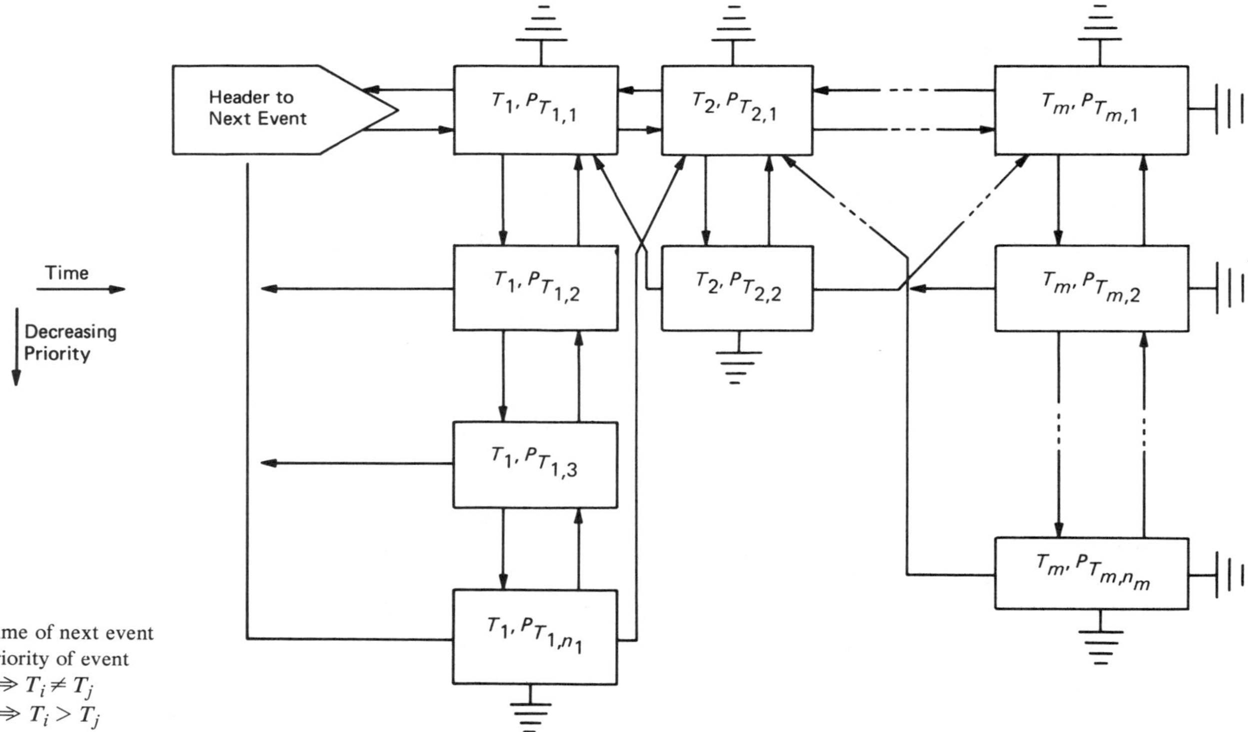

T_i: Time of next event
P_i: Priority of event
$i \neq j \Rightarrow T_i \neq T_j$
$i > j \Rightarrow T_i > T_j$
$K < l \Rightarrow P_{T_{i,k}} \geq P_{T_{i,l}}$
If $P_{T_{i,k}} = P_{T_{i,l}}$, secondary keys are used.

Figure 5–3. Data Structure Used in Event Scheduling

to change. For example, a single module can handle addressing at the host-node interaction level, so addressing functions can be identified and altered (replaced) witout affecting the remaining parts of the program. Although it produces flexibility, the modular structure may be inefficient at execution time. Specifically, because of the structure, activities at time t_i must schedule multiple other actions for time t_i. Moreover, to maintain the correctness of the model, the multiple events scheduled at a given time must occur in a specified order. The use of conventional data structures for event scheduling, such as the linear list, causes considerable overhead in the insertion or deletion of event notices when multiple events are scheduled for a given time. Furthermore, these structures do not handle properly the ordering of the execution of these simultaneous events. The nature of the model program suggests use of the two-dimensional data structure in figure 5–3, in which each activity-scheduling notice contains not only a primary key giving time of occurrence, T_i, but also a secondary key $P_{T_{i,j}}$, which determines its placement among the events scheduled at T_i. Furthermore, the priority value of a scheduled event cannot be static (that is, cannot be assigned a priori to the event type), but rather must be assigned when the event is scheduled. For example, the order of handling the simultaneous events "set node busy status" and "set channel busy status" differs depending on whether the system state is node transmission or node reception.

The two-dimensional structure in figure 5–3 aids the assignment of event priorities as well as the insertion and deletion of event notices by reducing the number of scans (of notices) from the number required by conventional data structures. The structure thus allows use of a modular model program structure without the penalty in execution time that conventional data structures would involve.

Input-Traffic Generators. A large number of network simulations are conducted assuming that arriving messages, at node i, obey a Poisson process with parameter λ_i. Typically, a simulation program satisfies this assumption by scheduling an "arrival" for each of the K nodes in the network. For large K, this adds significantly to the number of event notices and, hence, slows the insertion and deletion operations. A cleaner, more efficient approach is given by forming

$$\lambda = \sum_{i=1}^{K} \lambda_i$$

and scheduling a single stream of events, with interevent times drawn from the exponential distribution with parameter λ. Each occurrence of the event signals arrival, and the cumulative distribution of the λ_i can be used to determine the node at which *the* message has arrived. Specifically, a random number u is drawn, and if

$$(1/\lambda) \sum_{i=1}^{j-1} \lambda_i < u \leq (1/\lambda) \sum_{i=1}^{j} \lambda_i$$

the message is declared to have arrived at node j. The procedure works because of the ability to split a Poisson stream into multiple streams via a multibranch Bernoulli trial, and it serves to insure that one rather than $K \gg 1$ notice is in the event queue to signal message arrivals.

As a final note we point out that many access protocols can be modelled using scheduling functions, grouping functions, and connectivity matrices defined in chapter 3. A summary of usage and settings for these notions is given in table 5–2.

Distributed Simulation. Recently, the concept of distributed computing has been applied to simulation [52–56]. In conventional discrete-event simulation, a machine serially executes program instructions causing events. To mimic the order of events and their times of occurrence, an event set is

Table 5–2
Protocols Currently Captured by g (.), S(.), and DCM Configurations.

Protocol Name	*S(i,j)=*	*g(i)=*	*LOS/DCM*
ALOHA [23]	0	1	$d_{ij} = y$ non-LOS $x_{ij} = 1$ LOS
1-persistent CSMA p-persistent CSMA [28]	0	1	$x_{ij} = y$
Nonpersistent CSMA [28]	0	1	$x_{ij} = y$
Prioritized CSMA [39]	i	i	$x_{ij} = 0$
TDMA [40]	i packet transmission time	i	$x_{ij} = 1$
MSAP [16]	$(i - j - K) \bmod K$ $i \neq j$ 0 $i = j$	i	$x_{ij} = 0$
BRAM or Centralized Polling [22]	$(I - j + m) \bmod m$ $i \neq j$ m $i = j$	$1 \leq g(\mathrm{i}) \leq m$ $1 \leq m \leq K$	$x_{ij} = 0$,LOS case $d_{ij} = y$,non-LOS case
SUPBRAM [41–43]		$1 \leq g(i) \leq m$, arbitrary d_{ij} $1 \leq m \leq K$	

Note: Consult chapter 3 for definitions of S, g, DCM, and x_{ij}.
K = number of nodes in network; Y = topology-dependent value; LOS = within line of sight and range.

maintained by the control part of the simulation program. By advancing the simulated clock and associating its value with simulated event times, the changes in the system are executed at their proper simulated times. The organization of the program that executes these events differs according to the simulation-language world view used. Three views predominate: the event, the process interaction, and the activity-oriented views [35–37]. With all these approaches, however, state changes are executed (occur) sequentially, though possibly in an interleaved manner. Distributed processing offers the possibility of reducing execution times by using the natural parallelism inherent in computer networks. In fact, although distributed simulation requires coordination that is not necessary with centralized simulations, early results suggest that improvement in execution time can be obtained [52,53].

Hybrid Simulation. Hybrid simulation attempts to combine analytic and simulation techniques to realize a model. The general technique first requires identification of all system-state-change events (a necessary step for either simulation or analytic techniques). Next, events are categorized by frequency of occurrence. For example, a model of a computer system that employs a quantum-driven round-robin processor-scheduling mechanism has task arrivals to the processor queue that are low-frequency events as compared to the cyclic pattern of events of the assignments of the processor to tasks for a quantum and the event of their likely return to the processor queue following expiration of the quantum.

The hybrid approach [57,61] attempts to account for high-frequency events via analytic machinery, in a manner whereby the analytic results can be incorporated into a simulation model that captures the low-frequency events. The resulting hybrid model is more efficient than a simulation model that accounts for all events, as the cost of using a simulation model increases with the frequency of the most frequent events and is more tractable than an approach based solely on analysis. The approach has been demonstrated for models of stand-alone computer systems [57,61]. The resulting models may be approximate in that the analytic portions yield expected state-dependent measures rather than the distribution of state-dependent measures. Nonetheless, as shown in Schwetman [61], the results can be very good and at a significant reduction in simulation cost. In fact, the validity of the approach improves as the degree of interaction between the high-frequency and low-frequency events decomposes into nearly separate and independent phenomena, an attribute of so-called decomposable systems [62,63].

Testbed Approach

The testbed system is becoming a popular tool for network experimentation. A testbed system is a physical realization of a network, with hardware and software features to facilitate the design and realization of experiments and the collection of operational data.

The hardware components may be constructed so that a variety of topologies, access protocols, link level protocols and application modules can be accommodated. Additionally, special executive-software functionality is generally included to facilitate the generation of work requests (for example, a message-generation process based on a random-number generator) and the collection, reduction, analysis, and display of operational data. For data collection, elaborate passive mechanisms can be employed, which not only monitor channel traffic but also CIU registers, buffer contents, and processor states.

Additionally, these systems generally have a central node that controls experiments and data collection. The central node contains software-development tools (languages, editors, libraries of modules, and so on as well as mechanisms for down-loading application (experiment) modules and parameters to testbed nodes and mechanisms for starting and stopping experiments and requesting collected operational data from testbed nodes. Thus, although the central node facilities and monitors experiments, it does not participate in experiments and, hence, does not artificially cause a distributed system (see chapter 4) to become centralized. Chapter 6 contains an example of a low-cost yet flexible testbed system, designed to facilitate network-protocol and distributed-database-system investigations.

A Snapshot of Local-Network Modeling Results

Most local-network modeling efforts have concentrated on the access protocol, with expected-message delay D, throughput S, and capacity C as the measures of performance. Both analysis and simulation have been used to evaluate various access protocols. A few results exist for link-level protocols, and, because link-level protocols are somewhat more complex to capture with analytic machinery than are access protocols, most results were obtained by simulation.

Bus Access-Protocol Performance Evaluation

Various protocols directly applicable to the bus medium have been described in chapter 3. The various analytic models of these protocols are to a large extent based on some subset of the following modeling assumptions:

1. The channel is noiseless; in other words, messages can be damaged only due to collision.
2. There exists an independent acknowledgment channel, and node-acknowledgment processing-time requirements are negligible.

3. There is no capture effect; partial or total overlap of messages results in complete destruction of all messages involved.
4. The network consists of K nodes.
5. Each of the K nodes in the network is able to transmit or receive, but not simultaneously, and turnaround time between the two states is negligible (except for collision-detection protocols).
6. The nodes can detect the busy or idle status of the channel in a negligible time.
7. All nodes can sense the effect of all other nodes on the channel (by presence or absence of a carrier signal).
8. The message-transmission time is constant (that is, messages are packetized) and denoted by T.
9. The message-propagation delay d, normalized by T, is denoted by a.

Under these assumptions, relatively simple closed-form solutions can be obtained for several bus-applicable protocols:

Simple ALOHA

$$S = Ge^{-2G} \tag{5.28}$$

Slotted ALOHA

$$S = Ge^{-G} \tag{5.29}$$

Nonslotted nonpersistent CSMA

$$S = \frac{Ge^{-aG}}{G(1 + 2a) + e^{-aG}}$$

Slotted nonpersistent CSMA

$$S = \frac{aGe^{-aG}}{(1 - e^{-aG}) + a}$$

Nonslotted, 1-persistent CSMA

$$S = \frac{G[1 + G + aG(1 + G + aG/2)]e^{-G(1 \ll 2a)}}{G(1 + 2a) - (1 - e^{-aG}) + (1 + aG)e^{-G(1+a)}}$$

Slotted 1-persistent CSMA

$$S = \frac{G \exp\{-G(1 + a)\} [1 + a - \exp\{-aG\}]}{(1 + a)(1 - \exp\{-aG\}) + a \exp\{-G(1 + a)\}}$$

Results for p-persistent CSMA protocol are more complicated because of their dependence on the retransmission probability parameter p, and Kleinrock and Tobagi [28] should be consulted for an expression for S as a function of G.

MSAP and simple prioritized BRAM ($a \sim 0$)

$$S = 1 + G - \sqrt{1 + G^2}$$

MSAP and simple prioritized BRAM (a not negligible) [17, 22]

$$G = \frac{S(2 - S)}{2(1 - S)} + \frac{aS(K - S)}{K(1 - S)}$$

Figure 5–4 shows S as a function of G for a small propagation-delay value of $a = 0.01$ for a variety of protocols. Figures 5–5 and 5–6 give curves of delay D as a function of S for a similar set of protocols, assuming in all cases that messages are of constant length, that is, packets. Figure 5–7 compares thoughput for parametric BRAM with simple BRAM for a variety of a values. Figure 5–8 shows throughput as a function of delay for CSMA-CD, with γ giving the time (in a-slots) until all colliding nodes sense and terminate their transmissions.

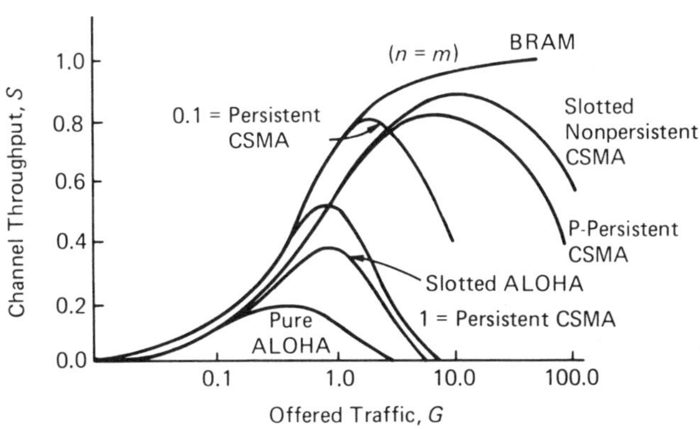

$K = 10$; $a = 0.01$.

Figure 5–4. Protocol Throughput Comparisons

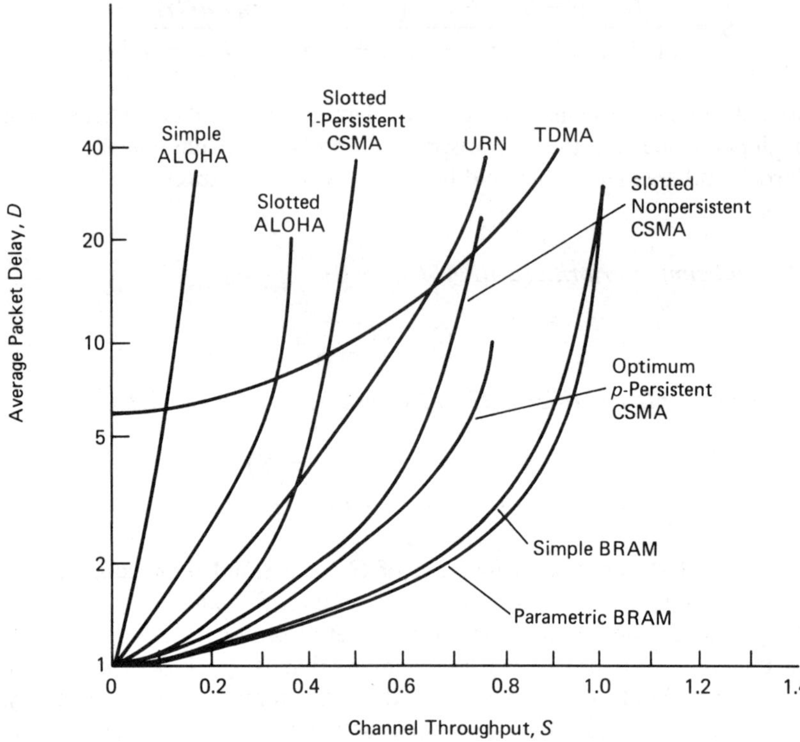

$K = 10; a = 0.01.$

Figure 5–5. Access-Protocol Delay Curves: $a = 0.01$

In some cases, delay expressions can be derived using analytic machinery; in others, they must be obtained by simulation.

For slotted ALOHA we have

$$D = 1 + \frac{E(d + 1)}{2}$$

where d is an integer giving maximum retransmission delay in a-slots, and

$$E = \frac{1 - y_n}{y_t}$$

with

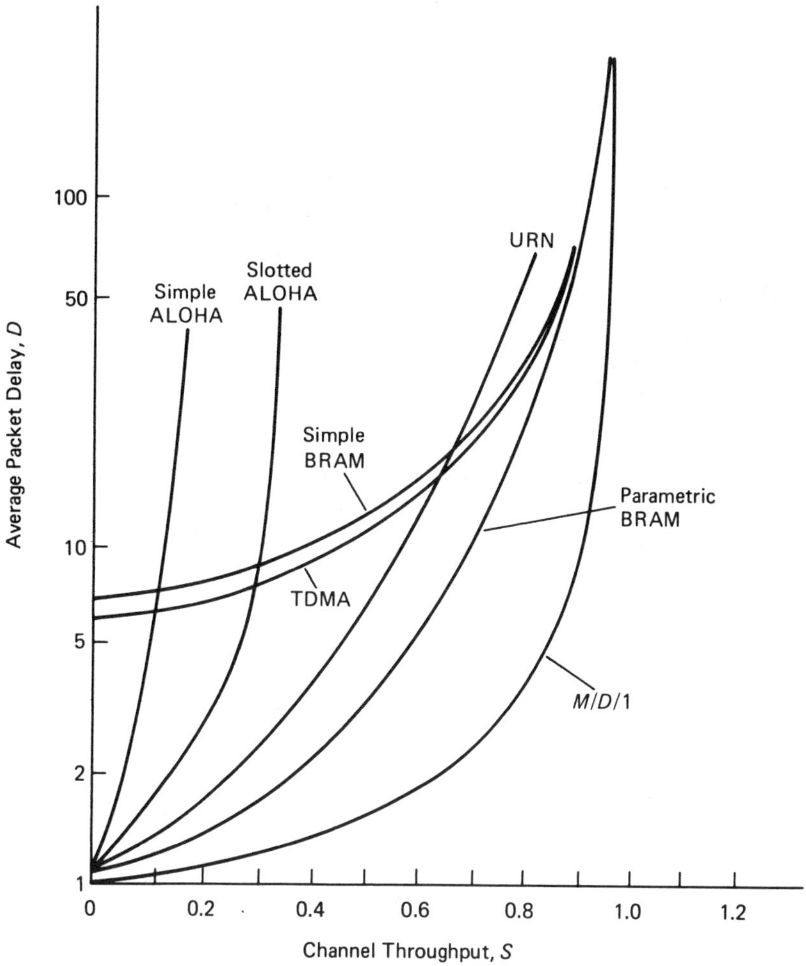

$K = 10; a = 1.$

Figure 5–6. Access-Protocol Delay Curves: $a = 1.0$

$$y_n = \left[e^{-G/d} + \frac{G}{d}e^{-G}\right]^d e^{-S}$$

and

$$y_t = \frac{e^{G/d} - e^{-G}}{1 - e^{-G}}\left[e^{-G/d} + \frac{G}{d}e^{-G}\right]^{d-1} e^{-S}$$

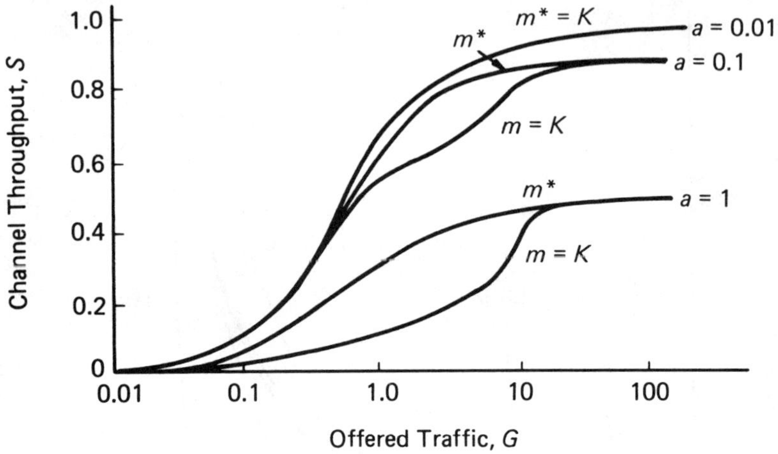

Figure 5–7. Comparison of Throughput in $m = K$ BRAM and Optimal m^*-Value Parametric BRAM for Various a-Values (Simulation Results)

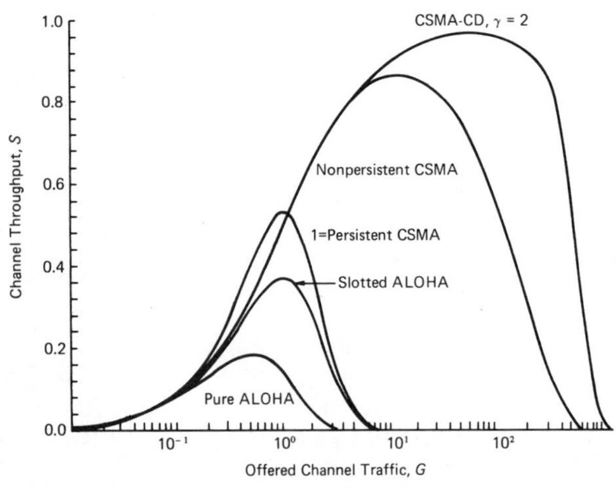

$a = 0.01$

Figure 5–8. Throughput versus Channel Traffic (Infinite-Population Model)

Delay results have also been generated for simple unslotted ALOHA, assuming that the interpacket arrival and retransmission-delay distributions are identical [64] and different [65]. Results for the more complex CSMA are given in Tobagi and Kleinrock [33].

TDMA with slots assigned in a round-robin fashion can be modeled as a collection of K $M/D/1$ queues with a rest period [16], to obtain:

$$D = 1 + K\left[\frac{S}{2(1-S)} + \frac{1}{2}\right]$$

Comparative analysis of both Frequency Division Multiple Access (FDMA) and TDMA protocols via a more general model has also been performed for satellite-like channels [103].

For negligible a values, we have, for MSAP and simple *BRAM, the* $M/D/1$ result

$$D = 1 + \frac{S}{2(1-S)}$$

For nonnegligible propagation-delay values a, we have, for prioritized BRAM,

$$D = 1 + \frac{S}{2(1-S)} + \frac{a}{2}(1 - \frac{S}{K})(1 + \frac{K}{1-S})$$

and

$$G = \frac{S(2-S)}{2(1-S)} + \frac{aS(K-S)}{K(1-S)}$$

Delay values for fair BRAM and nonnegligible a can only be obtained by simulation.

For the PSD protocol with message-based priorities, rather simple approximate analytic results can be obtained from the theory of priority queues. Approximate results [66] are obtained by viewing system behavior as obeying (approximately) $M/G/1$ queuing theory, with the message-class arrival rates given by $\lambda_i = \lambda P_i$ (see table 5–3) and the class i message-transmission times for node j given by

$$S_i^j \; (1 \le j < K),$$

with

$$\begin{aligned} S_1^j &= j \cdot a + 1_1/r + d_0 \text{ (alert)} \\ S_2^j &= (K + j)a + 1_2/r + d_0 \text{ (normal)} \\ S_3^j &= (2K + j)a + 1_3/r + d_0 \text{ (background)}, \end{aligned} \tag{5.30}$$

with 1_i the message length, d_0 the fixed delay, and r the speed of the channel. Assuming a uniform distribution on j, that is, on the node that captures the channel for any given class-i transmission, equation 5.30 yields:

$$E\,[S_1^j] = a(K+1)/2 + E(1_1)/r + d_0$$

$$E\,[S_2^j] = Ka + a(K+1)/2 + E(1_2)/r + d_0$$

$$E\,[S_3^j] = 2Ka + a(K+1)/2 + E(1_3)/r + d_0$$

Additionally, from $M/G/1$ theory, class-i use of the server (channel) is given by

$$\rho_i = \lambda_i E[S_i^j]$$

Finally, from equation 5.30 and the assumption of uniformity on j, $E[(S_i^j)^2]$ can be calculated to produce

$$W = \frac{1}{2}\sum_{i=1}^{3} \lambda\, E[S_i^j]^2$$

from which D_i, the $M/G/1$-predicted expected class-i message delay, can be had by:

$$D_i = W/[(1 - \sum_{j=1}^{i-1} \rho_j)(1 - \sum_{j=1}^{i} \rho_j)] \tag{5.31}$$

The results produced by equation 5.31 will be approximate, for two reasons. First, they bias the utilizations, ρ_i, upward by including the scheduling-period times in the transmission times, S_i^j. Second, $E[S_i^j]$, hence $E[(S_i^j)^2]$ are only approximate, because of the assumption of uniformity on j, which does not allow the magnitude of the scheduling-period length to shrink as λ grows. The second difficulty is inherent in the approximation. The first difficulty, that is, the biasing of λ_i, can be removed as follows. Specifically, instead of plotting the points (Di, ρ), with

$$\rho = \sum_{i=1}^{3} \rho_i$$

the points $(D_i, \hat{p})$ can be plotted, where

$$\hat{\rho} = \sum_{i=1}^{3} \hat{\rho}_i \text{ and } \hat{\rho}_i = \rho_i \frac{E[l_i]}{E[S_i^j]}$$

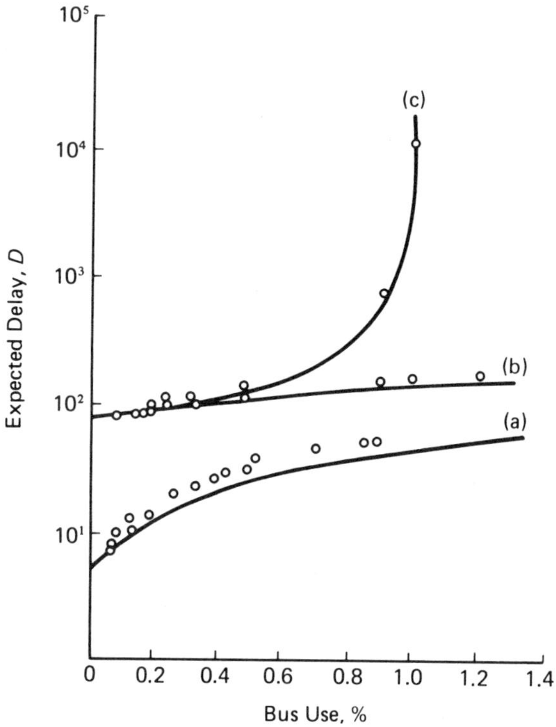

$K = 10$; $a = 0.01$; o = simulation results; solid line = analytically derived approximate results.

Figure 5–9. Message-Class Delay Curves; (a) Class 1; (b) Class 2; (c) Class 3

To assess the viability of the approximate model, we compare simulation-produced results with the values $(Di, \hat{\rho})$. As shown in figures 5–9 and 5–10, the comparison is very good for all three classes and is especially good for classes 2 and 3. (Figures 5–9 and 5–10 were produced assuming the parameterizations given in table 5–3.) The agreement between simulation and analytic results improves as

$$E[l_i]/E[S_i^j]$$

approaches unity, thus explaining why the approximation better fits class 2 and 3 results than it does class 1 results. The approximation is easily used, especially by comparison with simulation. In part, its viability stems from the fact that, even for $a = 0.04$, the collision rate is very low, as shown in figure 5–11. More exact analytic models of PSD with message-based priorities are difficult to construct. Analytic models of PSD are also given in [2].

Figure 5–8 shows throughput for CSMA-CD and for comparison also shows CSMA and ALOHA. Improvement in the channel capacity is

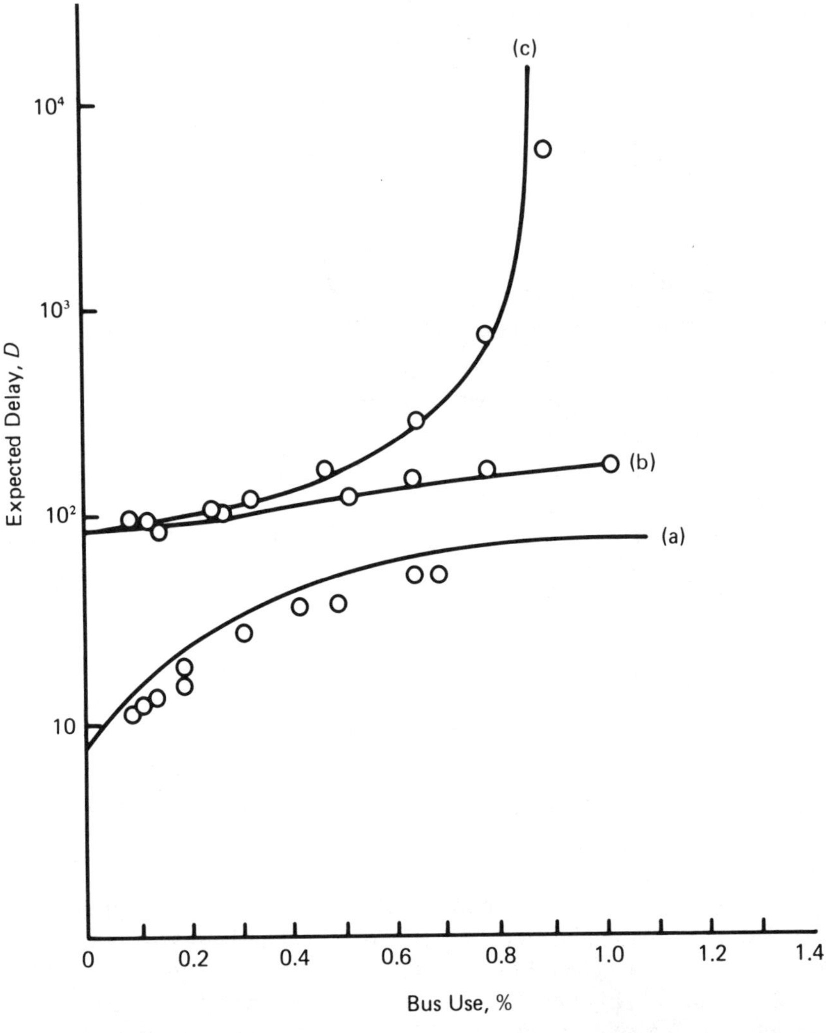

$K = 10$; $a = 0.04$; o = simulation results; solid line = analytically derived approximate results.

Figure 5–10. Message-Class Delay Curves: (a) Class 1; (b) Class 2; (c) Class 3

noticeable even for relatively small value, $a = 0.01$. The curve also suggests that CSMA-CD possesses an inherently more stable behavior than ALOHA or CSMA, because of the ability to produce very high throughput values over a relatively wide range of traffic loads.

Throughput-delay curves for CSMA-CD are shown in figure 5–12 for various ν values, with ν the probability that each backlogged user senses the

Table 5–3
Parameters Employed in PSD Analysis

Message Class i	*Message* length $E[1_i]$	*Distribution of Message Lengths*	*Percentage of Total Traffic from Class i*
	$E[1_i]$	$F_{1_i}[x]$	P_i
Alert $[i = 1]$	5	U [0,10]	10
Normal $[i = 2]$	86	U [0,172]	20
Background $[i = 3]$	86	U [0,172]	70

U = uniform distribution

Service (transmission) time S_i for messages from class i is given by $1_i/r$, with $E[S_i] = E[1_i]/r$, r the bus-transmission rate.

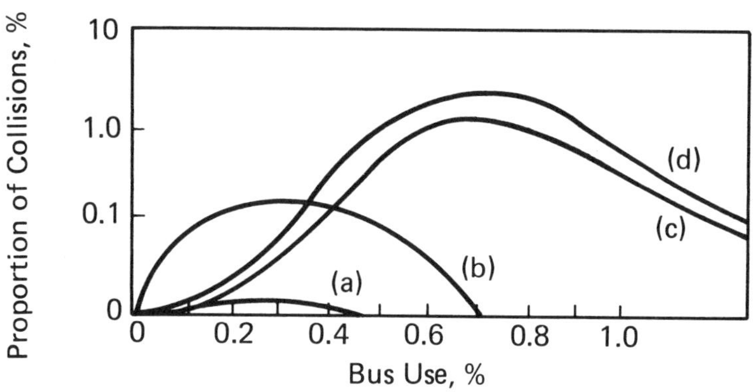

$K = 10$.

Figure 5–11. Percentage of Collisions Suffered: (a) $a = 0.01$ (3 scheduling periods); (b) $a = 0.04$ (3 scheduling periods); (c) $a = 0.01$ (1 scheduling period); (d) $a = 0.04$ (1 scheduling period)

channel in any given slot. The best performance can be maintained by choosing the value ν dynamically as a function of message load.

In Kleinrock [67], an interesting question was raised with respect to the possibility of having more than one access scheme share the multiaccess channel by splitting its bandwith and using a different access scheme in each part. The result from this question is a theorem that states that the mixing of two schemes cannot improve throughput or delay performance beyond those exhibited by either of the access methods alone [67]. The mixing of access philosophies to create more efficient protocols has been successfully done, however. In satellite schemes, a contention reservation and subsequent fixed allocation have been used, for example, to improve performance over both pure contention (ALOHA) and pure preallocation (TDMA) schemes.

As previously noted, expected delay D becomes unbounded as throughput S approaches C, the channel capacity. Consequently, most access

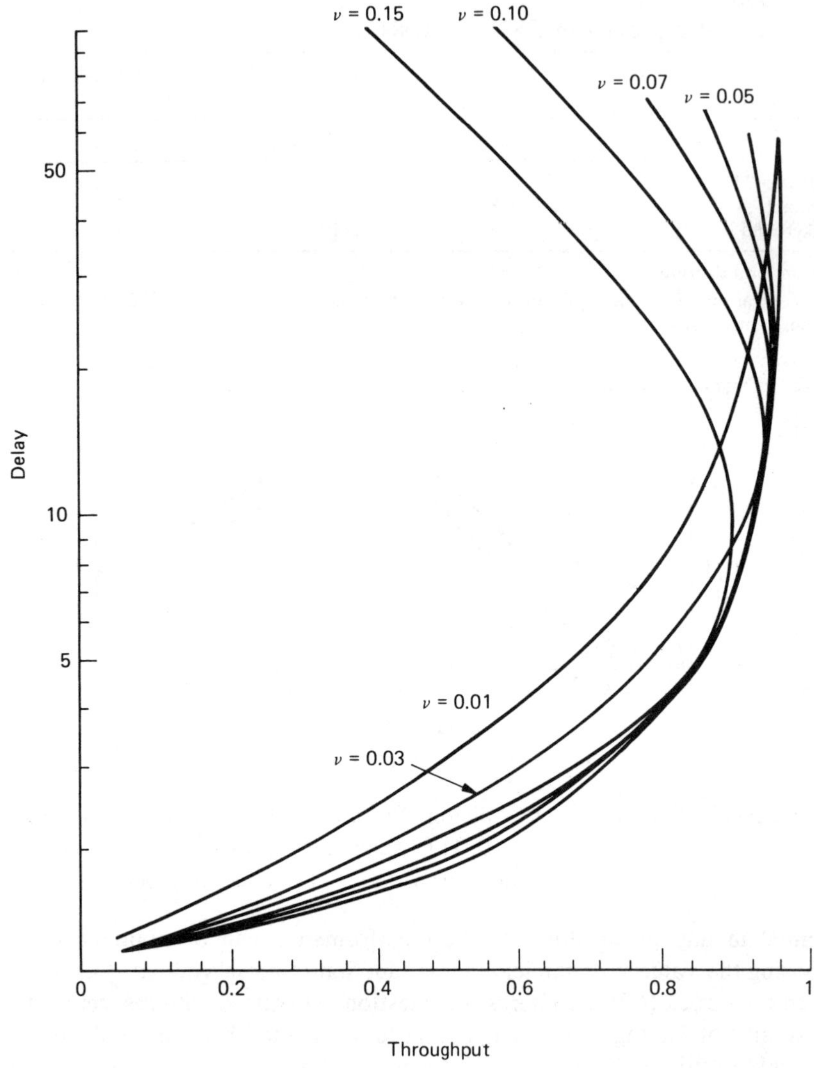

Figure5–12. The Throughput-Delay Trade-Off in CSMA-CD at Fixed ν

protocols cannot operate even near their capacity if a stable operation is to be maintained [68]. Nonetheless, capacity is an often-used performance indicator.

For many protocols, such as simple and fair BRAM and prioritized CSMA, we have

$$C = \frac{1}{1 + a}$$

because one a-slot is always dedicated in each scheduling period to the "first" node. For slotted and unslotted ALOHA, we have, as previously noted, $C = 1/e$ for slotted ALOHA and $C = 1/2e$ for the unslotted variant.

In protocols where a is a factor in determining the likelihood of collisions, as in CSMA, the capacity is a decreasing function of propagation delay. Furthermore, capacity is heavily dependent on the traffic model. For ALOHA, it was shown [28] that capacity far in excess of the $1/e$ value can actually be obtained. Figure 5–13 shows capacity curves as a function of the propagation delay, a, for a variety of access protocols.

Ring-Protocol Results

In a ring network, we are faced with a circumstance different from that of the bus. Consequently, the models used must be based on modeling assumptions and measure definitions that reflect the key ring-operational factors (which may be different from the factors found with busses). For example, with rings, the destination of messages and distribution of sources become important, as a ring is a collection of point-to-point links that connect all node pairs. For this reason, channel utilization may have to be computed incrementally over all ring segments. Furthermore, for certain ring-protocol approaches, the message (or packet) generation mechanism of each node is dependent on the state of the node. For instance, a simple exponentially driven packet-stream source is not easy to justify with the resister-insertion technique, since a node will be blocked while a message is in its register.

Considerations related to propagation delay are also different. A message circulating in a ring may encounter K propagation delays, for example, if it is returned to the source node. If K is large, the total delay can be significant even if the single-hop (that is, node-to-node) propagation delay is small. Thus, message-delay computations must account for total propagation. Additionally, message-delay computation must account for message delay encountered at each intermediate node. (Delays between source and destination or between source and source may occur, depending on how a message is removed from the ring. A message is removed either by the destination node or by the message-source node; both the average-delay and throughput measures must carefully account for such differences.)

For the token passing schemes [69], the average waiting-time delay, defined as the delay between the time a message reaches the top of a node-buffer queue until the time it is actually transmitted, has been derived assuming a single buffer [70] and assuming single or multiple buffers [71].

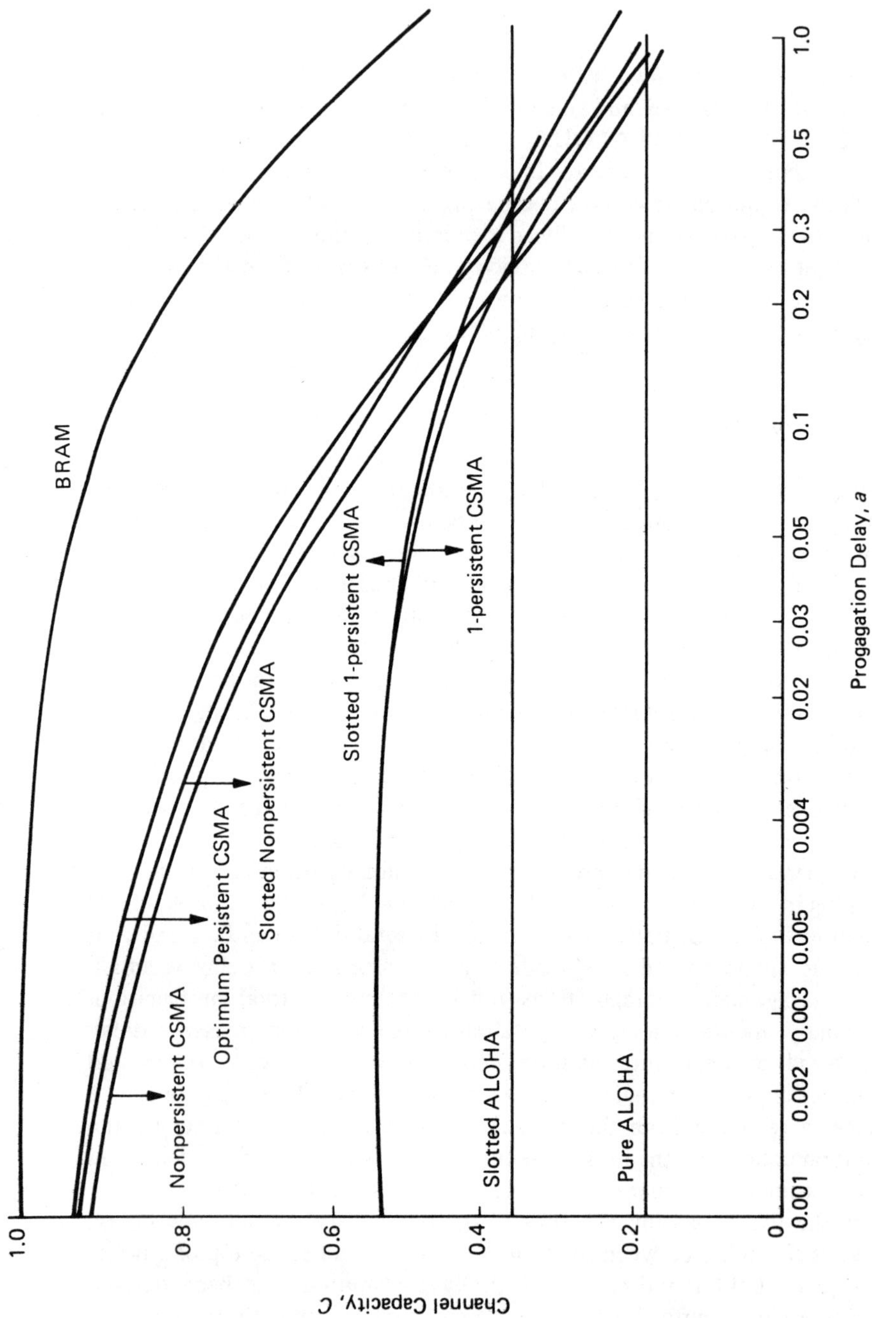

Figure 5–13. Protocol-Capacity Curves

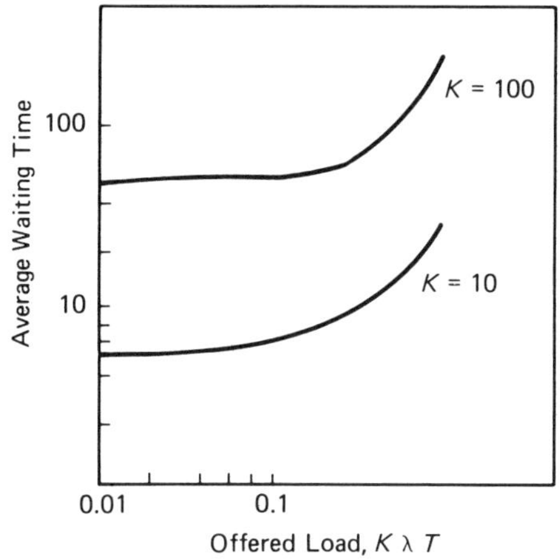

Figure 5–14. Delay versus Offered Load for Systems with 10 and 100 Nodes

Figure 5–14 shows sample delay results as a function of offered traffic, $k\lambda T$, assuming a single-node buffer, constant-size messages (packets), and homogeneous nodes. Similar analysis also appears in Labetoulle, Manning, and Peebles [72]. Analysis of token passing, assuming infinite-node buffer storage and assymetrical arrival rates [75], has shown that delay can be prevented from becoming unbounded up to loading values of 0.6, whereas, as shown in figure 5–14, delay becomes unbounded for loadings near 0.2 under previous assumptions.

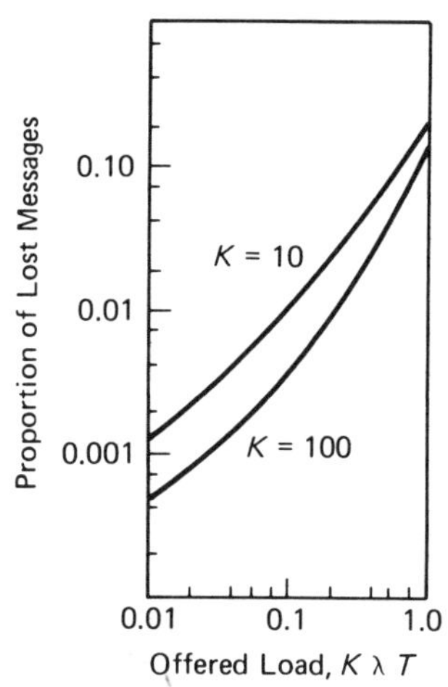

Figure 5–15. Proportion of Blocked Messages versus Offered Load

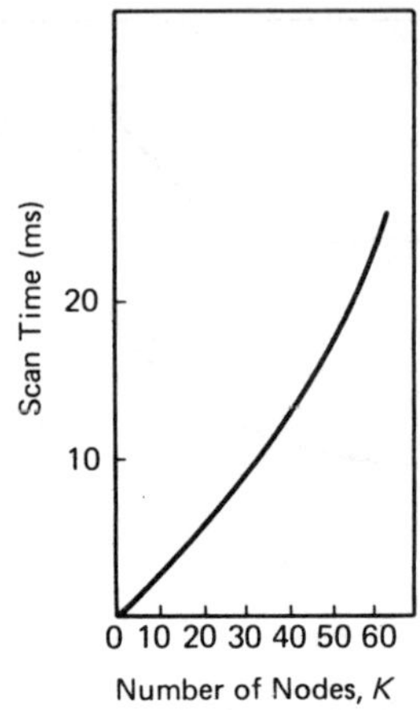

Figure 5–16. Scan Time versus Number of Nodes

Since channel access is related to token availability, the number of blocked messages becomes an important design measure. Figure 5–15 shows the proportion of blocked messages (that is, lost if a single-node buffer is assumed). Figure 5–16 shows the average delay from the time a packet reaches the top of a node queue until the time it is transmitted.

The message-passing-control scheme [73] is dependent on the availability of empty message slots. Its performance was studied using both analytic and simulation models [74–77]. For this protocol, the utilization can be twice as high as with the previous protocol, because, on the average, half of a message's journey is a nonproductive return journey to the source node. As a result, real throughput is bounded by 0.5. However, since more than one new packet can be in transit, the average packet delay can be improved using this protocol. (A possible disadvantage, which can be prevented by additional hardware, comes from the possibility of a monopolizing node with relatively high arrival rate blocking messages from other nodes.) In Spragins [78,79], the technique was analyzed for infinite buffers, negligible propagation delays, and assymetric arrival rates. In this system, only one central node issues and cancels free slots, which travel around the loop. Consequently, nodes closest to the controller will gain best performance by having the best access to empty slots. Figures 5–17 and 5–18 show delay and queue-length performance for a ten-node ring for various p values, with p giving the total number of packet slots needed by each node.

The register-insertion technique implemented in the distributed-loop computer network (DLCN) ring has been analyzed by simulation [80], assuming a single exponentially driven arrival mechanism, variable-length messages, infinite buffer storage, and a homogeneous six-node ring. Mathe-

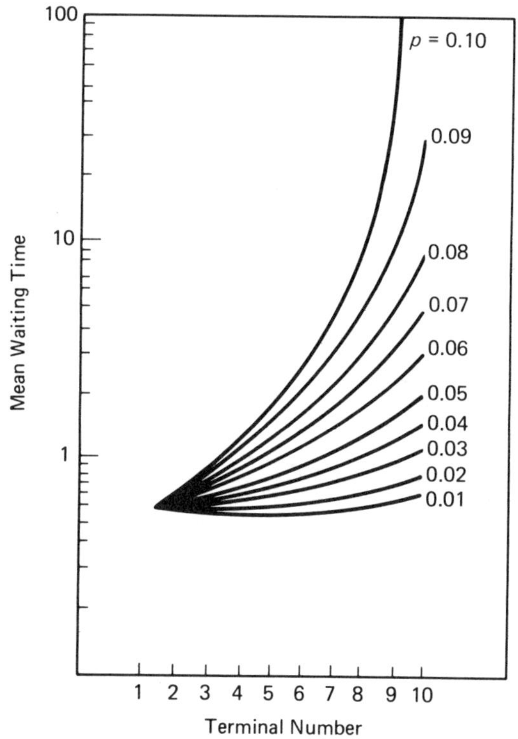

Figure 5–17. Mean Waiting Time versus Terminal Number

matical models [81] have also been constructed under the additional assumption that new messages always have highest priority for transmission.

Quantitative comparison studies for these techniques are limited in number [80,83,84] and seemingly lead to contradictory conclusions. In Penney and Baghdadi [85,86], an attempt is made to shed some light on the discrepancy in the reported results, but more comparative studies are needed.

Radio-Channel Access-Protocol Results

Radio-network protocol performance depends on the connectivity of the network nodes. With full connectivity, performance measures will not differ from those given for bus-based systems (which are fully connected). With hidden nodes, consequences of partial connectivity will be felt. That is, performance of access protocols not specifically designed for the hidden-node environment will deteriorate as the degree of disconnectness of the

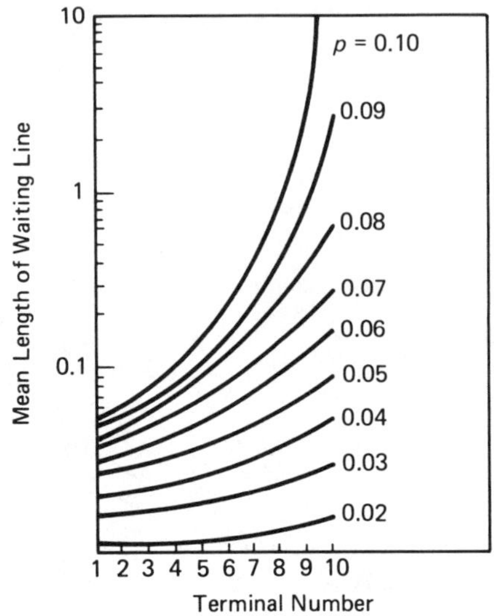

Figure 5–18. Mean Length of Queue versus Terminal Number for a Loop with Ten Identical Nodes Used in Pure Data-Collection Mode

network graph increases. Figures 5–19 and 5–20 quantify this point for certain sample protocols.

Figure 5–19 shows, for 1-persistent CSMA, the degradation in throughput S as a function of G, the total packet demand, for various values of β, which specifies, for each node in a set of nodes, the ratio of the number of nodes hidden from the node to the total number of nodes. For the circumstance shown, each node is hidden from the same number of nodes (the so-called symmetric-dependent group case), so that a single β value applies to all nodes.

We may also consider the case of independent groups, such that nodes within a group can hear each other while nodes in different groups cannot. If there are N such groups, and assuming a nonpersistent CSMA access protocol, it has been shown [87], assuming an exponentially driven stream of packets to each group, that:

$$\frac{s}{g} = e^{g(1-2a)}\left[\frac{e^{-g(1-a)}}{g(1+2a+e^{-ag}}\right]^{N}$$

where s and g reflect the group-dependent S and G values. Obviously, as N increases, the number of nodes in each group decreases and performance decreases. Formally, we may let $N \rightarrow \infty$ with $Ns \rightarrow S$ and $Ng \rightarrow G$ to obtain

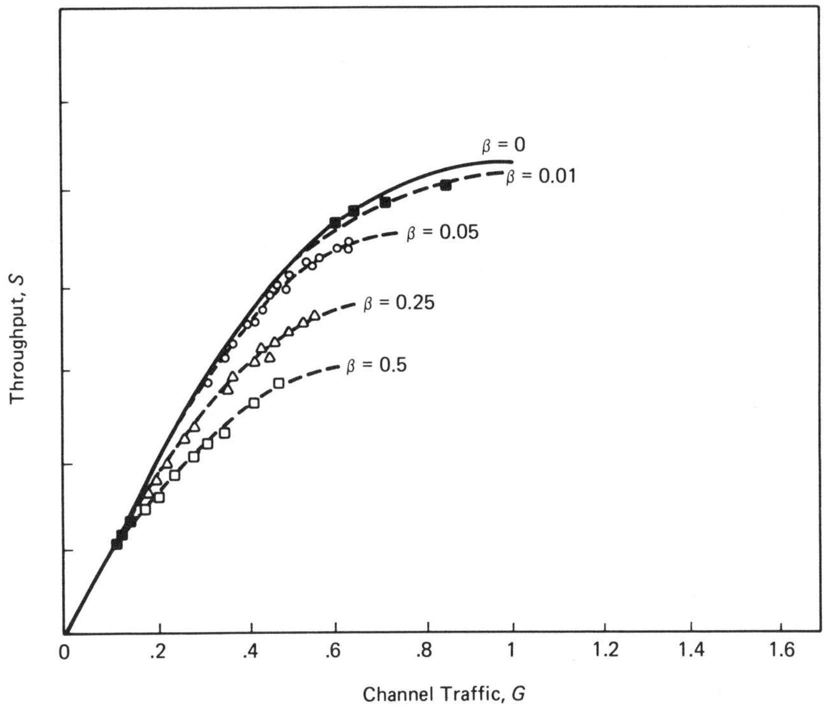

1-Persistent CSMA, Symmetric-Dependent Groups; $a = 0.01$; $K = 10$.

Figure 5–19. Symmetric-Dependent-Groups Configuration: Throughput versus Channel Traffic

$$\frac{S}{G} = e^{-2G}$$

reflecting the case of simple ALOHA.

Figure 5–20 shows (among other things) the capacity degradation for both 1-persistent and nonpersistent CSMA as a function of the value of R, the measure of connectivity defined in chapter 3. Figure 5–21 shows throughput as a function of total-packet-offered traffic for BRAM for various values of R. As might be expected, the curves cover the performance range from simple BRAM to simple ALOHA as R varies from 0 to 1. The optimal grouping algorithm improves BRAM performance, as was suggested in chapter 3, by eliminating some potential collisions; specifically, intergroup collisions are eliminated. Figures 5–22 and 5–23 [88] show the relative performance improvement obtainable by using BRAM with optimized

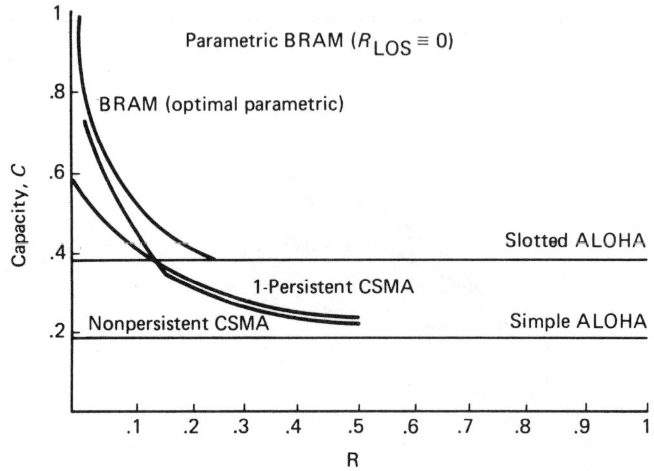

$a = 0.01$ is used because of CSMA figure published with this propagation delay value in Tobagi and Kleinrock [87]

Figure 5–20. Capacity as a Function of Connectivity

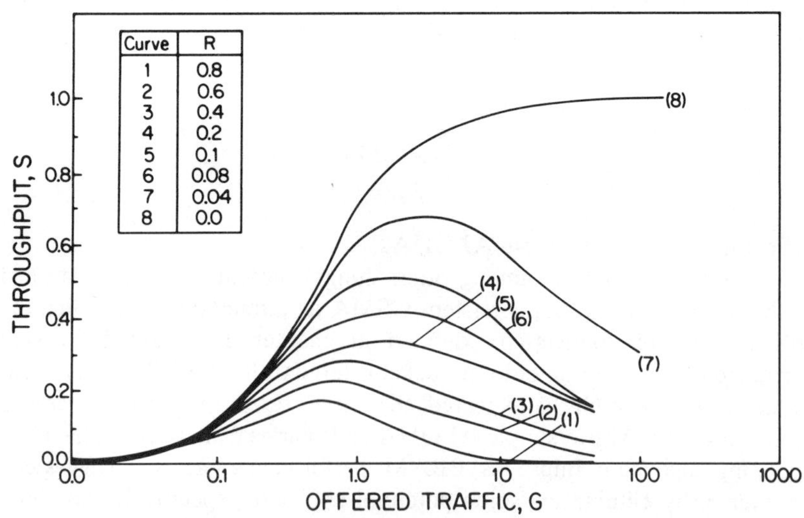

Figure 5–21. BRAM Throughput versus Connectivity

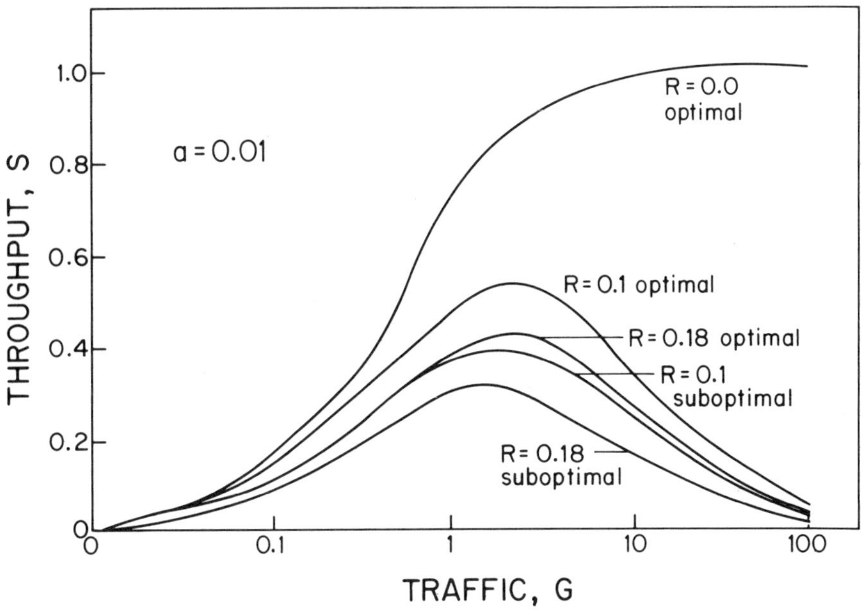

a = 0.01.

Figure 5–22. Optimal BRAM Node-Grouping Throughput Curves

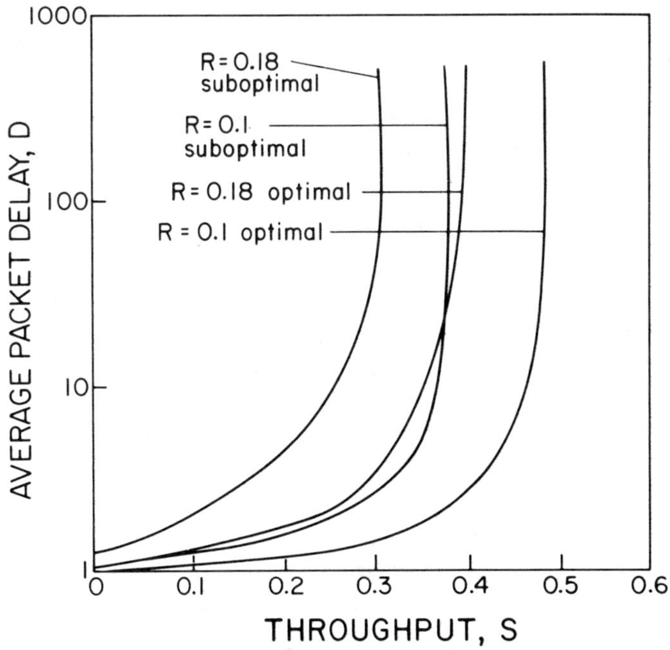

Figure 5–23. Optimal BRAM Node-Grouping Delay Curves

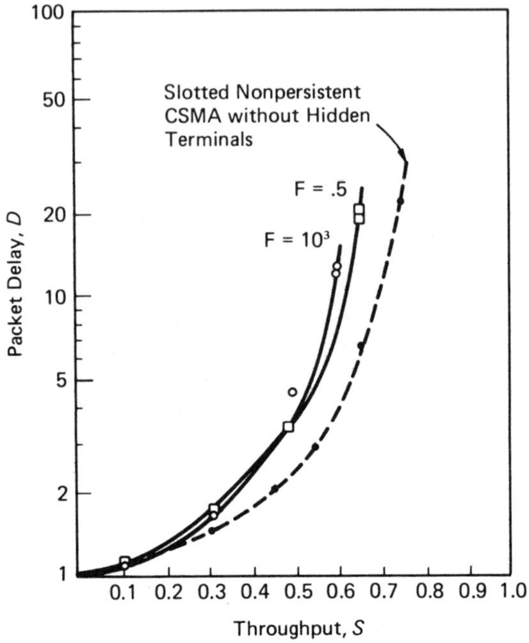

$a = 0.01$; $F =$ false-alarm probability.

Figure 5–24. BTMA Throughput-Delay Trade-offs (Propagation Delay)

grouping. Although improvement can be had, a performance degradation because of hidden nodes remains. Protocols designed to accommodate hidden nodes do better.

As explained in chapter 3, the BTMA protocol is specifically designed for the hidden-node environment, with a star connectivity graph. Recall that the busy tone (generated by the hub node) simulates the carrier signal used in fully connected network graphs, and that with the busy tone we can use any of the access protocols that employ a carrier signal. Figure 5–24 shows delay performance for BTMA, using slotted nonpersistent CSMA. For comparison, slotted nonpersistent CSMA results are also shown for a fully connected network. The curves plotted are in terms of F, a probability of false alarm, that is, the probability that a node incorrectly detects absence of the busy tone.

The SUPBRAM protocol, which relies on the single data channel to provide for collision-free node accesses in the face of hidden nodes, admits additional performance improvement. Figure 5–25 shows performance curves, taken from Chlamtac and Franta [42], for the network shown in Figure 5–26. The K^1 value, that is, the maximum number of hops required to span the network, is four; consequently, three different split-packet-delay

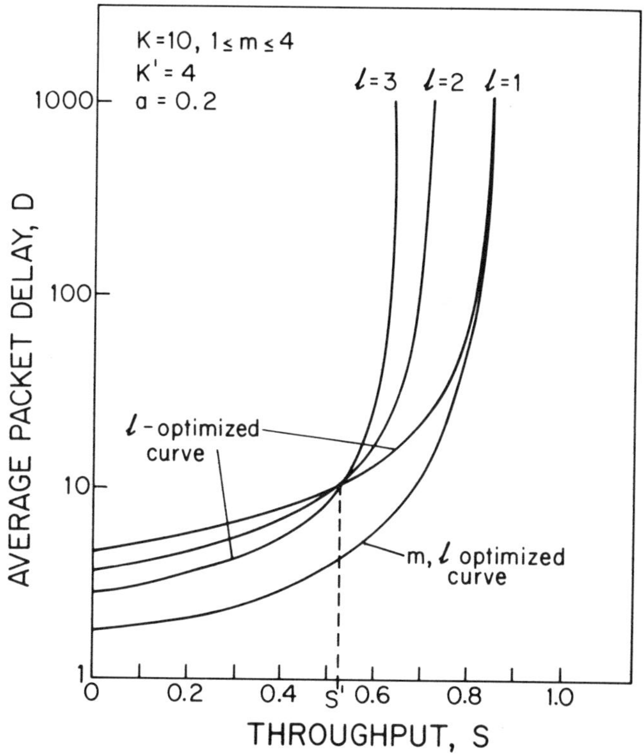

$K = 10$; $1 \le m \le 4$; $K' = 4$; $a = 0.2$.

Figure 5–25. Delay-Performance Comparison for Network of Figure 5–26

values are possible, and figure 5–25 gives a delay curve for each of these three values.

Expected delay for the protocol using the scheduling function of equation 3.6 is given by [42]:

$$D = 1 + la + \frac{S + Sla}{2(1 - S - Sla)} + \frac{a}{2}\left(1 - \frac{S + Sla}{K}\right)\left(1 + \frac{KK^1 - Kl}{1 - S - Sla}\right)$$

(An expression also exists for S as a function G [42].) When equation 3.5 is employed, results must be obtained by simulation [42].

In Chlamtac and Franta [42], it was shown that the curves for various l values intersect in a small interval of S values. Furthermore, it was shown that a best l value can be selected. Specifically, it is proven that:

Theorem: The l value, l^*, that minimizes D over all allowable l values is given by

$$l^* = \begin{cases} K^1 - 1 & \text{for } S < S^1 \\ 1 & \text{for } S > S^1 \end{cases}$$

where

$$S^1 = \frac{1}{2}(\hat{S} + T) - \frac{W}{3V} - \frac{1}{2}\sqrt{-3}\,(\hat{S} - T)$$

and

$$\hat{S} = (R + (Q^3 + R^2)^{1/2})^{1/3}$$
$$T = (R - (Q^3 + R^2)^{1/2})^{1/3}$$
$$R = (9WUV - 27ZV^2 - 2W^3)/54V^3)$$
$$Q = (3UV - W^2)/9V^2$$

and

$$U = aK^2(K^1)^2 - aK^1 - 2K(K^1 - 2) + K^2(K^1 - 2) - 2aKK^1 (K^1 - 2)$$
$$V = a(K^1 - 2) - 2aK^1 + a^2(2K^1 - (K^1)^2) - a^3K^1(K^1 - 1)$$
$$W = 3aK^1 - a(K - 2) - a^2(2K^1 - (K^1)^2) + K(K^1 - 2) + aKK^1 (K - 2) + a^2K(K^1 - 1)(K^1 - 2)$$
$$Z = 2K(K^1 - 2) - K^2(K^1 - 2)$$

Figure 5–25 also shows the l-optimized delay curve.

In Chlamtac and Franta [43], a generalized SUPBRAM is discussed in which, with a two-parameter optimization, it is possible to further improve performance. One parameter is l; the other, m, reflects the number of groups assembled to shorten scheduling periods. (The grouping algorithm is unlike the grouping algorithms presented for BRAM, and Chlamtac and Franta [43] should be consulted for an explanation.) The generalized protocol is adaptive in nature, and l and m change at a finite collection of S values to yield the m,l-optimized delay curves. Figure 5–25 shows the m,l-optimized delay curve for the network of figure 5–26. Finally, figure 5–27 shows delay curves for a variety of protocols, with a star connection graph.

The results given have assumed that data packets are only transmitted

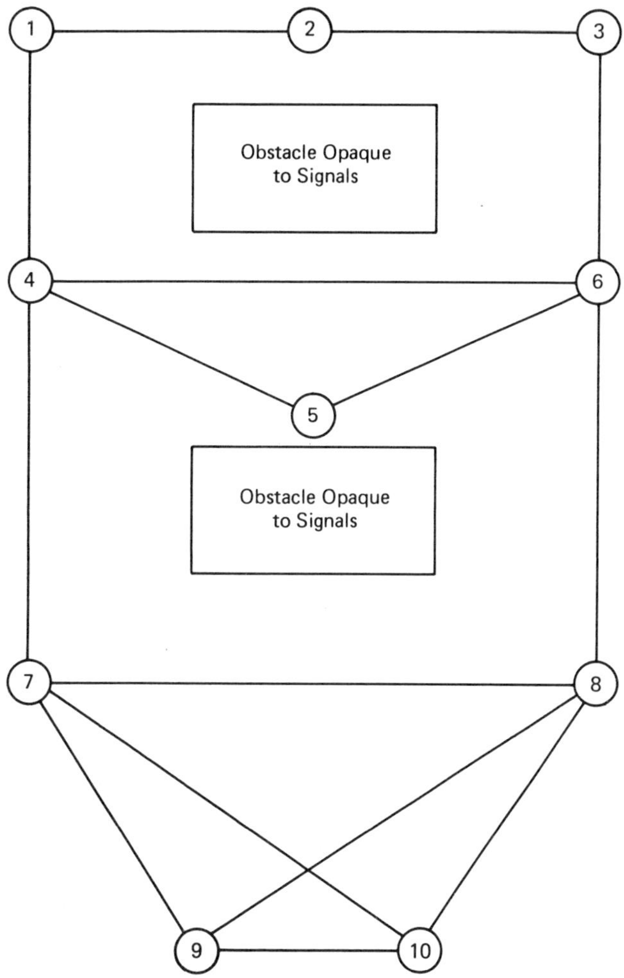

Figure 5–26. Sample Network

between connected nodes (while reservation packets in SUPBRAM are transmitted among nonconnected nodes). The actual traffic pattern in a distributed radio-packet network is not necessarily limited to transmissions between connected nodes. In many respects, the complications introduced to account for multihop transmission are the same as found in modeling end-to-end protocols in packet-switching networks [13], and the references should be consulted for pointers to the literature [71,74,89–91].

Finally, we have not given results for the most promising case, wherein multiple transmissions are permitted if they are noninterfering. Little is

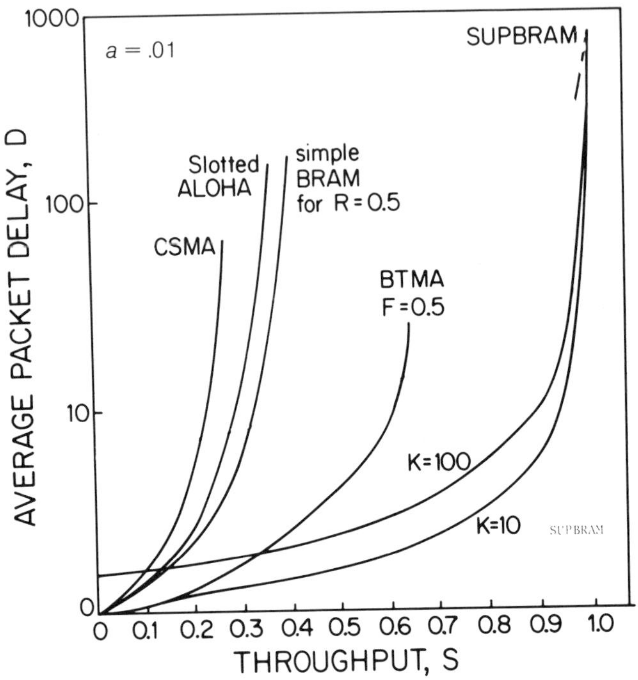

Figure 5–27. Comparison of Packet Delays for Various Protocols: Demonstration of the Effect of *K* on *S/D* SUPBRAM Performance

known about this class of protocols, and Kleinrock and Silvester [92] may be consulted for an example.

Satellite Access-Protocol Results

The multiaccess satellite channel is fully connected to the network nodes in the sense that all ground stations can "hear" all downlink transmissions.

As our examples in chapter 3 suggest, because of the very large end-to-end propagation delay of the satellite channel (0.27/sec), demand-assignment (reservation) and random-assignment protocols are the most attractive. Some protocols, such as ALOHA and R-ALOHA, are easy to implement but suffer from the drawbacks associated with collisions and instability. Certain reservation protocols, such as FIFO, R-TDMA, and CPODA, do not so suffer and offer better performance than random-access protocols (by the use of very short reservation packets). Given that a channel capacity of γ

is sacrificed for reservation packets, these protocols reduce data-channel capacity to $C = 1 - \gamma$. In Lam [93], γ is computed for several access protocols. It was found that the quality of performance for various protocols is related to the traffic load and type of traffic [93].

The same general observations apply to satellite channels as were given for bus systems. Specifically, fixed-assignment protocols, such as TDMA, are useful for nonbursty traffic. With bursty traffic, contention or reservation schemes are preferred. Furthermore, if the length of messages is sufficient to justify reservations, both contention and fixed-reservation channel scheduling can be used. Fixed scheduling causes overhead to increase with increases in the number of nodes but has the advantage of offering collision-free reservations.

Figures 5–28 through 5–30 show comparative delay-performance results for slotted ALOHA, TDMA, and the FIFO scheme, with both a slotted ALOHA and a TDMA reservation subchannel (where L gives average

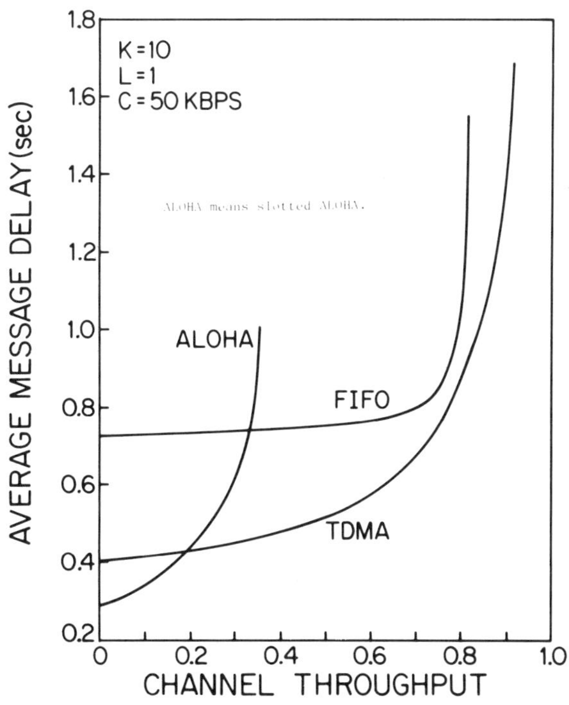

$K = 10$; $L = 1$; $C = 50$ kb/s

Figure 5–28. Delay-Throughput Trade-Off for Ten Nodes and Short Messages (One Packet per Message)

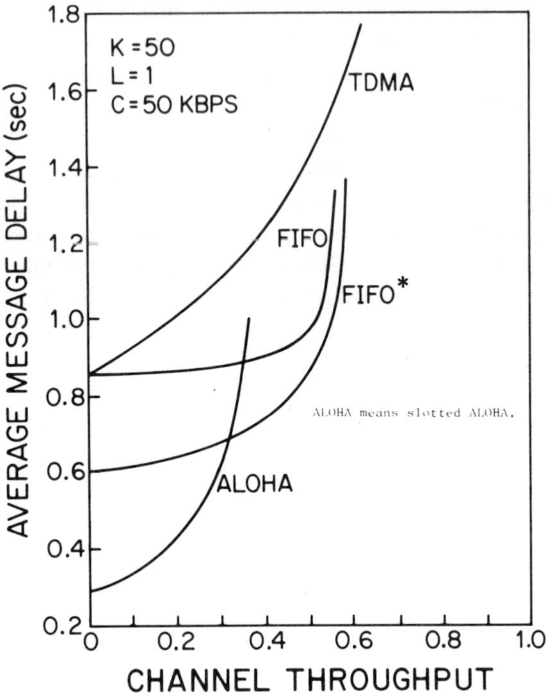

$K = 50$; $L = 1$; $C = 50$ kb/s.

Figure 5–29. Delay-Throughput Trade-Off for Fifty Nodes and Short Messages (One Packet per Message)

message length in packets). The results are as we might expect from our examination of bus-oriented access-protocol performance. For low channel loadings, particularly, ALOHA performs well. For high loadings, the reservation schemes (FIFO and FIFO*) perform best. These observations are easily explained when one remembers that, with FIFO schemes, a minimum delay of two round-trip times is required for all traffic loads, one for the reservation and one for the data packet.

In Borgonovo and Fratta [94], an access method is presented that requires only one round-trip delay, while still guaranteeing reservations for all but the first message from each node. This is done in a manner similar to FIFO (that is, TDMA reservations), but each reservation bit is followed in the same slot by the data packet.

The performance of such protocols as CPODA seems promising in offering improvement in delay performance over the schemes depicted in figures 5–28 through 5–30, and it is the subject of evaluation to be carried out on SATNET, an experimental packet satellite network [5].

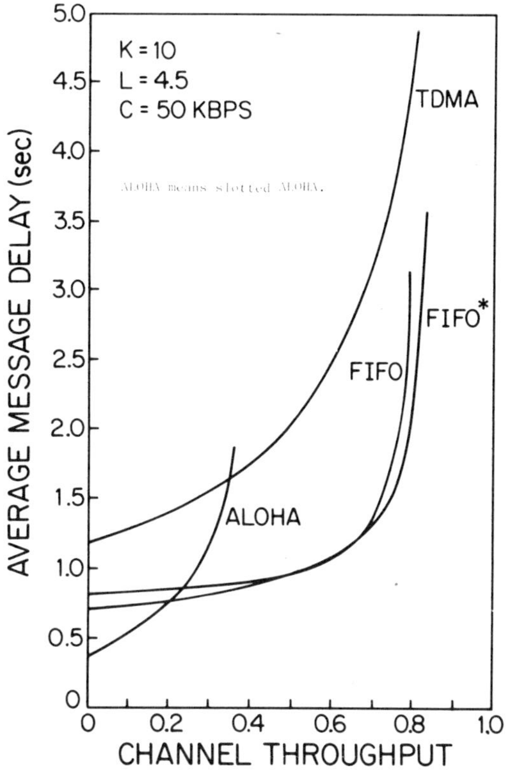

$K = 10$; $L = 4.5$; $C = 50$ kb/s.

Figure 5–30. Delay-Throughput Trade-Off for Ten Nodes and Multipacket Messages

Link-Level Protocols

The link-level protocol controls the flow of information between the communicating nodes and creates the illusion of an error-free communication. In performing these functions, considerable overhead is introduced. Factors contributing to the overhead include the length of frames, the use of fixed-length or variable-length frames, the windowing procedure, the physical characteristics of the channel (bandwidth, error rate, and so on), the acknowledgment policy, and the buffering and error detection or correction mechanisms.

To account for these factors, the model for a link-level protocol unit must account for the following:

1. The channel bandwidth;

2. The channel propagation delay;
3. The message-generation patterns (usually an exponentially driven source is assumed);
4. The channel-bit error probability;
5. Frame length;
6. The length of acknowledgment frames;
7. The maximum number of acknowledgments to be sent per message;
8. The acknowledgment-delay timeout interval;
9. The window size; and
10. Node-buffer availability.

It is not hard to observe that, even if packet destruction (because of channel-bit errors) is not accounted for, effective channel utilization is degraded by frame overhead, acknowledgment traffic, propagation time, and node-processing time. Consideration of the effect of channel errors complicates model development. Assuming no bit errors, channel utilization can theoretically be increased by increasing the size of transmitted frames. With errors assumed, a trade-off results. Specifically, the longer the frame, the higher the probability of error in a transmitted frame. Consequently, an optimum frame size exists, which balances the probability of error (in a frame) against effective utilization. This optimum-size frame has been derived for various protocols [102].

In this section, rather than pursuing such a general model, we concentrate on a model of a variant of the windowing protocol presented in example 3.5. Actually, several performance studies of link-level protocols exist. Most, however, concentrate on throughput efficiency for a saturated channel [95–98] but are applicable to a multiaccess channel. Channel efficiency and message delay have recently been studied (using both simulation and analysis) for certain protocol choices for unsaturated channel cases [99,100], but unfortunately only for a point-to-point channel. Here we concentrate on a model developed to predict channel-throughput efficiency for a satellite-communication channel [97].

In the Advanced Data Communication Procedure (ADCCP), High-level Data Link Control (HDLC), or Synchronous data link control (SDLC) protocols, damaged or lost messages are retransmitted until they are correctly received. To achieve this goal, the sender and the receiver monitor the flow of messages and use error-detecting codes, control commands, and timeouts to detect an error, in the manner discussed in chapter 3. To elaborate, the reject (REJ) and selective reject (SREJ) commands are sent by the receiver to the sender if errors are detected. The sender responds with one or more retransmissions. Since this sequence of actions is not failproof (for example, it cannot protect against loss of control messages), sender timeouts are also used. Before giving the full description of the satellite model, we point out that it represents a kind of worst-case analysis for most local networks, in that, in most local networks, propagation delays are short and message-arrival rates are generally lower. The model is developed [97], assuming that the recovery using REJ and SREJ is always successful. Furthermore, the model assumes that data are transmitted in information frames (I-frames), while control information is sent in supervisory frames (S-frames), and that each I-frame is numbered, using a sequence number, $N(S)$ modulo M, and carries a CRC for error detection, as discussed in chapter 3. Additionally, it is assumed that the receiver and sender alternate in sending information, that is, each can transmit without having to wait for the other. We also assume that the receiver always remembers the next expected message number, $N(R)$, and will either reject all other I-frames, when acting on a REJ exception condition, or store them, if acting on a SREJ exception condition. (The REJ command requests that all messages be retransmitted starting with the I-frame with number $N(R)$, while SREJ requests that only the I-frame numbered $N(R)$ be retransmitted. A description of the SREJ version is shown in figure 5–31.) Finally, for tractability, the following are assumed:

1. I-frames are of constant length such that I-frame transmission time is the basic time unit;
2. The error-generation process has no memory, and p is the probability of an error in an I-frame;
3. Zero frame-processing time is required by the nodes; and
4. The channel round-trip delay, d, includes both the transmission of an S-frame and round-trip channel-propagation delay.

The analysis proceeds by associating regeneration points with the sending of an REJ. Doing so allows definition of a stochastic process, with random variables describing the cycle length (the cycle time given by the time between two regeneration points) and A_j, the number of frames accepted in a cycle, j. The expected number of accepted frames before the first loss is given by $p/(1-p)$ (from the geometric distribution), and with B_j the number of additional frames accepted in the cycle, we have

$$E(A_j) = 1 + \frac{p}{1-p} + E(B_j)p \qquad (5.32)$$

The computation of $E(B_j)$ [97] gives

$$E[B_j] = \left(\frac{1}{1-p^d}\right)\left(2 + \frac{p}{1-p}\right)$$

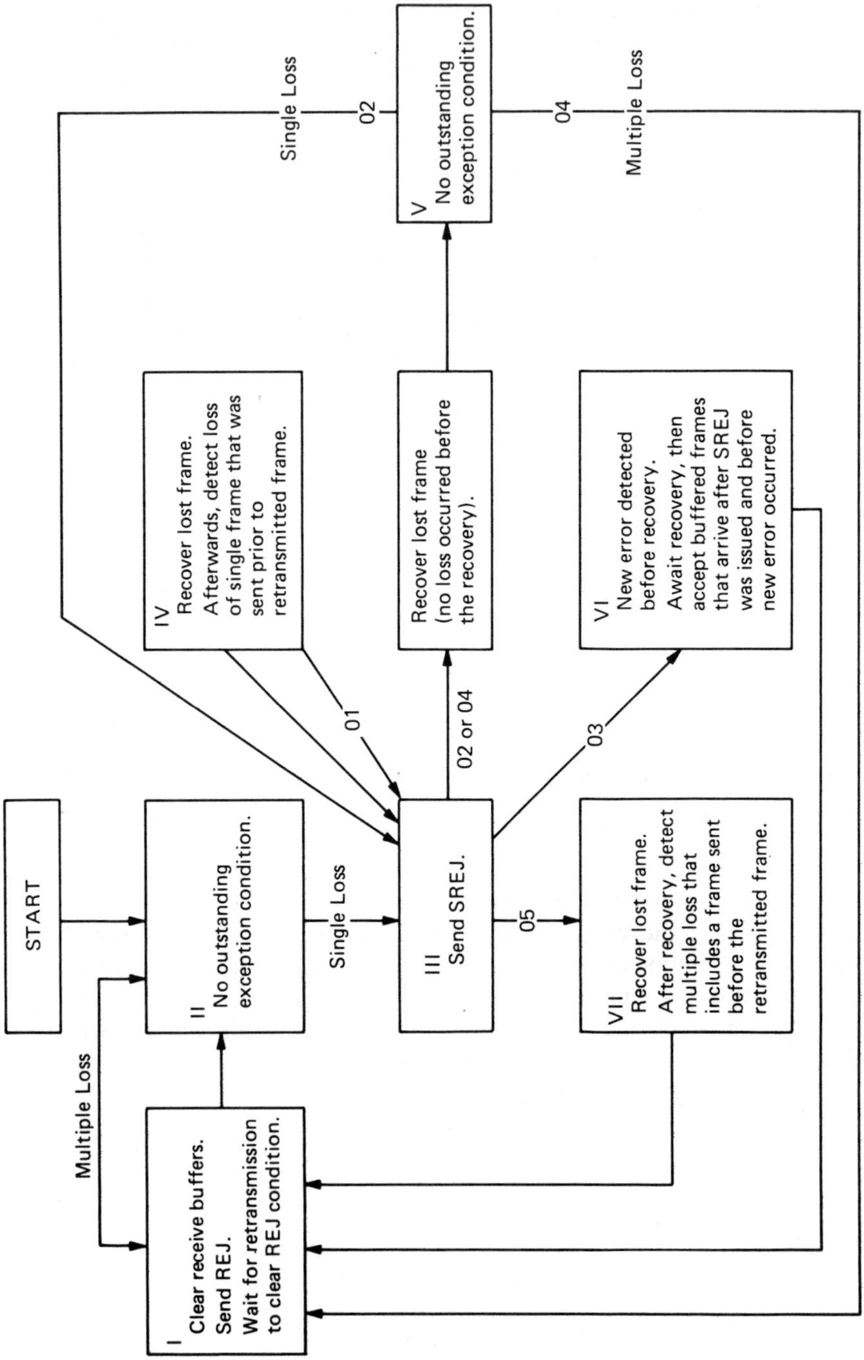

Figure 5–31. Basic SREJ Protocol

and substituting this expression into equation 5.32 gives:

$$E[A_j] = \frac{1}{1-p} + \frac{p}{1-p^d}\left(1 + \frac{1}{1-p}\right)$$

Computation of the cycle length, τ_j, gives

$$E[\tau_j] = d + 1 + 1/(1-p) + 1/p + E[Y_j]p$$

with Y_j standing for the number of frame times that pass from the time of entrance to Box III to the end of the cycle (see figure 5–31). Its expected value is given by

$$E(Y_j) = E(L)/(1 - p^d)$$

where $E(L)$ is the expected number of entries into Box III, a quantity computed in Easton [97]. Given these quantities, we define channel-throughput efficiency as follows: channel-throughput efficiency = frame efficiency × (1 − fraction of frame overhead), with frame efficiency given by:

$$\lim_{t \to a} F(t)/t$$

with $F(t)$ the number of frames accepted to time t. Using the expressions for $E(A_j)$, $E(\tau_j)$, $E(Y_j)$ and $E(L)$, frame efficiency becomes:

$$\frac{p[-p^d + p(2-p)]}{1 + (d+1)p(1-p^2) - p^d[p(d+1)(1-p) + 3] + p^{d-1}[2p^2 + 1]}$$

Figure 5.32 compares the above, "basic SREJ" model with other retransmission alternatives, which are explained in the figure. If the error rate is small (or even of moderate size), the advantage of SREJ is clear.

Other models of link-type protocols that make it possible to derive both throughput and delay measures have also been developed [100]. The central idea in this analysis is use of the $M/G/1$ queuing model (assuming an exponentially driven message-arrival process with parameter λ and use of REJ). Thus, channel throughput and message delays can be had in addition to the channel efficiency obtained from the previous model. To obtain a queuing model, the virtual transmission time, T_v, is defined as the time it takes for an arbitrary I-frame to be transmitted and successfully received,

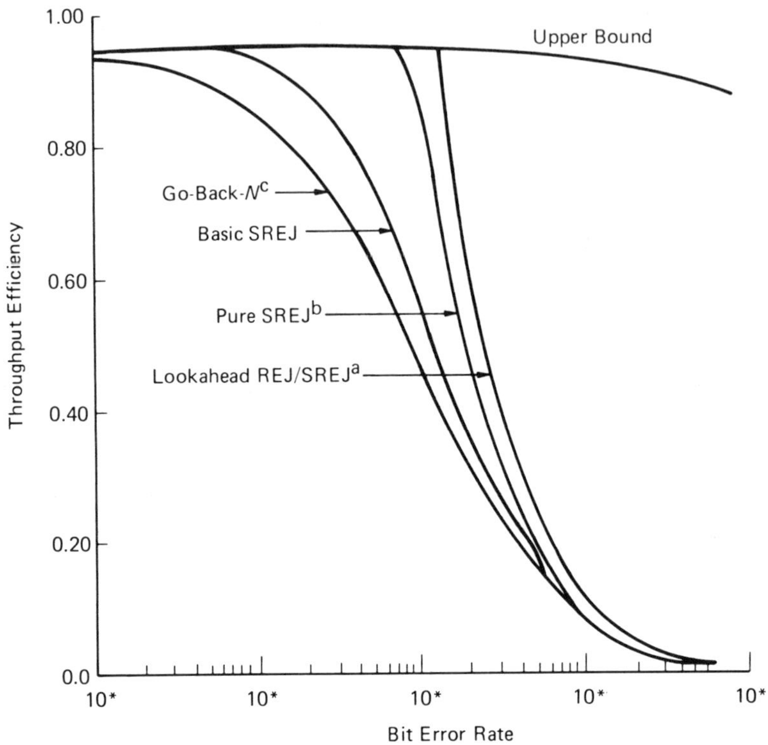

Bandwidth = 1.544 Mb/s; round = trip delay = 700 ms; number of bits in overhead = 56; number of bits in frame = 1,000.

Decision on sending REJ or SREJ is made by looking one frame ahead in the buffer when loss of frame is detected.

[b]SREJ is used as the only method of recovery.

[c]REJ is used as the only method of recovery.

Figure 5–32. Throughput Efficiency with 1,000-Bit Frames

which can include several retransmissions of the frame. After determining the distribution function of the virtual transmission time, expected delay, D_f, can be approximated by the Pollaczek-Khintchine formula [12]:

$$D_f = E[T_v] + \frac{\lambda E[T_v^2]}{2[1 - \lambda E[T_v]]}$$

For details of the analysis, the reader should consult Bux and Truong [100]. Figure 5–33 shows the throughput as a function of message length and bit-error rate, given in terms of the I-frame probability, P_B, with P_B given by:

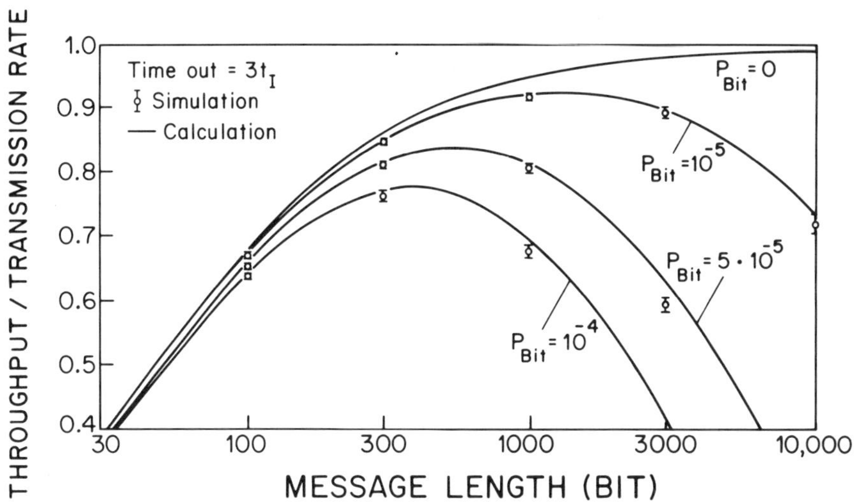

Timeout = $3t_{\mathrm{I}}$.

Figure 5–33. Throughput or Transmission Rate versus Message Length

$$P_B = l - (l - P_{\mathrm{bit}})^{l+y}$$

assuming a frame with l data bits and y overhead bits, and a bit-error probability P_{bit}. With $y = 48$, figure5–33 clearly shows the effect of short messages for various values of P_{bit}. Figure 5–34 shows message delay as a function of throughput for different bit-error probabilities (and a frame length of 1,000 bits). As expected, for very low bit-error probabilities, an *M/D/*1-type behavior is observed.

Finally, figure 5–35 shows mean buffer-occupancy time as a function of throughput (for a frame length of 5,000 bits) and various bit-error probabilities. It is interesting to note that, with the protocol version described and with a timeout value of three I-frame transmission times, the buffer requirements become unbounded at relatively low throughout values as the error rate increases. Consequently, choice of the optimal frame size must take into account the buffer constraints as well as throughput and delay performance.

Discussion

A definitive treatment of protocol-performance models would consume a volume. We make no suggestion, therefore, that our presentation is complete.

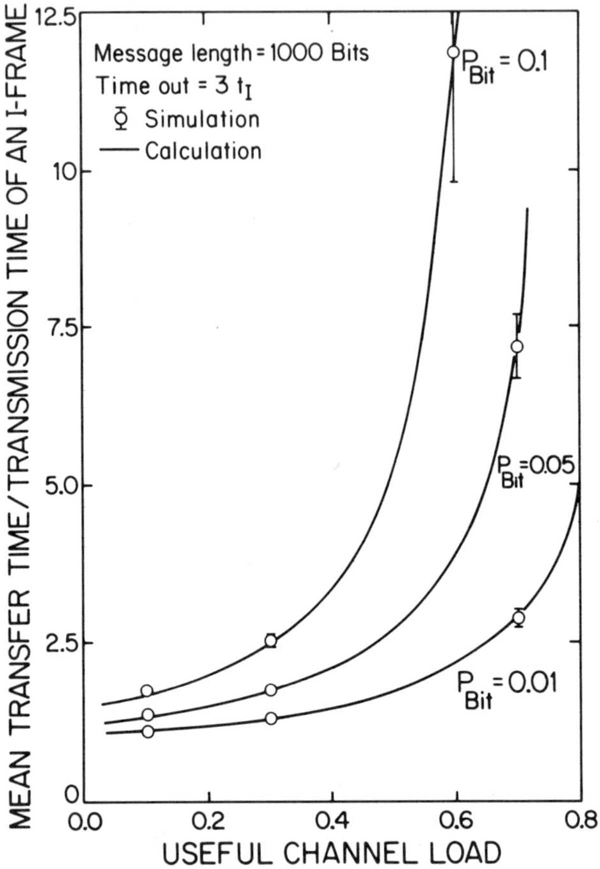

Timeout = $3t_I$.

Figure 5–34. Mean Transfer Time or Transmission Time of an I-Frame versus Throughput (Message Length = 1,000 Bits)

We hope we have given the reader a general notion of the often-used quantitative-performance measures and the approach taken in the development of performance models. From the curves presented (and the discussion included), one can reach general conclusions on the effectiveness of various protocols. We have made no effort, however, to rank protocols in terms of effectiveness, because considerations related to robustness, information required by the protocol, environment of applicability, and so forth, make such a task difficult if not impossible. Additionally, our rather liberal reference list supplies a substantial base for exploring the literature.

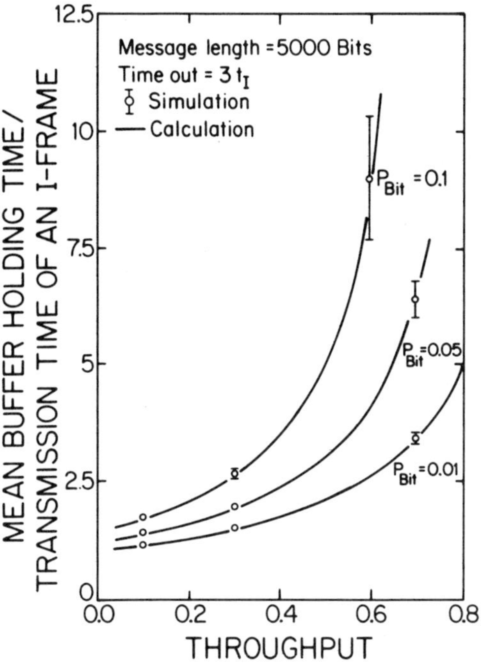

Timeout = $3t_I$.

Figure 5–35. Mean Buffer Holding Time or Transmission Time of an I-Frame versus Throughput (Message Length = 5,000 Bits)

References

1. Grubb, D.S., and Cotton, I.W. "Rating Performance." *Data Communications 1975*; also in *Computer Networks: A Tutorial*, IEEE Computer Society, 1978.
2. Christensen, G., and Franta, W.R. "Design and Analysis of the Access Protocol for HYPERchannel Networks." *Proceedings of the Third USA-Japan Computer Conference*. AFIPS, Montvale, N.J.,
3. Tobagi, F.A., Lieberson, SE.; and Kleinrock, L. "On Measurement Facilities in Packet Radio Systems." *Proceedings of the National Computer Conference, 1976*.
4. Kleinrock, L., and Naylor, W. "On Measured Behaviour of the ARPA Network." *AFIPS Conference Proceedings* 43 (May 1974):767–780.
5. Gerla, M.L.; Nelson, L.; and Kleinrock, L. "Packet Satellite Multiple Access: Models and Measurements." *Conference Record, NTC*, Los Angeles, December 1977.

6. Tobagi, F.A.; Gerla, M.; Peebles, R.W.; and Manning, E.G. "Modeling and Measurement Techniques in Packet Communication Networks. *Proceedings of the IEEE,* 66 (November 1978).
7. Shoch, J.F., and Hupp, J.A. "Performance of an Ethernet Local Network—A Preliminary Report." *Proceedings of the Local Area Communications Network Symposium.*, Boston, 7–9 May 1979.
8. Wells, W. "Front End Networking with Adaptors." *Proceedings of the University of Minnesota Local Networking Conference*, 23–24 October 1978.
9. Chlamtac, I., and Franta, W.R. "Aids to the Development of Network Simulators." *AFIPS Conference Proceedings* 48 (1979 National Computer Conference).
10. Chu, W.W. and Naylor, W.E. "Measurement and Simulation Results of C-PODA Protocol Performance." *NTC 78 Conference Record*, Birmingham, Ala., December 1978.
11. Gordon, G. *System Simulation*. Englewood Cliffs, N.J.: Prentice-Hall, 1969.
12. Kleinrock, L. *Queueing Systems, Vol. 1: Theory*. New York: Wiley, 1975.
13. Kleinrock, L. *Queueing Systems, Vol. II.: Computer Applications*. New York: Wiley Interscience, 1976.
14. Hillier, F.S., and Lieberman, G.J. *Operations Research*, 2nd ed. San Francisco: Holden-Day, 1974.
15. Kobayashi, H., and Konheim, A.G. "Queueing Models for Computer Communications System Analysis." *IEEE Transactions on Communications* COM-25 (January 1977).
16. Scholl, M.O. "Multplexing Techniques for Data Transmission over Packet Switched Radio Systems." Ph.D. dissertation, University of California at Los Angeles (Report No., UCLA-ENG-76123), December 1976.
17. Chlamtac, I. "Radio Packet Broadcasted Computer Network—The Broadcast Recognizing Access Methods." M.S. thesis, Tel Aviv University, 1976.
18. Konheim, A.G., and Meister, B. "Service in a Loop System." *JACM* 19 (January 1972):
19. Rothauser, E.H., Wild, D., "MLMA—A Collision-Free Multi-Access Method." *Proceedings of the IFIP Congress 1977*, pp. 431–436.
20. Martin, J. *Teleprocessing Network Organization*. Englewood Cliffs, N.J.: Prentice-Hall, 1970.
21. Tobagi, F.A., and Kleinrock, L. "Packet Switching in Radio Channels: Part III—Polling and (Dynamic) Split-Channel Reservation Multiple Access." *IEEE Transactions on Communications* COM-24 (August 1976): 832–845.

22. Chlamtac, I.; Franta, W.R.; and Levin, D. "BRAM: The Broadcast Recognizing Access Method." *IEEE Transactions on Communications* COM-27 (August 1979): 1183–1190.
23. Abramson, N. "The ALOHA-System—Another Alternative for Computer Communications." *AFIPS Conference Proceedings* 37 (1970):
24. Levin, K.D. "The Overlapping Problem and Performance Degradation of Mobile Digital Communication Systems." *IEEE Transactions on Communications* COM-23 (November 1975): 1342–1347.
25. Lam, S.S. "Packet Switching in Multi-Access Broadcast Channel with Application to Satellite Communication in a Computer Network." Ph.D. dissertation, University of California at Los Angeles, 1974.
26. Abramson, N. "The Throughput of Packet Broadcasting Channels." *IEEE Transactions on Communications* COM-25 (January 1977).
27. Abramson, N. "Packet Switching with Satellites." *Proceedings of the National Computer Conference*, 1973, pp. 695–702.
28. Kleinrock, L., and Tobagi, F. "Packet Switching in Radio Channels: Part I—Carrier Sense Multiple Access Modes and Their Throughput-Delay Characteristics." *IEEE Transactions on Communications* COM-23 (December 1975):1400–1416.
29. Hansen, L.W., and Schwartz, M. "An Assigned-Slot-Listen-before Transmission Protocol for a Multi-Access Data Channel." *IEEE Transactions on Communications* COM-27 (June 1979):846–857.
30. Feller, William. *An Introduction to Probability Theory and Its Applications*, Vol. I, 3rd ed. New York: Wiley, 1968.
31. Carleil, A.B., and Hellman, M.E. "Bistable Behavior of ALOHA-Type Systems." *IEEE Transactions on Communications* COM-23 (April 1975):401–410.
32. Kleinrock, L., and Lam, S. "Packet Switching in a Multi-Access Broadcast Channel: Performance Evaluation," *IEEE Transactions on Communications* COM-23 (April 1975):410–423.
33. Tobagi, F., and Kleinrock, L. "Packet Switching in Radio Channels: Part IV—Stability Considerations and Dynamic Control in Carrier Sense Multiple Access." *IEEE Transactions on Communications* COM-25 (October 1977):1103–1120.
34. Cohen, J.W. *The Single Server Queue*. New York: Wiley, 1969.
35. Franta, W.R. *The Process View of Simulation*. New York: Elsevier North-Holland, 1977.
36. Mihram, G.A. "The Modelling Process." *IEEE Transactions of Systems, Man and Cybernetics* SMC-2 (November 1972):621–629.
37. Fishman, G.S. *Principles of Discrete Event Simulation*. New York: Wiley, 1978.
38. Zeigler, B.P. *Theory of Modelling and Simulation*. New York: Wiley, 1976.

39. Franta, W.R., and Bilodeau, M. "Analysis of a Prioritized CSMA Protocol Based on Staggered Delays." *Acta Informatica* 13(1980): 299–324.
40. Schwartz, M. *Computer-Communication Network Design and Analysis*. Englewood Cliffs, N.J.: Prentice-Hall, 1977.
41. Chlamtac, I., and Franta, W.R. "A Description of the Supervisory Node Broadcast Recognizing Access Method (SUPBRAM)." TR-78-18, University of Minnesota, Department of Computer Science, August 1978.
42. Chlamtac, I., and Franta, W.R. "SUPBRAM Performance Analysis: Simple SUPBRAM and *l*-optimized SUPBRAM." TR-79-4, University of Minnesota, Department of Computer Science, February 1979.
43. Chlamtac, I., and Franta, W.R. "Generalized SUPBRAM: Protocol and Performance Analysis." TR-79-7, University of Minnesota, Department of Computer Science, April 1979.
44. Chan, T.F., and Lewis, J.Y. "Computing Standard Deviations: Accuracy." *CACM* 22 (September 1979):526–531.
45. West, D.W.D. "Updating Mean and Variance Estimates—An Improved Method." *CACM* 22 (September 1979):532–535.
46. Crane, M.A., and Iglehart, D.I. "Simulating Stable Stochastic Systems, I: General Multiserver Queues." *JACM* 21 (January 1974): 103–133.
47. Crane, M.A., and Iglehart, D.I. "Simulating Stable Stochastic Systems, II: Markov Chains." *JACM* 21 (January 1974):114–123.
48. Fishman, G.S. "Statistical Analysis for Queueing Simulations." *Management Science* 20 (1973):363–369.
49. Fishman, G.S. "Estimation in Multiserver Queueing Simulations." *Operations Research* 22 (1974):72–78.
50. Fishman, G.S. "Achieving Specific Accuracy in Simulation Output Analysis." *CACM* 20 (May 1977):310–314.
51. Coe, D.R., and Smith, W.L. *Queues*. London: Methuen, 1961.
52. Peacock, J.K.; Wong, J.W.; and Manning, E.G. "Distributed Simulation Using a Network of Processors." *Computer Networks* 3 (February 1979).
53. Peacock, J.K.; Wong, J.W.; and Manning, E.G. "A Distributed Approach to Queueing Network Simulation." *Proceedings Winter Simulation Conference*, December 1979.
54. Bryant, R,E. "Simulation of Packet Communication Architecture Computer Systems." MIT/LCS/TR-18, Massachusetts Institute of Technology Cambridge, Mass., November 1977.
55. Bryant, R.E. "Simulation on a Distributed System." *Proceedings of*

the First International Conference on Distributed Systems, October 1978.

56. Chandy, K.M.; Holmes, V.; and Misra, J. "Distributed Simulation of Networks." Technical Report 81, University of Texas at Austin, Department of Computer Science, 1979.
57. Kimbleton, S. "A Heuristic Approach to Computer Systems Performance Improvement, I:A Fast Performance Prediction Tool." *Proceedings of AFIPS 1975*, National Computer Conference 44 (1975) 839–846.
58. MacDougal, M. "Computer System Simulation: An Introduction," *Computing Surveys 2* (September 1970):191–210.
59. Brown, R.; Browne, J.; and Chandy, K. "Memory Management and Response Time." *CACM* 20 (March 1977):153–165.
60. Lasser, D. "Productivity of Multiprogrammed Computers—Progress in Developing an Analytic Prediction Method." *CACM* 12 (December 1969):678–684.
61. Schwetman, H.D. "Hybrid Simulation Models of Computer Systems." *CACM* 21 (September 1978).
62. Curtois, "Decomposability, Instabilities, and Saturation in Multiprogramming Systems." *CACM* 18 (July 1975):371–377.
63. Curtois, P.J. *Decomposability—Queueing and Computer System Applications*. New York: Academic Press, 1977.
64. Ferguson, M.J. "A Simple Upper Bound to the Delay Distribution in a 'Homogeneous' Unslotted ALOHA Network with Fixed Length Packets." ALOHA System Technical Report B76-5, March 1976.
65. Ferguson, M.J. "A Bound and Approximation of Delay Distribution for Fixed-Length Packets in an Unslotted ALOHA channel and a Comparison with Time Division Multiplexing (TDM)." *IEEE Transactions on Communications* COM-25 (January 1977):136–139.
66. Chlamtac, I., and Franta, W.R. "Message-Based Priority Access to Local Networks." *Computer Communications* 3 (1980):77–83.
67. Kleinrock, L. "Performance of Distibuted Multi-Access Computer-Communication Systems." *Proceedings of IFIP 77*, 1977.
68. Pippenger, N. "Bounds on the Performance of Protocols for a Multiple-Access Broadcast Channel." IBM Research Report, RC 7742 (#33525), IBM T.J. Watson Research Center, June 1975.
69. Farmer, W.D., and Newhall, E.E. "An Experimental Distributed Switching System to Handle Bursty Computer Traffic." *Proceedings of the ACM Symposium on Problems in the Optimization of Data Communications*, October 1969, pp. 1–33.
70. Kaye, A.R. "Analysis of a Distributed Control Loop for Data Transmission." *Symposium on Computer Communication Networks*

and Teletraffic, Polytechnic Institute of Brooklyn, April 1972, pp. 47–58.

71. Robillard, P.N. "An Analysis of a Loop Switching System with Multirank Buffers Based on the Markov Process." *IEEE Transactions on Communications* COM-22 (November 1974):1772–1778.
72. Labetoulle, J.; Manning, E.C.; and Peebles, R.W. "A Homogeneous Comuter Network: Analysis and Simulation." *Computer Networks* 1 (May 1977):225–240.
73. Pierce, J.R. "Network for Block Switches of Data." *Bell System Technical Journal* 51 (July/August 1972):1133–1145.
74. Kropfl, W.J. "An Experimental Data Block Switching System." *Bell System Technical Journal* 51 (July/August 1972):1147–1165.
75. Avi-Itzchak, B. "Heavy Traffic Characteristics of a Circular Data Network." *Bell System Technical Journal* 50 (October 1971):2521–2549.
76. Hayes, J.F., and Sherman, D.N. "Traffic Analysis of a Ring Switched Data Transmission System." *Bell System Technical Journal* 50 (November 1971):2947–2978.
77. Anderson, R.R., Hayes, J.F., and Sherman, D.N., "Simulated Performance of a Ring Switched Data Network." *IEEE Transactions on Communications* COM-20 (June 1972):576–591.
78. Spragins, J.D. "Loops Used for Data Collection." *Symposium on Computer Communications Networks and Teletraffic*, Polytechnic Institute of Brooklyn, April 1972, pp. 59–76.
79. Spragins, J.D. "Simple Derivation of Queueing Formulas for Loop Systems." *IEEE Transactions on Communications* COM-23 (April 1977):446–448.
80. Reames, C.C., and Liu, M.T. "Design and Simulation of the Distributed Loop Computer Network (DLCN)." *Proceedings of the Third Annal Symposium on Computer Architecture*, Florida, January 1976, pp. 124–129.
81. Babic, G.; Liu, M.T.; and Pardo, R. "Traffic Analysis of the Distributed Loop Computer Network (DLCN)." *Proceedings of the 1977 National Telecommunication Conference*, Los Angeles, December 1977, pp. 31:5/1–31:5/7.
82. Chlamtac, I., "Issues in Design and Measurement of Local Area Networks" Proceedings of the CMG International Conference, Boston, Mass., 1980, pp. 32–35.
83. Loomis, D.C. "Ring Communication Protocols." Technical Report No. 26, University of California, Irvine January 1973.
84. Liu, M.T.; Pardo, R.; and Babic, G. "A Performance Study of Distributed Control Loop Network." *Proceedings of the International Conference on Parallel Processing*, August 1977, pp. 137–138.

85. Penney, B.K., and Baghdadi, A.A. "Survey of Computer Communications Loop Networks: Part 1." *Computer Communications* 2 (August 1979):
86. Penney, B.K., and Baghdadi, A.A. "Survey of Computer Communications Loop Networks: Part 2." *Computer Communications* 2 (October 1979):
87. Tobagi, F., and Kleinrock, L. "Packet Switching in Radio Channels: Pat II—The Hidden Terminal Problem in Carrier Sense Multiple-Access and the Busy Tone Solution." *IEEE Transactions on Communications* COM-23 (December 1975):1417–1433.
88. Chlamtac, I., and Franta, W.R. "The Operational Performance of the Broadcast Recognizing Access Method in a Network with Hidden Nodes." *Proceedings of the ICC*, 1981.
89. Kunzelman, R.C. "Overview of the ARPA Packet Radio Experimental Network." *Proceedings of the ICC*, 1978, pp. 157–160.
90. Scott, J.D., and Sawinsky, G.K. "A New Way to Provide Telephone Services with Subscriber Radio." *ICC 1978*, pp. 451–453.
91. Stern, M., and Graziano, V. "Dyna Tac Update." *ICC 1978*, pp. 411–414.
92. Kleinrock, L., and Silvester, J. "Optimum Transmission Radii for Packet Radio Networks or Why Six is a Magic Number." *NTC 1978*, Birmingham, Ala.
93. Lam, S. "Satellite Packet Communication—Multiple Access Protocols and Performance." *IEEE Transactions on Communications* COM-27 (October 1979):
94. Borgonovo, F., and Fratta, L. "A New Technique for Satellite Broadcast Channel Communication." *Proceedings of the Fifth Data Communications Symposium*, 1977, pp. 2–1 to 2–9.
95. Traynham, K.C., and Steen, R.F. "SDLC and BSC on Satellite Links. A Performance Comparison, *ACM Computer Communications Review* 7 (October 1977):3–14.
96. Gelenbe, E.; Labetoulle, J.; and Fayolle, G. "Performance Evaluation of the Protocol HDLC." *Proceedings of the Symposium of Computer Network Protocols*, Liege, Belgium, February 1978, pp. G3.1–G3.5.
97. Easton, M.C. "Batch Throughput Efficiency of ADCCP/HDLC/SDLC Selective Reject Protocols." *IEEE Transactions on Communications* COM-28 (February 1980):187–195.
98. Kaul, A. "Performance of High-Level Data Link." *COMSAT Technical Review* 8 (Spring 1978):41–87.
99. Bux, W.; Kümerle, K.; and Truong, H.L. "Results on the Performance of Balanced HDLC Procedures." *NTC*, Birmingham, Ala., 4–6 December 1978, pp. 28.3.1–28.3.7.
100. Bux, W., and Truong, H.L. "A Queueing Model for HDLC-Controlled

Data Links." IBM Research Report, RZ954 (#33250), IBM Zurich Research Laboratory, June 1979.

101. Kahn, R.E.; Gronemeyer, S.A.; Burchfiel, J.; and Kunzelman, R.C. "Advances in Packet Radio Technology." *Proceedings of the IEEE* 66 (November 1978).
102. Tanenbaum, Andrew S. Computer Networks. Prentice-Hall, 1981.
103. Rubin, I. "Message Delays in FDMA and TDMA Communication Channels." *IEEE Transactions on Communications*, COM-27 (May 1979):769–777.
104. Fayolle, G.; Gelenbe, E.; and Labetoulle, J. "Stability and Optimal Control of the Packet Switching Broadcast Channels." *Journal of the Association Computer Machinery* 24 (July 1977):375–386.
105. Howard, R. *Dynamic Programming and Markov Processes*, Cambridge, Mass.: MIT Press, 1960.

6 Sample Components and Systems

Introduction

In previous chapters, we have examined a number of access protocols, interprocess mechanisms, and so forth, and have proposed a hierarchy of protocols applicable to local networks, all without reference to any particular systems or systems components, such as CIUs. As we have suggested earlier, a number of local networks have been realized. Many of these realizations are one-of-a-kind systems, produced by companies or university groups to meet particular needs or to examine a particular set of local-networking issues. Recently, however, a number of local-network systems and system components have become commercially available, and the number of companies producing local-network components or services is steadily increasing. Many of the offered components are designed to employ extant operating-system structures and therefore do not follow the ISO reference model [1] (just as we did not in chapters 3 and 4). For summary and comparison, a number of protocol (network) models are depicted in figure 6–1. The ISO model is depicted in figure 6–1a, the DECNET (Digital Equipment Corporation) DNA model [2] is shown in figure 6–1b, and SNA (IBM's system network architecture) [3], is shown in figure 6–1c. The notions of the X.25 protocol are depicted in figure 6–1d, and figure 6–1e depicts the relationship between SNA, ISO, and the layers of X.25.

Table 6–1 summarizes the systems and components presented in this chapter as examples. The table is not meant to provide a definitive listing of commercially available systems and components. The primary reasons for presenting the systems listed include (1) a desire to include examples of both ring and bus systems; (2) a desire to include systems federating microcomputer elements as well as those federating maxicomputers or supercomputers; and (3) author familiarity. Each example shown in table 6–1 is discussed in this chapter, and, if possible, the system is presented in an appendix to the chapter via a reprint of original reports.

Ethernet

The Ethernet System (appendix 6A) was originally developed by Xerox and presented in Metcalfe and Boggs [4]. It is designed to accommodate the

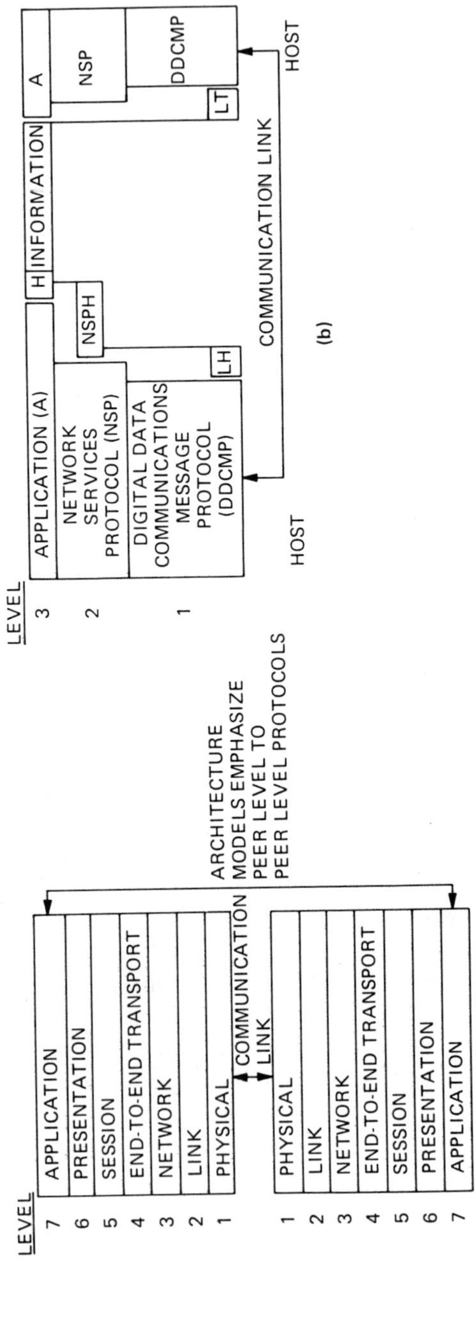
LEVEL
7 APPLICATION
6 PRESENTATION
5 SESSION
4 END-TO-END TRANSPORT
3 NETWORK
2 LINK
1 PHYSICAL
COMMUNICATION LINK
1 PHYSICAL
2 LINK
3 NETWORK
4 END-TO-END TRANSPORT
5 SESSION
6 PRESENTATION
7 APPLICATION
ARCHITECTURE MODELS EMPHASIZE PEER LEVEL TO PEER LEVEL PROTOCOLS
(a)
LEVEL
3 APPLICATION (A)
2 NETWORK SERVICES PROTOCOL (NSP)
1 DIGITAL DATA COMMUNICATIONS MESSAGE PROTOCOL (DDCMP)
HOST
H INFORMATION
NSPH
LH
LT
A
NSP
DDCMP
COMMUNICATION LINK
HOST
(b)

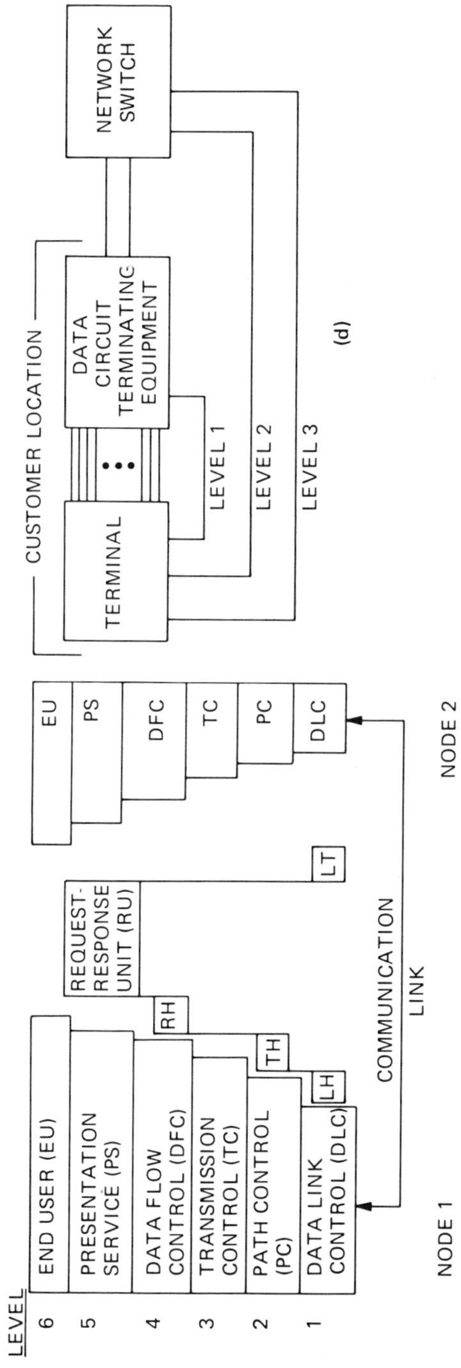
LEVEL
6
5
4
3
2
1
END USER (EU)
PRESENTATION SERVICE (PS)
DATA FLOW CONTROL (DFC)
TRANSMISSION CONTROL (TC)
PATH CONTROL (PC)
DATA LINK CONTROL (DLC)
NODE 1
LH
TH
RH
REQUEST-RESPONSE UNIT (RU)
LT
COMMUNICATION LINK
EU
PS
DFC
TC
PC
DLC
NODE 2
CUSTOMER LOCATION
TERMINAL
DATA CIRCUIT TERMINATING EQUIPMENT
NETWORK SWITCH
LEVEL 1
LEVEL 2
LEVEL 3

(c)

(d)

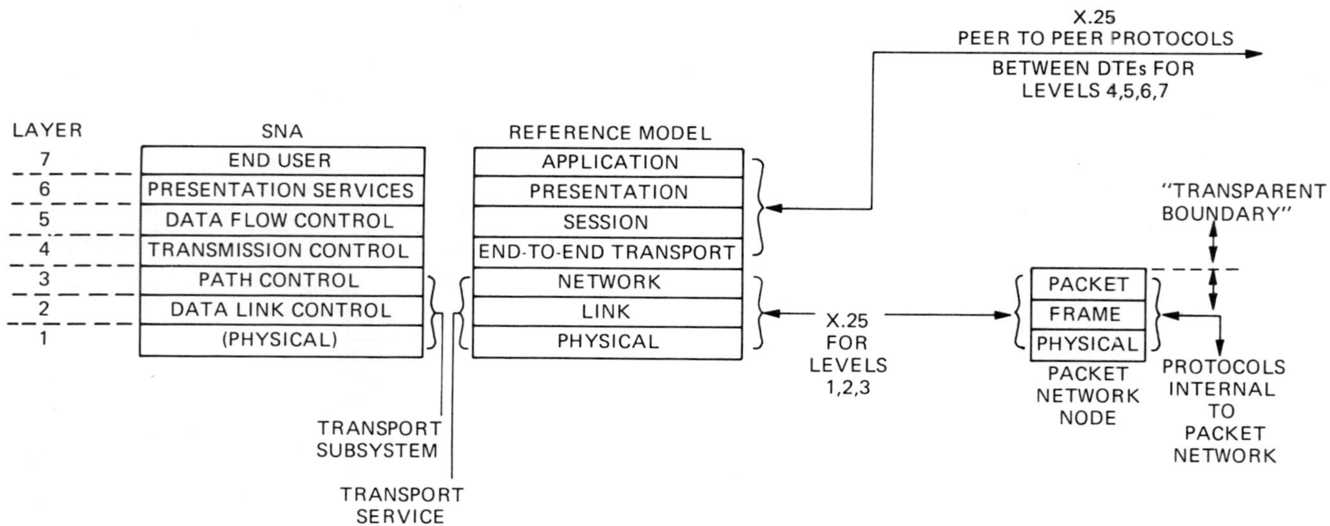

(e)

Figure 6–1. Common Protocol Models: **(a)** ISO Reference Model; **(b)** DNA; **(c)** SNA; **(d)** X.25 Concept; **(e)** SNA/ISO Reference Model-X.25 Comparison

Table 6–1
Some Commercially Available Systems and Systems Components

System or Component Name	*Supplier*	*Topology*	*Element Types*	*Medium*	*Access Protocol*	*Maximum Number of Nodes per Segment*	*Channel Speed*	*Systems or System Components*
Ethernet	Originally Xerox Corporation, now Digital, Xerox, Intel	Bus (tree)	Secondary-storage devices, graphics terminals, work stations	Cable, fiber optics	CSMA-CD	1024	1–10 Mb/s (cable)	Both
HYPERchannel	Network Systems Corporation	Bus (tree)	Minis, maxis, device controllers, microwave, etc., links	Cable, fiber optics	PSD	64 per segment	50 Mb/s (cable)	Components
LCN (Loosely Coupled Network)	Control Data	Bus	Minis, maxis, super computers	Cable	Rotating priorities (has elements of both BRAM and PSD)	32 per segment	50 Mb/s	Components
RINGNET	Prime Computer Corporation	Ring	Minis	Cable, fiber optics	Token passing	255	$\leq$ 10 Mb/s	Systems
Cambridge Ring	Cambridge University Computer Laboratory	Ring	Microcomputers	Cable	Packet train	—	10 Mb/s	
PERQ-net	Three Rivers Company	Bus	Micros	Cable	Nonpersistent CSMA	64	10 Mb/s	Systems
CHIMPNET: Network Testbed	Honeywell Corporate Technology Center	Arbitrary, including bus, ring, etc.	Minis, micros	Cable	Arbitrary, including token passing, CSMA, CSMA-CD etc.	Arbitrary, but realistically $\leq$ 20	1–10 Mb/s	Components

automated office environment and federate a collection of work stations [5], hardcopy devices, and shared secondary storage. In late 1980, Digital Equipment Corporation, Intel Corporation, and Xerox banded together to define and market Ethernet products and services, including an Ethernet CIU on a chip. As part of the activity, the companies have jointly produced a specification of the Ethernet system up through the link-level protocol layer. The specification is a candidate for the IEEE Standard (see chapter 3), and Hewlett-Packard Company (HP) has announced [6] that it will adapt the Ethernet specification for its own products, a move made as a result of HP's realization of the benefits of a standard [7]. Although the final specification of Ethernet may differ from version 1.0, available at the time of publication of this book we offer it a an example of a very complete specification through the link level (including flowcharts and Pascal code), as an explanation of Ethernet, and as a strong contender for the standard. In addition to the material given in appendix 6A, performance data can be found in [18], and practical design considerations are given in [17].

HYPERchannel

HYPERchannel CIUs are offered by Network Systems Corporation, Minneapolis, Minnesota. This company was among the first to offer local network CIUs and remains among the few that offer CIUs at transmission rates attractive for the interconnection of supercomputers. In Network Systems Corporation terminology, a CIU is known as an *adapter* and a shared cable channel is known as a *trunk*. The material presented in appendix 6B is taken from an eleven-section document [8].

Loosely Coupled Network

The Control Data Loosely Coupled Network (LCN) Bus Interface Unit (BIU) has not yet appeared in the marketplace. It has much of the flavor of the network-systems offering (50 Mb/s, up to four channels per BIU, and so on) but differs in a number of ways. A block diagram of the BIU is shown in chapter 2.)

A full description of the LCN [10] is given in appendix 6C.

Ringnet

Ringnet [11] is a commercially available 8MHz packet-switched communication system designed to connect hosts in the same building, usually less than several hundred feet apart, although it can also be used for loosely coupled multiprocessor systems. Control of the network is completely decentralized and depends only on a circulating token for arbitration of the communication medium. Appendix 6D describes the hardware and software architecture of the network and discusses some of the design principles used in its implementation.

Cambridge Ring

The Cambridge ring [12,13,37] is not a commercially available product. It is interesting in that it was designed to realize a conventional time-sharing system using microcomputers. In essence, the system is intended to support the application given in the section entitled "The Cambridge Model Distributed System" in chapter 2. To complete the presentation begun in chapter 2, we offer additional material in appendices 6E and 6F.

The appendixes discuss the implementation of means whereby a user can log in to the system and be allocated the use of a computer. The implementation is achieved partly by software in the VDU concentrator and partly by the program known as the Resource Manager, which runs in a computer of its own.

PERQ

The term PERQ refers to a sophisticated personal computer or work station that has microcode and software that allows it to serve as a CIU for network interaction (except for the cable tap and serialization or deserialization functions that are part of the tap hardware). A PERQ supports Pascal, a virtual-storage operating system, and software tools for microcode development. See appendix 6G for a full description of the PERQ system.

CHIMPNET: A Networking Testbed

CHIMPNET [14] is a testbed system. It is an inexpensive, flexible interconnection of microprocessors to support experiments with distributed systems, including studies of distributed-database management systems using various interconnection topologies and access protocols. Appendix 6H presents system hardware and software features, including interface hardware and experiment-control mechanisms.

Table 6–2
Other Available Systems and Components

System or Component Name	*Supplier*	*Topology*	*Element Types*	*Medium*	*Access Protocol*	*Maximum Number of Nodes*	*Channel Speed*	*System or Components Supplied*
Z-NET	Zilog, Inc.	Bus	Microprocessor	Cable	Ethernet	255	800 kbps	Both
NET/ONE	Ungerman-Bass, Inc.		RS-232 serial or 8-bit parallel compatible devices	Cable	Nonpersistent CSMA	200 per segment, ≤ 4 devices per node	4–8 Mb/s	Components and software
System 20 (local net)	Network Resources Corporation	Bus	Terminals, RS-232C compatible devices	Cable	CSMA/CD and frequency-division multiplexing to provide 120 channels	120 channels, 200 nodes per channel	9600 b/s per channel	Components and software
Hyperbus	Network Systems Corporation	Bus	R2232C and RS366 compatible devices, minis	Cable	PSD	≤ 500	1–10 Mb/s	Components and software
Litton Adaptive Transfer Modular Network	Litton Industries	Ring	Minis (UYK family), peripherals (real-time control)	Fiber optics	Token passing	192	20 Mb/s	Components
Spectrum	Foxboro Company	Bus	Controllers, consoles, etc. for real-time control	Cable	—	100 per segment (including clusters)	1 Mb/s	Components
Cluster/One	Nestar Systems, Inc.	Bus, tree star	Microcomputers, e.g., Apple II	Cable	—	64	—	Components and software

Other Systems and Components

Table 6–2 lists the characteristics of other commercially available systems. Certainly there are still others, including the commercially available versions of the Honeywell HXDP system [15] and the Univac Shinpads system [16]. Additionally, a number of testbed systems are under development. As a consequence of the ever-widening use of these systems and components, it is only natural to want to interconnect networks, and interconnection is the subject of our final chapter.

Appendix 6A: The Ethernet

A Local Area Network: Data Link Layer and Physical Layer Specifications

Important Information and Disclaimers

1. This specification includes subject matter relating to a patent(s) of Xerox Corporation. No license under such patent(s) is granted by implication, estoppel or otherwise as a result of publication of this specification. Applicable licenses may be obtained from Xerox Corporation.
2. This specification is furnished for informational purposes only. Digital, Xerox, and Intel do not warrant or represent that this specification or any products made in conformance with it will work in the intended manner, nor do they assume responsibility for any errors that it may contain or have any liabilities or obligations for damages, including but not limited to special, indirect or consequential damages arising out of or in connection with the use of this specification in any way. This specification shall not necessarily apply to any product that may be developed by Digital, Xerox, or Intel. Any such products that may be developed shall be sold under the then current terms and conditions of sale.

Preface

This document contains the specification of the Ethernet, a local area network developed jointly by Digital Equipment Corporation, Intel Corporation, and Xerox Corporation. The Ethernet specification arises from an extensive collaborative effort of the three corporations, and several years of work at Xerox on an earlier prototype Ethernet.

This specification is intended as a design reference document, rather than an introduction or tutorial. Readers seeking introductory material are directed to the reference list in Section 2, which cites several papers describing the intent, theory, and history of the Ethernet.

Digital Equipment Corporation, Intel Corporation, Xerox Corporation, "The Ethernet: A Local Area Network: Data Link Layer and Physical Layer Specifications," Version 1.0, September 30, 1980. Reprinted with Permission.

This document contains 7 sections, falling into three main groups:

Sections 1, 2, and 3 provide an overall description of the Ethernet, including its goals, and the scope of the specification.

Sections 4 and 5 describe the architectural structure of the Ethernet in terms of a functional model consisting of two layers, the Data Link Layer and the Physical Layer.

Sections 6 and 7 specify the two layers in detail, providing the primary technical specification of the Ethernet.

Readers wishing to obtain an initial grasp of the organization and content of the specification will be best served by reading Sections 1, 3, and 4. Readers involved in actual implementation of the Ethernet will find Sections 5, 6, and 7 to contain the central material of the specification. Section 2 provides references, and the appendices provide supplementary material.

The approach taken in the specification of the Data Link Layer in Section 6 is a procedural one; in addition to describing the necessary algorithms in English and control flow charts, the specification presents these algorithms in the language Pascal, [21]. This approach makes clear the required behavior of Data Link Layer, while leaving individual implementations free to exploit any appropriate technology.

Because the procedural approach is not suitable for specifying the details of the Physical Layer, Section 7 uses carefully worded English prose and numerous figures and tables to specify the necessary parameters of this layer.

Some aspects of the Ethernet are necessarily discussed in more than one place in this specification. Whenever any doubt arises concerning the official definition in such a case, the reader should utilize the Pascal procedural specification of the Data Link Layer in Section 6.5, and the detailed prose specification of the Physical Layer in Sections 7.2 through 7.9.

One aspect of an overall network architecture which is not addressed by this specification is network management. The network management facility performs operation, maintenance, and planning functions for the network:

Operation functions include parameter setting, such as address selection.

Maintenance functions provide for fault detection, isolation, and repair.

Planning functions include collection of statistical and usage information, necessary for planned network growth.

While network management itself is properly performed outside the Ethernet Data Link and Physical Layers, it requires appropriate additional interfaces to those layers, which will be defined in a subsequent version of this specification.

1. Introduction

The Ethernet local area network provides a communication facility for high speed data exchange among computers and other digital devices located within a moderate-sized geographic area. Its primary characteristics include:

Physical Layer:

Data rate: 10 Million bits/sec

Maximum station separation: 2.5 Kilometers

Maximum number of stations: 1024

Medium: Shielded coaxial cable, base-band signalling

Topology: Branching non-rooted tree

Data Link Layer:

Link control procedure: Fully distributed peer protocol, with statistical contention resolution (CSMA/CD)

Message protocol: Variable size frames, "best-effort" delivery

The Ethernet, like other local area networks, falls in a middle ground between long distance, low speed networks which carry data for hundreds or thousands of kilometers, and specialized, very high speed interconnections which are generally limited to tens of meters. The Ethernet is intended primarily for use in such areas as office automation, distributed data processing, terminal access, and other situations requiring economical connection to a local communication medium carrying bursty traffic at high peak data rates. Use in situations demanding resistance to hostile environments, real-time response guarantees, and so on, while not specifically excluded, do not constitute the primary environment for which the Ethernet is designed.

The precursor to the Ethernet specified in this document was the "Experimental Ethernet," designed and implemented by Xerox in 1975, and used continually since that time by thousands of stations. The Ethernet defined here builds on that experience, and on the larger base of the combined experience of Digital, Intel, and Xerox in many forms of networking and computer interconnection.

In specifying the Ethernet, this document provides detailed definitions of the lowest two layers of an overall network architecture. It thus defines what is generally referred to as a *link-level* facility. It does not specify the higher level protocols needed to provide a complete network architecture. Such higher level protocols would generally include such functions as internetwork communication, error recovery, flow control, security measures (e.g. encryption), and other higher level functions that increase the power of the communication facility and/or tailor it to specific applications. In particular, it should be noted that all error recovery functions have been relegated to higher level protocols, in keeping with the low error rates that characterize local networks.

One of the main objectives of this specification is *compatability*. As stated in Section 3, it is intended that *every implementation of the Ethernet be able to exchange data with every other implementation*. It should be noted that higher level protocols raise their own issues of compatability over and above those addressed by the Ethernet and other link-level facilities. This does not eliminate the importance of link-level compatibility, however. While the compatibility provided by the Ethernet does not guarantee solutions to higher level compatibility problems, it does provide a context within which such problems can be addressed, by avoiding low level incompatibilities that would make direct communication impossible.

2. References

[The original report contained references here. They are collected in the references for the chapter.]

3. Goals and Non-Goals

This section states the assumptions underlying the design of the Ethernet.

3.1 Goals

The goals of the Ethernet design are:

Simplicity: Features which would complicate the design without substantially contributing to the meeting of the other goals have been excluded.

Low cost: Since technological improvements will continue to reduce the overall cost of stations wishing to connect to the Ethernet, the cost of the connection itself should be minimized.

Compatibility: All implementations of the Ethernet should be capable of exchanging data at the data link level. For this reason, the specification avoids optional features, to eliminate the possibility of incompatible variants of the Ethernet.

Addressing flexibility: The addressing mechanisms should provide the capability to target frames to a single node, a group of nodes, or to all nodes on the network.

Fairness: All nodes should have equal access to the network when averaged over time.

Progress: No single node operating in accordance with the protocol should be able to prevent the progress of other nodes.

High speed: The network should operate efficiently at a data rate of 10 Megabits per second.

Low delay: At any given level of offered traffic, the network should introduce as little delay as possible in the transfer of a frame.

Stability: The network should be stable under all load conditions, in the sense that the delivered traffic should be a monotonically non-decreasing function of the total offered traffic.

Maintainability: The Ethernet design should allow for network maintenance, operation, and planning.

Layered Architecture: The Ethernet design should be specified in layered terms to separate the logical aspects of the data link protocol from the physical details of the communication medium.

3.2 Non-Goals

The following are *not* goals of the Ethernet design:

Full duplex: At any given instant, the Ethernet can transfer data from one source station to one or more destination stations. Bi-directional communication is provided by rapid exchange of frames, rather than full duplex operation.

Error control: Error handling at the data link level is limited to detection of bit errors in the physical channel, and the detection and recovery from collisions. Provision of a complete error control facility to handle detected errors is relegated to higher layers of the network architecture.

Security: The data link protocol does not employ encryption or other mechanisms to provide security. Higher layers of the network architecture may provide such facilities as appropriate.

Speed flexibility: This specification defines a physical channel operating at a single fixed data rate of 10 Megabits per second.

Priority: The data link protocol provides no support of priority station operation.

Hostile user: There is no attempt to protect the network from a malicious user at the data link level.

4. Functional Model of the Ethernet Architecture

There are two important ways to view the Ethernet design, corresponding to:

Architecture, emphasizing the logical divisions of the system, and how they fit together.

Implementation, emphasizing the actual components, and their packaging and interconnection.

Figure 6A–1 illustrates these two views as they apply to a typical implementation, showing how each view groups the various functions.

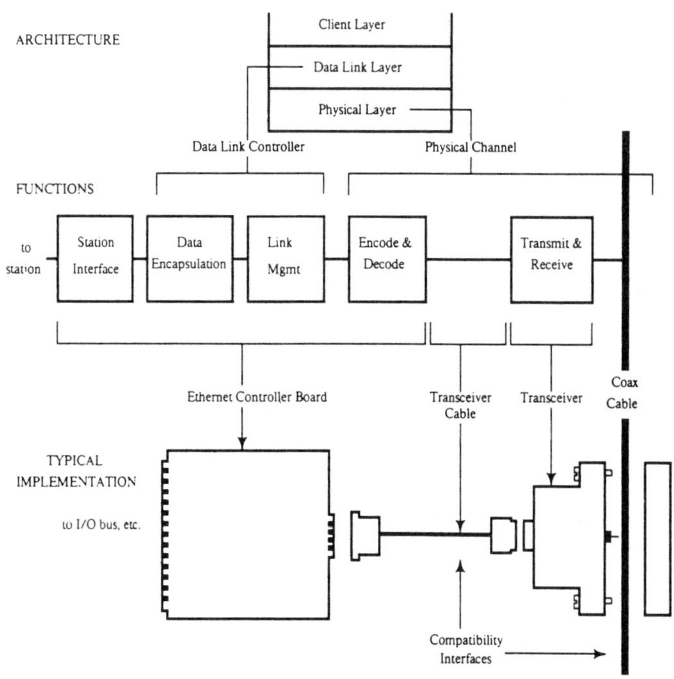

Figure 6A–1. Ethernet Architecture and Typical Implementation

This document is organized along *architectural* lines, emphasizing the large-scale separation of the Ethernet system into two parts: the *Data Link Layer* and the *Physical Layer*. These layers are intended to correspond closely to the lowest layers of the ISO Model for Open Systems Interconnection [1,19]. Architectural organization of the specification has two main advantages:

Clarity: A clean overall division of the design along architectural lines makes the specification clearer.

Flexibility: Segregation of medium-dependent aspects in the Physical Layer allows the Data Link Layer to apply to transmission media other than the specified coaxial cable.

As is evident in figure 6A–1, the architectural model is based on a set of interfaces different from those emphasized in the implementations. One crucial aspect of the design, however, must be addressed largely in terms of the implementation interaces: *compatibility*. Two important compatibility interfaces are defined within what is architecturally the Physical Layer:

Coaxial cable interface: To communicate via the Ethernet, all stations must adhere rigidly to the exact specification of coaxial cable signals defined in this document, and to the procedures which define correct behavior of a station. The medium-independent aspects of the Data Link Layer should not be taken as detracting from this point: *communication via the Ethernet requires complete compatability at the coaxial cable interface.*

Transceiver cable interface: It is anticipated that most stations will be located some distance away from their connection to the coaxial cable. While it is necessary to place a small amount of circuitry (the *transceiver*) directly adjacent to the coaxial cable, the majority of the electronics (the *controller*) can and should be placed with the station. Since it is desirable for the same transceiver to be usable with a wide variety of stations, a second compatibility interface, the *transceiver cable interface*, is defined. While conformance with this interface is not strictly necessary to insure communication, it is highly recommended, since it allows maximum flexibility in intermixing transceivers and stations.

4.1 Layering

The major division in the Ethernet Architecture is between the Physical Layer and the Data Link Layer, corresponding to the lowest two levels in the

ISO model. The higher levels of the overall network architecture, which use the Data Link Layer, will be collectively referred to in this document as the "Client Layer" since, strictly speaking, the identity and function of higher level facilities are outside the scope of this specification. The intent, however, is that the Ethernet Physical and Data Link Layers support the higher layers of the ISO model (Network Layer, Transport Layer, etc.).

The overall structure of the layered architecture is shown in figure 6A–2. In the architectural model used here, the layers interact via well defined interfaces.

> The interface between the Client Layer and the Data Link Layer includes facilities for transmitting and receiving frames, and provides per-operation status information for use by higher-level error recovery procedures.

> The interface between the Data Link Layer and the Physical Layer includes signals for framing (carrier sense, transmit initiation) and contention resolution (collision detect), facilities for passing a pair of serial bit streams (transmit, receive) between the two layers, and a wait function for timing.

These interfaces are described more precisely in Section 5.

As mentioned in the preface, additional interfaces are necessary to allow a higher level network management facility to interact with the Data Link

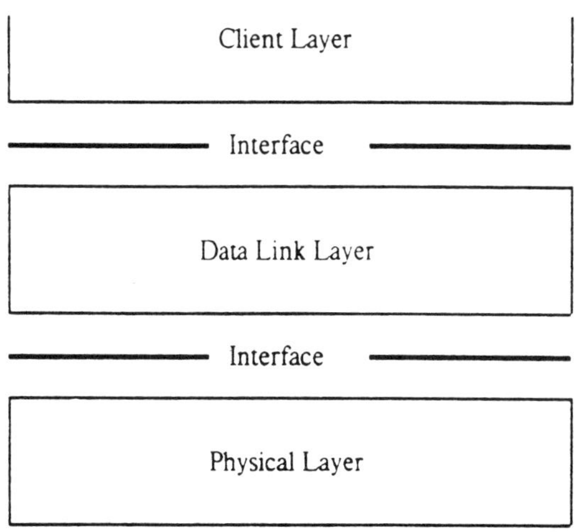

Figure 6A–2. Architectural Layering

Layer and Physical Layer to perform operation, maintenance and planning functions.

4.2 *Data Link Layer*

The Data Link Layer defines a medium-independent link level communication facility, built on the medium-dependent physical channel provided by the Physical Layer. It is applicable to a general class of local area broadcast media suitable for use with the channel access discipline known as carrier-sense multiple-access with collision-detection (CSMA-CD). Compatibility with non-contention media (e.g., switched lines, token-passing rings, etc.), while a worthwhile topic for further research, is not addressed in this specification.

The Data Link Layer specified here is intended to be as similar as possible to that described in the ISO model. In a broadcast network like the Ethernet, the notion of a data link between two network entities does not correspond directly to a distinct physical connection. Nevertheless, the two main functions generally associated with a data link control procedure are present:

Data encapsulation

—framing (frame boundary delimitation)

—addressing (handling of source and destination addresses)

—error detection (detection of physical channel transmission errors)

Link management

—channel allocation (collision avoidance)

—contention resolution (collision handling)

This split is reflected in the division of the Data Link Layer into the Data Encapsulation sub-layer and the Link Management sub-layer, as shown in figure 6A–3.

In terms of the ISO model, the Ethernet Data Link Layer provides a multi-endpoint connection between higher-layer entities wishing to communicate. The connection provided is called a *data link*, and is implemented between two or more Data Link Layer entities called *data link controllers* via a Physical Layer connection called the *physical channel*.

4.3 *Physical Layer*

The Physical Layer specified in this document provides a 10 MBit/sec physical channel through a coaxial cable medium. Because one purpose of

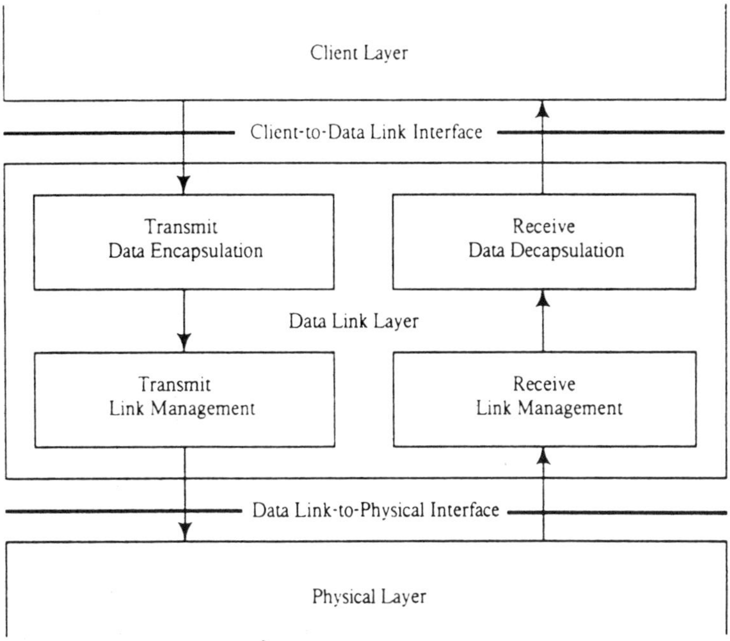

Figure 6A–3. Data Link Layer Functions

the layered architecture is to insulate the Data Link Layer from the medium-specific aspects of the channel, the Physical Layer completely specifies the essential physical characteristics of the Ethernet, such as data encoding, timing, voltage levels, etc. Implementation details are left unspecified, to retain maximum flexibility for the implementor. In all cases, the criterion applied in distinguishing between essential characteristics and implementation details is *guaranteed compatibility*: any two correct implementations of the Physical Layer specified here will be capable of exchanging data over the coaxial cable, enabling communication between their respective stations at the Data Link Layer.

The Physical Layer defined in this specification performs two main functions generally associated with physical channel control:

Data encoding

—preamble generation/removal (for synchronization)

—bit encoding/decoding (between binary and phase-encoded form)

Channel access

—bit transmission/reception (of encoded data)

—carrier sense (indicating traffic on the channel)

—collision detection (indicating contention on the channel)

This split is reflected in the division of the Physical Layer into the Data Encoding sub-layer and the Channel Access sub-layer, as shown in figure 6A–4.

4.4 Ethernet Operation and the Functional Model

This section provides an overview of frame transmission and reception in terms of the functional model of the architecture. This overview is descriptive, rather than definitional; the formal specifications of the operations described here are given in Sections 6 and 7.

4.4.1 Transmission Without Contention. When the Client Layer requests the transmission of a frame, the Transmit Data Encapsulation component of the Data Link Layer constructs the frame from the client-supplied data and appends a frame check sequence to provide for error detection. The frame is then handed to the Transmit Link Management component for transmission.

Transmit Link Management attempts to avoid contention with other traffic on the channel by monitoring the *carrier sense* signal and *deferring* to passing traffic. When the channel is clear, frame transmission is initiated

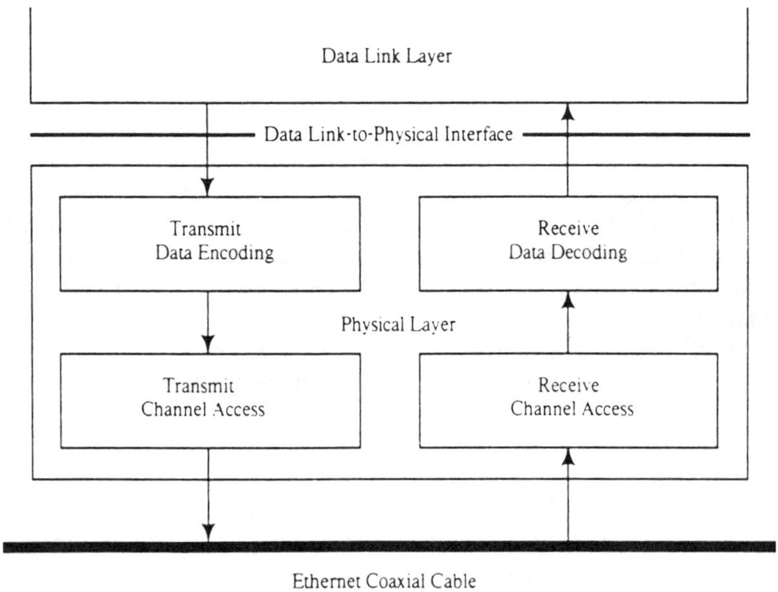

Figure 6A–4. Physical Layer Functions

(after a brief interframe delay to provide recovery time for other data link controllers and for the physical channel). The Data Link Layer then provides a serial stream of bits to the Physical Layer for transmission.

The Data Encoding component of the Physical Layer, before sending the actual bits of the frame, sends an encoded preamble to allow the receivers and repeaters along the channel to synchronize their clocks and other circuitry. It then begins translating the bits of the frame into encoded form and passes them to the Channel Access component for actual transmission over the medium.

The Channel Access component performs the task of actually generating the electrical signals on the medium which represent the bits of the frame. Simultaneously, it monitors the medium and generates the *collision detect* signal, which, in the contention-free case under discussion, remains off for the duration of the frame.

When transmission has completed without contention, the Data Link Layer so informs the Client Layer and awaits the next request for frame transmission.

4.4.2 Reception Without Contention. At the receiving station, the arrival of a frame is first detected by the Receive Channel Access component of the Physical Layer, which responds by synchronizing with the incoming preamble, and by turning on the carrier sense signal. As the encoded bits arrive from the medium, they are passed to the Receive Data Decoding component.

Receive Data Decoding translates the encoded signal back into binary data and discards the leading bits, up to and including the end of the preamble. It then passes subsequent bits up to the Data Link Layer.

Meanwhile, the Receive Link Management component of the Data Link Layer, having seen carrier sense go on, has been waiting for the incoming bits to be delivered. Receive Link Management collects bits from the Physical Layer as long as the carrier sense signal remains on. When the carrier sense signal goes off, the frame is passed to Receive Data Decapsulation for processing.

Receive Data Decapsulation checks the frame's destination address field to decide whether the frame should be received by this station. If so, it passes the contents of the frame to the Client Layer along with an appropriate status code The status code is generated by inspecting the frame check sequence to detect any damage to the frame enroute, and by checking for proper octet-boundary alignment of the end of the frame.

4.4.3 Collisions: Handling of Contention. If multiple stations attempt to transmit at the same time, it is possible for their transmitting data link controllers to interfere with each others' transmissions, in spite of their attempts to avoid this by deferring. When two stations' transmissions overlap, the resulting contention is called a *collision*. A given station can experience a collision during the initial part of its transmission (the "collision window"), before its transmitted signal has had time to propagate to all parts of the Ethernet channel. Once the collision window has passed, the station is said to have *acquired* the channel; subsequent collisions are avoided, since all other (properly functioning) stations can be assumed to have noticed the signal (via carrier sense) and to be deferring to it. The time to acquire the channel is thus based on the *round-trip propagation time* of the physical channel.

In the event of a collision, the Transmit Channel Access component of a transmitting station's Physical Layer first notices the interference on the channel and turns on the collision detect signal. This is noticed in turn by the Transmit Link Management component of the Data Link Layer, and collision handling begins. First, Transmit Link Management *enforces* the collision by transmitting a bit sequence called the *jam*. This insures that the duration of the collision is sufficient to be noticed by the other transmitting station(s) involved in the collision. After the jam is sent, Transmit Link Management terminates the transmission and schedules a retransmission attempt for a randomly selected time in the near future. Retransmission is attempted repeatedly in the face of repeated collisions. Since repeated collisions indicate a busy channel, however, Transmit Link Management attempts to adjust to the channel load by *backing off* (voluntarily delaying its own retransmissions to reduce its load on the channel). This is accomplished by expanding the interval from which the random retransmission time is selected on each retransmission attempt. Eventually, either the transmission succeeds, or the attempt is abandoned on the assumption that the channel has failed or has become overloaded.

At the receiving end, the bits resulting from a collision are received and decoded by the Physical Layer just as are the bits of a valid frame. In particular, collisions do *not* turn on the receiving station's collision detect signal, which is generated only during transmission. Instead, the fragmentary frames received during collisions are distinguished from valid frames by the Data Link's Receive Link Management component, by noting that a collision fragment is always smaller than the shortest valid frame. Such fragments are discarded by Receive Link Management.

5. Inter-Layer Interfaces

The purpose of this section is to provide precise definitions of the interfaces between the architectural layers defined in Section 4. In order to provide such a definition, some precise notation must be adopted. The notation used here is the Pascal language, in keeping with the procedural nature of the formal Data Link Layer specification (see 6.5). Each interface is thus described as a set of procedures and/or shared variables which collectively provide the only valid interactions between layers. The accompanying text describes the meaning of each procedure or variable and points out any implicit interactions among them.

Note that the description of the interfaces in Pascal is a notational technique, and in no way implies that they can or should be implemented in software. This point is discussed more fully in 6.5, which provides complete Pascal declarations for the data types used in the remainder of this section. Note also that the "synchronous" (one frame at a time) nature of the frame transmission and reception operations is a property of the architectural interface between the Client Layer and the Data Link Layer, and need not be reflected in the implementation interface between a station and its controller.

5.1 Client Layer to Data Link Layer

The two primary services provided to the Client Layer by the Data Link Layer are transmission and reception of frames. The interface through which the Client Layer uses the facilities of the Data Link Layer therefore consists of a pair of functions.

Functions:
TransmitFrame
Receive Frame

Each of these functions has the components of a frame as its parameters (input or output), and returns a status code as its result.

The Client Layer transmits a frame by invoking *TransmitFrame:*

```
function TransmitFrame (
    destinationParam: AddressValue;
    sourceParam: AddressValue;
    typeParam: TypeValue;
    dataParam: DataValue): TransmitStatus;
```

The *TransmitFrame* operation is synchronous, in the sense that its duration is the entire attempt to transmit the frame, so that when the operation completes, transmission has either succeeded or failed, as indicated by the resulting status code:

```
type TransmitStatus = (transmitOK, excessive CollisionError);
```

Successful transmission is indicated by the status code *transmitOK*; the code *excessiveCollisionError* indicates that the transmission attempt was aborted due to excessive collisions, because of heavy traffic or a network failure. Implementations may define additional implementation-dependent status codes if necessary.

The Client Layer accepts incoming frames by invoking *ReceiveFrame*:

```
function ReceiveFrame (
    var destinationParam: AddressValue;
    var sourceParam: AddressValue;
    var typeParam: TypeValue;
    var dataParam: DataValue): ReceiveStatus;
```

The *ReceiveFrame* operation is synchronous, in the sense that the operation does not complete until a frame has been received. The fields of the frame are delivered via the output parameters, along with a status code:

```
type ReceiveStatus = (receiveOK, frameCheckError, alignmentError);
```

Successful reception is indicated by the status code *receiveOK*. The code *frameCheckError* indicates that the frame received was damaged by a transmission error in the physical channel. The code *alignmentError* indicates that the frame received was damaged, and that in addition, its length was not an integral number of octets. Implementation may define additional implementation-dependent status codes if necessary.

5.2 Data Link Layer to Physical Layer

The interface through which the Data Link Layer uses the facilities of the Physical Layer consists of a function, a pair of procedures and three Boolean variables.

Function:	Variables:
ReceiveBit	*collisionDetect*
Procedures:	*carrierSense*
TransmitBit	*transmitting*
Wait	

During transmission, the contents of an outgoing frame are passed from the Data Link Layer to the Physical Layer via repeated use of the *TransmitBit* operation:

```
procedure TransmitBit (bitParam: Bit);
```

Each invocation of *TransmitBit* passes one new bit of the outgoing frame to the Physical Layer. The *TransmitBit* operation is synchronous, in the sense that the duration of the operation is the entire transmission of the bit, so that when the operation completes, the Physical Layer is ready to accept the next bit immediately. (Note: this does not imply that all invocations of *TransmitBit* are of exactly equal duration; for example, if the Physical Layer must perform some initial processing—e.g., preamble generation—before transmitting the first bit of a frame, the first invocation of *TransmitBit* may take significantly longer.)

The overall event of data being transmitted is signaled to the Physical Layer via the variable *transmitting*:

var transmitting: Boolean;

Before sending the first bit of a frame, the Data Link Layer sets *transmitting* to *true*, to inform the Physical Link that a stream of bits will be presented via the *TransmitBit* operation. After the last bit of the frame has been presented, the Data Link Layer sets *transmitting* to *false* to indicate the end of the frame.

The presence of a collision in the physical channel is signaled to the Data Link Layer via the variable *collisionDetect*:

var collisionDetect: Boolean;

The *collisionDetect* signal remains *true* during the duration of the collision. (Note: Since an entire collision may occur during the first invocation of *TransmitBit*—e.g., during preamble removal—the Data Link Layer must handle this possibility by monitoring *collisionDetect* concurrently with its transmission of outgoing bits. See 6.5 for details.)

The *collisionDetect* signal is generated only during transmission and is never *true* at any other time; in particular, it cannot be used during frame reception to detect collisions between overlapping transmissions from two or more other stations.

During reception, the contents of an incoming frame are retrieved from the Physical Layer by the Data Link Layer via repeated use of the *ReceiveBit* operation:

function ReceiveBit: Bit;

Each invocation of *ReceiveBit* retrieves one new bit of the incoming frame (i.e., not including any preamble bits) from the Physical Layer. The *ReceiveBit* operation is synchronous, in the sense that its duration is the entire reception of a single bit. (As with *TransmitBit*, the first invocation of

ReceiveBit make take significantly longer—e.g., due to preamble removal). Upon receiving a bit, the Data Link Layer must immediately request the next bit until all bits of the frame have been received. (See 6.5 for details.)

The overall event of data being received is signaled to the Data Link Layer via the variable *carrierSense*:

```
var carrierSense: Boolean;
```

When the Physical Layer sets *carrierSense* to *true*, the Data Link Layer must immediately begin retrieving the incoming bits via the *ReceiveBit* operation. When *carrierSense* subsequently becomes *false*, the Data Link Layer can begin processing the received bits as a completed frame. Note that the *true/false* transitions of *carrierSense* are not defined to be precisely synchronized wit the beginning and end of the frame, but may precede the beginning and lag the end, respectively. If an invocation of *ReceiveBit* is pending when *carrierSense* becomes *false*, *ReceiveBit* returns an undefined value, which should be discarded by the Data Link Layer. (See 6.5 for details.)

The Data Link Layer must also monitor the value of *carrierSense* to defer its own transmissions when the channel is busy.

The Physical Layer also provides the procedure *Wait*:

```
procedure Wait (bitTimes: integer);
```

This procedure waits for the specified number of bit times. This allows the Data Link Layer to measure time intervals in units of the (physical-channel-dependent) bit time.

Another important property of the Physical Layer which is an implicit part of the interface presented to the Data Link Layer is the *round-trip propagation time* of the physical channel. This figure represents the maximum time required for a signal to propagate from one end of the network to the other, and for a collision to propagate back. The round-trip propagation is primarily (but not entirely) a function of the physical size of the network. The round-trip propagation time of the Physical Layer is defined to be at most 450 bit times (see 7.1.2).

6. Ethernet Data Link Layer Specification

6.1 Data Link Layer Overview and Model

As defined in Section 4, the Ethernet Architecture consists of the Data Link Layer, and below it, the Physical Layer. Furthermore, the Data Link Layer is divided into two sub-layers (see figure 6A–3).

Data encapsulation

—framing

—addressing

—error detection

Link management

—channel allocation

—contention resolution

This model is used throughout this section to structure the detailed specification of the Data Link Layer. An English description of the Data Link Layer is given in 6.2–6.4. A more precise algorithmic definition is given in 6.5, which provides a procedural model for the Data Link Layer in the form of a program in the language Pascal. Note that whenever there is any apparent ambiguity concerning the definition of some aspect of the Data Link Layer, it is the Pascal procedural specification in 6.5 which should be consulted for the definitive statement.

6.2 Frame Format

The data encapsulation function of the Data Link Layer comprises the construction and processing of frames. The subfunctions of framing, addressing, and error detection are reflected in the frame format as follows:

Framing: No explicit framing information is needed, since the necessary framing cues (*carrierSense* and *transmitting*) are present in the interface to the Physical Layer.

Addressing: Two address fields are provided to identify the source and destination stations for the frame.

Error detection: A Frame Check Sequence field is provided for detection of transmission errors.

Figure 6A–5 shows the five fields of a frame: the addresses of the frame's source and destination, a type field for use by higher layers (see 6.2.2), a data field containing the transmitted data, and the frame check sequence field containing a cyclic redundancy check value to detect transmission errors. Of these five fields, all are of fixed size except the data field, which may contain any integral number of octets between the minimum and maximum values specified below (see 6.2.5). Relative to figure 6A–5, octets of a frame are

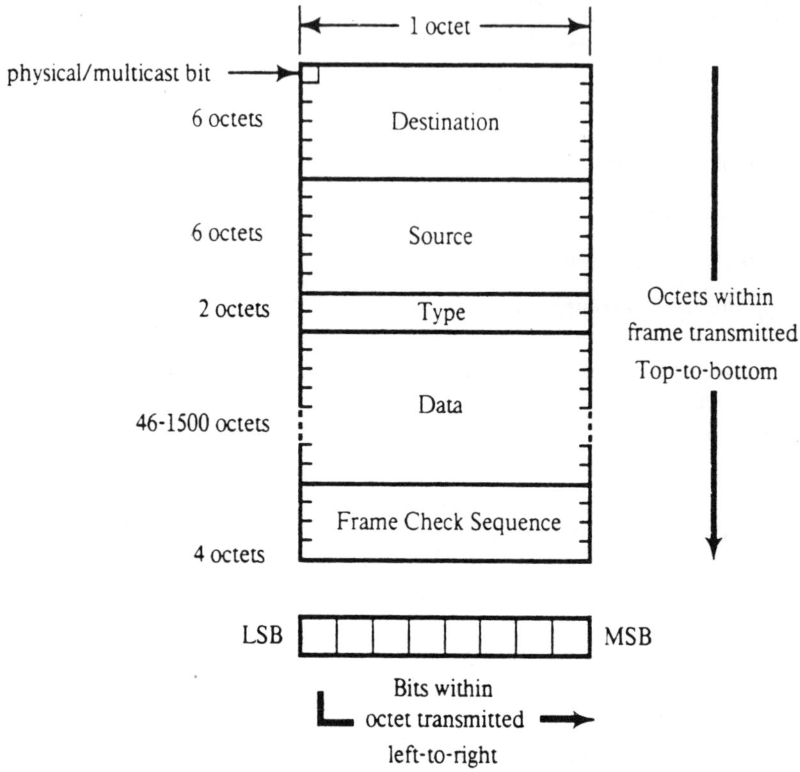

Figure 6A–5. Data Link Layer Frame Format

tranmsmitted from top to bottom, and the bits of each octet are transmitted from left to right.

NOTE

This document does *not* define an order of transmission for the octets of standard multi-octet data types (strings, integers, etc), since no values of such data types appear in the data link frame format. The order in which implementations of the Ethernet store the octets of a frame in computer memory, and the manner in which higher level protocols interpret the contents of the data field as values of various multi-octet data types, are beyond the scope of this specification.

The Ethernet itself is also totally insensitive to the interpretation of bits within a octet as constituting the digits of an 8-digit binary numeric value. Since some uniform convention is helpful, however, in avoiding needless incompatibility among different station types, the interpretation is arbitrarily defined to be that the left-most bit (first transmitted) is the low-order (2^0) digit and the right-most bit (last transmitted) is the high-order (2^7) digit.

6.2.1 Address Fields. Data link addresses are 6 octets (48 bits) in length. A data link address is of one of two types:

Physical address: The unique address associated with a particular station on the Ethernet. A station's physical address should be distinct from the physical address of any other station on *any* Ethernet.

Multicast address: A multi-destination address, associated with one or more stations on a given Ethernet. There are two kinds of multicast address:

—*Multicast-group address:* An address associated by higher-level convention with a group of logically related stations.

—*Broadcast address:* A distinguished, predefined multicast address which always denotes the set of *all* stations on a given Ethernet.

The first bit of a data link address distinguishes physical from multicast addresses:

0 → physical address

1 → multicast address

In either case, the remainder of the first octet and all of the subsequent octets form a 47-bit pattern. In the case of the broadcase address, this pattern consists of 47 one-bits. There is no standard "null" address value.

The procedures for assigning suitably unique values for physical and multicast addresses are discussed in Appendix B.

6.2.1.1 Destination Address Field. The destination address field specifies the station(s) for which the frame is intended. It may be a physical or multicast (including broadcast address. For details of address recognition by the receiving station(s), see 6.4.1.2.

6.2.1.2 Source Address Field. The source address field specifies the station sending the frame. The source address field is not interpreted at the Data Link Layer. It is specified at the data link level because a uniform convention for the placement of this field is crucial for most higher level protocols.

6.2.2 Type Field. The type field consists of a two-octet value reserved for use by higher levels (in particular, to identify the Client Layer protocol associated with the frame). The type field is uninterpreted at the Data Link Layer. It is specified at this level because a uniform convention for the placement and value assignment of this field is crucial if multiple higher level protocols are to be able to share the same Ethernet network without conflict. Appendix B discusses the assignment of type field values.

6.2.3 Data Field. The data field contains a sequence of n octets, where $46 \leq n \leq 1500$ Within this range, full data transparency is provided, in the sense that any arbitrary sequence of octet values may appear in the data field.

6.2.4 Frame Check Sequence Field. The frame check sequence (FCS) field contains a 4-octet (32-bit) cyclic redundancy check (CRC) value. This value is computed as a function of the contents of the source, destination, type and data fields (i.e., all fields except the frame check sequence field itself). The encoding is defined by the generating polynomial:

$$G(x) = x^{32} + x^{26} + x^{23} + x^{22} + x^{16} + x^{12} + x^{11} + x^{10} + x^{8} + x^{7} + x^{5} + x^{4} + x^{2} + x + 1$$

(This polynomial is also used in the Autodin-II network; its properties are investigated in [22,23].)

Mathematically, the CRC value corresponding to a given frame is defined by the following procedure:

1. The first 32 bits of the frame are complemented.
2. The n bits of the frame are then considered to be the coefficients of a polynomial M(x) of degree $n - 1$. (The first bit of the destination address field corresponds to the x^{n-1} term and the last bit of the data field corresponds to the x^0 term.)
3. M(x) is multiplied by x^{32} and divided by G(x), producing a remainder R(x) of degree ≤ 31.
4. The coefficients of R(x) are considered to be a 32-bit sequence.
5. The bit sequence is complemented and the result is the CRC.

The 32 bits of the CRC value are placed in the frame check sequence field so that the x^{31} term is the leftmost bit of the first octet, and the x^0 term is the rightmost bit of the last octet. (The bits of the CRC are thus transmitted in the order $x^{31}, x^{30}, \ldots, x^1, x^0$)

Appendix C discusses CRC implementation issues.

6.2.5 Frame Size Limitations. Given the limitations on the size of the data field specified in 6.2.3 and the 18 octet total size for the other four fields, the smallest valid frame contains 64 octets and the largest valid frame contains 1518 octets.

6.3 Frame Transmission

The Data Link frame transmission and reception are as follows:

Frame transmission includes data encapsulation and link management aspects:

> *Transmit Data Encapsulation* includes the assembly of the outgoing frame (from the values provided by the Client Layer) and frame check sequence generation.
>
> *Transmit Link Management* includes carrier deference, interframe spacing, collision detection and enforcement, and collision backoff and retransmission.

The performance of these functions by a transmitting data link controller interacts with corresponding actions by other data link controllers to jointly implement the Ethernet data link protocol.

6.3.1 Transmit Data Encapsulation.

6.3.1.1 Frame Assembly. The fields of the data link frame are set to the values provided by the Client Layer as arguments to the *TransmitFrame* operation (see 5.1), with the exception of the frame check sequence, which is set to the CRC value generated by the data link controller.

6.3.1.2 Frame Check Sequence Generation. The CRC value defined in 6.2.4 is generated and inserted in the frame check sequence field, following the fields supplied by the Client Layer. Appendix C discusses CRC implementation.

6.3.2 Transmit Link Management.

6.3.2.1 Carrier Deference. Even when it has nothing to transmit, the data link contoller monitors the physical channel for traffic by watching the *carrierSense* signal provided by the Physical Layer. Whenever the channel is busy, the data link controller *defers* to the passing frame by delaying any pending transmission of its own. After the last bit of the passing frame (i.e., when *carrierSense* changes from true to false), the data link controller continues to defer for 9.6 μsec to provide proper interframe spacing (see 6.3.2.2). At the end of that time, if it has a frame waiting to be transmitted, transmission is initiated independent of the value of *carrierSense*. When transmission has completed (or immediately, if there was nothing to transmit) the data link controller resumes its original monitoring of *carrierSense*.

When a frame is submitted by the Client Layer for transmission, the transmission is initiated as soon as possible, but in conformance with the rules of deference stated above.

6.3.2.2 Interframe Spacing. As defined in 6.3.2.1, the rules for deferring to passing frames insure a minimum interframe spacing of 9.6 μsec. This is intended to provide interframe recovery time for other data link controllers and for the physical channel.

Note that 9.6 μsec is the minimum value of the interframe spacing. If necessary for implementation reasons, a transmitting controller may use a larger value with a resulting decrease in its throughput. The value should not exceed 10.6 μsec.

6.3.2.3 Collision Handling. Once a data link controller has finished deferring and has started transmission, it is still possible for it to experience contention for the channel. As discussed in 4.4.3, collisions can occur until acquisition of the network has been accomplished through the deference of all other stations' data link controllers.

The dynamics of collision handling are largely determined by a single parameter called the *slot time*. This single parameter describes three important aspects of collision handling:

It is an upper bound on the acquisition time of the network.

It is an upper bound on the length of a frame fragment generated by a collision. (See 6.4.2.1.)

It is the scheduling quantum for retransmission (See 6.3.2.3.2.)

In order to fulfill all three functions, the slot time must be larger than the sum of the Physical Layer round-trip propagation time (450 bit times; see 7.1.2) and the Data Link Layer maximum jam time (48 bit times, see 6.3.2.3.1). The slot time is defined to be 512 bit times.

6.3.2.3.1 Collision Detection and Enforcement. Collisions are detected by monitoring the *collisionDetect* signal provided by the Physical Layer. When a collision is detected during a frame transmission, the transmission is not terminated immediately. Instead, the transmission continues until at least

32 (but not more than 48) additional bits have been transmitted (counting from the time *collisionDetect* went on). This collision enforcement or "jam" guarantees that the duration of the collision is sufficient to insure its detection by all transmitting stations on the network. The content of the jam is unspecified; it may be any fixed or variable pattern convenient to the data link controller implementation, but should not be the 32-bit CRC value corresponding to the (partial) frame transmitted prior to the jam.

6.3.2.3.2 Collision Backoff and Retransmission. When a transmission attempt has terminated due to a collision, it is retried by the transmitting data link controller until either it is successful, or 16 attempts (the original attempt plus 15 retries) have been made and all have terminated due to collisions. Note that all attempts to transmit a given frame are completed before any subsequent outgoing frames are transmitted. The scheduling of the retransmissions is determined by a controlled randomization process called "truncated binary exponential backoff". At the end of enforcing a collision (jamming), the data link controller delays before attempting to retransmit the frame. The delay is an integral multiple of the slot time. (See 6.3.2.3.) The number of slot times to delay before the nth retransmission attempt is chosen as a uniformly distributed random integer r in the range $0 \leq r < 2^k$ where $k = \min(n, 10)$. If all 16 attempts fail, this event is reported as an error.

Note that the values given above define the most aggressive behavior that a station may exhibit in attempting to retransmit after a collision. In the course of implementing the retransmission scheduling procedure, a station may introduce extra delays which will degrade its own throughput, but in no case may a station's retransmission scheduling result in a lower average delay between retransmission attempts than the procedure defined above.

6.4 Frame Reception

Frame reception includes both data decapsulation and link management aspects:

> *Receive Data Decapsulation* comprises framing, address recognition, frame check sequence validation, and frame disassembly to pass the fields of the received frame to the Client Layer.
>
> *Receive Link Management's* main function is the filtering of collision fragments from complete incoming frames.

The performance of these functions by a receiving data link controller interacts with corresponding actions by other data link controllers to jointly implement the Ethernet data link protocol.

6.4.1 Receive Data Decapsulation.

6.4.1.1 Framing. The data link controller recognizes the boundaries of an incoming frame by monitoring the *carrierSense* signal provided by the Physical Layer. There are two possible length errors that can occur, which indicate ill-framed data: the frame may be too long, or its length may not be an integral number of octets.

6.4.1.1.1 Maximum Frame Size. The receiving data link controller is not required to enforce the frame size limit specified in 6.2.5, but it is allowed to truncate frames longer than 1518 octets and report this event as an (implementation-dependent) error.

6.4.1.1.2 Integral Number of Octets in Frame. Since the format of a valid frame specifies an integral number of octets, only a collision or an error can produce a frame with a length that is not an integral multiple of 8. Complete frames (i.e., not rejected as collision fragments; see 6.4.2.1) that do not contain an integral number of octets are truncated to the nearest octet boundary. If frame check sequence validation (see 6.4.1.3) detects an error in such a frame, the status code *alignmentError* is reported.

6.4.1.2 Address Recognition. The Ethernet data link controller is capable of recognizing physical and multicast addresses as defined in 6.2.1.

6.4.1.2.1 Physical Addresses. The data link controller recognizes and accepts any frame whose destination field contains the physical address of the station.

The physical address of each station is set by network management to a unique value associated with the station, and distinct from the address of any other station on any Ethernet. The setting of the station's physical address by network management allows multiple data link controllers connected to single station all to respond to the same physical address. The procedures for allocating unique addresses are discussed in Appendix B.

6.4.1.2.2 Multicast Addresses. The data link controller recognizes and accepts any frame whose destination field contains the broadcast address.

The data link controller is capable of activating some number of multicast-group addresses as specified by higher layers. The data link controller recognizes and accepts any frame whose destination field contains an active multicast-group address. An active multicast-group address may be deactivated.

6.4.1.3 Frame Check Sequence Validation. FCS validation is essentially identical to FCS generation. If the bits of the incoming frame (exclusive of the FCS field itself) do not generate a CRC value identical to the one received, an error has occurred and is reported as such. Implementation issues are discussed in Appendix C.

6.4.1.4 Frame Disassembly. The frame is disassembled and the fields are passed to the Client Layer via the output parameters of the *ReceiveFrame* operation (see 5.1).

6.4.2 Receive Link Management.

6.4.2.1 Collision Filtering. As specified in 6.2.5, the smallest valid frame must contain at least 64 octets. Any frame containing less than 64 octets is presumed to be a fragment resulting from a collision and is discarded by the receiving data link controller. Since occasional collisions are a normal part of the link management procedure, the discarding of such a fragment is not reported as an error to the Client Layer.

6.5 The Data Link Layer Procedural Model

6.5.1 Overview of the Procedural Model. The functions of the Ethernet Data Link Layer are presented below, modeled as a program written in the language Pascal [20]. This procedural model is intended as the primary specification of the functions to be provided in any Ethernet Data Link Layer implementation. It is important to distinguish, however, between the model and a real implementation. The model is optimized for simplicity and clarity of presentation, while any realistic implementation must place heavier emphasis on such constraints as efficiency and suitability to a particular implementation technology or computer architecture. In this context, several important properties of the procedural model must be considered.

6.5.1.1 Ground Rules for the Procedural Model.

a) First, it must be emphasized that the description of the Data Link Layer in a programming language is in no way intended to imply that a data link controller must be implemented as a program executed by a computer. The implementation may consist of any appropriate technology including hardware, firmware, software, or any combination.
b) Similarly, it must be emphasized that it is the *behavior* of Data Link Layer implementations that must match the specification, *not* their internal structure. The internal details of the procedural model are useful only to the extent that they help specify that behavior clearly and precisely.
c) The handling of incomimg and outgoing frames is rather stylized in the

procedural model, in the sense that frames are handled as single entities by most of the Data Link Layer and are only serialized for presentation to the Physical Layer. In reality, many data link controller implementations will instead handle frames serially on a bit, octet or word basis. A serial implementation would typically perform the required functions (address recognition, frame check sequence generation/validation, etc.) in an overlapped, pipelined fashion. This approach has not been reflected in the procedural model, since this would only complicate the description of the functions without changing them in any way.

d) The model consists of algorithms designed to be executed by a number of concurent processes; these algorithms collectively implement the Ethernet data link control procedure. The timing dependencies introduced by the need for concurrent activity are resolved in two ways:

   Processes vs. External events: It is assumed that the algorithms are executed "very fast" relative to external events, in the sense that a process never falls behind in its work and fails to respond to an external event in a timely manner. For example, when a frame is to be received, it is assumed that the data link procedure *ReceiveFrame* is always called well before the frame in question has started to arrive.

   Processes vs. Processes: Among processes, no assumptions are made about relative speeds of execution. This means that each interaction between two processes must be structured to work correctly independent of their respective speeds. Note, however, that the timing of interactions among processes is often, in part, an indirect reflection of the timing of external events, in which cast appropriate timing assumptions may still be made.

   It is intended that the concurrency in the model reflect the parallelism intrinsic to the task of implementing the Ethernet data link, although the actual parallel structure of the implementations is likely to vary.

6.5.1.2 Use of Pascal in the Procedural Model. Pascal was chosen for the procedural model because of its relative simplicity and clarity, and its general acceptance.

Several observations need to be made about the way in which Pascal is used for the model, including:

a) Some limitations of the language have been circumvented in order to simplify the specification:

   1) The elements of the program (variables, procedures, etc) are presented in logical groupings, in top-down order. Certain Pascal

ordering restrictions have thus been circumvented to improve readibility.

2) The **process** and **cycle** constructs of the Pascal derivative Concurrent Pascal [21] have been introduced to indicate the sites of autonomous concurrent activity. As used here, a process is simply a parameterless procedure that begins execution at "the beginning of time" rather than being invoked by a procedure call. A cycle statement represents the main body of a process and is executed repeatedly forever.

3) The lack of variable array bounds in the language has been circumvented by treating frames as if they are always of a single fixed size (which is never actually specified). In fact, of course, the size of a frame depends on the size of its data field, hence the value of the "pseudo-constant" *frameSize* should be thought of as varying in the long-term, even though it is fixed for any given frame.

4) The use of a variant record to represent a frame (both as fields and as bits) follows the letter but not the spirit of the Pascal Report, since it allows the underlying representation to be viewed as two different data types. (It also assumes that this representation is as shown in figure 6A–5.

b) The model makes no use of any explicit interprocess synchronization primitives. Instead, all interprocess interaction is done via carefully stylized manipulation of shared variables. For example, some variables are set by only one process and inspected by another process in such a manner that the net result is independent of their execution speeds. While such techniques are not generally suitable for the construction of large concurrent programs, they simplify the model and more nearly resemble the methods appropriate to the most likely implementation technologies (e.g. microcode, hardware state-machines, etc.)

6.5.2 Procedural Model. The procedural model used here is based on five cooperating concurrent processes. Of these, three are actually defined in the Data Link Layer. The remaining two processes are provided by the Client Layer and utilize the interface operations provided by the Data Link Layer. The five processes are thus:

Client Layer:

Frame Transmitter Process **Frame Receiver Process**

Data Link Layer:

Bit Transmitter Process **Bit Receiver Process**
Deference Process

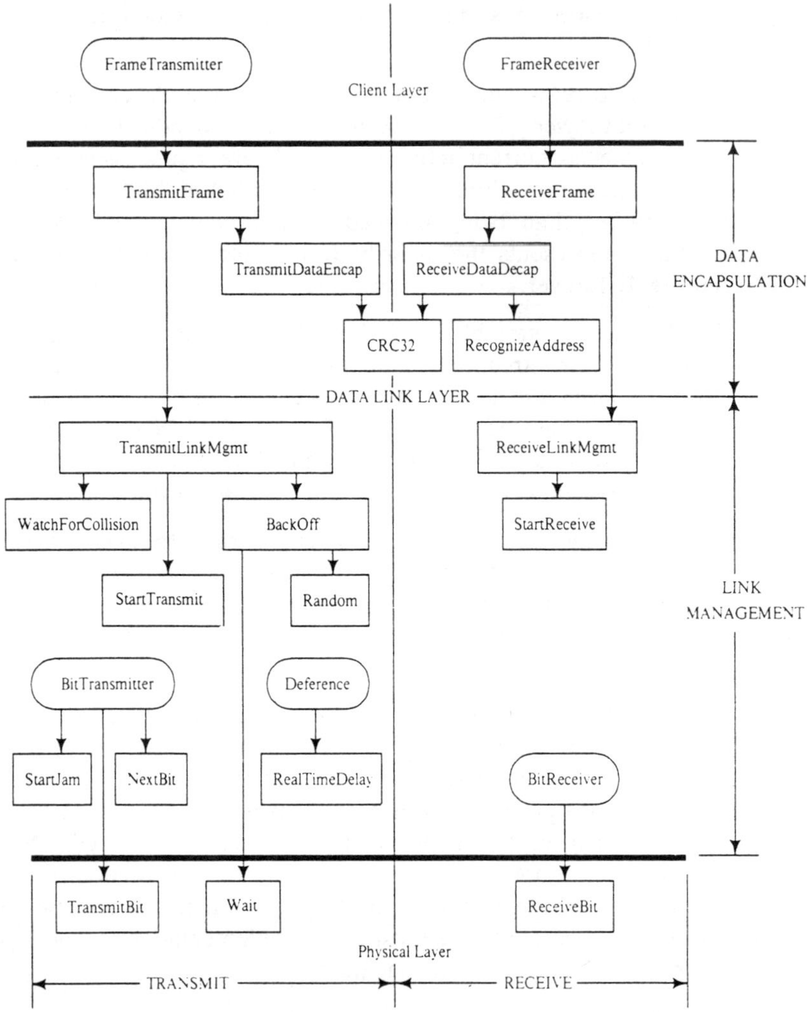

Figure 6A–6. Structure of the Data Link Procedural Model

This organization of the model is illustrated in figure 6A–6, and reflects the fact that the communication of entire frames is initiated by the Client Layer, while the timing of collision backoff and of individual bit transfers is based on interactions between the Data Link Layer and the Physical-Layer-dependent bit-time.

Figure 6A–6 depicts the static structure of the procedural model, showing how the various processes and procedures interact by invoking each other.

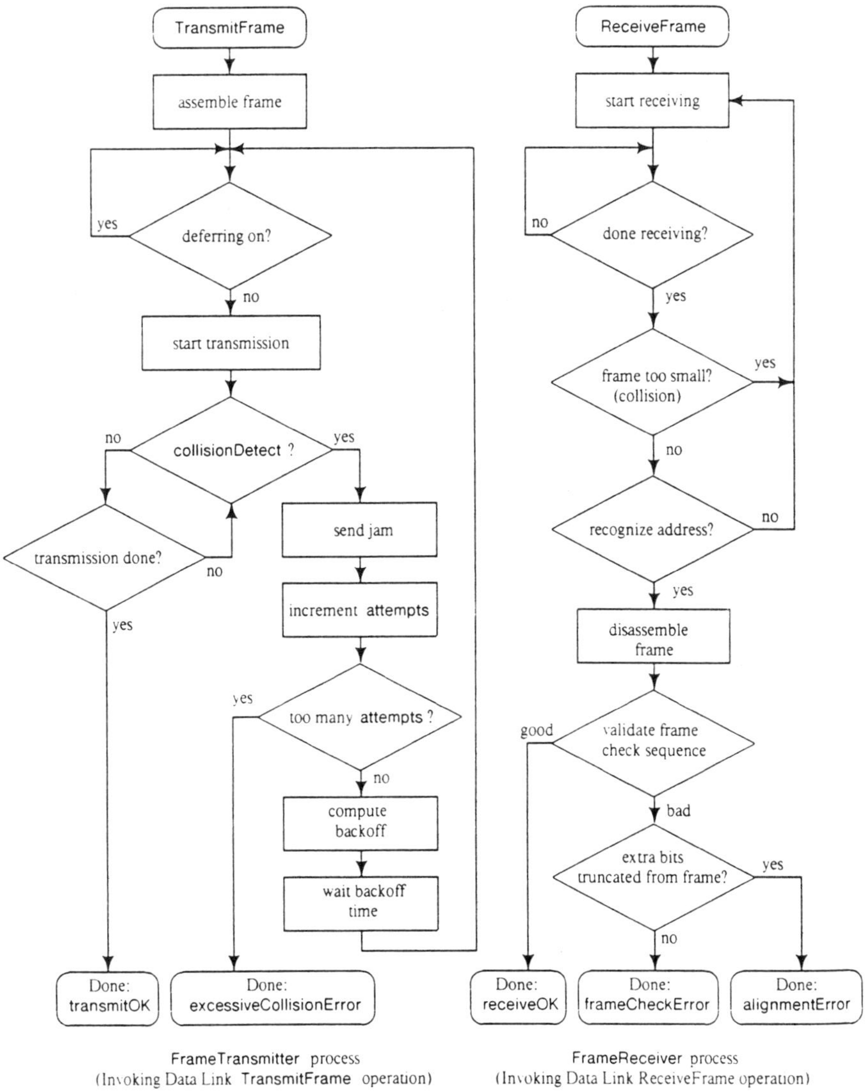

Figure 6A–7. Control Flow Summary—Client Layer Processes

Figures 6A–7 and 6A–8 summarize the dynamic behavior of the model during transmission and reception, focusing on the steps that must be performed, rather than the procedural structure which performs them. The usage of the shared state variables is not depicted in the figures, but is described in the comments in 6.5.2.1.

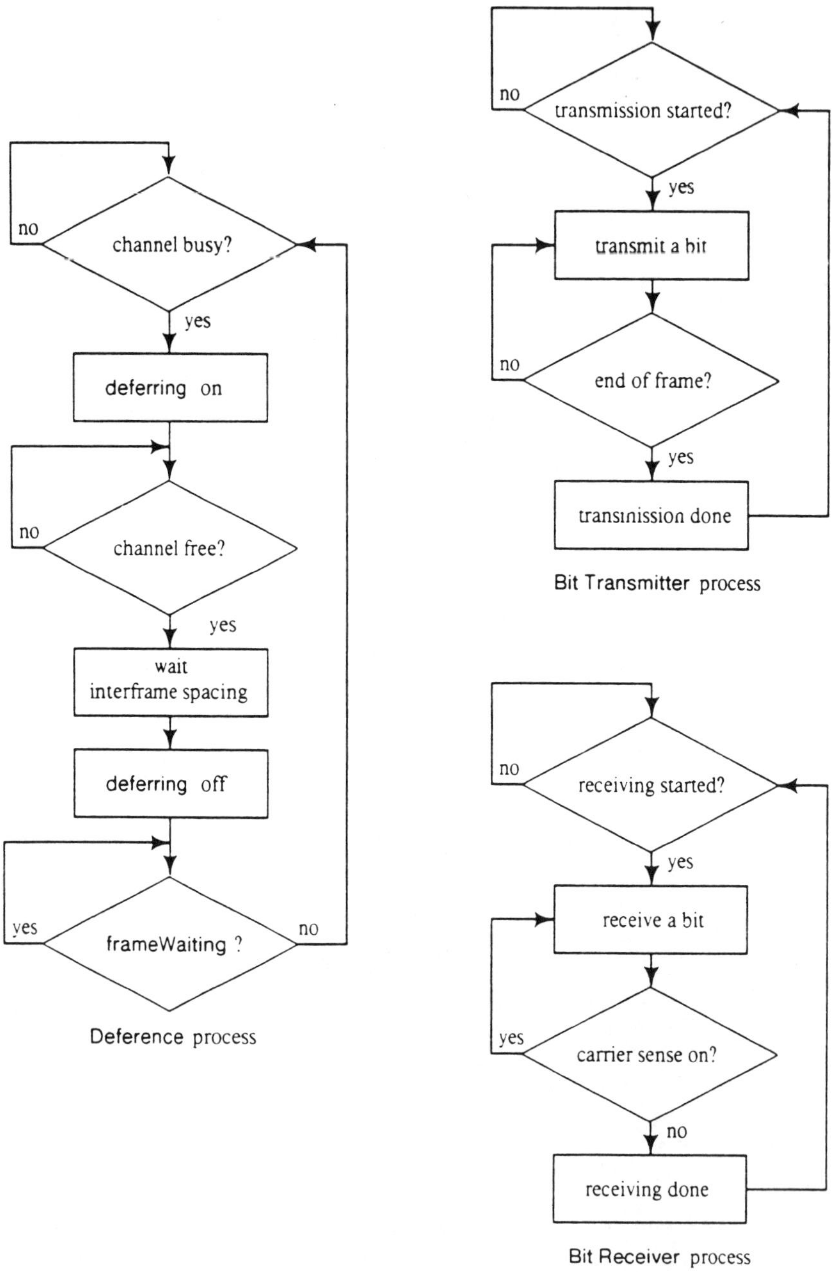

Figure 6A–8. Control Flow Summary—Data Link Layer Processes

6.5.2.1 Global Declarations.

6.5.2.1.1 Common Constants and Types. The following declarations of constants and types are used by the frame transmission and reception sections of each data link controller:

```
const
    addressSize = 48; {48 bit address = 6 octets}
    typeSize = 16; {16 bit protocol type = 2 octets}
    dataSize = ...; {see 6.5.1.2, note 3}
    crcSize = 32; {32 bit CRC = 4 octets}
    frameSize = ...; {= 2*addressSize + typeSize + dataSize +
      crcSize...see 6.5.1.2, note 3}

    slotTime = 512; {unit of time for collision handling}

type
    Bit = 0..1;
    AddressValue = array [1..addressSize] of Bit;
    TypeValue = array [1..typeSize] of Bit;
    DataValue = array [1..dataSize] of Bit;
    CRCValue = array [1..crcSize] of Bit;

    ViewPoint = (fields, bits); {Two ways to view the contents of a
      frame}

    Frame = record {Format of data link frame }
        case view: ViewPoint of
          fields: (
            destinationField: AddressValue;
            sourceField: AddressValue;
            typeField: TypeValue;
            dataField: DataValue;
            fcsField: CRCValue);
        bits: (
            contents: array [1..frameSize] of Bit)
    end; {Frame}
```

6.5.2.1.2 Transmit State Variables. The following items are specific to frame transmission. (See also 6.5.2.1.4 on interfaces)

```
const
    interFrameSpacing = 9.6; {minimum time between frames, in
      microseconds}
```

```
    attemptLimit = 16; {Max number of times attempt trans-
      mission}
    backOffLimit = 10; {Limit on number of times to back off}
    jamSize = 32; {jam may be 32 to 48 bits long}

var
    outgoingFrame: Frame; {The frame to be transmitted}
    currentTransmitBit, last TransmitBit: 1..frameSize; {Positions
      of current and last outgoing bits in outgoingFrame}
    deferring: Boolean; {True implies any pending transmission
      must wait for the channel to clear}
    frameWaiting: Boolean; {Indicates that outgoingFrame is
      deferring}
    attempts: 0..attemptLimit; {Number of transmission attempts
      on outgoingFrame}
    newCollision: Boolean; {Indicates that a collision has oc-
      curred but has not yet been jammed}
    transmitSucceeding: Boolean; {Running indicator of whether
      transmission is succeeding}
```

6.5.2.1.3 Receive State Variables. The following items are specific to frame reception. (See also 6.5.2.1.4 on interfaces)

```
var
    incomingFrame: Frame; {The frame being received}
    currentReceiveBit: 1..frameSize; {Position of current bit in
      incomingFrame}
    receiving: Boolean; {Indicates that a frame reception is in
      progress}
    excessBits: 0..7; {Count of excess trailing bits beyond octet
      boundary}
    receiveSucceeding: Boolean; {Running indicator of whether
      reception is succeeding}
```

6.5.2.1.4 Summary of Interlayer Interfaces. The interface to the Client Layer, defined in 5.1, is summarized below:

```
type
    TransmitStatus = (transmitOK, excessiveCollisionError); {Re-
      sult of TransmitFrame operation}
    ReceiveStatus = (receiveOK, frameCheckError, alignment-
      Error); {Result of ReceiveFrame operation}
```

```
function TransmitFrame (
    destinationParam: AddressValue;
    sourceParam: AddressValue;
    typeParam: typeValue;
    dataParam: DataValue): TransmitStatus; {Transmits one
      frame}

function ReceiveFrame (
    var destinationParam: AddressValue;
    var sourceParam: AddressValue;
    var typeParam: TypeValue;
    var dataParam: DataValue): ReceiveStatus; {Receives one
      frame}
```

The interface to the Physical Layer, defined in 5.2, is summarized below:

```
var
    carrierSense: Boolean; {Indicates incoming bits}
    transmitting: Boolean; {Indicates outgoing bits}
    collisionDetect: Boolean; {Indicates channel contention}
procedure TransmitBit (bitParam: Bit); {Transmits one bit}
function ReceiveBit: Bit; {Receives one bit}
procedure Wait (bitTimes: integer); {Waits for indicated number of
  bit-times}
```

6.5.2.1.5 State Variable Initialization. The procedure *Initialize* must be run when the Data Link Layer begins operation, before any of the processes begin execution. *Initialize* sets certain crucial shared state variables to their initial values. (All other global variables are appropriately reinitialized before each use.) *Initialize* then waits for the channel to be idle, and starts operation of the various processes.

```
procedure Initialize;
begin
    frameWaiting := false;
    deferring := false;
    newCollision := false;
    transmitting := false; {In interface to Physical Layer; see
      below]
    receiving := false;
    while carrierSense do nothing;
```

```
    {Start execution of all processes]
end; {initialize}
```

6.5.2.2 *Frame Transmission.* The algorithms in this section define data link frame transmission.

The function *TransmitFrame* implements the frame transmission operation provided to the Client Layer:

```
function TransmitFrame (
    destinationParam: AddressValue;
    sourceParam: AddressValue;
    typeParam: typeValue;
    dataParam: DataValue): TransmitStatus;
procedure TransmitDataEncap;...{nested procedure; see body
  below]
begin
    TransmitDataEncap;
    TransmitFrame : = TransmitLinkMgmt
end; {TransmitFrame}
```

First, *TransmitFrame* calls the internal procedure *TransmitDataEncap* to construct the frame. It then calls *TransmitLinkMgmt* to perform the actual transmission. The *TransmitStatus* returned indicates the success or failure of the transmission attempt.

TransmitDataEncap builds the frame and places the 32-bit CRC in the frame check sequence field:

```
procedure TransmitDataEncap;
begin
    with outgoingFrame do
    begin {assemble frame}
        view : = fields;
    destinationField : = destinationParam;
        sourceField : = sourceParam;
        typeField : = typeParam;
        dataField : = dataParam;
        fcsField : = CRC32(outgoingFrame);
        view : = bits
    end {assemble frame}
end; {TransmitDataEncap}
```

TransmitLinkMgmt attempts to transmit the frame, deferring first to any passing traffic. If a collision occurs, transmission is terminated properly and retransmission is scheduled following a suitable backoff interval:

```
function TransmitLinkMgmt: TransmitStatus;
begin
    attempts := 0; transmitSucceeding := false;
    while attempts < attemptLimit and not transmitSucceeding
      do
    begin {loop}
        if attempts > 0 then BackOff;
        frameWaiting := true;
        while deferring do nothing; {defer to passing frame, if any}
        frameWaiting := false;
        StartTransmit;
        while transmitting do WatchForCollision;
        attempts := attempts + 1
    end; {loop}
    if transmitSucceeding then TransmitLinkMgmt := transmit-
      OK
    else TransmitLinkMgmt := excessiveCollisionError
end; {TransmitLinkMgmt}
```

Each time a frame transmission attempt is initiated, *StartTransmit* is called to alert the *BitTransmitter* process that bit transmission should begin:

```
procedure StartTransmit;
begin
    currentTransmitBit := 1;
    lastTransmitBit := frameSize;
    transmitSucceeding := true;
    transmitting := true
end; {StartTransmit}
```

Once frame transmission has been initiated, *TransmitLinkMgmt* monitors the channel for contention by repeatedly calling *WatchForCollision*:

```
procedure WatchForCollision;
begin
    if transmitSucceeding and collisionDetect then
    begin
        newCollision := true;
        transmitSucceeding := false
    end
```

```
end: {WatchForCollision}
```

WatchForCollision, upon detecting a collision, updates *newCollision* to insure proper jamming by the *BitTransmitter* process.

After transmission of the jam has completed, if *TransmitLinkMgmt* determines that another attempt should be made, *BackOff* is called to schedule the next attempt to retransmit the frame.

```
var maxBackOff: 2..1024; {Working variable of BackOff}

procedure BackOff;
begin
    if attempts = 1 then maxBackOff := 2 else if attempts ≤
      backOffLimit then maxBackOff := maxBackOff*2;
    Wait(slotTime*Random(0, maxBackOff))
end; {BackOff}
function Random (low, high: integer): integer;
begin
    Random := ...{uniformly distributed random integer r such
that low ≤ r < high}
end; {Random}
```

BackOff performs the truncated binary exponential backoff computation and then waits for the selected multiple of the slot time.

The *Deference* process runs asynchronously to continuously compute the proper value for the variable *deferring*.

```
process Deference;
begin
    cycle {main loop}
        while not carrierSense do nothing; {watch for carrier to
          appear}
        deferring := true; {delay start of new transmissions}
        while carrierSense do nothing; {wait for carrier to dis-
          appear}
        RealTimeDelay(interFrameSpacing);
        deferring := false; {allow new transmissions to proceed}
        while frameWaiting do nothing {allow waiting transmis-
          sion (if any)}
    end {main loop}
end; {Deference}

procedure RealTimeDelay (usec: real);
begin
```

```
        {Wait for the specified number of microseconds}
end; {RealTimeDelay}
```

The *BitTransmitter* process runs asynchronously, trnsmitting bits at a rate determined by the Physical Layer's *TransmitBit* operation:

```
process BitTransmitter;
begin
    cycle {outer loop}
        while transmitting do
        begin {inner loop}
            TransmitBit(outgoingFrame[currentTransmitBit]);
              {send next bit to Physical Layer}
            if newCollision then StartJam else NextBit
        end {inner loop}
    end {outer loop}
end; {BitTransmitter}

procedure NextBit;
begin
    currentTransmitBit := currentTransmitBit + 1;
    transmitting := (currentTransmitBit ≤ lastTransmitBit)
end; {nextBit}

procedure StartJam;
begin
    currentTransmitBit := 1;
    lastTransmitBit := jamSize;
    newCollision := false
end; {StartJam}
```

BitTransmitter, upon detecting a new collision, immediately enforces it by calling *StartJam* to initiate the transmission of the jam. The jam may contain 32 to 48 bits of arbitrary data. (*StartJam* uses the first 32 bits of the frame, merely to simplify this program).

6.5.2.3 *Frame Reception.* The algorithms in this section define data link frame reception:

The procedure *ReceiveFrame* implements the frame reception operation provided to the Client Layer:

```
function ReceiveFrame (
        var destinationParam: AddressValue;
    var sourceParam: AddressValue;
```

```
        var typeParam: TypeValue;
        var dataParam: DataValue): ReceiveStatus;
    function ReceiveDataDecap: ReceiveStatus;...{nested func-
      tion; see body below}
begin
    repeat
        ReceiveLinkMgmt;
        ReceiveFrame : = ReceiveDataDecap;
    until receiveSucceeding
end; {ReceiveFrame}
```

ReceiveFrame calls *ReceiveLinkMgmt* to receive the next valid frame, and then calls the internal procedure *ReceiveDataDecap* to return the frame's fields to the Client Layer if the frame's address indicates that it should do so. The returned *ReceiveStatus* indicates the presence or absence of detected transmission errors in the frame.

```
function ReceiveDataDecap: ReceiveStatus;
begin
    receiveSucceeding : = RecognizeAddress
        (incomingFrame.destinationField);
    if receiveSucceeding then with incomingFrame do
    begin {disassemble frame}
        view : = fields;
        destinationParam : = destinationField;
        sourceParam : = sourceField;
        typeParam : = typeField;
        dataParam : = dataField;
        if fcsField = CRC32(incomingFrame) then ReceiveData-
        Decap : = receiveOK
        else if excessBits = 0 then ReceiveDataDecap : =
          frameCheckError
        else ReceiveDataDecap : = alignmentError;
        view : = bits
    end {disassemble frame}
end; {ReceiveDataDecap}
```

```
function RecognizeAddress (address: AddressValue): Boolean;
begin
    RecognizeAddress : = ...{Returns true for the set of physical,
      broadcast, and multicast-group addresses corresponding
      to this station}
end; {RecognizeAddress}
```

ReceiveLinkMgmt attempts repeatedly to receive the bits of a frame, discarding any fragments from collisions by comparing them to the minimum valid frame size:

```
procedure ReceiveLinkMgmt;
begin
    repeat
        StartReceive;
        while receiving do nothing; {wait for frame to finish
          arriving}
        excessBits : = frameSize mod 8;
        frameSize : = frameSize − excessBits; {truncate to octet
          boundary}
        receiveSucceeding : = (frameSize ≥ slotTime); {reject
          collision fragments}
    until receiveSucceeding
end; {ReceiveLinkMgmt}

procedure StartReceive;
begin
    currentReceiveBit : = 1;
    receiving : = true
end; {StartReceive}
```

The *BitReceiver* process run asynchronously, receiving bits from the channel at the rate determined by the Physical Layer's *ReceiveBit* operation:

```
process BitReceiver;
    var b: Bit;
begin
    cycle {outer loop}
        while receiving do
        begin {inner loop}
            b : = ReceiveBit; {Get next bit from physical link}
            if carrierSense then
            begin {append bit to packet}
                incomingFrame[currentReceiveBit] : = b;
                currentReceiveBit : = currentReceiveBit + 1
            end; {append bit to packet}
            receiving : = carrierSense
        end {inner loop}
    end {outer loop}
end; {BitReceiver}
```

6.5.2.4 Common Procedures. The function *CRC32* is used by both the transmit and receive algorithms to generate a 32 bit CRC value:

```
function CRC32 (f: Frame): CRCValue;
begin
    CRC32 : = {The 32-bit CRC as defined in 6.2.4)
end; {CRC32}
```

Purely to enhance readability, the following procedure is also defined:

```
procedure nothing; begin end;
```

The idle state of a process (i.e., while waiting for some event) is cast as repeated calls on this procedure.

7. Ethernet Physical Layer Specification: Baseband Coaxial System

7.1 Physical Channel Overview and Model

The Ethernet physical channel (henceforth referred to as the channel) provides the lowest layer in the Ethernet architecture. It performs all the functions needed to transmit and receive data at the physical level, while supporting the Data Link to Physical Layer Interface described in 5.2.

This section describes the requirements for interface and compatibility with a baseband coaxial implementation of the channel.

7.1.1 Channel Goals and Non-Goals. This section states the objectives underlying the design of the channel.

7.1.1.1 Goals. The following are the goals of the channel:

1. Provide a means for communication between Ethernet Data Link Entities.
2. Define physical interfaces which can be implemented compatibly among different manufacturers of hardware.
3. Provide all clocks, synchronization, and timing required for both itself and the Ethernet Data Link.
4. Provide high bandwidth and low bit error rates.
5. Provide for ease of installability and serviceability.
6. Provide for high network availability.

7. Support the Ethernet Data Link to Physical Link interface.
8. Low cost

7.1.1.2 Non-Goals. The following are not goals of the baseband coaxial channel design:

1. Operation at data rates other than 10 megabits per second.
2. Operation with media other than the specified coaxial cable.
3. Simultaneous use of the channel by transmitters using signals not specified in this document.
4. Protection against a malicious user or a malfunctioning Data Link Entity is not provided by the channel as specified. However, higher layers (above the Data Link) and/or physical security means may be employed to achieve this.

7.1.2 Characteristics of the Channel. The channel provides (and the data link assumes) the following characteristics:

1. The ability to send and receive information (non-simultaneously) between any two or more data link entities on the same network.
2. The ability to detect the presence of another station's transmission while not transmitting (carrier sense).
3. The ability to detect the presence of another station's transmission while transmitting (collision detect).
4. A total worst-case round trip signal propagation delay (including actual propagation time, synchronization time for all intervening electronics, and signal rise time degradation) of 450 bit times (equal to 45 μs for this 10 Mbit channel).

7.1.3 Functions Provided by the Channel. The channel hardware provides the following functions in the performance of its role:

1. Means for transmitting and receiving serial bit streams between the data link layer and the media.
2. Generation of clock for synchronization and timing.
3. Means for detecting carrier (non-idle channel).
4. Means for detecting collisions (simultaneous transmission attempts by multiple stations).
5. Coding and decoding of the data link bit stream into a self-synchronizable sequence of electrical signals suitable for transmission on the media provided by the channel.
6. Generation and removal of coding-specific preamble information (a

synchronizing header sequence inserted before the first bit of the frame) to ensure that all channel electronics are brought to a known steady-state before the data link frame is transmitted.

7.1.4 Implementation of the Channel. The physical channel specification is implementation dependent; most of the channel hardware is fully specified, and little leeway is given to the individual designer. This is done in the interest of compatibility; any system which allows different implementors to use different channel cables, connectors, clock speeds and the like will not be compatible across manufacturer boundaries. Only the design of channel components which are not critical to system compatibility is left to the implementor.

7.1.4.1 General Overview of Channel Hardware. The channel minimally consists of the following functional blocks:

1. The passive broadcast medium (coaxial cable),
2. The transceiver (transmitter-receiver for the coaxial cable),
3. The means for connecting transceivers to a coaxial cable segment and for connecting coaxial cable segments together,
4. The channel clock,
5. The channel data encoder and decoder,
6. The preamble generator and remover,
7. The carrier and collision detect circuits.

the coaxial medium is the only element common to the entire network. A transceiver is required for each station connected to the medium. The transceiver must be located adjacent to the coaxial cable. The latter four components are generally located within, and tightly coupled to, the station hardware implementing the data link function.

It may be useful to be able to physically separate the transceiver from the rest of the channel hardware. This allows topological flexibility, packaging advantages, and improved system availability, as well as allowing for independent manufacture of station hardware and transceivers. To ensure that compatibility is maintained, a physical interface (known as the *transceiver cable*) is identified and specified to connect the trnsceiver to the station.

Finally, it may be necessary to add *repeaters* to the system, to reach the maximum allowable distance between stations, and to provide additional topological flexibility. Repeaters are implemented using standard transceivers, plus a simple, non-buffered finite state machine.

7.1.4.2 Compatibility Interfaces. There are a number of possibilities for implementing systems or subsystems compatible in whole or in part with this specification. It is important that all implementations be compatible at some point, so that heterogenous systems from different manufacturers' implementations can be interconnected on the same medium. It is not necessary in every case to implement all of the components described herein; e.g., it is possible to design an integrated station/transceiver (without requiring the transceiver cable). The implementor must make the required trade-offs between topological flexibility, system availability, configurability, user needs, and cost when designing the system.

For a device to be considered compatible, it must meet the applicable requirements at either the transceiver cable or the coaxial cable interface, as appropriate, in addition to the Data Link compatibility required for all stations connected to the network.

All Ethernets must be compatible at the coaxial cable.

If a transceiver cable is used, it should be the one specified in this document. This allows device manufacturers to build hardware compatible with the Ethernet at the transceiver cable level, without concerning themselves with the details of transceiver implementation. Devices implementing transceiver cable compatibility should be capable of using transceivers designed and built by another manufacturer, on the specified coaxial cable.

Equipment designed for connection to the specified coaxial cable either without a physically separate transceiver or with a non-standard transceiver cable interface will be capable of communication. However, a sacrifice may have been made with respect to interchangeability with other stations.

This scheme of multiple compatibility interfaces allows individual designers some flexibility in making system tradeoffs, yet allows cable manufacturers, transceiver manufacturers and systems manufacturers to use standard commodity parts to produce a compatible communications system.

7.1.5 Channel Configuration Model. Certain physical limits have been placed on the physical channel. These revolve mostly around maximum cable lengths (or maximum propagation times), as these affect the slot time as defined in the data link. While the precise specification (in later sections) specify these maxima in terms of propagation times, they were derived from the physical configuration model described here.

The maximum configuration is as follows:

1. A coaxial cable, terminated in its characteristic impedance at each end, constitutes a cable *segment*. A segment may contain a maximum of 500 meters of coaxial cable.
2. A maximum of 2 repeaters in the path between any two stations. Repeaters do not have to be located at the ends of segments, nor is the user limited to one repeater per segment. In fact, repeaters can be used

not only to extend the length of the channel, but to extend the topology from one to three-dimensional. Repeaters occupy transceiver positions on each cable segment and count towards the maximum number of transceivers on a segment just as do the logically distinguishable stations.

3. A maximum total coaxial cable length along the longest path between any two transceivers of 1500 meters. The propagation velocity of the coaxial cable is assumed to be 0.77 c worst-case. (c is the velocity of light *in vacuo*; 300,000 kilometers per second.) The total round-trip delay for all the coaxial cable in the system is therefore 13 μs worst-case.
4. A maximum of 50 meters of transceiver cable between any station and its associated transceiver. Note that in the worst case the signal must pass through six 50 meter transceiver cables, one at the transmitting station, one at the receiving station, and 2 at each repeater (two repeaters possible). The propagation velocity of the transceiver cable is assumed to be .65 c worst-case. The total round-trip delay for all the transceiver cables is therefore 3.08 μs worst-case.
5. A maximum of 1000 meters of point-to-point link anywhere in the system. This will typically be used as a way of linking cable segments in different buildings. Note that a repeater with this internal point-to-point link can be used to repeat signals between segments many hundreds of meters apart. The worst-case propagation velocity of the link cable is assumed to be .65 c; the round-trip propagation delay for 1000 meters is 10.26 μs.

Table 6A–1 summarizes the allocation of the round-trip propagation delay to the individual components in the channel. Figure 6A–9 shows a minimum, typical, and large-scale channel configuration.

7.1.6 Channel Interfaces. The channel specification hinges around three well-defined entities; the transceiver and coaxial cables (shown as compatibility interfaces in figure 6A–1), and the logical interface between the physical channel and the data link controller (shown in figure 6A–4). Note that the former two are physical interfaces specific to the channel, and are specified in the interest of compatibility. The latter is provided as a means by which the data link controller can interact with the physical channel.

The channel access component of the logical interface (discussed in 4.4.1) comprises the collision and carrier detect functions described in 7.5.2 and 7.5.3, as well as the actual transmission of signals on the media. The data encoding and decoding functions described in 4.4.1 comprise the generation and decomposition of encoded signals suitable for transmission (described in 7.5.1), the generation and removal of code-specific preamble (described in 7.5.1.3 and 7.5.4.1), and the serial bit stream interface between the layers.

Section 5 describes the interface between the data link and physical

Table 6A–1
Physical Channel Propagation Delay Budget (Note 1)

Element	*Unit Steady-State Delay*	*Unit Startup Delay*	*# Units Forward Path (Note 2)*	*# Units Return Path*	*Total Delay*
Encoder	0.1 μS	0	3	3	0.60 μS
Transceiver Cable	5.13 nS/M	0	300 M	300 M	3.08 μS
Transceiver (transmit path)	0.50 μS	0.2 μS	3	3	1.50 μS
Transceiver (receive path)	0.50 μS	0.5 μS	3	0	1.65 μS
Transceiver (collision path)	0	0.5 μS	0	3	1.50 μS
Coaxial Cable	4.33 nS/M	0	1500 M	1500 M	13.00 μS
Point-to-Point Link Cable	5.13 nS/M	0	1000 M	1000 M	10.26 μS
Repeater (repeat path)	0.8 μS	0	2	0	1.60 μS
Repeater (collision path)	0.2 μS	0	0	2	0.40 μS
Decoder	0.1 μS	0.8 μS	2	0	1.80 μS
Carrier Sense	0	0.2 μS	3	0	0.60 μS
Collision Detect	0	0.2 μS	0	3	0.60 μS
Signal Rise Time (to 70% in 500 M) (Note 3)	0	0.1 μS	3	0	0.30 μS
Signal Rise Time (50% to 94% in 500 M) (Note 4)	0	2.7 μS	0	3	8.10 μS
		Total Worst-Case Round-Trip Delay			44.99 μS

Note 1: All quantities given are worst-case (both number of units and unit delays per unit).

Note 2: The propagation delay has been separated into "forward-path" and "return path" delay. This is because in one direction it is carrier sense which is being propagated through the channel, and in the return direction it is collision detect which is being propagated. The two signals have different propagation delays.

Note 3: In the worst-case, the propagated signal must reach 70% of its final value to be detected as valid carrier at the end of 500 meters of coaxial cable. This rise time must be included in the propagation delay budget.

Note 4: In the worst-case the propagated collision on the return path must reach 94% of its final value to be detected as a collision at the end of 500 meters of coaxial cable.

layers as a series of Pascal procedures, functions, and shared variables. The data link specification in Section 6 shows how the data link uses this interface to communicate between client layers. However, this specification will not attempt to model the operation of the physical channel in Pascal. The interface between layers is supported by the physical hardware which provides the ability to send and receive bit streams, provide timing, and signal carrier sense and collision detect to the data link.

The remainder of this section specifies the requirements for compatibility

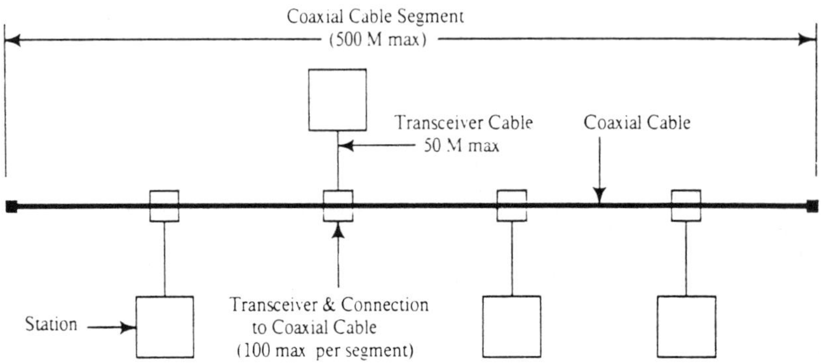

Figure 6A–9a. A Typical Medium-Scale Configuration

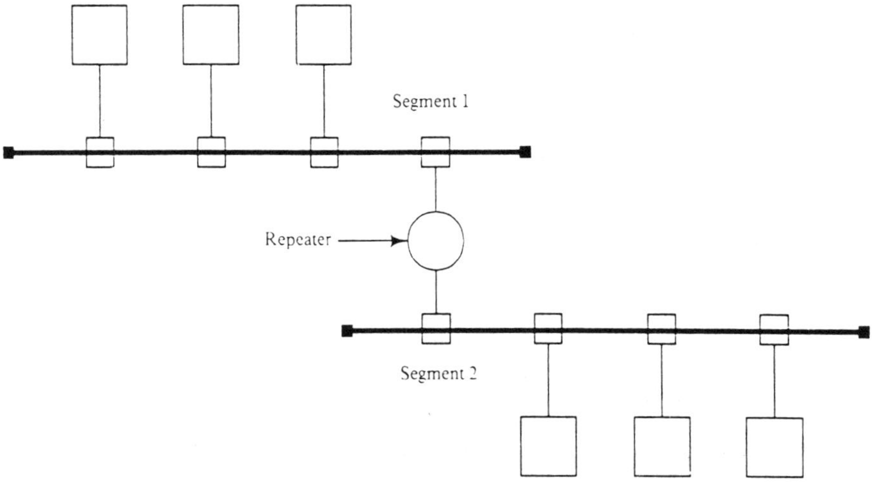

Figure 6A–9b. A Typical Medium-Scale Configuration

at both the transceiver cable and the coaxial cable. In addition, the specifications for the transceiver, which interfaces the transceiver cable to the coaxial cable is given, as well as the specification for the logic required between the transceiver cable and the interface to the data link.

7.2 Transceiver Cable Compatibility Interface Specifications

The transceiver cable is the means by which a physically separate transceiver is connected to a station. It provides one of the compatibility interfaces described in 7.1.4.2.

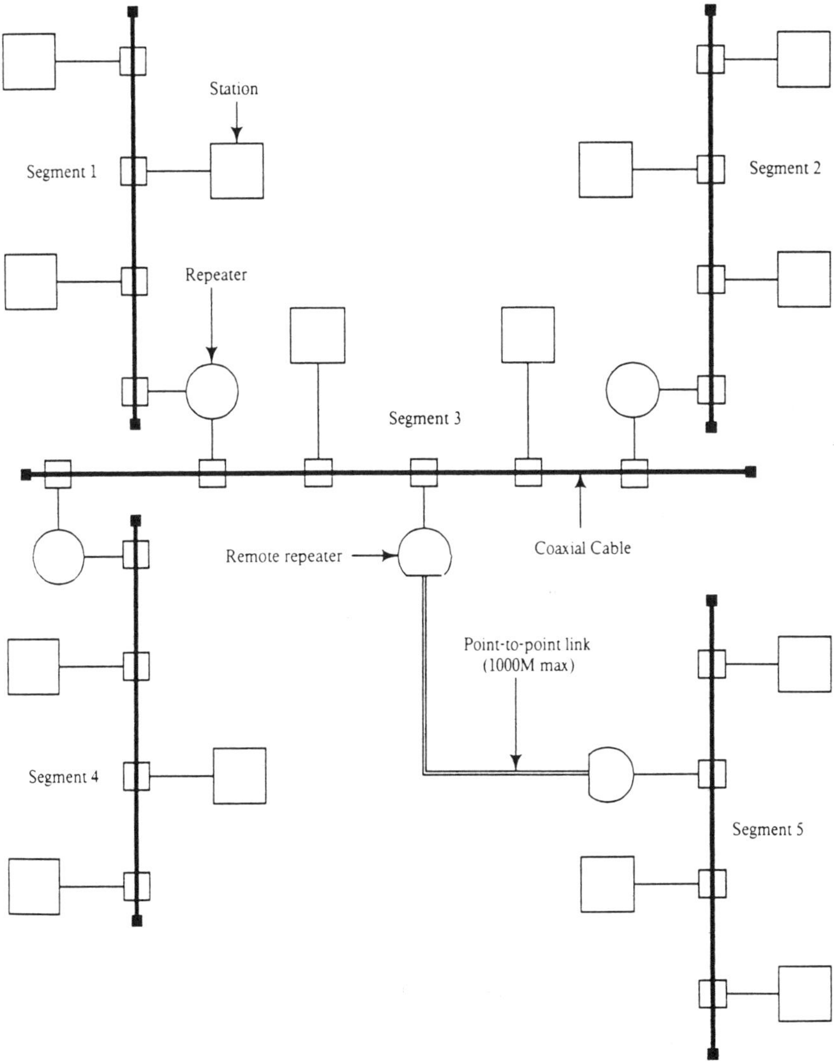

Figure 6A–9c. A Typical Large-Scale Configuration

7.2.1 Transceiver Cable Signals. The transceiver cable carries four signals: Transmit, Receive, Collision Presence, and Power. Each signal is carried on a twisted pair of conductors in the cable.

7.2.1.1 Transmit Signal. The transmit pair carries encoded data for which the data link is requesting transmission on the channel. This signal is generated by the data encoder, with the transceiver cable drive characteristics specified in 7.2.4.

7.2.1.2 Receive Signal. The receive pair carries encoded data from the transceiver to the station. It typically goes to the data decoder and the carrier sense circuitry. In the steady-state, all transitions and lack of transitions on the coaxial cable become transitions and lack of transitions on the receive pair, with the transceiver cable drive characteristics specified in 7.2.4. (During start-up, the first few bits may be absorbed by the transceiver to attain steady-state.)

In the case of a station transmitting without collision interference, the station's own transmit transitions on the coaxial cable will also appear on the receive pair, after a delay due to propagation through the transceiver. During collisions (whether or not that transceiver is involved in the collision) transitions on the receive lead are undefined; they may or may not meet decoder phase requirements, or they may not be present at all for extended periods. Thus the receive signal on the transceiver cable cannot be used alone to deterministically generate the carrier sense signal. This is described in more detail in 7.5.3.

7.2.1.3 Collision Presence Signal. The collision presence pair is used by the transceiver to indicate the presence of multiple transmission attempts on the coaxial cable. This is done by transmitting a square wave with a 10MHz fundamental frequency through the standard transceiver cable driver (described in 7.2.4). An oscillator is used instead of a simple level shift to allow AC coupling at the transceiver. Transceivers use the collision presence signal to indicate one of two conditions: the transceiver is transmitting and there is an attempt by another station to transmit at the same time, or there is a simultaneous transmission attempt by three or more stations regardless of whether the transceiver in question is transmitting.

7.2.1.4 Power. A pair of wires is designated for providing power to the transceiver. When the transceiver cable is implemented, the station end of the cable must supply a voltage between +12 and +15 Vdc ± 5% with at least 0.5 Amperes available to the cable for remotely powering the transceiver. The power source must meet applicable requirements for UL Class 2 wiring devices.

7.2.2 Transceiver Cable Parameters.

7.2.2.1 Mechanical Configuration. The transceiver cable consists of four stranded, twisted pair conductors, plus an overall shield and insulating jacket. The conductor and jacket insulating material may be polyethylene or other suitable material. The flammability characteristics of the insulating material must be suitable for the installed environment.

7.2.2.2 Characteristic Impedance. The differential mode characteristic impedance of all pairs shall be 78 Ω, ± 5 Ω, in the configuration.

7.2.2.3 Attenuation. The signal attenuation of any pair shall not exceed 3 dB (measured at 10 MHz) for the total length between the transceiver and the station.

7.2.2.4 Velocity of Propagation. The minimum velocity of propagation of the transceiver cable shall be 0.65 c.

7.2.2.5 Pulse Distortion. Pulse distortion shall not exceed ± 1 nS at the end of 50 meters of cable when driven with random 10 Mbit data encoded in accordance with 7.5.1.

7.2.2.6 Resistance. The resistance of the conductors used for the power pair shall not exceed 40 milliohms per meter.

7.2.2.7 Transfer Impedance. The common mode transfer impedance of the transceiver cable shall not exceed the values shown in figure 6A–10 as a function of frequency. The differential mode transfer impedance of the cable with respect to any pair shall be 20 dB lower than the specified common mode transfer impedance.

7.2.3 Transceiver Cable Connectors. The connectors used at the ends of the transceiver cable shall be 15 conductor 'D' subminiature types (Cinch type DASM-15 or equivalent). The end of the cable that mates with the transceiver must use a female connector with a slide lock assembly (Cinch type DA 51220-1 or equivalent). The transceiver must provide a mating male connector with locking posts. The other end of the transceiver cable (which mates with a female connector at the station) must use a male connector with locking posts (Cinch type D 53018 or equivalent). The station must provide a female connector with the slide lock assembly.

Because of the end-to-end matching of the connectors, transceiver cables may be extended by concatenating transceiver cable sections. (The transceiver cable sections function as 'extension cords'.) A cable with multiple sections must still meet the cable loss characteristics of 7.3.1.1.2.

The pin assignment is given in the following table:

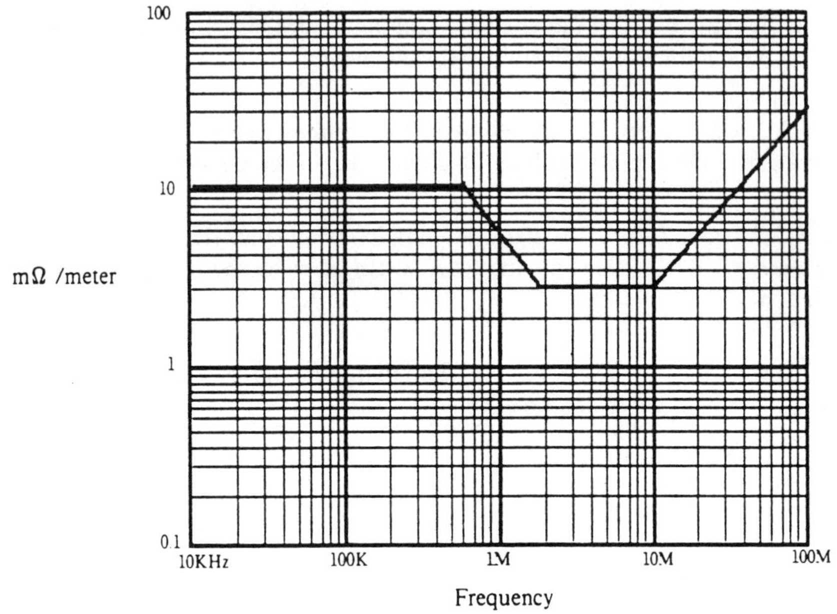

Figure 6A–10. Transceiver Cable Transfer Impedance

Transceiver Cable Connector Pin Assignment

1. Shield (See note)	
2. Collision Presence +	9. Collision Presence −
3. Transmit +	10. Transmit −
4. Reserved	11. Reserved
5. Receive +	12. Receive −
6. Power return	13. Power
7. Reserved	14. Reserved
8. Reserved	15. Reserved

Note: Shield must be terminated to connector shell as well as pin 1.

Metal, metallized plastic, or otherwise shielded connector backshells must be used to ensure shield integrity.

7.2.4 Transceiver Cable Drive. This section describes the requirements for driving any of the signal pairs in the transceiver cable: transmit, receive, and collision presence.

The AC signal levels presented to the transceiver cable shall be $\pm$ 700 mV nominal, balanced differential drive into 78 $\pm$ 5 Ω. The common mode

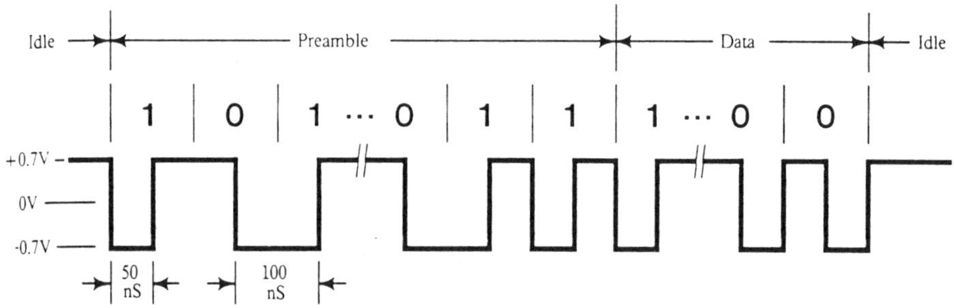

1. Voltages are measured differentially at output of transceiver cable driver.
2. Rise and fall times meet 10,000 series ECL requirements.

Figure 6A–11. Typical Transceiver Cable Waveform

voltage presented to the transceiver cable shall not exceed that allowed at the receiver, as specified in 7.2.5.2. Signal waveform shall be as shown in figure 6A–11.

The transceiver cable driver must be capable of maintaining the specified minimum differential signal into the worst case low cable impedance (73 Ω differential, 18.5 Ω common mode) in the environment specified in section 7.7.

The idle state of the output shall be high (+700 mV nominal); the first transition presented is negative-going, the last transition must be positive-going. Note that the presence of AC coupling may cause the voltage as specified at the output of the transceiver cable drive circuit not to appear on the transceiver cable in the idle state.

A typical transceiver cable drive circuit is given in Appendix D.

7.2.5 Transceiver Cable Receive. The following sections specify the requirements for receiving signals from any signal pair in the transceiver cable: transmit, receive, and collision presence. The circuit must be capable of receiving the signals from the transceiver cable driver specified in 7.2.4 through the cable specified in 7.2.2 in the worst case. A typical receive circuit is given in Appendix D.

7.2.5.1 Load Impedance and Termination. The termination impedance shall be 78 Ω ± 1% differential mode, and 18.5 Ω minimum common-mode, over the frequency range of 3–20 MHz.

7.2.5.2 Common Mode and CMRR. The common mode range and the common mode rejection ratio shall be sufficient to maintain a 5:1 signal to noise ratio in the environment specified in 7.7, measured at the input to the transceiver cable receiver. The common mode DC voltage at the input of the receiver shall be in the range of zero to +5 Vdc..

7.3 Coaxial Cable Compatibility Interface Specifications

The coaxial cable is the common, shared broadcast medium through which stations communicate. It provides one of the compatibility interface points described in 7.1.4.2.

7.3.1 Coaxial Cable Component Specifications. The cable is of constant impedance, coaxial construction. It is terminated at each end by a *terminator* (specified in 7.3.1.3), and connection provided for each transceiver. Coaxial cable connectors are used to make the connection from the cable to the terminators, and between cable sections (if needed). The cable has various electrical and mechanical requirements which must be met to ensure proper operations.

7.3.1.1 Coaxial Cable Parameters.

7.3.1.1.1 Characteristic Impedance. The average characteristic impedance of the cable shall be $50 \pm 2\ \Omega$, measured according to Mil. Std. C17-E. Periodic variations in impedance along a single piece of cable may be up to $\pm 3\ \Omega$ sinusoidal, centered around the average value, with a period < 2 meters. Note that the proper operation of the network is dependent upon the cable characteristic impedance; its value and tolerance are critical.

7.3.1.1.2 Attenuation. The attenuation of a cable segment shall not exceed 8.5 dB measured at 10 MHz, nor 6.0 dB measured at 5 MHz.

7.3.1.1.3 Velocity of Propagation. The minimum acceptable velocity of propagation is 0.77 c..

7.3.1.1.4. Mechanical Requirements. The cable used should be suitable for routing in various environments, including but not limited to, dropped ceilings, raised floors, and cable troughs. The jacket must provide insulation between the cable sheath and any building structural metal. Also, the cable must be capable of accepting coaxial cable connectors, described in 7.3.1.2. The cable must in addition conform to the following requirements:

1. The center conductor must be 0.0855±'' .0005'' diameter solid, tinned copper,
2. The core dielectric material must be foamed,

3. The inside diameter of the innermost shield must be .242″ minimum,
4. The outside diameter of the outermost shield must be .326″ ± .007″,
5. The outermost shield must be greater than 90% coverage tinned copper braid,
6. The jacket O.D. must be 0.405″ nominal,
7. The cable concentricity must be 90% minimum.

The cable must also meet applicable flammability criteria and local codes for the installed environment. Different (e.g., polyethylene and Teflon dielectric) types of cable sections may be interconnected, while meeting the sectioning requirements of 7.6.1.

7.3.1.1.5 Pulse Distortion. Pulse distortion shall not exceed ± 7 nS at the end of 500 meters of cable when driven with random 10 Mbit data encoded in accordance with 7.5.1.

7.3.1.1.6 Jacket Marking. The cable jacket must be marked with annular rings in a color contrasting with the background color of the jacket. The rings must be spaced at 2.5 meter ± 5 cm regularly along the entire length of the cable. It is permissible for the 2.5 meter spacing to be interrupted at discontinuities between cable sections joined by connectors. (See 7.6.2. for transceiver placement rules which mandate cable markings.)

7.3.1.1.7 Transfer Impedance. The transfer impedance of the cable shall not exceed the values shown in figure 6A–12 as a function of frequency.

7.3.1.2 Coaxial Cable Connectors. Coaxial cable connectors are used to join cable sections and attach terminators. Three types of connectors may be necessary; male plugs, female jacks, and female-to-female barrels. Plugs are used exclusively at the ends of all cable sections. Jacks are used to house cable terminators. Barrels are used to join cable sections.

All connectors are N series, 50 Ω constant impedance types. Since the frequencies present in the transmitted data are well below UHF range (being band-limited to approximately 20 MHz), military versions of the connectors are not required (but are acceptable).

Means must be provided to ensure that the connector shell (which connects to the cable sheath) does not make contact with any building metal, or other unintended conductor. A sleeve or boot to be slid over the connector at installation time is suitable.

7.3.1.3 Coaxial Cable Terminators. Coaxial cable terminators are used to provide a termination impedance for the cable equal in value to its characteristic impedance, thereby eliminating any reflection from the ends of the cables. Terminators shall be packaged within an inline female jack

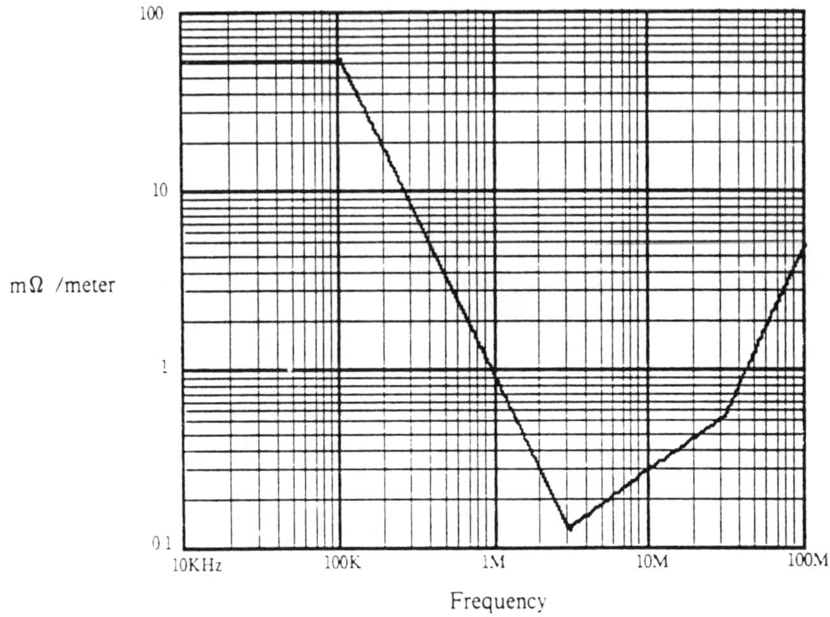

Figure 6A–12. Maximum Coaxial Cable Transfer Impedance

connector. The termination impedance shall be 50 Ω ± 1% measured from 0–50 MHz, with the magnitude of the phase angle of the impedance not to exceed 5 degrees. The terminator power rating shall be 1 watt or greater.

7.3.1.4 Transceiver-to-Coaxial Cable Connections. A means must be provided to allow for attaching a transceiver to the coaxial cable. The connection must disturb the transmission line characteristics of the cable as little as possible; it must present a predictably low shunt capacitance, and therefore a negligibly short stub length. For this reason, the transceiver must be located as close to its cable connection as possible; they are normally considered to be one assembly. Long (greater than 3 cm) connections between the coaxial cable and the input of the transceiver are not acceptable.

The transceiver-to-coaxial cable connection shall present less than 2 picofarads shunt capacitance to the coaxial cable, not including any transceiver electronics. If the design of the connection is such that the coaxial cable must be severed to install the transceiver, the coaxial cable segment must still meet the sectioning requirements of 7.6.1. Any coaxial connectors used on a severed cable must be type N, as specified in 7.3.1.2.

7.3.2 Coaxial Cable Signaling. The AC component of the signal on the coaxial cable due to a single transceiver as measured on the coaxial cable immediately adjacent to the transceiver connection shall be ± 16 mA nominal (14 mA min, 19 mA max). The DC component shall be one-half the AC component, plus 4.5 mA (4 mA min, 5 mA max). The actual current measured at a given point on the cable is a function of the transmitted current and the cable loss to the point of measurement. Positive current is defined as current out of the center conductor of the cable (into the transceiver). Cable loss is specified in 7.3.1.1.2.

The 10%–90% rise and fall times shall be 25 ± 5 nsec. Figure 6A–13 shows typical waveforms present on the cable. Harmonic content generated from a 10 MHz fundamental periodic input shall meet the following requirements:

Second and Third Harmonics:	−20 dB min
Fourth and Fifth Harmonics:	−30 dB min
Sixth and Seventh Harmonics:	−40 dB min
All Higher Harmonics:	−50 dB min

The signals as generated from the encoder (described in 7.5.1.1) shall appear on the coaxial cable without any inversions.

7.4 Transceiver Specifications

The following sections specify the requirements for a transceiver.

7.4.1 Transceiver-to-Coaxial Cable Interface. The following sections describe the interface between the transceiver and the coaxial cable. Positive current is defined as current into the transceiver (out of the center conductor of the cable).

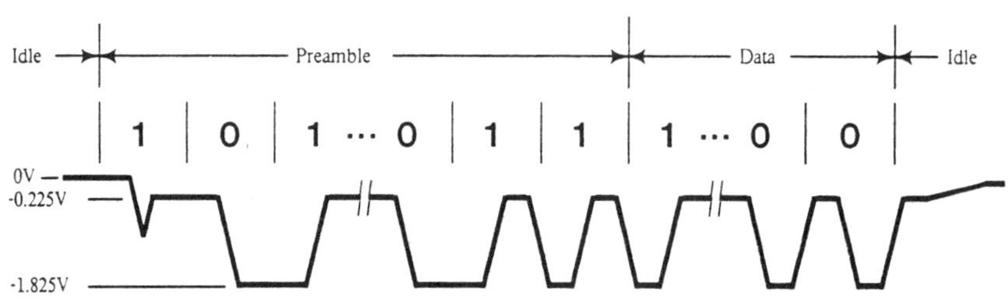

1. Voltages given are nominal; worst case is given in text.
2. Rise time is 25 nS nominal.
3. Voltages are measured on coaxial cable adjacent to transceiver.

Figure 6A–13. Typical Coaxial Cable Waveform

7.4.1.1 Input Impedance. The shunt capacitance presented to the coaxial cable by the transceiver circuitry (not including the means of attachment to the coaxial cable) shall not exceed 2 picofarads. The shunt resistance presented to the coaxial cable shall be greater than 50 KΩ.

These conditions must be met in both the power off and the power on, not transmitting states.

7.4.1.2 Bias Current. The transceiver must draw between −2 and +50 uA in the power-off and the power-on, not transmitting states.

7.4.1.3 Transmit Output Levels. Signals received from the transceiver cable transmit pair must be transmitted onto the coaxial cable with the characteristics specified in 7.3.2. Note that 7.3.2 specifies the current level on the coaxial cable. Since the coaxial cable proceeds in two directions away from the transceiver, the current into the transceiver is actually twice the current measured on the coaxial cable.

Transmitted output asymmetry shall not exceed 2 ns for a 50/50 duty cycle input on the transceiver cable transmit pair.

7.4.2 Transceiver-to-Transceiver Cable Interface.

7.4.2.1 Transmit Pair. The transceiver must present the transceiver cable receive characteristics specified in 7.2.5 to the transmit pair. At the start of a frame transmission, no more than 2 bits (two 100 ns bit cells) of information may be received from the transmit pair and not transmitted onto the coaxial cable. The steady-state propagation delay between the transmit pair input and the coaxial cable output shall not exceed 50 ns. There are no signal inversion between the transceiver cable transmit pair and the coaxial cable.

7.4.2.2 Receive Pair. The transceiver must present the transceiver cable transmit characteristics specified in 7.2.4 to the receive pair. Asymmetry as seen on the receive pair shall not exceed 1 ± 2 nsec for a ± 200 mV peak sinusoidal input from the coaxial cable.

The signal from the coaxial cable shall pass through AC coupling with an appropriate time constant before proceeding to the receive pair. The time constant should compensate for the coaxial cable pulse distortion.

At the start of a frame reception from the coaxial cable, no more than 5 bits (five 100 ns bit cells) of information may be received from the coaxial cable and not transmitted onto the receive pair. In addition, it is permissible for the first bit sent over the receive pair to contain encoding phase violations or invalid data, however all successive bits of the frame shall be valid and meet encoding rules. The steady-state propagation delay between the coaxial cable and the receive pair output shall not exceed 50 ns. There are not signal inversions between the coaxial cable and the transceiver cable receive pair.

7.4.2.3 Collision Presence Pair. The transceiver must present the transmitter characteristics specified in 7.2.4 to the collision presence pair. The signal presented to the collision presence pair shall be a periodic waveform with a 10 MHz ± 15% frequency. This signal shall be presented to the collision presence pair no more than 5 bit times (500 nS) after the average signal on the coaxial cable at the transceiver exceeds either that which could be produced by two transceiver outputs in the worst case (if the transceiver in question is not transmitting), or that which could be produced by that transceiver alone in the worst case (if that transceiver is transmitting).

7.4.2.4 Power Pair. The transceiver cable provides power which may be used for operation of the transceiver electronics. The power available shall be as described in 7.2.1.4. The distribution impedance of the transceiver cable is 4 Ω maximum, for a 50 meter cable with the resistance specified in 7.2.2.6. In order for the transceiver to derive its operating power from the power pair, circuitry must be employed to provide the required electrical isolation specified in 7.4.3.

7.4.3 Electrical Isolation. The transceiver must provide electrical isolation between the transceiver cable and the coaxial cable. The isolation impedance shall be greater than 250 KΩ, measured between any conductor (including shield) of the transceiver cable and either the center conductor or shield of the coaxial cable, at 60 Hz. The breakdown voltage of the isolation means provided shall be at least 250 VAC, rms.

7.4.4 Reliability. No single nor double component failure within the transceiver electronics shall impede communication among other transceivers on the coaxial cable. Connectors and other passive components comprising the means of connecting the transceiver to the coaxial cable shall be designed to minimize the probability of total network failure.

7.5 Channel Logic

The following sections describe the functions that must be performed to properly interface between the data link and the transceiver cable. They are normally implemented as logic, typically within the same device implementing the data link layer.

7.5.1 Channel Encoding. The channel shall use Manchester phase encoding, with a data rate of 10 Mbps, ± .01%, measured at the encoder clock. Thus, each bit cell is 100 ns long.

The following section describes the requirements for encoding and decoding signals to be transmitted on, or received from the coaxial or transceiver cables.

7.5.1.1 Encoder. The encoder is used to translate physically separate signals of clock (synchronization) and data into a single, self-synchronizable serial bit stream, suitable for transmission on the coaxial cable by the transceiver.

During the first half of the bit cell time, the serial signal transmitted is the logical complement of the bit value being encoded during that cell. During the second half of the bit cell time, the uncomplemented value of the bit being encoded is transmitted. Therefore, there is always a signal transition (either positive-going or negative-going, depending on the bit being encoded) in the center of each bit cell. A timing diagram for a typical bit stream is given in figure 6A–14.

The encoder output drives the transmit pair of the transceiver cable, and ultimately, the coaxial cable through the transceiver. The encoder output asymmetry must not exceed 0.5 ns. The encoder shall provide the defined output for the first (and all subsequent) bits presented to its input. All information submitted for encoding shall appear at the output of the encoder.

7.5.1.2 Decoder. The decoder is used to separate the incoming phase encoded bit stream into a data stream and a clock signal. The decoder must be able to provide data and clock signals usable by the data link under the asummetry imposed by the worst case system configuration. The decoder must provide usable output (clock and data) after no more than 8 bit cell times after reception of an encoded signal. The first signals received from the transceiver at the beginning of frame reception may not constitute a valid, properly encoded bit; it is possible for the time from the first transition seen to the first true mid-bit cell transition to assume any value from zero to 100 nS.

The decoder input is normally derived from the coaxial cable, through the transceiver cable receive pair. It is not necessary for the decoder to provide

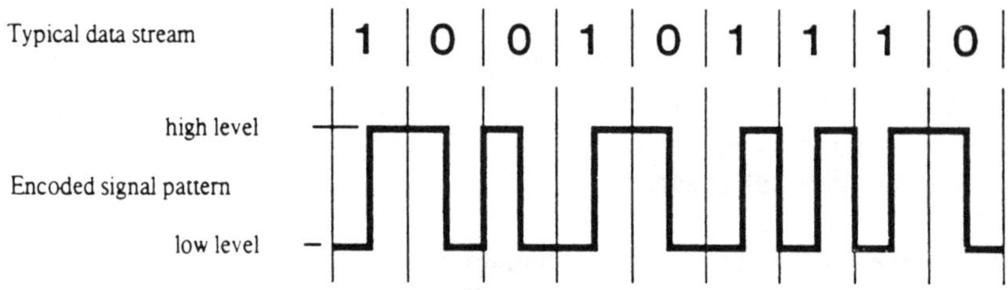

Figure 6A–14. Manchester Encoding

usable output when there is a collision on the coaxial cable, regardless of whether the station using that decoder is involved in the collision.

7.5.1.3 Preamble Generation. Because most of the channel circuitry is allowed to provide valid output some number of bit times after being presented valid input, it is necessary for a preamble to be sent before the start of data link information, to allow the channel circuitry to reach its steady-state, with valid outputs throughout the system. Upon request by the data link to transmit the first bit of a new frame, the channel shall first transmit the preamble; a predetermined bit sequence used for channel stabilization and synchronization. If, while transmitting the preamble, the channel log asserts the collision detect signal as specified in 7.5.2, any remaining preamble bits shall not be sent. The channel should immediately proceed with the transmission of the bit submitted by the data link.

The preamble is a 64 bit pattern to be presented to the channel encoder in the same manner as data link information. The pattern is:

10101010 10101010 10101010 10101010 10101010 10101010
10101010 10101011.

The bits are transmitted in order, from left to right. The nature of the pattern is such that when encoded, it appears as a periodic waveform on the cable, with a 5 MHz frequency. Excepting the final two bits, the only transitions present in the waveform are in the center of the bit cells. This is depicted in figure 6A 15. The last two bits of the preamble contain transitions at both the bit cell centers and the edges, and are used to indicate the end of the preamble, and the beginning of the data link encapsulation portion of the frame. The next bit transmitted is the bit originally submitted by transmission by the data link.

Preamble removal on reception is discussed in 7.5.4.1.

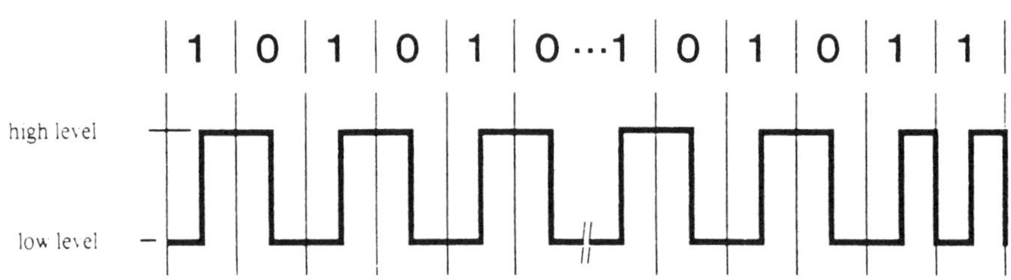

Figure 6A–15. Preamble Encoding

7.5.2 Collision Detect Signal. The channel must indicate to the data link when the signals on the coaxial cable imply simultaneous transmission attempts by more than one station. This is normally indicated through the collision presence pair in the transceiver cable, described in 7.2.1.3.

The channel logic must assert the collision detect signal within 2 bit times (200 ns), following the onset of collision presence. This collision detect signal shall be asserted only when the data link is transmitting. A functional logic description of the collision detect signal is shown in figure 6A–16.

Following the loss of collision presence information, the channel must deassert the collision detect signal within 1.6 bit cell times (160 ns).

7.5.3 Carrier Sense Signal. The channel must indicate to the data link the presence of carrier, a signal transmission attempt on the coaxial cable by a station. This is normally indicated through both the receive and collision presence pairs in the transceiver cable, described in 7.2.1.

The carrier sense signal shall be asserted when one or more station is attempting transmission on the cable, regardless of whether the station sensing carrier is transmitting at that time. The channel logic must assert the carier sense signal within 2 bit times (200 ns) following the onset of carrier presence information. A functional logic description of these signals is shown in figure 6A–17.

Following the loss of carrier presence information (receive transitions and collision presence information) the channel must deassert the carrier signal within 1.6 bit cell times (160 ns).

7.5.4 Channel Framing. During reception, the channel must provide the data link with signals to indicate beginning and end of frame.

7.5.4.1 Beginning-of-Frame Sequence. The channel logic recognizes the presence of activity on the medium through the carrier sense signal. This is

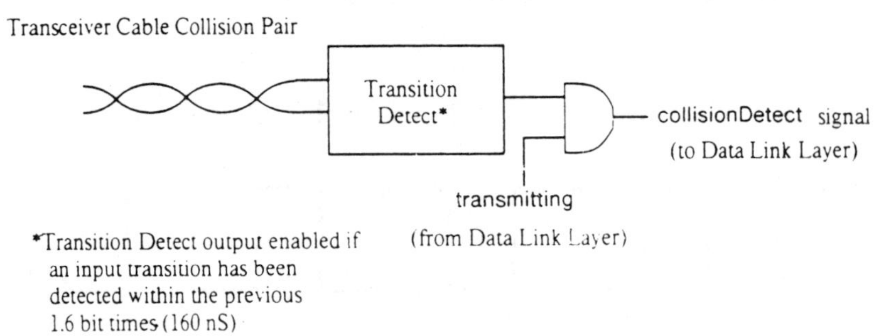

Figure 6A–16. Functional Logic of *collisionDetect* Signal

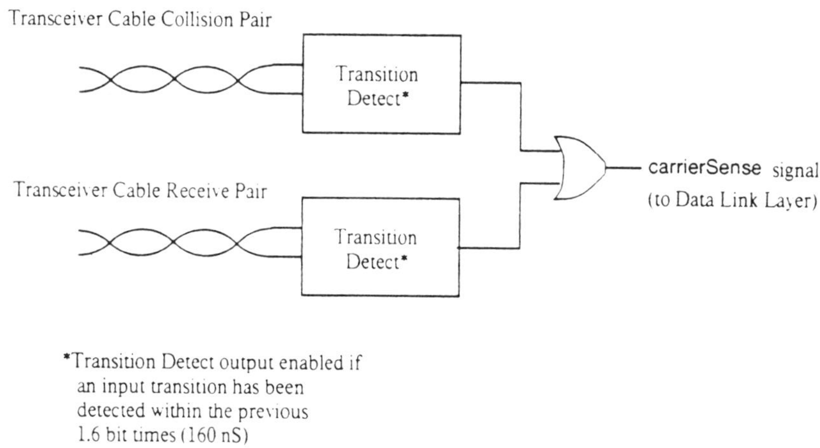

Figure 6A–17. Functional Logic of *carrierSense* Signal

the first indication that the frame reception process should begin. However, dependent upon the physical configuration of the system, there are some number of preamble bits to be received by the channel before the start of the data link frame as indicated by the double-1 at the end of preamble. In addition, the first signals received from the decoder may be invalid due to the first bit allowance of the transceiver (see 7.4.2.2). The channel must wait no less than 8 bit times (800 nS) before monitoring the output of the decoder for the "double-1" indicating end of preamble, and beginning of data link frame. Upon reception of the double-1, the channel shall begin passing successive bits to the data link through the defined receive bit strem interface. If, after waiting the required 8 bit times, a "double-0" is encountered, the physical channel shall not pass any bits of the current frame to the data link. Normal operation of the data link and channel shall resume on the subsequent frame.

7.5.4.2 End-of-Frame Sequence. As specified in 7.5.3, the carrier sense signal must be deasserted no later than 1.6 bit times (160 ns) after the cessation of activity on the coaxial cable as seen by the channel logic. The channel ensures that no extraneous bits will appear at the end of a frame following the last valid bit.

7.6 Channel Configuration Requirements

7.6.1 Cable Sectioning. The 500 meter maximum length coaxial cable segment need not be made from a single, homogeneous length of cable. The boundary between two cable sections (joined by coaxial connectors; two male plugs and a barrel) represents a signal reflection point due to the impedance discontinuity caused by the batch-to-batch impedance tolerance of the cable. Since the worst-case variation from 50 Ω is 2 Ω (see 7.3.1.1.1), a possible worst-case reflection of 4% may result from the joining of two cable sections. The configuration of long cable segments (up to 500 meters) from smaller sections must be made with care. The following recommendations apply, and are given in order of preference:

1. If possible, the total segment should be made from one homogeneous (no breaks) cable. This is feasible for short segments, and results in minimal reflections from cable impedance discontinuities.
2. If cable segments must be built up from smaller sections, it is highly desirable to ensure that all the sections are from the same manufacturer and lot. This is equivalent to using a single cable, since the cable discontinuities are due to extruder limitations, and not extruder-to-extruder tolerances. There are no restrictions in cable sectioning if this method is used. However, if a cable section in such a system is later replaced, it must be replaced either with another cable from the same manufacturer and lot, or with one of the standard lengths described below.
3. If uncontrolled cable sections must be used in building up a longer segment, the lengths should be chosen such that reflections, when they occur, do not have a high probability of adding in phase. This can be accomplished by using lengths which are odd integral multiples of a half-wavelength in the cable at 5 MHz; this corresponds to using lengths of 23.4, 70.2, and 117 meters (± 0.5 meters) for all sections. These are considered to be the standard lengths for all cable sections. Using these lengths exclusively, any mix or match of cable sections may be used to build up a 500 meter segment without incurring excessive reflections.
4. As a last resort, an arbitrary configuration of cable sections may be employed, if it has been confirmed by analysis or measurement that the worst-case signal reflection due to the impedance discontinuities at any point on the cable does not exceed 7% of the incident wave when driven by a transceiver meeting the specifications of 7.4.

7.6.2 Transceiver Placement. Transceivers and their associated connections to the cable cause signal reflections due to their non-infinite bridging impedance. While this impedance must be implemented as specified in 7.3.1.4 and 7.4.1, the placement of transceivers along the coaxial cable must also be controlled to insure that reflections from transceiver do not add in phase to a significant degree.

Coaxial cables marked as specified in 7.3.1.1.6 have marks at regular 2.5 meters spacing; a transceiver may be placed at any mark on the cable. This guarantees both a minimum spacing between transceivers of 2.5 meters, as well as controlling the relative spacing of transceivers to insure non-alignment on fractional wavelength boundaries.

The total number of transceivers on a cable segment shall not exceed 100.

7.6.3 System Grounding. The sheath conductor of the coaxial cable shall not make electrical contact with any earth reference, building structural metal, ducting, plumbing fixture, or other unintentioned conductor. Insulators may be used to cover any coaxial connectors used to join cable sections and terminators, to insure that this requirement is met. A sleeve or boot attached at installation time is acceptable.

The sheath conductor of the transceiver cable shall be connected to the earth reference or chassis of the device housing the station logic.

7.6.4 Repeaters. Repeaters are used to extend the channel length and topology beyond that which could be achieved by a single coaxial cable segment. (See the channel configuration model in 7.1.5.) A repeater requires a transceiver on each of the segments between which it is repeating signals. These transceivers must be as specified in 7.4, and must be counted towards the maximum specified in 7.6.2.

A maximum of two repeaters may be in the signal path between any two transceivers on the channel.

7.6.4.1 Carrier Detect and Transmit Repeat. Repeaters must implement the carrier sense function as specified in 7.5.3 for both segments between which it is connected. Upon detection of carrier from one segment, the repeater must retransmit all received signals from that segment onto the other segment. Signals shall be retimed and amplified as specified in 7.6.4.3. The maximum steady-state propagation delay through the repeater for the repeated signal (not including startup delays, carrier sense delay or retiming delays) shall not exceed 800 nS.

7.6.4.2 Collision Detect and Collision Repeat. Repeaters must implement the collision detect function as specified in 7.5.2 for both segments between which it is connected. If, while repeating signals as specified in 7.6.4.1, collision is detected on either side, the repeater must ensure that all stations involved in the collision recognize the event as a collision, regardless of which side of the repeater the station is on. The maximum time between the recognition of the collision and the repeating of the collision indication (not including carrier sense of retiming delays) shall not exceed 200 nS.

7.7 Environment Specifications

The following sections specify the physical environment in which all channel components must operate to be considered compatible.

7.7.1 Electromagnetic Environment. The physical channel hardware shall meet its specifications when operating in the following ambient plane-wave fields:

2 Volts/Meter from 10 KHz through 30 MHz

5 Volts/Meter from 30 MHz through 1 GHz

7.7.2 Temperature and Humidity. All physical channel hardware, with the possible exception of the channel logic components shall operate over the ambient temperature range of 5 to 50 degrees Celsius, and humidity range of 10% to 95% non-condensing. The channel logic components are normally part of the station hardware, and are thus subject to individual station product requirements. Hardware which does not meet the temperature and humidity requirements specified must state so in its published product specification.

Appendix A: Glossary

This section defines some of the essential terminology associated with the Ethernet.

baseband coaxial system: A system whereby information is directly encoded and impressed on the coaxial transmission medium. One information signal at a time can be present on the medium without disruption (see collision).

binary exponential backoff: The algorithm used to schedule retransmissions after a collision. So called because the interval from which the retransmission time is selected is expanded exponentially with repeated collisions.

broadcast: Describes the class of media for which the Ethernet is designed, in which all stations are capable of receiving a signal transmitted by any other station. Also, describes the mode of usage of such a medium by the Data Link Layer in which all stations are instructed to receive a given frame.

carrier sense: A signal provided by the Physical Layer to the Data Link Layer to indicate that one or more stations are currently transmitting on the channel.

channel logic: The logical functions provided between the transceiver cable and the Data Link, which support the defined interface between the data link and the physical layers.

Client Layer: Collective term used to describe any layer of a network architecture, which use the Ethernet Data Link and Client interface.

coaxial cable: A two-conductor, concentric, constant impedance transmission line.

coaxial cable interface: The electrical, mechanical, and logical interface to the shared coaxial cable medium. This is a mandatory compatibility interface, which must be correctly implemented by every Ethernet implementation.

coaxial cable section: An unbroken piece of coaxial cable, fitted with coaxial connectors at its ends, used to build up coaxial cable segments.

coaxial cable segment: A length of coaxial cable made up from one or more coaxial cable sections and coaxial connectors, terminated at each end in its characteristic impedance. A 500 meter segment is the longest configuration possible without repeaters.

collision: The result of multiple transmissions overlapping in the physical channel, resulting in garbled data and necessitating retransmission.

collision detect: A signal provided by the Physical Layer to the Data Link Layer to indicate that one or more other stations are contending with the local station's transmission. It can be true only during transmission.

collision enforcement: Transmission of extra, encoded "jam" bits after a collision is detected, to insure that the duration of the collision is sufficient to guarantee its detection by all transmitting stations.

compatibility interfaces: The *coaxial cable interface*, and the *transceiver cable interface*, the two points at which hardware compatibility is defined to allow connection of independently designed and manufactured components to the Ethernet.

contention: Interference between colliding transmissions (see collision). Resolution of occasional contention is a normal part of the Ethernet's distributed link management procedure (see CSMA-CD).

controller: The implementation unit which connects a station to the Ethernet, typically comprising part of the Physical Layer, much or all of the Data Link Layer, and appropriate electronics for interfacing to the station.

CSMA-CD: Carrier Sense Multiple Access with Collision Detection, the generic term for the class of link management procedure used by the Ethernet. So called because it a) allows multiple stations to access the broadcast channel at will, b) avoids contention via carrier sense and deference, and c) resolves contention via collision detection and retransmission.

Data Link Layer: The higher of the two layers in the Ethernet design, which implements a medium-independent link level communication facility on top of the physical channel provided by the Physical Layer.

deference: A process by which a data link controller delays its transmission when the channel is busy to avoid contention with ongoing transmissions.

frame check sequence: An encoded value appended to each frame by the Data Link Layer to allow detection of transmission errors in the physical channel.

interframe spacing: An enforced idle time between transmission of successive frames to allow receiving data link controllers and the physical channel to recover.

jam: An encoded bit sequence used for collision enforcement.

Manchester encoding: A means by which separate data and clock signals can be combined into a single, self-synchronizable data stream, suitable for transmission on a serial channel.

multicast: An addressing mode in which a given frame is targeted to a group of logically related stations.

physical address: The unique address value associated with a given station on the network. An Ethernet physical address is defined to be distinct from all other physical addresses on all Ethernets.

Physical Channel: The implementation of the physical layer.

Physical Layer: The lower of the two layers of the Ethernet design, implemented by the physical channel using the specified coaxial cable medium. The Physical Layer insulates the Data Link Layer from medium-dependent physical characteristics.

preamble: A sequence of 64 encoded bits which the Physical Layer transmits before each frame to allow synchronization of clocks and other Physical Layer circuitry at other sites on the channel.

repeater: A device used to extend the length and topology of the physical channel beyond that imposed by a single segment, up to the maximum allowable end-to-end channel length.

round-trip propagation time: In bit times, the time required in the worst-case for a transmitting station's collision detect signal to be asserted due to normal contention for the channel. This delay is the primary component of the slot time.

slot time: A multi-purpose parameter which describes the contention behavior of the Data Link Layer. It serves as a) an upper bound on the collison vulnerability of a given transmission, b) an upper bound on the size of the frame fragment produced by a collision, and c) the scheduling quantum for collision retransmission.

station: A single addressable site on the Ethernet, generally implemented as a computer and appropriate peripherals, and connected to the Ethernet via a controller and a transceiver.

transceiver: The portion of the Physical Layer implementation that connects directly to the coaxial cable and provides both the electronics which send and receive the encoded signals on the cable and the required electrical isolation.

transceiver cable: A four pair, shielded cable used for the transceiver cable interface.

transceiver cable interface: The electrical, mechanical and logical interface which connects the transceiver to the controller. The standard transceiver cable is a recommended compatibility interface.

Appendix B: Notes on Address and Type Assignment, and Licensing

Address and Type Assignment

The address and type fields will be administered by Xerox Corporation.

A block of addresses will be assigned to each licensee of Ethernet patents (see below). Others may obtain an address block or type field assignment by request. A nominal fee to cover administrative costs will be charged.

Submit written requests to:

Xerox Corporation
Ethernet Address Administration Office
3333 Coyote Hill Road
Palo Alto, CA 94304

Licensing

Ethernet incorporates features that are protected by one or more patents assigned to Xerox Corporation. Questions on the need for licensing particular uses of this specification should be directed to:

Xerox Corporation
Director of Licensing
Long Ridge Road
Stamford, CT 06904

Appendix C: CRC Implementation

Every frame contains, in its frame check sequence field, a 32-bit cyclic redundancy check (CRC) code. Because the formal mathematical definition of this code (see 6.2.4) is not suggestive of an appropriate implementation,

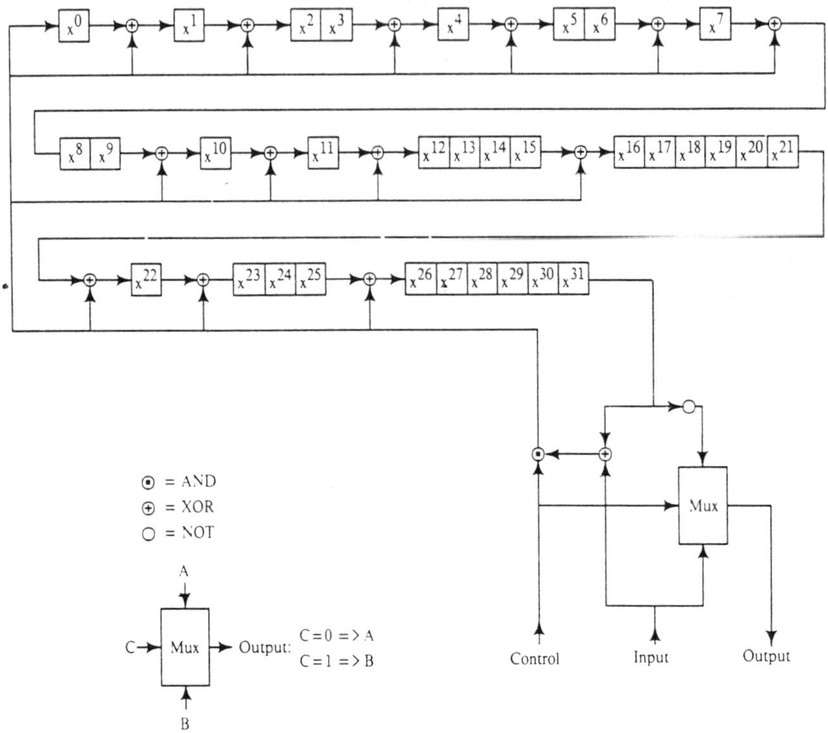

Figure 6A–18. CRC Implementation

this appendix outlines one possible implementation in terms of a feedback shift register. This type of implementation is likely to be common in practice, but is not a mandatory part of the specification.

The feedback shift register (see figure 6A–18) is used to represent division of the pre-scaled message by the generating polynomial. The 32-bit register is accessed via the three signals Input, Output, and Control. When Control = 1, Input bits are shifted into the feedback shift register and also fed directly back to Output. When Control = 0, the feedback paths are disabled and the shift register shifts the complement of its contents to Output.

Before CRC generation at the transmitting end, initialization logic (not shown in figure 6A–18) preloads the shift register to all 1's. Control is then held at 1 while the address, type and data fields of the outgoing frame are shifted into Input and the CRC is generated. Meanwhile, the same bits emerging at Output are transmitted over the network. When the last bit of the data field has been processed, Control is set to 0 and the complemented CRC is shifted out for transmission, starting with the x^{31} term (see 6.2.4).

CRC checking at the receiving end also begins with the shift preloaded to all 1's. Control is then held at 1 while the incoming bits are shifted into Input to regenerate the CRC. When the last bit of the data field has been processed, the shift register should contain the CRC whose binary complement is about to arrive on the network. Since this field boundary cannot be recognized by the receiver, however, Control remains at 1 and the bits of the CRC continue to feed into the shift register until the end of the entire frame is reached. If the two CRCs match, the final contents of the shift register is the value:

11000111 00000100 11011101 01111011

(where the leftmost bit corresponds to the x^{31} term of the polynomial and the rightmost to the x^0 term). Any other final value indicates a detected error. (The extra logic to test for this value is not shown in figure 6A–18.)

One potential problem which is avoided in this implementation is insensitivity of the shift register to incoming zero-bits when it is in the all-zero state. Following standard practice, this state is avoided at the beginning and end of the frame by preloading the shift register with all 1-bits, and by inverting each bit of the final CRC. Logically, these correspond, respectively, to the complementing of the first 32 bits of the frame and to the final complementing of the remainder, as specified in the mathematical definition in 6.2.4. See also [22] for further discussion.

Appendix D: Implementation of Transceiver Cable Driver and Receiver

This appendix presents circuit diagrams for typical implementations of the transceiver cable drivers and receivers. The use of these exact circuits is not necessary for conformance to the specification; equivalent circuits may be used as long as the relevant specifications are met.

Figure 6A–19 depicts an implementation of the transceiver cable driver specified in 7.2.4. It is suitable for use at either end of the transceiver cable, as necessary; i.e., it would be located at the station end to drive the transmit pair, and at the transceiver end to drive the receive and collision presence pairs. In addition, it is capable of driving suitable isolation circuits required to be located within the transceiver.

Figure 6A–20 depicts an implementation of the transceiver cable receiver specified in 7.2.5. It is suitable for use at either end of the transceiver cable, as necessary; i.e., it would be located at the station end to receive from the receive and collision presence pairs, and at the transceiver to receive from the transmit pair. It is capable of operating through suitable isolation circuits required to be located within the transceiver.

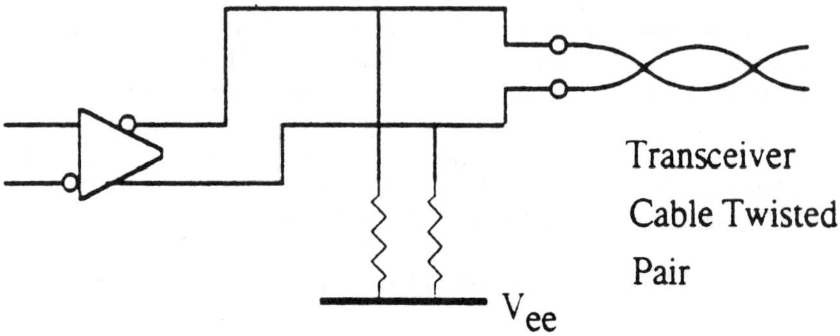

Figure 6A–19. Typical Transceiver Cable Driver

Appendix E: Interframe Recovery

It is important that data link controller implementations be able to receive a frame that arrives immediately after another frame has been transmitted or received. Here, "immediately" means 9.6 μsec, based on the minimum interframe spacing provided as recovery time for the data link. (See 6.3.2.2.) It is important that the data link controller be able to resume reception within that time.

Reception of multiple closely spaced incoming frames is a very desirable capability, and is crucial for stations which tend to communicate with several other stations concurrently. There is one important case in which a data link controller implementation cannot reasonably be expected to receive closely

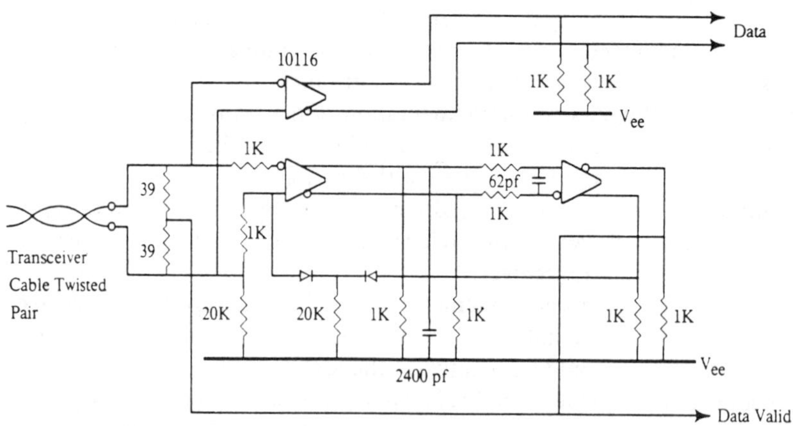

Figure 6A–20. Typical Transceiver Cable Receiver

spaced incoming frames: if the station hardware (e.g. I/O bus) is intrinsically unable to accept the bits of a frame at the rate at which they arrive over the network, each incoming frame must be buffered to allow the station to accept it at some lower rate. Assuming limited buffering resources (e.g. a one frame buffer), reception of subsequent frames cannot occur until sufficient buffer space is available. This mode of operation is allowed for low performance stations.

Reception of an incoming frame immediately after transmission of an outgoing frame is a very important capability, even for stations which do not tend to communicate with several other stations concurrently. All stations, low performance to high performance, should allow reception of an incoming frame immediately after transmission of an outgoing frame.

Appendix 6B: Systems Description: HYPERchannel Network Adapters

1. INTRODUCTION

The Network Systems HYPERchannel Network Adapters provide a unique capability for the interconnection of resources in a computing installation. Central processors, front-end processors, storage subsystems, and unit record subsystems from different manufacturers can be interconnected in a short-haul, high-speed local network.

The application of an adapter network can make the difference between a collection of computing equipment and an effective computing site by providing:

- interconnection of equipment from various manufacturers.
- high performance communication between processors.
- a sharing of peripheral systems between multiple processors.
- realistic physical location of interconnected equipment.
- increased utilization of interconnected equipment.
- increased tolerance to individual equipment failures.

Adapter Network

The adapter network utilizes single coaxial cable data trunks which provide reliable communication from 50 million bits per second at 1000 feet to 1.5 million bits per second at 1 mile. Greater distances can be achieved through the use of lower loss coax as shown in the following performance table:

Network Trunk Performance

Speed (nominal) / *Cable Dia.*	*0.3 in.*	*0.6 in.*	*0.9 in.*
50 megabits/sec	1,000 ft.	2,000 ft.	4,000 ft.
25 megabits/sec	1,500 ft.	3,000 ft.	6,000 ft.
12 megabits/sec	2,000 ft.	4,000 ft.	8,000 ft.
6 megabits/sec	3,000 ft.	6,000 ft.	12,000 ft.
3 megabits/sec	4,000 ft.	8,000 ft.	16,000 ft.
1.5 megabits/sec	5,000 ft.	10,000 ft.	20,000 ft.

Network Systems Corporation, "Systems Description: HYPERchannel Network Adapters," Publication No. A01-0000-02, January 1978. Reprinted with permission.

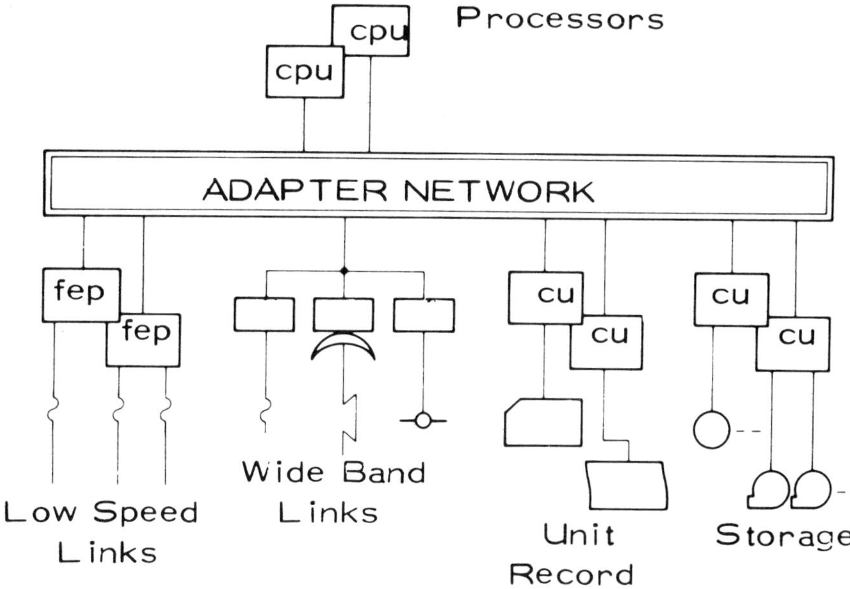

Figure 6B–1. Site Interconnect: A network of high-speed, short-haul installation data paths

Network Adapters interface individual equipment to the network of data trunks. Different adapter models provide an electrical and logical interface to specific processors and peripheral systems from various manufacturers. The adapters at each equipment contain a microprocessor and control and data buffering. The adapters implement a sophisticated network data movement protocol.

Each adapter can attach up to four independent network trunks. Each trunk may be of a different performance. An adapter network can therefore be configured to match a specific installation and provide for:

- incremental expansion
- an interconnect cost which is linear
- no single point of failure

Adapter Types

There are two basic types of network adapters:

- Processor Adapter
- Device Adapter

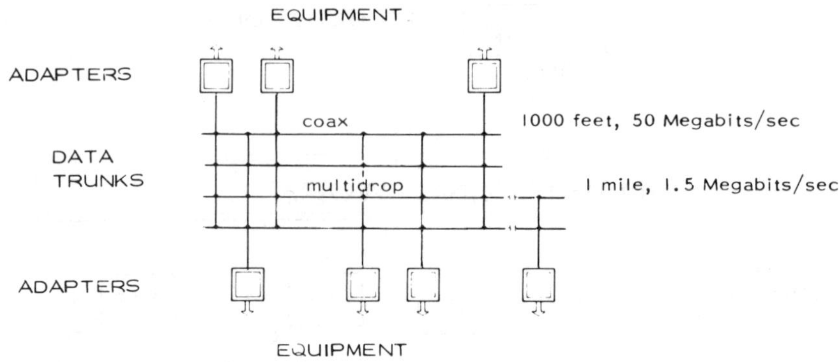

Figure 6B–2. Adapter Network: Multidrop single coaxial cable data trunks with intelligent, buffered adapters at each equipment

Processor Adapter

A processor adapter interfaces a computer data channel to the network of data trunks. It functions as a buffered communications controller to move messages on the network. In operation, the computer communicates with the adapter buffers at its own rate and asynchronous with transmissions on the data trunk. The adapter TRANSMITS data stored in its buffers on the selected data trunk, providing the transmission format and protocol required. The processor adapter RECEIVES data from the data trunk into its buffers and responds to the transmitting adapter with its status. The computer attached to the receiving adapter may then access the received data.

Device Adapter

A device adapter functions as a remote channel creating a computer data channel for the attachment of peripheral control units. It is driven by messages from the data trunks. The adapter RECEIVES messages containing device command stacks, data and control information. It GENERATES messages containing status or device data. In operation, the remote channel executes a stack of commands against a specified attached device. The adapter will block multiplex operations on the attached devices from multiple operations on the attached devices from multiple processors and provides for reservation of the attached devices.

Another class of device adapter is the Adapter/Controller which provides for direct attachment of peripheral devices and performs the dual function of network adapter and device controller. The Link Adapter is an adapter which interfaces wide band data links.

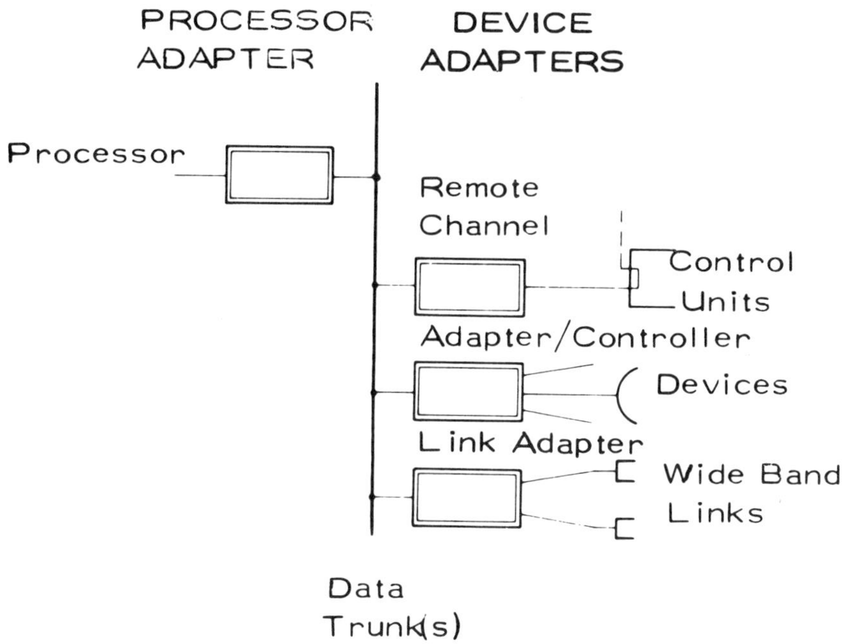

Figure 6B–3. Adapter Types: Specific adapter models provide an exact interface to individual manufacturers equipments

Applications

The Network Adapters have a wide range of applications in creating an effective local computing installation. Several examples are described below.

Channel to Channel Network

Adapters are used to implement a very high speed channel to channel network between processors. They are uniquely useful when the processors are from different manufacturers. The decoupling provided by the adapter buffering creates very efficient operations especially when the processors have different channel rates.

A specific application of the channel to channel network is the interconnection of front-end communications processors, or other special processors, to multiple central processors. In this application the adapters can be effective in reducing the amount of time and memory space ultimately required in these smaller processors to implement an effective, high speed data path with the central processors.

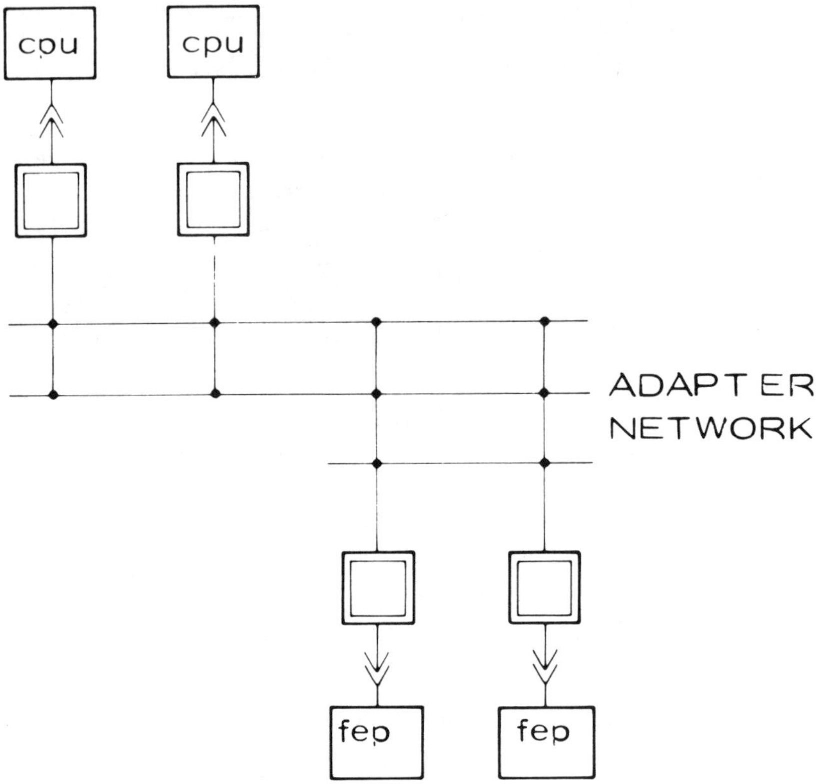

Figure 6B–4. Channel to Channel Network: High speed, buffered links between processors, including different CPU manufacturers

Extended CPU I/O Capability

The evolution from batch to terminal type user access and the increased demand for on-line mass storage has overwhelmed the I/O capability of conventional processors in many installations. The adapter network can provide specific capabilities in solving this problem by providing for:

- Attachment of larger numbers of peripherals.
- Effective simultaneous operation of multiple peripherals.
- Location of equipment at longer distances.
- Increased utilization of the processor data channels.

The network of data trunks allows many devices to be attached, provides for

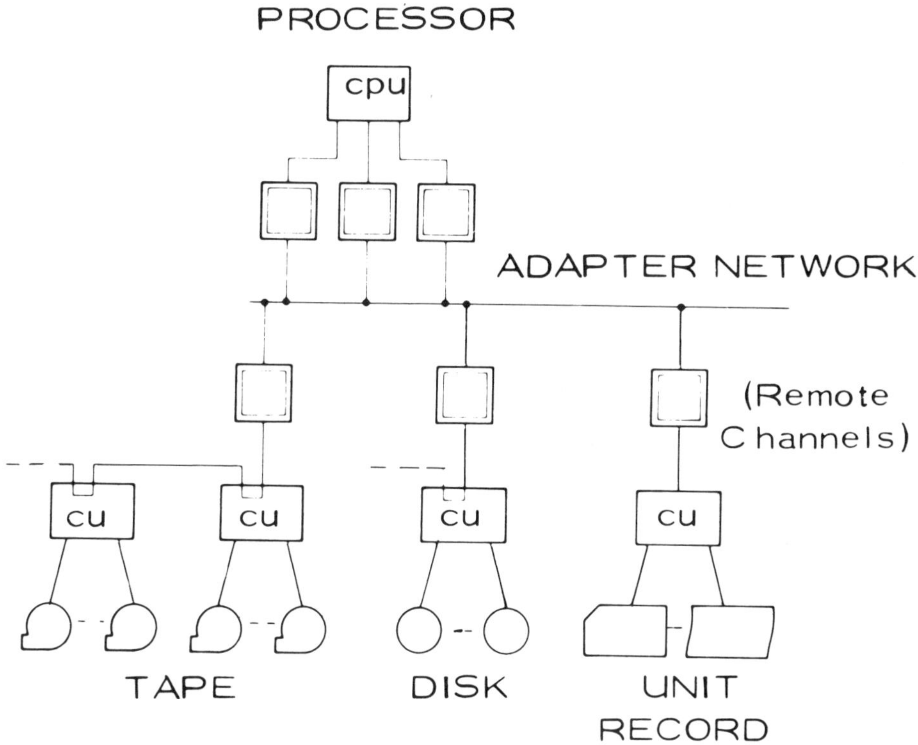

Figure 6B–5. Extended I/O Capability: Adapters as remote channels providing increased I/O capability, attachment of peripherals from different manufacturers and remote location of peripherals

the access to the devices from a number of channels and allows for the equipment to be placed at longer distances from the CPU.

The remote data channels allow an expansion of the capability for parallel device operation.

Most CPU channel transfers can proceed at full channel rate regardless of the speed of the attached equipment. The buffering in the processor adapters allows data blocks to be received and buffered in adapters and transferred to the processor at full channel rate.

Pooling of Peripherals

The adapter network provides an effective access to multiple peripherals from multiple processor.

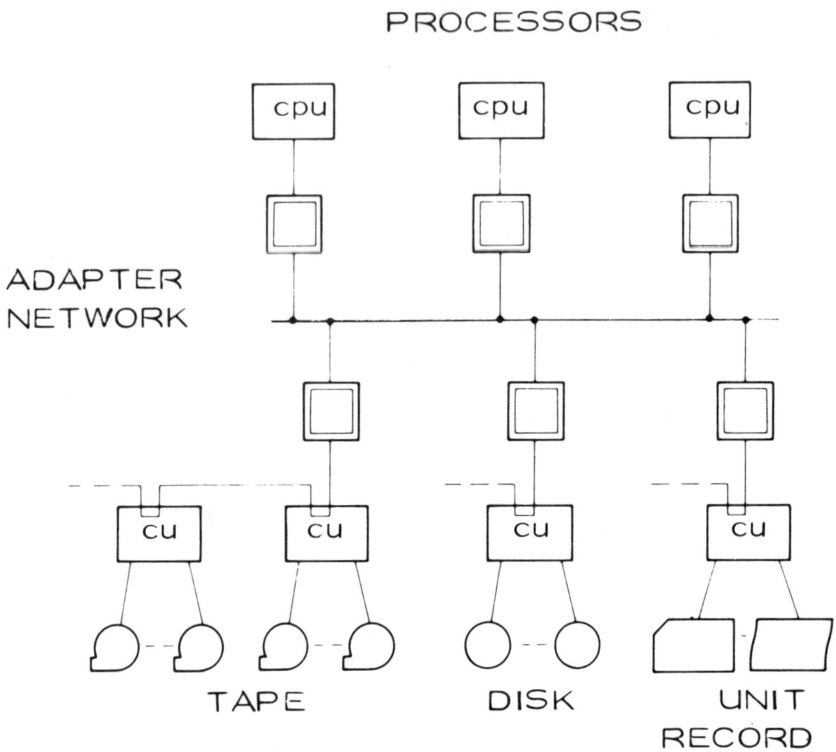

Figure 6B–6. Pooling of Peripherals: Shared, remote channel capability of the adapters providing for the effective sharing of peripherals in an installation

This pooling of peripherals can provide access to resources where needed and when needed at a low cost. The peripherals and processors can be from different manufacturers and cap be located at long distances from each other without affecting performance. Especially useful is the capability to introduce a new technology device into an installation when the device is not normally compatable with the existing system.

A single device adapter provides for the multiplexing of I/O operations on its attached devices by different processors, thus allowing very efficient utilization of the attached peripheral subsystem. By virtue of the complete set of interconnections, a processor may control the data access in the network yet allow the data itself to proceed directly between another processor and the peripheral subsystem.

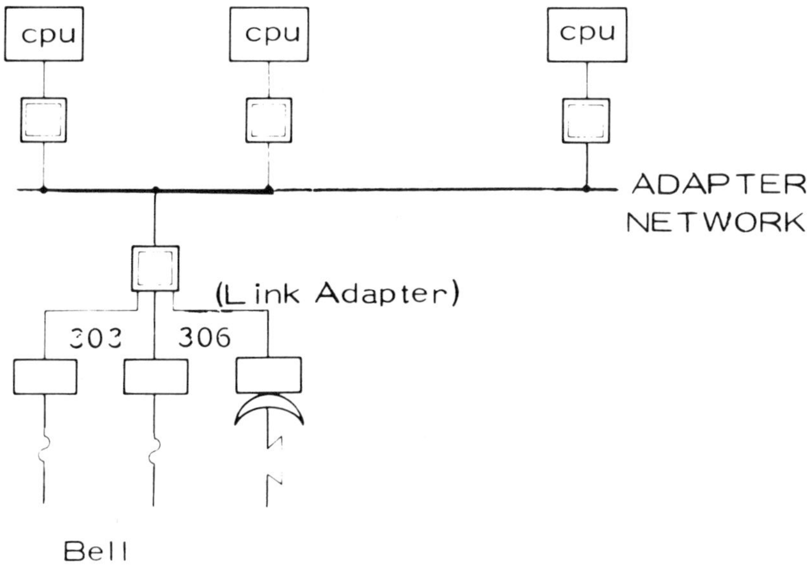

Figure 6B–7. Access to Wide Band Links: Link adapters interfacing the local network to common carrier wide band links

Access to Wide Band Links

The high speed serial data envelope and the data movement control provided by adapters for the data trunks makes it logical to interface to a wide band data link, such as Bell T1 or Microwave Links. In addition, the link adapters are designed to interface multiple wide band data links to the local adapter network for access by all processors.

Physical Characteristics

Dimensions and Weight:
- Height: 12¾ in. [32.4 cm]
- Width: 19 in. [48.3 cm]
- Depth: 20½ in. [52.1 cm]
- Weight: 140 lb [63.5 kg]

Power Requirements:
- Voltage and Frequency: 105v min, 125v max; 50–63 Hz
- Total Current Requirement: 15 amp max

Operating Humidity Range: 30 to 90% RH

Ambient Temperature:
Storage: −22 to 185 F [−30 to 85 C]
Operating: 59 to 95 F [15 to 35 C]

Cooling Method: Forced Air (Internal Blower)

TECHNOLOGY

Data Trunks

The serial coaxial data trunks are a combination of the technologies of data communications and high performance electronics. The data trunks provide:

- high reliability
- long local distances
- economical interconnections
- adaptability to various equipments
- high performance

Transmission Medium

The data trunks use 75 ohm coaxial cable for reliability, noise rejection, and performance. The data trunk scheme has been designed and is specified against economical industry standard CATV type coaxial cable. If application demands, special coaxial cables for extreme physical and electrical environment are available.

Transmission Scheme

The data trunks use a base-band, phase modulation technique. This transmission technique allows data clocking to be recovered from the transmission and eliminates complex timing synchronization between units.

Interconnect

The data trunks ac couple into each drop. The impedance seen by the coax line at a drop is carefully matched to the line allowing multiple drops on the

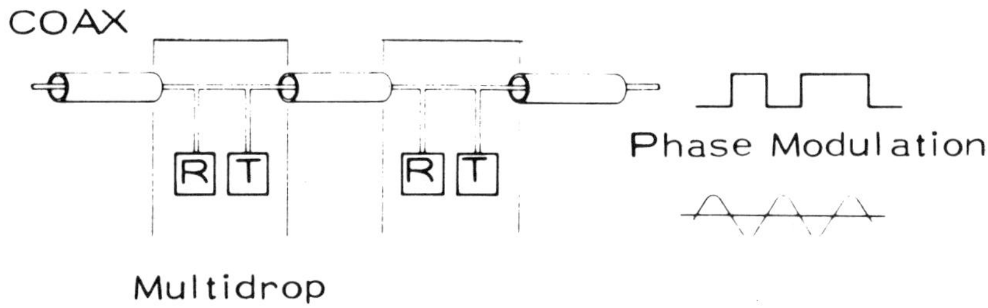

Figure 6B–8. Data Trunk

line while maintaining a high performance and reliability of data transmission. The ac coupling allows transmission between different grounding and power systems. It also does not require that each drop be powered-up to maintain line continuity.

Cyclic Redundant Checkwords

The data transmission takes place in a serial communications type envelope. This envolope protects all communications, control and data, by 16-bit cyclic redundant checkwords. Because of the high speed of transmission and the local distances, these codes have been chosen for maximum error detection capability. Independent checkwords on control and data are used to further decrease error effects.

Network Addressing

The transmission envelope contains 8-bit physical adapter addresses for both destination and source as required in a network. Physical addressing is used to maximize the efficiency of maintenance of the network.

Access Codes

The trunk transmission envelope contains a 16-bit access code independent of network addressing, which is used in conjunction with a locked physical switch code at each adapter. This code provides positive control at each adapter over access ability to individual trunk transmissions.

Transmission Protocol

The adapters implement a complete data transmission protocol. A response is made by the receiving adapter to each transmission before the transmitting adapter releases the transmission data. Interlock flags in each adapter are used to control and synchronize data movement between adapters.

Trunk Allocation

The trunks are allocated on a demand basis. Trunk allocation is accomplished by blocking an adapter from transmitting on a data trunk when a transmission is already taking place. Following the end of a transmission other adapters continue to be temporarily blocked from transmitting giving priority to a responding adapter. Variable delays in each adapter give each adapter a time slot in which it may initiate transmission when a trunk becomes free.

Data Buffering

The trunk transmission is buffered at each end. This buffering decouples the data rate at each equipment from the trunk data rate. The high reliability of a fixed trunk transmission rate is maintained and the utilization of the attached processor data channels and peripheral equipment, and the trunk itself can be significantly increased.

Adapter Technology

The adapter uses the latest technology consistent with industry standard availablity and demonstrated reliability.

Packaging

The adapter is contained in a stand-alone package with integral power supplies and cooling. The package can be mounted in RETMA standard 19″ rack cabinets, taking about 14″ in height.

Power

The adapters use a switched regulator power supply allowing a wide range of power sources with a high degree of logic voltage stability.

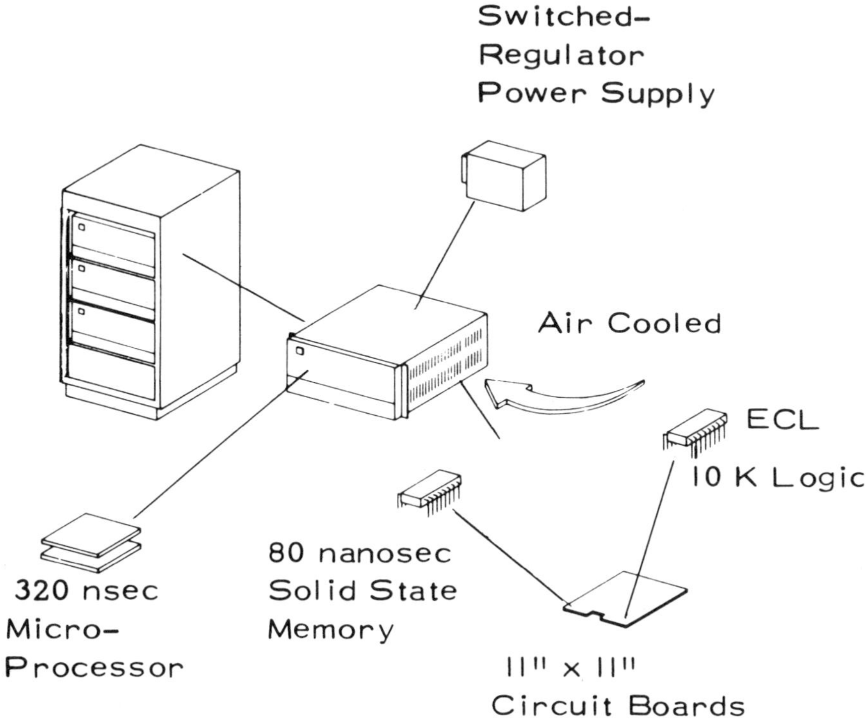

Figure 6B-9. Adapter Technology: Industry standard, high performance technology

Cooling

The adapter is air cooled with separate cooling paths provided for the logic and the power supply. The cooling system is designed to support high altitude applications and to account for residual heat build up without damage on power failure. Over temperature warning and power shut down, plus air flow sensing are provided.

Circuit Boards

11" × 11½" circuit boards are used in the adapter with approximately 100 chips per board. The boards are multilayer circuit boards with high capacity power and ground layers buried and the logic layers exposed. The proximity of logic lines and ground plane across the board provide the transmission characteristics required with high speed logic. All interconnect between boards is twisted pair for maximum reliability.

Logic and Memory

The adapter uses industry standard 10,000 series ECL logic and solid state memory. The speed of the ECL circuitry is conservatively used to eliminate circuit selection and to maximize reliability.

Configuration

The adapter is physically configured to house 12 circuit boards. Figure 2–3 describes the board slots occupied by the functional elements of the Adapter. The Equipment Interface section consists of either 1 or 2 boards depending upon the specific adapter model. The twelfth slot is reserved for a plug-in maintenance function. A careful mapping between physical location and function has been maintained to allow maximum efficiency of diagnostics and repair including maximum commonality between adapter models.

3. ADAPTER ARCHITECTURE

The adapter is divided into four logical sections; the Trunk Interfaces, the Buffer and Control Logic, the Microprocessor, and the Equipment Interface.

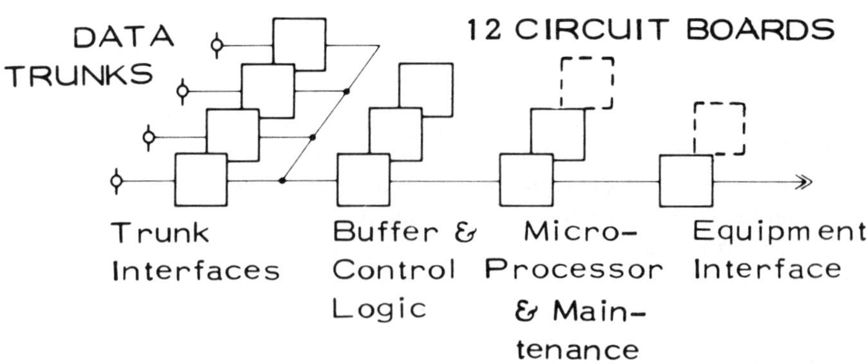

Figure 6B–10. Physical Configuration: Strict mapping between circuit board and logical function decreases maintenance complexity

Trunk Interface

The adapter contains up to 4 trunk interface boards. Each board attaches one data trunk. It provides the transmitting and receiving electronics and the high speed logic to manage the trunk transmission envelope-checkwords, access code, and network address. Each trunk interface board has the ability to generate a Busy or Reserved response if the adapter is busy with another trunk or is unavailable to receive a transmission.

Buffer and Control Logic

The adapter contains a single set of buffer and control logic. The Buffer and Control Logic in conjunction with the Trunk Interfaces accomplish the very high speed control of the tunk transmissions. There are two buffers—a 1024 8-bit byte control buffer, normally used for stacking control information, and a data buffer containing optionally from 4096 to 8192 8-bit bytes. This section also contains a 16-bit flag register plus registers to specify buffer address and length of data transmission with the data trunk. Other registers provide network addressing information. The buffer and control section contains the logic to resolve contention for its use between trunk interfaces and the equipment interface. The buffers and registers are accessable simultaneously by the trunk control logic in the Buffer and Control section and the Equipment Interface section. The 100 megabit/second buffers allow a 50 megabit data movement with the data trunks simultaneous with a 50 megabit data movement with the attached equipment.

Microprocessor

The micro-processor handles equipment functions and responses and manages the data flow on the direct data paths between the equipment and the adapter buffers. The micro-processor has a 320 nanosecond cycle time. It has a 4096 16-bit word read-only instruction memory. It executes instructions against 16 immediate and 256 extension registers, all 8-bits in length. The extension registers provide access to the Buffer and Control Logic, the Equipment Interface, and registers for control of the direct data path.

The direct data path, with hardware ready resume, allows high speed block transfers between the adapter buffers and the attached equipment unlimited by the micro-processor.

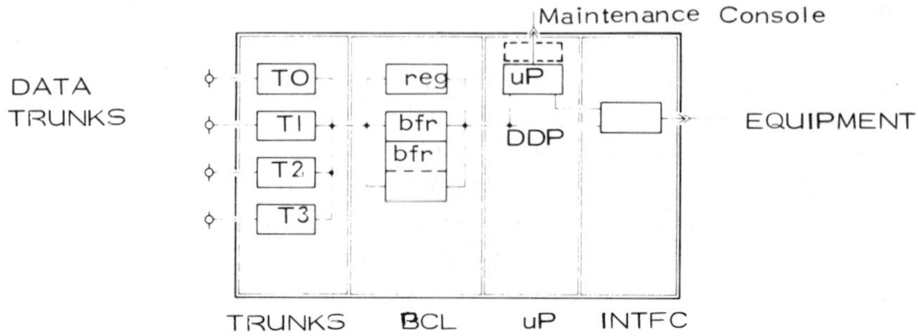

Figure 6B–11. Adapter Block Diagram

Equipment Interface

The Equipment Interface provides the electrical and cable interface to the specific attached equipment. In some cases it also provides assembly/disassembly, holding registers and hardware ready-resume logic.

4. SYSTEM OPERATION

Communication between computing equipment via the adapter network takes place in a network message which has a defined format in the first fields to direct the message in the network.

A PROCESSOR ADAPTER transmits and receives network messages between the attached processor and the network of data trunks. The messages are generated by the attached processor. The processor adapter receives the complete message for transmission from the processor and delivers the complete received message to the processor.

A DEVICE ADAPTER, on the other hand, is operated by and generates network messages. It interprets received network messages and accomplishes the specified function internally or with its attached devices. It generates messages in response to actions initiated by received messages. The Network Adapters accomplish major tasks in the management and control of the network utilizing a sophisticated transmission protocol within the network without burdening the attached equipment. The adapter tasks include:

- Interpreting the first fields of the messages to determine network destination, data trunks to try and access code to use.
- Implementing the internal network data framing and data movement protocol.

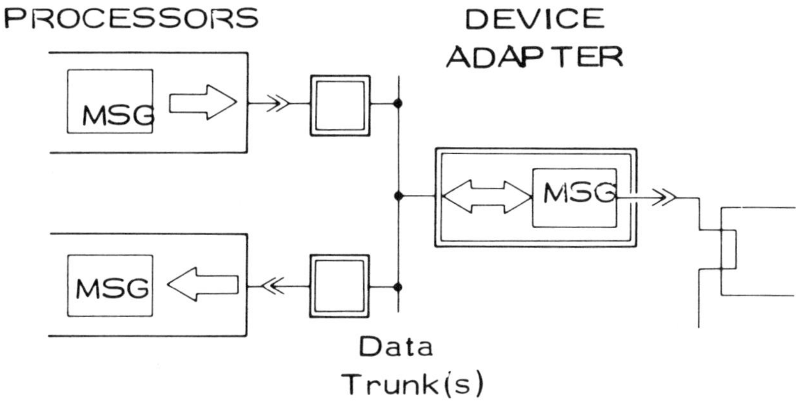

Figure 6B–12. Message Generation

- Managing the adapter buffers for maximum data movement efficiency; i.e., use of alternating buffers to provide a continuous data flow with long data streams, sensing and adjusting to the size of the receiving adapters buffer.
- Verifying each transmission and retrying on error conditions.

Network Message

The network message consists of two sections; the message proper and, optionally, associated data. The length of the message proper may be up to 64 bytes. The length of the associated data is not limited.

The first fields of the message proper have a fixed format and are interpreted by adapters to direct the original message and a response message in the network. A Processor adapter interprets the fields from a network message presented for transmission. A Device adapter interprets the fields in a network message it receives to generate the response message (TO and FROM words are turned around).

Control

Trunk Control (bits 0–3)—These bits specify to an adapter which trunks, out of the four possible trunks attached to an adapter, to use. The trunk number is associated with the physical location of the trunk interface board in the adapter. An adapter will try on trunk 0, 1, 2, 3, 0, 1, etc. for which the

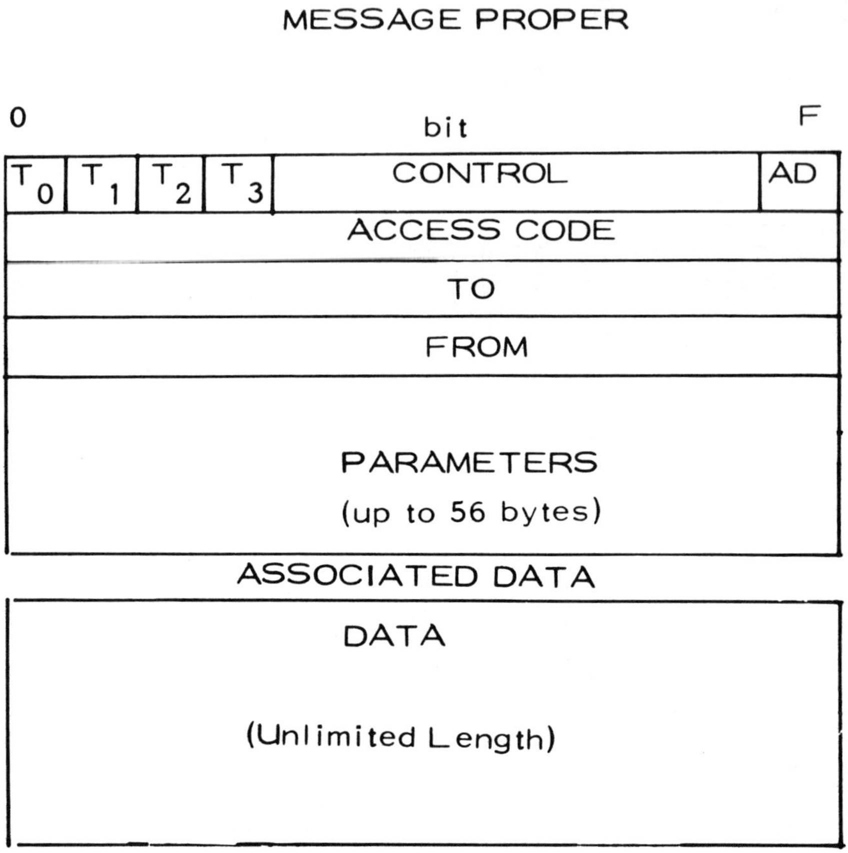

Figure 6B–13. Network Message

corresponding bits are set until a nonbusy trunk is found on which the addressed receiving adapter responds.

Associated data (bit F)—This bit, when set, indicates that there is associated data with the message.

The remaining control bits are specified by individual adapter models.

Access Code

This 16 bit word is logically combined with the physical access code of the transmitting adapter to form the access code used on all transmissions associated with this network message. (See Section 8)

To

This 16 bit word is used to define the destination of this network message. Bit 0–7 are used by a transmitting adapter as the physical network address of the receiving adapter. Bit 8–F are used by specific adapters or are available to a receiving processor to define an internal destination.

From

This 16 bit word is not interpreted by a transmitting processor adapter but can be used by a receiving processor to indicate the source of a message. It is used by a device adapter to generate and transmit a response message.

Parameters

This field is used by device adapters to define the basic function of the message.

5. PROCESSOR ADAPTER OPERATION

Function

A processor adapter interfaces a processor data channel to the network of data trunks. It functions to send and receive network messages with other adapters in the network.

A processor adapter is designed to appear as a peripheral control unit to the processor, accepting commands and providing status under the protocol of the specific processor channel.

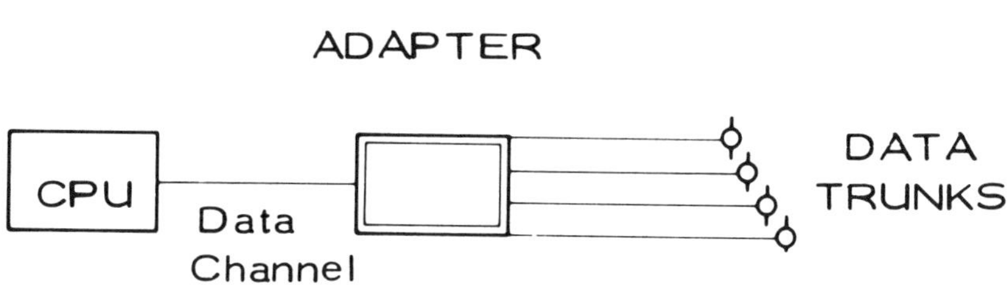

Figure 6B–14. Processor Adapter

Operations

A processor adapter can be directed to accomplish these basic operations:

TRANSMIT MESSAGE/DATA
INPUT MESSAGE/DATA
TEST
STATUS

Transmit Message

The adapter accepts the processor output as the network message proper to be transmitted. It interprets the first fields of the message to determine the trunks to try, the access code to use, and the destination network address.

The message proper is limited to 64 8-bit bytes in length. The adapter moves the message at channel rate into its control buffer. It locates a non-busy specified trunk, transmits the message, and receives a response from the receiving adapter.

The processor adapter will take the following action:

- Trunks—If all trunks are busy it will keep trying until a non-busy trunk is found. If no response is received on any of the specified trunks it will abort the operation.
- Receiving Adapter—If the receiving adapter is reserved by another adapter or busy receiving a transmission from another adapter, the processor adapter will keep trying until the transmission is completed. If the receiving adapter is not in receive mode, the processor adapter will continue to try until it goes into receive mode. If the receiving adapter is reserved by its attached equipment (indicating the attached equipment is in the process of transmitting itself) the processor adapter will go into receive mode temporarily and then retry the transmission.
- Errors—If a transmission error is indicated by the receiving adapter the message will be retransmitted.

In general, the adapter will continue to try to transmit the message unless it cannot receive a response on any trunk or until it is commanded to stop attempting to transmit. Status information is made available to the processor channel and an End Operation command to the adapter is provided to terminate a transmit operation.

Transmit Data

Data associated with a message is preceded by a specific command, Transmit Data, or some other channel mechanism which indicates that the following output is data associated with the previous Transmit Message operation. Associated data is buffered in the adapter's data buffer. The adapter uses an alternating buffer scheme. It accepts data from the processor channel into its data. When the buffer is half full, it initiates transmission of that amount of data. Simultaneous with the transmission of data on the data trunk it continues to accept data from the processor channel into the other half of the adapter data buffer. This continues until the processor data channel output is exhausted. The adapter uses the same trunk, access code, and destination as the preceding Transmit Message operation. Multiple Transmit Data operations can be used.

Input Message

This command causes the processor adapter to send a received network message to the processor channel. The actual receiving of a message is a background mode in the processor adapter. The adapter accepts received network messages, and stacks them in its control buffer. The processor adapter will continue to receive and accept network messages to the limit of its available space in its control buffer.

If a message is received which has associated data, the associated data is buffered in the adapter's data buffer and the adapter will not receive more messages until the associated data is serviced by the processor.

The adapter will present received messages to the processor data channel on a First-In-First-Out basis.

Input Data

This command causes the processor adapter to send the associated data to the processor channel. The processor may accept and input the associated data or may reject all or part of the associated data by an End Operation command.

Test

For testing purposes the processor channel is provided explicit access to the adapter Control and Data Buffers and the trunk control registers.

This access is provided only when the adapter is not actively transmitting or receiving. The functions used include:

- Set Address/Length
- Write Adapter
- Read Adapter

Status

Status commands provide adapter status to the attached processor. Typical status bytes include:

- Operational Status
    - Function Rejected
    - Operation Aborted
    - Adapter Memory Parity Error
- Last Function
- Trunk Status

6. DEVICE ADAPTER OPERATION

Function

A device adapter interfaces the network of data trunks to a specific manufacturer's line of peripheral control units by creating that manufacturer's data channel.

Specific device adapter models create an electrically and logically identical channel allowing all similar control units from that manufacturer to be attached and allowing multiple control units to be attached under that manufacturers rules for multiple control unit attachments.

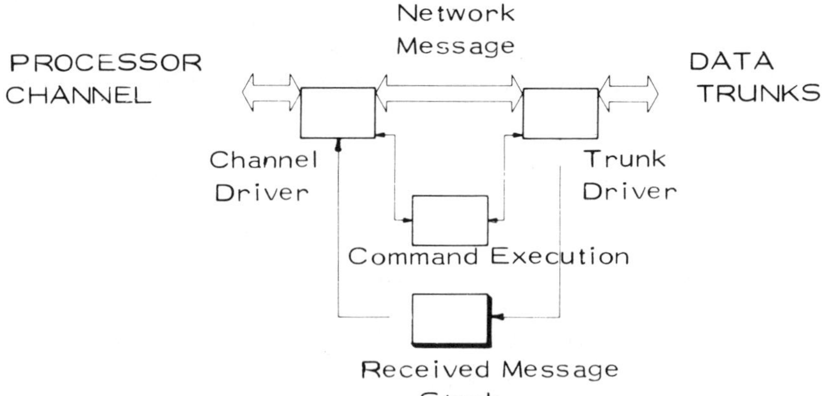

Figure 6B–15. Processor Adapter Functions

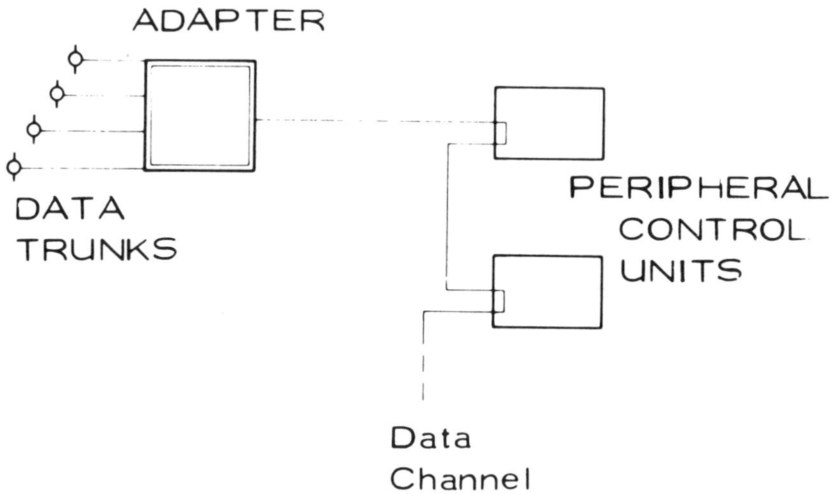

Figure 6B–16. Device Adapter—Remote Channel

Network Messages

The device adapter is driven by network messages from another adapter on the network of data trunks and responds by generating network messages. A device adapter functions as a remote channel unit. It will execute a channel program; i.e. a stack of functions. It will multiplex the execution of several device channel programs when there is latency or other wait times with the associated equipment. These programs being multiplexed may be from different processors in the network.

The adapter maintains a reserve table to allow a processor to reserve a peripheral device or a logical label on a specific device.

Channel programs may be preloaded into the adapter and may be shared by several executions.

Received Messages

A device adapter receives the following messages to direct its operation:

SET/CLEAR PROGRAM
RESERVE/RELEASE DEVICE
START I/O
DATA
CLEAR DEVICE/ADAPTER
SENSE DEVICE/ADAPTER

Channel Programs

A Set Program message provides a channel program to the adapter. Clear Program releases a program. A Channel Program may be held by the adapter for repeated use. These programs consist of a sequence of channel or device command words. These command words indirectly point to parameters allowing a channel program to be used with various parameters and addresses.

Reserve Device

The adapter maintains a device reserve table. A specific device or a device label may be reserved for the FROM field of the message executing a reserve.

A START I/O message will not be accepted for a device/label which is reserved by a FROM address different from the FROM address of the START I/O message. A reserve message can specify that the sender be notified when the present reserve is released.

The device number normally relates to a specific physical device. The label, however, is a logical entity for reservation purposes only.

Start I/O

The START I/O message initiates the execution of a channel program against a specific device. This message contains the parameters to be used by the channel program for this I/O operation. The adapter will execute the channel program until it is completed or until an abnormal condition is detected by the adapter.

The adapter will suspend execution of a channel program on detection of a WAIT condition in the associated device. During this suspension the adapter can initiate a START I/O against another device or can reinitiate execution on a suspended I/O operation on detection of the end of the device WAIT condition.

Data

The adapter will generate a message to the initiator of the START I/O when I/O execution requires data. The initiator must then respond with a Data message and the data.

Clear

Messages are available to clear either a specific device and I/O operation or the adapter and all devices on the adapter.

Sense

A message is available to generate a status response message for a specific device. A message is also available to generate a sense response message for the adapter returning detailed status on the adapter itself.

Response Messages

The adapter generates two basic response messages:

STATUS
DATA

Status contains the reason for the initiation of the status, a status of the I/O execution and in the case of faults, a detailed status of the adapter. Status messages are initiated in response to command messages, as indicated by specific channel command words or occurrence of any abnormal condition in an I/O execution or upon completion of an I/O execution. Data messages are initiated by the execution of a read channel command word.

Channel Programs

Channel Programs consist of a sequence of individual Channel Command Words (CCW). See figure 6B–18. The channel command word specifies the command and the data address and length associated with the command. It also specifies by its flag field:

- Chain Command—continue with next command upon successful completion of this command.
- Chain Data—upon depletion of the data length in this channel command word use the address and length of the next CCW as a chained data area moving the command field.
- Inhibit Trunk Transfer—do not move data on the trunk for a read command.
- Initiate Status—initiate a status message when this command is encountered. Does not affect command execution.

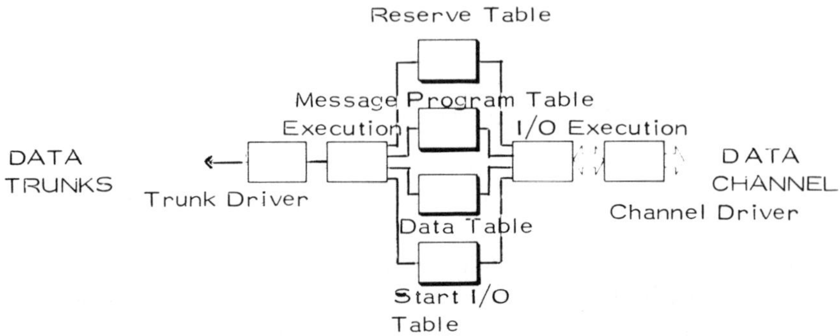

Figure 6B–17. Device Adapter Functions

Program Multiplexing

The device adapter can share itself across several I/O executions when there is a wait associated with a specific device. The wait condition is normally a specific fixed status from the attached peripheral controller or device. In some cases a specific channel command is available to initiate suspension of a channel program.

Other Device Adapters

For some specific peripheral devices, Network Systems provides another type of adapter which interfaces the peripheral device directly and performs the dual function of both an adapter and device controller. The operation of this adapter type is similar to the remote channel adapters described above.

The link adapter is another type adapter which directly interfaces wide band links to the adapter network.

7. INTERNAL NETWORK OPERATION

Data Movement

Data movement in the network takes place in three asynchronous steps:

- Sending equipment to sending adapter buffer.
- Sending adapter buffer to receiving adapter buffer.
- Receiving adapter buffer to receiving equipment.

COMMAND	FLAGS	DATA ADDRESS	DATA LENGTH

Figure 6B–18. Channel Command Word

The data rates of the attached equipments and of the data trunks are decoupled by the adapter buffers.

All three data movement steps can take place simultaneously. With long data streams an alternating buffer scheme is used in the adapter to maintain a continuous data stream through the adapter. As each segment of a sending adapter is filled, it is "burst" on the data trunk to the receiving adapter buffer. The data trunk itself is therefore only used during actual data transmission and can be shared by other adapter to adapter data movements.

The adapters implement a complete protocol of data movement between adapter buffers in the network. This protocol is decoupled from the attached equipment by the adapter logic and microprocessor routines and is invisible outside the network.

Internal Frames

Within this internal network protocol commands, responses and data segments are moved between adapters as Frames in a communications type envelope.

INTERNAL FRAME FORMAT

Sync	— 24 bits
Frame Code	— 8 bits
Access Code	— 16bits
To	— 8 bits
From	— 8 bits
Function/Response	— 16 bits
Length Count	— 16 bits
Header Checkword	— 16 bits
Data	— n bits
Data Checkword	— 16 bits
Sync	— 56 bits

Sync—a sync pattern is transmitted on the message front end to synchronize the receiver and is used as a pad in the trailing end of the message to supply clock to the receiver. The Sync pattern consists of the alternating 1's and 0's.

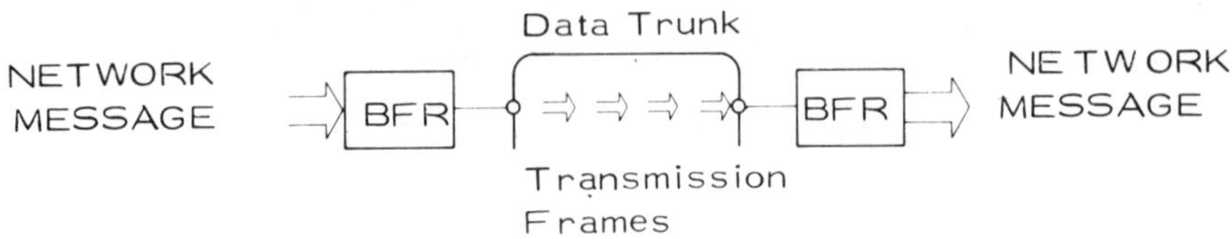

Figure 6B–19. Data Movement: Data movement in the network takes place in three asynchronous, simultaneous steps separated by the adapter buffers

Frame Code—The frame code indicates the start of the message or the response. The code is 99 for a transmit message and 96 for a response message and is included in the header checkword.

Access Code—Each Adapter has an externally appplied 16-bit access number used to control access to transmissions on a common data path. Each frame transmitted by an Adapter contains its access number as the transmission frame's access code. This transmission frame is accessible only by Adapters with a corresponding access number. (See Section 8)

To–From—An externally applied 8-bit unit number indicates each Adapter's physical address in the network. The adapter transmits its unit number as the frame's FROM field and compares its unit number with the TO field in received frames.

Function/Response—This field contains the function code in initial transmission and the status and response in response transmissions.

Length Count—The length count is inserted by the transmitter and indicates the number of eight bit bytes in the data field.

Checkwords—The 48 bits of the header and the data field are independently checked by a 16 bit cyclic checkword.

Data—Both the initial and the response frames have an optional data field which can be any number of bits in length.

Internal Frame Function Codes

The function code of the frame is directed to and is executed by the receiving adapters Buffer and Control Logic hardware. The Buffer and Control Logic receiving a frame executes the frame function and immediately generates a response frame containing its status and optionally requested registers or data.

Reserve—Reserves the Adapter for the Adapter unit number initiating the function.

Copy Registers—Returns the contents of specified Adapter registers via the data field of the response frame.

Load Registers—Loads the data field of this frame into specified Adapter registers.

Flag Bits—Test-and-Set or Test-and-Clear specified Adapter flag bits.

Return Data—Directs the Adapter to transmit as the data field in the response frame data from the Adapter's control or data buffers.

Receive Data—Directs the Adapter to load the data field of this frame into the Adapter's control or data buffers.

The execution of a frame function is conditioned on a flag in the Buffer and Control Logic of the receiving adapter. Flag 0 is nonexistent and provids for unconditional execution.

Transmit Sequence

The movement of a data block between adapters is accomplished by a sequence of frames between adapters which clears and set flags, copies control registers and moves data blocks. These frame sequences and the flags provide a complete interlock of operations between adapters. Coping registers allows coordination of the transmitting and receiving buffer sizes. Since each data block movement is immediately responded to, data error detection and retransmission is immediate .The adapters are reserved to other adapters in the network during a message movement to limit the effect of control frame faults on other adapters in the network.

Message Data Rate

The effective data rate of an individual message movement in the adapter network is reduced from the actual trunk rate by:

- The frame sequence protocol
- The frame envelope
- The trunk length
- The data buffer size

8. NETWORK ADDRESSES AND ACCESS CODES

Network Address

Each adapter has an 8-bit physical network address. This address is selected by two hexidecimal thumbwheel switches on each adapter. Each adapter in the network is normally assigned a unique network address to reduce complexity and enhance maintenance. The network address, however, may be duplicated if the duplicated address is on a separate trunk.

Data Trunks

A data trunk is referenced by an adapter by the physical position of the trunk interface board in the adapter to which the data trunk is attached. Although it is not necessary, each data trunk is normally attached at each connected adapter at the same trunk interface position. This will give the data trunk a consistent number across connected adapters reducing complexity and enhancing maintenance. It is not necessary to fill the trunk interface positions in an adapter in order.

Access Code

Each adapter has a 16-bit physical access code. This code is set by 4 locked hexidecimal thrumbwheel switches on each adapter. All frames transmitted by an adapter contain this access code as the first frame field. An adapter will not accept or respond to frames which contain an access code which does not compare to its physical access code, regardless of the network address.

The physical access code is treated as four 4-bit characters. A zero character is a "don't care" character. Where an adapter's access code contains a zero character, the adapter will accept a frame access code with any character in this position.

FF07 Physical Access Code
F370 Received Frame Access Code
$C\bar{C}C\bar{C}$ C = Compare

The access code mechanism can be ignored by setting the access code on each adapter to all zeros.

When directed to Transmit, the adapter combines the message access code with the adapters physical access code to generate the frame access code. Wherever there is a zero character in the physical access code, the message access code character will be used.

FF00 Physical Access Code
F370 Message Access Code
FF70 Transmitted Frame Access Code

An adapter which has no zero characters in its physical access code can generate and will accept a single access code, the physical access code.

An adapter which has zero characters in its physical access code can generate and will accept a *set* of access codes.

The following physical access code assignment example provides each CPU with a private disk plus access to a common disk.

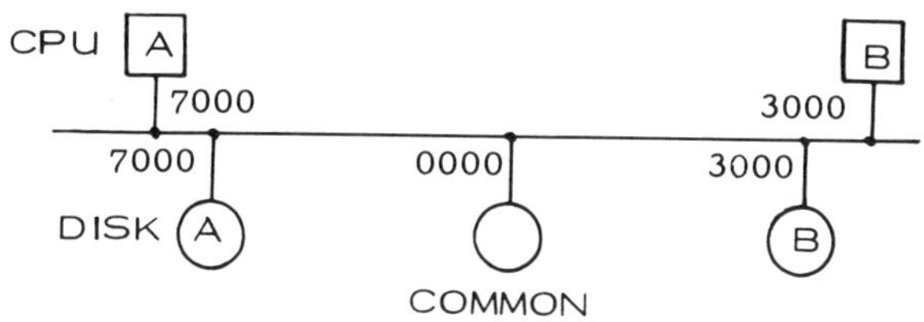

CPU A cannot access disk B nor can CPU B access disk A, yet both CPU's can access the common disk . In this arrangement the CPU's cannot communicate with each other. By making the following physical access code assignment, disk A and B remain private but the CPU's can now communicate because they can each generate an access code for their own disk and the other CPU.

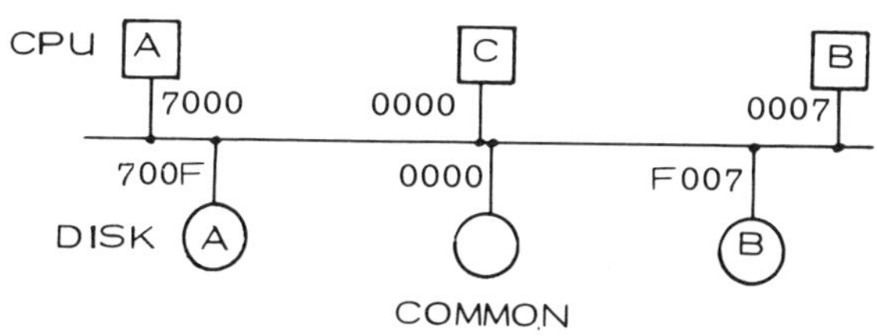

Also shown is CPU C which, because it can generate any access code, can communicate with any adapter on the network.

Trunk Allocation

When directed to transmit, an adapter contends for the use of a network trunk via one of its trunk interfaces. There are three mechanisms involved in allocating a trunk to multiple transmitt requests.

Trunk Busy

If a trunk is busy (another adapter's transmission is detected on the trunk) the trunk interface hardware will not initiate a transmission.

Fixed Delay

Each trunk interface contains a hardware delay from the time it senses the trunk not busy until it is enabled to transmit. This delay allows a response frame transmission, or following transmissions by the adapter which had the trunk, to take priority on the trunk. The fixed delay is the same in all adapters and depends on the length of the trunk:

Fixed delay—4 ns (trunk length in feet)

A 1000-foot trunk, therefore, requires a 4 microsecond fixed delay.

N Delay

Following the trunk going not busy and the expiration of the fixed delay, each adapter generates a unique time pulse, referred to as n delay, at which time it may initiate transmissions on the trunk and capture the trunk without contention.

An adapter's n delay is a function of its physical position on the trunk and is determined by the following calculation.

n delay = (n-1 delay) + 4 nsec (distance between n-1 and n in feet)
n = 0 uses 0 delay

The n delay is selected at installation in each adapter. It is not necessarily related to the adapters network address.

The following example illustrates the selection of n-delay on a trunk.

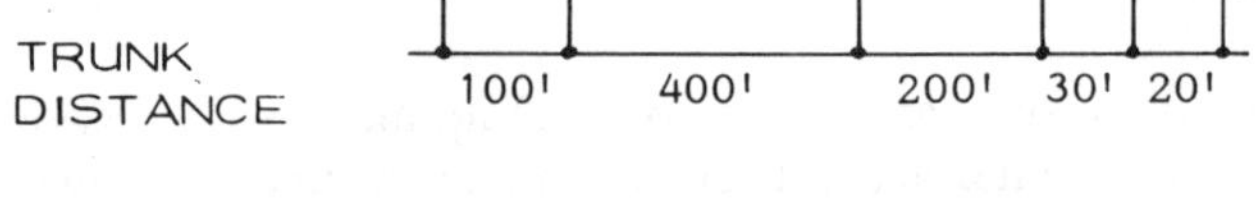

ADAPTER n	*DELAY TIME (n delay)*
0	0 nsec
1	0 + 4 nsec (750′) = 3.00 usec

2	3.00 usec + 4 nsec (730′) = 5.92 usec
3	5.92 usec + 4 nsec (30′) = 6.04 usec
4	6.04 usec + 4 nsec (200′) = 6.84 usec
5	6.84 usec + 4 nsec (400′) = 8.44 usec

Contention

Two or more adapters could simultaneously initiate transmission because of the propagation delay between adapters. If this occurs, all frames will be garbled and no responses will be generated by the intended receiving adapters. As a result of this trunk activity the n delay mechanism will be initiated. Both transmitting adapters will initiate retry and one of the adapters will capture the trunk first due to the priority established by the n delay mechanism.

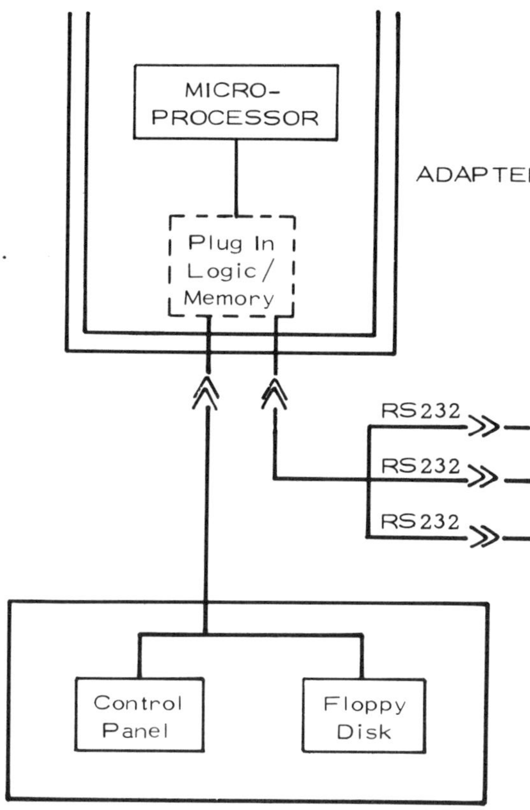

Figure 6B–20. Maintenance Console

9. Maintenance Console

The adapter maintenance console is a separate physical package which is portable and which plugs into an adapter to provide testing capability.

The console consists of a logic/memory board, containing 4096 16-bit words of Read/Write memory, which plugs into a board slot in an adapter. There is a direct interface to a control panel and four RS232 interfaces. One of the RS232 interfaces are used to attach the floppy disk. The remaining three RS232 interfaces are available for attachment of other devices such as a display terminal.

The console control panel provides the following capabilities:

- Start/Stop/Step/Clear the adapter microprocessor.
- Breakpoint the adapter microprocessor.
- Cause the adapter microprocessor to execute out of the console Read/Write memory instead of the adapter Read-Only memory.
- Load and dump the console Read/Write memory with the floppy disk.

By loading test routines into the console Read/Write memory and executing the adapter microprocessor from this memory, a wide variety of test capabilities are available:

- Diagnostic routines for the adapter microprocessor, buffer and control logic, trunk interfaces, and equipment interface.
- Diagnostic routines for the equipment attached to the adapters.
- Diagnostic routines to test the network and other adapters in the network.
- Driving of a terminal display/keyboard and primer.

10. Adapter Models

The following is a list of Adapters which are currently in production or under development. Additional adapter models will be scheduled for development as the demand dictates:

PROCESSOR ADAPTERS		
MODEL	PROCESSOR MANUFACTURER/MODEL	INTERFACE CONNECTION
A110	CDC/6000, CY70, CY170	PPU Data Channel
A120	CDC/7600, CY176	7000 Type PPU
A130	CRAY/CRAY-1	16 bit High Speed Asynchronous Channel
A140	UNIVAC/1100 Series, 494, 418 III	Word Channel
A220	IBM/360/370/303X or IBM Compatible Processors	Selector or Block Mux Channel
A410	DEC/PDP-11 Series	DR11-B
A420	Data General/Eclipse or NOVA	Directly to "I/O BUS"
A430	ModComp/I, II or IV Series	Directly to "Modular BUS"
A440	Interdata/6, 7 or 8 Series	Directly to "I/O BUS"
A460	DEC/DEC 10	To be Defined
A470	SEL/32/35, 32/55 or 32/75	HSD 9132 or HSD 73-9132

DEVICE ADAPTERS		
MODEL	MANUFACTURER/CHANNEL	DEVICE CONNECTION
A510	IBM/Block MUX Channel	All devices compatible with the Block MUX
A520	CDC/6000, CY70, CY170 PPU Data Channel	All devices compatible with the PPU Data Channel.
A540	CDC/3000 Series Data Channel	All devices compatible with the 3000 Data Channel.

OTHER DEVICE ADAPTERS		
MODEL	DISK FORMAT	DEVICE CONNECTION
A320	18 Sectors/Track with 512 64-bit words. Compatible with Cray Disk Controller.	Controls the CDC 819 Disk or NSC D300 Disk.
A327	20 Sectors/Track with 512 60-bit words. Compatible with CDC Disk Controller.	Controls the CDC 819 Disk or NSC D300 Disk.

Appendix 6C: Loosely Coupled Network

Introduction

The Control Data Loosely Coupled Network (LCN) provides a form of two-party cooperative communications. Put another way, LCN acts as an agent for Multi-Mainframing and distributed processing by providing a means for interconnection of, and information exchange amongst, a collection of mainframes or mainframes and peripherals (all referred to as "hosts" in the remainder of this paper).

LCN appears in a host as that software which provides network services to applications. These services include permanent file transfer, queued file transfer, application to (remote) application chit-chat, and shared rotating mass storage.

An equipment called a Network Access Device (NAD), attached to a host using the channel protocol native to that host, is the hardware entry point to the network. NADs in turn are interconnected by bit-serial trunks. Up to 32 NADs can be attached to a trunk; up to four trunks may be attached to a NAD. The combination of NADs and trunks provide the interconnection between hosts, and thus the hardware path for information exchange amongst hosts.

A set of protocols define and control LCN activities. They are shown in figure 6C–1, as they relate to the ISO Open System Interconnection Reference model [1]. Levels read down the page from the highest (application) to the lowest (physical). The remainder of this paper is limited to the protocols of the lower four levels.

Virtual Channel

Conventionally two hosts have been coupled in one of three ways.

a) common memory storage
b) channel-to-channel (a variation is shared disk)
c) communication lines

William C. Hohn, "The Control Data Loosely Coupled Network Lower Level Protocols," *Proceedings of the National Computer Conference*, May 1980, pp. 129–134. Reprinted with permission.

ISO (Open Systems Architecture) *Model*	*LCN*
Application	Application
Presentation	Network Block PROTOCOL
Session	CYBER/NAD PROTOCOL
Transport	Transport
Network	Network
Data Link	Data Link
Physical	Physical

Figure 6C–1. Protocol Levels

in order of descending performance. In addition, operating systems tend to be cognizant of these variations since data rates and response times vary dramatically with the form of coupling. What differentiates LCN from the traditional interconnect schemes are the characteristics of the interconnect.

A host NAD, which interfaces a host to the remainder of LCN, is designed to the channel specifications native to the host—including the maximum data rate of the channel.

NADs in turn are interconnected by shared trunks. The amount of trunk bandwidth available to a given NAD to NAD transfer is dependent on the loading of the trunk, varying from a maximum of 50 megabits (minus overhead) down to some minimum but nonzero value as trunk loading increases. Loading refers to how many NADs are attempting to use the trunk simultaneously.

From an operating systems point of view, a NAD to NAD transfer can occur at maximum channel rate, or at some lesser rate down into the realm of communication lines. This effect is analogous to virtual memory in that as the number of jobs mapped onto real memory exceeds the size of real memory, the execution time for each job increases.

A second parallel to virtual memory is that NAD to NAD transfers replace what is otherwise a system bottleneck with a slow transition. For example, coupling synchronous transfer rates of different value. The analogy in virtual memory is the mapping of a 10 million word program onto a half million word real memory without reprogramming for overlays or special I/O techniques.

In summary, LCN appears as neither a channel extension nor as a communications scheme, but rather as a virtual channel.

Protocol Design Considerations

A design decision was made that the NAD should incorporate the lower protocol levels up to and including the transport level, primarily because of the problems associated with resource contention. Other factors influenced by and therefore favoring this decision included error recovery, performance of the network, simplicity of design, commonality throughout the network, and integration with existing hardware. Inspection of these factors with greater resolution revealed that the implementation had to:

a) meet design goals at low cost
- connectivity — # units, distance, data rates
- accessibility — controlled access, multi-path
- performance — overhead
- dependability — detect errors, graceful degradation
- maintainability — fault trace

b) which translate into givens
- serial trunk — low cost
- buffering — data rate matching
- communication like protocol — messages vs ready/resume
- intelligence — to manage it all

c) and avoiding these self-inflicted pains
- single point of failure — centralized network management
- dead box deadlock — also called "united we fall"
- throttling — slow host throttles fast host
- missing message — lost data
- spoofing — security breach
- global autoload — load one—load all
- the "bully" — fixed trunk access priority
- daisy chain — NAD to trunk connection
- resource deadlock — no closure
- error prone transmission — requires higher level protocol

d) and recognizing the inherent problems
- error retrys — how many
- resource allocation — single path or multipath
- host/trunk (real/virtual channel) — performance matching
- the "missing ACK" — resynchronization in the face of errors

Although the detailed analysis of these attributes is beyond the scope of this paper, they are shown to indicate considerations made in arriving at a working implementation.

LCN Site Protocol

Strictly speaking, Site Protocol is not one of the layers given in the ISO Open System Interconnection document. But it is presented to show that connectivity and accessibility are not the same thing. The configuration of trunk/NAD interconnects, together with assignment of physical addresses and access codes, constitute the site protocol.

Connectivity

An example of LCN hardware is shown in figure 6C–2, where MF = mainframe and P = peripheral. The NAD can interface with one to four trunks, some examples of which are shown in figure 6C–1. The NAD connects its attached device to the network, but the interconnect pattern of the NADs/trunks defines the connectivity between devices. Note that attaching a device to the network does not imply connectivity with all other devices attached to the network. For example, MF/B cannot connect with P/C, P/D, or MF/E. Another example is MF/F, which can connect to all other devices except P/C.

Addressing

The hardware which interfaces a NAD to a trunk is called a Trunk Control Unit (TCU).

Each TCU is identified by an 8-bit physical address. The destination field of a message must match the physical address in order for the message to be accepted by the NAD.

The site protocol requires that all TCUs on a given NAD must have the same physical address.

Set Identifier

Each NAD/trunk interface includes a 16-bit set identifier (the access code). The access code field of a message must match the switch selectable access code of the TCU in order for the message to be accepted by the NAD. The access code allows sets of NADs to share the same trunk yet be independent.

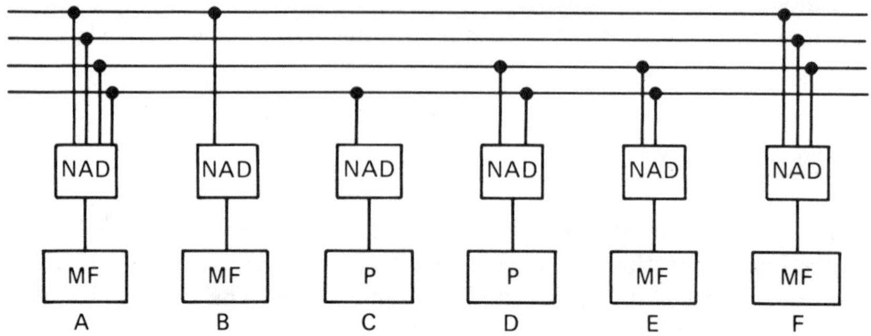

Figure 6C–2. LCN Connectivity

All NADs of a set may access all other NADs within the set, but no others. Messages directed to a NAD outside of the set are not accepted by that NAD. [Note that a NAD may be a member of more than one set.] Access code transmission and matching are hardware functions.

Accessibility

These three characteristics (network connection, physical address, and set identifier or access code) constitute the accessibility of a NAD (and hence its attached host) to all other network NADs.

Transport Control Protocol

The Transport Control Protocol provides the method by which mutually accessible hosts exchange information. This protocol is defined independently of, yet with consideration for, the broad range of hosts considered likely LCN candidates.

Data Path

The primary means for information exchange is the data path. A data path is a logical, bi-directional "channel" terminating at each end in a host. Data path creation and deletion is performed by the NAD as directed by its host. A path normally is created between two different hosts, but the protocol allows a host to create a path to itself. Furthermore, some NADs are designed to have multiple attached hosts. When generating a path between hosts on the same NAD, or when a host creates a path to itself, the path is contained solely within the associated NAD since that NAD is attached to both path-end hosts.

No more than one data path may exist between a pair of NADs.

A NAD can support up to 128 paths. However, since each path requires a small dedicated area in memory for path control (not including data buffers), the maximum number of paths supported by a NAD varies with its hardware configuration.

Information is passed on a path in the form of data, marks, or as a code.

Data Path—Connect

Path creation is initiated by a host. A successful connect requires acceptance by the local and remote NADs (path control resource allocation), and by the destination host. That means the three intelligent entities—NADs and destination host—all have the opportunity to deny the request. Put another way, the three must cooperate in order to complete the connect. Once connected, a path exists until explicitly disconnected by either of the hosts, or until an unrecoverable error, such as a broken trunk occurs.

At connect time the host presents the routing parameters to its NAD, or receives them from its NAD, depending on path-end. Both hosts also are given a path ID by their respective NADs. Thence forward, the hosts refer to the path by ID, and the necessary routing is automatically performed by the NAD.

Data Path—Data Exchange

By definition, data transfers are bi-directional on a data path. Host transfers are "blocked" by the NAD before transmission on the trunk in order to (a) decouple the host channel rate from the trunk rate and thereby allow unused trunk time to be used by other NADs, (b) to provide a mechanism whereby the data buffer area of NAD memory can be allocated dynamically across several paths, (c) to provide concurrent bi-directional transfer, and (d) to segment a long transfer for lower probability of induced errors.

The amount of data transferred is unlimited, but the effective rate of transfer is limited by buffer availability (real and path threshold) in the associated NADs, as well as by trunk loading (the "virtual channel" characteristic). A special data transfer mode is provided in which the trunk is not released between data blocks. In this mode only the two NADs involved can use the trunk, all other NADs being locked out. In this mode trunk loading is removed as a factor, and the network appears as a dedicated point-to-point connection. Transfer rates are then limited by the host channel and trunk rates and overhead.

Data Path—Mark

A mark is a special form of data ,analogous to an end of record mark. A mark may be sent at any time. The data and interspersed marks are delivered in the same order as sent.

Data Path—Code

In addition to data and marks, a very short (32 bit) message may also be transmitted down a path. This message (CODE) is different from data and marks in two ways. First, the data path CODE buffers at each end are permanently allocated and, hence, always available (unlike data buffers which are dynamically allocated). Second, CODE messages are not queued at the receiving end; rather each CODE message "overwrites" the previously received one.

Data Path—Disconnect

A path may be disconnected by either path end host. The NAD performing the disconnect first transmits all of its outstanding output data, marks, and code; then sends a disconnect message to the other NAD. Residual input is discarded in the NAD initiating the disconnect.

The disconnect is queued at the receiving NAD and is presented to the attached host after all data (and marks) in front of it have been presented.

Control Message

The control message (DATAGRAM) is an alternate means for information exchange. Control Messages are self-contained, meaning they have fixed length, they contain routing information, and they are not associated with data paths. The host supplies the Control Message to the NAD, and the NAD simply sends it to the destination (NAD). A Control Message, which for any reason cannot be delivered to the destination NAD, is returned to the host.

The control message format is shown in Figure 6C–3.

Summary

Transport Control Protocol uses data paths and Control Messages for information exchange between mutually accessible hosts. Since data paths

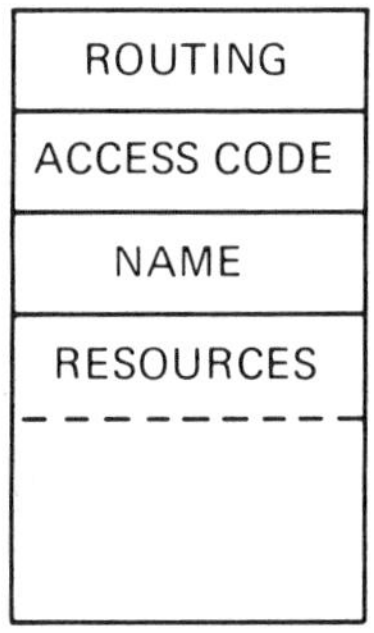

Figure 6C–3. Control Message

exist as logical "channels," a host and its attached NAD may have many paths assigned and serviceable concurrently (but not simultaneously). At the same time the Control Message ,independent of data paths, is avaialable for flow control, status, functional requests of a higher level, or just general chit-chat.

Network Control Protocol

This protocol level defines information flow control between NADs. In order for a host with a dedicated NAD to exchange information with any other host, the transfer obviously requires traversing a trunk from NAD to NAD. Hosts sharing a NAD, however, communicate with each other through their shared NAD, but with other hosts across a trunk (and another NAD).

A primary task for the Network Control Protocol is recognizing and processing these routing varitions .

Command/Response Message Modes

Three modes are defined for communications between NADs. Each mode is tailored to a specific work function ,to effectively use the trunk and NAD resources.

In the following three sections, the graphic conventions listed below are used.

The Command Message and Response Message, which always occur in pairs, are illustrated as a pair of boxes connected by a line.

The left hand box is always a command message, and the right hand box is always a response message. The interconnecting line represents the interval during which the receiving NAD processor examines the command message and determines the appropriate response message to return. The trunk remains captured until the processor signals the trunk interface to transmit the response message.

Mode 1—Control

Mode 1 consists of one command/response message pair. CONTROL is directed to the host, and has meaning defined by a higher level protocol, or is a flow control message directed to and processed by the NAD processor.

Mode 1 Command Messages

** Control Message

** Connect

Pathcode

Path Mark

Disconnect

Double Purge

Connect Accept

Connect Reject

Status Change

**These are the only messages (of all three modes) which are generated by the host.

Mode 1 Response Messages

ACK

WAITNAK

Sequence Error

Illegal Command Message

Illegal Path

Mode 2—Data Transfer

Mode 2 is a two command/response message set used for transmission of data. The first command, Path Request, identifies the path and the buffer size. The receiving NAD returns an ACK if the data transfer is permissible. The sending NAD then immediately transmits the data, a closing ACK is returned, and the trunk is released.

If the receiving NAD cannot accept the data, it will return a NAK, following which the trunk is released.

Mode 2 Command Messages

Path Request

Path Data

Mode 2 Response Messages

ACK

Queue Full NAK

Illegal Command Message

Illegal Path

Sequence Error

Mode 3—Captured Trunk (Streaming Mode) Data Transfer

Mode 3 is a special form of data transfer in which trunk multiplexing is temporarily halted by capturing the trunk (streaming) for the duration of a multi datablock transfer. Consequently, total trunk bandwidth is allocated to the path capturing the trunk. Two useful effects result. First, the data path transfer rate is maximized since trunk loading has been eliminated and protocol overhead minimized. Second, all other NADs (and their hosts) on the trunk have had their intercommunication momentarily suspended, which implies an interlock capability.

Mode 3 Command Messages

Enable Stream Path Request

Disable Stream

Path Data

Path Mark

Path Code

Wait

Mode 3 Response Messages

ACK

BLOCK SEQUENCE ERROR

Illegal command message

Illegal Path

Disconnect

Ready

Nak

Message Transmission Retry

As explained in the Link Control Protocol section, all transmisions consist of a command and response message pair. A normal transmission consists of a TCU receiving a command message addressed to it, and returning a response to the TCU originating the command.

Transmission Abnormality

A transmission abnormality occurs when no response is forthcoming to the command. Listed below are the main reasons for no response occurring:

1. Addressed a nonexistent NAD (actually TCU)
2. Command message garbled on the trunk causing
   a. Destination Field to address a nonexistent NAD
   b. Check sum error at receiver (no answer if check sum error)
3. Command message received correctly but the response message was garbled giving a similar effect as (2).

When a transmission abnormality occurs, the command message is retransmitted (with the same sequence number), up to 256 times, until a response message is received. If no response message is received after 256 retries, a fatal error has occurred. The disposition of the unsuccessfully transmitted command message depends on its type.

During retry the controlware will not attempt to send any command messages other than the one enduring the transmission abnormality. The controlware, however, will accept incoming command messages.

Destination Busy

The status of the responding NAD (TCU) is included in a response message. One of these status bits is the "Memory busy" bit. The "Memory busy" status signals that, although the command message was received by the destination TCU correctly, it could not be passed on to NAD memory. Hence, the response returned its likewise not from memory but generated by the TCU. Since the NAD processor at the destination did not receive the command, it must be retransmitted.

Provided the remainder of the response status is correct, the command message is queued for retry, and will be retransmitted until accepted by the destination NAD memory (or until a fatal error occurs).

The retry queue is serviced on a fixed interval basis. Other command messages may be sent during this interval.

Destination Fatal Error

Other NAD status bits in a response message include NAD processor not running, sequence errors, and other indicators of fatal errors at the destination NAD.

If the response status indicates a fatal error, the command message is not retransmitted. Marked "fatal error," the message is disposed of according to type.

Fatal Message Errors

Fatal message errors are those which are caused by hardware errors during the transmission of a trunk command/response. These errors can be caused by:

- trunk interface failures at either NAD
- trunk/data set failures
- NAD failures

Link Control Protocol

The LCN Link Control Protocol defines a format and sequence of bits impressed upon the trunk to facilitate the transmission of information. The vehicle for all command and response information on the trunk is called a message. Each transmission on the trunk consists of only one message frame. In all cases, communication between two elements X and Y consists of a pair of message transmissions: a command message transmitted from X to Y and a response message transmitted from Y to X.

Command Message Frame Structure

A valid command message is a minimum of ten 8-bit bytes in length following the frame synchronization sequence and must conform to the following structures: P, F, T, FUN, A1, A2, RP, S L1, L2, FC1, FC2, I, FC3, FC4 where,

P = preamble of all ones preceding sync frame

F = message frame synchronizing byte

T = destination address byte

FUN = function byte

A1, A2 = access code bytes

RP = resync parameter byte

S = source address byte

L1, L2 = length field bytes

FC1, FC2 = header frame check sequence bytes

I = information field, variable length

FC3, FC4 = information frame check sequence bytes

Response Message Frame Structure

A valid response message is a minimum of ten 8-bit bytes in length following the frame synchronization sequence and must conform to the following structure: P, F, T, FUN, P1, P2, P3, S, L1, L2, FC1, FC2, I, FC3, FC4 where,

P1 = not used

P2 = TCU/TCI status byte

P3 = not used

and all other elements are identical to the command message elements.

Physical Level Protocol

The transmission scheme employs carrier modulation of self clocked data, with the NADs attaching to a coaxial trunk via a T-tap. The measured error rate of the combination (including data sets) is 10^{-12} or better within the configuration limitations.

Access to the trunk is governed by Trunk Reservation and Contention Elimination (TRACE) priority hardware. TRACE is a rotating priority scheme in which every NAD is given access to the trunk in turn. (Author's note: The access protocol has elements of both BRAM and PSD. Details may be found in [9].)

Appendix 6D: Ringnet

Introduction

As the name implies, local area networks [4,25,29] offer a means of providing high-bandwidth communications between hosts that are relatively close (10 to 1000 meters) and usually in the same building. Many of these are based on packet switched technology [31] and have been in existence for several years in various universities and industrial laboratories. However, the technology is sufficiently new that commercially available packet switched local networks are still rare. This paper presents the architecture of a communication subsystem built by Prime Computer for local networking, although it could also be used in loosely coupled multiprocessing [32].

System Overview

A Ringnet local area network is comprised of two or most host[1] nodes, each node containing an interface that connects to the transmission medium, a node controller that plugs into a standard Prime I/O bus, and network software that interfaces to the Prime Operating System (PRIMOS) as shown in figure 6D–1. The node interface, or junction box, consists of an electronically operated relay controlled by the node controller. When deselected by the controller or by a failure of system power, it offers a straight through connection that bypasses the node; otherwise, it connects the transmission lines to receiving and transmitting circuits in the node controller. Although the basic topology is that of a ring and seemingly might not lend itself to convenient incremental extension and reconfiguration, a slight modification in the wiring of node interfaces [30] would allow a host interconnection topology of an unrooted tree, so that a local network of hosts could be extended from any of its points in any direction.

Control of the network is completely decentralized in order to eliminate the requirement of a particular node having to be operational to arbitrate the communication medium and operates by passing a control token sequentially around a loop, much like that of the Distributed Computing System [27, 28].

R.L. Gordon, W.W. Farr, and P. Levine, "Ringnet: A Packet Switched Local Network with Decentralized Control," *Computer Networks* 3 (December 1979) :373–379. Reprinted with permission.

[1]A host node can be any one of several Prime models, in particular, either a P-400, P-500, P-350/450/550/650/750. Each of these models is normally thought of as being in the "Super-mini" class of machines since they support a large address space (2**29 bytes) and multiple users (up to 64).

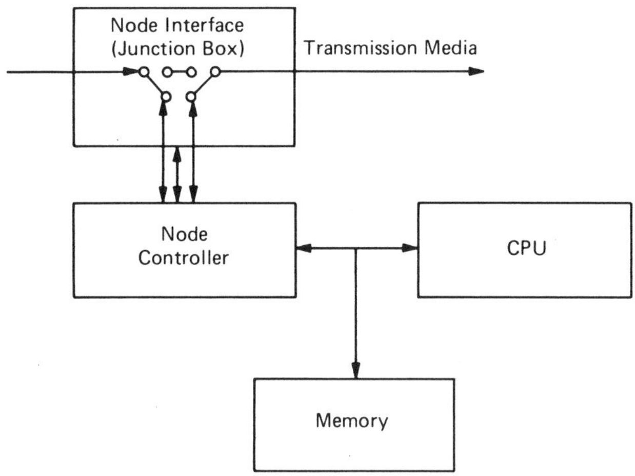

Figure 6D–1. Ringnet Components

Since Ringnet is a uni-directional loop network, each operational node normally retransmits the incoming bit stream. This repeating of the bit stream at each node required engineering tradeoffs to be made between the signalling media, the signalling rate, and the transmitter to receiver separation, a process that resulted in Ringnet using a low-loss "off the shelf" shielded twinex cable as the transmission medium. At a signalling speed of 10 MHz, the chosen medium provides for a maximum active node to node (or node to repeater) cable length of 230 meters (750 feet), although longer separations between active nodes are possible at lower signalling speeds. Each hardware node controller may be programmed to recognize one of 255 node addresses; however, it will always respond to an address of all ones (address 255) that can be used for broadcasting [26].

In order to facilitate running of application software on three different kinds of networks; (local, long-haul or point to point synchronous, and public data networks), PRIMENET[2] provides the user with three network services common to all three types of networks: Interactive Terminal Support (ITS), an Interprocess Communication Facility (IPCF), and a transparent network File Access Method (FAM).

The interprocess communication facility provides a virtual circuit capability at the program level, (i.e. a set of operating system calls for X.25 services) upon which the other two network services are based. In practice, the remote file access and the interactive terminal support offer a user flexible access to most of the computing resources of a local network. The full

[2]PRIMENET is Prime's trademark for all of its networking products, both local and longhaul.

use of these services allows any terminal connected to a node of a local network to be used to login to any other node, and the free sharing of all host files by all local network users. However, the level of sharing may be altered by a system administrator from that of full access to all resources to that of access by each node to only its local resources.

System Hardware

Overview

Each message on the network is sent as one or more packets, where a packet consists of a header field, a data field, and a trailer field. Data bits and some of the header information are passed to the node controller (under program control) by the host, while the rest of the header bits and the trailer bits are handled exclusively by the node controller hardware. Packets may vary in size from a minimum of 4 bytes (header only) up to a maximum of 2048 bytes (header plus 2044 data bytes). A transmitting node will interrupt its host when a packet has been transmitted and acknowledged by one or more nodes, if its buffer is full, or if a network fault has occurred; a receiving node will interrupt the host only when a packet has been correctly received.

Control of the network is maintained by passing a special bit pattern known as a "token" around the loop. If a node controller has a packet pending for transmission and detects a "free" token (one not associated with a message), it may remove the token and put a packet on the loop. Packets are placed onto and removed from the network *only* by the transmitting node. During this time the other active nodes are operating in a "transceive" mode and are responsible for receiving, retransmitting and copying messages if necessary.

Separate provisions are made for initially establishing a token and recovering from damaged tokens due to nodes connecting and disconnecting.

Packet Format and Framing

The detailed link level format of a Ringnet packet is shown in figure 6D–2. Only the second through sixth fields are accessible by host software, all others are managed solely by the node controller. The "TO" field contains the address of the node intended to receive the packet or an address of all ones which implies that all nodes should copy the packet, thus providing a natural broadcast capability for the network when needed. The "FROM" address contains the address of the transmitting node, while the packet "TYPE" field is used by the software and the node controller to distinguish

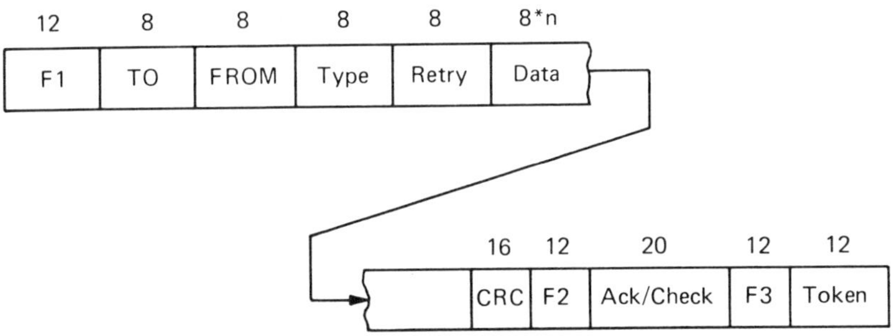

Figure 6D–2. Link Protocol Packet Format (field width is in bits)

different packet types such as a data packet or a status packet. Trailer fields consist of a 16-bit cyclic redundancy checksum (CRC), a delimiting synch frame, and an acknowledge/check frame that is modified by the receiving node(s) and sent back to the transmitting node. Packet frames F1, F2, F3 and the token are special bit patterns that cannot be duplicated in the rest of the packet due to the particular encoding scheme[3] used.

Token Management

It is important that at least one token is circulating, since messages can only be inserted into the network if the node controller detects a "free" token. However, because of the autonomous operation of the nodes (see [33] for a discussion of the importance of allowing autonomous operation of hosts) a token may get destroyed by the closing of a relay in the node interface when a node is being connected or disconnected. Also, tokens must be inserted when the network is initially powered up, and occasionally multiple tokens may be present when two or more nodes simultaneously attempt to initiate tokens. Recovery from and control of these conditions is called "token management" and is a cooperative hardware and software effort as described below.

Before requesting the node controller to transmit a packet, the host control software sets a software timer, just in case the node controller will not respond. Next, an instruction is issued that not only notifies the node controller a packet is ready for transmission but also resets several status bits in the controller such as the "token detected" status bit, the "multiple token detected" status bit, and the "packet did not return" status bit.

[3]A key design decision was to use a local clock in each controller rather than a master clock, this requiring a solution to the problem of synchronizing the transmitter and receiver pairs. A particular four out of five encoding scheme was chosen to guarantee uniqueness of special bit patterns such as synchronizing characters packet frames, tokens, etc., resulting in an effective bit rate of 8 MHz, even though the signalling rate is 10 MHz.

When a node controller begins transmitting, it takes all the received data off the network, a procedure known as "stripping" the incoming bit stream, and begins searching in one of two ways for the packet it launched. The first search is conducted by a node controller for its own "FROM" address plus the three packet frame characters F1, F2 and F3. Failing the first search, it attempts to detect a token on the receive side immediately after transmission stops on the transmit side, since whenever the controller finishes launching a packet, it transmits a token followed by some fill bits. If some other token or packet arrives before the one it just launched, the controller sets the "packet did not return" status bit. Thus multiple tokens are removed during a transmit cycle along with any extraneous messages. Of course, messages associated with the duplicate tokens will have to be retransmitted.

Failure to complete transmission of the packet for any number of reasons (e.g. no token circulating or a failure of the intended recipient) will cause the software timer to expire and the host control software to interrogate the status of the controller. If a "no token detected" status is indicated, the control software assumes that nothing is circulating, for if the packet was in any way corrupted, the "packet did not return" bit in the transmit status would have been set. In either case, the control software initiates a new token, resets the timer, and attempts a retransmission of the packet.

It is possible that two or more hosts holding traffic may attempt this procedure at the same time and simultaneously launch tokens. To reduce this possibility, each host waits a different amount of time (based on its address) before attempting to initiate a new token. Even so, there is a small probability that multiple tokens may be initiated. However, multiple tokens circulating are not a problem since they are "stripped" during transmission as already described.

Error Recovery

At the time the network was designed there was very little operational experience with respect to the kinds and frequency of errors that occur in a local network environment. For these reasons the controller preserves enough status for the software to be aware of different kinds of transmission errors, token management problems, and retransmissions. Three different diagnostic modes were designed in so that the node controller could be operationally verified under program control without disrupting normal network traffic. They are:

1) Digital circuit loop back—single step
2) Analog loop back—full speed on the controller
3) Analog loop back—full speed on the network

In the first two modes the controller is not connected to the network and is essentially transmitting to itself. Under these condtions a variety of error modes can be forced such as CRC errors, NACK, Check Character Error, etc., in order to check out the controller. In the third mode the controller is sending messages around the loop to itself in order to verify loop integrity.

This level of control over the node controller by a host allows an interesting heuristic to be used for maintaining network availability and locating a faulty node. Inability to successfully deliver any packets for an extended time can automatically result in disconnecting a node from the network and initiating node-node controller diagnostics. When a controller passes all of the "on-board" diagnostics, it reconnects. Since all affected hosts initiate the same action, a faulty host will not reconnect and the network will return to normal service with only "healthy" nodes.

If the failure was not mapped out by the above procedure, a cable or connector was probably at fault. Since one of the diagnostic modes designed into the node controller allows it to send a packet without a token to another node, the fault can be isolated by a cooperative effort where all the nodes send packets to all other nodes. A comparison of the physical mapping to the received packets shows where the failure occurred.

Software Architecture

Overview

PRIMENET software is an optional enhancement to the PRIMOS[4] operating system that provides users with the three network services previously mentioned. It is intended that running a program on a remote host from a terminal connected to a local host, or accessing remote files from a local host should require not reprogramming of application software or retraining of users. The same file system calls to the operating system used for local file access are also used for remote file access, and login procedures are similar for local and remote hosts.

Both the transparent remote file facility and the remote login facility are based on the use of "virtual circuits." Virtual circuits can be managed at the user program level by the proper use of a collection of subroutine calls to PRIMOS and provide a "Level 3, X.25 Interprocess Communication Facility (IPCF). Packets using a local network route are enveloped differently at the lower levels than for a long-haul synchronous path because of different link control and hardware protocols, however it was desired to

[4]PRIMOS is the name of Prime's multi-user, multi-environment operating system used on all Prime computers.

support only one level three protocol for the three different types of networks in use. Since the link protocol for Ringnet was previously described in the hardware section, only the "Level 3" enveloping, the operating system calls, and the FAM services will be described here.

The visible resources of a network can be controlled over a broad range by a system administrator, from full access to every file of every host on a local network to only those attached to a user's local host. In fact, two or more "logically independent" local networks can be configured to share the same physical loop. This control is supported through the use of an intereactive program that aids an administrator in configuring a network.

X.25 Enveloping

Messages presented to the operating system for transmission over a network are handled as a series of "packets" by the network control software and passed to the appropriate link control module depending on whether or not it is local or long-haul traffic. Routing information is established during circuit initialization and is readily determined from a "virtual circuit identifier" presented along with each message. Virtual circuit identifiers are obtained from an initial connection dialogue described in the section on X.25 Services.

Once a virtual circuit has been established, messages are prepared as a series of fixed length packets (if they are larger than the maximum packet size for the circuit being used, a term called "packetizing") and have prefixed to them a four byte header as shown in figure 6D–3. The header consists of an extra byte reserved for future use, a 4-bit format type field, a 12-bit logical channel number, and two bytes of flow control information (sequence numbers) as provided for in the X.25 "Level 3" data packet format standards [24]. Ringnet packets are then queued for handling by the node controller interface module after the logical channel number is mapped into a physical node number and the link protocol frames are added.

X.25 Services

Virtual circuit services are provided to users by a collection of network subroutines that are calls into the PRIMOS operating system. The major

8	4	12	7	1	7	1
Reserved	Format Type	Logical Channel	Packet # Rcvd	More Data	Packet # Sent	0

Figure 6D–3. Level 3 Data Packet Header (field width is in bits)

services provided are for forming a connection, breaking a connection and transmitting or receiving data. Generally, two different forms of a service are provided. The first form is an abbreviated calling sequence, with only a minimum amount of information needed to be supplied by a user in order to establish and use a virtual circuit. The second form is a more detailed one that allows a user full access to all fields of the X.25 "Level 3" defined packet formats. The latter form is intended primarily for users wishing to form X.25 connections to non-Prime hosts on Public Data packet networks.

The addressability defined in the basic X.25 specifications refer only to a single 14-digit address per host, although it is not uncommon for a host (like PRIMOS) to handle multiple processes and users. Therefore, in order to decide which user or operating system service should control a connection, each incoming "call request packet" in PRIMENET must specify a network "port." This port, coupled with the 14-digit address of the target system, designates a target process.

Each host in Ringnet has a pool of 255 available ports that may be assigned to any process on the first come, first served basis by a call on the operating system. However, only ports 1 through 99 are available for users; the rest are reserved for system use. Permanent port assignments to a process are possible by controlling the order in which processes are initiated just after system startup; otherwise, there is no absolute guarantee that a particular process is associated with a given port number.

The short form of the initial connection protocol uses an ASCH host name (e.g. "ENG.15") instead of the long 14-digit address and a port number previously acquired by the target process. The "connect" function is typical of the IPCF primitives and the request for it is shown as a partial example of how a circuit is formed at the program level.

```
CALL X$CONN(VCID, PORT, ADR, ADRL, VC_STAT)
```

The variable ADR points to a string containing the name of the intended host (i.e. ENG.15), ADRL contains the length of the name (6), and VC_STAT represents the status of the requested service. Upon completion of a successful connection, a "virtual circuit identifier" (VCID) is returned that can be used for the subsequent transmission of data. Incoming calls for a particular port in a host are queued on a first come first served basis. Information concerning a call request at the head of a port queue can be obtained via a system call, so that connections can be accepted, refused, cleared, etc. Calls are kept pending for 90 seconds, during which the requestors' status is that of "connection in progress." Other X.25 services are provided to users that allow for waiting on the completion of a network event, accepting or clearing a call, passing off a virtual circuit to another process in the same host, and obtaining status information about a particular circuit.

FAM and LOGIN Services

The File Access Manager (FAM) is a PRIMOS subsystem that extends the functions of the PRIMOS file system to a network of hosts. Virtualization of the file system is accomplished by permanently assigning a port (255) to the local FAM process of each host, over which virtual circuits to neighbouring FAMs are used to accomplish remote file operations on behalf of a user.

A FAM process in a host fields requests from local users for file operations on remote hosts, handles incoming file requests from remote hosts, and maintains status and update information concerning the current state of network connections and file system devices. When the PRIMOS supervisor decides that a particular user request is destined for a remote device, it queues the request for the local FAM process and suspends the user. FAM packages this request in a message and passes it off to the appropriate remote FAM, which performs the requested file operations on behalf of the user. The remote FAM process sends the original request and the requested data back to the local FAM, which copies the returned values into the user's address space and causes the user to be rescheduled. Because certain file primitives are guaranteed to the "atomic" operations, all file functions are performed to completion just as if they occurred locally, even if they require multiple messages or updating of local supervisor tables.

Since both local and remote operations on a particular file are handled through the file system of the host that owns the particular file, all of the normal file protection and other mechanisms, such as locking a particular record while writing, are automatically accomplished. Applications using remote data as well as local data run without change.

In a similar fashion, the ability of a user to "remotely log-in," as if their terminal were attached to the host of their choice, is achieved by the operating system multiplexing all remote terminal traffic through port "O." when a user "logs in," they may designate a system to be attached to as:

LOGIN SMITH—ON ENG.15

At this point the local login server establishes a virtual circuit to the target host and requests the initiation of, and connection to, a process in the remote host. From then on the local terminal buffers are effectively diverted to the input and output buffers of the remote process running on the selected node.

Resource Configuration

Control over user available resources are managed at the system level through a network configuration procedure that is invoked when a system is initially installed or whenever major changes to a network are made. An interactive program (NETCFG) is used to insure that all of the relevant parameters have the proper values set. During this procedure the logical extent of a local network is determined by specifying which hosts know about each other. For example, in a Ringnet that has six hosts attached (A, B, C, D, E, and F), hosts A, C, E, and F can be configured as one local network, and hosts B and D can be configured as another. Under this arrangement, none of the resources of B and D can be accessed by A, C, E, and F.

Other configuration parameters under administrative control are the maximum number of processes in PRIMOS that are reserved for serving remote users and whether local disks can be used by a particular remote host. Once permission for remote access to the local disks is given, then those disks may be "added" to the disk lineup of a remote host. The FAM process in each host maintains a table of disks that are active, and access to a disk (on a host by host basis) is controlled through system administrator commands that access these tables.

It should be noted that network resources are not automatically made available to all users: A user must be "known" to the local login server on the host they wish to connect to and must have proper access rights to the remote files they wish to use, in exactly the same way they would on a stand-alone system.

Conclusions

Ringnet is currently being used extensively in various local network configurations to share peripheral resources and serve large communities (several hundred) of users. Tens of thousands of hours of reliable Ringnet operation, supporting both remote login service and remote file access, has proven the soundness of many of the design decisions and provided a base for new network applications. The particular emphasis on decentralized control which allows for the autonomous operation of each node of the local network is well placed, since this simplifies operational schedules and provides for smooth system extensibility.

Appendix 6E: The Cambridge Model Distributed System

Since all communication takes place via the same medium, namely the ring, it is necessary to provide means whereby the VDU concentrator and the computer allocated to it shall be able to reject unwanted packets addressed to them, accidentally or mischievously, from computers under the control of other users. This is done by maintaining, in the interfaces to computers in the computer bank and in the VDU concentrators, lists of ring stations from which packets are acceptable. These are known as *acceptance lists*. As a refinement, a system of port numbers is implemented and a separate acceptance list is maintained for each port. Any packet which arrives from a source that does not figure in the appropriate acceptance list, or is addressed to a nonexistent port, is thrown away.

The acceptance list in the VDU concentrator is set up as part of the operation of opening the byte streams needed for communication with other parts of the system. The Resource Manager has an acceptance list which is unspecific as to source machine but specific as to port number, and communication with it is initially established through one of these ports. The same system is used for communication with servers.

When the VDU concentrator is first switched on, it refers to the name server to ascertain the address of the Resource Manager. When a VDU becomes active, the concentrator is then in a position to open a byte stream connection to the Resource Manager. This connection is used to conduct the type of dialogue familiar in time-sharing systems. The user's password and other particulars are checked and, if they are in order, a computer is allocated to him assuming, of course, that one is available. The Resource Manager advises the concentrator of the identity of the computer allocated and warns it to be prepared to accept a byte stream connection. It then causes the computer to be loaded with a suitable program and tells it which VDU it is to work with. The first action of the computer is to open a byte stream to the VDU concentrator which is, of course, expecting it. Once the connection has been established, the VDU user is in control of the computer just as effectively as if his VDU were directly connected to it. Anything he types will normally pass straight to that computer. He can, however, direct messages to the Resource Manager by typing a suitable escape character.

The user's computer may stop and special provision must be made to enable him to reboot it, since he is not in positon to press a button on the

---

M.V. Wilkes and R.M. Needham, "The Cambridge Model Distributed System," *Operating Systems Review* 14 (January 1980) :21–29. Reprinted with permission.

processor panel. Special provision must similarly be made for him to use the debugging facilities in his computer interface. It is being arranged that the user can call on the Resource Manager for help in these situations. This is thought to be better than encumbering the VDU concentrator with software that is unconnected with its main role, and which would have to be replicated for each type of computer in the bank.

Access to Servers. The principle adopted in CMDS is that a user need establish his identity once only, namely with the Resource Manager. It is then the responsibility of the Resource Manager to put him in a position to access the various servers and to obtain from them services to which he may be entitled. It is necessary that there should be available, somwhere in the system, information about the user and his entitlements and it is further necessary that accounting information should be maintained. No firm decision has yet been taken as to whether this information should be partly held in the various servers.

It is essential that, once a user's credentials have been established with any server, the requests for service that follow should be recognised as valid without the repetition of the entire validation procedure. Unfortunately, this cannot be done at low level by a system of acceptance lists such as that just described for the VDU concentrators and users' computers. Instead, each packet arriving at a server must be examined by high level software. There is a danger that, under certain circumstances, a server may be bombarded with an excessive number of unwanted packets. This could arise, for example, if a computer under the control of one of the users got out of hand. It is not known how serious this problem is likely to be in practice. If necessary, ways could be implemented whereby the server could appeal to the Resource Manager, which would then restrain the offending computer.

Discussion

Bootstrapping the Boot Server. The boot server provides bootstrapping services for computers throughout the system, but is unable to provide these services for itself. The Problem may be solved by providing the boot server with some form of nonvolatile memory, for example, a floppy disc or, perhaps, a bubble memory. Alternatives to be considered are making the boot server load itself from the file server, or combining in one computer the functions of file server and boot server.

Low Level Protocol for Communication with the Printer. The use of a computer on the ring as a printing server, with the printer itself separately interfaced to the ring, calls for some comment. The more obvious arrangement would be to have the printer connected as a peripheral to the server. When the scheme adopted was first conceived, it was envisaged that communication between the printing server and the printer proper would be at a very low level of protocol, using a single independent minipacket for each byte transmitted. In such circumstances the interface between the ring and the printer could be extremely simple. Since one printing server could serve a number of printers in different location, it was thought the scheme would prove to be economical.

However, it was soon discovered that a Z80A microcomputer with 4K bytes of memory could easily accommodate a program that would implement the byte stream protocol, together with the underlying packet protocol. The byte stream protocol is very convenient from the software writer's point of view and is a standard throughout the system. Once it was realised that it could be implemented in the printer interface, there seemed no point in using anything else. If, as is possible, it ultimately turns out that the entire software for a printing server could be accommodated in a Z80A, then the present argument for a separate printing server falls to the ground. The development of special silicon chips for ring interfaces might, however, change the situation, especially if a single chip interface for printers and other devices became available. In the meanwhile, it has been thought consistent with the objects of a program of research in distributed computing that, in the first instance at any rate, functions should be distributed as widely as possible.

An Editing Server. Editing, like compiling, is considered as one of the operations for which a user will use the computer allocated to him and, for this reason, no mention of it has so far been made. If, however, the view is taken that editing is a system function then it would be natural to provide an *editing server* for the purpose. The presence of such a server would enable a user to create and edit files without requesting the allocation of a computer. This capability might be of value in an environment in which a good deal of file editing went, on, possibly for word processing purposes. The presence of an editing server would also enable a user to create and edit files while a program was running in the computer that had been allocated to him.

An editor designed to run in an editing server and to be used simultaneously by a number of users could not offer the same performance as one running in a dedicated computer with plenty of memory available. There would, however, be nothing to prevent a user, who required a better performance than a system editing server afforded, requesting the allocation of a computer of his own and loading it with the editor of his choice.

Other Servers. Whenever a situation arises in which a number of users need to perform the same task, using the same program, then the option of providing a special server is open. The server need not run in a computer permanently dedicated to the purpose since any one of the computers available in the computer bank could be temporarily commandeered. If a distributed system of the kind described here were used in a business data processing environment where transaction processing was the order of the day, then many opportunities for the multiple use of a computer in this way would arise.

Intelligent Terminals. The reader will have noticed that in CMDS the users' VDUs are connected to the system through concentrators which provide the minimum of echoing or editing facilities. This is indeed an essential feature of the system. Once logged-in, the user is provided with a whole computer—or, if necessary, with more than one computer— for his exclusive use. It is not, therefore, necessary for computing power to be available in his terminal, nor indeed if it were would it have any clearly differentiated role to play.

Notwithstanding what has just been said, a user with a minicomputer in his own office, who wished to have it attached to the system could readily be accommodated. Such a user would not normally be a candidate for having one of the system computers allocated to him; what he would be interested in would be making use of the file server, of a hard copy server and, possibly, of other servers as well. Apart from the satisfaction of owning his own computer and having it always available, such a user would not be in a markedly different position from that of a user who was allocated one of the computers in the bank. Perhaps the most important point to make in this connection is that, in a truly distributed system, based on a communication system of adequate bandwidth and reliability, it is of little importance from the user's point of view where particular items of equipment or software are located. In planning a distributed system the considerations affecting this issue are likely to be cost, economy of maintenance, utilization of space, and preservation of the continuity of service in the face of failure of individual components. The latter subject is discussed in the next section.

Failure of System Components. If a computer allocated to a user fails, he can report this to the Resource Manager and have another one allotted to him. He will thus suffer temporary inconvenience but no more. Failure of the computer holding the name server or failure of that holding the Resource Manager would very soon have the effect of bringing the system down. It would be possible to provide a second name server and to arrange that all relevant software should try first one, then the other. Similarly, it would be possible to provide more than one Process Manager. Each would run its own computer and be assigned an order of precedence. Normally, the Resource Manager of highest precedence which was in working order would control the system and would send periodic signals to the others to prevent them from coming into action. If the running Resource Manager failed, the signals would stop and the others would attempt to take over; only the one having the highest precedence would succeed in doing so. In order to avoid having to keep tables up to date in the non-operational Resource Managers (and the hazards to their taking over successfully which this involves) the ring interfaces could be so designed that a Resource Manager could ascertain by polling them what the state of the system was. It should be pointed out, however, that whereas the supervisors in TYMNET run under time-sharing in separate computers and those not in active mode consume very little in the way of resources, in the case of the distributed system a separate computer must be dedicated to each supervisor and the cost of providing the standby facility is therefore not negligible. It might be observed that the name server in particular can run in quite a small microcomputer whose intrinsic reliability is likely to be high. Possibly, therefore, the best policy would be to accept the chances of its failing, in the same way that one accepts the chance of a ring repeater failing. The Resource Manager needs a somewhat larger computer but it is, nevertheless, probably that duplicating it would only be necessary when an extremely high degree of availability was required.

This system is supported by the hardware described in appendix 6F.

Appendix 6F: The Cambridge Digital Communication Ring

The design study for the digital communication ring now operating was begun in 1974 [34]. At that time a clear need was seen for a system that would allow the interconnection of computers and similar devices within a building and be capable of operating at a data rate substantially in advance of that provided by conventional telecommunication techniques. A ring had the advantage of conceptual simplicity and it was felt that this simplicity could be preserved in a practical design. A system was proposed in which information would be sent in very small fixed-length packets. The acceptance at the destination of each packet would be verified independently of other packets and there would be minimum of protocol built in at the hardware level. Importance was, however, attached to choosing a system that would be intrinsically proof against the hogging of the ring by one station. Since it was felt that the bandwidth readily obtainable over short distances was more than ample for the purpose, making the best possible use of a given bandwidth was no part of the terms of reference against which the design was done.

The design study led to the proposal to use a packet containing a byte giving the destination, a byte giving the source, two bytes of data, and a few bits for control purposes. It appeared at the time that the objectives outlined in the previous paragraph could be achieved by the use of the *register insertion* mode of operation [35]. The packet would be shifted out and from that moment the shift register would carry the entire traffic of the ring. The packet would be copied at its destination and would eventually arrive back in the shift register where it would be recognized by its source address. The shift register would then be switched out of the ring and the traffic on the ring would once more bypass it. There can be no hogging in such a system, since any station whose shift register is not already in circuit can insert a packet between any two packets passing in the ring.

The register insertion system, however, suffers from the disadvantage that a fault developing in a shift register can disrupt the entire action of the ring. Moreover, if the fault were to develop in an inactive station, the fact that it had done so would not become apparent until the station began to transmit. An alternative to the register insertion system is the *empty packet* system, in which packets continually circulate and each carries a leading bit to indicate whether it is full or empty. A station assembles a packet it wishes to transmit

---

M.V. Wilkes and D.J. Wheeler, "The Cambridge Digital Communication Ring," *Proceedings of the Local Area Communications Network Symposium*, Boston, May 1979, pp. 47–61. Reprinted with permission.

in a shift register as before and shifts the information into the first available empty packet that comes along. A breadboard model of a station working on the register insertion principle had already been constructed when it was realized that, if packets were allowed to make a complete circuit of the ring, the empty packet system would have similar anti-hogging properties to the register insertion system. The packet would be copied at the destination and would return to the source where it would be marked as empty. The station would not, however, be allowed to refill that packet, but would be required to pass it downstream.

Simultaneously, it was realized that there would be no need for the returning packet to be recognized by its source byte, since the number of packets circulating in the ring is fixed and the station has only to count packets as they go by to know when its own packet has returned. The significance of this observation is that it is not necessary; to have an additional shift register permanently connected in series with the ring at each station in order that the full/empty bit will not have left the station by the time the source bytes are recognized. There need, in fact, be no more delay at each station than is necessary to regenerate the pulses. Thus, the amount of equipment in series with the ring is reduced to a minimum and the reliability may be expected to increase proportionately. A fault developing in a shift register at a particular station will affect transmission from that station, but will not affect the performance of the ring as a whole. It was found that the original breadboard could readily be modified for the new system and that the total count of TTL packages was the same.

The fact that packets always make a complete circuit of the ring would appear at first sight to imply that half the transmission capacity is wasted. This, however is not the case, since the returning packet can convey information as to whether the packet was successfully copied at its destination. Otherwise, special measures would have to be taken to indicate this, such as the launching from the destination of a separate packet addressed to the original source. Allowing packets to make a full circuit of the ring enables a very simple hardware protocol to be implemented in which the transmission of each packet and the verification of the fact that it has been received is independent of the transmission of other packets.

In both the register insertion system and the empty packet system it is necessary to provide a *monitor station* which will have the effect of removing from the ring packets that circulate indefinitely in consequence of some fault condition. In the case of the empty packet system all that is necessary is to include in the packet a monitor bit which is unset when the packet is launched and is set at the monitor station. The monitor station marks as empty any packet which reaches it with the monitor bit already set. Errors which can cause packets to circulate indefinitely are very rare in the form of the empty packet system adopted. An example is the full/empty bit in an empty packet becoming accidentally reversed. Corruption of the source byte in a packet would not cause the packet to circulate indefinitely since, as explained above, this byte plays no part in the recognition by the source of the returning packet.

The monitor station may also conveniently provide the means whereby the ring is initialized on switching on or re-initialized after a failure. It can also be designed to keep statistics of ring performance and loading.

It is desirable that there should be some feature whereby a station may render itself deaf to stations from which it does not wish to receive packets. It was decided to incorporate in the station unit a single byte register known as the *source select register*. When this register contains all ones, the station will receive a packet addressed to it from any source. When the register contains all zeros, the station will not receive packets from any source. Otherwise the station is open to receive packets only from the source whose address is specified by the number standing in the register.

Provision for Maintenance

It was early realized that some aid would be necessary to enable breaks in the ring to be readily located. The first ring to be built had an echo feature. It was possible to launch from the monitor station an interrogating packet which would be recognized as such by the station to which it was addressed. The station would then respond by sending a signal along a logically separate low bandwidth channel to the monitor station. Valuable, however, as this feature might be in the location of hard faults, it would not help with the location of intermittent or rarely occurring faults, or with the identification of places at which noise was finding its way into the ring. A proposal for continuously monitoring the ring and reporting errors to a *logging station* was made by Wheeler and Hopper [36]. This proposal was so attractive that the ring was rebuilt to implement it.

In the new system each packet has an additional trailing bit used as a parity bit. As the packet leaves each station, including the station at which it is launched, this bit is set so that the packet has even parity. When a packet enters a station, the parity is checked by separate circuits. If it is found to be correct no action is taken. If it is incorrect, the station that has discovered the error proceeds itself autonomously to launch a reporting packet to a logging station, which has address zero. Thus, if one of the repeaters develops an intermittent or marginal fault, or if noise enters the ring from outside, the logging station will begin to receive reporting packets from the station immediately downstream of the trouble. The faulty packet continues on its way, but since the parity bit is reset as it leaves each station, the stations downstream of that at which the parity was found to be wrong will not give rise to further reporting packets.

The logging station is replaced just ahead of the monitor station and reporting packets are launched with the monitor bit already set so that they are removed by the monitor station without making a complete circuit of the ring. As an alternative to providing a separate logging station, facilities for recording information arriving in reporting packets may be built into the monitor station.

The monitor station fills empty packets with random digits and these packets are subjected to the procedure just described in exactly the same way as the full ones. The functioning of the ring is thus continuously monitored whether or not it is carrying traffic. The staff responsible for the maintenance of the ring can thus receive immediate intimation that trouble is occurring and is in no way dependent on reports received from users. It is suggested that this should be a design requirement for any digital communication system from which a high degree of reliability is expected.

The leading digit in a packet is always a "one" so that a station can never in normal operation receive a long unbroken stream of zeros. If this situation does occur the design of the station is such that it will emit a sequence of reporting packets as long as the condition persists. At the same time it passes downstream that will appear to the next station to be packets of normal parity. Thus the reporting system enables breaks in the ring, as well as intermittent faults, to be located.

Description of the Present Ring

A station consists of a *repeater* and a *station unit* (see figure 6F–1). These are identical for all stations except that the station unit has inserted into it a plug specifying its address. In addition, there is an *access box* which must be specially built to interface a particular type of computer or a particular device to the ring.

In the present ring the plug has also wired into it an indication of how many packets there are in the ring. In the earlier ring, the number of packets was determined dynamically by the framing circuits. This feature was removed for reasons of expediency when the ring was rebuilt, but is likely to be reinstated in future designs.

The ring is composed of two separate channels which, between them, carry information at a data rate of 10 Mbits/sec in one direction only. In all of the sectors but one, two twisted pairs in ordinary telephone cables are used. Included in the repeaters are transformers which remove any common mode interference or low frequency noise, and screening of the twisted pairs is not found to be necessary. The repeater design was thoroughly tested with

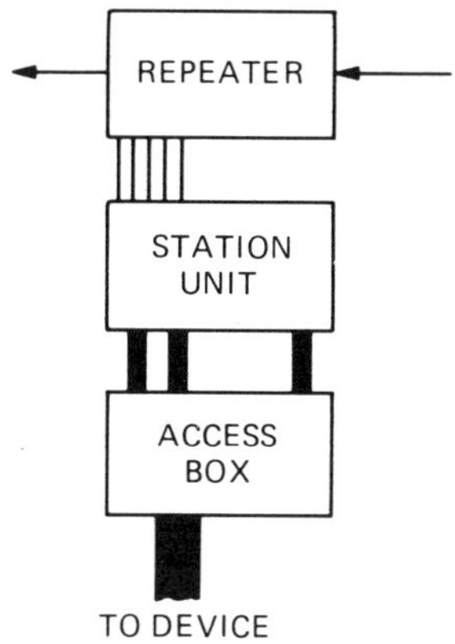

Figure 6F–1. Station Components

200 metres of cable between repeaters but, to be on the safe side, 100 metres has so far been regarded as the upper limit. Many repeaters are, of course, very much closer together than this. On one sector a pair of fibre optic cables are used. These run for 200 metres although the attenuation and dispersion are so low that the upper limit would be several kilometres at least.

The use of two channels enables a simple self-clocking system of modulation to be used. In each pulse interval a transition on both channels denotes a one and a transition on one or other of the channels only denotes a zero. The waveform on each channel is fully balanced and, as compared with the well-known phase or frequency modulation systems on a single channel, there is no half-pulse ambiguity. Each repeater incorporates a phase-locked oscillator for the generation of a local clock. The twisted pairs used for pulse transmission are also used to carry DC power at 50 volts for the repeaters, each repeater having in it a step down DC transformer.

Power is injected into the ring at two or three points as necessary. Power to the station unit and access box is normally supplied from the associated computer. The advantage of this system is that the repeaters, being independent of local sources of power, continue to work when the station units are de-energized.

The packet format is shown in figure 6F–2. The first bit is always a "one", the second bit indicates whether the packet is full or empty, and the third is the monitor bit. After that come the destination and source bytes, followed by two bytes of data. These are followed by two response bits which are both set to one when the packet is launched. If the destination is absent they will be unchanged when the packet returns to its source; otherwise they are changed by the destination according to the code shown and indicate whether the packet was accepted, was rejected because the station was busy, or rejected because the station was deaf to the particular source. Finally, but not shown in figure 6F–2, is the parity bit already referred to. This is not copied at the destination and is used solely by the error reporting system.

The packets follow one another head to tail up to the capacity of the ring. The train of packets is terminated by two or three zeros referred to as *gap digits*. These zeros, together with the leading one in the packets, are used for packet framing and packet counting. It might here be mentioned that the delay in each repeater is very small—about 1½ pulse times—so that the total number of packets circulating in the ring is also small. As the ring is operating at present this number is only two and even this requires a shift register of about 20 digits in length in the monitor station in order to increase the length of the ring artificially.

Four lines constitute the interface between a repeater and a station unit. Two of the lines are data lines. One passes the digit stream received from the ring continuously to the station unit and the other enables the station unit to pass digits to the repeater for transmission along the ring.

The fourth line carries a control waveform originating in the station unit; this waveform determines whether the repeater is to pass on the digits that it receives from the ring or whether it is to insert digits sent to it from the station unit. In order that the repeater may be completely isolated when the station unit is switched off, this line is routed through a normally open relay in the repeater energized from the same power supply that feeds the station unit. It is only the control waveform that passes through the relay, not the traffic on the ring.

There is a further control line going into the repeater which enables the frequency of the phase-locked oscillator to be controlled directly. This is only used at the monitor station and provides the means whereby the frequency of the phase-locked oscillator may be correctly set when the ring is initialized or re-initialized.

The station unit contains framing circuits that synchronize themselves to the passing packets using the leading ones and the gap digits. It also contains the parity generating and checking circuits, and the circuits for dispatching a

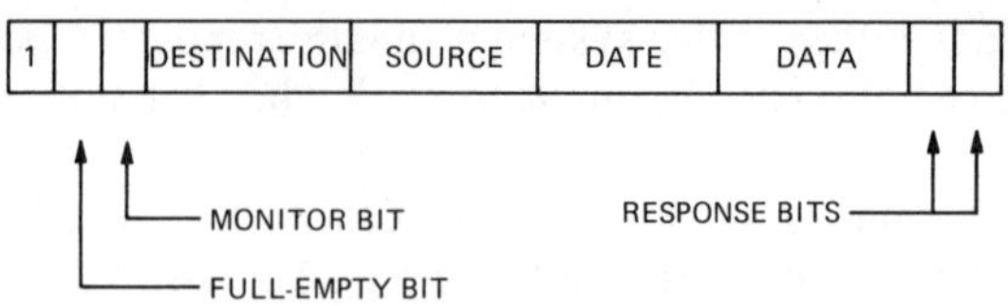

ON RETURN OF A PACKET THE RESPONSE BITS HAVE THE FOLLOWING VALUES:

11 DESTINATION ABSENT
01 PACKET ACCEPTED
10 DESTINATION DEAF
00 DESTINATION BUSY

Figure 6F–2. Frame Format

reporting packet when one is necessary. The reporting packet is easy to generate since, apart from the sourct byte and the full/empty bit, all of its bits are zeros.

The transmission and reception circuits in the station unit are independent of each other and permit full duplex operation. On the receiving side there are circuits which continuously monitor the digit stream received from the repeater and which are capable of recognizing packets addressed to the station. As long as the station is free—that is, not busy dealing with a previously received packet—the digit stream flows into a receiving shift register. When a packet addressed to the station is recognized, a note is made of the fact and, if it subsequently appears that the packet has come from a source to which the station is not deaf, shifting ceases. When it is known whether or not the packet is to be accepted, the front part of it will already have passed the repeater; however, there is plenty of time for the packet to be marked as accepted or rejected, since the response bits which carry this information come at the end. If the packet is accepted, it remains in the receiving shift register until that register is cleared by a signal from the access box. If any further packets addressed to the station arrive before this has happened they are marked busy .

There is a separate shift register for transmission. The destination and data bytes are written into this in parallel from the access box and on an appropriate signal from the access box are launched into the ring to fill the first empty packet to arrive, the source byte and control bits being added automatically. The transmitting shift register is circular and retains a copy of the transmitted packet. The packet can, therefore, be retransmitted if necessary without reloading the shift register. It was decided to take further advantage of the fact that a copy of the transmitted packet is retained and to provide circuits for checking bit by bit that the data and address bytes in the returned packet are identical with those transmitted. Two additional TTL packages were required for this purpose. We have, however, had second thoughts on the desirability of doing this and we will return to the point later.

When the packet has returned, 5 bits are available for reading by the access box; they correspond respectively to busy, unselected, acccepted, unrecognized, and returned packet in error. These bits, or some of them, must be inspected before the decision can be made whether to resend the packet that has just returned or whether to send a new one. It is, therefore, not possible for the access box to fill the packet immediately after the one that has returned, even if it is empty. When allowance is made for this and for the fact that a packet carries nearly 60% overheads, it is found that the maximum data rate at which a station can transmit is approximately $0.4/(n + 2)$ Mbits/sec., where n is the number of packets in the ring. For the special case of 2 packets circulating this comes out to slightly over 1 Mbit/sec.

The interface between the station unit and the access box consists of two 16-bit busses, the digits of which are denoted by TB0 through TB15 and RB0 through RB15, respectively, and 17 control lines CS1 through CS17. There is also a disabling line used only during switching on and switching off. The functions of the various control signals are given below. All the control lines are normally high so that an absent cable will not generate a spurious signal.

CS1 sets the 8-bit source select register from RB0–7.

CS2 gates the first data byte from the receiving shift register to RB0–7.

CS3 gates the second data byte from the receiving shift register to RB8–15.

CS4 gates the source address from the receiving shift register to RB0–7.

CS5 gates the source select register to RB0–7.

CS6 gates a one to RB6 if the station has rejected a packet from an unselected source at any time since the source select register was last set.

CS7 echoes the logical OR of CS1–6 and CS16 (handshake response to access box).

CS8 sets the first data byte in the transmitting shift register from TB0–7.

CS9 sets the second data byte in the transmitting shift register from TB8–15.

CS10 sets the destination byte in the transmitting shift register from TB0–7.

CS11 gates the response bits for last packet returned to TB0–4; these bits are not valid until CS14 has gone up.

CS12 echoes the logical OR of CS8–11 and CS13 (handshake response to access box.)

CS13 causes the packet in the transmitting shift register to be transmitted or retransmitted (transmit command).

CS14 falls at the end of CS13 and rises again when the transmitted packet has returned (packet returned signal).

CS15 falls at the end of CS16 and rises again when a packet has arrived in the receiving register (packet received signal).

CS16 discards the information in the receiving shift register and prepares the station unit to receive (receive command).

CS17 signals appearing on this line indicate that the ring is up and working.

Traffic Control

Although the anti-hogging provision means that a station is guaranteed its proportionate share of the ring capacity, nevertheless in certain circumstances a station would have an adverse effect on the performance of the ring if it were repeatedly to address packets to a busy station. This could happen, for example, if a computer were to attempt to send information to a teletype at a very much greater rate than the teletype could absorb it. Although it can be argued that to use the ring for busy waiting in this way represents poor software design and should not occur, it was nevertheless thought wise to include in the design of the ring a feature that would mitigate its consequences. Accordingly, it is arranged that, if a packet returns repeatedly marked busy or rejected, the appearance of the signal on the control line CS14 is progressively delayed, the delay eventually amounting to about 16 ring circulation times. The transmitting shift register may, however, be reloaded earlier if the user likes to do his own timing.

We no longer think in terms of connecting slow devices directly to the ring without any buffering and the case for providing the traffic control feature just described has perhaps become less strong. However, it is useful for preventing the ring being accidentally polluted by false traffic.

Higher Level Protocols

This paper is primarily concerned with the hardware level but something might be said about how the ring is used. One must be very cautious in taking over to a local area communications system, with an extremely low error rate, experience obtained in operating over public telephone lines where the error rate is high and variable. Usually, errors are controlled by some form of redundancy checking followed by retransmission if necessary. Even if the error rate is very low, error control is still necessary, but the retransmission unit can be large.

It is important not to lose flexibility and efficiency by insisting on the use of the same transmission protocol under circumstances. Even single packets are adequate in some circumstances, for example, for verifying that a particular computer is switched on or for acknowledging the receipt of information.

A protocol for the transmission of *basic blocks* has been defined by R.M. Needham and has come into general use. A basic block consists of a header giving the number of data packets that will follow, together with an indication of whether or not the block will carry a check sum at the end. Normally the basic block will include a check sum, but this is not insisted on by the protocol. The header also contains a *port number* for use within the computer that will receive the basic block. Basic blocks can be of any length up to 2K bytes. Basic blocks are what most people would call packets, and it is perhaps unfortunate that the term was used to describe the unit in which information is transmitted at the ring hardware level. The subject of higher level protocols and their relationship to the hardware facilities of the ring will be reported on more fully elsewhere.

[Three sections of original omitted. References that were contained in the original are collected in the references for the chapter.]

Appendix 6G: The PERQ System

The PERQ system (figure 6G–1) is a highly integrated set of components designed to provide a complete computing environment for a single user. PERQ is a personal computer with sufficient power and facilities to perform a wide variety of tasks found in offices, research facilities, business and government. The key to the small size and low cost of PERQ is that all components of the system were designed together, with the goal of minimizing the *system* complexity.

To support the wide bandwidth requirements of the CPU display, disk and network, the PERQ memory system is designed for a 200 megabit per second aggregate memory bandwidth. The memory plane is organized as 64K of 64 bit wide words. Memory cycles are split between the display and the rest of the system with 50% of the bandwidth available to the display. The display controller is completely integrated into the memory controller, resulting in a compact, low cost design. The memory connects to the CPU and IO channel controller with a 3 bus design (Address, Data In, Data Out) which can transfer 16 bits every 680 ns. The IO channel multiplexes 4 high bandwidth devices (network, disk, and two optional controllers) which can deliver 10 M bits per second to each device with all 4 devices running simultaneously.

For lower speed devices, an 8 bit microprocessor is included in the system to provide a low cost method of interfacing simple peripherals. Incorporating a standard uP permits the use of off the shelf LSI components to reduce the cost and complexity of, for example, the RS-232 channel and the IEEE-488 bus interface. The high speed controllers and the μP communicate with the CPU via a 16 bit I/O bus.

The microprogrammed CPU performs many of the housekeeping tasks for the I/O devices. Microcode for the disk, for example, implements device control block (DCB) dequeuing, buffer manipulation, track seek operations, etc. Using microcode in this manner reduces controller complexity significantly. The disk controller itself is comprised of less than 40 integrated circuits. The CPU is a horizontally microprogrammed processor with a 48 bit wide microword. The processor includes a 256 word dual ported general purpose file, a 16 level hardware implemented expression evaluation stack, and barrel shift and mask logic. Special hardware in the processor provides an extremely efficient mechanism for emulating byte coded instruction sets. Simple 1 byte instructions can execute a single microcycle. Hardware support for the RasterOp bit map manipulation primative allows bit ad-

Material supplied by Three Rivers Computer Corporation.

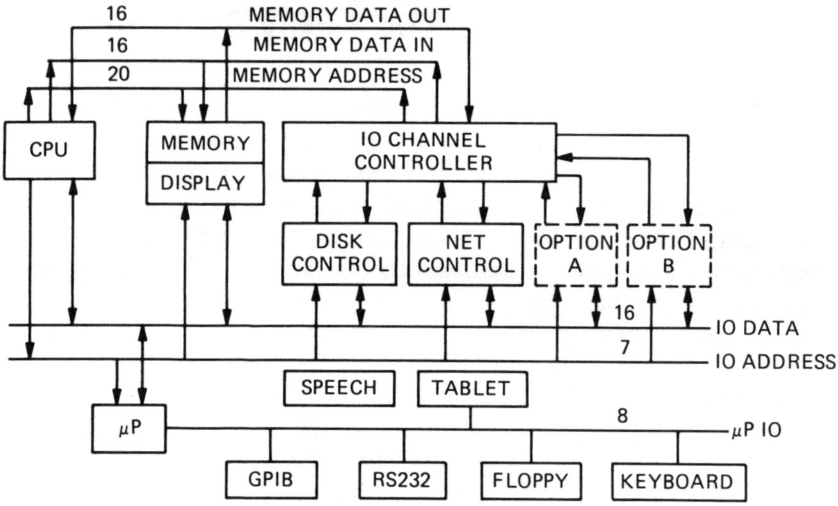

Figure 6G–1. PERQ Schematic

dressed raster data to be streamed at 64 bits per memory cycle. The microprogram sequencer implements two way and multiway conditional branches, loops, and micro subroutine with a 4 level call stack.

In order to service the needs of the I/O controllers, the microengine can be interrupted (microinterrupt) which is implemented with a multiple priority, zero overhead change of microstate.

The microengine is designed to be user microprogrammed. The data and control structures are very straightforward, with few baroque quirks, so that user microprogramming is easy. The 4K writable control store is fully supported with assembler, loader and debugger, and is expected to be a popular option.

PERQ's Virtual Memory System features a segmented 32 bit virtual address space mapped into a 20 bit physical address (1 megaword). (The Pascal compiler allows the user to group functions and procedures into code segments.) Each code segment can be up to 64K bytes of instructions (P-codes). A dictionary at the beginning of a code segment supplies offsets relative to the code segment base to each procedure contained in the segment. A procedure call (at the P-code level) is of the form CALL P,S where P is a procedure number and S is a segment number. The system maintains a Process Segment Table (PST) for each process which contains a pointer to the System Segment Table (SST) for each segment. The SST contains the location in physical memory for the segment (if resident), its location on the disk and an active process count Implementing a two-level table (PST and SST) allows sharable code segments among processes and provides a means to efficiently implement separately compiled segments. The dictionary on each segment allows separately compiled segments to call procedures without knowing their location within the segment. Since SST has physical addresses, no relocations are necessary in the complier or linker. Code segments are read-only and re-entrant and always occupy contiguous real memory (when resident). A process can have as many as 64K segments, each up to 64K bytes long. This means that there are no practical limits on program size other than the size of the SST and PST. The compiler optimizes intrasegment procedure calls to avoid the overhead of the SST and PST references. The compiler also recognizes segment numbers and procedure numbers less than 256 and uses short forms of the CALL P-code with one byte parameters.

For data, PERQ distinguishes between statically allocated data (globals and locals), and dynamically allocated data (Pascal new operator). Static data is allocated on a stack segment. Each process can have only one stack segment which can be up to 64K words long. Locals are allocated in a straightforward stack discipline with mark stacks and dyamic and static chains.

Global data is allocated at the base of the stack segment. It is accessed through a Global Pointer Table (GPT) which is subdivided into sections for each code segment. This allows separately compiled code segments to access globals declared by another segment without knowing about all declared globals. All offsets in the stack segments are 16 bits. The compiler sorts local accesses by static reference count and assigns the eight most frequently used locals to low memory addresses. A similar algorithm is used on globals. These favorite locals and globals are loaded/stored with single byte P-codes. All common load/store opcoded have 8 and 16 bit offset forms for maximum code density.

Dynamically allocated data is accessed through pointers. Pointers in PERQ are 32 bit virtual addresses. In the initial release of the PERQ system, the new operation will return 16 bit data segment number and a 16 bit offset with the segment. Data segments have entries in the SST and are limited to 64K words per segment. A process may have multiple data segments. Segments are swappable. A space allocator manages segments to allocate and de-allocate space as needed within a segment. Since a segment is limited to 64K words, there is an upper limit on the size of an allocated data type.

A subsequent implementation of the PERQ system will implement a paging system with 256 word pages. The new operators will then return a true 32 bit virtual address and the limitations of 64K segments will be eliminated.

Finally, it should be noted that the processor has 20 bit internal data paths so that it can manipulate real addresses without resorting to double precision arithmetic. The programmer does not see this, it merely improves efficiency.

The Packet Stream Network is a system for communications among processors utilizing packet broadcasting along a coaxial cable.[1]

Packets are protected by a hardware implemented cyclic redundancy check (CRC). It is possible that two nodes will broadcast packets at the same time; therefore, a collision occurs. The CRC will fail if a collision occurs and all nodes will ignore the data. Packets are acknowledged by the intended recipient. Failure to receive an acknowledgment within some dynamically chosen interval will trigger retransmission of the packet by the sender.

Nodes attempt to avoid collisions by using a statistical distribution scheme. A node wishing to transmit a packet listens on the net to see if another transmission is in progress. If it is, the node waits a random amount of time (dynamically determined), then checks to see if the net is still busy. When the net is free the node transmits its packet.

Collisions arise when two or more stations listen for prior traffic at the same time while the net is quiescent. Since they both believe the net is available, they would simultaneously initiate transmission and collide. Each time a node wishing to send a packet listens on the net and finds it busy, the range (interval) of its random number generator increases. The "randomness" of the delay increases as traffic increases, which distributes the probes.

---

[1]The PERQ network will be Ethernet compatible.

Appendix 6H: CHIMPNET: A Networking Testbed

Introduction

The CHIMPNET (Cheaply Interconnected Multiple Processor NETwork) system is a testbed for experiments with various networking and distributed system applications. CHIMPNET experiments apply to environments in which system speed is not a major concern. The system's flexibility permits development of experiments using arbitrary interconnection topologies, arbitrary access protocols (compatible with the topologies) and diverse applications. An experimental system may be expanded by adding nodes to the CHIMPNET system. CHIMPNET experiments are instrumented and controlled from a central node using software tools contained in the kernel resident in each system node. The CHIMPNET system is inexpensive, using off-the-shelf components and subsystems whenever possible. Despite its low cost, CHIMPNET supports realistic models of interesting distributed computing systems and therefore it facilitates experiments directed at distributed system design choices.

In this paper we present both the general CHIMPNET structure and details of specially-designed hardware and software system components.

Project Goals

The first major goal of this project was to develop a low-cost, flexible testbed system that could be expanded or altered by adding or deleting nodes, communication links, or hosts, to support non-time-critical experiments in distributed computing. These experiments might involve investigations into distributed database concurrent update algorithms or into communication protocols, and might be directed to questions of logical correctness and robustness of these algorithms. The second major goal was to design and implement a comprehensive instrumentation system which would maximize the utility of CHIMPNET as a research tool.

The general strategy followed in the CHIMPNET system design is that the interconnections be provided through flexibly cabled serial communications links connecting electrically similar nodes. A designated node (the instrumentation node) controls the experiments and collects data, both by

---

R.Y. Kain, W.R. Franta, and G.D. Jelatis, "CHIMPNET: A Networking Testbed," *Computer Networks* 3 (December 1979):447–457. Reprinted with permission.

observing system state changes and by passing data collection requests to nodes within the system under study. The system design must insure that timing constraints peculiar to the CHIMPNET implementation do not influence experiment results: this requires that software controlling the experiments be written in a "correct" manner so that instrumentation activities do not impact experiment results. These goals are met by the techniques described in succeeding sections.

General System Hardware Structure

CHIMPNET systems are assembled from a set of identical microprocessor based nodes constructed from identical hardware units. Node software distinguishes one node, the instrumentaion node (I-node), from the system nodes (S-nodes). Node structural details are presented in the following section. Here we illustrate how CHIMPNET nodes can be interconnected for some typical experimental configurations.

Figure 6H-1 depicts the general CHIMPNET system. Each node presents a set of pairs of unidirectional serial interfaces (transmit and receive) for interconnection purposes. One bidirectional interface pair is connected to the bus used by the I-node to instrument and control the experiment. This "instrumentation bus" is shown on the left side of the diagram. The remaining serial interfaces from the S-nodes are interconnected to construct the system under study (SUS). Additional serial interfaces in the I-node may be used to monitor or observe the traffic on the SUS serial links. The I-node would not drive the SUS serial links, except possibly to inject "noise" into the SUS.

The communications protocols used on these two classes of interconnections—the instrumentation bus and the SUS links—are managed independently, and will generally differ. All transactions on the instrumentation bus are controlled by software in the I-node, which enforces a strict master-slave protocol with fixed message formats. These transactions are supported by basic CHIMPNET software in the I-node's RAM and in S-node ROM. Placement of this software in S-node ROM (rather than RAM) insulates the system control protocols from possibly faulty SUS software. Details of I-bus transactions are discussed in a later section.

The CHIMPNET I-node uses the instrumentation bus to control the experiment and to collect data on the SUS. It may digest this data or it may simply pass it along to a host computer for further processing. By software convention the I-node may request that S-nodes emulate various failure modes, thus allowing the CHIMPNET system to be used to study faults and their effects on the SUS. The I-node also controls experiment time so that the processing time required for traffic generation and other functions not a part

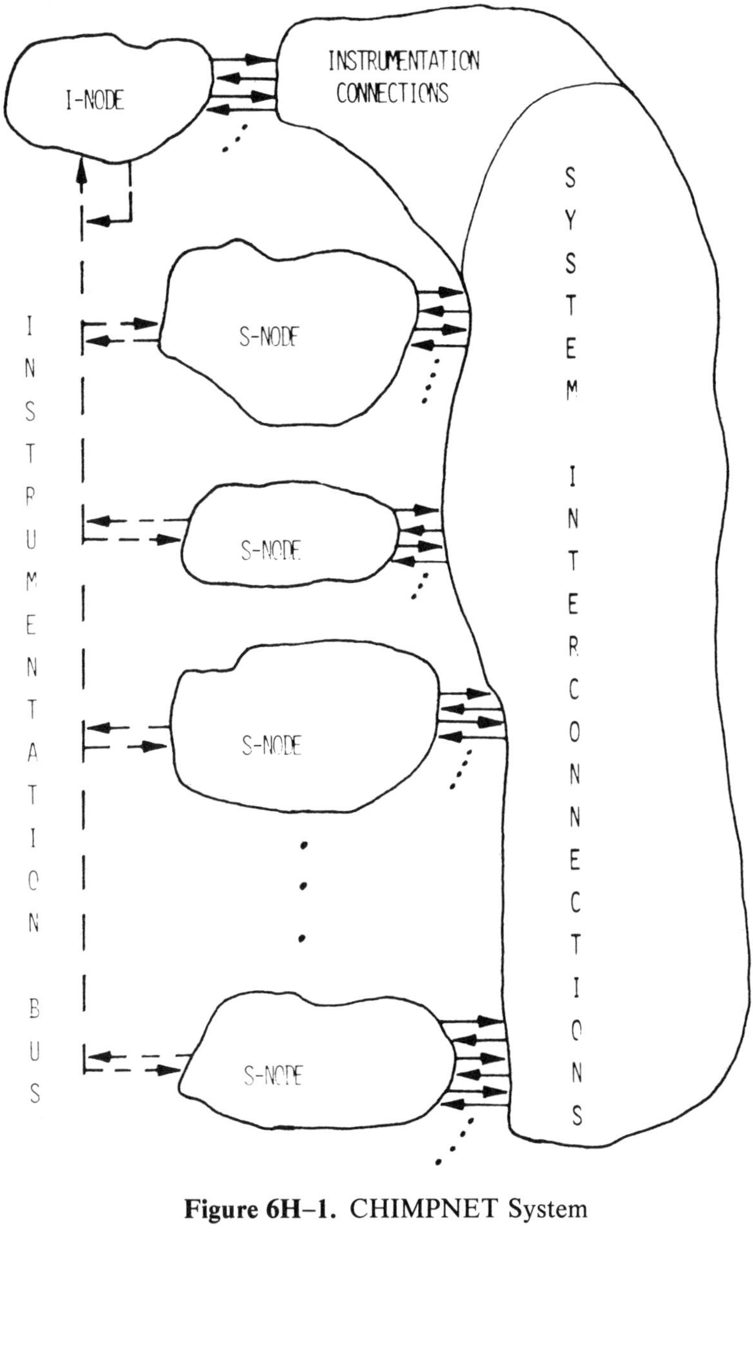

Figure 6H–1. CHIMPNET System

of the system under study are "transparent", i.e. they do not affect measuremets of SUS behavior. This transparency is accomplished by suspending (i.e. stopping) the experiment clock when necessary.

CHIMPNET S-nodes control the communications along all links in the

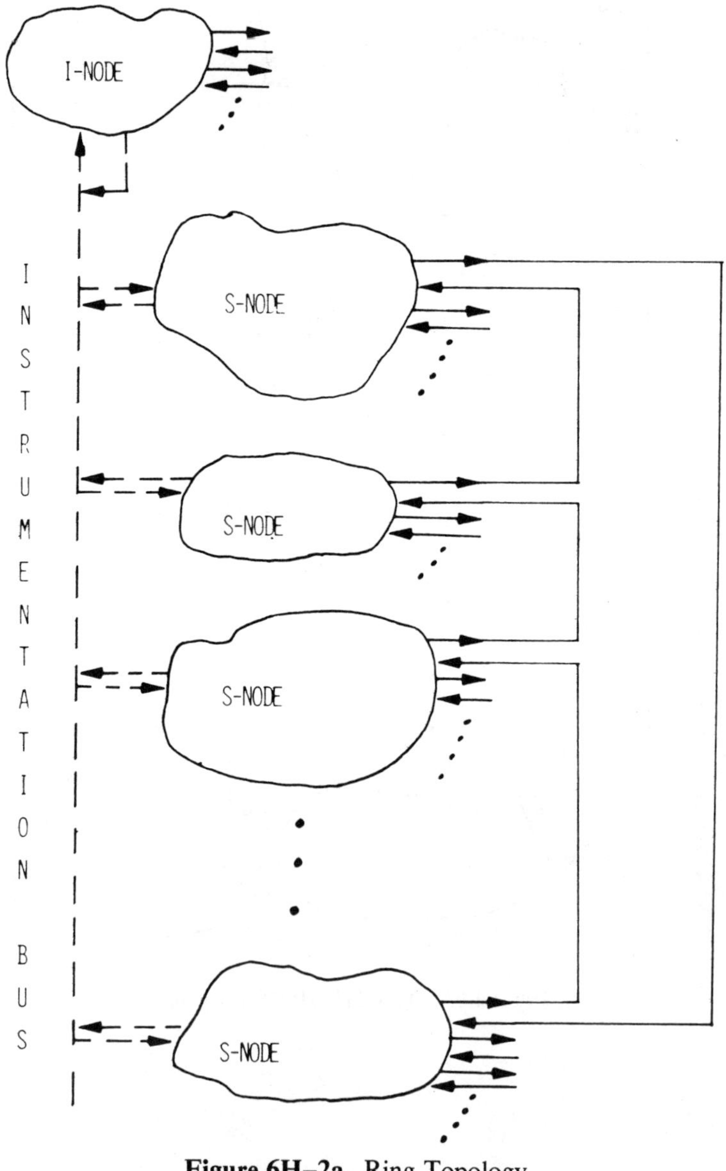

Figure 6H–2a. Ring Topology

system under study. They control the access protocol, message formats, and message generation.

Figure 6H-2 illustrates how S-nodes can be interconnected to give the SUS ring, star, and bus topologies. For simplicity, I-node connections to

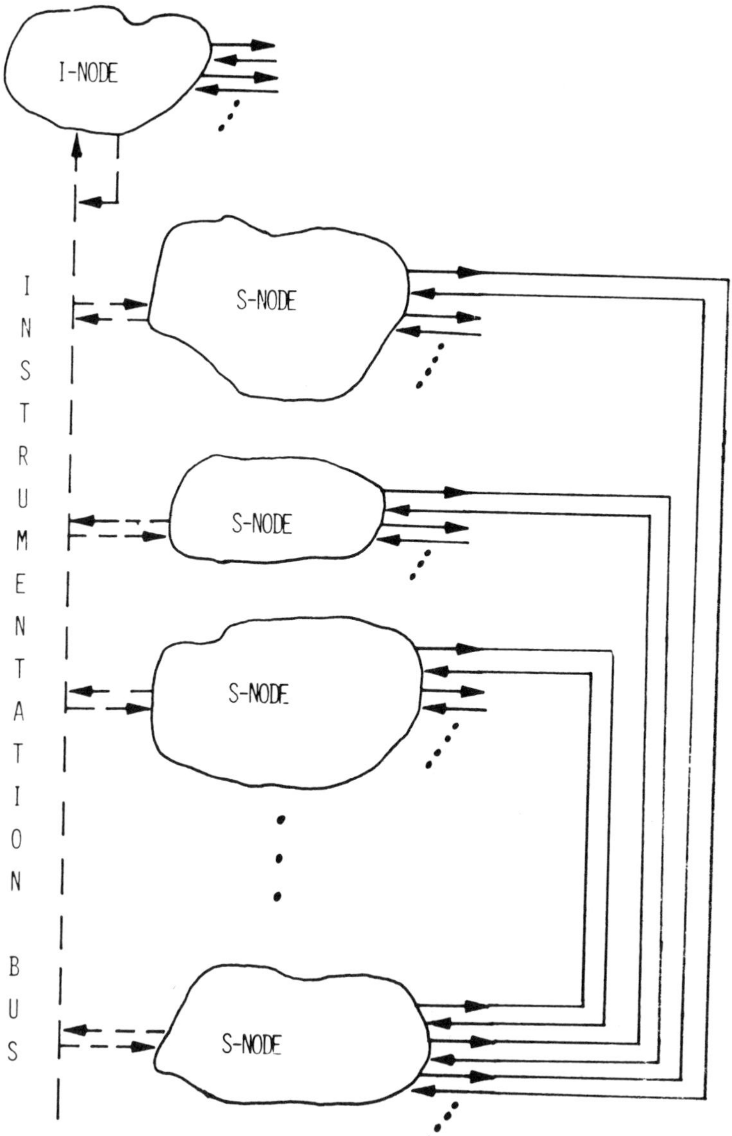

Figure 6H–2b. Star Topology

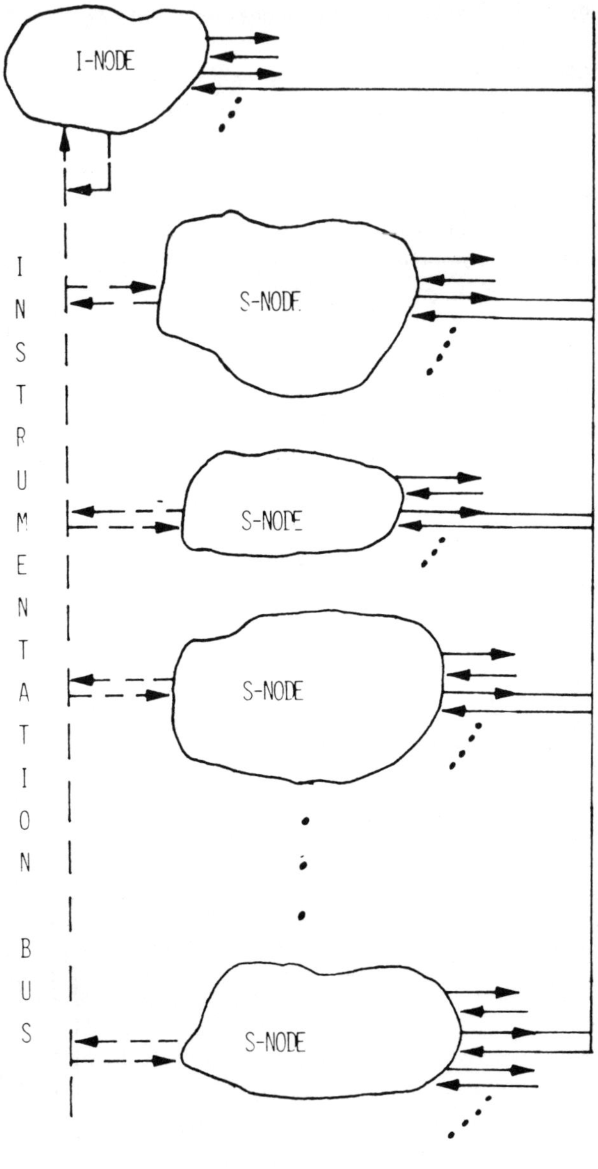

Figure 6H–2c. Bus Topology

links of the SUS are not shown in all of these drawings, but the I-node can be connected to observe the traffic on any desired link. Other topologies, including those using a node as a "gateway" between sub-nets can also be configured from the system components.

Experiment Control Timing

The CHIMPNET I-node controls all timing in the system under study and thus controls the progress of the experiment or simulation. When the system is "correctly" configured, the timing of all links in the SUS, as well as all counters used in the SUS for experiment timing, are controlled by the experiment clock (eclock), which is a global timing signal from the I-node. The transition rate of this timing signal is controlled by a constant which is loaded, by experiment control software, into a counter on an interface chip in the I-node. This rate can be adjusted to compensate for mismatches between the speed of the SUS software and the speed of data transfers on communication links. Furthermore, the I-node can suspend experiment progress indefinitely by repeatedly loading a large number into the rate-determining counter. When it is appropriate to resume the progress of the SUS, the I-node software reloads the previous constant into the rate-determining counter. Signals from S-nodes to the I-node convey requests to suspend and resume the experiment timing signal.

While it is clearly possible to write experiment programs which rely on the existence of a global clock and the resulting synchrony of all S-nodes, this is *not* intended. Each S-node has local counter-timer hardware, clocked by the experiment clock, which provides a local view of global time and should be used as such by S-node software. If these local timers are used only to provide event sequencing information across nodes, then they are logically equivalent to asynchronous (but stable) clocks at each node augmented by synchronizing messages to achieve sequencing of time-stamped events [42]. Only the instrumentation software should use the fact that these local counters are all in synchrony.

CHIMPNET Node Hardware

As noted earlier, a CHIMPNET system is constructed from a set of identical microprocessor based nodes. The unique I-node is distinguished from the S-nodes of the SUS by software, firmware (ROM) and special cabling. Figure 6H-3 depicts the structure and components of a typical CHIMPNET node.

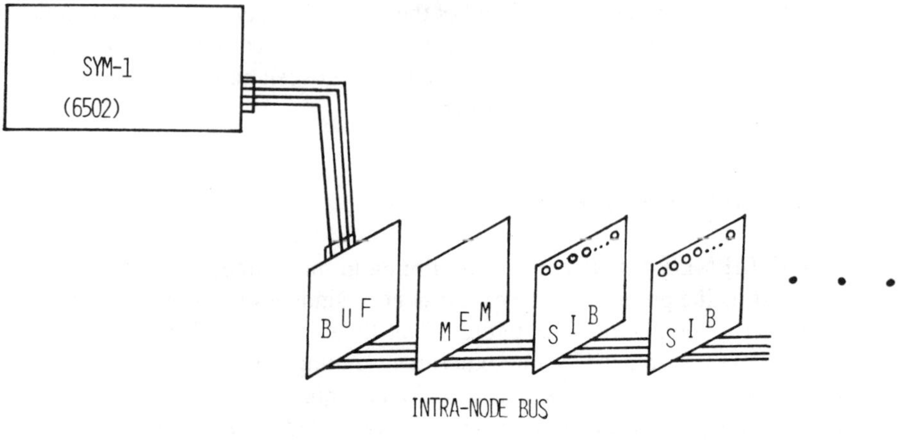

Figure 6H–3. Node Structure

The CHIMPNET node processor is a 6502 based SYM-1 [44]* board microcomputer. A special "buffer board" is used to electrically buffer address, data and control lines from the SYM-1's expansion (E) connection into a Motorola EXORcisor ® bus cardcage. The cardcage intra-node bus allows each node to have additional memory (RAM) and several special "serial interface boards" (SIBs) which provide the serial interface and counter/timer functions. The use of a standard microprocessor bus permits convenient expansion of node capabilities using available hardware.

The hardware components used are either "off the shelf" boards and assemblies or special purpose boards of logically simple, straightforward design. The only change made to the standard SYM-1 boards involves the addition of a jumper to allow software system reset, and the addition of an EPROM to hold S-node experiment control software. All other features needed to implement the CHIMPNET design are realized by plugging special boards into the extended processor (or intra-node) bus. Before we describe these special boards we must briefly discuss some features of the SYM-1 board that are important for the CHIMPNET design.

SYM-1 Features: Several programmable interface chips are available on the SYM-1 board: One of the outputs of each interface chip can be programmed to generate a square-wave like signal, with the interval between transitions controlled by constants loaded into the chip from the program. This feature is used in the I-node to generate the global clock signal that controls experiment time. Interface chip leads are also used to implement the S-node to I-node attention lines, which allow an S-node to cause an I-node interrupt.

* Following preparation of this paper the M6809 replaced the 6502.

A SYM-1 system is normally reset by pressing a button on its control keyboard. To allow the I-node to reset all S-nodes, thus establishing a consistent system state before experiments begin, we have added a jumper so that one interface chip output on each S-node SYM-1 board drives the reset line on that board. A special I-node to S-node message will cause the execution of a ROM instruction sequence in each S-node which will set this output to a logic "one" and thus cause a hardware reset at each node.

SYM-1 Extensions: All extensions to the SYM-1 system are connected to an intra-node bus that is interfaced to the processor board by a specially designed buffer board. The logic on this board provides buffering signals from the processor, including disabling the SYM-1 address outputs when DMA operation is desired within the card cage. In addition, several useful functions are provided, including buffer amplifiers with external inputs and outputs and a free-running oscillator that can be used for timing (though this feature is not used in system configurations supported by basic CHIMPNET software).

The most important extension to the SYM-1 is the serial interface board (SIB) which plugs into the intra-node bus to provide serial communication and timing functions. Many features of this board are directly derived from the features of the two LSI devices resident on the board: the Signetics 2652 Multiple Protocol Communications Controller (MPCC) [43] and the Intel 8253 triple counter [39]. Other SIB features are provided by additional TTL logic and are included to support a wider range of possible access protocols. The SIB design includes a large number of coaxial connectors to allow the flexible inter-node cabling necessary to realize different S-node interconnection topologies as mentioned previously. Figure 6H-4 shows a block diagram of the SIB board, including significant details of the MPCC and counter devices.

A SYM-1 processor sees each SIB board as a set of sixteen contiguous memory locations; twelve of these locations correspond directly to registers on the MPCC and counter chips, while four others act as SIB status and control registers.

The SIB design allows the execution speed of experiment software in the S-nodes to be independent of the speed of the serial communications used in the experiment; this capability can be achieved through S-node software that uses the counters on the SIB board to determine the timing of all experiment events.

Addiltional SIB board flexibility is provided by the MPCC chip, which supports numerous serial communications protocols through proper setting of its control registers. Different character lengths, error checking, and control character selections can, for example, be controlled in this manner. CHIMPNET software will generally use a fixed subset of the chip options. (We note again that this flexibility is not used on the SIB boards interfacing with the instrumentation bus, which operates under a fixed protocol.)

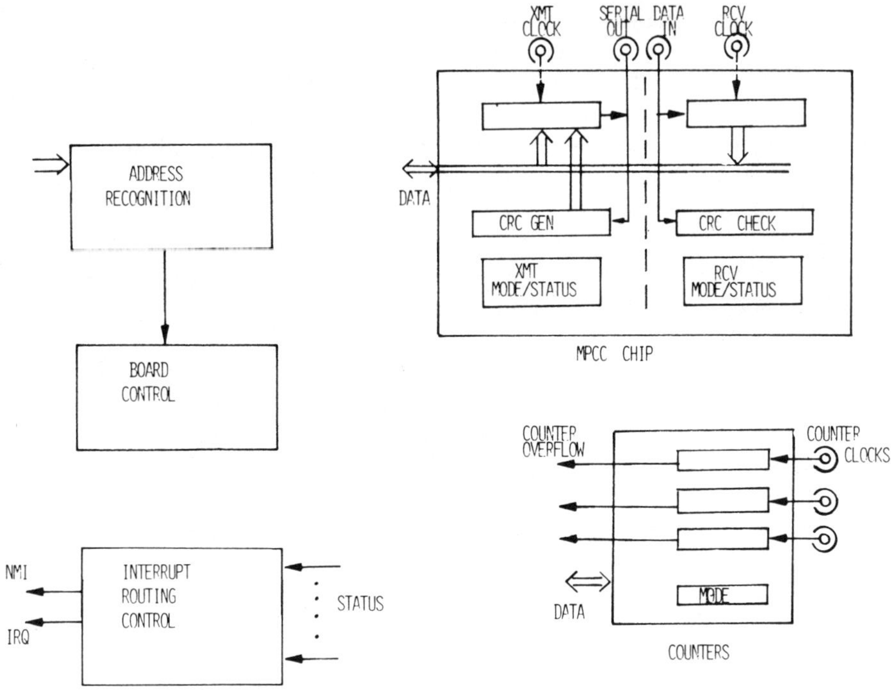

Figure 6H–4. SIB Board Structure

The SIB board control logic also provides software control and use of condition signals from the MPCC chip, the counter chip, and several external signals. All of these condition signals are always available to the processor as bits of the SIB status registers. Interrupt routing control logic on the SIB allows software selectively either to enable each condition signal to cause a non-maskable interrupt or a maskable interrupt when it becomes "true," or to disable each signal. An interrupting SIB is identified by a polling interrupt routine in the SYM-1, and the cause of the interrupt is determined by reading the interrupting SIB's status registers.

Interconnection Hardware

Interconnections among CHIMPNET nodes are made through sets of coaxial cables that can be reconnected to change experiment parameters or the topology of the system under study. CHIMPNET's basic software support system assumes that all counters and communications links in the

SUS are timed by the single global experiment clock signal produced by the I-node.

The instrumentation bus (see figure 6H-1) also uses cables to interconnect the transmitters and the receivers of a single designated SIB at each S-node and at the I-node. This bus is timed by a free-running clock whose speed can be adjusted. The I-node's control over the system depends on this bus topology.

The SIB boards provide three extra signals useful in emulating certain special protocols. One such signal, the SIB EXTERNAL INTERRUPT, can be used by special CSMA hardware interfaces to allow modulated carrier broadcast communications (the basic CHIMPNET system uses "baseband" communications); the SIB EXTERNAL INTERRUPT would signal the presence of a carrier on the link. The second signal, BUS FREE, is used to allow study of CSMA systems without such special hardware; this signal is normally high and is forced low when any transmitter connected to the link is turned on—thus a logic test on the signal can be used to determine when the bus becomes free (this signal is generated by logic on each SIB and may be routed to processor interrupt lines). Finally, circuitry on the SIB board senses whether two transmitters are simultaneously transmitting conflicting signals on the link; the resulting Transmitter Conflict signal can be used as an interrupt source and the event CONFLICT can be tested by board readout as discussed above.

System Software

The CHIMPNET system software provides a small set of fairly powerful and general support functions to aid the development of event driven or time driven application and instrumentation software for distributed computing experiments. (Events are predefined system state changes.) The software for a particular experiment will depend upon several factors, including network topology, access protocol and instrumentation plan. Because of this variability, the system software does not presume any particular hardware configuration or operational scheme for the system under study.

The system software is embodied in the S-node kernel (all S-nodes have the same kernel software) and the I-node kernel (which differs from the S-node kernel). Certain key parts of the S-node software reside in read only memory, primarily to guarantee the survivability of the instrumentation-bus communications software at each S-node and thus insure the integrity of the instrumentation system. This kernel software will provide a support environment for:

a) event driven S-node software,

b) time driven S-node software,
c) instrumentation, including data collection, noise introduction and experiment initiation and control and
d) inter-node message passing.

S-node Kernel

The S-node kernel code and data structures enable it to provice functions to:

1) manage the slave side of the I-bus communications protocol,
2) effect experiment control at I-node request,
3) schedule processes for dispatching by using kernel-calls (k-calls) to associate them with an event or time,
4) dispatch processes for execution in response to event or time-generated interrupts,
5) manage a run-time environment supporting processes executing pure procedures (ie. re-entrant code).

These functions enable the S-nodes to provide a flexible, effective experiment environment at a reasonable level of abstraction. The design is a compromise between our desire to provide very general abstractions and the real limitations imposed by microprocessor scale, speed and functionality.

Kernel-Calls

The interface to the S-node kernel is a set of k-calls (table 6H-1) used to control the existence and scheduling of processes. Process scheduling is associated either with the passage of experiment time (e-time or with the occurrence of events related to S-node state changes. When a process associated event occurs or time interval elapses, that process is dispatched into the ready list for execution. Whether or not the process should be executed while e-time is accumulating is specified by the type of association (table 6H-2).

Processes are created by *create*. A process consists of a process descriptor and an activation record. A process terminates its execution and releases both its descriptor and its activation record viat *terminate*. Via *quit* a process may terminate its execution but leave its data structures intact, i.e., the process continues to exist under the name given by *create*. Thus *quit* is equivalent to a *terminate*; *create* sequence, with a guarantee that the old and new process names are the same. Via *destroy* the activation record and descriptor of a named process are released, and the process name is cleared.

Table 6H–1.
Kernel-Call Summary

Process-Event association k-calls

on <event_name> *do* <process_call>
qon <event_name> *do* <process_call>
after <event_name> *do* <process_call>

Process-Time association k-calls

beforet <e-time_interval> *do* <process_call>
ont <e-time_interval> *do* <process_call>
qont <e-time_interval> *do* <process_call>
aftert <e-time_interval> *do* <process_call>

Cancel association k-call

cancel {*on* | *qon* | *after*} <event_name>
cancel {*beforet* | *ont* | *qont* | *aftert*} <process_name>

Process creation and destruction k-calls

<process_name_var> := *create* <module_name>
destroy <process_name>
terminate

Process initiation and completion k-calls

initiate{*o* | *q* | *a*} <process_call>
(This corresponds to
{*ont* | *qont* | *aftert*} <zero_interval> *do* <process_call> as described above.)
quit

Process synchronization k-calls

wait
signal <process_name>
await {<event_name> | <e-time_interval>}

Notation

<process_call> := <process_name>[(<pparameter_list>)]

Certain associations are established conveniently by *initiate*{*o* | *q* | *a*}. Synchronization via semaphores is provided by *wait* and *signal*, and *await* allows event synchronization.

The keywords *on*, *qon* and *after* (*beforet*, *ont*, *qont* and *aftert*) specify the scheduling of the process relative to the named event (e-time). The semantics of the various process-event associations are summarized in table 6H-2; examples of usage are also cited. All times cited in the table are experiment times. Those cases specifying process completion before a specified time may require stopping the e-clock. The system must support three process classes (column 4 of table 6H-2). The classes are based on the timing constraints, scheduling restrictions and whether or not the e-clock is running

Table 6H–2.
Timing and Usage of Process Associations

Nature of Association	*Process may be executed with e-clock on*	*off*	*Process Scheduling Class*	*Timing Restrictions*	*Example of Anticipated Usage*
beforet	yes	yes	1,3	$t_a \leq t_s; t_f \leq t_a + (T - 1)$	artificial traffic generation process
qont	yes	no	2	$(t_a + T) \leq t_s \leq t_f$	retransmit after timeout
ont	no	yes	1	$(t_a + T) = t_s = t_f$	periodic data collection
qon	yes	no	2	$t_a \leq t_e \leq t_s \leq t_f$	receive message
on	no	yes	1	$t_a \leq t_e = t_s = t_f$	handle exception
aftert	yes	yes	3	$(t_a + T) \leq t_s$	periodic data collection
after	yes	yes	3	$t_a \leq t_e \leq t_s$	response to other than time-critical status change

T = e-time interval
t_a = e-time when association is established
t_e = e-time when event occurs
t_s = e-time at which process starts execution
t_f = e-time when process finishes execution

(columns 2 and 3 of table 6H-2). Within each process class, processes are run to completion on a FCFS basis, with two exceptions. First, the scheduler may interrupt a process for the execution of a process of another priority class. Second, a process may suspend itself when it executes an *await* or a *wait*. Note that *beforet* processes are shown in two classes; initially they are in class 3, but they must be promoted to class 1 if their time intervals are about to expire and they have not yet completed execution.

There is a strong interaction between process dispatching and the running of the e-clock. When the e-clock is off, processes of classes 1 or 3 may execute, with class 1 having priority. When the e-clock is on, processes of classes 2 or 3 may execute, with class 2 having priority. The e-clock will be turned off whenever any processor indicates that it has a class 1 process ready for execution and will be turned on again as soon as no processor has a class 1 process to run.

The appendix presents an example of the use of these constructs to transmit messages under an ALOHA-CD protocol. Examples of both transmit and receive can be found in [40].

There is a fixed set of events with which processes may be associated (table 6H-3). An event-process association remains in effect until explicitly cancelled by a *cancel* k-call or superceded by the creation of a new

Table 6H–3.
Events with Which Processes May Be Associated
(There Is One Set of Events for each SIB)

	Event Number	*Event Name or Description*
	1	MPCC receiver buffer full
	2	MPCC transmitter buffer empty
	3	Timer 0 interval expired
	4	Timer 1 interval expired
Handled	5	Timer 2 interval expired
by	6	BUS FREE
Class 1 or 2	7	CONFLICT
Processes	8	MPCC transmit buffer underrun*
	9	MPCC receiver status change
	10	EXTERNAL INTERRUPT to SIB
	11	SYNC or flag char received
Handled	12	Message received
by	13	MPCC receiver abort
Class 3	.	.
Processes	.	.
	.	.

* Transmitter buffer not being filled fast enough to maintain transmission.

association between the event and another process. A time-interval-process association interval can be explicitly cancelled by a *cancel* k-call, specifying the process name, before the interval expires. When the process is dispatched for execution, the time association is cancelled. Several processes may be associated with intervals ending at the same e-time, but not with the same event. Processes that happen to be associated in the same way with the same time will be executed in an arbitrary order.

System Control Software

While the experiment control and instrumentation functions are largely resident in the I-node, some cooperating system control software must reside in each S-node kernel. Specifically, the routines to support I-bus communications, to respond to commands from the I-node and to request attention from the I-node must all reside in every S-node (probably in EPROM).

By judicious use of the scheduling constructs, it is possible to construct two logically distinct software subsystems in each S-node. Specifically, all instrumentation software can be scheduled with the e-clock off, and will thus not affect the experiment results. Stopping the global e-clock involves the entire system and can only occur under the control of the I-node. Experiment software in a distributed system will be largely message driven, so many of the events are defined in terms of changes in SIB state. Thus we can see that both instrumentation and communication functions will require just the sort of flexible asynchronous scheduling mechanisms described above.

I-bus Protocols

Experiment control and some instrumentation functions are implemented by message exchanges between the I-node and the S-nodes using the I-bus. All instrumentation bus transactions begin with a message sent from the I-node to an S-node. The I-node thus controls traffic on the I-bus. An S-node may transmit on the I-bus only when it is required to respond to a message received from the I-node; an S-node can, however, effectively initiate an I-bus dialogue by signalling on the attention lines.

Messages on the I-bus are fixed format, serial, synchronous bit streams. A bit oriented protocol is used which provides

messages framed by flag bytes (FF),

transparency by automatic zero insertion/deletion,

cyclic redundancy checks and

secondary station addressing.

These protocol conventions are supported by the MPCC device on the SIB, and are selected by setting its control registers. There are four classes of control messages used on I-bus:

1) System reset: initializes all S-node hardware;
2) S-node load: Transfers binary data from the I-node to specified memory locations in a specified S-node;
3) S-node dump: Transfers binary data from specified memory locations in a specified S-node to the I-node;
4) Experiment control functions, including those to start, pause, and resume the experiment.

These four message classes, together with the I-node's ability to control the experiment clock, are sufficient for the I-node to control SUS experiments, including the collection of performance data.

Summary

CHIMPNET is a flexible, inexpensive, extensible, instrumented, testbed system for investigating problems of distriuted computing. It provides minimal but sufficient functionality for the design, implementation and execution of models of distributed computer systems. Further, it supports experimentation with instrumentation facilities which allow performance data to be collected without disturbance to the system under study.

Appendix

To clarify module structure and demonstrate the use of k-calls, we present module organization for the transmit portion of an ALOHA-CD (collision detection) [38,41,45] scheme. Figure 6H-5 shows the modules involved and their relationships. The module at the tail of a dotted arrow establishes the event-process association shown on the arrow for the module pointed to by the arrow. Solid line arrows trace the execution sequences followed for message transmissions.

"driver" process code fragment

⋮

xmproc := *create* xmtmsg;

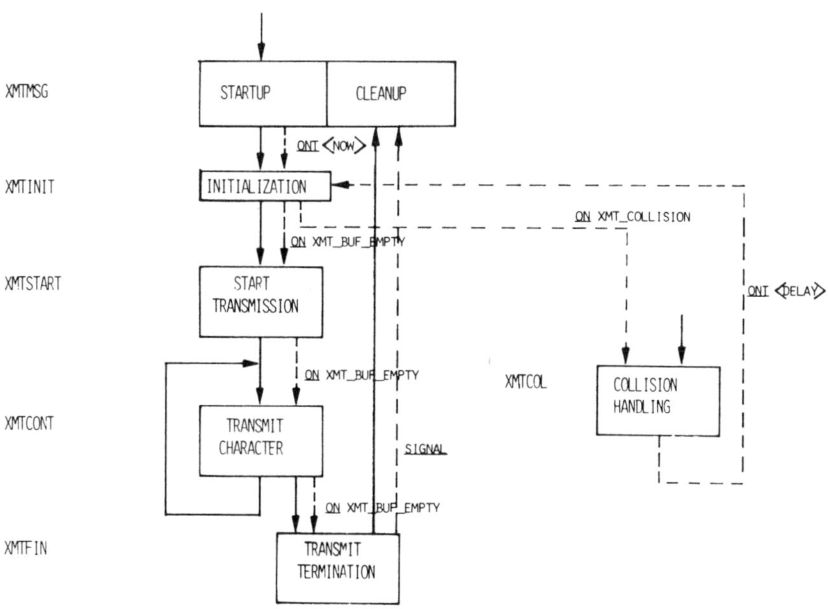

Figure 6H–5. Example Module Structures

```
    initiateo xmproc( buffer, this__process__name, source, dest, num);
      :
      :

module xmtmsg( buffer: pointer;
               driver: process name;
               source, dest, num: integer);
constants
  xm = 1; xi = 2; xs = 3; xc = 4; xf = 5; xcol = 6;
types
  process__name__table = array 1..6 of process name;
variables
  pnt: process__name__table;
  begin
    pnt[xm] := this__process__name; (*system function*)
    pnt[xi] := create xmtinit;
    pnt[xs] := create xmtstart;
    pnt[xc] := create xmtcont;
    pnt[xf] := create xmtfin;
    pnt[xcol] := create xmtcol;
    initiateo pnt[xi]( buffer, pnt, source, dest, num);
    wait;
    <disable SIB[source] transmitter>;
    cancel on SIB[source].xmt__collision;
    destroy pnt[xi];
    destroy pnt[xs];
    destroy pnt[xc];
    destroy pnt[xf];
    destroy pnt[xcol];
    signal driver;
    terminate
  end (*xmtmsg*);

module xmtinit( buffer: pointer;
                pnt: process__name__table;
                source, dest, num: integer);
  begin
    on SIB[source].xmt__collision
      do pnt[xcol]( buffer, pnt, source, dest, num);
    on SIB[source].xmt__buf__empty
      do pnt[xs]( buffer, pnt, source, dest, num);
    <enable SIB[source] transmitter>;
    <set SIB[source] start__of__message__flag>;
    quit
  end (*xmtinit*);
```

```
module xmtstart( buffer: pointer;
                 pnt: process__name__table;
                 source, dest, num: integer);
variables
  out: integer;
  begin
    SIB[source].xmt__buf := dest; (* 1st char is destination *)
    out := 0; (*init buffer out index *)
    on SIB[source].xmt__buf__empty
      do pnt[xc](buffer, pnt, source, num, out);
    <clear SIB[source] start__of__message flag>;
    quit
  end (*xmtstart*);

module xmtcont( buffer: pointer;
                pnt: process__name__table;
                source, num, out: integer);
  begin
    SIB[source].xmt__buf := buffer↑.[out];
    out := out + 1;
    (*xmtcont is executed once for each msg char*)
    if out = num  (*last char sent*)
      then on SIB[source].xmt__buf__empty
        do pnt[xf]( pnt, source);
    quit
  end (*xmtcont*);

module xmtfin( pnt: process__name__table;
               source: integer);
  begin
    <set SIB[source] xmt__end__of__message flag>;
    cancel on SIB [source].xmt__buf__empty;
    await SIB[source].xmt__buf__empty;
    <clear SIB[source] xmt__end__of__message flag>;
    signal pnt[xm];
    quit
  end (*xmtfin*);

module xmtcol( buffer: pointer;
               pnt: process__name__table;
               source, dest, num: integer);
  begin
    <set SIB[source] xmt__abort flag>;
    cancel on SIB[source].xmt__buf__empty;
```

```
    await 2*char_time;
    <disable SIB[source] transmitter>;
    aftert short_delay
      do pnt[xi]( buffer, pnt, source, dest, num);
    <clear SIB[source] xmt_abort flag>;
    quit
  end (*xmtcol*);
```

References

1. Zimmerman, H. "OSI Reference Model—The ISO Model of Architecture for Open Systems Interconnection." *IEEE Transactions on Communications* COM-28 (April 1980):

2. Wecker, Stuart. "DNA: The Digital Network Architecture." *IEEE Transactions on Communications*. COM-28 (April 1980):510–526.

3. IBM "Systems Network Architecture General Information." IBM Publication No. GA27-3102; or *IBM Systems Journal* 18 (1979), entire issue.

4. Metcalfe, R.M., and Boggs, D.R. "Ethernet: Distributed Packet Switching for Local Computer Network." *CACM* 19 (July 1976):

5. Thacher, C.P.; McCreight, E.M.; Lampson, B.W.; Sproull, R.F.; and Boggs, D.R. "Alto: A Personal Computer." In *Computer Structures: Readings and Examples*, edited by Siewiorek, Bell, and Newell, forthcoming.

6. Greitzer, John. "HP to Adapt Ethernet Controller for Its Local Computer Network." *Computer Business News* 3 (15 September 1980):1.

7. Schultz, Brad. "Converging with Ethernet, IEEE Group Drafting Local Net Standard." *Computerworld*, 25 August 1980, pp. 49–50.

8. Network Systems Corporation. "Systems Description: HYPERchannel Network Adapters." Publication No. A01-0000-02, January 1978.

9. Burke, R.G. "Eliminating Conflicts on a Contention Channel." *Proceedings of the Fourth Conference on Local Computer Networks*, 22–23 October 1979, pp. 48–55.

10. Hohn, William C. "The Control Data Loosely Coupled Network Lower Level Protocols." *Proceedings of the National Computer Conference*, June 1980, pp. 129–134.

11. Gordon, R.L.; Farr, W.W.: and Levine, P. "Ringnet: A Packet Switched Local Network with Decentralized Control." *Computer Networks* 3 (December 1979):373–379.

12. Wilkes, M.V., and Needham, R.M. "The Cambridge Model Distributed System," *Operating Systems Review* 14 (January 1980):21–29.

13. Wilkes, M.V., and Wheeler, D.J. "The Cambridge Digital Com-

munication Ring," *Proceedings of the Local Area Communications Network Symposium*, Boston, May 1979, pp. 47–61.

14. Kain, R.Y.; Franta, W.R.; and Jelatis, G.D. "CHIMPNET: A Networking Testbed." *Computer Networks* 3 (December 1979):447–457.

15. Franta, W.R.; Jensen, E.D.; Kain, R.Y.; and Marshall, G.D. "Real Time Distributed Systems." In *Advances in Computers*, ed. M. Yovits. Vol. 20. New York: Academic Press, 1981.

16. Kahns, R.C., and Shoquist, M.C. "A Serial Databus System for Local Processing Networks." *COMPCON* 79 Spring.

17. Crane, R.C., and Taft, E.A. "Practical Considerations in Ethernet Local Network Design." Presented at Hawaii International Conference on System Sciences, January 1980.

18. Shoch, J.F., and Hupp, J.A. "Measured Performance of an Ethernet Local Network." Presented at Local Area Communications Network Symposium, Boston, May 1979.

19. International Organization for Standardization (ISO). "Reference Model of Open Systems Interconnection." Document No. ISO/TC97/SC16 N227, June 1979.

20. Jensen, K., and Wirth, N., *Pascal User Manual and Report*, 2nd ed. Springer-Verlag, 1974.

21. Brinch Hansen, P. "Concurrent Pascal Report." Technical Report CIT-IS-TR 17, California Institute of Technology, 1975.

22. Hammond, J.L.; Brown, J.E.; and Liu, S.S. "Development of a Transmission Error Model and an Error Control Model." Technical Report RADC-TR-75-138, Rome Air Development Center, 1975.

23. Bittel, R. "On Frame Check Sequence (FCS) Generation and Checking." ANSI Working Paper X3-S34-77-43, 1977.

24. "Provisional Recommendations X.3, X.25, X.28 and X.29 on Packet Switched Data Transmission Services." CCITT, Geneva 1978.

25. Clark, D.C.; Pogran, K.T.; and Reed, D.P. "An Introduction to Local Area Networks." *Proceedings of the IEEE* 66 (November 1978):1497–1517.

26. Dalal, Y.K. "Broadcast Protocols in Packet-Switched Computer Networks." Ph.D. dissertation, Stanford University. Digital Systems Laboratory Technical Report 128, April 1977.

27. Farber, D.J., Larson, Kenneth C., "The Distributed Computing System." *Digest of Papers, COMPCON 73*, February 1973, pp. 31–34.

28. Farber, D.J. "A Ring Network." DATAMATION 21 (February 1975):44–46.

29. Freeman, H.A., Thurber, K.J. "Issues in Local Computer Networks," *International Conference on Communications* 2 (10–14 June 1979):20.3.1–20.3.5.

30. Gordon, R.L., and Nelson, D.L. "The Use of Rings in High

Availability Local Networks." *Proceedings of the Louisiana Computer Exposition*, University of Southwestern Louisiana, Lafayette, 2–3 March 1979, pp. 126–142.

31. Kahn, R.E.; Uncapher, K.W.; and VanTrees, H.L. (eds.). *Special Issue: Packet Communication Networks Proceedings of the IEEE* 66 (November 1978):1497–1517.

32. Nelson, D.L., and Gordon, R.L. "Computer Cells—A Network Architecture for Data Flow Computing." *COMPCON 78 Fall*, September 1978, pp. 296–301.

33. Svobodova, L.; Lisov, B.; and Clark, D. "Distributed Computer Systems: Structure and Semantics." Massachusetts Institute of Technology Report, MIT/LCS/TR-215, March 1979.

34. Wilkes, M.V. "Communication Using a Digital Ring." *Proceedings of the PACNET Conference,* Sendai, Japan, 1975.

35. Hofner, E.R.; Nenadel, Z.; and Tschanz, M. "A Digital Loop Communication System." *IEEE Transactions on Communications* COM-22 (1974):877.

36. Wheeler, D.J., and Hopper, A. "Maintenance of Ring Communication Systems." *IEEE Transactions on Communications* COM-27 (1979):760.

37. Hopper, A. "Data Ring at Computer Laboratory, University of Cambridge." In *Computer Science Technology: Local Area Networking*, Washington, D.C., NBS Special Publication 500–31, 1978, p. 11.

38. Abramson, N. "The ALOHA System—Another Alternative for Computer Communications." *AFIPS Conference Proceedings*, 1971, 281–285.

39. Intel. *8253 Programmable Interval Timer*. Intel Component Data Catalog, Intel Corporation, Santa Clara, California, 1979, pp. 11.32–11.42.

40. Kain, R.Y.; Franta, W.R.; and Jelatis, G.D. "CHIMPNET: A Networking Testbed." *Proceedings of the Fourth Conference on Local Area Networks*, October 1979.

41. Kleinrock, L., and Lam, S. "Packet Switching in a Multiaccess Broadcast Channel: Performance Evaluation." *IEEE Transactions on Communications* COM-23 (April 1975).

42. Lamport, L. "Time, Clocks and the Ordering of Events in a Distributed System." *CACM* 21 (July 1978):558–565.

43. Signetics. *Signetics Multi-Protocol Communications Controller (MPCC/SDLC) 2652*. Signetics Corporation, Sunnyvale, California, 1979.

44. Synertek, *SYM Reference Manual*. Synertek Systems, Santa Clara, Calif., 1978.

45. Tobagi, F.A., and Hunt, V.B. "Performance Analysis of Carrier Sense Multiple Access with Collision Detection. "Report No. TR173, Computer Systems Laboratory, Stanford University, Palo Alto, June 1979.

7 Interconnecting Local Networks

Introduction

The basic motivation for network interconnection is the same as that which led to networking in the first place: a desire to interconnect devices, mainframes, and so forth, to promote or allow sharing of resources and communication among nodes (and ultimately users). In a sense, then, internetting creates the illusion of a single large network.

Three types of interconnection can be identified:

1. Interconnections among homogeneous local networks;
2. Interconnections among heterogeneous local networks;
3. Interconnection between a local network and a long-haul (public) network.

The first type obtains when, for example, homogeneous but geographically dispersed segments of a network are connected via microwave, satellite, or telecommunications link. The situation may also obtain when two technologicically homogeneous but functionally nonhomogeneous networks are connected (by the aforementioned means to accommodate occasional traffic between them). The second type of interconnection need arises from a number of obvious circumstances (for example, different company, division, or department networks), and the third obtains when, for example, a local network is connected to the Arpanet. For this latter case, it is often functionally both more reasonable and more cost-effective to interconnect elements locally and provide a single gateway to a long-haul network than it is to connect elements individually to a long-haul network.

The Interconnection Problem

Interconnection involves providing the hardware and software so that nodes on one network can easily, conveniently, and effectively communicate with nodes on another network (in order to support some application activity). Interconnection is facilitated by gateway nodes (see figure 7–1) that map internet communications (messages) from one network-protocol hierarchy to another and then forward messages. Thus, the problem of internetting is one of examining alternative strategies for mapping and forwarding so as to realize flexible, simple, and efficient gateway functionality. Issues involved in selecting and comparing strategies concern the kinds of services supported—for example, datagram or virtual circuit—as well as addressing, error-control, flow-control, and routing strategies in the networks being connected.

Additionally, issues must be addressed [1] concerning data security, regulation of the flow of messages into and out of a local network (across a gateway), and validation and generation of accounting and audit trail information.

As figure 7–1 suggests,a gateway node is two-faced. It converses in the protocol associated with the local network of which it is a node, but it is also conversant (for heterogeneous and local-to-long-haul interconnections) in the protocol levels of one or several other protocol hierarchies to effect internetting. Usually not all levels in the hierarchy are affected by internetting. Specifically, user levels are so complex that interconnection of different protocols at these levels is unlikely [3]. Correspondingly, physical levels are unique to specific networks and are not affected. What remains are the levels responsible for datagram and virtual-circuit support, and these levels must provide for internet-mapping flow control, error control, and so forth. In this regard, two kinds of gateways can be identified [3,4]: media-conversion (translators) and protocol-translation gateways.

Media gateways receive messages (datagrams) from one network, perhaps remove the envelope, generate a new envelope and routing information,

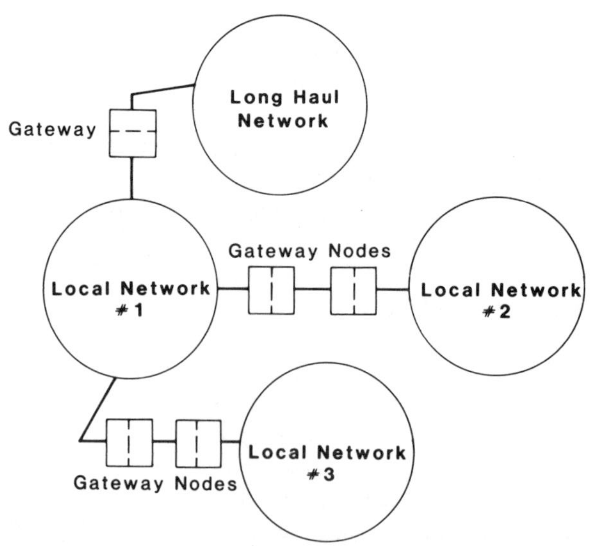

Figure 7–1. Interconnected Local Networks

and forward the message to another network. The name obtains from the fact that the media channels used by the different networks may be different. A media gateway is at the core of an internet datagram service.

Protocol-translation gateways translate a protocol used in one network to that used in another, generally for two networks with protocols of similar semantics. It does so by mapping messages from one protocol to those of another, a task that increases in difficulty as we rise in the protocol hierarchy and simple one-for-one mappings become unlikely. One approach to this mapping is had by providing gateways that map from a network-dependent protocol to a standard internetwork protocol, and the reverse (see figure 7–2).

Datagrams versus Virtual Circuits

A datagram service is really simpler to provide than a virtual-circuit service [8]. Many local-network functions are adequately served by a datagram service, whereas many long-haul networks are based on a virtual-circuit service [9,14]. Thus, datagram mappings by media gateways are simple, and in some pass-through situations the mapping is provided by an *encapsulation* process, whereby a datagram is wrapped in an outer envelope on entry to a network and is stripped of its outer envelope upon exit from the network. For interconnections involving long-haul networks, virtual circuits are generally employed, as they guarantee delivery of messages and ensure the order of delivery for a stream of messages. In these cases, the ISO recommendation for internetting, that is, the X.75protocol [12], may be used.

Naming, Addressing, and Routing

For a data object to be transported in an internetting environment, the message-data object must be identified and its placement determined. Next, the placement of the destination object must be ascertained, and a path that moves the message-data object from source to destination must be determined. To this end [4], *names* identify the objects; *addresses* serve to

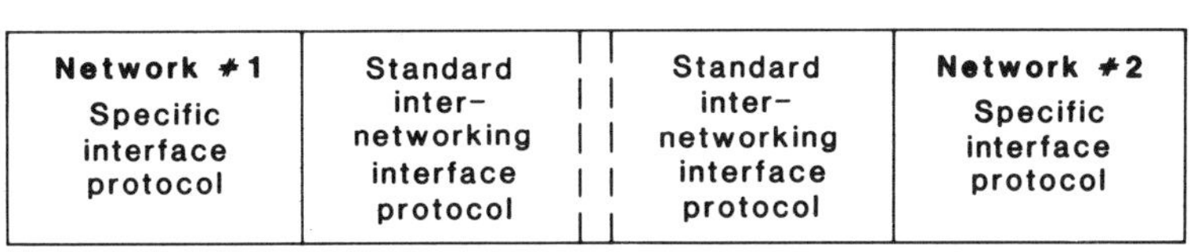

Figure 7–2. Gateway

determine their locations; and a *route* specifies a path from sender to destination. The communication requires mapping from name to location, and from location of the destination object to determination of route. These functions are served by hierarchical addressing [4,7], that is, by addresses of the form:

$$\begin{bmatrix} \text{destination} & & \text{destination} & & \text{destination} \\ \text{network} & : & \text{element} & : & \text{object} \end{bmatrix}$$

Internet routing employs the first element, whereas the last two are used to route the data object within the destination network. Hierarchical addressing is best served if all networks employed are the same structure.

Routing is served by both static and adaptive routing strategies [10]. With static strategies, a single route is always used to forward messages from a given source to a given destination.

With adaptive strategies, the route taken by a message for a given source-destination pair is not fixed but changes dynamically as a function of prevailing network conditions. In this manner, deadlocks and local congestions can be avoided and best use of communication resources becomes possible. The drawback of adaptive strategies stems from the need to constantly update the routing tables required, a procedure that requires that routing-control information be passed between the network nodes and that reasonably complicated update algorithms be executed. With local-network interconnection, however, these overheads are easily offset by the low price of processing and transmission of information. The routing process may consist of choosing the best route for a message, a decision that is based on the destination address and gateway routing tables. Both centralized and decentralized routing strategies are possible.

Flow and Congestion Control

As defined in chapter 3, flow control is concerned with regulation of the flow of messages between a source-destination pair [11]. Internet congestion control is concerned with ensuring that gateways are not excessively burdened with excessive message traffic, a task that is linked to internet routing strategies and may involve gateway rejection of receive (forwarded) messages.

Other Issues

In addition to naming, routing flow, and congestion control, internetting requires that attention also be given to fragmentation, privacy, and security issues [1,13,15]. Fragmentation arises when internetting connects two networks with differing packet sizes or connects a network that transmits packets with one that transmits messages. Because of the differing sizes of the units transmitted, larger units must be segmented and transmitted as multiple smaller units. Fragmentation can be handled by gateways or by in-network nodes, as in the Arpanet.

Finally, internetting requires attention to security and privacy issues. As mentioned earlier, gateways can protect networks from unauthorized traffic, and internetting can employ encryption as necessary to guarantee security.

Experience with internetting is being gained [2,4,5,6], and internet standards have been proposed [12].

Example 7.1

As an example, we abstract material that originally appeared in Boggs et al. [4].[a]

The work described in this paper represents one internetwork architecture, known as *Pup*, in widespread regular use within Xerox. The name referred originally to the abstract design of a standard ilnternetwork datagram (the PARC Universal Packet), but has expanded in usage to include the whole hierarchy of internetwork protocols as well as a general style for internetwork communication.

To assist in understanding the design of the Pup protocols, it is useful to characterize briefly the environment in which this architecture has evolved.

The computational environment includes a large number of "Alto" minicomputers [16,17] and other personal computers capable of high-quality interaction with human users. Supporting these are various specialized server systems that are shared among many users and provide access to expensive peripherals such as large disks, magnetic tapes, and high-quality printers. Additionally, there are several general-purpose time sharing systems providing customary services for terminal users.

The communications environment includes several different individual network designs. The dominant one is the "Ethernet" communications network, a local-area broadcast channel with a bandwidth of 3 megabits per second [19]. Long-haul communication facilities include the Arpanet, the ARPA Packet Radio network, and a collection of leased lines implementing an Arpanet-style store-and-forward network. These facilities have distinct native protocols and exhibit as much as three orders of magnitude difference in bandwidth.

[a]D.R. Boggs, J.F. Shoch, E.A. Taft, and R.M. Metcalfe, "Pup: An Internetwork Architecture," *IEEE Transactions on Communications* COM-28 (April 1980):612–623. Reprinted with permission.

The applications to be supported include a wide range of activities: terminal access to the time sharing services, electronic mail, file transfer, access to specialized data bases, document transmission, software distribution, and packet voice, to name just a few. We would also like to facilitate more ambitious explorations into the area generally referred to as "distributed computing."

The basic function provided bythe Pup internet is the transport of datagrams; this simple abstraction is the foundation of Pup. The internet does not guarantee reliable delivery of datagrams (called "Pups"); it simply gives its "best efforts" to deliver each one, and allows the end processes to build protocols which provide reliable communications of the quality they themselves desire [18]. The internet has no notion of a connection. It transports each Pup independently, and leaves consruction of a connection—if that is the appropriate interprocess communication model—to the end processes. Keeping fragile end-to-end state out of the packet transport system contributes to reliability and simplicity.

A Layered Hierarchy of Protocols

Layering of protocols is one of the most effective means for structuring a network design: each level uses the functions of the lower level, and adds some functionality of its own for possible use by the next level. Provided that suitable interfaces are maintained, an implementation at one level can be modified without impacting the overall structure; this helps to simplify both the design and the implementation.

Pup protocols are organized in a hierarchy, as shown in figure 7–3. A level represents an abstraction, to be realized in different ways in different hosts. There are four levels of interest, but there may be more than one protocol at any level except level 1, representing a different use of the underlying layers. (The numbering of layers—and, indeed, the choice of points at which to divide the layers—is arbitrary; there is no relationship between Pup's numbering and that of other designs such as the Open Systems Architecture.)

The level 0 abstraction is a packet transport mechanism. There are many realizations: an Ethernet channel, the Arpanet, the ARPA Packet Radio Network, our store-and-forward leased line network, and others. Level 0 protocols include specifications such as hardware interfaces, electrical and timing characteristics, bit encodings, line control procedures, and network-dependent packet formatting conventions. Associated with each packet transport mechanism is a convention for encapsulating Pups.

The level 1 abstraction is an internet datagram. The realization of this abstraction consists of the format of a Pup, a hierarchical addressing scheme,

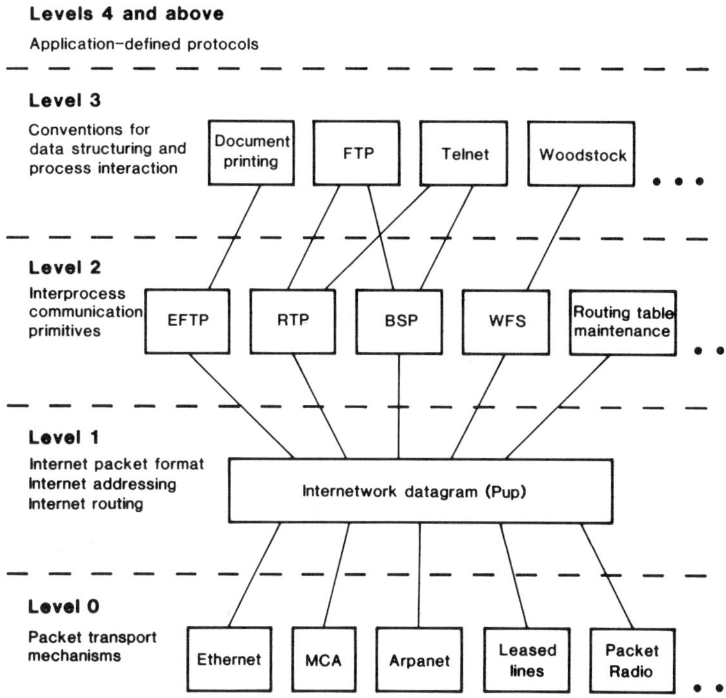

Figure 7–3. Pup Protocol Hierarchy

and an internetwork routing algorithm. There is only one box at level 1: the internet datagram protocol; it is this layer of commonality which unifies all of the different networks that might be used at level 0, and which makes available a uniform interface to all of the layers above. It is the purpose of this level to provide media independence while maintaining the common properties of the underlying packet networks.

The level 2 abstraction is an interprocess communication mechansim: a way to move bits without saying much abou their form or content. Various level 2 protocols provide many combinations of reliability, throughput, delay, and complexity. These protocols can be divided into two classes acording to the amount and lifetime of state information kept by the communicating end processes. Connectionless protocols support short-lived interactions; the end processes maintain little state, and usually only during the exchange of a few Pups—no more than a few seconds. Connection-based protocols support sustained interactions, generally requiring substantial state to be maintained at both ends, and for longer periods—minutes to hours.

Level 3 adds structure to the data moved at level 2, as well as conventions for how processes interact. For example the File Transfer Protocol (FTP) consists of a set of conventions for talking about files and a format for sending them through a level 2 byte stream protocol connection. These are sometimes referred to as function-oriented protocols [20].

Above level 3 the dividing lines become blurred, and individual applications evolve with their own natural decomposition into additional layers. With respect to layering of protocols, Pup is similar in many ways to the ARPA Internet and TCP design [22] and the Open Systems Architecture [21]. Unlike the Open Systems Architecture (and others), Pup often has several alternative boxes which all rest on a lower level and offer different functionality and interfaces to the next higher level.

An address field, as contained in a Pup, is one of the important elements of commonality in the internet design. An end process sends and receives Pups through a *port* identified by a hierarchical address consisting of three parts: a *network number*, a *host number*, and a *socket number*. This structure reflects the attitude that the communicating parties are the end processes, not the host's protocol handlers; among other things, this permits alternate implementations of a higher-level protocol to coexist in a single machine.

The actual process of routing a packet through the Pup internet uses a distributed adaptive routing procedure. The source process specifies only the *destination address* and not the *path* from source to destination. The internetwork gateways rout Pups to the proper netwok, a network then routes Pups to the proper host, and a host routes Pups to the proper socket.

This routing process is associated with Level 1 in the protocol hierarchy, the level at which packet formats and internet addresses are standardized. The software implementing level 1 is sometimes referred to as a *router*. Thus the routing table itself is kept at level 1; a very simple host (or gateway) would need only levels 0 and 1 in order to route Pups. But the routing table also requires periodic updating, as gateways exchange and distribute their current routing information; this *routing table maintenance* protocol is found logically at level 2 of the hierarchy.

Gateways provide internet routing tables to individual hosts as well as to each other. Hosts use this routing information to decide where to send outgoing packets destined other than to a directly-connected network.

Flow Control and Congestion Control

The Pup datagram-based internet model does not require that the internet successfully deliver every packet that has been accepted. Therefore, an intermediate gateway which suddenly encounters a period of severe congestion is free to discard packets, although the system should be engineered to make this an uncommon event.

If a gateway is forced to discard an incoming packet because of congestion, it should attempt to return some information to the source: an *error Pup* (negative acknowledgment) indicating that a packet had to be discarded in mid-route. This error Pup is simply returned to the source port, as identified in the discarded Pup; this a good illustration of the value of including the socket number as part of the standard internet address. The source process can use this information to modify its transmission strategies—for example, to reduce its offered load (the rate at which it attempts to send Pups along the congested path) and thereby help to relieve the congestion.

Long-term congestion should eventually be reflected in the routing information exchanged among gateways, discouraging subsequent traffic from attempting to pass through a badly congested area.

Implementation

The preceding section has outlined some of the important properties of the Pup architecture and the internetworking issues it addresses. What follows is a more detailed description of the present design of the four major layers in the system.

Level 0: Packet Transport

An individual network moves network-specific packets among hosts; the addressing schemes, error characteristics, maximum packet sizes, and other attributes of networks vary greatly. An internetwork packet transport mechanism, however, moves Pups between hosts. The level 0 code which transforms a network into an internet packet transport mechanism is called a *network driver*.

A machine connected to a single network, therefore, has one level 0 network driver; a gateway has one driver for each directly-connected network. Only the driver knows about the peculiarities of a network's hardware interface and low-level protocol.

The interface between levels 0 and 1 is very simple. Level 1 passes down a Pup and a network-specific host address, and the driver encapsulates the Pup and does its best to deliver it to the specified host. When a Pup arrives at a host, the driver decapsulates it and passes it up to level 1; if for any reason the Pup looks suspicious (as determined by network-specific error checking), the driver discards it.

Every packet transport mechanism must be able to accept a maximum-size Pup; if the actual network cannot directly encapsulate a packet of that size for transmission, the driver must include some form of intranetwork fragmentation.

A network driver may also be asked to broadcast a packet to all other hosts on that net. On some networks this is straightforward; on others it may require use of a reverse-path forwarding algorithm [23] or brute-force replication of the packet to each destination.

The transport mechanisms do not have to be perfectly reliable, but they should be successful most of the time—a packet loss rate of less than 1 percent is usually acceptable. A network operating for a short time in a degraded mode with a higher loss rate is harmless, so long as the probability is low that Pups will transit more than one net that is in this condition. However, if a network's inherent error characteristics are unfavorable, the driver should take steps to improve its performance, perhaps by incorporating a network-specific low-level acknowledgment and retransmission protocol.

To date, there have been five major types of networks integrated into the Pup architecture, each with a different level 0 driver.

Ethernet. Local Ethernet facilities can very easily serve as transport mechanisms for Pups: a Pup fits in an Ethernet packet with only a few additional words of encapsulation (see figure 7–4), and requires no frag-

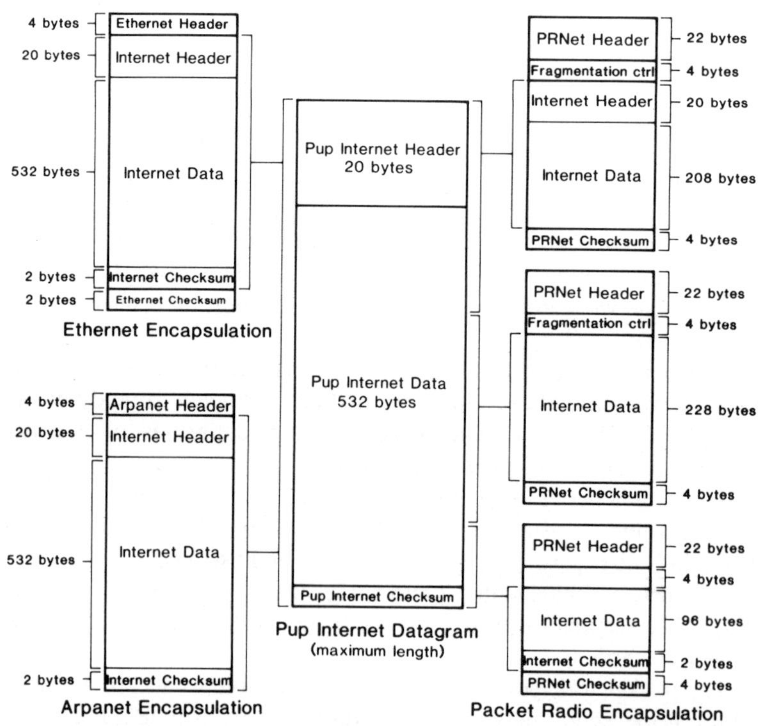

Figure 7–4. Pup Encapsulation in Various Networks

mentation. These systems have good reliability, high speed, and can send broadcast packets [19,24,25].

MCA. The Multiprocessor Communications Adapter (MCA), a parallel TDM bus, serves as a local network tying together a limited number of Nova computers [26]. It has good reliability and requires no fragmentation, but does not support broadcast packets. Broadcasts are accomplished by the brute-force method—sending a copy of a broadcast packet to each of the possible hosts.

Arpanet. To cover longer distances, Pups can be routed through the Arpanet; the format for encapsulating a Pup in an Arpanet message is shown in figure 7–4. (Note that Arpanet Pup transport is based on Host-IMP protocol messages, not on Host-Host protocol streams.) Because the standard maxium Pup length is less than that of an Arpanet message, the driver itself need not fragment Pups; however, the Arpanet does perform network-specific fragmentation internally: one "message" containing a Pup may become multiple "packets" within the Arpanet. Furthermore, the Arpanet provides increased reliability through the use of its own internal acknowledgment and retransmission protocols. The Arpanet does not presently support broadcast packets; rather than sending packets to all possible Arpanet hosts, the network driver does not implement broadcasts at all.

Leased Line Store-and-Forward Network. More frequently, different local networks are interconnected over long distances through the use of a private store-and-forward network constructed using leased telephone circuits. Similar in spirit to the Arpanet, this system is used to connect internetwork gateways. Unlike the Arpanet, the system does not use separate packet switches (IMP), but instead switches packets through the hosts themselves—that is, the connected hosts include network-specific drivers that implement a store-and-forward network. This network has its own adaptive routing procedure, independent of the internetwork routing. The system is fairly reliable and does not require low-level acknowledgments. At present, the network drivers do not fragment Pups, but they do promote small packets to the front of transmission queues at intermediate points to help improve performance for interactive traffic.

Packet Radio Network. On an experimental basis, the ARPA Packet Radio network [27] has been used to carry traffic among local networks in the San Francisco Bay area. The Packet Radio network was integrated into the system by building a suitable level 0 network driver [28]. The system provides good reliability; but due to the relatively small maximum packet size (232 bytes), the driver must perform fragmentation and reassembly (see figure 7–4. Though using a broadcast medium, the Packet Radio protocols do not support broadcast packets. In this case, the low-level driver includes a procedure to periodically identify Packet Radio hosts that might be running Pup software; when asked to broadcast a packet, the driver sends copies of it to all such hosts.

To date we have not used any public packet-switched networks, such as Telenet, as packet transport mechanisms. These systems usually provide only a virtual circuit interface (X.25) that requires a user to pay for functionality that may not be needed. Compared to our existing leased line network, a Telenet-based packet transport mechanism would not be cost-effective except under conditions of very light traffic volume. We would prefer to use a service that provided simple, unreliable datagrams; if there were an appropriate interface, we could dismantle our leased line store-and-forward network.

Level 1: Internetwork Datagrams

This is the level at which packet formats and internetwork addresses are standardized. It is the lowest level of process-to-process communication.

Pup Format

The standard format for a Pup is shown in figure 7–5. The following paragraphs highlight the sorts of information required at the internet datagram level.

The *Pup length* is the number of 8-bit bytes in the Pup, including internetwork header (20 bytes), contents, and checksum (2 bytes).

The *transport control* field is used for two purposes: as a scratch area for use by gateways, and as a way for source processes to tell the internet how to handle the packet. (Other networks called this the "facilities" or "options" field.) The *hop count* subfield is incremented each time the packet is forwarded by a gateway. If this ever overflows, the packet is presumed to be travelling in loop and is discarded. A *trace bit* is specified, for potential use in monitoring the path taken by a packet.

The *Pup type* is assigned by the source process for interpretation by the destination process and defines the format of the Pup contents. The 256 possible types are divided into two groups. Some types are *registered* and have a single meaning across all protocols; Pups generated or interpreted within the internet (e.g., by gateways) have types assigned in this space. Interpretation of the remaining *unregistered* types is strictly a matter of agreement between the source and destination processes.

The *Pup identifier* is used by most protocols to hold a sequence number. Its presence in the internetwork header is to permit a response generated

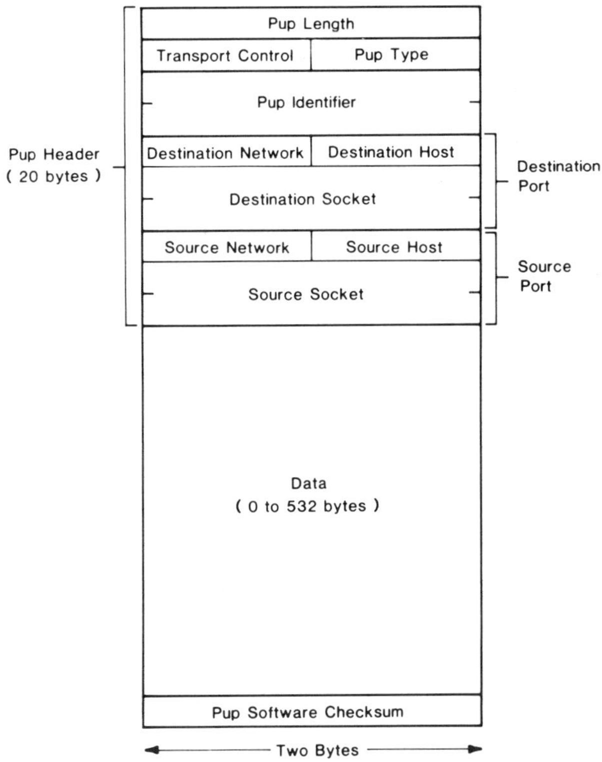

Figure 7–5. Pup Internet Datagram

within the internet (e.g., error or trace information) to identify the Pup that triggered it in a manner that does not depend on knowledge of the higher-level protocols used by the end processes.

Pups contain two addresses: a *source port* and a *destination port.* These hierarchical addresses include an 8-bit network number, an 8-bit host number, and a 32-bit socket number. Hosts are expected to know their own host addresses, to discover their network numbers by locating a gateway and asking for this informtion, and to assign socket numbers in some systematic way not legislated by the internet protocol.

There are some important conventions associated with the use of network addresses. A distinguished value of the network number field refers to "this network" without identifying it. Such a capability is necessary for host initialization (since most hosts have no permanent local storage and consequently no *a priori* knowledge of the connected network number), and to permit communication to take place within a degenerate internet consisting of an unidentified local network with no gateways. A distinguished value of the destination host address is used to request a broadcast. Certain values of the socket number field refer, by convention, to "well-known sockets" associated with standard, widely-used services, as is done in the Arpanet.

The *data* field contains up to 532 data bytes. The selection of a standard maximum packet length must reflect many considerations: error rates, buffer requirements, and needs of specific applications. A reasonable value might range anywhere from 100 to 4000 bytes. In practice, much of the internet traffic consists of packets containing individual "pages" of 512 bytes each, reflecting the quantization of memory in most of our computers. But just carying the data is not enough, since the packet should accommodate higher-level protocol overhead and some identifying information as well. Allowing 20 additional bytes for such purposes, we arrive at 532 bytes as the maximum size of the data field (a somewhat unconventional value in that it is not a power of two). Thus, there may be between 0 and 532 content bytes in a Pup, so its total length will range from 22 to 554 bytes. Pups longer than 554 bytes are not prohibited and may be carried by some networks, but no internetwork gateway is required to handle larger ones.

The optional *software checksum* is used for complete end-to-end coverage—it is computed as close to the source of the data and checked as close to the ultimate destination as is possible. This checksum protects a Pup when it isn't covered by some network-specific technique, such as when it is sitting in a gateway's memory or passing through a parallel I/O path. Most networks employ some sort of error checking on the serial parts of the channel, but parallel data paths in the interface and the I/O system often are not checked.

The checksum algorithm is intended to be straightforward to implement in software; it also allows incremental updating so that intermediate agents which modify a packet (gateways udating the hop count field, for example) can quickly update the checksum rather than recomputing it. The checksum may (but need not) be checked anywhere along a Pup's route in order to monitor the internet's integrity.

Routing

Accompanying the packet format defined at level 1 are the protocols for internetwork routing. Each host, whether or not it is a gateway, executes a routing procedure on every outgoing Pup, as illustrated in figure 7–6. This procedure decides, as a function of the Pup destination port field, upon which *directly-connected network* the Pup is to be transmitted (if there is more than one choice), and it yields an *immediate destination host* which is the address on that network of either the ultimate destination or some gateway believed to be closer to the destination. Each routing step employs the same algorithm based on local routing information, and each Pup is routed independently.

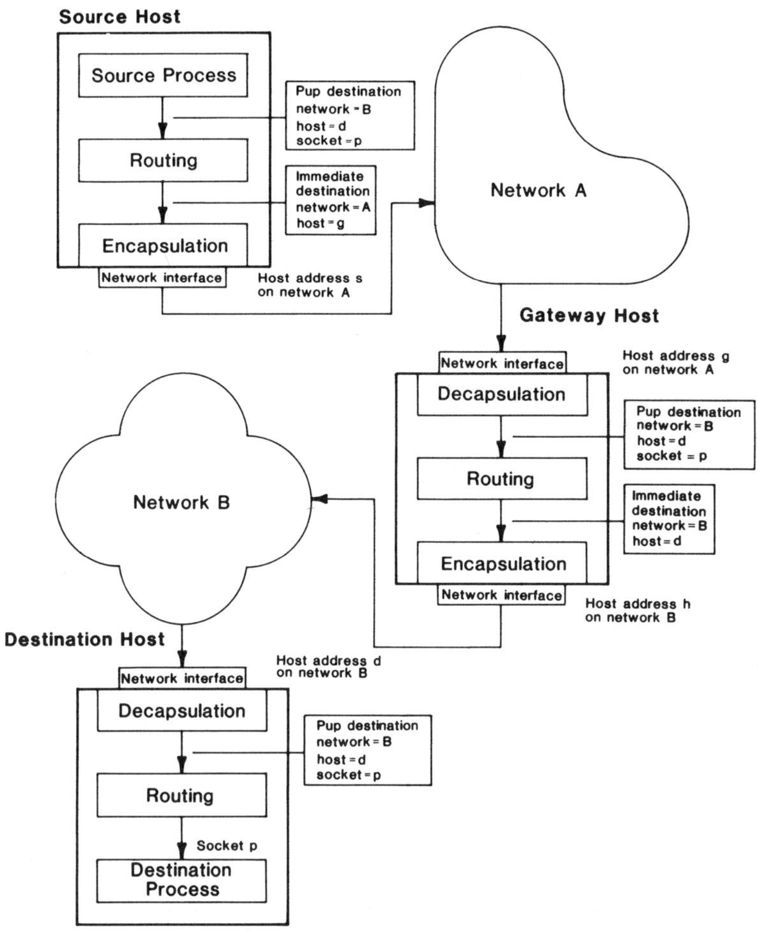

Figure 7–6. Internetwork Routing

Routing information is maintained in a manner very similar to the Arpanet-style adaptive procedures [29]. The initial metric used for selecting routes is the "hop count"—the number of intermediate networks between source and destination. The protocol for updating the routing tables involves exchanging Pups with neighboring gateways and rests logically at level 2 of the protocol hierarchy. This is an example of a connectionless protocol which doesn't require perfectly reliable transmission for correct operation. Changes in internetwork topology may cause different gateways' routing tables to become momentarily inconsistent, but the algorithm is stable in that the routing tables rapidly converge to a consistent state and remain that way until another change in topology occurs.

A host which is not a gateway still implements a portion of this level 2 routing update protocol: it initially obtains an internetwork routing table from a gateway on its directly-connected network, and it obtains updated information periodically. If there is more than one gateway providing connections to other networks, the host can merge their routing tables and thus be able to select the best route for packets directed to any network.

Level 2: Interprocess Communication

Given the raw datagram facility provided at level 1, we can begin to build data transport protocols, tailored to provide appropriate levels of reliability or functionality for real applications.

These protocols generally fall into two categories: those in which a connection is established for a sustained exchange of packets, and those in which individual packets are exchanged on a connectionless basis. Connection-style protocols usually transport data very reliably, and transparently.

EFTP: The Easy File Transfer Protocol. This is a very simple protocol for sending files. Each data Pup gives rise to an immediate acknowledgment, and there is at most one Pup outstanding at a time. This protocol is an indirect descendent of the one outlined in [19]. Its simplicity makes this piece of communication mechanism easy to include under conditions of very limited resources. For example, we have implemented a complete EFTP receiver in 256 words of assembly language, for use in a network-based bootstrap and down-line loading process.

Rendezvous & Termination Protocol (RTP). This is a general means to initiate, manage, and terminate connections in a reliable fashion [30]. In normal use, an RTP user initiates a connection by communicating with a well-known socket at some server. That server wil spawn a new port to actually provide the service, and the RTP will establish contact with this port. It employs a non-reusable *connection identifier* to distinguish among multiple instantiations of the same connection and to cope with delayed packets without making assumptions about maximum packet lifetimes. RTP also synchronizes Pup identifiers for use in managing the connection.

Byte Stream Protocol (BSP). This is a relatively sophisticated protocol for supporting reliable, sequenced streams of data. It provides for multiple outstanding packets from the source, and uses a moving window flow control procedure. User processes can place *mark bytes* in the stream to identify logical boundaries and can sent out-of-band *interrupt* signals. RTP and BSP combined perform a function similar to that of the TCP, with which they share a certain degree of common ancestry [3,22].

Connectionless protocols do not attempt to maintain any long-term state; they usually don't guarantee reliability, but leave it up to the designer to construct the most suitable system. Their simplicity and ease of implementation make them extremely useful.

Echo. A very simple protocol can be used to send test Pups to an *echo server* process, which will check them and send back a reply. Such servers are usually embedded in gateways and other server hosts, to aid in network monitoring and maintenance. The server is trivial to implement on top of the level 1 facilities.

Name Lookup. Another server provides the mapping from string names of resources to internetwork addresses; this is accomplished by a single exchange of packets. This service is often addressed with a broadcast Pup, since it is used as the first step in locating resources. (The name lookup service itself, of course, must be located at a well-known address. To be useful, it must be widely available; therefore it is typically replicated at least once per network.)

Routing Table Maintenance. The internetwork routing tables are maintained by Pups exchanged periodically among internetwork gateways and broadcast for use by other hosts.

Page-Level File Access. The Woodstock File Server (WFS), one of the family of file servers available on the internet, provides page-at-a-time access to a large file store [31]. The protocols used for this do not require establishment of a connection, but merely exchange request and response Pups that each carry both commands and file data. This arrangement supports random-access, transaction-oriented interactions of very high performance—frequently better than that obtained using local file storage, because the file server's disks are much faster than those typically connected to personal computers.

Gateway Monitoring and Control. There is no single network control center, but individual gateways may be queried from a monitoring program run on any user machine. With suitable authentication, the user may assume remote control of the gateway so as to perform operations such as changing parameters and loading new versions of the software.

Other connectionless protocols are used to access a *date and time server*, an *authentication server*, and a *mail check server* integrated with an on-line message system. These protocols are designed to be as cheap as possible to implement (i.e., without connection overhead) so that such servers may be replicated extensively and accessed routinely without consuming excessive resources. For example, instances of some of these servers are present in all gateway hosts so as to maximize their availability.

Level 3: Application Protocols

Armed with a reasonable collection of data transport protocols at level 2, one can begin to evolve specific applications at level 3. These are supported by various function-oriented protocols [20].

Telnet. Terminal access to remote hosts is provided with an internetwork Telnet protocol, which makes use of the combination of the Rendezvous & Termination Protocol (RTP) and the Byte Stream Protocol (BSP) at level 2. Using the notion of a virtual terminal, Telnet implementations map characteristics of actual terminals into a network-independent representation; a mark byte in the stream and an out-of-band interrupt, for example, are used to signal an "attention." (This approach is a subset of the Arpanet Telnet protocol, without any of its options such as RCTE [32,38]).

FTP. The RTP and BSP are again combined as the foundation for an internetwork File Transfer Protocol (FTP), supporting stream-oriented access to files. The underlying byte streams provide reliable communication, and the major taks of FTP is to communicate commands and responses and to sort out different represenations of data in different file systems. FTP implementations have been embedded within existing time-sharing systems, and also constitute the core of dedicated, high-capacity file servers.

Printing. Among the important shared resources in the internet are high-quality printing servers. Rather than using the fully developed BSP and FTP, the specialized task of sending unnamed, standard format document files to a printer makes use of the more restricted but much simpler EFTP.

CopyDisk. Given high-performance networks and simple gateways that can forward Pups among them efficiently, it is perfectly reasonable to copy entire disk packs through the internet. The CopyDisk protocol negotiates between the participating machines to ensure that the disks are compatible, and handles error recovery should something break down.

Remote Graphics. Personal display-oriented computers such as the Alto can be used to provide a convivial front end for large programming systems such as Interlisp. The Alto Display protocol is used for exchanging descriptions of graphical structures as well as text; it is similar to the ARPA Network Graphics Protocol, but with extensions to support raster-scanned graphics [33,34,35].

Additional applications have included cooperative editing of common documents from multiple machines, audio communication and packet voice, and many others.

As users create new applications, these systems tend to develop their own natural layering of function. Some may require new protocol designs in the existing hierarchy; the Pup architecture permits this degree of flexibility down to the level of the simple internetwork datagram. As we gain experience with new systems, common pieces of design will begin to emerge that might be of more general use; they will eventually find their way into an appropriate place in this hierarchy of communications protocols.

Evolution, Actual Experience, and Performance

The Pup architecture emerged against a background of Arpanet protocols. Many of its important—and those of its key relative, TCP—first appeared during the course of a series of meetings of the International Network Working Group (IFIP TC-6 WG6.1) during 1973. Pup and TCP share a number of important principles, most notably that of reliable end-to-end transmission through an internet. Pup subsequently diverged from TCP as the desire for implementation within Xerox required decoupling it from TCP's long and sometimes painful standardization process.

The fundamentals of the Pup design crystallized in 1974 and have remained essentially unchanged since then. During this interval many higher-level protocols have been developed, the implementations have evolved considerably, and the internetwork system has grown to include approximately 1000 hosts, attached to 25 networks of 5 different types, using 20 internetwork gateways. The system is in regular use, is quite stable, and requires little regular maintenance or attention.

From a functional point of view, this internetwork architecture has been able to fulfill the needs of a very diverse community. While the bulk of all traffic is carried by means of a few standard protocols, it has proven extremely valuable to be able to define new protocols—aiming at different points in the space of performance, cost, and functionality—and to fit them into the internet protocol hierarchy at any of several levels.

In terms of performance, the internetwork gateways impose very little overhead because they are so simple. In regions of the internet where multiple high-bandwidth local networks are interconnected directly by a single minicomputer-based gateway, there is almost no noticeable difference between intranet and internet performance. Total throughput in an individual gateway is high, ranging from 400 to 1000 kilobits per seconds (depending on the perticular implementation), and the typical delay experienced by maximum-length Pups in the case just mentioned is 2 to 5 milliseconds.

These figures don't represent limits to what is achievable—even with the relatively low-powered machines now being used as gateways—because the gateway software has not been highly tuned for this application but rather is based on general-purpose software packages that are also used in many other hosts. But the current performance is adequate because the internetwork traffic load is typically only a tiny fraction of the capacity of the underlying local network channels. There exists one Alto-based gateway that interconnects three 3-megabit per second Ethernet channels as well as several 9.6-kilobit per second leased lines and a Packet Radio interface. In general the bottlenecks are not the gateways but rather the slower communication channels; discard of Pups due to congestion in gateways is almost exclusively due to overload of the 9.6-kilobit per second lines.

As might be expected, most of the traffic in our local networks is intranetwork—that is, consisting of Pups whose source and destination are on the same network. For example, measurement of one such network has shown a typical volume of 2.2 million packets per day, 72 percent of which are intranetwork packets [24]. Furthermore, of the remaining 28 percent, more than half consist of traffic to or from another nearby local network connected via a single gateway. (This site is served by multiple local networks because it is too large to cover with a single one using existing Ethernet technology, and also because it would exhaust a single network's address space.) The rest of the traffic—some 250,000 packets per day—is transported to or from other campuses in the internet, mostly via the leased line network.

The higher-level protocols, such as the Byte Stream and FTP, are generally limited in performance by the processor capacity or the secondary storage bandwidth at the source and destination. For example, our BCPL implementation of BSP can maintain a data stream at the rate of about 500 kilobits per second between end processes running on Alto minicomputers, at which point both machines are CPU-bound. While it is certainly adequate for most applications, we find this performance somewhat disappointing, and we view it as an indication that BSP—though substantially simpler than, say TCP—is still too complicated a protocol for high-performance communication.

The Pup architecture allows individual networks to be added to the internet system on an *ad hoc* basis, with no need for central control or coordination except to assign new network numbers. Users sharing a local network can assemble gateways and lease lines to other nearby gateways; they are encouraged to make multiple intergateway connections to provide alternate routes and thereby reduce the probability of being isolated. The gateway software has evolved to the point where if one starts a copy of it on a host having at least one connection to the existing internet, it will automatically obtain the files and other information it needs, announce its availability to the rest of the internet, and begin forwarding Pups.

A Retrospective Critique, Possible Improvements, and Future Research

While the architecture works extremely well, there are some lessons to be learned from this experience.

Addressing and Routing

The size of address fields is a question of continuing controversy. An eight-bitnetwork number supports up to 256 nets; that is fine for now, but eventually it should be made larger. To date, 256 hosts per net has not been a problem, though it is likely to become one (for example, when the Arpanet's new 24-bit addressing convention starts to receive wide use). We have avoided variable-length address fields in the Pup design because they increase per-packet processing costs.

If an internetwork system becomes extremely large, the number of networks becomes so great that it is no longer practical for all hosts to keep routing table entries for all possible destination networks. Area routing strategies may be employed to attack this problem [29]. Alternatively, one may adopt a scheme in which the local routing table becomes a cache of recently used routing information, with routes to specific networks computed and maintained as needed. The problem of locating routes to distant parts of the internet is an area of current research.

One could consider revising the entire notion of a hierarchical address space. Under the current design, it is sometimes necessary to change the host number of a machine which is moved from one net to another—an operational annoyance. It is conceivable that every host could be given a unique address within a flat address space; a more sophisticated mechanism would then be needed to map addresses into routes, since there would no longer be a network number as part of the address (except perhaps as a hint, to improve performance).

We view with some disfavor non-hierarchical organizations in which internet addresses consist of a concatenation of network-specific addresses [36]. Such arrangements have the effect of fixing the *path* to a given destination and blur the distinction between addressing and routing.

Socket numbers, which are now 32 bits wide, could easily shrink to 16. Originally, 32 bits were assigned to allow inclusion of a unique subfield to distinuish among multiple instantiations of a connection; we now recognize that a better approach is to use a distinct connection identifier at the time a connection is established, as mentioned earlier in the presentation of the Rendezvous & Termination Protocol.

Using hop counts as the metric for routing decisions has worked remarkably well. An obvious drawback, however, is that it considers a hop through a 9.6-kilobit per second phone line equally as good as a hop through a 3-megabit per second Ethernet link. As the topology becomes more richly connected, this will increasingly become a problem. We intend eventually to change the routing algorithms to reflect some consideration of bandwidth and delay, using known techniques based on research into adaptive distributed routing algorithms in the Arpanet and elsewhere.

We have given little consideration to source routing or other forms of advice (e.g., class of service) provided to the internet routing procedures by source processes. In providing such facilities, one must take great care not to compromise the simplicity of the basic internet datagrams or violate the layering of protocols.

Congestion Control and Utilization of Low-Bandwidth Channels

The current congestion control techniques must be regarded as primitive. Discarding Pups and (where possible) notifying the source process when congestion occurs has the virtue of simplicity, and we believe it is a good general approach; but the present design has several defects. Insufficient information is returned to the source process to enable it to make an informed decision about how to proceed; further, the discard of Pups is haphazard, and no provision is made for fairness. Congestion occurs most often at the entry to slow channels, and under overload conditions the perceived performance of paths through those channels is highly variable.

This is a situation in which it would be appropriate to perform a relatively large amount of computation per packet in order to optimize the utilization of the communication bandwidth. For example, the network-specific driver for a leased telephone circuit could examine the source and destination addresses of Pups to deduce the existence of "conversations", and use this information to share the slow channel more effectively. (The Arpanet IMP deduce conversations in precisely this way, though for purposes having to do primarily with flow control rather than congestion control.)

In the same vein, techniques such as code compression, elimination and regeneration of identical internet headers in successive packets, ets., may be implemented in the network-specific drivers for the slow channels, with minimal impact on the end-to-end protocols. Such techniques are used widely in virtual circuit designs, and their applicability is sometimes cited as an advantage of virtual circuits over datagrams [37]. But there is no reason they can't be employed in a datagram-based internet, so long as the necessary additional computation is done in the right place.

The important point is that optimizing the utilization of the communication channel is appropriate only when the channel bandwidthis scarce compared to the computation required to perform such optimization. Where the processing capacity of the end machines is itself the scarce resource—as we have observed in the local network environment—such techniques are highly inappropriate.

Pup Types in the Internet Header

The distinction between registered and unregisterd Pup types at the level of internet datagrams has not turned out to be particularly useful, except in a few cases: Pups of type "error" and "trace" may be generated from within the internet without knowledge of the higher-level protocols being employed by the end processes.

Performance of Reliable End-to-End Protocols

Present implementations of the Byte Stream Protocol include fairly sophisticated adaptive flow control heuristics that also try to take note of any packets lost due to internet congestion. This approach has worked reasonably well in enabling a source to adapt to the conditions encountered along the path to a particular destination. However, use of networks with highly variable behavior—such as the wide-ranging delays experienced when using the Packet Radio network—can confound these heuristics. Under unusual circumstances, the flow control procedures have been observed to move suddenly into very unfavorable operating regions. The difficulty involving the Radionet has since been solved, but the general design of simple, effective flow control and congestion control procedures is just a very hard problem—particularly procedures intended to adapt dynamically to and make good use of different networks whose performance may vary by nearly three orders of magnitude.

The step from raw Pups to a byte stream may be too large. The Byte Stream Protocol does too much for many applications; it is complex enough that few systems have ever implemented the entire specification. As discussed previously, performance of the BSP—when compared to some other systems—is reasonable; but it does not give a user the full capacity of the underlying networks. In a high-bandwidth local network environment, paying attention to per-packet processing overhead is of extreme importance.

We have considered—but have not yet implemented—a proposal for an intermediate level of functionality: a Reliable Packet Protocol (RPP) that takes care of connection establishment and processes flow control information, but tries not to dictate how a client program should do buffer management. It ensures reliable delivery (i.e., each packet once and only once), but may deliver packets to the client out of order, and does not deliberately attempt to hide packet boundaries. A BSP connection—where that is what is desired—may then be re-implemented as a veneer on top of an RPP connection.

Access to the Internet

The present Pup architectue can be characterized as "open": users and applications are permitted—and indeed encouraged—to take advantage of the internet for routine communication. Access to the internet is uncontrolled; as in many network designs, responsibility for access control rests with the host systems, and whatever accounting is performed is for the services rendered by individual servers. In our research and development environment this is ideal, but obviously in some other environments it might not be.

Conclusions

The success of Pup as an internetwork architecture depends on a number of important principles. Key among these is the layering of function in such a way that applications may make use of the internet at any of several levels, with the ability to choose among alternative protocols at each level or to develop new ones where necessary. Simple internetwork datagrams constitute the level at which media independence (through encapsulation) is achieved; they are also the unit of direct process-to-process communication. This is crucial both to flexibility and to performance, particularly in an internetwork environment dominated by relatively lightweight hosts and high-bandwidth local networks.

During 1976 the Pup internet reached a level of functionality roughly equivalent to that provided by the standard Arpanet protocols—byte streams, Telnet, and FTP. From that time to the present we have concentrated on building servers and constructing applications to access them through the internet. We are just beginning to explore that area of interprocess communication traditionally considered the domain of multiprocessors. Some interesting opportunities arise from the availability of 100 or so minicomputers interconnected by a 3-megabit per second broadcast channel, and by 10 or so similar clusters, all interconnected by a store-and-forward network. We believe that the Pup architecture serves as a good foundation for such investigations.

References

1. Cerf, V.G., and Kirstein, P.T. "Issues in Packet-Network Interconnection." *Proceedings of the IEEE* 66 (November 1978):1386–1408.

2. Clark, D.C.; Pogran, K.T.; and Reed, D.P. "An Introduction to Local Area Networks." *Proceedings of the IEEE* 66 (November 1978):1497–1517.

3. Postel, J.B. "Internetwork Protocol Approaches." *IEEE Transactions on Communications* COM-28 (April 1980):604–611.

4. Boggs, D.R.; Shoch, J.F.; Taft, E.A.; and Metcalfe, R.M. "Pup: An Internetwork Architecture." *IEEE Transactions on Communications* COM-28 (April 1980):612–623.

5. Sunshine, Carl A. "Interconnection of Computer Networks." In *Computer Networks and Simulation*, edited by S. Schoemaker. North-Holland Publishing Company, 1978; also in *Computer Networks* 1 (February 1977):175–195.

6. Sunshine, Carl. "Network Interconnection." Workshop summary, *Proceedings of the Local Area Computer Network Symposium*, Boston, May 1979.

7. CCITT. "Recommendation X.121—International Numbering Plan for Public Data Networks." Study Group VII, Temporary Document 76-E, International Telecommunications Union, Geneva, April 1978.

8. Pouzin, L. "Virtual Circuits vs. Datagrams—Technical and Political Problems." *Proceedings of the National Computer Conference* 1976, pp. 483–494.

9. Roberts, L.G. "International Connection of Public Packet Networks." *Proceedings of the Third International Conference on Computer Communications*, Toronto, 1976, pp. 239–245.

10. Schwartz, M., and Stern, T.E. "Routing Techniques Used in Computer Communication Networks." *IEEE Transactions on Communications* COM-28 (April 1980):539–552.

11. Kleinrock, L., and Gerla, M. "Flow Control: A Comparative Survey." *IEEE Transactions on Communications* COM-28 (April 1980):539–552.

12. CCITT. "Recommendation X.75—Terminal and Transit Call Control Procedures and Data Transfer System on International Circuits between Packet-Switched Data Networks." Study Group VII, Temporary Document 132-E, International Telecommunications Union, Geneva, 25 April 1978.

13. Mathison, S.L. "Commercial, Legal, and International Aspects of

Packet communications." *Proceedings of the IEEE* 66 (November 1978): 1527–1539.

14. "Recommendation X.25—Interface between Data Terminal Equipment (DTE) and Data Circuit-Terminating Equipment (DCE) for Terminals Operating in the Packet Mode on Public Data Network." In *CCITT Orange Book*, Vol. 7, International Telephone and Telegraph Consultative Committee, Geneva, Switzerland.

15. Gien, M., and Zimmerman, H. "Design Principles for Network Interconnection." *Proceedings of the Sixth Data Communications Symposium*, Monterey, Calif., November 1979, pp. 109–119.

16. Kay, Alan C. "Microelectronics and the Personal Computer." *Scientific American* 237 (September 1977).

17. Thacker, C.P.; McCreight, E.M.; Lampson, B.W.; Sproull, R.F.; and Boggs, D.R. "Alto: A Personal Computer." *Computer Structures: Readings and Examples*, edited by D. Siewiorek, G. Bell, and Newell. 1981.

18. Metcalfe, Robert M. "Packet Communication." Ph.D. thesis, Harvard University, MIT Project MAC TR-114, December 1973.

19. Metcalfe, Robert, and Boggs, David. "Ethernet: Distributed Packet Switching for Local Computer Networks." *Communications f the ACM* 19 (July 1976).

20. Crocker, S.D.; Heafner, J.F.; Metcalfe, R.M.; and Postel, J.B. "Function-oriented Protocols for the ARPA Computer Network." *AFIPS Conference Proceedings (SJCC)* 40 (1972).

21. Zimmerman H., "OSI Reference Model—the ISO Model of Architecture for Open Systems Interconnecton." IEEE Transactions on Communications COM-28 (April 1980).

22. Cerf, Vinton, and Kahn, Robert. "A Protocol for Packet Network Interconnection." *IEEE Transactions on Communications* COM-22 (May 1974).

23. Dalal, Yogen K., and Metcalfe, Robert M. "Reverse Path Forwarding of Broadcast Packets." *Communications of the ACM* 21 (December 1978).

24. Shoch, John F., and Hupp, Jon A. "Performance of an Ethernet Local Network—a Preliminary Report." *Local Area Network Symposium*, Boston, May 1979.

25. Shoch, John F. "Internetwork Naming, Addressing, and Routing." *Seventeenth IEEE Computer Society International Conference (COMPCON)*. September 1978.

26. Data General Corporation. *Type 4038 Multiprocessor Communications Adapter*. Technical Reference 014-000002-01, September 1971.

27. Kahn, R.E.; Gronemeyer, S.A.; Burchfiel, J.; and Kunzelman, R.C.

"Advances in Packet Radio Technology." *Proceedings of the IEEE* 66 (November 1978).

28. Shoch, John F., and Stewart, Lawrence. "Interconnecting Local Networks via the Packet Radio Network." *Sixth Data Communications Symposium*, Pacific Grove, Calif., November 1979.

29. McQuillan, John M. "Adaptive Routing Algorithms for Distributed Computer Network." Ph.D. thesis, Harvard University. Bolt, Beranek and Newman, Report No. 2831, May 1974.

30. Sunshine, Carl, and Dalal, Yogen. "Connection Management in Transport Protocols." *Computer Networks* 2 (1978).

31. Swinehart, Dan; McDaniel, Gene; and Boggs, David. "WFS: A Simple Shared File System for a Distributed Environment." *Operating Systems Review* 13 (November 1979).

32. Davidson, J.; Hathaway, W.; Postel, J.; Mimno, N.; Thomas, R.; and Walden, D. "The Arpanet Telnet Protocol: Its Purpose, Principles, Implementation, and Impact on Host Operating System Design." *Fifth Data Communications Symposium*, Snowbird, Utah, September 1977.

33. Sproull, Robert, and Thomas, Elaine. "A Network Graphics Protocol." *Computer Graphics* 8 (Fall 1974).

34. Teitelman, Warren. "A Display-Oriented Programmer's Assistant." *Fifth International Joint Conference on Artificial Intelligence*, Cambridge, Mass., August 1977; also available as Xerox PARC Technical Report CSL-77-3.

35. Sproull, Robert F., and Cohen, Dan. "High-Level Protocols." *Proceedings of the IEEE* 66 (November 1978).

36. Sunshine, Carl. "Source Routing in Computer Networks." *ACM Computer Communications Review* 7 (January 1977).

37. Roberts, Lawrence G. "The Evolution of Packet Switching, *Proceedings of the IEEE* 66 (November 1978).

38. Feinler, E., and Postel, J. (eds.). "Telnet Protocol Specification." *Arpanet Protocol Handbook*, January 1978.

8 Epilogue

Introduction

An epilogue offers the opportunity to comment on topics neglected in previous chapters. Those topics begging for mention here include:

PBX based systems,

Broadband based systems,

Standardization efforts,

Network-users-association activity, and

Miscellaneous notes.

We begin with a summary of Private Branch Exchange (PBX) based networks and broadband based networks, two rivals of the baseband systems discussed throughout the previous chapters.

Broadband Based Networks

The action to date in the local networking area has revolved around baseband communication, but future action may revolve around broadband communication. The key reason for this potential stems primarily from broadband's ability to simultaneously accommodate analog video and voice, and digital data transmissions over greater distances than baseband digital data transmissions. Broadband provides these features by supporting multiple channels on the coaxial cable (via frequency division multiplexing), while baseband communication can accommodate only one channel. Although a baseband bandwidth of 175 MHz or more is possible, broadband based systems (using CATV technology) can achieve bandwidths in the 300–400 MHz range. Thus with broadband a given bandwidth (typically in the 300 MHz range) can be divided into a number of bands (channels) that can be used for different purposes (as long as the sum of the channel bandwidth is less than or equal to the total available bandwidth of, say, 300 MHz). The individual channels are separate, thus providing a measure of security or privacy for certain communications. Figure 8–1 shows a possible frequency division mapping. Note that for those frequency segments devoted to a multiaccess

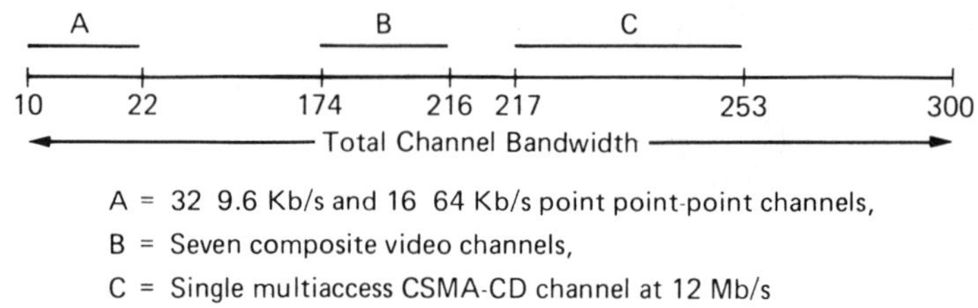

Figure 8–1. Possible Frequency Division Mapping

channel most of the access strategies discussed in chapter 3 (and associated with baseband systems) can be used.

As mentioned in chapter 2, the penalty for this flexibility is the need for a head-end (central) retransmission node as CATV is based on a directional broadcast transmission. All transmissions (except those emanating at the head-end node) must be broadcast in one frequency range to the head-end, where they are relayed in a second frequency range (see figure 8–2) to all other nodes.

CBX Based Networks

The Private Branch Exchange (PBX) or CBX (Computerized Branch Exchange) also provides a vehicle for the transmission of both analog voice and digital data. Systems in this class employ installed voice telephone lines connected to a computerized switching computer, thus realizing a star network topology. The capacity of a single switching computer is extended by interconnecting switching computers to (generally) realize a mesh connected network. With PBX (CBX) systems a user can dial-up either a digital or voice connection. With a digital connection the digital bit sequence may be

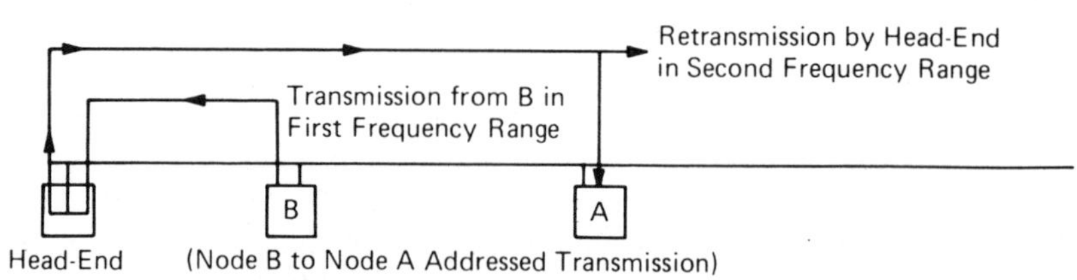

Figure 8–2. CATV Head-End Relays

constructed by switching computer (by sampling an analog signal associated with an RS232 link) or directly by the local device that initiated the dial-up connection. Digital connections are generally in the 9.6 Kb/s and 19.2 Kb/s ranges, although higher rates (for example, 56 Kb/s) can also be had. A typical PBX (CBX) system is shown in figure 8–3. The switching computer performs switching, control, call processing, digitization (if necessary), call routing, and connections to communication services outside the local network via the interconnected set of switching computer. Generally each switching computer can handle several thousand connections and, via interface devices, connections to baseband and broadband local-network segments and satellite channels.

Standards Efforts

While, as indicated in chapter 2, a number of organizations are pursuing development of network standards, the most action has come from the IEEE 802 Committee.

The touted benefits of standardization revolve around the derived ability to use networking equipment from multiple vendors in a single local network, if all vendors subscribe to the same set of standards. From the material

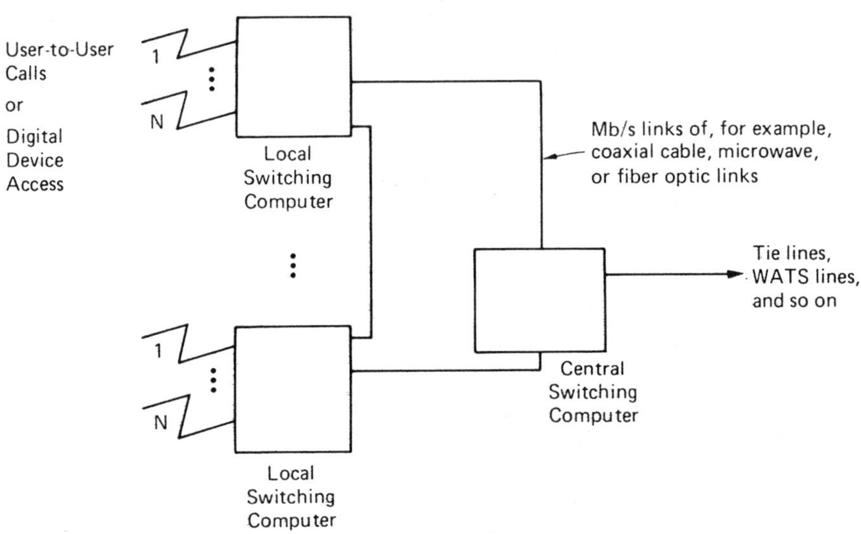

Figure 8–3. PBX Based Local Network

presented especially in chapter 6, it is obvious that a standard is now nonexistent. Additional reinforcement for this statement can be found by consulting the series of comparative diagrams given in [3]. Products differ in their:

Use of baseband, broadband;

Data encoding strategy;

Electrical connection requirements;

Data rates;

Access protocol;

Use of access priority;

Collision handling (Backoff strategy);

Frame structuring; and

Protocol layering.

The 802 Committee is addressing these issues and more. While some considerations are noncontentious and therefore relatively easily standardized, others are not. Among the more contentious issues are those related to the access protocol embraced by the standard. Current plans call for the standard to embrace two access protocols, CSMA-CD for bursty traffic environments, and a token passing strategy for deterministic environments. Put differently, network operation obeys (theoretically speaking) probabilistic rules when CSMA-CD is used, and deterministic rules when token passing is used. In some environments probabilistic bahavior is unacceptable. These and other standards issues are discussed in [4].

As of this writing an 802 draft standard exists, [5]. It addresses what we have termed low speed (less than 20 Mb/s) networks, and contains specifications for:

CSMA/CD and token access methods,

CIU capabilities,

Framing structures,

Addressing field sizes, and

Link-level services.

In each category the draft standard embraces a number of options so that "devices built to this standard may not be directly interoperable" [5]. The functional specification against which the standard is being developed is contained in appendix 8–A.

Miscellany

New communication equipment (CIU) workstations and local-network software offerings are announced almost daily, and the number of companies offering baseband, broadband, or PBX local-network products and services is growing rapidly. Interested parties can keep abreast of local-network products by monitoring [1]. Additionally, a network users association has been formed to promote standards, exchange information, and so on [2].

References

1. The LocalNetter, published monthly by Architecture Technology Corporation, P.O. Box 24344, Minneapolis, MN 55424.
2. For information on the Network Users Association, contact Sheldon Blauman, BCS, MIS 9C-59, P.O. Box 24346, Seattle, WA 98124.
3. Hsi, Peter, and Lissack Tsvi, "Local Networks' Consensus: High Speed," *Data Communications*, December 1980, pp. 56–66.
4. Mokhoff, Nicolas, "Local Data Nets: Untying the Office Knot," *IEEE Spectrum*, April 1981, pp. 57–59.
5. 802 Committee, "The IEEE 802 Local Network Standard, Draft 1," July 4, 1981.

Appendix 8A: IEEE 802 Project Functional Requirements Document (Version 5.2)

Introduction

This document defines the interface and protocol functional requirements for a specific set of Local Area Networks. These requirements include the uses, environments, and specific functions of, as well as the required performance for such networks. These requirements will be used to define an interface and protocol standard or a set of standards.

A Local Area Network is a data communications system that allows a number of independent data devices to communicate with each other. It is distinguished from other types of data networks in that the communication is usually confined to a moderate-sized geographic area such as a single office building, a warehouse, or a campus, and can depend on a physical communication channel of moderate to high data rate that has a consistently low error rate. This is in contrast to long-distance networks that interconnect facilities that may be in different parts of the country, and networks of data devices within a single piece of equipment.

Scope

The applications environment for the Local Area Network is intended to be commercial and light industrial. Use of the Local Area Network in home or heavy industrial environments, while not precluded, is not considered specifically within the scope of this document. Similarly, the use of the Local Area Network for process control and other real-time, high-reliability, or high-security applications, while not precluded, is not specifically considered here. No data equipment or application will be specifically excluded from connection to, or use of the Local Area Network as long as it conforms to all mandatory requirements of the Local Area Network Standard.

This Local Area Network Functional Requirements Document does not make any assumptions regarding network architecture or topology.

The Local Area Network is intended to have a wide applicability to many environments. To this end, the network should support applications processes and services such as:

File Transfer and Access Protocols,

Graphical Applications,

Word Processing,

Electronic Mail,

Remote Data Base Access, and

Digital Voice Applications.

The Local Area Network shall support the use of digitized voice services where this service is similar to that of normal digital data traffic. Typical services might include: voice messages, low traffic-volume intercom facilities, public-address facilities, and limited teleconferencing facilities. The Local Area Network is not required to support high-volume real-time interactive voice capabilities normally associated with Private Branch Exchange facilities, although conforming system designs that can provide such capability are not precluded.

The Local Area Network is intended to support various data devices, such as:

Computers,

Terminals,

Mass-Storage Devices,

Printers/Plotters,

Photo- and Telecopiers,

Monitoring and Control Equipment, and

Bridges and Gateways to Other Networks.

The foregoing lists are intended to show typical applications and devices and, as such, are not intended to be exhaustive, nor do they constitute a set of required items.

Objectives

The objective of the Local Area Network Standard is to ensure compatibility between equipment made by different manufacturers, such that data communication can take place between the equipment with minimum effort on the part of the equipment users or the builders of a system containing the equipment. To accomplish this, the standard will provide specifications that establish common interfaces and protocols for local data communications networks.

The Local Area Network will provide an architecture that permits the efficient interconnection of moderately priced devices and is, in itself, a moderately priced network.

These specifications will be defined in terms of a layered architecture that corresponds, as much as possible, to the Reference Model for Open Systems Inerconnection, as proposed by the American National Standards Institute (ANSI) and the International Organization for Standardization (ISO). The layers will be defined in such a way as to be relatively device and application independent. In addition, the end result of the application of the Local Area Network Standards developed by IEEE Project 802 shall also also conform to the ISO Reference Model. The intent of the layering in the Local Area Network architecture is to allow individual protocol and service layers to be replaced as needed without requiring changes in other parts of either the network or its individual nodes.

Functional Requirements

The Local Area Network shall provide a service to deliver, with a high probability, link-level data units to one or more addressed destinations using peer-to-peer communication. The delivery mechanism must provide both a connection-oriented and transaction-oriented service.

The Local Area Network shall be described in terms of, and designed to be in conformance with layered services and protocols, including those of the physical and link layers, as defined in the ISO document entitled, "Reference Model of Open Systems Interconnection" (ISO document ISO/TC97/SC16/N537).

In order to accommodate a number of present and potential future physical signal transmission technologies, the Local Area Network Standard shall define a physical interface between the data device and the medium-access unit, as shown in figure 8–4. The standard will define at a minimum:

1. The service provided by *L* to the higher layers,
2. The *LL peer protocol,*

3. *The LP′* interface,
4. The *P′P′* signalling protocol,
5. The *P′P′* physical interface,
6. A *P′P′* peer protocol,
7. A *PP* signalling protocol, and
8. A *PP* physical interface.

Additional *PP′* protocols and *PP* physical interfaces and signalling protocols for the Local Area Network medium will be defined as they evolve and will be included in the standard at that time.

Items 4 and 5 will be specified in such a way as to provide minimum constraint on (1) the topology of the Local Area Network, (2) the medium used with the Local Area Network, and (3) the link-layer logical protocol, *LL*.

Physical Characteristics

The Local Area Network shall provide for data transparency; that is, the data paths through the network shall be insensitive to unique combinations of the character codes or bit patterns used by higher levels in the architecture.

The architecture of the Local Area Network shall not preclude direct data interchange between any two data devices using the network. It should be possible to transmit data units between any two data devices without requiring store-and-forward via a third data device, unless that device is

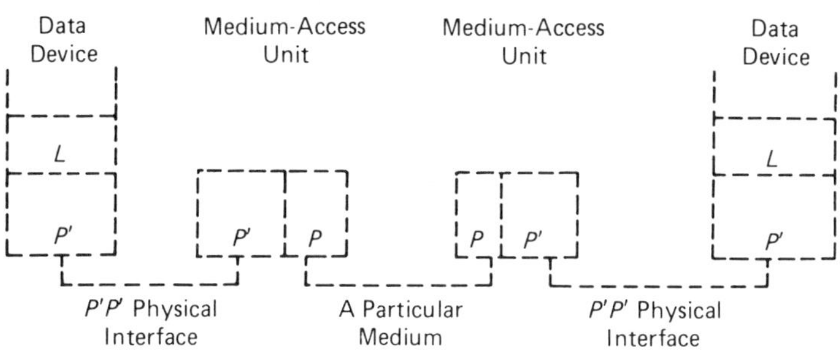

Figure 8–4. OSI Representation of Local Network

needed to provide a conversation or translation of class of service between corresponding data devices.

The Local Area Network shall be capable of supporting at least 200 connected devices distributed along a communication medium of at least two kilometers in length. Repeaters may be used as part of the network implementation. Note that a specific reference to this section should specify maximum values (for example, up to 200 devices).

The data rate over the Local Area Network medium shall lie in the range of 1,000,000 bits per second to 20,000,000 bits per second.

The Local Area Network shall be designed so that user data devices and medium-access units can be easily added or deleted. The connection to, or the disconnection from the Local Area Network of data devices shall not introduce a transient fault lasting more than one second.

Where the various nodes of the Local Area Network have the need to share resources such as media bandwidth, media access, and multiplexed user ports, the Local Area Network shall provide a mechanism to arbitrate and manage the use of these shared network resources in a manner construed to be "fair" to all network nodes.

In the case where a physically separate medium access unit is used to provide the interface between the data device and the medium, the cable and interface between the data device and the medium-access unit must be capable of supporting a separation between the two devices of at least fifty meters. If the medium is such that a medium-access unit is not required, then this functional requirement is not applicable.

The Local Area Network shall provide protection from lightning and galvanic effects both for itself and for connected data services.

Link Characteristics

The addressing mechanisms of the Local Area Network shall include the capability to simultaneously address a given message to more than one receiving station and shall include the capability to simultaneously address all stations connected to the Local Area Network.

For certain classes of service, the Local Area Network should permit end users to administer part or all of their address space.

The link data units shall be composed of an integral number of octets; that is, the data unit shall be exactly 8**n bits in length, where n* is an integer.

Errors, Failures, and Maintenance

The Local Area Network should have an undetected bit error rate, at the link-service interface, of less than one erroneous link-level data unit per year, assuming a data-unit size of 200 bytes and a data rate, at the link-service interface, of 5 Mbits/sec. This amounts to an undetected bit error rate of approximately one part in 10**14, at the link-service interface. In performing this calculation, the following assumptions should be made:

1. At the physical-layer service interface, the bit error rate is less than one part in 10**8. Assume further that the physical layer will provide a burst error detection capability that will eliminate 90 percent of the total number of erroneous bits. The resulting bit error rate, as seen by the link level, will be one part in 10**9.

2. Each data device connected to the Local Area Network shall be designed such that a single failure in the data device shall not cause more than a transient failure of the Local Area Network as a whole except as related only to the failed data device. The loss of power to any data device shall not cause more than a transient failure of the Local Area Network as a whole. The Local Area Network shall be capable of recovering from the effects of such transient failures. For the purposes of this document, "transient" is defined as an event having a duration of about one second.

A statement concerning reliability of the Local Area Network will be provided at a later time.

The Local Area Network shall include features that facilitate Network maintenance, diagnostics, and service.

Miscellaneous

Where necessary and appropriate, the Local Area Network shall conform to the mandatory requirements of relevant regulating and licensing agencies.

Any material used in the Local Area Network standard must be non-proprietary or must be available on a reasonable and nondiscriminatory basis.

Where possible and appropriate, the Local Area Network shall be defined to comply with existing, and in cognizance of emerging standards.

Where possible and appropriate, the Local Area Network shall be so defined as to use standard and commercially available, multiple sourced component parts.

The Local Area Network should be such that it can be easily interfaced to other networks or to common carrier facilities.

The data device interface (the *P'P'* interface) in the Local Area Network should be kept as simple and as economical as possible.

Where possible and appropriate, the Local Area Network Standard shall permit the use of high-volume Large Scale Integration (LSI) circuitry.

Index

About the Authors

W.R. Franta is associate professor of computer science and associate director of the University Computer Center at the University of Minnesota. He was formerly a research Fellow and manager for operation software at the University Computer Center. His research interests include queueing theory, simulation methodology, computer-performance evaluation, and local networking. He is the author of *The Process View of Simulation*. Dr. Franta received the B.S. and the M.S. in mathematics and the Ph.D. in computer science at the University of Minnesota.

Imrich Chlamtac is currently employed by Digital Equipment Corporation in engineering local networks. He has served as a consultant and project manager in computer-aided system analysis with the Israeli government from 1975 to 1976, an instructor in the Department of Mathematics at Tel Aviv University during 1977, a teaching associate in the Computer Science Department at the University of Minnesota and a member of the Special Interactive Computation Laboratory at the University Computer Center from 1977 to 1979, and a member of the faculty of the Computer Science Department of the University of Minnesota from 1979 to 1981. Dr. Chlamtac received the B.Sc. and M.Sc. from Tel Aviv University and the Ph.D. in computer science from the University of Minnesota. His interests include multiple-access communications, simulation, and computer-network modeling and analysis.